Small Group Research:
A Handbook

Printed in the United States of America.

Library of Congress Cataloging-in-Publication Data

Small group research / A. Paul Hare . . . [et al.].
    p. cm.
    Includes bibliographical references and indexes.
    ISBN 0-89391-692-7   0-89391-952-7 (ppk)
    1. Small groups. 2. Social psychology — Research — Methodology.
  I. Hare, A. Paul (Alexander Paul), 1923-
  HM133.S646   1992
  302.3′4 — dc20   91-40016
                                                                    CIP

Ablex Publishing Corporation
355 Chestnut Street
Norwood, New Jersey 07648

Small Group Research:
A Handbook

**A. Paul Hare,
Herbert H. Blumberg,
Martin F. Davies,
M. Valerie Kent**

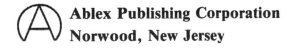 **Ablex Publishing Corporation
Norwood, New Jersey**

Small Group Research: A Handbook

A. Paul Hare, Herbert H. Blumberg, Martin F. Davies, and M. Valerie Kent

BRIEF TABLE OF CONTENTS

DETAILED TABLE OF CONTENTS

Preface

When we set out to prepare a new edition of Hare's (1976) *Handbook of Small Group Research*, we found that there has been a small flood of new material since the mid-1970s, including a potential set of about 6000 journal articles alone. It therefore seemed best to limit ourselves primarily to studies and reviews published in the period from 1975 to 1988, thereby complementing the Second Edition rather than replacing it. Thus the two volumes, taken together, provide a review of small group research "from its beginnings to the present." The chapters in the present volume do, however, contain enough information about the gist of earlier work that they can be read independently of the earlier volume.

Many of the articles and books cited in this volume were read in full. However, for most of the articles and books, the *Psychological Abstracts* or *Sociological Abstracts* or a book review was our primary source of information concerning the relevance of the research for the analysis of interpersonal behavior in small groups. Our emphasis has not been on an evaluation of current research, but rather to call attention to available works that might be relevant for a person wishing to do further research in some specified area. For this reason we also refer to other reviews of parts of this literature that may provide a somewhat different perspective and perhaps include citations selected on different criteria. Thus our intention has been to produce a reference work rather than an introductory text, although we will be pleased if the present work is used as a text, as was the case with the previous edition of the *Handbook of Small Group Research*.

The organization of the first 10 chapters in this volume follows that of our two-volume selection of readings on *Small Groups and Social Interaction* (H. H. Blumberg, Hare, Kent, & Davies, 1983). The organization of the material in Chapters 11 and 12 is similar to that in the earlier *Handbook* under the same chapter headings. The focus is on the content of research, calling attention to sets of studies in the same general area. When a study deals with more than one major variable or effect, it may be cited in several chapters. (However, if one is interested in both aspects of a "joint topic" such as sex differences in conformity, it may be worth checking two different chapters as well as the index.) If a study has a methodological emphasis it is cited in the Appendix under research methods or, if it applies primarily to a particular type of group, it is cited in the Appendix under Special Types of Groups. Some cases of research that illustrate a particular trend are summarized in more detail in one or two paragraphs. However, since the volume of research to be covered is so large, we have not included long summaries of research with figures and tables. Where an item of research is cited with only a word or two of information describing the content, or as part of a list of relevant research, the reader may usually obtain more information by referring to the *Psychological Abstracts* or *Sociological Abstracts*. Where we had information about the abstract number, the number is given at the end of the entry in the References. However, we did not attempt to locate in the *Abstracts* the numbers for all items discovered in our direct search of journals or of books, especially recent ones.

The present canvas of the literature includes all the references since the 1976 *Handbook*, using the same kinds of source material. In some cases we have also cited studies from the period previously covered — for example, if we refer to a work which provided the impetus for later research.

In the course of this scan, *Psychological Abstracts* have been checked from Volume 52 (1974) to 75(6) (June 1988) — including all entries classified as experimental social psychology plus selected topics from the subject indexes. *Sociological Abstracts* have been checked from 1974 to mid-1988.

Canvassing the literature and initially deciding on the allocation of journal references to topics was done by all four authors. Keeping track of the references and checking the citations was done mainly by Herbert Blumberg and Martin Davies.

In order to compile a list of books to check, we consulted (1975 to mid-1988): *Contemporary Psychology*, *Contemporary Sociology*, and, under selected headings, the *National Union Catalog* (Books: Subject Index).

We used the *Social Sciences Citation Index* to check for additional articles and books by "key" authors — people who have been very heavily cited either in the *Handbook of Small Group Research*, Second Edition, or in selected chapters of various recent social psychological texts.

In addition, the following journals were checked issue by issue from 1975 to mid-1988 (or, in the case of ceased or new journals, for whatever part of that period a particular journal was published): *Advances in Applied Social Psychology*, *Advances in Experimental Social Psychology*, *Advances in Group Processes*, *American Journal of Sociology*, *American Psychologist*, *American Sociological Review*, *Annual Review of Psychology*, *Applied Social Psychology Annual*, *Basic and Applied Social Psychology*, *Behavioral Science*, *British Journal of Psychology*, *British Journal of Social and Clinical Psychology*, *British Journal of Social*

Psychology, British Journal of Sociology, Canadian Journal of Behavioral Science, Current Sociology, European Journal of Social Psychology, Human Organization, Human Relations, International Journal of Small Group Research, Journal of Abnormal Psychology, Journal of Applied Behavioral Science, Journal of Applied Psychology, Journal of Applied Social Psychology, Journal of Conflict Resolution, Journal of Consulting Psychology, Journal of Educational Psychology, Journal of Experimental Social Psychology, Journal of Personality, Journal of Personality and Social Psychology, Journal of Psychology, Journal of Social Issues, Journal of Social Psychology, Organizational Behavior and Human Decision Making, Organizational Behavior and Human Performance, Personality and Social Psychology Bulletin, Progress in Applied Social Psychology, Psychological Bulletin, Psychological Reports, Psychological Review, Psychology Today, Representative Research in Social Psychology, Review of Personality and Social Psychology, SASP [Society for the Advancement of Social Psychology] Newsletter, Small Group Behavior, Social Behavior and Personality, Social Forces, Social Psychology Quarterly, Social Research, Sociological Inquiry, Sociology and Social Research, and *Sociometry.* The *European Review of Social Psychology* commenced publication after our search was completed.

Because of the large number of potential references, we have had to be comparatively stringent in limiting ourselves to studies involving—or having fairly immediate relevance to—face-to-face social interaction.

The present large body of small-groups research has been described by Fred Strodtbeck as being carried out in an "incrementalist" period of research. Much of the work is "paradigmatic" in that it concerns the (sometimes) systematic exploration of conditions under which previously found phenomena are particularly strong or weak or even reversed. We hope that readers will find it useful to have the present body of material organized and described in a single work.

A. Paul Hare
Herbert H. Blumberg
Martin F. Davies
M. Valerie Kent

Note added in proof: Because of unexpected delays in the publishing and printing process, there has been a substantial time lag between our completion of the literature search for this volume and its publication. Because new developments have not altered the structure of the field, though the scope of findings continues to expand, we have decided not to alter the volume, which would cause further delay.

Acknowledgment

We would like to thank Caroline Kelly, Aron Siegman, Fred Strodtbeck, and Brian Young for their helpful comments on a draft of the manuscript. We wish to thank our publishers for their support, advice, and help. We also very much appreciate the assistance received, and use of facilities, at the Boston Public Library, British Library, Library of Congress, and the libraries of Ben-Gurion University, Goldsmiths' College, Harvard University, and the Open University.

Introduction

A. Paul Hare

DEFINITION OF A SMALL GROUP

Groups are "small" if they have from 2 to 30 members. However there is no definite cutting point between a "small" group and a "large" group, or indeed a whole organization or larger social entity. The distinctive characteristics of a group, in contrast to a collection of individuals who may have similar traits or be close together in the same physical location, are that: (a) group members have a set of shared values that help them to maintain an overall pattern of activity, (b) they acquire or develop resources and skills to be used for their activity, (c) they conform to a set of norms that define roles to be played in the activity and have a sufficient level of morale to provide "cohesiveness," and (d) they have a specific goal or set of goals that they wish to achieve and the leadership necessary to coordinate their resources and roles in the interest of the goal or goals (Hare, 1976, pp. 4–5, 12–13).

Bales (1950, p.33), who provided one of the earliest definitions of a small group, suggested that a group was "small" if, after a session of face-to-face interaction, each member could remember something about the contributions of every other member. In general small groups are less likely to contain subgroups with different value systems, find it easier to share common resources, are more cohesive, and can control their activities with a more democratic, in contrast to authoritarian, form of leadership. However some small groups can have the more "formal" characteristics of a larger organization and some groups of 30 or more persons, especially if they have lived and worked together for a period of time, can be as "informal" as a smaller group.

A group is different from a "network," in that pairs of persons or small sets of persons who form the links in a network may have the characteristics of a small group, but the network may include persons who are more than one link removed and who never meet in a face-to-face situation. In recent years the term "minimal group" has appeared in the literature to refer to a set of persons who have, or who are told that they have, some common characteristic, such as ethnic or political background. Persons so defined may well exhibit common attitudes toward members of another set of persons defined as an "out group," but they do not constitute a group in the sense that we are using the term in this volume.

J. DeLamater (1974) has reviewed the definition of "group" used in the social-psychological literature and notes that the definitions usually include the characteristics of shared interaction, perceptions, affective ties, and interdependent roles. Fine (1979) shows how small groups, such as Little League baseball teams in the United States, develop their own "ideocultures." M. E. Shaw (1981) provides one of the most comprehensive summaries of research on the dynamics of small groups.

THEORIES

The 1976 edition of the *Handbook of Small Group Research* did not include a section with references to then-current theories of social interaction in small groups with the exception of a brief introduction to functional theory in Chapter 1. Chapters in *Small Groups and Social Interaction* (H. H. Blumberg, Hare, Kent, & Davies, 1983) include an outline (by Kent) of some of the theories and more extensive introductions to others, such as equity, functional analysis, FIRO, SYMLOG, and frame analysis. Hare (1982) gives brief introductions to some aspects of functional theory, four dimensions of interaction, dramaturgical theory, and exchange theory. As A. Pepitone (1981) has noted in his review of the metatheoretical perspectives and the theory/research areas that have constituted the main history of social psychology in the United States, most of the theories center on the individual in a social situation rather than group or collective phenomena. K. K. Smith and White (1983) suggest that the social-psychological study of groups could benefit by incorporating issues and concepts from other group traditions. Mullen and Goethals (1987) have edited reviews of eight psychological theories that can be used to understand aspects of group behavior: social comparison, cognitive dissonance, self-presentation, drive, social impact, self-attention, social cognition, and transactive memory. J. C. Turner (1985, 1987) proposes a "self-categorization" theory.

The most comprehensive new theoretical perspective to be introduced since 1976 is that of A System for the Multiple Level Observation of Groups (SYMLOG) developed by Bales and his colleagues (Bales & Cohen, 1979; Bales, 1984, 1985). The theory assumes that all interpersonal behavior can be understood in terms of a three dimensional space, where the three dimensions are Upward-Downward (Dominance vs. Submission), Positive-Negative, and Forward-Backward (Task oriented and conforming vs. Expressive and anticonforming). In addition to providing hypotheses concerning individual effectiveness in groups, the theory and associated methods have the additional advantage of providing for the analysis of the relationship of individuals to the group and subgroups to each other. Examples of applications of the theory for the study of small groups are found, especially, in the *International Journal of Small Group Research* (see, for example, Parke & Houben, 1985, and L. Kelly & Duran, 1986, on group types) and in the collection of papers edited by Polley, Hare, and Stone (1988). Polley (1983) indicates the relationship between the SYMLOG space and that proposed by Eysenck. Polley (1987) suggests the revision of some items of the factor scales, but Bales, Koenigs, and Roman (1987) indicated that the relationship between the items on the scales depends on one's ideal. Hare and Naveh (1985) give examples of the application of the theory for the analysis of negotiation. Results of analyses of interpersonal behavior that result in factors that are similar to some of those in the SYMLOG space are reported by: Ahlgren & Walberg (1978); Golding & Knudson (1975); Isenberg & Ennis (1981); Moxnes & Engvik (1973); and Wish, Deutsch, & Kaplan (1976). The items listed above represent only a small sample of the research using the SYMLOG theory and related methods. A review of research on SYMLOG is given by Hare (1989).

The dramaturgical perspective, often associated with the work of Goffman, since the publication of his work on *The Presentation of Self in Everyday Life* (1959), continues to attract advocates. When social interaction is viewed as drama the focus in on the behavior of actors and audience on stage and off stage. The perspective can be used for the analysis of instances of collective behavior as well as small groups. Hare (1985) and Hare and Blumberg (1988) review the literature.

Buss and Briggs (1984) and Giddens (1984) use Goffman's concepts as a starting point but also elaborate his approach. Morrione (1985) emphasizes the importance of the actors definition of the situation, Perinbanayagam (1985) the importance of motives, and Mangham and Overington (1982) the significance of the alternation between performing and rehearsing. R. H. Levine (1977) observes that two modes of communication, speech and non- speech, are not adequately synthesized by the "rule-role" model that is part of the dramaturgical perspective. Pryor and Merluzzi (1985) and T. D. Wilson and Capitman (1982) provide examples of "scripted" behavior in "boy-meets-girl" relationships and McLeod (1984) recommends the use of the dramaturgical approach for the analysis of group therapy.

For additional research related to the dramaturgical perspective see: Abelson, 1976, 1981; Collett, 1977; Ditton, 1980; J. D. Douglas, Adler, Adler, Fontana, Freeman, & Kotarba, 1980; Forgas, 1979; Goffman, 1974, 1981, 1982; Harré, 1979; Lofland, 1978; Schlenker, 1980; Vernon, 1978.

New perspectives, or revisions of old perspectives, are continually being introduced in the literature (T. M. Mills, 1979). Some of these are discussed by Steiner (1986). C. L. Cooper (1975b) has collected a number of papers which explore theories and methods, especially for experiential groups. However in this section we have only included references to those articles or books that emphasize theory rather than substantive results. Examples of this type of article are those of A. Pepitone (1976) who calls attention to the importance of group values and beliefs, Neidhardt (1979) and Tesser (1980b) who both propose theories that place more emphasis on conflict, Rossignol (1975) and Diamond and Allcorn (1987) who base their hypotheses on psychoanalytic theory, J. C. Turner (1981) who advances a social-cognitive theory, Wisdom (1978) who suggests that Bion's theory has more general application than Freud's, and Tubbs (1984) who uses a systems approach. Fine (1986) provides a "reintegration" of Lewinian field theory. For consideration of cognitive balance in groups, see Kimberly (1984). For social and sociological aspects of attribution theory see: Crittenden, 1983; Hewstone, 1984.

If Buys (1978a) was correct in his conclusion, after reviewing the small groups literature, that "humans would do better without groups," then there would be no need for further theory. However not everyone agreed with his conclusions (L. R. Anderson, 1978; R. B. Green & Mack, 1978; Kravitz, Cohen, Martin, Sweeney, McCarty, Elliott, & Goldstein, 1978; L. S. Shaffer, 1978). In a rejoinder, Buys (1978b) explained his position by asserting that: "Clearly, many forms of groups are beneficial, if not essential, to humans. Indeed, it seems nonsensical to search for alternatives to human groups."

SUMMARIES OF RESEARCH AND COMMENTS ON THE FIELD

Summaries of recent research on small groups, comments, and bibliographies are given by: Blake & Mouton, 1981; Brandstätter, Davis, & Stocker-Kreichgauer, 1982; C. L. Cooper, 1975b; Denzin, 1984; D. G. Ellis, Werbel, & Fisher, 1978; Forsyth, 1983; Hare, 1982; Herskin, 1979; Johnstad, 1980; Katovich, 1984; Maines, 1984; McGrath, 1984; McGrath & Kravitz, 1982; Maines, 1984; T. M. Mills, 1984; Napier & Gershenfeld, 1985; Nixon, 1979; Paulus, 1983, 1989; R. L. Peterson, 1973; G. M. Phillips & Erickson, 1970; Steiner, 1986; Stone, 1984; Ridgeway, 1983; Thibaut & Kelley, 1986; Zander, 1977, 1979a, 1979b; Zlate, 1983. See also Dimock (1987), and see below, the last few paragraphs of this section.

A. A. Harrison and Connors (1984) provide a review of research on "groups in exotic environments," including polar camps, space capsules, supertankers, weather stations, and simulations of these settings. Since many of these groups are relatively small, especially those in outer space, the authors are able to examine the structures and processes of small groups with clear task goals and minimal direct association with members of other groups. The same variables are found to be important for groups in these exotic environments as in more everyday settings. However problems that occur because of intermember incompatibility, task overload, or sensory deprivation, for example, have a more obvious relationship to the success of the group's mission.

For a review of cross-cultural studies of small groups, see L. Mann (1980).

Reviews of the use of small groups as they have been used as intervention techniques and in various forms of social engineering are given by Back (1974) and Graebner (1986). The qualitative analysis of human interaction has been reviewed by Lofland (1976).

Several authors comment on the apparent decline in research on small groups after a peak of activity in the late 1950s and early 1960s (Borgatta, 1981; Denzin, 1984; Goodstein & Dovico, 1979; Steiner, 1974). However, Back (1979) concludes that research on small groups is still necessary since it provides a bridge between the individual and the surrounding society and Zander (1985b) assumes that there will be a continuing need for understanding behavior in groups. Concurrent with the "apparent decline," there has been a substantial increase in the actual amount of research on small group topics.

Some areas of research have not attracted as much interest in the recent period as they did in the period up to 1974 — for example, personality variables and race (probably as a result of the decline in interest in the United States in civil rights). Some areas, that have been of interest since the earliest research at the turn of the century continue, such as social facilitation and inhibition, and compliance with group norms. In the case of compliance, recent studies focus on the kinds of requests a salesperson might make approaching a customer and on the influence of the minority on the majority. Differences in behavior between men and women continue to be of interest, although now there is more concern with women as leaders and the extent to which traditional gender roles reflect status differences.

Interest in leadership has also continued, but now with an emphasis on the style of leadership appropriate for different situations.

Research that formerly appeared under the heading of sociometry or friendship has now attracted considerable attention under the heading "intimate relationships." For a classified bibliography of the 1974–1988 literature on attraction and friendship, see Davies and Blumberg (1988).

Some topics that were relatively new at the time of publication of the previous *Handbook* continue to be researched in detail. These include: choice shift, especially in simulated juries, cooperation and competition, especially with collective dilemmas, and various games and simulations, especially the Prisoners' Dilemma. The main new emphasis in research is on nonverbal behavior with contributions from persons in speech and language departments studying paralanguage and linguistic factors not formerly considered by psychologists and sociologists. This includes an interest in the topics of self disclosure and deceptive communication. Along with the current interest in the effect of environment, there is also a new concern for factors contributing to environmental stress and human spatial behavior, including personal space and crowding.

A number of authors have suggested a more comprehensive approach for the study of small groups, especially placing the small group in a wider situational context: R. G. Barker, 1978; Battegay, 1977; Boyd, 1983; Burlingame, Fuhriman, & Drescher, 1984; Dies, 1985; Fuhriman, Drescher, & Burlingame, 1984; R. A. Kane, 1975; König, 1983; Latta & Gorman, 1984; Maines, 1984; Moscovici, 1979; Munne, 1985; Neidhardt, 1983; K. K. Smith & Berg, 1987b; Stone, 1984; Tajfel, 1979; Tubbs, 1984; Von Cranach, Ochsenbein, & Valach, 1986.

Some texts, readers, and annual publications include sections on the small group or related material, for example: Alblas, 1983; Argyle, Furnham, & Graham, 1981; Atkinson, Atkinson, Smith, & Hilgard, 1987, Chapter 18; Berkowitz, 1984, 1986; Blumberg, Hare, Kent, & Davies, 1983; Bootzin, Bower, Zajonc, & Hall, 1986, Chapter 27; R. Brown, 1986; R. J. Brown, 1988; Deaux & Wrightsman, 1988; T. Douglas, 1983; Forgas, 1985; C. Hendrick, 1987a, 1987b; Johnstad, 1980; Jungk & Müllert, 1981; Lawler, 1985 (and other annual volumes of *Advances in Group Processes*); Lindzey & Aronson, 1985; Luft, 1984; Milgram, 1977; Mullen & Goethals, 1987; Napier & Gershenfeld, 1983; Oskamp & Spacapan, 1987; Paulus, 1983; M. Robinson, 1984; Shaver, 1985; K. K. Smith & Berg, 1987a; Tedeschi & Lindskold, 1976; J. C. Turner, 1987; S. Wilson, 1978; Zander, 1985a.

Some books and other sources, especially in the "group dynamics" tradition, have an emphasis on application: Miles, 1980; M. Robinson, 1984; Schindler-Rainman & Lippitt, 1975; G. T. Solomon & Winslow, 1983; G. L. Wilson & Hanna, 1986; Zander, 1982.

OVERVIEW OF VOLUME

Because of the large number of potential references, we tried to limit our review to studies involving face-to-face interaction in small groups or those having special relevance for small group processes. Thus topics such as individual tendencies to help or hurt (see M. V. Kent & Blumberg, 1988a, 1988b) or to make friends, that might be covered in whole chapters or whole books in other volumes on social psychology, only appear here as parts of chapters. We have also limited our review to human groups. For research on groups of infrahuman primates see two works (recommended by S. Perloe in a personal communication): Hinde (1983) and Smuts, Cheney, Seyfarth, Wrangham, and Struhsaker (1987) — and see also DeWaal (1983) and Kellerman, Buirski, & Plutchik (1974).

The organization of Parts I through V follows the rationale used in our collection of readings on *Small Groups and Social Interaction* (H. H. Blumberg, Hare, Kent, & Davies, 1983). Progressively more sources of influence on the individual and the group are brought "on stage." In part I we review research on the influence of the physical situation (Chapter 1) and the individual's personality and social characteristics (Chapter 2). Part II includes the influence of others on the individual, both by their presence (Chapter 3) and by pressures toward conformity

(Chapter 4). Part III deals with group structure, both with roles and relationships in general (Chapter 5) and the specific role of leader (Chapter 6). Part IV summarizes research on group process, including social interaction (Chapter 7) and decision making and choice shift (Chapter 8). Part V considers some interaction modes: cooperation, competition, and conflict resolution (Chapter 9) and games, bargaining, and coalitions (Chapter 10).

The last two chapters, in Part VI, are similar to those in the second edition of the *Handbook of Small Group Research* (Hare, 1976). They provide a summary of the research on small groups with the emphasis on productivity. Chapter 11 compares the productivity of an individual with that of a group on the same task and Chapter 12 compares groups with different types of structure and process.

In an appendix we cite references to research methods that have special relevance for research on small groups and to some of the literature on special types of groups. The list of references covers social-psychological research on small groups from 1975 through 1988.

Part I

THE SITUATION AND THE PERSON

Chapter 1

The Physical Situation

Martin F. Davies

Fish are proverbially the last to realize that they live in a liquid environment. Until quite recently, psychologists had also overlooked the role of the environment in human affairs—witness the creation of an environmental psychology section as late as 1973 in the *Annual Review of Psychology* (Craik, 1973; followed by Stokols, 1978; J. A. Russell & Ward, 1982; Holahan, 1986).

For reviews of the environment and behavior, see: Altman, 1975; Altman & Chemers, 1980; Altman, Rapoport, & Wohlwill, 1980; Altman & Wandersman, 1987; Altman & Werner, 1985; Altman & Wohlwill, 1976, 1977, 1978, 1983; Altman, Vinsel, & Brown, 1981; Altman, Wohlwill, & Everett, 1982; R. G. Barker & Associates, 1978; Baum & Singer, 1982; Baum, Singer, & Valins, 1978; Canter & Craik, 1981; Feimer & Geller, 1983; J. D. Fisher, Bell, & Baum, 1984; J. H. Harvey, 1981; Heimstra & McFarling, 1974; Proshansky, Ittelson, & Rivlin, 1976; Stokols, 1977; Stokols & Altman, 1987; W. P. White, 1978; Wohlwill & Weisman, 1981.

The physical situation in which an individual or group is located consists of: the *ambient environment*—such as the noise level and temperature; the *human environment*—such as the number and density of people present (real or imagined) and their spatial arrangement; and *material aspects* of the environment—such as room design, architecture, fixtures and fittings.

These three aspects of the environment can influence behavior in various ways, but Darley and Gilbert (1985) suggest that the single most important influence of a setting, situation, or place is its *perceived purpose*. For example, the sorts of behavior associated with a classroom—and expected of its occupants—are different from the sorts of behavior associated with a factory assembly line, a library, or a bar room.

Though social psychologists usually speak of the "situation" as having some sort of direct influence on social behavior, environmental psychologists prefer to view the physical situation in terms of how it *facilitates* or *hinders* behavior. Stokols (1978) noted that an important theme in environmental psychology is the idea of *human-environment optimization*. People do not simply subsist in environments, they select "optimal" environments or try to change their existing environment so as to maximize their well-being, their needs, and the fulfillment of their plans and goals. Often, however, people are unable to attain such optimal environmental conditions, in which case they try to adapt to the less-than-ideal conditions.

ENVIRONMENTAL STRESS

When environmental conditions are such that a person's adaptive and coping resources are strained or taxed, the environment is not only less than optimal, it is also stressful. Examples of environmental *stressors* include noise, heat, cold, pollution, and crowding or density (crowding and density are reviewed in a separate section of this chapter under Human Spatial Behavior). Stressors that are intense, prolonged, unpredictable, and uncontrollable are particularly distressing and debilitating (Baum, Singer, & Baum, 1981; S. Cohen, 1980; Fleming, Baum, & Singer, 1984). First of all, unpredictable and uncontrollable stressors make heavy demands on attentional and information-processing capacity because of the effort required to "tune out" the distracting aspects of the stimulus and/or to monitor the threatening aspects of the stimulus. Prolonged exposure to such stressors results in *cognitive fatigue* and a depletion of attentional resources that persists even after the stressful experience has ended (S. Cohen, 1978). Second, exposure to unpredictable and uncontrollable stressors can lead to *learned helplessness* (M. E. P. Seligman, 1975) where people come to believe that their inability to cope with the existing stressful situation is indicative of a general inability to influence, control, or cope with life-tasks and events—with resultant motivational, emotional, and cognitive deficits.

For reviews of the effects of environmental stress, see: J. M. Campbell, 1983; S. Cohen, 1980; S. Cohen, Evans, Stokols, & Krantz, 1986; G. W. Evans, 1981, 1982; Selye, 1976.

Noise

S. Cohen's (1978) cognitive-fatigue hypothesis suggests that unpredictable, uncontrollable noise should lead to a reduction in people's sensitivity to social cues. Consistent with this idea, S. Cohen and Lezak (1977) showed slides of people in either mundane or dangerous situations (e.g., a slide showing a man paying for oil at a gas station vs. another showing a man trying to rob a gas station) to students while they were learning nonsense syllables either in quiet or noisy conditions. When subsequently questioned about the slides, students in the noisy condition could recall fewer of the situations as being dangerous, presumably because they had not attended to the "danger" aspect of the situations. Rotton, Olszewski, Charleton, and Soler (1978) found that loud speech, noise, and increased task load reduced subjects' subsequent ability to discriminate between which people occupied particular social roles. J. M. Siegel and Steele (1980) similarly found that noise interfered with interpersonal and social discrimination.

Attentional deficits may account for the finding that people are less helpful after exposure to noise. K. E. Mathews and Canon (1975) had an experimental confederate drop a box of books on a city street. In one condition, the confederate's arm was in a plaster cast, in the other condition not. The incident was staged either under noisy conditions (a nearby power mower) or quiet conditions. When the street was quiet, passers-by were much more likely to help the confederate with an arm cast than the confederate without a cast. Under noisy conditions, not only was there less helping overall, but passers-by were also no more likely to help the confederate with the arm cast than the confederate without the cast, because passers-by in the noisy compared with the quiet condition were less likely to notice that the confederate's arm was in a cast. Page (1977) also found that loud noise decreased helping. A confederate of the experimenter, acting as a pedestrian carrying packages, staged the dropping of the packages near a construction site. When the site noise was particularly loud significantly fewer passers-by stopped to help the confederate. Boles and Hayward (1978), R. H. Feldman and Rezmovic (1979), Korte, Ypma and Toppen (1975), Wiener (1976), and Yinon and Bizman (1980) but not Geller and Malia (1981) obtained similar results. For a related area of research, see the section on *Urban Overload*.

The role of *perceived control* in moderating the after-effects of noise stress was highlighted by Sherrod and Downs (1974a, 1974b). Subjects worked on a task under one of three noise conditions. In one condition, subjects were exposed to soothing sounds; in a second condition, subjects were exposed to distressing sounds which could not be terminated (no control), while in a third (perceived control) condition, subjects were also exposed to distressing sounds but could turn off the noise if they wished. After completion of the task and on their way out of the laboratory, subjects were asked by a second experimenter for help in a research project. Subjects who had been exposed to the soothing sounds volunteered the most, subjects exposed to the uncontrollable distressing sounds volunteered least, and subjects exposed to controllable distressing sounds showed an intermediate amount of helping.

Looking at hurtfulness rather than helpfulness, E. Donnerstein and Wilson (1976) had subjects work on a math task while exposed to either quiet conditions, uncontrollable loud noise, or controllable loud noise (the noise could be terminated). Subsequently, half the subjects were made angry by an experimental confederate and half were not. Angry subjects in the uncontrollable noise condition showed most aggression toward the confederate, whereas angry subjects in the controllable noise condition were no more aggressive than angry subjects in the quiet condition. Interestingly, these findings are not consistent with a learned helplessness explanation of uncontrollable stress, since an *increase* in motivation was found rather than a motivational *deficit*. If anything, the findings appear more consistent with reactance theory. Geen (1978) and Konecni (1975) provide additional evidence that noise increases aggression.

For reviews of the effects of noise, see: S. Cohen & Spacapan, 1984; S. Cohen & Weinstein, 1981.

Temperature

It might seem intuitively plausible that unpleasantly hot temperatures should result in more negative affect and negative behavior. Early studies by Griffitt (Griffitt, 1970; Griffitt & Veitch, 1971) in laboratory settings did indeed find that subjects liked a fictitious stranger (described in a dossier) less under hot and humid conditions (100*F/60%) than under normal conditions (see also P. A. Bell, 1980). However, subsequent studies did not find that high temperatures lead to disliking of a stranger (P. A. Bell & Baron, 1974). P. A. Bell, Garnand, and Heath (1984) found that hot room temperatures led to more negative affect and that the environment was evaluated more negatively in hot conditions when students sat adjacent to rather than opposite each other. However, these negative effects were not mirrored in measures of interpersonal attraction.

Kenrick and Cialdini (1977) and Kenrick and Johnson (1979) argued that the presence of others *reduces* the aversive arousal of stressful situations such that another's presence is reinforcing, leading to greater attraction to a stranger in aversive conditions—a *shared stress* effect. They argued that laboratory studies of heat and attraction which found decreased attraction to strangers under aversive conditions used a paradigm where the stranger (fictitious or real) was not present and so did not share the same aversive conditions. In Kenrick and Johnson's study, students were exposed to either stressful or comfortable conditions. Half the students indicated how much they liked a stranger who was physically present in the same room, the other half indicated their liking for a fictitious stranger described in a dossier. The physically-present stranger was liked more under aversive conditions than under comfortable conditions, whereas the fictitious stranger was liked less under aversive than under comfortable conditions.

Notwithstanding these setbacks to our intuitions, it might nevertheless seem plausible that high temperatures should lead to more arousal, activity, and energy, and hence to greater aggressive — even violent — activities (everyday sayings exhort us to: "keep your cool, man!" and "don't get hot under the collar!"). But, in a series of laboratory studies (R. A. Baron, 1978a; R. A. Baron & Bell, 1975, 1976a; P. A. Bell & Baron, 1976, 1977) a *curvilinear* relation between negative feelings (affective state) and aggressive behavior was found. Up to a certain point, an increase in negative state — whether caused by heat, insult, or provocation — increased aggression. Beyond this point, however, further increases in negative state led to reductions in aggression, apparently because the motivation to aggress was supplanted by other motivations—such as how to escape, avoid, or reduce the aversive conditions. Accordingly, incidences of collective violence were predicted by R. A. Baron and Ransberger (1978) to be more likely when the weather was moderately hot rather than extremely hot. Support for this curvilinear relationship was obtained from archival analysis of 102 riots in the United States between 1967 and 1971, and meteorological reports of the prevailing weather conditions.

However, Carlsmith and Anderson (1979) argued that Baron and Ransberger had failed to take account of how many days there were at particular temperatures. If it turned out that there were more days in a year at moderately hot temperatures than at very hot temperatures, then there would simply be more *opportunities* for riots to occur. The appropriate analysis, therefore, would be to test whether there are *relatively* more riots at moderately hot than at cooler or hotter temperatures. When Carlsmith and Anderson calculated the probability of a riot conditional upon temperature, they found strong evidence for a *linear* rather than a curvilinear relation. C. A. Anderson and Anderson (1984) also found a linear relation between ambient temperature and violent crime (murder and rape) and argued that laboratory studies of heat and aggression are subject to artifactual explanations. For example, high temperatures in the lab are artificially created and, unlike moderate conditions, are quickly—and suspiciously—noticed by subjects. When subsequently insulted by a confederate, subjects might well guess the experimenter's intentions and not hold the confederate personally responsible for the insult. Similar findings of a linear relation between ambient temperature and violence have been reported by DeFronzo (1984), Harries and Stadler (1983), Rotton and Frey (1985).

Note that research on heat stress has examined people's reactions and behavior occurring *during* the presence of the stressor rather than the *after-effects* of the stress (unlike the research on noise stress).

Related to the research on temperature, M. R. Cunningham (1979) found that, at comfortable temperatures, people are more generous the more the sun shines—a "sunshine samaritan" effect. An annotated bibliography of research on meteorological variables and behavior can be found in D. E. Campbell and Beets (1977).

For additional studies on heat and temperature, see: R. A. Baron, 1976; Calvert-Boyanowski, Boyanowski, Atkinson, Gaduto, & Reeves, 1976; Kenrick & MacFarlane, 1986; F. W. Schneider, Lesko, & Garrett, 1980.

Other Stressors

Some research has been done on air or atmospheric *pollution*. For example, Rotton, Barry, Frey, and Soler (1978) looked at the effects of atmospheric pollution on liking for an attitudinally similar or dissimilar fictitious stranger. In one study, they found—contrary to predictions—that liking for a similar stranger was greatest in a polluted atmosphere (ammonium sulfide) compared with a neutral (no odor) control condition. This suggested a *shared stress* effect (previously discussed in the *Temperature* section). In a second study, subjects were told they were alone in the lab and would not meet the (bogus) stranger. This had the effect of producing the expected relation between an aversive stressor (air pollution) and disliking for a stranger as well as disliking for the environment. Similar findings were obtained by Rotton (1983). As with lab studies on heat and aggression, Rotton, Frey, Barry, Mulligan, and Fitzpatrick (1979) found a curvilinear relation between pollution (unpleasantness of odor) and aggression.

Bleda and Sandman (1977) found that nonsmokers liked a person who smoked in their presence less than a person who did not smoke, and Bleda and Bleda (1978) found that people moved away faster from a smoker who invaded their personal space than from a nonsmoker. J. W. Jones and Bogat (1978) found that subjects delivered higher levels of noise to a confederate when they were exposed to smoke regardless of whether they had been provoked or not. Similar results were obtained by Rotton, Frey, Barry, Mulligan, and Fitzpatrick (1979) and Zillmann, Baron, and Tamborini (1981).

Generally, however, little is known about the effects of air pollution on social behavior (G. W. Evans & Jacobs, 1981). If it operates like other stressors, then unpredictable, uncontrollable, and intense pollution should lead to: impaired task performance, learned helplessness deficits, attentional deficits and insensitivity to the needs of others, and negative mood or arousal. For additional studies on air pollution, see: Evans, Jacobs, & Frager (1982).

Other important, but relatively under-researched, environmental stressors are: *natural hazards and disasters* (I. Burton & Kates, 1978); *disasters caused by human action or inaction* (Baum, Fleming, & Davidson, 1983; Baum, Gatchel, & Schaeffer, 1983); and the *threat of nuclear war and nuclear accidents* (Blackwell & Gessner, 1983; Escalona, 1982; Fiske, Fischhoff, & Milburn, 1983; J. D. Frank, 1980; M. D. Newcomb, 1986). Little is known about the effects of these stressors on interpersonal and social behavior.

HUMAN SPATIAL BEHAVIOR

Just as an observer from Mars would notice that humans are spaced around the environment in particular ways, so psychologists have investigated human spatial behavior or *proxemics*. Included under proxemics are: *territory*—the occupancy, marking, and defense of a place or an object; *personal space*—the interpersonal distance at which people prefer to converse and interact; *spatial arrangements*—the ways in which people space themselves in a group environment; and *crowding*—the stress and negative feelings experienced when there are felt to be too many people in a particular place. For a review of spatial behavior, see Baldassare (1978).

Privacy

An important concept underlying ideas about spatial behavior is privacy. There have been a number of analyses of privacy. Kelvin (1973) suggested that privacy allows us to control what other people know about our actions, and serves as a way of limiting other people's power over us. Similarly, S. T. Margulis (1977) suggests that the important function of privacy is control over information.

The most influential approach to privacy is Altman's (1975, 1976) *boundary-regulation* model. Altman's analysis of privacy emphasizes the dialectic quality of social interaction (see Altman, Vinsel, & Brown, 1981), where forces serve both to bring people together and to push them apart. According to Altman's model, people try to achieve an optimal level of social contact or stimulation—a desired level of privacy. Privacy is not simply an urge to keep people out; if the level of stimulation is sufficiently low, then people will actively seek the company of others. The desire for social contact varies over time, present company, personality, particular settings, and other circumstances.

Privacy is an immediate, current, and ever-changing balancing of forces designed to increase or decrease access to the self. If, at a given point in time, there is too much social contact, a person may feel crowded or intruded upon. If there is too little social contact, the person will feel lonely or isolated. In order to increase or reduce the amount of social contact to achieve the desired level of privacy, Altman suggests people use various *privacy-regulation* or *boundary-regulation* mechanisms. These mechanisms include verbal, nonverbal, as well as spatial behaviors.

People can regulate the amount of social stimulation and contact they receive by exerting control over particular places in the environment—*territories*—where control is exerted by employing or deploying markers and signs, either explicit ("keep out!") or implicit (leaving personal effects on a train or library seat). In casual encounters, people can regulate the amount of stimulation they receive from others by varying the openness/closedness of their self-boundary (or in the case of groups, the group-boundary). This can be achieved through *interpersonal distancing* (sitting or standing close or far from other people), nonverbal behavior (more open or closed postures, more or less eye contact), and verbal behavior (talking more or less, or talking about more or less intimate topics). In group settings, desired levels of privacy can be achieved by selecting suitable *seating positions*, such as central positions for high levels of stimulation or peripheral positions for low levels. Finally, *crowding* can be seen to be a *consequence* of a failure to achieve an optimal level of privacy (rather than a privacy-regulation *mechanism*). When the density of people is such that a higher-than-desired level of social stimulation is received, people feel crowded. (Crowding is discussed here rather than under Environmental Stress because it constitutes a central component of any model or explanation of spatial behavior.)

In contrast to some analyses, which emphasize the closed nature of privacy (reducing social contact, cutting down communication), Altman sees privacy regulation as a bi-directional process, *increasing* access to the self when social stimulation is *low, reducing* access to the self when social stimulation is *high.*

Additional research on privacy can be found in: Altman, 1977; Archea, 1977; W. H. Foddy, 1984; Laufer & Wolfe, 1977; N. J. Marshall, 1974. For an update on Altman's position, see: Altman, Vinsel, & Brown, 1981; and D. A. Taylor & Altman, 1983.

Territories

In territories, boundaries are regulated by the marking and demarcation of a place to indicate ownership and occupancy. Altman (1975) classified territories into three types: primary, secondary, and public.

Primary territories—such as bedrooms, apartments, family homes—are owned and exclusively occupied on a regular and long-term basis by individuals and groups. There is a high degree of control over access to such territories, ensuring a high degree of privacy for personally important or intimate activities.

Secondary territories are places used by groups on an intermittent basis, such as local pubs, clubs, and bars, meeting rooms, work premises, communal areas of student dormitories, and apartment buildings. The group members do not own such places on a legal basis, but they still claim proprietary rights and restrict access to and use of such places. For example, residents of an apartment building may confront nonresidents (intruders) in communal areas of the building; regular patrons of a bar may discourage use of it by outsiders.

Public territories—such as restaurant tables, park benches, or library seats—are not owned by the occupants, and are used only for a short time. There is usually little control over access to such places, and there is little privacy.

For a territorial claim to be successful, other people must recognize and respect the proprietary rights of the occupant (McAndrew, Ryckman, Horr, & Solomon, 1978). In public territories, people use territorial "markers" to reserve their places. These markers are often artifactual and symbolic, but sufficiently personalized that anyone who comes across a folded scarf on a chair seat or a fountain pen lying on an open book can understand the message (F. D. Becker, 1973; D. R. Shaffer & Sadowski, 1975). However, if, for some reason, another person does invade or intrude upon a "marked" space, there is not much evidence that people are willing to defend the territory or confront the invader (F. D. Becker, 1973).

Haber (1980) found that people whose seat was occupied in their absence were more likely to challenge the invader if the seat was centrally rather than peripherally located in a classroom (see also D. R. Shaffer & Sadowski's similar findings for areas of "high interaction potential"). Those who defended their seat stared more at the invader. In subsequent sessions, the invadees turned up earlier than usual to occupy or reoccupy their seats, perhaps to preempt further invasions. The agonistic nature of staring was investigated by D. E. Campbell and Lancioni (1979) who found that invasion of a church pew was more successful if the invader stared at the occupant of the pew. Ruback (1987) expected that people would feel more at ease alone in a library aisle than in the presence of another person, so that they would leave the aisle sooner when another person turned up than when left alone. In fact, the opposite was found. However, it is possible that the presence of a newly-arrived person was distracting and interfered with task completion (e.g., searching for a library reference).

Edney and Jordan-Edney (1974) investigated *group territories* on public beaches and discovered that the larger the group, the less space per person was claimed. Male groups claimed more territory than female or mixed-sex groups (see H. W. Smith, 1981, for a cross-cultural replication). In addition, the longer the group stayed, the more space was claimed. Edney and Grundmann (1979) replicated these findings and found that groups of friends claimed less space than groups of strangers. However, only groups of 2 to 4 persons were observed.

In secondary territories, proprietary rights are more variable and uncertain, since they are located somewhere between the free and common access of public spaces and the exclusive and singular ownership of primary territories. Consequently, there are more likely to be conflicts over the use of secondary territories. O. Newman (1972) analyzed crimes in public-housing projects and found that crimes against the person often occurred in secondary territories such as hallways, stairwells, and elevators. Residents considered these areas too difficult to defend and came to treat the areas as public territories. Newman suggested that such areas could become *defensible spaces* by making appropriate architectural alterations; allowing easier surveillance by residents of the high-risk areas, and building smaller residential units so that there would be a small number of users who would be able to recognize one another and spot intruders (see Bynum & Purri, 1984).

B. B. Brown and Altman (1983) discovered that compared with nonburglarized residences, burglarized residences had fewer defensive barriers (such as gates and fences) and displayed fewer symbolic markers of territory (such as address plates or hedges). Territorial marking and defense may not only deter intruders but may have a beneficial psychological effect on the residents. A. H. Patterson (1978), for example, found that elderly residents who displayed territoriality (defensive barriers and symbolic markers) felt less fear of crime. This was confirmed by Pollack and Patterson (1980) for elderly but not for nonelderly people. Normoyle and Lavrakas (1984) found that fear of crime in the elderly was associated with lack of perceived control over territory and also a general lack of perceived control over life events. It may be that those with a high degree of perceived control take appropriate measures to defend their territory and so feel safer against intruders. R. B. Taylor, Gottfredson, and Brower (1980) predicted that territorial cognitions would be related to the social climate of urban neighborhoods. They found that the more congenial and stable the neighborhood was perceived to be, the greater the perceived control, the easier it was to distinguish between insiders and outsiders, and the greater the felt responsibility for the area.

Primary territories are not only the most central arenas of people's lives, they can also be said to constitute extensions of the self—especially homes (C. Cooper, 1974). Consequently, people might personalize their primary territories, particularly if they feel attached to them. Hansen and Altman (1976) discovered that university dropouts displayed fewer signs of personalization of their college rooms (e.g., posters and pictures) than nondropouts. Vinsel, Brown, Altman, and Foss (1980), however, found that dropouts tended to decorate their rooms more, but the decorations showed a low association with the present university setting.

Sebba and Churchman (1983) identified four different areas of family homes. There were *individual* areas such as studies and single bedrooms; *shared* areas were used by subgroupings within the family, for example, bedrooms shared by two or more children; *jurisdiction* areas were used by all the family but proprietary rights tended to reside in one member; and *public* areas were used by all the family (living rooms, lounges, hallways, bathrooms). In an outdoor environment, van den Berghe (1977) mapped territorial behaviors of families in an outdoor recreational (angling) club and found three levels of territoriality. Club members defended the entire area against nonmember intrusions. Families defended their plots against other families and other club members. And within families, individuals and guests defended their own eating and sleeping areas.

For reviews of territories, see: B. B. Brown, 1987; Edney, 1974. For additional studies of territories, see: Arenson, 1977; Bar-Tal & Kubzansky, 1987; Brower, Dockett, & Taylor, 1983; Calsyn, 1976; Conroy & Sundstrom, 1977; Edney, 1975; Edney & Uhlig, 1977; Guyot, Byrd, & Caudle, 1980; Haring, 1976; Jason, Reichler, & Rucker, 1981; E. O'Neal, Caldwell, & Gallup, 1977; Mercer & Benjamin, 1980; Lindskold & Wayner, 1981; Lindskold, Albert, Baer, & Moore, 1976; Rosenblatt & Budd, 1975; Shah & Dembla, 1985; R. B. Taylor & Brooks, 1980; R. B. Taylor & Ferguson, 1980; R. B. Taylor & Lanni, 1981; Truscott, Parmelee, & Werner, 1977.

Personal Space

The study of personal space and interpersonal distance has proved to be an enormously popular research topic. Hayduk (1978) defined personal space as the area individuals maintain around themselves into which others cannot intrude without arousing discomfort—a sort of "portable" territory that people carry round with them. The shape of personal space is not exactly circular; frontal distances are slightly larger than rear distances (Aono, 1981; Ashton & Shaw, 1980; S. J. Beck & Ollendick, 1976; Hayduk, 1981a, 1981b; Hayduk & Mainprize, 1980; Strube & Werner, 1982), although some studies fail to find such differences (Leventhal, Schanerman, & Matturro, 1978; Roger & Schaelerkamp, 1976; Whalen, Flowers, Fuller, & Jernigan, 1975).

Theories and models. A number of theories or models of interpersonal spacing have been developed. The earliest was Argyle and Dean's (1965) *equilibrium* theory. In any interaction, there are various "approach" forces that pull people together (such as need for affiliation or contact) and "avoidance" forces that push people apart (such as fear of social embarrassment or rejection). Argyle and Dean suggested that for a particular interaction there is a (perceived) appropriate level of intimacy between interactants. Greater eye contact, more open postures, warmer voice tone, more intimate topics of conversation, and closer interaction distances all contribute to increasing the intimacy of the encounter. If the level of intimacy is either lower or higher than the desired or appropriate level, then the interactants may modify one or more of these verbal and non-verbal behaviors to achieve the desired level of intimacy. Moreover, interactants can use *compensatory* means of regulating deviations from the desired level of intimacy. If it is felt that the interpersonal distance is too close, this increased intimacy can be compensated by either gazing less at the other, adopting a more closed posture, or changing to a less intimate topic. Similarly, if one person feels the other person is introducing too intimate topics into the discussion, this can be compensated by reducing eye contact, closing up the posture, or moving further away.

Support for this intimacy equilibrium model has been obtained by: Buchanan, Goldman, & Juhnke, 1977; Coutts & Schneider, 1976; Coutts & Ledden, 1977; Dietch & House, 1975; J. G. Ford, Cramer, & Owens, 1977; M. Goldberg & Wellens, 1979; P. Greenbaum & Rosenfeld, 1978; C. I. Greenberg & Firestone, 1977; C. F. Johnson & Dabbs, 1976; M. L. Patterson, 1977. However, a number of other studies do not support or offer qualified support (Carr & Dabbs, 1974; A. J. Chapman, 1975a; Kleinke, Staneski, & Pipp, 1975; Lockard, McVittie, & Isaac, 1977; Russo, 1975; F. W. Schneider & Hansvick, 1977). The clearest evidence for compensatory reactions is observed in the relation between interpersonal distance and eye contact.

Small variations in intimacy level may be insufficient to produce disequilibrium and hence compensatory reactions (Aiello & Thompson, 1980b; J. K. Burgoon & Jones, 1976; M. L. Patterson, 1976, 1977). Conversely, extremely large changes in intimacy level may also not produce compensation because equilibrium cannot be established by sufficient changes in compensatory behaviors (Aiello, 1977a, 1977b; Aiello & Thompson, 1980a). For example, decreasing eye contact — or even eliminating it — may not be sufficient to compensate for extremely close (touching) interaction distances (Aiello, 1977a, 1977b). In such cases, the encounter is likely to be terminated rather than continue in a state of disequilibrium.

In attempting to account for some of the contradictory findings, M. L. Patterson (1976) devised a theory that predicts *reciprocal* as well as compensatory changes. Patterson argued that changes in intimacy level produce changes in nonspecific *arousal* (Middlemist, Knowles, & Matter, 1976) that accentuates existing feelings. This arousal may be felt as a negative state (anxiety, embarrassment, discomfort) or as a positive state (attraction, comfort, warmth) depending on the setting, the other person, the relationship, and individual differences. If one person increases the intimacy of the encounter, and this produces negative feelings in the other person, the other person will compensate and try to reduce the arousal by lowering the intimacy level. But, if a positive feeling is produced, the other person will attempt to maintain or increase the intimacy level by a *reciprocal* reaction. For example, compensation is more likely in interaction with a stranger than with a friend. A friend is less likely to induce anxiety, and, assuming a "friendly" interaction ensues, increases in intimacy are likely to be reciprocated. Support for Patterson's model has come from Foot, Chapman, and Smith (1977), M. L. Patterson (1977, 1978), R. J. Smith and Knowles (1978, 1979), and Whitcher and Fisher (1979). In a related manner, Schiffenbauer and Schiavo (1976) and Storms and Thomas (1977) provide evidence that close physical distances intensify existing feelings. Recently, M. L. Patterson (1982) has altered his model to take account of the fact that the functional bases of interaction are variable. In addition to the intimacy function, included in his revised nonverbal exchange model are social-control and service-task functions.

Age. The size of personal space increases with age until the early twenties (Aiello & Thompson, 1980a; Dean, Willis, & LaRocco, 1976; G. H. Price & Dabbs, 1974; Smetana, Bridgeman, & Bridgeman, 1978), but this may simply be due to increasing body size.

Sex differences. Hayduk's (1983) review notes that 27 studies found significant sex differences in personal space, 54 obtained mixed evidence, and 29 studies found no sex differences. Some studies find that personal space is greatest between two males, followed by one male and one female, with the shortest space between two females (e.g., Brady & Walker, 1978). However, quite a few studies find one or the other of these differences to be reversed (e.g., Ahmed, 1979; Giesen & Hendrick, 1977; Giesen & McClaren, 1976; Willis, Carlson, & Reeves, 1979). Hayduk argued that it is unlikely that there are simple biological sex differences in personal space. Rather, the influence of sex differences is likely to be mediated by a host of other variables, such as status, plans, fears, urges, needs, objectives, and behavioral style. One view, for example, is that large male spaces and small female spaces simply serve to reinforce traditional sex roles (Frieze & Ramsey, 1976). Ickes and Barnes (1977) suggest that some of the apparent sex differences in spacing may be due to body size. Using "nearest-point-of-body" measures, they found no sex differences in spacing. However, when distance between "body-midline" was used, male-pair distances were larger than female-pair distances.

Individual differences. Although there are large individual differences in personal space, which are fairly stable over time (Eberts & Lepper, 1975), attempts to correlate them with personality variables have not produced any strong or consistent findings (e.g., Ickes & Barnes, 1977; K. E. Mathews, Canon, & Alexander, 1974). Personality *disorders* seem to provide stronger relationships (e.g., Loo, 1978). D. R. Gilmour and Walkey (1981) confirmed an earlier finding by Kinzel (1970) that violent prisoners have larger personal spaces than nonviolent prisoners. Booraem, Flowers, Bodner, and Satterfield (1977) found that personal space was largest for criminals convicted of personal crimes, smallest for criminals convicted of victimless crimes, and intermediate for those convicted of property crimes.

Cultural differences. E. T. Hall (1966) described Arabic, Mediterranean, and Latin American cultures as being "contact cultures," where touching and close interpersonal distances were common, whereas North American and North European cultures were "noncontact cultures," where touching and close interpersonal distances were not common. There have not been that many studies of true cross-cultural differences (as opposed to ethnic differences in the same culture). Noesjirwan (1977, 1978) reported that Indonesian students preferred closer distances than Australian students, and Shuter (1976) found that Costa Ricans preferred closer distances than Colombians or Panamanians. However, two studies of distances between male strangers seated on park benches obtained no differences between Kenya, Morocco, Spain, and the United States (Mazur, 1977; C. F. Keating & Keating, 1980). So, support for E. T. Hall's analysis is equivocal. In fact, Shuter (1976) found large differences in preferred spacing across different Latin American countries which are all supposed to be contact cultures. Reviewing subcultural differences, Aiello and Thompson (1980a) confirmed Hall's contact analysis for Hispanic vs. Anglo-Americans, but did not find support for blacks' having closer spacing (four studies finding larger spaces for blacks than whites, seven showing no differences, two finding blacks have smaller spaces than whites, and five showing conditional effects). Other studies include: J. L. Sanders, Hakky, & Brizzolara, 1985; N. M. Sussman, & Rosenfeld, 1982.

Situational factors. E. T. Hall's (1959, 1966) influential analysis of personal space suggested that interpersonal distance is heavily dependent on the particular setting, interaction, and relationship. *Intimate* distances (0–1.5 feet) are appropriate for intimate, private activities, such as lovemaking. *Personal* distances (1.5–4 feet) are appropriate for conversations between friends. *Social* distances (4–12) are appropriate for casual encounters between strangers. And, *public* distances (over 12 feet) are appropriate for a speaker addressing an audience.

Among other findings, people prefer more space when they are in an anxiety- or stress-provoking situation (Brady & Walker, 1978; G. T. Long, 1984; G. T. Long, Selby, & Calhoun, 1980; Ugwuegbu & Anusiem, 1982), in vertically restricted areas (Cochran, Hale, & Hissam, 1984; Cochran & Urbanczyk, 1982), or in the corner rather than in the center of a hallway (G. H. Price & Dabbs, 1974).

Acquaintance. According to Altman's privacy-regulation theory, personal boundaries should be larger with friends than with strangers. Although both male and female friends show smaller spaces than strangers, the evidence is not overwhelming (e.g., Ashton, Shaw, & Worsham, 1980; J. W. Burgess, 1983; Coutts & Schneider, 1976; J. G. Ford, Knight, & Cramer, 1977; E. Sundstrom, 1978b).

Reactions to close distances. Numerous studies have documented the aversive nature of close interpersonal distances or personal space "violations." People feel aroused or stressed after space violations (J. G. Ford, Knight, & Cramer, 1977; Kanaga & Flynn, 1981) and they may withdraw or avoid interaction with the intruder (Bleda & Bleda, 1978; B. Harris, Luginbuhl, & Fishbein, 1978; Konecni, Libuser, Morton, & Ebbesen, 1975; D. M. Pedersen & Sabin, 1982; Peery & Crane, 1980; Reid & Novak, 1975). R. J. Smith and Knowles (1978) found that a person who invaded another's personal space was perceived as unpleasant, rude, hostile, and aggressive. Although it might seem reasonable to expect that people would form negative impressions of an invader, there is evidence that close spacing can lead to *positive* feelings. Dooley (1978), Loo and Smetana (1978), R. J. Smith and Knowles (1978), and Stires (1980) found negative affective reactions, whereas Banziger and Simmons (1984), J. K. Burgoon (1978), J. K. Burgoon and Aho (1982), Kahn and McGaughey (1977), Kmiecik, Mausar, and Banziger (1979), Schiffenbauer and Schiavo (1976), Skolnick, Frasier, and Hadar (1977), and Storms and Thomas (1977) found both negative and positive reactions. It appears that if the invader is attractive or if the interaction turns out to be pleasant, then shortening the interpersonal distance may lead to liking, whereas if the invader is unattractive or the interaction is unpleasant, then a closer distance will lead to disliking.

Polit and LaFrance (1977) found that females withdrew more quickly than males when their personal space was invaded. However, Krail and Leventhal (1976) did not obtain such effects; using latency of compensatory reactions, they found that subjects reacted quickest to a same-sex invasion (see also Mahoney, 1974; M. L. Patterson & Mahoney, 1975). Noting from research on interpersonal attraction that males tend to prefer to sit face to face across from a friend, whereas females prefer to sit beside a friend, J. D. Fisher and Byrne (1975) found that males felt more discomfort when someone invaded their personal space from the front, whereas females felt more discomfort when invaded from the side. They also found that males erected barriers of books and jackets in front of them on a library table whereas females erected barriers to the side of them.

It is important to distinguish between invasions that are unintentional or unavoidable (such as in a crowded elevator) and those that are deliberate. Murphy-Berman and Berman (1978) found that male invaders were evaluated more negatively and female invaders more positively, the more the invasion appeared intentional and personally directed. Skolnick, Frasier, and Hadar (1977) studied invasions on a Los Angeles beach and found that females evaluated a male invader positively (and even welcomed the invasion). Cross-sex invasions of the deliberate kind were more likely to be seen as sexual overtures, whereas same-sex invasions were more likely to be attributed to loneliness (see also Jason, Reichler, & Rucker, 1981).

Ernest and Cooper (1974) found that compliance with a request from a person in need was greater with close distances. R. A. Baron (1978b), however, found that agreeing to help an invader was inhibited when the invader's apparent need was low, but was facilitated when the invader's need was great (see also R. A. Baron & Bell, 1976b; R. J. Smith & Knowles, 1979).

For other studies of space violations, see: Ahmed, 1980; E. Baker & Shaw, 1980; Caplan & Goldman, 1981; DeBeer-Keston, Mellon, & Solomon, 1986; Edney, Walker, & Jordan, 1976; Giesen & Hendrick, 1974; Mishara, Brawley, Cheevers, Kitover, Knowles, Rautiala, & Surjian, 1974; Sobel & Lillith, 1975; Soper & Karasik, 1977; E. Sundstrom & Sundstrom, 1977; N. M. Sussman & Rosenfeld, 1978.

Group space.   Knowles, Kreuser, Haas, Hyde, and Schuchart (1976) observed that pedestrians walked further away from a group than from an individual, and that an interacting-group's space increases with group size. Interestingly, Knowles and Bassett (1976) found that passers-by approached an aggregation of experimental confederates more closely if it was engaged in crowd (random) activity than in group (organized) activity, yet Lindskold, Albert, Baer, and Moore (1976) found that pedestrians took more divergent paths around a group, the more a group was interacting (a passive audience produced the least diversion). M. L. Patterson and Schaeffer (1977) found that group interaction distances were closest for all-female groups, furthest for all-male groups, with mixed-sex groups intermediate. D. M. Pedersen (1977) reported that personal space was smaller, toward groups not containing men, for groups of females coming from behind, and for groups facing away. Group size did not produce a simple effect but interacted with sex and orientation of the group. D. M. Pedersen (1978) found that females maintained greater distances than males towards group.

For reviews of personal space, see: Aiello & Thompson, 1980b; Altman & Vinsel, 1977; Codol, 1978a, 1978b; Hayduk, 1978, 1983; Knowles, 1980; Mishra, 1983; D. M. Pedersen & Shears, 1973; E. Sundstrom & Altman, 1976.

Additional research on personal, group space, and interpersonal distance can be found in: L. L. Adler & Iverson, 1974, 1975; Balgooyen, 1984; Barrios & Giesen, 1977; Beach & Sokoloff, 1974; Bouska & Beatty, 1978; C. E. Brown, 1981; Buchanan, Juhnke, & Goldman, 1976; J. W. Burgess, 1983; Ciolek, 1982, 1983; Ciolek & Furnham, 1980; Dean, Willis, & Hewitt, 1975; Domachowski, 1980; Duke, 1977; J. G. Ford & Hoebeke, 1980; J. G. Ford & Maloney, 1982; Gifford, 1982b, 1983; Grossnickle, Lao, Martoccia, Range, & Walters, 1975; Guardo, 1976; Hamid, 1974; Hartnett, Bailey, & Hartley, 1974; Hayduk & Mainprize, 1980; M. Hendricks & Bootzin, 1976; R. D. Hill, Blackham, & Crane, 1982; Jorgenson, 1975; K. J. Kaplan, 1977; K. J. Kaplan, Firestone, Klein, & Sodikoff, 1983; Kleinke, Staneski, & Pipp, 1975; Kline & Bell, 1983; Knowles & Brickner, 1981; Knowles & Johnsen,

1974; Kunzendorf & Denney, 1982; Latta, 1978; Leventhal, Matturro, & Schanerman, 1978; Lomranz, 1976; Louvet, Mogenet, Vienat, & Lemaine, 1977–1978; Love & Aiello, 1980; Mandal & Maitra, 1985; Matson, 1978; McGrew & McGrew, 1975; McKenzie & Strongman, 1981; E. C. O'Neal, Brunault, Marquis, & Carifio, 1979; E. C. O'Neal, Brunault, Carifio, Troutwine, & Epstein, 1980; A. H. Patterson & Boles, 1974; D. M. Pedersen & Shears, 1974; Petri, Huggins, Mills, & Barry, 1974; W. G. Powers & Guess, 1976; Rivano-Fischer, 1984; Roger, 1976; Roger & Reid, 1978; P. Rogers, Rearden, & Hillner, 1981; N. Rumsey, Bull, & Gahagan, 1982; Ryen & Kahn, 1975; Sarafino & Helmuth, 1981; S. E. Scherer, 1974; Schiavo, Schiffenbauer, & Roberts, 1977; J. A. Scott, 1974; Seta & Schkade, 1976; Skotko & Langmeyer, 1977; Sykes, Larntz, & Fox, 1976; Tennis & Dabbs, 1975, 1976; D. E. Thompson, Aiello & Epstein, 1979; Veno, 1976; J. W. Walker & Borden, 1976; Wellens & Goldberg, 1978; M. J. White, 1975; Wittig & Skolnick, 1978; Worthington, 1974.

Spatial Arrangements

Seating preferences.   Early research by Sommer (1959, 1962, 1969) concluded that people prefer particular seating arrangements for different types of interpersonal activities. For casual conversations, people prefer to sit at right angles (at 90 degrees to each other) or face to face. In cooperating situations, people prefer to sit side by side, whereas in competing situations, they prefer a face to face arrangement. In coacting situations, seating arrangements that reduce intimacy are preferred such as diagonally opposite corners of a table. Questionnaire responses revealed that people select particular seating arrangements in order to optimize task efficiency. In a field study of social settings, Leventhal, Lipshultz, and Chiodo (1978) observed that opposite-sex pairs selected a side-by-side arrangement, whereas same-sex pairs, especially males, adopted a face-to-face (opposite) arrangement. In nonsocial settings, individuals selected the side by side arrangements regardless of sex. This study did not, however, provide information as to the types of activity engaged in. Ryen and Kahn (1975) examined the *after-effects* of different intergroup orientations on seating preferences. After intergroup cooperation, subjects sat near both in-group and out-group members with a slight bias in favor of own group. After intergroup competition (but without win-lose feedback), group members sat near in-group members and far from out-group members. After intergroup competition with win-lose feedback, members of the winning group tried to sit closer to members of the losing group, but the losing group members tried to sit far from the winning group. After working alone or in coacting groups, members chose random seating arrangements.

Some of these findings on seating preferences may be explained in terms of privacy. Koneya (1977) discussed seating arrangements from the point of view of *privacy regulation.* Particular seat locations in a group produce greater or lesser verbal participation rates and visual accessibility among group members, resulting in more or less social stimulation and contact. Group members' seating choices may therefore indicate their desired level of privacy.

Seating arrangements and interaction. An important regulator of social interaction is eye contact. Osmond (1957) suggested that certain sorts of seating arrangements encourage conversation and interaction by increasing the possibility of eye-contact (*sociopetal spaces*), whereas other arrangements discourage conversation (*sociofugal spaces*). For example, in waiting areas, rows of seats which face away from each other are sociofugal, whereas rows of seats which face each other would be sociopetal (as long as the distance between the rows is not so great as to make conversation difficult). Holahan (1974) investigated the effects of sociofugal, sociopetal, mixed sociofugal and sociopetal, and freely-chosen seating arrangements on social interaction in psychiatric hospitals. Sociopetal and mixed seating facilitated social interaction, whereas sociofugal and free seating inhibited it. Types of conversation were also affected by seating arrangements.

J. Greenberg (1976) reviewed research on seating position and group interaction and concluded that (a) centrally-located people are able to maintain eye contact with the most group members, thereby increasing their ability to interact with the group and their likelihood of emerging as group leader, (b) tasks requiring interpersonal communication are associated with close seating arrangements, and (c) physical closeness enhances friendship formation and is a reliable sociometric index of friendship choices in groups. In an observational study of naturally occurring triads (Silverstein & Stang, 1976), it was found that members with the greatest visual centrality spoke most often. However, Michelini, Passalacqua, and Cusimano (1976), investigating the roles of central seating position and visual access in group participation, found that high *visibility* leads to *receiving* communications, whereas *centrality* is associated with *initiating* communications. Caproni, Levine, O'Neal, McDonald, and Garwood (1977) varied the position of an instructor in graduate seminars and observed that students seated in high eye-contact areas participated more than those in low eye-contact areas. C. S. Green (1975) conducted a longitudinal observational study of committee meetings at a mental hospital and found that increased member participation in the meetings was associated with sitting closer to the chairperson, but not with a narrower angle between chairperson's line of sight and member's seating position.

Seating arrangements and leadership. It has often been observed that the leader of a group takes the most prominent position, such as at the head of a table, and that people who take prominent positions are perceived as leaders (Strodtbeck & Hook, 1961). Lecuyer (1976b) found that people assigned to be leaders of groups took up their position at the head of a rectangular table. Leaders in rectangular arrangements participated more in group discussion than ordinary members, but this did not occur for leaders in a circular arrangement (where there is no dominant position). In the rectangular arrangement, leaders spent more time on task activities, whereas in the circular arrangement, leaders spent more time on socioemotional activities. Cummings, Huber and Arendt (1974) had 3-, 4-, or 5- person groups seated in either leader-centered (where one seating position stood out from the group) or neutral arrangements. The neutral arrangement resulted in better performance on complex tasks and greater consensus. Roger and Reid (1978, 1982) investigated the seating arrangements that evolve during role differentiation processes in small (4-person) groups by measuring the spacing between chairs after a group problem-solving session. It was found that ordinary group members sat closer to those judged to be leaders than to those judged to be nonleaders (who had contributed least to the group); these nonleaders were relatively isolated from the group.

Haber (1982) observed that members of dominant social groups (in this case Anglo-Saxon protestants) were more likely to occupy the spatial center of college classroom groupings than marginals (defined in terms of religion, ethnicity, and race), and that the greater a person's marginality, the higher the likelihood that a peripheral position would be taken up.

Additional research on spatial arrangements can be found in: Ciolek, 1978; Ciolek & Kendon, 1980; Collett & Marsh, 1980; L. R. Greene, 1976; Hiers & Heckel, 1977; Ingham, 1974; Kendon, 1976; Koneya, 1978; Lecuyer, 1976b; D. W. Levine, O'Neal, Garwood, & McDonald, 1980; M. L. Patterson, Roth, & Schenk, 1979; M. L. Patterson, Kelly, Kondracki, & Wulf, 1979; Rime, 1974; Rime & Leyens, 1974; J. C. Russell, Firestone, & Baron, 1980; G. M. Stephenson & Kniveton, 1978; Strodtbeck & Lipinski, 1985.

Crowding

Early studies of animal behavior (e.g., Calhoun, 1962) suggested that overcrowding might lead to a variety of physical, psychological, and social pathological conditions in humans. However, Freedman claimed there was little reliable support for the view that lack of space is harmful either to humans (J. L. Freedman, 1975) or to animals (J. L. Freedman, 1979). (Freedman's analyses have been questioned by R. M. Baron and Needel, 1980, but reaffirmed by J. L. Freedman, 1980). Studies of human populations have found little evidence of a relation between household density and social pathology when important confounding factors, such as socioeconomic status, ethnicity, and so on, were controlled for (J. L. Freedman, Heshka, & Levy, 1975; Galle & Gove, 1979; Gove, Hughes, & Galle, 1979; Kirmeyer, 1978). Rohe (1982) reported significant negative effects of household density on attitudinal and behavioral measures of well-being (but not on measures of health), particularly for residents in close social contact and for people with a history of high-density living.

Research on prison populations (Cox, Paulus, & McCain, 1984; McCain, Cox, & Paulus, 1976; Paulus, Cox, McCain, & Chandler, 1975; Paulus, McCain, & Cox,

1978) does indicate a link between density (total number of inmates, and number of inmates per cell) and pathology (higher suicide and death rates, greater illness complaints, and psychiatric conditions). Of course, prisons are not designed for congenial lifestyles, and, unlike households, apartments, or student dormitories, crowding in prisons is usually long term, intense, and inescapable.

High population density (persons per unit of space) does not invariably lead to crowding—defined as an unpleasant or stressful feeling or experience. Early laboratory studies of density which failed to find crowding effects were criticized by Paulus, Annis, Seta, Schkade, and Matthews (1976) for employing either insensitive test tasks or density levels which were insufficient to create stressful situation. However, people can adapt to stressful situations as long as they are not too intense, prolonged, unpredictable, or uncontrollable (S. Cohen, 1978). If people are expecting a situation to be crowded, they can marshal their adaptive resources to cope with the anticipated crowding (Ditton, Fedler, & Graefe, 1983; C. I. Greenberg & Baum, 1979; K. Klein & Harris, 1979; Shelby, Heberlein, Vaske, & Alfano, 1983). In some cases, high density may enhance pleasant experiences (J. L. Freedman, 1975)—such as might occur at parties, discos, concerts, or football matches (assuming your team isn't being taken to the cleaners).

Definitions have been a problem in research on crowding and density. Stokols (1972) pointed out the difference between *density* (a physical quantity) and *crowding* (a negative psychological state). High density may be a necessary but not a sufficient condition for crowding to occur, that is, feeling crowded depends on individual, social, and situational factors in addition to conditions of high density.

Density itself is not a particularly straightforward or unidimensional concept. Amos Rapoport (1975) suggests that *functional* density rather than *physical* density is the important factor; that is, the number of people present who directly affect a person's feelings or behavior rather than all the people present. Loo (1973) and Stokols (1976) argued that *social* density (variations in the number of people in a given space) is conceptually different from *spatial* density (variations in the amount of space available to a given number of people). The effects of high density could therefore be due to the number of people present (social density), the lack of space available (spatial density), or both. On the one hand, F. J. Smith and Lawrence (1978) varied spatial restrictions on single males (alone in a chamber) and found that the greater the spatial restriction, the greater the feelings of being crowded. On the other hand, Paulus, Cox, McCain, and Chandler (1975) concluded that crowding in prisons was mainly due to social rather than spatial density. In a lab setting, Nogami (1976) found that perceptions of crowding were mainly due to group size, and to a lesser extent room size, but not density (space-per-person). However, Paulus, Annis, Seta, Schkade, and Matthews (1976) found that group size, room size, and *interpersonal distance* all had significant effects on task performance.

Knowles (1978b, 1983) proposed a measure of density based on the *proximity of others*, specifically, the sum of the reciprocals of the distances from any one individual to each of the other individuals in the group. According to this, people close to an individual should have a much greater influence on crowding than people further away, and by extension, people at the periphery of a group or crowd should feel less crowded than people in the center. Defined in this way density effects begin to look like personal space effects. In fact, McClelland and Auslander (1978) found that people's perceptions of crowdedness across a range of different settings correlated -0.40 with interpersonal spacings after social and spatial density had been controlled for. A number of authors (J. D. Fisher, 1974; C. I. Greenberg & Firestone, 1977; Walden & Forsyth, 1981; Worchel & Teddlie, 1976; Worchel & Yohai, 1979) have suggested that interpersonal distance is the main determinant of perceptions of crowding, and it has been found that people with large personal spaces are more affected by crowded conditions than those with smaller personal spaces (Aiello, DeRisi, Epstein, & Karlin, 1977; Dooley, 1978).

A number of theories have been developed to account for when and why high density will lead to feelings of crowding. Early theoretical accounts of crowding separated into those that emphasized "output" processes (behavioral constraint/ social interference) and "input" processes (information or cognitive overload).

Behavioral constraint.   This theory suggests that people will feel crowded when density results in interference, restriction, or inhibition of ongoing activities (Schopler & Stockdale, 1977) or future behavioral options (Proshansky, Ittelson, & Rivlin, 1976). Thus, Stokols, Rall, Pinner, and Schopler (1973) found that people felt more crowded in competitive than in cooperative groups; in competitive groups, there is more interference and inhibition than in cooperative groups. Sundstrom (1975) suggested that high density can disrupt interpersonal or group interactions and this disruption produces crowding stress. However, if density does not disrupt interactions then crowding will not occur. J. F. Heller, Groff, and Solomon (1977) found that high density led to interference in group performance only when a high degree of physical interaction between group members was required in group activities. When physical interaction was minimal, high density did not lead to interference and crowding.

Information overload.   With increasing levels of environmental stimulation, greater demands are made on a person's attentional capacity. This can have adverse effects on current tasks and activities. Prolonged exposure to high information loads can result in a shrinkage in attentional capacity that continues to have adverse effects long after the period of stimulation has ended (S. Cohen, 1978). Under conditions of high social or spatial density, the information or cognitive load may be sufficiently high to produce feelings of crowding and adverse behavioral effects.

Thus, Saegert (1973) reported that customers in a department store recalled fewer details of the store under high-density than under low-density conditions. Likewise, Mackintosh, West, and Saegert (1975) found reduced recall of environmental information in high-density conditions, particularly when subjects had to scan the surroundings and interact in the setting. Valins and Baum (1973) found that students rated corridor-style dormitories as more crowded than suite-style dormitories, and suggested that the former are less effective at screening out unwanted social contact and stimulation. Baum and Greenberg (1975) discovered that subjects *anticipating* a crowded experience took steps to reduce the impact of crowding before its onset — such as choosing more socially isolated seats, and avoiding eye contact with others present (similar results were obtained by Baum and Koman, 1976). D. McCarthy and Saegert (1978) found that residents of high-rise apartments came into contact with more people in communal areas of the building than did residents of low-rise apartments, with the consequence that the high-rise residents felt greater social overload, unwanted social contact, and negative feelings associated with crowding.

Altman's *boundary-regulation* model of privacy can be seen to be a variant of the information-overload theory. When current levels of social contact or stimulation exceed the desired level of stimulation, people feel stressed and crowded.

Arousal-Attribution. This theory suggests that high density produces increased levels of physiological and psychological arousal (G. W. Evans, 1978), such as high blood pressure and heart rate (D'Atri, 1975; G. W. Evans, 1979; Paulus, McCain, & Cox, 1978) and increased skin conductance (Aiello, Epstein, & Karlin, 1975). This increased arousal may be due to close interpersonal distances (G. W. Evans, 1978) or fear of being physically harmed in some way (Paulus, 1980).

Whether such arousal is experienced as a feeling of being crowded depends on whether the cause of the arousal is attributed to density or not. If the arousal is attributed to density, then people will feel crowded; if it is attributed to non-density factors, then people will not feel crowded.

Worchel and Teddlie (1976) manipulated spatial density (room size), interaction distance (close or far), and presence/absence of visual distractors (pictures hanging on the wall). Feelings of crowding were greatest with high density, close interpersonal distances, and no visual distractors. However, feelings of crowding were significantly reduced when picture distractors were present. Worchel and Teddlie argued that the arousal caused by close interpersonal distances was attributed solely to room density when no distractors were present, but when picture distractors were present, attention was diverted away from room density, felt arousal was attributed in part to the picture distractors, and so feelings of crowding were reduced. Similar findings were obtained by Aiello, Thompson, and Brodzinsky (1983) and Worchel and Yohai (1979). Anything that highlights density conditions should increase feelings of crowding (cf. Paulus & Matthews, 1980b, and the physical interaction effects found by J. F. Heller, Groff, & Solomon, 1977, and the crowd-scanning effect found by Mackintosh, West, & Saegert, 1975).

M. L. Patterson's (1976) model of interpersonal distance (see section on Personal Space) is of the arousal-attribution type; arousal produced by the intimacy of close interpersonal distances is experienced as pleasant or unpleasant depending on the existing situation and the attributions made for the arousal (see also Schaeffer and Patterson, 1980). Similarly, J. L. Freedman's (1975) *density-intensity* model of crowding suggests that density intensifies existing pleasant or unpleasant feelings. However, Freedman's model only applies to social behaviors, whereas arousal-attribution models apply to any behavior (see J. L. Freedman & Perlick, 1979; J. L. Freedman, Birsky, & Cavoukian, 1980).

Perceived control. For reviews of perceived control and crowding, see R. M. Baron and Rodin (1978), and Baum and Valins (1979). Currently, the most popular conceptualization of the link between density and crowding is in terms of perceived or personal control; when density results in a reduction of perceived control, people experience feelings of crowding. Indeed, D. E. Schmidt and Keating (1979) claimed that all the major theories of crowding can be interpreted in terms of personal control. For example, when high density interferes with ongoing activities (behavioral constraint), resultant feelings of crowding may be due to perceived loss of control rather than to the interference or restriction per se. And, as noted earlier under Environmental Stress, S. Cohen (1978) argued that the cognitive fatigue induced by information overload is particularly acute for unpredictable and uncontrollable stressors. Reviewing the literature on field studies of crowding, Y. M. Epstein (1981) concluded that the adverse effects of high density are greatest when level of control and social cooperation are lowest. Crowding appears to be most severe in prisons, intermediate in dormitories, and least in family residences, a progression in keeping with increasing degrees of personal control.

In an early study by Sherrod (1974), subjects worked in groups of eight in either small (high density) or large (low density) rooms. After an hour, subjects were moved to a large reception area and were given a number of tests. Those subjects who had previously worked under high-density conditions showed less tolerance for frustration than those who had worked under low-density conditions. However, the adverse after-effects of high density were ameliorated for a third group of subjects (perceived control) who had worked in the small room but who had the option of leaving to work in a larger room, though no one had actually used this option (hence perceived rather than actual control). Rodin, Solomon, and Metcalf (1978) found that subjects who stood next to the control panel in an elevator felt less crowded and felt the elevator was larger than subjects standing far from the control panel. In a second study, subjects assigned the role of initiating or terminating group activities felt less crowded than those without this behavioral option.

There are other types of control apart from *behavioral* control (Averill, 1973). Paralleling the above findings on behavioral control, there have been a number of studies on the beneficial effects of *informational* control on crowding stress. Providing people with information about the causes, consequences, reactions, and feelings associated with a stressful experience has been found to reduce unpleasant reactions (as in surgical procedures; see J. E. Johnson, 1986). The more information a person has about the causes and consequences of dense situations, the less should be crowding-stress reactions. Thus, Langer and Saegert (1977) found that people felt less uncomfortable and crowded when they were told before entering a crowded supermarket about the likely feelings they would experience. Baum, Fisher, and Solomon (1981) obtained similar results for students about to enter a crowded college bookstore (see also J. D. Fisher & Baum, 1980). Wener and Kaminoff (1983) documented fewer reports of crowding by prison visitors when information was provided about where telephones, toilets, drinking water, and other amenities could be found.

Long-term exposure to high density conditions can lead to *learned helplessness* particularly when crowding stress is unpredictable and uncontrollable. Rodin (1976) found that children from crowded homes showed less task persistence following a standard learned helplessness pretreatment (insoluble task) than children from uncrowded homes. Baum, Aiello, and Calesnick (1978) found that residents of long-corridor dormitories experienced more frequent unwanted contact with unfamiliar neighbors and felt more crowding than did residents of short-corridor dormitories. Initially, the long-corridor residents showed evidence of attempting to reassert control, but over a longer period, they became withdrawn and exhibited symptoms of loss of control and learned helplessness.

In addition to the findings mentioned above, there have been many other studies investigating density and crowding.

Sex differences.   As with studies of personal space, the findings on sex difference in crowding are not clear-cut. J. E. Marshall and Heslin (1975) found that females but not males in mixed-sex groups preferred large to small groups and crowded to uncrowded conditions, but for same-sex groups these findings for females were reversed. Paulus, Annis, Seta, Schkade, and Matthews (1976) found negative effects of group size and interpersonal distance on task performance for both males and females, but effects of room size were only found for males. Schettino and Borden (1976) found that density produced aggressiveness in males but nervousness in females. Y. M. Epstein and Karlin (1975) found that crowding in male groups led to a competitive, fragmented group orientation, whereas females formed cohesive, cooperative groups. Leventhal and Levitt (1979) found that the addition of posters to a room under high-density conditions led to greater feelings of crowding in males but not in females, suggesting sex differences in reactions to information overload.

Dabbs (1977) sounded a warning that studies of sex differences in crowding using same-sex groups do not separate effects due to sex of subject from those due to sex of other people present. And, Karlin, McFarland, Aiello, and Epstein (1976) argued that those findings indicating that males respond to spatial restrictions negatively while females react positively are not due to simple biological sex differences, but are due to differences in normative expectations (see the section on *Personal Space* for a similar argument about traditional sex-role expectations).

Individual differences.   As mentioned earlier a number of studies (Aiello, DeRisi, Epstein, & Karlin, 1977; Dooley, 1978) have found that people (adults) with large personal spaces feel more crowded than people with small personal spaces (in children, the findings are more equivocal; Loo, 1979; Loo & Kennelly, 1979; Loo & Smetana, 1978). Bharucha-Reid and Kiyak (1979) reported that people with an internal locus of control felt more stressed in uncontrollable crowded situations than people with an external locus of control. Similarly, Burger, Oakman, and Bullard (1983) found that people scoring high on desire for control reported greater discomfort and perceived the room as more crowded than did low scorers.

Cultural differences.   Iwata (1974a) concluded that Japanese were more sensitive to crowding and density than Caucasians, and that Japanese (but not Caucasian) males were more sensitive than females. Six, Martin, and Pecher (1983) found that Germans were more comfortable than North Americans with large group sizes. D. E. Schmidt (1983) found that personal control had similar effects in the mediation of density and crowding in the United States and Singapore.

Arousal, discomfort, and stress.   The bulk of research on crowding suggests that high density produces unpleasant or stressful experiences (Aiello, Epstein, & Karlin, 1975; Aiello, Thompson, & Brodzinsky, 1983; R. M. Baron, Mandel, Adams, & Griffen, 1976; D'Atri, 1975; Y. M. Epstein & Karlin, 1975; Y. M. Epstein, Woolfolk, & Lehrer, 1981; G. W. Evans, 1979; Nicosia, Hyman, Karlin, Epstein, & Aiello, 1979; Paulus & McCain, 1983; Paulus, McCain, & Cox, 1978; Walden & Forsyth, 1981). As previously noted, these adverse effects of density can be ameliorated if (a) density does not disrupt or interfere with ongoing or future activities, (b) density cues do not contribute to information overload, or (c) density does not lead to a reduction in personal control. And, if the existing situation, interaction, or experience is perceived to be pleasant, increased density can increase pleasant feelings (J. L. Freedman, 1975).

Task performance.   Most research on crowding suggests adverse effects of density on task performance either as a result of short-term acute crowding, or long-term chronic crowding, with the same qualifications as those noted in the previous subsection (L. P. Clark & Arenson, 1980; Glassman, Burkhart, Grant, & Vallery, 1978; Karlin, Rosen, & Epstein, 1979; Kuykendall & Keating, 1984; H. Lange, Mueller, & Donnerstein, 1979; Paulus, Annis, Seta, Schkade, and Matthews, 1976). Some studies find adverse effects for *complex* but not for simple tasks (G. W. Evans, 1979; Nagar & Pandey, 1987) suggesting information-overload effects — performance deficits only appear when attentional capacity is exceeded (S. Cohen, 1978). By similar reasoning, it would be expected that crowding and density would impair performance least at the end of a task session, when familiarity with the task has been acquired through practice, and attentional demands are least. This was confirmed by Paulus and Matthews (1980a), but Peay and Peay (1983) found *more* adverse effects at the end of an experimental session. Emiley (1975) and Leventhal and Levitt (1979) reported no effects of density on task performance.

Intragroup relations. A number of studies have shown that residential density produces characteristic intragroup relations and group formations—particularly coalitions and social isolates. Baum, Shapiro, Murray and Wideman (1979) found that in overcrowded dormitories, 3-person ("tripled") roommate groups produced 2-person coalitions and an isolate—who felt crowded and generally disconsolate. D. M. Reddy, Baum, Fleming, and Aiello (1981) also found in 3- and 4-person roommate groups that isolated compared with nonisolated members felt: more crowded, greater dissatisfaction with living arrangements, a lack of control, and difficulties in regulating social interactions. Gormley and Aiello (1982) found that "tripled" roommates who experienced negative interpersonal relationships exhibited even more crowding stress than "twinned" roommates who had negative personal relationships.

For reviews of density and crowding, see: R. M. Baron, 1979; Baum & Epstein, 1978; Dean, Pugh, & Gunderson, 1978; Y. M. Epstein, 1981; Lawrence, 1974; Paulus, 1980; E. Sundstrom, 1978a.

Additional studies of density and crowding include: Aiello, Nicosia, & Thompson, 1979; Baum, Harpin, & Valins, 1975; Baum, Calesnick, Davis, & Gatchel, 1982; J. C. Baxter & Rozelle, 1975; Bossley, 1976; Burch & Walker, 1978; Calsyn & Becker, 1976; J. L. Cohen, Sladen, & Bennett, 1975; Ditton, Fedler, & Graefe, 1983; Duckitt, 1983; D. J. Edwards, 1980a, 1980b; Eoyang, 1974; Fagot, 1977; J. D. Fisher, 1974; Gochman & Keating, 1980; Gramann, 1982; Hammitt, 1983; Iwata, 1974b, 1980; Jorgenson & Dukes, 1976; J. P. Keating & Snowball, 1977; Leventhal & Matturro, 1980; Levitt & Leventhal, 1978; Li, 1984; Loo & Smetana, 1978; R. W. Matthews, Paulus, & Baron, 1979; McCain, Cox, Paulus, Luke, & Abadzi, 1985; R. McCallum, Rusbult, Hong, Walden, & Schopler, 1979; McClelland, 1976; S. Miller & Nardini, 1977; S. Miller, Rossbach, & Munson, 1981; Montano & Adamopoulos, 1984; Morasch, Groner, & Keating, 1979; Prerost, 1981, 1982; Reichner, 1979; R. Robinson, 1978; Sadalla, Burroughs, & Staplin, 1978; M. J. Smith, Reinheimer, & Gabbard-Alley, 1981; R. B. Taylor, 1981; Thalhofer, 1980; B. Webb, Worchel, Riechers, & Wayne, 1986; Wolfe, 1975; Zeedyk-Ryan & Smith, 1983; Zuckerman, Schmitz, & Yosha, 1977.

THE BUILT ENVIRONMENT

In addition to ambient factors and human spatial factors, architectural aspects of the environment can affect social behavior in a number of ways, for example, by making places pleasant or unpleasant for interaction, by helping or hindering behavior, or by increasing or decreasing privacy.

Urban Overload

Milgram (1970) suggested that the experience of living in cities is one of sensory or information overload, including noise, bright lights, and crowds of people. To cope with this, city dwellers filter out a lot of environmental stimulation, and thereby become less attentive to and less inclined to interact with other people (the vast majority of whom are likely to be total strangers, unlike a rural village, where everyone knows everyone else; McCauley & Taylor, 1976).

In support of this *urban incivility* effect, it has been found that the larger the town or city, the lower the levels of eye contact between strangers (Amato, 1980; J. Newman & McCauley, 1977), the lower the likelihood of accepting a handshake (Milgram, 1977), or helping another person (Amato, 1983b; Korte & Kerr, 1975; Milgram, 1970; Rushton, 1978). However, F. W. Schneider and Mockus (1974) did not find any urban-rural differences in helpfulness, and Korte, Ypma, and Toppen (1975) failed to find differences in helping between Dutch cities and towns, but observed differences as a function of environmental input level (sound level, traffic count, pedestrian count, and building count). For areas of low input level in both cities and towns, there was greater helping of a stranger. Similarly, Holahan (1977) found less helping the higher the environmental input but no effects of urban size per se. However, Amato (1983a) observed less helping in larger cities, but obtained no evidence that urbanites were more helpful in low-density settings than in high-density settings. M. Goldman, Lewandowski and Carrill (1982) also found no urban-nonurban differences in helpfulness, but they did find less helping in the business areas of both cities and small towns than in the residential areas; people in the business areas were, not surprisingly, too busy to help. House and Wolf (1978) did not find that urban and rural dwellers differed in their *attitudes* to helping others, but did find differences in their helping *behavior*. Yet, this unwillingness to help strangers was not found to be related to population size, density, or urban overload, but rather to the crime rate.

In a meta-analytic review of urban-rural differences in helping behavior, Steblay (1987) concluded that there was consistent evidence that helping behavior is more likely in non-urban than in urban contexts, and that this was due not to subject variables (e.g., urbanites having less helpful attitudes than their country cousins) but to situational factors (e.g., the environment is more likely to facilitate helping in rural than in urban areas); see Korte, 1980, for a similar conclusion. However, the relationship between population size and helping was not found to be linear. For nonurban areas (defined as fewer than 50,000 people), there was an unexpected *positive* relation between population size and helping.

For other studies of urban overload, see: Hansson, Slade, & Slade, 1978; McKenna, 1976; Weiner, 1976.

Residential Design

As discussed previously under *Territories*, residences vary in their defensible space (O. Newman, 1972), particularly for secondary territories of apartment buildings, and, within family homes, particular areas differ in their privacy and territorial exclusivity (Sebba & Churchman, 1983; J. D. Fisher, Bell, & Baum, 1984). Residents of high-rise compared with low-rise apartment buildings feel crowded, less safe, and experience feelings of low control and low privacy due to the prevalence of unwanted social contact in the communal (secondary territory) areas of the building (D. McCarthy & Saegert, 1978). Similarly, Wilcox and Holahan (1976) found that there was less involvement, cohesion, and emotional support among student residents of high-rise than low-rise university dormitories.

However, Weckerle (1976) found high levels of neighborhood and residential satisfaction among the inhabitants of a high-rise singles complex, presumably due to their age similarity and shared preference for making social contacts. Also, Williamson (1981) found that high-rise buildings did not lead to feelings of crowding when the apartments were well designed and residents enjoyed good relations with their neighbors. Churchman and Ginsberg (1984) found that residents of high-rise buildings felt there were advantages (large variety of people they could meet) and disadvantages (building height) of high-rise living.

In a programmatic series of studies of university dormitory design, Baum and Valins have investigated the effects of living in corridor-style dorms and suite-style dorms. In both types of dorm there were about the same number of students living on each floor, and room sizes and room designs were comparable. However, they differed in that each corridor-style dorm housed 34 students in double bedrooms either side of a long corridor, whereas the suite-style dorm housed only six students in a suite of three bedrooms situated around a central lounge area. Students in corridor-style dorms experienced more unwanted contact with unfamiliar neighbors and felt more crowded than students in suite-style dorms (Baum, Aiello, & Calesnick, 1978; Valins & Baum, 1973). They were also less likely to seek social contact, spent more time away from the dorm, and avoided the communal dormitory areas (such as lounges)—all to avoid unwanted social contact (Baum & Valins, 1977).

Away from the dormitory setting, in a laboratory setting, corridor-style residents showed signs of withdrawal in their social interactions—such as reduced eye contact and other interpersonal intimacy (Baum, Harpin, & Valins, 1975). After the first weeks housed in corridor-style dorms, it seemed that such coping strategies were successful; in laboratory games, the students showed evidence of asserting control (greater competitiveness). However, over a longer period, the corridor-style residents showed evidence of a failure to cope and showed signs of a loss of control and learned helplessness (Baum, Aiello, & Calesnick, 1978; Baum & Gatchel, 1981). By a simple architectural intervention—simply separating the one long corridor into two halves by creating a central lounge area—Baum and Davis (1980) found that some of the problems associated with corridor-style living were relieved. For reviews of work on residential design, see: Aiello & Baum, 1979; Baum & Valins, 1977.

Office and Classroom Design

A major innovation in the design of offices and classrooms in the 1960s was the open-plan design, which did away with internal walls altogether or replaced them with a few partitions. The idea behind the open-plan design was that it would facilitate communication, heighten accessibility between people, and minimize hierarchical barriers. One problem was that it did nothing for people's attempts at privacy regulation. Workers in open-plan offices complained about the lack of visual and acoustic privacy compared with workers in conventionally-walled offices (Boyce, 1974; F. D. Becker, Gield, Gaylin, & Sayer, 1983; A. Hedge, 1982; Marans & Spreckelmeyer, 1982; E. Sundstrom, Herbert, & Brown, 1982; Wineman, 1982).

In school classrooms, open-plan designs resulted in environmental distractions which were found by teachers to be particularly annoying (Ahrentzen & Evans, 1984; Ahrentzen, Jue, Skorpanich, & Evans, 1982). However, open-plan designs were found to increase contact between teachers of different classes which provided a mutually-supportive environment (Ahrentzen & Evans, 1984).

For further studies on architectural factors and social behavior, see: Amato, 1981a, 1981b; D. E. Campbell, 1979; Holahan, 1976; Keeley & Edney, 1983; Reizenstein & Ostrander, 1981; Sommer, 1974, 1983; E. Sundstrom, Town, Brown, Forman, & McGee, 1982.

Research on aspects of the physical situation not covered in this chapter can be found in: Bakeman & Beck, 1974; S. Bochner, Duncan, Kennedy, & Orr, 1976; J. W. Burgess, 1984; Ebbesen, Kjos, & Konecni, 1976; Emurian, Brady, Meyerhoff, & Mougey, 1983; Forgas & Brown, 1977; D. C. Jones, 1975; Nahemow & Lawton, 1975; M. W. Segal, 1974; Sossin, Esser, & Deutsch, 1978; Worchel & Norvell, 1980.

SUMMARY

The physical situation in which an individual or group is located consists of the ambient environment (noise, temperature), presence of others (density, spatial arrangement), and material aspects (architecture, room design). These environmental factors influence behavior in various ways, by facilitating or hindering ongoing activities, but perhaps the single most important influence of a setting, situation, or place is its perceived purpose.

An environment becomes stressful when an individual's or group's resources are not sufficient to cope, and this can lead to cognitive fatigue or learned helplessness. Excessive noise can reduce a person's sensitivity to social cues. An increase in temperature can move people to become angry and violent, unless the temperature is so high that they only wish to escape the heat. Unpredictable, uncontrollable, and intense air pollution (for example, a smoky atmosphere) may have similar effects.

The analysis of human spatial behavior (proxemics) includes: territory (occupancy, marking, and defense of an area), personal space (preferred interpersonal distance), spatial arrangements (positions of individuals in a group), and crowding (the feeling that there are too many people in a place). All of these variables can be seen to reflect an individual's concern for privacy, and an attempt to maintain an optimal level of social contact or stimulation.

Territories can be classified as primary (homes or other areas used on a long-term and exclusive basis), secondary (social or work areas used on an intermittent basis), and public (areas open to anyone on a short-term basis). In public places, such as libraries, individuals may place personal objects as "markers" to define their territory as areas they are willing to defend. The amount of territory claimed by a group in a public place varies with the sex composition and degree of friendship of the members. Conflicts are more likely in secondary areas, since proprietary rights are more variable and uncertain. In residential areas, crimes are less likely in places that appear to be defended.

Personal space is slightly larger in front of a person than in back, since most people feel more uncomfortable being approached from the rear. Although personal space has not been found to be consistently associated with the sex, personality, or friendship of the individual, there do appear to be cultural differences. In the United States, situational factors may determine whether the interpersonal distance is intimate (0–1.5 feet), personal (1.5–4 feet), social (4–12 feet), or public (over 12 feet). For a particular interaction there is an appropriate level of intimacy, indicated by the amount of eye contact, openness of posture, warmth of tone of voice, intimacy of conversational topic, and closeness of distance between persons. If the level of intimacy is either lower or higher than the desired or appropriate level, the individuals may modify one or more of these variables.

Seating arrangements vary with the type of task and the degree of closeness desired, with closer seating indicating greater intimacy. For casual conversation, seating at right angles or face to face is preferred, for cooperation, seating side by side, and for competition, seating face to face. Persons occupying central seats that are close to and in full view of others are better able to maintain eye contact with other group members. Leaders tend to take more prominent seats and persons who do take prominent positions are perceived as leaders.

Feelings of being crowded can result from having a large number of people in a space in relation to its size or having only a small space available for an individual, or both. Persons who prefer larger interpersonal distances are more likely to feel crowded, especially when the density of people in a place interferes with their activity, reduces their perception of control, and produces an overload of information. Anything that highlights the density conditions increases arousal, and in turn increases feelings of crowding. The relationship between individual differences, cultural differences, and task performance have also been explored.

Architectural design in cities, apartments, and homes, and offices and classrooms can affect social behavior by making places pleasant or unpleasant, helping or hindering behavior, or increasing or decreasing privacy. High-density cities, apartments, dormitories, and work places produce adverse effects in individuals and groups if they result in prolonged unwanted social stimulation or reduced privacy.

Chapter 2

Personality and Social Characteristics

Martin F. Davies

Groups are more than mere aggregates of human units or elements. The characteristics of each group member can have a significant influence on group functioning. Personal attributes, such as age, sex, personality, and abilities affect how group members interact and interrelate with each other. In addition, particular combinations of group members can affect individual and group functioning through group composition effects; for example, a group composed of highly dominant individuals will function differently from a group composed of individuals varying in dominance.

As a reflection of the bulk of reported research, the present chapter is limited to personality and social characteristics. However, other aspects of the person, such as brain regulatory mechanisms and other physiological phenomena, may be closely related to the social systems of small groups (Barchas, 1986).

PERSONALITY CHARACTERISTICS

This review of research on personality and interpersonal/group behavior is probably less exhaustive in coverage than other sections of the book, because the scanning of the group research literature was confined mainly to the Experimental Social Psychology section rather than the Personality section of Psychological Abstracts.

For representative reviews of personality research, see: Aronoff & Wilson, 1985; Buss, 1986; Helson & Mitchell, 1978; D. J. Kiesler, 1983; Lanyon, 1984; Loevinger & Knoll, 1983; Pervin, 1985; Phares & Lamiell, 1977; Ryff, 1987; Sechrest, 1976.

Over the years, a large number of personality traits have been identified and investigated; R. D. Mann (1959) found that over 500 different personality measures had been used in group research alone. Researchers have looked at the relationships between personality traits to see if there is some underlying structure that might represent basic personality dimensions. Cattell (1947) discovered 16 main factors. Norman (1963), however, found only five (surgency, agreeableness, conscientiousness, emotional stability, and culture), whilst Peabody and Goldberg (1989) identified three major factors and three minor ones.

Hare (1976) chose A. S. Couch's (1960) four-dimensional scheme of interpersonal behavior as a framework for reviewing research on personality variables in small groups. However, since 1960, a significant development in group research has been the SYMLOG theory of personality and group dynamics (Bales & Cohen, 1979; Bales, 1984, 1985; Hare, 1989). In this theory, there are three principal interpersonal dimensions: Upward-Downward (Dominant vs. Submissive), Positive-Negative (Friendly vs. Unfriendly), and Forward-Backward (Accepting vs. Opposing Established Authority). Accordingly, the following review uses the SYMLOG scheme as the framework for presenting the research on personality variables and interpersonal/group functioning.

Since Hare's review of research, there have been a number of changes in the way personality is viewed in relation to behavior. These changes stemmed from Mischel's (1968) critique of the validity of personality traits. Mischel's basic argument was that personality traits have low predictive utility in accounting for behavior across different situations, and that situational forces are much more influential than personality dispositions. At its extreme, this idea suggests that an extravert, for example, may emit extraverted behavior only in some situations, whereas in other situations introverted behavior may occur. Ever since Mischel's critique, debate has raged about the relative contribution of personality and situation in accounting for behavior. Various resolutions of this debate have been suggested.

As K. Lewin (1935) recognized, behavior is a function of the person and the situation. The interactionist position is that, although personality or the situation may on their own explain some behavior, most behavior is determined by the interaction of personality and situation (for reviews, see Endler & Magnusson, 1976; Magnusson & Endler, 1977; Magnusson, 1981).

Bem and Allen (1974) argued that personality traits predict the behavior of some people, some of the time, but not all people, all of the time. Thus, some people's level of trait extraversion might be predictive of their behavior across a wide range of situations, whereas, for other people, extraverted behavior might be quite inconsistent across situations. A related argument is that people behave consistently in some types of situation but not in others (template-matching; Bem & Funder, 1978). However, Mischel and Peake (1982) report findings indicating that the cross-situational predictive validity of personality traits does not increase when the consistency of people and situations are taken into account.

Others (e.g., S. Epstein, 1979) have argued that low correlations between personality and behavior are due to unreliable behavioral measurement. Typically, only single-act or single-occasion measures are taken so it is unrealistic to expect a personality trait to predict behavior under such circumstances. Just as personality traits are measured using a variety of test items, so multiple behavioral measures should be taken to produce an aggregate score for behavior, which will then be found to be correlated more highly with personality (but see Mischel & Peake, 1982).

Finally, some researchers (e.g., N. Cantor, Mackie, & Lord, 1984; M. Snyder, 1983) suggest that laboratory studies of personality and social behavior present subjects with social situations which were not freely chosen or entered into by the subject. When subjects actively select situations in which to interact, personality characteristics should be more closely reflected in behavior.

Having said this, very few studies of personality and group behavior have taken account of these developments, and most continue to view personality in terms of the old trait approach. In contrast to the theoretical efforts in personality research, empirical research on personality and interpersonal/group behavior shows little systematic or programmatic progression. Most studies are one-off investigations of a particular idea which does little to provide a coherent picture of the role of personality factors in group functioning. Often, experimental investigations of group processes include personality variables merely as a side issue to increase reportable results.

Dominance-Submission

People who are assertive, dominant, aggressive, outgoing, high on self-esteem, and so on, typically participate more in group and interpersonal situations, whereas people who are unassertive, submissive, unaggressive, introverted, and low on self-esteem participate less (Hare, 1976).

Assertiveness. J. M. Williams and Warchal (1981) found that less assertive students were more conforming in the Asch paradigm than more assertive students. Alden and Cappe (1981) found that nonassertiveness was associated with negative self-evaluation rather than social skills deficits. Relative to assertive people nonassertive people evaluated requests as more reasonable, rated themselves as less able to handle requests, and expected poorer outcomes from assertive responses (Chiauzzi & Heimberg, 1986). R. J. Delamater and McNamara (1986) reviewed the social impact of assertiveness. For additional studies, see: Hull & Schroeder, 1979; Kuperminc & Heimberg, 1983; W. L. Robinson & Calhoun, 1984; J. M. Williams, 1984.

Dominance. Aries, Gold, and Weigel (1983) found within all-male and all-female groups that trait dominance was highly correlated with an overall pattern of dominance-related behaviors, but not with any single behavior. In mixed-sex groups however, there was little relation between trait dominance and dominant behavior. E. C. Bell and Blakeney (1977) found that trait aggression and dominance were correlated with "fronting" and "forcing" modes of conflict resolution. For additional studies, see: Courtright, Millar, & Rogers-Millar, 1979; Roger & Schumacher, 1983; Mason & Blankenship, 1987.

Extraversion. Extraversion has been found to be strongly associated with assertiveness (Vestewig & Moss, 1976) and speaking more than introverts (A. Campbell and Rushton, 1978). Furnham (1981) reported that extraverts have a significantly different pattern of activity preferences than introverts. Graziano, Feldesman and Rahe (1985) reasoned that since introverts are more responsive to punishment than extraverts, then introverts may recall past aversive social encounters more vividly. In two studies, introverts overestimated the aversiveness/unpleasantness of past and future encounters.

Machiavellianism. Machiavellians (Machs) are able to manipulate interpersonal encounters so that they influence and control social situations for their own ends.

In group discussions, high Machs were found to be frequent participators and provided much specific task information, indicating that they influence the group at critical phases of discussions (A. P. Bochner, Di Salvo, & Jonas, 1975). In a management simulation game, R. E. Jones and White (1983) discovered that high Mach groups were more successful than low Mach groups due to high Machs making better strategic and operating decisions. It might be expected that high Machs would tend to be made leader more often than low Machs. However, on a model-building task, medium Machs were rated as leaders more than high or low Machs especially when the task was unstructured (Gleason, Seaman, & Hollander, 1978).

One way in which Machs might exert their influence and control is by deception. Thus, high Machs make more convincing liars than low Machs (Geis & Moon, 1981). DePaulo and Rosenthal (1979) also found that Machs were effective liars and tended to use a histrionic lying strategy (hamming) — which turns out to be a very effective strategy in deceiving others — but Machs were not particularly good at detecting lying in others. Falbo (1977) reported that Machiavellianism was associated with the use of indirect and nonrational power strategies. W. H. Jones, Nickel, and Schmidt (1979) found that high Machs disclosed more information in cooperative as opposed to competitive interactions, whereas low Machs disclosed more in competitive interactions. This suggests a strategic motive behind the self-disclosures of high Machs. The manipulative nature of high Machs would seem to be contradicted by a study by Wolfson (1981), which provided evidence that low Machs helped more in an emergency than high Machs, mainly in a condition where group members could communicate with each other (compared with noncommunicating groups, or an alone condition). However, Wolfson suggested that the findings could be better explained by differences in low and high Mach communication patterns rather than by differences in their sympathy for a fellow human being.

For other studies on Machiavellianism, see: S. Cooper & Peterson, 1980; Drory

& Gluskinos, 1980; W. R. Fry, 1985; Gleason, Seaman, & Hollander, 1978; Harrell, 1980; Harrell & Hartnagel, 1976; Hunter, Gerbing, & Boster, 1982; Okanes & Stinson, 1974; Sheppard & Vidmar, 1980.

Self-monitoring. Self-monitoring resembles Machiavellianism in some ways — at least in terms of strategic motives underlying social interactions. High self-monitors are concerned about their public impression, and regulate their expressive self-presentation to create favorable impressions (M. Snyder, 1974, 1979; M. Snyder & Gangestad, 1986). Studies have shown that high self-monitors change their behavior to suit the prevailing situation much more than do low self-monitors (Lippa, 1976; M. Snyder & Monson, 1975).

M. Snyder and Gangestad (1982) had participants choose whether or not to enter a situation that called for behavioral expressions of extraversion. For high self-monitors, willingness to enter depended on situational factors (how well the extraverted nature of the situation was defined), whereas, for low self-monitors, willingness to enter depended on dispositional factors (how extraverted they were). D. R. Shaffer, Smith, and Tomarelli (1982), in a study of reciprocity of self-disclosures, found high self-monitors were more likely to reciprocate intimacy, emotionality, and descriptive content of the other's self-disclosures, confirming the idea that high self-monitors are more likely to tailor their behavior to fit the existing situation. This "chameleon-like" ability should make high self-monitors more persuasive in social interaction. W. Douglas (1984) found that high self-monitors differed from low self-monitors on initial interaction scripts and also on their descriptions of these scripts. High self-monitors were more linguistically competent partly because their understanding of contextually appropriate conversation was more extensive than low self-monitors. Ickes and Barnes (1977) observed that high self-monitors, in unstructured interaction with a same-sex stranger, were more likely to initiate conversation, were perceived both by themselves and their partners as having a greater need to talk, perceived themselves as having been guided more by their partner's behavior, but were perceived by partners as having been more directive. Dyads composed of one high and one low self-monitor experienced particular interaction difficulties, apparently due to their very different interpersonal styles. Dabbs, Evans, Hopper, and Purvis (1980) found that the pace of speaking, pausing, and interrupting in dyadic conversations suggested that high self-monitors were more facile speakers. Contrary to Ickes and Barnes, high and low self-monitors conversed easily together.

The prospect of future interaction with a (bogus) partner in the Prisoner's Dilemma game increased the cooperation of high but not low self-monitors, indicating the strategic self-presentational nature of high self-monitors (Danheiser & Graziano, 1982). Sypher and Sypher (1983) examined the relationship between measures of interpersonal effectiveness and job level in the headquarters of a large corporation. Self-monitoring was found to be related to perceived persuasive ability and to perceived communication effectiveness. Job level in the organization was positively related to self-monitoring and to perceived communication effectiveness. Garland and Beard (1979) found that high self-monitors emerged more often as leaders than low self-monitors in female brainstorming groups but not in male brainstorming groups.

Like Machiavellians, high self-monitors might make good liars. Siegman and Reynolds (1983b) found that the extraversion and acting subscales of self-monitoring correlated with deception ability in unfeigned lying situation, but only the acting subscale correlated with successful feigned lying. Riggio and Friedman (1983) expected high self-monitors to be better at disguising deception due to their being better able to control leakage of deception cues, but in fact self-monitoring was not found to be related to better control of nonverbal behaviors or to being perceived as truthful.

Self-monitoring differences have been linked to differences in interpersonal attraction, friendship, dating and romantic relationships. Jamieson, Lydon, and Zanna (1987) tested the hypothesis that self-monitoring may moderate the attitude similarity-attraction effect and the activity preference similarity-attraction effect in initial interpersonal attraction. As predicted, for low self-monitors, attitude similarity influenced initial attraction to a stimulus person more than did activity preference similarity. By contrast, for high self-monitors, activity preference similarity influenced initial attraction more than did attitude similarity. Low and high self-monitors attend to different types of information when first forming impressions of others, reflecting the different interaction goals of low and high self-monitors. M. Snyder, Gangestad, and Simpson (1983) found that high self-monitors chose friends as activity partners on the basis of their friends' particular skills in the activity domain. Low self-monitors chose friends as activity partners on the basis of general feelings of liking for their friends. In a second study on preferences for social worlds, high self-monitors preferred relatively partitioned and compartmentalized social worlds in which they would engage in particular activities only with specific partners. Low self-monitors preferred relatively homogeneous and undifferentiated social worlds in which they would spend time with friends who were globally similar to them.

M. Snyder, Berscheid, and Glick (1985) found that differences in self-monitoring resulted in distinctly different orientations in the initiation of dating relationships. In two studies, involving males choosing a female partner for a date, low self-monitors paid a greater amount of attention to and placed comparatively more weight on information about interior personal attributes than did high self-monitors, who paid more attention to and placed greater weight on exterior physical appearance. M. Snyder and Simpson (1984) found that high self-monitors were willing to end their current relationships in favor of alternative partners. For those involved in multiple dating relationships, high self-monitors reported having dated a greater number of partners than low self-monitors. For those involved in steady, exclusive dating relationships, low self-monitors reported having dated their current partner for much longer than high self-monitors. These findings suggest that high self-monitors adopt an uncommitted and low self-monitors a committed orientation toward dating relationships.

For other studies on the relation between self-monitoring and interpersonal/ group behavior, see: Furnham & Capon, 1983; Lippa, 1978; McCann & Hancock, 1983; Miell & le Voi, 1985; Santee & Maslach, 1982; Schlenker, Miller, & Leary, 1983.

Self-esteem. P. A. Cohen and Sheposh (1977) found that low self-esteem subjects took significantly greater risk when performing alone than when performing in front of an audience. Crocker and Schwartz (1985) found no evidence for more in-group favoritism among low self-esteem subjects, but low self-esteem subjects rated both in-group and out-group less favorably than high self-esteem subjects. In a study of group problem solving, subjects were given bogus feedback about the group's performance (Schlenker, Soraci, & McCarthy, 1976). High self-esteem individuals felt that their solutions to the problems had not been influenced by other group members in success conditions, but that their solutions were influenced by other group members in failure conditions. Thus, high self-esteem individuals managed to shift relative credit for group success to themselves and relative blame for failure away from themselves. Low self-esteem individuals felt equally influenced in all conditions. Other research indicates that people low in self-esteem are more susceptible to the influence of social cues because they are uncertain about the appropriateness of their behavior or beliefs, such that they are more likely to imitate others (H. M. Weiss, 1977, 1978; Brockner, O'Malley, Hite, & Davies, 1987).

Anxiety. Researchers have distinguished between a number of types of anxiety: communication anxiety or apprehension, social anxiety, test anxiety, and manifest or general anxiety. Anxiety has been found to affect interpersonal behaviors in a number of ways—usually negative. Halford and Foddy (1982) found that high socially-anxious subjects produced a higher frequency of self-statements concerned with disapproval by others in social interactions (see also J. V. Clark & Arkowitz, 1975). Steffen and Reckman (1978) found that, contrary to predictions, high and low anxious subjects did not selectively attend to positive or negative social cues. However, high anxious subjects felt the other person would prefer to interact less with them in the future than did the low anxious subjects. Anxious people tend to exhibit more inhibition, disruption, or withdrawal in verbal and nonverbal behaviors (Booth-Butterfield & Butterfield, 1986; Daly, 1978).

For other studies on anxiety, see: Benton, 1975a; Daibo, Sugiyama, & Yoshimura, 1975; Fouts, 1979; Jablin, 1981; Poteet & Weinberg, 1980; Prokop, 1983; V. P. Richmond, 1978; Wine, 1975.

Depression. Negative affect and effects are also associated with depression. In dyadic interactions, depressives communicate relatively high levels of self-devaluation, sadness, dependency, distrust, helplessness, and general negative content (S. R. Blumberg & Hokanson, 1983; Hokanson, Loewenstein, Hedeen, & Howes, 1986).

Not surprisingly, the negative feelings and behaviors exhibited by depressives may spread to other nondepressed people. Howes, Hokanson, and Loewenstein (1985) found that, after living together for a few weeks, the roommates of depressives had significantly increased depression scores. Possible causes for this induction of depressive affect include direct induction due to day-to-day contact, a modeling effect, or increased dysphoria associated with an unhappy roommate relationship. Subjects who interact with depressives on a short-term basis show anxiety, depression, and hostility (Strack & Coyne, 1983; but not Gotlib & Robinson, 1982), smile less often, show less arousal and pleasantness in facial expression, less positive and more negative content in conversation, and make fewer statements of support to their partners (Gotlib & Robinson, 1982).

Zemore and Dell (1983) found that subjects with poor interpersonal problem-solving skills were more depression-prone than those with good problem-solving skills.

In group situations, depressed subjects talked less, were rated as less important contributors, and were selected as leaders in group settings less often than nondepressed subjects (Petzel, Johnson, Johnson, & Kowalski, 1981). Haley and Strickland (1986) found that depressed subjects who experienced interpersonal betrayal in a Prisoner's Dilemma game were more critical of their performance on a subsequent task than nondepressed subjects or depressed subjects who experienced a cooperative interaction. Depressed subjects in the betrayal condition also behaved more aggressively toward the betraying partner. These results suggest that the negative schemas of depressed subjects can be altered by interpersonal experiences.

Friendly-Unfriendly

Compared with the Dominance-Submission dimension, far fewer studies associated with the Friendliness-Unfriendliness dimension were unearthed. Included in this section are studies of sociability, affiliation motive, intimacy motive, and loneliness.

Strictly speaking, loneliness is not a personality variable per se, but it is included in this section because of its inverse relationship with intimacy and friendliness.

Sociability, affiliation, and intimacy.   Gifford and Gallagher (1985) found that sociability (measured as amount of participation in group-conversation) was significantly related to personality (affiliation) and to a complex interaction involving personality (affiliation, dependence), social context (level of friendship), and physical setting (seating arrangement). Sorrentino and Sheppard (1978) discovered that approval-oriented swimmers had faster swimming speeds in group than in individual competition, whereas rejection-threatened swimmers had slower swimming speeds in group than in individual competition. Mason and Blankenship (1987) reported that highly stressed women with a high need for affiliation and low activity inhibition were most likely to use infliction of abuse as a means of resolving intimate interpersonal conflicts on their partner. O'Malley and Schubarth (1984) found that people high in need for achievement showed a general appreciation for performance differences and tended to allocate rewards equitably. Affiliation-oriented subjects, however, appeared to focus on the response tendencies of their partner and behave in kind; they divided points equitably with an equitable partner, equally with an egalitarian partner, and self-interestedly with a self-serving partner. Results were explained in terms of the competitive and cooperative interpersonal styles of achievement-oriented and affiliation-oriented people.

Intimacy motivation is associated with warm and communicative interpersonal exchanges (McAdams & Powers, 1981) and the expression of more interpersonal thoughts (McAdams & Constantian, 1983). People high on intimacy motivation are perceived as sincere, likeable, loving, and natural (McAdams & Powers, 1981). Whereas affiliation motivation is associated with wishing to be with others when alone, intimacy motivation is negatively associated with wishing to be alone when with others (McAdams & Constantian, 1983).

Loneliness. Compared with people not experiencing loneliness, lonely people show more inhibition in social interactions, speaking less, being less intimate, and using simple attentiveness rather than familiarity modes of conversation (Sloan & Solano, 1984). W. H. Jones, Hobbs, and Hockenbury (1982) suggested that loneliness may stem from social skills deficits. Lonely students were found to pay less attention to their partner in heterosexual conversations, and an intervention designed to increase attention to partner resulted in significant decreases in loneliness in these lonely students. In addition to conversational and interactional deficits, lonely people interpret the actions and intent of others more negatively than people not experiencing loneliness (Hanley-Dunn, Maxwell, & Santos, 1985). Wheeler, Reis, and Nezlek (1983) found for both males and females that loneliness was negatively related to the amount of time spent with females and to the meaningfulness of interaction with males and females. However, meaningfulness with males was more important than meaningfulness with females. Femininity was negatively related to loneliness for both sexes, and partially mediated the above relationships.

Hansson and Jones (1981) found that lonely persons were less confident in their opinions and less willing than nonlonely persons to advance their opinions publicly. Lonely males were also less conforming to a social consensus, and were less influenced by the behavior of a helpful model in an altruism experiment. Lonely females, however, were more conforming and more influenced.

Accepting vs. Opposing Authority

Only one personality variable has attracted sufficient attention from researchers to be included in this section.

Authoritarianism. Authoritarians have a respect — even a need — for power or authority systems and hierarchies, and when in a position of power or authority they act in an authoritarian manner — domineering, directive, and punitive. However, when they are in subordinate positions, their acceptance of the power or authority systems makes them act in a submissive and conformist way.

In dyads, members supposed to be authority figures who failed to behave in an authoritative manner were evaluated less favorably by high than by low dogmatics (dogmatism is a close relative of authoritarianism). Members supposed to be anti-authority figures who behaved in a socially acceptable fashion were evaluated more favorably by high than by low dogmatics (Bord, 1976a, 1976b).

A number of studies have investigated the implications of authoritarian punitiveness in jury trials. Mock-jury studies have found that authoritarian jurors are more likely to convict defendants (Werner, Kagehiro, & Strube, 1982) and award longer sentences (R. M. Friend & Vinson, 1974) than nonauthoritarians. Bray and Noble (1978) also found that high authoritarian jurors and juries reached guilty verdicts more frequently and imposed more severe punishments than low authoritarians. In addition, high authoritarians showed more pre- to postdiscussion verdict changes than low authoritarians. Deliberations produced a shift toward greater severity of punishment for high authoritarians but toward increased leniency for low authoritarians. In a simulated trial setting, high authoritarians were more influenced than lows by extralegal factors, such as defendant's sex and moral character (J. M. Siegel & Mitchell, 1979) or defendant-juror attitude dissimilarity (H. E. Mitchell & Byrne, 1973). Authoritarians report being more influenced by prosecution than by defense testimony (Sue, Smith, & Pedroza, 1975).

Other studies on authoritarianism and dogmatism include: K. S. Berg & Vidmar, 1975; T. B. Davis, Frye, & Joure, 1975; F. C. Hatfield, 1978; Raden, 1980; D. R. Shaffer & Case, 1982; D. R. Shaffer, Plummer & Hammock, 1986.

Other Personality Variables

Field dependence. Field dependence-independence is a cognitive-personality variable reflecting the extent of autonomous self-functioning or reliance on internal vs. external referents in judgment and behavior. Compared with field-dependent persons, field-independent persons have a more highly developed sense of separate identity, such that attitudes, values, and motives are felt to belong uniquely to the self and distinct from others. According to Witkin and Goodenough's (1977) review of studies of the relation between field dependence and interpersonal behavior, field-dependents make greater use of external social referents (such as in conformity) but only when the situation is ambiguous (e.g., L. R. Greene, 1979; A. Nadler, Goldberg, & Jaffe, 1982; but not DeBiasio, 1986). Under such conditions, field-independents function with more autonomy. Field-dependents are more attentive to social cues and have a general interpersonal orientation; they show strong interest in others, prefer closer interaction distances (R. Carli & Guerra, 1974; L. R. Greene, 1976), are more emotionally open (L. R. Greene, 1976), and are more attracted to social situations. They also show greater social skills and effective interpersonal relationships than field-independents (e.g., Oltman, Goodenough, Witkin, Freedman, & Friedman, 1975; but see Sabatelli, Dreyer, & Buck, 1983, for a contrary view). Field-independents have an impersonal orientation; they are not so interested in other people, show both physical and psychological distancing from people, and prefer nonsocial situations.

For other studies on field dependence, see: Donoghue, McCarrey & Clement, 1983; Lockheed, 1977; R. J. Simon, 1974.

Locus of control. People who are "internal" on locus of control tend to see their behavior as governed by internal forces (such as personality, abilities, effort, motivation) whereas people who are "external" on locus of control tend to see their behavior as governed by forces outside themselves (such as other people and agencies, fate, luck, the weather).

Lefcourt, Martin, Fick, and Saleh (1985) found that internals for affiliation (who attribute social consequences to internal factors) were more attentive listeners than externals, and on a variety of indicators, internals were more socially skilled than externals. Rajecki, Ickes, and Tanford (1981) found that, in unstructured dyadic interaction with a stranger, externals talked more and looked more than internals. The findings were interpreted to mean that externals were more socially dependent than internals, and that their behavior represented an attempt to clarify an ambiguous situation. Lord, Phillips, and Rush (1980) found that locus of control was significantly associated with leader emergence, influence, and power in small groups. Hrycenko and Minton (1974) led subjects to believe that they possessed either high or low power in a triadic communication network. It was found that satisfaction with power position was dependent on the degree of congruence between locus of control and amount of power possessed for males but not for females.

Burger (1987) investigated *desire* for control, and found that people low in desire for control were more likely to agree with a persuasive message which was supported by public opinion, whereas those high in desire for control were less persuaded by the message when not given information about public opinion. In a second study using the Asch paradigm, subjects low in desire for control were more likely to agree with confederates' ratings of cartoons than those high in desire for control.

For other studies on locus of control and interpersonal/group behavior, see: Abdel-Halim, 1981; C. R. Anderson & Schneier, 1978; D. Cole & Cole, 1974.

Studies of other personality variables can be found in: Biesse, Hlavsa, & Thormannova, 1979; Bixenstine, Lowenfeld & Englehart, 1981; Borucki, 1981; Brodt & Zimbardo, 1981; J. K. Burgoon & Burgoon, 1974; Cartwright, Howard, & Reuterman, 1980; Cegala, 1984; J. A. Cunningham & Strassberg, 1981; B. B. Ellis

& Penner, 1983; Faraone & Hurtig, 1985; Firth, Conger, Kuhlenschmidt, & Dorcey, 1986; Fodor, 1984; Gifford, 1981; Heretick, 1984; D. W. Johnson, Johnson, Roy, & Zaidman, 1986; Karabenick, 1977; Kello & Ruisel, 1979; Kernis & Reis, 1984; M. Kohn & Parnes, 1974; Liebrand, 1984; Lord, De Vader, & Alliger, 1986; Moran & Comfort, 1982; J. J. Morse & Caldwell, 1979; Neville, 1983; Orive, 1984; Pareek & Banerjee, 1976; Perju-Liiceanu, 1977; Pleck, 1976; Pratt, Uhl, & Little, 1980; Rim, 1977; Roco, 1977; Sacks & Bugenthal, 1987; Samerotte & Harris, 1976; K. S. Schneider, 1977; M. E. Shaw & Harkey, 1976; Slugoski, Marcia, & Koopman, 1984; Sorensen & McCroskey, 1977; Sosnowski, 1978; Stephen & Harrison, 1985; A. J. Stewart & Rubin, 1976; Stolte, 1983; Varca & Levy, 1984; Varghese, 1982; B. A. Walker & Robinson, 1979; Yinon & Sharon, 1985.

Personality Composition

Groups with members who have compatible personalities are likely to be happier (more cohesive), more efficient, and more productive than groups with incompatible members. One reason for this is that, in incompatible groups, interactions among group members are disrupted or inhibited resulting in deleterious effects on task and socioemotional activities. One of the most influential analyses of group compatibility is Schutz' (1958) theory of interpersonal behavior (FIRO). Schutz suggested that three needs underlie interpersonal behavior — inclusion, control, and affection. Some combinations of needs produce compatibility, and others produce incompatibility. In addition, Schutz suggested three types of compatibility — interchange, originator, and reciprocal — and that these different types of compatibility are linked to group cohesiveness and productivity.

Hewett, O'Brien, and Hornik (1974) found that compatible groups (interchange compatibility on FIRO-B) operating under participatory rather than supervisory leadership had higher productivity than incompatible groups. Contrary to Schutz' theory, R. E. Hill (1975) found that incompatible groups were more productive than compatible groups, and he suggested that a moderate amount of tension within groups, rather than complete group harmony, may result in greater productivity and effective group functioning.

Meyer and Pepper (1977) found that need compatibility in married couples was associated with better marital adjustment. However, Burke, Firth and McGrattan (1974) found that husband-wife compatibility (interchange, originator, and reciprocal compatibility on the FIRO-B) was not strongly related to measures of occupational and life stress management.

J. P. Wilson, Aronoff, and Messé (1975) examined the influence of personality composition and group structure on group productivity. They formed homogeneous three-person groups composed of either safety-oriented or esteem-oriented individuals and had them work under either a hierarchical or an egalitarian social structure. They predicted an interactive association between motive (orientation) and group structure, such that lower group productivity would occur when motivational orientation and group structure was incongruent. In line with their predictions, J. P. Wilson, Aronoff, and Messe found lower productivity when safety-oriented individuals worked under egalitarian conditions and when esteem-oriented individuals worked under hierarchical conditions.

Other studies on personality composition are: Aamodt & Kimbrough, 1982; Bixenstine & Rivera, 1981; Bixenstine & Abascal, 1985; Fromme & Close, 1976; LaFollette & Belohlav, 1982; Leonov & Lebedev, 1972; D. C. Lundgren, 1975; D. C. Lundgren & Knight, 1977; Obozov & Obosova, 1981; Roger & Schumacher, 1983; Vraa, 1974; Yantis & Nixon, 1982.

SOCIAL CHARACTERISTICS

Research on the role of social variables in group functioning has tended to proceed in much the same way as has research on the role of personality variables — with little direction, or cumulative purpose. One exception to this is the research on status characteristics and expectation states.

Status Characteristics and Expectation States

When people are brought together in groups, a pattern of differential influence and participation quickly develops; group members talk more or less, receive more or less agreement and acceptance, and direct or lead the group with varying degrees of success (Bales, 1970). J. Berger, Cohen, and Zelditch (1966) suggested that these inequalities ("interaction disabilities") are due to differences in "performance-expectation states" — beliefs about the likely task ability of each group member. An important aspect of group process is to sort out each member's likely contribution to the group, and task ability is a key element of this contribution. Therefore, early on, group members make judgments about each others' relative task abilities based on existing information, such that a picture of the performance expectations of each group member is built up. It is differences in performance expectation states that leads to the observed pattern of unequal influence and participation; those who are judged to have high ability are encouraged to contribute more to the group process, whereas those of low perceived ability are discouraged.

Some of the information about performance expectation states comes from initial group interaction, when impressions of each group member can be assessed. However, important information also comes from external status characteristics — attributes that people bring with them to the group, such as age, sex, race, occupation, and so on. These characteristics determine performance expectations even before interaction has begun. J. Berger, Fisek, Norman, and Zelditch (1977) distinguish between *diffuse* characteristics like age, sex, and race — whose contribution to performance expectations is unlimited—and *specific* characteristics like occupation—whose contribution to performance expectations is more specific, depending on the match between the particular occupational skills (e.g., manual dexterity) and the particular task skills required (e.g., policy making). Given that many social characteristics or dimensions have status value, how is a group member's overall performance expectation determined? Initial evidence suggested that different status cues (gender and competence) are averaged (J. Fox & Moore, 1979; Webster & Driskell, 1978; Zelditch, Lauderdale, & Stublarec, 1980), but Hembroff (1982; Hembroff & Myers, 1984) found evidence for a weighted average, where more weight is attached to attributes, the more closely they are related to task performance.

There are three important points about expectation-states theory. Firstly, the pattern of influence and activity in a group is likely to be heavily determined from the start by stereotypical beliefs rather than by direct evidence of ability. In accordance with the self-fulfilling prophecy, when group members have formed their expectations about each other based on status cues, subsequent group interaction is likely to provide behavioral confirmation of these expectations as the group members act in a fashion consistent with their expectations. Thus, a white, middle-aged male is likely to be more influential than a young, black female regardless of actual task ability. Secondly, the effects of different social characteristics may not be due to the particular characteristics per se but to their status value; apparent sex differences in group performance, for example, may not be so much due to biological sex as to status value differences. Thirdly, the fact that different social characteristics can be reduced to a common denominator (status) means that the many and various findings of their effects on group behavior can be integrated in a coherent manner.

Meeker and Weitzel-O'Neill (1977) compared the expectation-states explanation of sex differences in group behavior with the sex-role explanation. The former suggests that females are assigned lower status than males in task groups, and that passive, submissive, reactive behavior is expected of low status positions, whereas active, dominating, proactive behavior is expected of high status positions (see Eagly & Wood, 1982; Lockheed & Hall, 1976; W. Wood & Karten, 1986). The sex-role explanations suggest that males and females are socialized differently from birth, such that males are trained to behave in active, dominating, proactive fashion, whereas females are trained to behave in passive, submissive, reactive fashion. Meeker and Weitzel-O'Neill concluded from their review that inferred status differences provide a better account of the findings on sex differences than the sex-role explanation. However, M. T. Lee and Ofshe (1981) claimed that status is determined by behavioral style rather than expectation states, such that sex, race, or occupation are associated with status or dominance through demeanor. However, their experiment has been criticized by a number of authors on methodological grounds (J. Berger & Zelditch, 1983; S. J. Sherman, 1983), but reaffirmed by Ofshe and Lee (1983). In an earlier study, Rosa and Mazur (1979) suggested that the participation hierarchy which develops in groups is mediated by dominance signals. They found that a person's initial eye-glance rank predicted their eventual position in the status hierarchy. When eye contact was prevented, the first person to speak emerged as top of the status hierarchy. Ridgeway, Berger, and Smith (1985) argued that it is expectation states that determine nonverbal status cues. They found that subjects' verbal latency and initial gaze varied with the expectation advantage created by differences in the status characteristic of sex.

One way of increasing status and influence in a group might be simply to behave in a dominating or assertive manner. However, this approach can lead to status or dominance struggles in groups. I. Katz (1970) found that giving blacks assertiveness training did produce some increase in participation in mixed-race groups, but it also resulted in hostility and aggressiveness. Similarly, women who act in a dominant fashion in mixed-sex groups find themselves in status conflict with males (Meeker & Weitzel-O'Neill, 1977). Ridgeway (1978, 1982) suggested that members' perceived motivation toward the group may be an important determinant of the influence and status they attain in task-oriented groups. People who enter a group with low status characteristics can use the communication of group-oriented motivation ("we orientation") in combination with reasonably competent task performance to overcome the status inequality and improve their influence in the group. In experimental confirmation, it was found that females in male-dominated groups achieved fairly high influence and status when they appeared to be group-oriented, but very low status when self-oriented ("me orientation"). As expected, males in female groups achieved high influence regardless of their motivation.

If status expectations account for inequalities in group influence and participation, then rectifying the interaction disabilities of low-status members does not require changes in society's socialization practices. A number of studies have been carried out to test whether interventions designed to add or increase the status characteristics of low status members result in greater group participation and influence. Studies of mixed-race groupings (E. G. Cohen & Roper, 1972; E. G. Cohen, 1982; Riordan & Ruggiero, 1980; Webster & Driskell, 1978) have found that adding high-status characteristics (high task ability) to blacks and low-status characteristics (low task ability) to whites reduces interaction disabilities and inequalities. One method involves giving blacks special training at a task and then demonstrating the superior performance of blacks over whites. Similarly, in mixed-sex groupings, females' participation and influence can be increased by augmenting their demonstrated task ability and competence (Bradley, 1980; Pugh & Wahrman, 1983; W. Wood & Karten, 1986). However, other studies have not shown that such status interventions affect participation and influence rates (Webster, 1977; Lockheed, Harris, & Nemceff, 1983). Pugh and Wahrman (1983) and Markovsky, Smith, and Berger (1984) have shown that status interventions designed to eliminate status disadvantages transfer from the original group and task to other group tasks and group members. Reviewing research on sex and social influence, Lockheed (1985) concluded that when information about specific abilities or competences is absent, invariably males are accorded the highest status and are more dominant than females. When it is known that males and females are equal on specific abilities or competences, female dominance appears in about 40 percent of cases. And when there is evidence for female superiority on specific task abilities, females are accorded high status and are dominant in a large number of cases. W. Wood and Karten (1986), however, sound a note of caution in extrapolating from lab studies of status interventions. They note that many group tasks are highly sex-typed in real life; enhancing female status by providing task-related ability information may not therefore be of much use in minimizing gender differences.

Other studies of status characteristics are: K. A. Adams, 1980, 1983; J. Berger, Rosenholtz, & Zelditch, 1980; J. Berger, Webster, Ridgeway, & Rosenholtz, 1986; Bonacich & Light, 1978; Cansler & Stiles, 1981; Crosbie, 1979a; K. L. Dion, 1979; Entwisle & Webster, 1974; Finchilescu, 1986; Gleason & Harris, 1975; Greenstein & Knottnerus, 1980; R. Humphreys & Berger, 1981; Karuza & Brickman, 1981; Knottnerus & Greenstein, 1981; Lawler, 1975a, 1975b; H. J. Martin & Greenstein, 1983; M. W. Martin & Sell, 1985; F. G. Miller, Hurkman, Robinson, & Feinberg, 1979; Sell & Freese, 1984; R. T. Stein, 1980; Thune, Manderscheid, & Silbergeld, 1980; Van Kreveld, Willigers, Gloudemans, Rancuret, van der Wiel, & Poot, 1974; D. G. Wagner, & Berger, 1982.

Sex and Sex Roles

Sex and gender differences have attracted a great deal of research interest since the Second Edition of the Handbook in 1976, no doubt due in large part to the influence of the feminist movement. For reviews of sex and sex roles, see: Deaux, 1985; Mednick & Weissman, 1975; Lipman-Blumen & Tickamyer, 1975; Spence, Deaux, & Helmreich, 1985.

Sex differences have been explained in a number of ways, including: *biological differences* — men and women behave in different ways because of innate, immutable, biological differences; *sex-role socialization* — men and women behave differently because they are subject to differing sex-role influences during their upbringing; *status differences* — men and women are influenced by their differential status in social situations. Current conceptions of sex differences have tended to favor the social, rather than the psychological or biological: typically, explanations in terms of status differences have tended to supplant explanations in terms of sex-role or socio-biological differences.

Social interaction.   The findings on sex differences reported in Hare's (1976) review paint a picture of male and female behavior consistent with contemporaneous ideas about sex-role socialization; males typically task-oriented, engaging in instrumental behaviors, females typically expressive, engaging in socioemotional behaviors. These differences in interaction style have been confirmed in reviews by

L. R. Anderson and Blanchard (1982) and J. E. Baird (1976) of studies of small group behavior; males engage in more active task behavior (e.g., giving opinions or information), whereas females engage in more positive socioemotional behavior (e.g., agreeing and being friendly).

However, M. L. Barnes and Buss (1985) found a more complex pattern of sex differences in interpersonal behaviors reported by self and spouse in married couples. They found four dimensions of sex differences. One dimension ("Initiative") was similar to the instrumental, task-oriented interaction style typical of males, in that males were found to engage in more acts of enterprise and agency than females. A second dimension ("Communal") was similar to the positive socioemotional style typical of females, in that females were found to engage in more kind, thoughtful, considerate, and generous acts than males. However, a third dimension ("Coercive-Manipulative") indicated that females also engaged in more hostile, critical, demanding, and antagonistic acts than males, suggesting that the greater expressiveness in female behavior can exhibit *negative* aspects. One reason why most studies have found greater positive socioemotional but not greater negative socioemotional behavior in females than in males might be that such studies involved interactions between strangers engaged in task-oriented activities under lab conditions. Normally in such circumstances the intensity of interaction does not reach levels where people cry, nag, refuse to speak, or engage in other demanding and antagonistic acts that occur in marital interaction. (The fourth dimension found by Barnes and Buss — "Flashy Attire" — indicated that females were more likely than males to engage in acts of wearing flashy or seductive clothing.) Barnes and Buss also found that standard masculinity-femininity scales were quite successful in predicting the dimensions of behavior on which males and females were found to differ, but were not successful in predicting differences on these dimensions of behavior *within* each sex, suggesting that variations in "masculine" or "feminine" behavior within a given sex are not the same as the behavioral differences between males and females.

Somewhat different conclusions were reached in a study by Jose and McCarthy (1988). They found that sex-role orientation alone predicted task-oriented activity; individuals of both sexes who had high masculinity scores were perceived to have talked more in group discussions and to have had good ideas. This failure to find the expected sex difference could be explained by the sex-neutral nature of the group discussion tasks allowing females to take a more active role in task activities without conflicting with their low status position (see Meeker & Weitzel-O'Neill, 1977; W. Wood & Karten, 1986; W. Wood, Polek, & Aiken, 1985). Gender and sex-role orientation (femininity) were, as expected, found to be predictors of positive socioemotional behavior.

With respect to amount of talking or participation rates in groups, men appear to talk more than women (Aries, 1976; J. A. Kelly, Wildman, & Urey, 1982). This may simply reflect the fact that the priority of most group studies concerns the attainment of task goals (rather than expressive or socioemotional activities) and men are more likely to engage in task-oriented activities. In dyadic interaction, there is some evidence that, at least in same-sex dyads, women talk more than men (Ickes & Barnes, 1977; Markel, Long, & Saine, 1976) but this may be because, in such brief unstructured dyadic interaction with strangers in the lab, there is little explicit task-achievement activity; much of the time is devoted to socioemotional activities ("getting acquainted").

Intimacy and disclosure. Given that females engage in more socioemotional and expressive behavior, it would be expected that their interactions would involve greater intimacy and self-disclosure (Jourard, 1971). This has been confirmed in same- and mixed-sex dyads of strangers (Grigsby & Weatherley, 1983; Reis, Senchak, & Solomon, 1985; D. A. Taylor & Hinds, 1985). Somewhat surprisingly, Hacker (1981) reported no sex differences in self-disclosure in same-sex friendships, and that men were more confiding than women in mixed-sex friendships. With respect to sex-roles, Grigsby and Weatherley (1983) found that masculinity was negatively related to self-disclosure intimacy, but that femininity was not related. Stokes, Childs, and Fuehrer (1981) found that androgynous subjects reported more self-disclosure than other sex-role types. Results suggested that intimate self-disclosure requires both assertiveness (associated with the traditional masculine role) and sensitivity (associated with the traditional feminine role).

Nonverbal behavior. Similar findings on sex differences in intimacy have been found in nonverbal behaviors. In same-sex dyads, females show greater involvement and immediacy in their encounters than males, such as orienting their bodies more directly toward each other, gazing and gesturing more, as well as talking more (Ickes & Barnes, 1977). Sex-role orientation also has a significant influence on immediacy and involvement in both same-sex dyads (Ickes, Schermer, & Steeno, 1979) and mixed-sex dyads (Ickes & Barnes, 1978). Males and females who were stereotypically sex-typed (masculine/feminine) showed least involvement and had the most difficulty in interaction—less gazing, gesturing, smiling, laughing, and talking than less sex-typed pairs—and, at the end of the encounter these sex-typed pairs expressed least satisfaction and liking. These findings suggest that interactional involvement requires both traditionally "masculine" (instrumental) and "feminine" (expressive) capacities; with such instrumental and expressive skills, social interaction is more rewarding.

LaFrance and Ickes (1981) obtained a significant interaction between sex composition and sex-role composition in dyadic postural "mirroring." Among sex-typed pairs, females displayed more postural mirroring than males, but among androgynous pairs, the effect was reversed. Results showed a surprising negative relation between mirroring and rapport as well as a negative correlation between mirroring and verbalization. It was concluded that individual action (talking) and communal engagement (mirroring) may represent different modes of being involved in an interaction.

Women appear to be better at encoding and decoding nonverbal cues (J. A. Hall, 1984) possibly due to the capability of a less powerful group (women) to predict the behavior of a more powerful group (men). Henley (1977) suggested that perceived power and status differences might underlie observed sex differences in visual dominance behavior in mixed-sex interaction. In same-sex female dyads, Ellyson, Dovidio, Corson, and Vinicur (1980) found that the higher status person engaged in similar amounts of look-speak and look-listen behavior, while the lower status person showed more look-listen than look-speak behaviors. Lamb (1981) examined sex differences in three methods of nonverbal control of social interactions; initial eye-gaze dominance, initial speaking order, and time consumed while speaking. Findings indicated that females were as consistent as males in using these forms of control with members of the same sex, suggesting that power rather than sex is the important factor in nonverbal and paraverbal modes of communication. There was a tendency for females to avert initial gaze as they simultaneously spoke first. Males, however, were more likely to maintain the initial gaze as they spoke first.

For a review of sex differences in nonverbal behavior, see Mayo and Henley (1981). For other studies of sex differences in nonverbal behavior, see: Frances, 1979; Jaspars, van den Oever, & van Gils, 1974; Kimble, Yoshikawa, & Zehr, 1981; Roger & Nesshoever, 1987; Roger & Schumacher, 1983; Russo, 1975.

Related to research on nonverbal behavior, there have been numerous studies of sex differences in human spatial behavior. For reviews of this research, see the subsection on *personal space* in Chapter 1 (The Physical Situation).

Behavioral confirmation. D. Christensen and Rosenthal (1982) investigated the occurrence of the self-fulfilling prophecy in same- and mixed-sex interview dyads. Results showed that males were more biased by preinteraction expectations and produced stronger behavioral confirmation in their interviewees than females, and that female interviewees more readily showed behavioral confirmation than males. Zanna and Pack (1975) tested the idea that a person's behavior conforms explicitly to the sex-role stereotype that attractive others have regarding the person's gender. Females described themselves to a male partner who was either desirable or undesirable and whose stereotype of the ideal woman conformed closely to the traditional female stereotype or its opposite. When the partner was desirable, females portrayed themselves as more or less conventional in terms of sex role, depending on whether the partner's stereotypic view of women was traditional or not (see also von Baeyer, Sherk, & Zanna, 1981). In an extension of M. Snyder, Tanke, and Berscheid's (1977) study of the self-fulfilling nature of stereotypes, sex-typed and androgynous subjects of each sex engaged in getting-acquainted telephone conversations with supposedly attractive and unattractive members of their own or the opposite sex (S. M. Andersen & Bem, 1981). Although females were found to be more socially responsive than males, the sexes did not differ in their responsiveness to physical attractiveness nor in their responsiveness to cross-sex and same-sex interaction. Sex-typed people were rated as more responsive toward allegedly attractive than unattractive partners. In contrast, androgynous men did not differentiate on the basis of physical attractiveness, and androgynous women actually led allegedly unattractive partners to be rated as more socially attractive than allegedly attractive partners, thereby disconfirming the physical attractiveness stereotype.

Patterns of affiliation. Latané and Bidwell (1977) observed more females than males in the company of others in public places. Females were more likely to plan to eat with others, or, if unable to find someone, to forego lunch. Wheeler and Nezlek (1977) found that early on in their first semester at college, female first-year students decreased the amount of time per day engaged in social interaction more than males, mainly by reducing length of interactions, and they reported decreased satisfaction with these interactions. In interactions with same-sex best friends, females also decreased length more than males but maintained a higher level of satisfaction. Number of interactions with same-sex friends decreased markedly for females but not for males. These results suggest that females socialize more intensely than males in new environments and make use of same-sex best friends to deal with the social stimulation. Deaux (1978) found that men and women did not differ in their overall patterns of affiliation, except for same-sex groups, where males spent more time than females. Women spent more time engaged in conversation than men.

Aggression. Another aspect of sex-role socialization in Western society is that males should be assertive and aggressive, whereas females should be unassertive and unaggressive. Eagly and Steffen (1986) have provided a meta-analytic review of sex differences in adult aggressive behavior, mainly experimental lab studies of brief encounters between strangers. They took the view that aggression can be seen as role behavior regulated by the social norms that apply to people based on the roles they occupy. The male gender role includes norms encouraging many forms of aggression. Research on gender stereotypes for example shows that men are rated as more aggressive, assertive, and competitive than women, and that these qualities are seen as more desirable in men than in women (T. L. Ruble, 1983; Spence & Helmreich, 1978). The chivalric aspect of the male gender role however may temper aggression towards the weak and subordinate. By contrast, aggression is not part of the female gender role, since the nurturant and caring qualities are incompatible with aggression. Less traditional male and female gender roles modify these gender differences somewhat; less aggression in men, more assertiveness in women. Other sorts of social role may be differentially associated with the sexes, such as competitive sports in males or the different social status of men vs. women. Another possibility is that the sexes may differ in the perceived consequences of aggression with females judging the consequences more negatively than males (Frodi, Macaulay, & Thome, 1977).

Eagly and Steffen (1986) found that men aggress more and receive more aggression than women, although the differences were not that large compared with, for example, sex differences in helping, and there was also inconsistency across studies. In addition, the sex differences were more pronounced for aggression that produces pain or physical injury than for aggression that produces psychological or social harm. Women reported more guilt and anxiety as a consequence of aggression, they were more vigilant about the harm aggression may cause, and were more concerned about retaliation. Sex of researcher did not affect the size of the sex difference in aggression. Similar conclusions were reached by Frodi, Macaulay, and Thome (1977) except that they discounted the importance of fear of retaliation as a factor underlying sex differences. For other reviews, see: Hyde, 1984, 1986; Macaulay, 1985; Towson & Zanna, 1982; J. W. White, 1983.

For additional studies of aggression, see: J. Archer & Westeman, 1981; D. E. Barrett, 1979; Borden, 1975; Brinkerhoff & Booth, 1984; da Gloria & de Ridder, 1979; Frodi, 1978; Gaebelein, 1977a, 1977b; Golin & Romanowski, 1977; Hoppe, 1979; Hynan & Esselman, 1981; Kool & Kumar, 1979; Lando, 1976; Lando, Johnson- Payne, Gilbert, & Deutsch, 1977; Nirenberg & Gaebelein, 1979; D. C. Richardson, Bernstein, & Taylor, 1979; S. P. Taylor & Smith, 1974; H. L. Thompson & Richardson, 1983; Yinon, Jaffe, & Feshbach, 1975.

Helping. Eagly and Crowley (1986) also employed social-role theory to account for sex differences in helping; the male gender role fosters helping that is heroic and chivalrous, whereas the female gender role fosters helping that is nurturant and caring. They noted that research on helping has not been represen tative of helping in natural settings. Helping has been studied almost exclusively in brief encounters with strangers and not in long term role relationships within families, small groups, or organizations: Such conditions would favor male-role helping over female role helping. This led to their prediction that studies of helping should show overall greater male helping than female helping and females receiving help more often than males.

In a meta-analysis of research findings, Eagly and Crowley found more helping by men than women and women receiving more help than men, but there was inconsistency in sex differences across studies. In accordance with the male-role idea, men helped women more than men, and women were especially likely to receive help when an audience of onlookers was present (increased pressure on men to conform to a chivalry norm). It was also found that men helped more than women to the extent that male respondents believed themselves to be more competent and comfortable in helping than female respondents believed themselves to be. Such findings support the idea that sex differences in helping also depends on the sex-typed skills needed for helping. The preponderance of studies involving the administration of aid or succor to strangers in brief encounters might be explained by a male bias to portray men favorably, since most researchers were men. However, unlike Eagly and Carli's (1981) findings for conformity, Eagly and

Crowley did not find that male authors reported larger sex differences favoring men helping than female authors.

For additional studies of helping, see: Austin, 1979; L. D. Baker & Reitz, 1978; Balls & Eisenberg, 1986; R. D. Barnes, Ickes, & Kidd, 1979; Begin, 1978; P.L. Benson, Karabenick, & Lerner, 1976; Bickman, 1974a; R. D. Clark, 1974; Colaizzi, Williams, & Kayson, 1984; Dertke, Penner, & Ulrich, 1974; Dovidio, 1982; Fedler, 1984; Feinman, 1978; Fink, Rey, Johnson, Spenner, Morton, & Flores, 1975; Frydman & Foucart, 1983–1984; M. B. Harris & Bays, 1973; M. B. Harris & Ho, 1984; W. Howard & Crano, 1974; Kleinke, MacIntire, & Riddle, 1978; Latané & Dabbs, 1975; R. M. Lerner & Frank, 1974; Lesk & Zippel, 1975; Lindskold, Forte, Haake, & Schmidt, 1977; McGovern, Ditzian, & Taylor, 1975; Pandey & Griffitt, 1977; Rotton, 1977; Senneker & Hendrick, 1983; Siem & Spence, 1986; A. Simon, 1976; Skolnick, 1977; R. D. Taylor, Messick, Lehman, & Hirsch, 1982; West, Whitney, & Schnedler, 1975; D. W. Wilson & Kahn, 1975.

Conformity and influence.   Reviews by H. M. Cooper (1979), Eagly (1978), and Maccoby & Jacklin (1974) found little evidence for overall sex differences in influenceability, although sex differences were found to exist in some situations, notably, group pressure situations such as in the Asch paradigm.

One possible reason for greater influenceability in females than in males — first suggested by Sistrunk and McDavid (1971) — is that the sort of tasks typically employed favor male expertise and interests. However, this idea has not really been tested directly. Eagly and Carli (1981) had subjects rate their interest in and knowledge of topics employed in previous studies of sex differences in conformity and influenceability. They found no sex differences in rated interest or expertise, but they caution that their subjects' ratings may have differed from the ratings that might have been given by the subjects who originally served in the studies. Eagly and Carli's meta-analysis of studies showed that males were less influenced than females, particularly in situations involving surveillance by the influencing agent, but the differences were quite small. They also found that male researchers were more likely to find greater female influenceability than female researchers. This may have come about because male and female researchers behaved differently either in designing the experiments, implementing the experimental designs, or reporting sex difference findings.

Analyses of observations reported by L. Carli (1989) indicate that women receive more agreement and positive social behavior than men, which in turn yields more agreement from the receiver.

Eagly (1978) concluded from her narrative review that one likely explanation for the greater influenceability of females is that there is a propensity to yield inherent in the female sex role. However, a second explanation — that women tend to be more oriented towards interpersonal goals in groups than men — was also found to be plausible. Women may conform more than men in order to maintain group harmony and cohesiveness, consistent with their sex-role orientation. However,

Eagly, Wood, and Fishbaugh (1981) did not find that concern for group harmony accounted for greater female conformity. If anything, their results indicated that sex differences in conformity might be better described as a tendency to *nonconformity* in men rather than conformity in women under group surveillance. This is consistent with findings (Ridgeway & Jacobson, 1977; Ridgeway, 1981; Wahrman & Pugh, 1974) that nonconformity in men is likely to lead to more influence rather than rejection in groups, whereas women must exhibit initial conformity in order to be influential (building up "idiosyncrasy credit": Hollander, 1958).

Sex differences in conformity might be better explained by expectation-states theory (see the earlier section on *Status Characteristics and Expectation States*). Women in groups are accorded lower status than men, such that they are expected to have lower task ability and competence. Higher status group members are expected and indeed allowed to exert more influence and to be less influenceable than members of lower status.

Assertiveness, competitiveness, dominance, and power. Assertiveness, competitiveness, dominance, and power are all characteristics associated with masculine behavior in Western society. Once again, expectation-states theory suggests that women in mixed-sex groupings are not expected and not encouraged to be assertive or dominant.

K. A. Adams and Landers (1978) found that men were more likely than women to withstand challenges to their opinions on a joint decision-making task. This study was carried out with white students. However, for black students the reverse was found—black females being more dominant than black males—in accordance with the stereotype of the black female being active and assertive, and the black male being passive and submissive (K. A. Adams, 1980, 1983). In work settings, males report using more dominance behaviors toward female co-workers than females do toward male co-workers (Radecki & Jennings, 1980).

Instone, Major, and Bunker (1983) investigated whether women in positions of equal power differ in the strategies they use to influence subordinates. Although gender differences consistent with general sex-role stereotypes were found, most differences were weak and only of marginal significance. Relative to males, females made fewer influence attempts, used a more limited range of influence strategies, used fewer rewarding strategies, particularly promises of pay increases, and used more coercive strategies, especially pay deductions. Females displayed lower levels of self-confidence than did males, and sex-linked differences in self-confidence explained much of the gender difference observed in the frequency with which influence attempts were made and the extent to which coercive strategies were used. In intimate relations, Falbo and Peplau (1980) found that females employ unilateral and indirect power strategies whereas males employ direct and bilateral power strategies (see also Cowan, Drinkard, and MacGavin (1984).

Alagna (1982) investigated the effects of sex-role identity and peer evaluation on the responses of males and females in a competitive situation. Results showed that masculine and androgynous groups had higher expectancies for performance than feminine groups, better objective performance, and greater perceived success than feminine or undifferentiated groups of either sex. Males and females in masculine and androgynous groups did not differ from each other in performance, affect, or cognitions. Women responded more positively on all measures to approval than disapproval, whereas men were largely unaffected. Valle, DeGood, and Valle (1978) examined the relationship between a subject's sex and his/her behavior in competition in three different tasks. Results were not consistent with the idea of fear of success in females. Competition with either sex increased performance level for both sexes in all three tasks. Weisfeld (1986) reviewed the literature on female behavior in mixed-sex competition. Results from several performance comparisons of females in same-sex and mixed-sex competition indicate that, when competing against males, some of the females depressed performance levels, resulting in loss to male competitors, whereas others elevated performance levels. Depressed performance levels were more likely to occur in naturalistic situations than in highly-controlled lab studies. Females who competed vigorously against males were characterized as being masculine or androgynous, having more internal locus of control, and preferring nontraditional roles. Data on female physiological responses in competitive situations suggest that conflicting social demands raise anxiety levels for some female competitors.

For other studies, see: J. M. McGuire & Thomas, 1975.

Leadership. It is often noted how few women are found in important leadership positions in society. The popular sex-role stereotype is that leadership in mixed-sex groups is not a suitable role for females and that males make more effective leaders (Bartol & Butterfield, 1976; Massengill & DiMarco, 1979; O'Leary, 1974; B. Rosen, Jerdee, & Prestwich, 1975). However, comparatively little research has been done on sex differences in leadership; the vast majority of research has involved all-male groups. In laboratory studies of mixed-sex discussion groups, males usually take the lead (Fleischer & Chertkoff, 1986; H. H. Frank & Katcher, 1977; Golub & Canty, 1982; Nyquist & Spence, 1986; L. B. Rosenfeld & Fowler, 1976; Snodgrass & Rosenthal, 1984). Gender differences in leadership effectiveness may be due more to self-fulfilling beliefs than to actual sex differences in leadership ability or behavior. If group members do not believe women make good leaders, then they will be more resistant to being led by a leader (S. L. Cohen, Bunker, Burton, & McManus, 1978), and the woman leader herself may also hold the same belief, so that she will be less confident in her leader behavior (Lenney, 1977; O'Leary, 1974; Terborg, 1977). In addition, apparently successful leadership by women is attributed to luck, whereas successful leadership by men is attributed to ability (R. W. Rice, Bender, & Vitters, 1980).

Expectation-states theory suggests that, in the absence of any other status cues, females are accorded lower status than males because it is assumed that they have less task ability or competence than males. Those of low status (low perceived task ability) are not encouraged by other group members in their attempts at influence, leadership, or other active task behaviors. In the case of appointed leaders, group members react more negatively to female than to male leaders, believing that female leaders are less competent and effective than male leaders — even when there are no apparent differences in leaders' or group performance (B. Rosen & Jerdee, 1974) — and making it more difficult for females to lead effectively. For females to be elected leaders in mixed-sex groups, they must somehow overcome their low status by demonstrating their value to the group. This could be done directly by engaging in more task-relevant activity and influence, but, firstly, there would be resistance to this from other group members, and, secondly, there would be status conflict with the male members (Meeker & Weitzel-O'Neill, 1977). Ridgeway (1978, 1982) suggests that one way for females to overcome their status disadvantage is to demonstrate a group-oriented motivation (rather than an individualistic orientation) at the same time as engaging in task activities. Another way is to show evidence of task ability and competence (Bradley, 1980; Pugh & Wahrman, 1983; W. Wood & Karten, 1986).

In the case of emergent leadership, by the time the emergence occurs, the leader must already have been able to exert influence and have had their task-contributions accepted by other group members. As with elected leaders, females should have demonstrated task ability and/or a group-orientation to overcome their initial status disadvantage. Perhaps one difference with elected leadership is that in emergent leadership (a) sex might not be so perceptually prominent as a status cue, since group members are not being asked to focus on each other's attributes and diffuse status characteristics might not be given the same weight as specific status characteristics (like task ability), and (b) status-conflict might not be as obvious for similar sorts of reasons.

Hollander and Yoder (1980) and Hollander (1983, 1985) conclude from their reviews that in studies where the leader is assigned or appointed (typically in laboratory studies), males tend to be more effective and to behave differently than females. Yet, in studies of existing leaders who emerged into the leadership role (typically in field settings), few sex differences are found, and it appears that individual characteristics are more important than gender (Bartol, 1978; Schneier & Bartol, 1980; Schneier & Goktepe, 1983). Thus, how people achieve leadership seems to be an important qualifier of any sex differences. Complementing this distinction, Dobbins and Platz (1986) found that men were more effective leaders than women in lab settings, but not in field settings. Appointed male leaders engage in more active task behaviors than appointed women leaders (Eskilson & Wiley, 1976). The tendency for women in groups to engage in less active task behavior than men could be linked to their likelihood of becoming leader because of the well-known link between participation rates (particularly task behaviors) and leadership (R. T. Stein & Heller, 1979). However, studies of emergent leaders show that behavior in the process of emergence is similar for both males and females (Bartol, 1974, 1978; Schneier & Bartol, 1980), and emergent leaders of both sexes have low LPC scores (high task-orientation)(Schneier, 1978).

Research shows that women are more reluctant to assume leadership (Eskilson & Wiley, 1976; Mamola, 1979). Because of their relatively low status, women may be less confident or may have less expertise in making leadership attempts, and both these factors are linked to emergent leadership (R. T. Stein & Heller, 1979). In addition, a lot of the tasks used in leadership research favor the interests and expertise of men (see W. Wood, 1987). Eskilson and Wiley (1976) attempted to improve appointed women leaders' belief in themselves by telling them that they had been made leader on the basis of their greater task-relevant skills. These women subsequently showed more leaderlike behavior and greater task performance than women appointed randomly. By contrast, men leaders were not influenced by such a manipulation (presumably because they already believed they had good task-relevant skills).

For other studies of sex differences in leadership, see: Alagna & Reddy, 1985; L. R. Anderson & McLenigan, 1987; Bartol & Wortman, 1979; V. Brown & Geis, 1984; Bullard & Cook, 1975; Bussey & Bandura, 1984; D. A. Butterfield & Powell, 1981; J. B. Chapman, 1975; Deaux, 1979; Denmark, 1977; Dobbins, Pence, Orban, & Sgro, 1983; Ferber, Huber, & Spitze, 1979; Geis, Boston, & Hoffman, 1985; L.R. Greene, Morrison, & Tischler, 1981; Inderlied & Powell, 1979; M. B. Jacobson & Koch, 1977; P. Johnson, 1976; J. A. Kelly, Wildman, & Urey, 1982; Kremer & Mack, 1983; Kushell & Newton, 1986; Larwood & Blackmore, 1978; Larwood & Lockheed, 1979; Leary & Schlenker, 1980; Linimon, Barron, & Falbo, 1984; Offermann, 1984; Osborn & Vicars, 1976; Porter, Geis, Cooper, & Newman, 1985; G. N. Powell & Butterfield, 1980, 1982, 1984; Reed, 1983; R. W. Rice, Instone, & Adams, 1984; Spillman, Spillman, & Reinking, 1981; Stake, 1981; Stitt, Schmidt, Price, & Kipnis, 1983; Yerby, 1975.

Reward allocation. Based on sex-role socialization, it might be expected that females would allocate rewards equally (due to their socioemotional orientation), whereas males would allocate equitably (due to their task orientation). Kahn, O'Leary, Krulewitz, and Lamm (1980) reviewed evidence on achievement motivation and behavior showing that the equity norm is consistent with the goals of Western males, whereas the equality norm is consistent with the goals of Western females. Equitable allocations reinforce competitive (agentic) success and equal allocations reinforce social (communal) success. Kahn, Nelson, and Gaeddert (1980) confirmed that women allocate rewards equally whereas men allocate equitably due to differences in interpersonal orientation (socioemotional vs. task oriented). Kidder, Bellettirie, and Cohn (1977) found that men and women allocate rewards equitably and equally, respectively, under public conditions, whereas, in private they would reverse themselves, each preferring the opposite option (indicating childhood socialization and adult constraints on sex-role performance).

Major and Adams (1983) also found that women allocate rewards more equally than men, but, contrary to Kahn, O'Leary, Krulewitz, & Lamm (1980), they did not find that men and women differed in interpersonal orientation. However, people high on interpersonal orientation did allocate more equally than did people low on interpersonal orientation, but only in private, not public, conditions. Contrary to Kidder, Bellettirie, and Cohn (1977), both women and men allocated rewards more equally when allocations were public than when they were private, and when future interaction was expected than when it was not (cf. Sagan, Pondel, & Wittig, 1981).

Reis and Jackson (1981) argued that previous studies finding that males allocate equitably whereas females allocate equally may have been due to the use of masculine sex-linked tasks. In two studies, Reis and Jackson found that males allocated equitably and females equally with same-sex partners on a masculine task. On a sex-appropriate task, both sexes allocated equitably. It was also found that both sexes allocated more generously to an opposite-sex partner than to a same-sex partner regardless of task type.

Stake (1985) investigated sex differences in allocating rewards under instructions to be fair, to increase productivity, or to improve worker relationships. Females allocated rewards more equally than males under pressure to improve worker relationships, whereas males were more equitable than females under pressure to increase productivity. Females were more likely to attribute a lower productivity rater to internal constraints and to quality of workmanship, and men were more likely to attribute a lower productivity rate to lower motivation. It was argued that sex differences in attributions of worker performance are a basis for the observed differences in allocation behavior. In a similar study, Stake (1983) however did not find sex differences in reward allocations.

For other studies on reward allocation, see: Austin & McGinn, 1977; M. A. Barnett & Andrews, 1977; Major & Adams, 1984; Messé & Callahan-Levy, 1979; Watts & Messé, 1982.

Group performance. W. Wood's (1987) review of sex differences in group performance (in particular, group productivity) noted that sex differences in group productivity are likely to occur if the particular group task suits the interest, experience, or ability of one sex more than the other. For example, women tend to be better than men at a variety of verbal tasks, whereas men tend to be better than women at a variety of quantitative, motor, and visual-spatial tasks (Maccoby & Jacklin, 1974). Second, men may be better motivated than women at problem-solving tasks (Meeker & Weitzel-O'Neill, 1977). Some factors, however, may uniquely affect *group* rather than *individual* performance, such as the way men and women interact in same-sex groups. As previously discussed, men's style is active task behavior whereas women's style is positive social behavior. Thus, it might seem plausible that men's greater task activity should facilitate group productivity, whereas women's greater socioemotional behavior should impair task completion.

On the other hand, Wood notes that positive socioemotional behavior might improve performance by increasing group cohesion and the involvement of all members in the task, especially if the task is conjunctive (group performance depends on the performance of the least able member) rather than disjunctive (group performance depends on the performance of the most able member). The effect of sex may vary with type of task depending on whether task performance is facilitated by active task behavior or positive social behavior (W. Wood, Polek, & Aiken, 1985). However, there is little direct evidence that sex differences in interaction style is responsible for sex differences in group performance.

Both W. Wood (1987) and M. E. Shaw (1981) note that most of the research in this area has been done on same-sex groups. Hoffman (1965) suggested that mixed-sex groups are more effective than same-sex groups because of the differing skills brought to the task by men and women. Hare (1976) argued that same-sex groups are more efficient than mixed-sex groups because same-sex groups spend less time on socioemotional activities. M. E. Shaw (1981) suggested that both these conclusions may be correct; mixed-sex groups may be more effective than same-sex groups when task solution requires differing perspectives, but mixed-sex groups can be less efficient if the presence of members of the opposite task distracts from task performance.

The results of W. Wood's (1987) meta-analysis showed that overall men's performance was superior to women's performance on both individual and group tasks, suggesting that the sex differences are attributable to factors such as task content or experimental contexts that favor men's interests and abilities over women's. Wood cautioned that the extent to which the results from the her sample of studies might generalize to real-world groups is unclear since the representativeness of the experimental tasks and settings used was not known. Specific group-level factors—in particular, interaction style—were found to be implicated in sex differences. For tasks judged to require a high level of task-oriented activity, males were superior to females in both individual and group performance. Contrary to expectation, however, the male superiority was only slightly greater for group than for individual performance, suggesting that men's interaction style contributes only a little to successful group performance. Wood suggested that men's high level of task activity is designed to enhance or maintain their status or influence in the group with the consequence that the selection of optimal task solutions is not the first priority. By contrast, for tasks judged to require a high level of social activity, men outperformed women in individual performance, but showed no superiority in group performance. This implies that *women's* interaction style facilitates group performance.

W. Wood's (1987) review turned up few findings relating to sex composition and group performance. What findings there were provided slight evidence that mixed-sex groups outperform same-sex groups, but it was unclear what contributed to this effect. P. Y. Martin and Shanahan (1983) also reviewed research on sex composition in groups, noting that there are three explanations for sex differences in same- and mixed-sex groups; sex-role differentiation, expectation states, and Kanter's (1977) numerical proportion model. It was concluded that research confirms the effectiveness of manipulating the proportions of males to females in mixed groups to improve the group experience for females, but that additional interventions are required for females to receive results and benefits equal to males.

When there are few women in a mixed-sex group, they may be thought of as "token" women. In a study of organizations, Kanter (1977) found that token women were perceived to be more salient and were perceived as being closer to the female stereotype ("assimilation") than women in more balanced mixed-sex groups, and perceived sex differences were found to be heightened ("polarization") (see also Cota & Dion, 1986). Heightened salience appeared to generate pressures for women to perform better, assimilation led to "role entrapment" (women found it difficult to change the role perceived by men to be appropriate for females), and polarization resulted in men strengthening their group boundaries (men forming subgroups that excluded women). Finigan (1982) tested Kanter's idea that a numerical minority in an unbalanced sex-ratio group will be inhibited in its group performance. Participant observation of decision making groups provided confirmation of Kanter's ideas for both male and female minorities. However, the effect was most pronounced for females in male-dominated groups. Izraeli (1983) also confirmed Kanter's ideas and also found that changes in the sex-proportion of groups had a stronger impact on stereotypical views of women than of men. Crocker and McGraw (1984) examined the consequences of solo status for women in mixed-sex groups, and found that solo females were unlikely to be group leaders, overall group satisfaction was lowest when a solo female was present, and gender-related issues were most likely to be raised in groups containing a solo female. Solo males, however, were integrated into the groups as leaders, resulting in smoother group functioning.

Aries (1976) found that men were more personally oriented, addressed individuals (as opposed to the group as a whole) more often, and spoke about themselves and their feelings more often in mixed-sex groups. By contrast, in all-male groups, they were more concerned with status and competition. Women in mixed-sex compared with same-sex groups were less dominant; they tended to let men dominate.

Other studies of group composition include: Mabry, 1985; J. E. Marshall and Heslin, 1975; D. N. Ruble & Higgins, 1976; J. A. Wall, 1977a; Vallacher, Callahan-Levy, & Messé, 1979.

For other studies of group performance, see: Bouchard, Barsalou, & Drauden, 1974; Bray, Kerr, & Atkin, 1978; Eskilson & Wiley, 1976; Fennell, Barchas, Cohen, McMahon, & Hildebrand, 1978; D. C. French, Brownell, Graziano, & Hartup, 1977; Graziano, French, Brownell, & Hartup, 1976; Harkins, Latané, & Williams, 1980; M. B. Jacobson & Effertz, 1974; N. L. Kerr, 1983; N. L. Kerr, & Bruun, 1981; N. L. Kerr, & Bruun, 1983; N. L. Kerr, & Sullaway, 1983; Lane, Mathews, Chaney, Effmeyer, Reber, & Teddlie, 1982; R. C. Mathews, Lane, Reber, Buco, Chaney, & Erffmeyer, 1982; M. E. Rosenbaum, Moore, Cotton, Cook, Hieser, Shovar, & Gray,

1980; S. F. Rosenthal, 1978; T. M. Schwartz, Wullwick, & Shapiro, 1980; M. E. Shaw & Ashton, 1976; M. E. Shaw & Harkey, 1976; M. A. Swanson & Tjosvold, 1979. For studies of other sex differences in interpersonal/group behavior, see: Alfgren, Aries, & Olver, 1979; Auerbach, Kilmann, Gackenbach, & Julian, 1980; Babinec, 1978; M. A. Barnett & Andrews, 1977; P. W. Berman, 1976; Brockner & Adsit, 1986; M. Burgoon, Dillard, & Doran, 1983; Cacioppo & Lowell, 1981; Callahan-Levy & Messé, 1979; N. L. Cantor & Gelfand, 1977; M. L. Clark, 1983; Coet & McDermott, 1979; Currant, Dickson, Anderson, & Faulkender, 1979; Dalton, 1983; K. L. Dion, 1979; B. A. Fisher, 1983; P. S. Fry, 1976; Gielen, Dick, Rosenberg, Kelly, & Chiafettelli, 1979; Gormally, 1982; Grush & Yehl, 1979; Hamby, 1978a, 1978b; M. B. Harris, 1977; E. A. Hartman, 1980; Kahn, Nelson, & Gaeddert, 1980; Klopfer & Moran, 1978; Kraft & Vraa, 1975; Khatschenko, 1982; Kollock, Blumstein, & Schwartz, 1985; Kushell & Newton, 1986; Linimon, Barron, & Falbo, 1984; Maruffi, 1985; McCarrick, Manderscheid, & Silbergeld, 1981; McKillip, DiMiceli, & Luebke, 1977; McLaughlin, Cody, Kane, & Robey, 1981; Pruitt, Carnevale, Forcey, & Van Slyck, 1986; R. W. Rice, Bender, & Vitters, 1980; Rokach, 1982; S. F. Rosenthal, 1978; Sagan, Pondel, & Wittig, 1981; Sissons, 1981; H. W. Smith & George, 1980; Snodgrass, 1985; Spoelders-Claes, 1973; Stake, 1985; Stingle & Cook, 1985; Toder, 1980; Tuma & Hallinan, 1979; Tuthill & Forsyth, 1982; N. M. Webb, 1984a; R. F. Weiss, Weiss, Wenninger, & Balling, 1981; J. A. Williams, 1984; J. T. Wood, 1981; F. Wright, 1976; Yamada, Tjosvold, & Draguns, 1983.

Race

In contrast to sex differences, research interest in race and ethnic group differences seems to have declined during the 1970s and 1980s from the highpoint of the 1960s, possibly because of waning public interest in civil rights issues in the United States. As a consequence, this section of the present chapter is considerably shorter than the previous one on sex and sex roles.

Nonverbal behavior. Some differences have been found in interactional and conversational styles as a function of race (mainly black/white). In employment interviews, whites tended to maintain more visual interaction than blacks with both white and black interviewers (Fugita, Wexley & Hillery, 1974). Gielen, Dick, Rosenberg, Kelly, & Chiafettelli (1979) found that white male dyads and black-white female dyads visually interacted the most while black-white male and male-female dyads visually interacted the least. A. Smith (1983) investigated nonverbal behavior in same-sex, same-race dyads and found that black females looked less often than white females, and leaned synchronously more often than white females and black males. However, LaFrance and Mayo (1976) did not find differences in overall amount of gazing, but found racial differences in patterns of gaze during conversations. Whites tended to gaze more at the other person when listening than when speaking, whereas blacks tended to gaze more when speaking than when listening. This difference in patterns of gaze produced interactional difficulties in turn taking; white listeners were cued to speak by the gazing of black speakers when the blacks had not yielded the floor, and black listeners frequently failed to be cued to speak by the gazing of white speakers. Zimmerman and Brody (1975) found that black children talked significantly less together during play, faced each other less directly, and interacted at greater interpersonal distance than white children. Racially mixed dyads were intermediate in social distance, talk, and body axis. Ickes (1984) examined the initial, unstructured interactions of interracial (black/white) dyads, and found that whites showed more interactional involvement than their black partners but experienced the interactions as more stressful and uncomfortable. Whites predisposed to avoid interaction with blacks looked and smiled less at their partners than those predisposed to initiate interaction. Not surprisingly, both black and white members of these avoidant dyads reported greater feelings of anxiety and concern about the interaction. It was suggested that black-white partner effects were due to differing amounts of cross-race contact typically experienced by blacks and whites.

Liking, attraction, and friendship. Given the existence of racial prejudice, it would be expected that attraction and friendship would be greater between members of the same race or ethnic group (for a review of black/white racial prejudice and discrimination, see Crosby, Bromley, & Saxe, 1980). Bartel, Bartel, and Grill (1973) found in integrated open classrooms that white children held other white children in high esteem and black children in very low esteem, whereas black children held other black children in low esteem. Tuma and Hallinan (1979) found that schoolchildren's existing friendship choices were associated with being the same sex and race as the other child. However, the formation of new friendships was not associated with sex and race and appeared to be almost random. S. Bochner and Orr (1979) used Milgram's small world technique to identify interpersonal bonds among members of a university international house, and it was found that both race similarity and academic status congruence contributed to affiliation with race similarity more salient for graduates and academic status more salient for undergraduates. F. A. Blanchard, Weigel, and Cook (1975) found less attraction for a black groupmate when he performed less competently than when he performed competently, but found no difference in attraction for a white teammate as a function of competence. Liking for both black and white teammates was greater after group success than after group failure, but this was especially so for less competent black teammates, who were liked and respected least after group failure, suggesting a scapegoating effect. F. A. Blanchard, Adelman, and Cook (1975) found greater attraction for groupmates after group success than after group failure conditions, but found no differences in attraction as a function of race (black/white) or amount of participation in the group's decision making (high/low).

Aggression. Racial prejudice would be expected to rear its ugly head in the form of aggression. Whites' aggression towards blacks appears to be moderated by normative constraints on overt racial prejudice. When subjects' behavior in an experiment was recorded on videotape to be viewed by white experimenters, whites were found to be less aggressive than when their behavior was not videotaped (and hence anonymous); aggression towards whites, however, was the same whether or not behavior was videotaped (E. Donnerstein & Donnerstein, 1973; M. Donnerstein & Donnerstein, 1978). R. W. Rogers and Prentice-Dunn (1981) similarly found that nonangered whites showed less aggression towards blacks than towards other whites, but, when angered, whites showed more aggression towards blacks than towards other whites.

Fear of retaliation also moderates interracial aggression. Whites' show more direct aggression (shock intensity) towards blacks when they believe the victim can retaliate than when they believe the victim cannot retaliate (E. Donnerstein & Donnerstein, 1975; M. Donnerstein & Donnerstein, 1977), whereas aggression towards other whites is unaffected by fear of retaliation (E. Donnerstein & Donnerstein, 1973). However, opportunity for victim-retaliation increases indirect aggression (shock duration) (E. Donnerstein & Donnerstein, 1972), especially if the black victim is perceived to be attitudinally dissimilar to whites (E. Donnerstein & Donnerstein, 1975), suggesting that whites' hostility towards blacks is suppressed in the direct aggression condition by fear of retaliation. However, L. Wilson and Rogers (1975) found that black females were more aggressive toward whites than blacks on a measure of direct aggression (shock intensity), suggesting that passive accommodation toward whites had been replaced by a readiness to display overt aggression. On a measure of impulsive but indirect measure of aggression (shock duration), black females were less aggressive towards whites than blacks. In a competitive situation, race (black/white) of the opponent was not found to differentially affect the aggressive behavior of either high or low prejudiced whites (Leonard & Taylor, 1981). However, when confronted with a nonaggressive competitor, high-prejudiced whites did attack the black opponent more than the white opponent. But when the competitor's nonaggressive intentions were made clear at the outset, this difference in aggression towards own- and other-race opponent by high-prejudiced whites disappeared. Thus, in the presence of a clear threat, prejudice increases aggression indiscriminately, but selective aggression occurs in the presence of an ambiguous threat.

Similarly in a study of aggression as a function of race of opponent (Jews of Western or Oriental origin) and prejudice, Schwarzwald and Yinon (1978) did not find, contrary to expectations, that the attitudes of Jews of Western origin towards Oriental Jews affected aggressive behavior. When the opponent was not expected to reciprocate aggression, both high- and low-prejudiced subjects were more aggressive towards an opponent of Oriental than of Western origin. For other studies on aggression, see: R. A. Baron, 1979.

Helping. These somewhat qualified findings on race and aggression are to some extent mirrored in studies of race and helping. Gaertner (1973) found that politically liberal whites were more likely to terminate a request for help from a black than from a white. However, when the request for help was completed, both conservative and liberal whites helped a white more than a black, with the conservatives helping more than liberals. However, Gaertner (1975) and Gaertner and Dovidio (1977) failed to find any link between prejudice towards blacks and helping a black vs. a white in an emergency. Dovidio and Gaertner (1981) also found no relation between prejudice and helping. They found that whites were more likely overall to help blacks than other whites, but there was an interaction with status, such that whites were less likely to help high-status blacks than low-status blacks. It has been suggested that whites' motives with respect to blacks and other minority ethnic groups are a mixture of feelings of sympathy for the underdog and feelings of aversion (Dutton & Lennox, 1974; Gaertner, 1975; Gaertner & Dovidio, 1977; I. Katz, Cohen, & Glass, 1975; I. Katz, Glass, Lucido, & Farber, 1979). On attitude measures, whites may show little prejudice, but in interaction with blacks their prejudice may be expressed in terms of aversion. In addition, whites are less helpful to blacks when nonhelping is justifiable or appropriate according to the prevailing situational norms (Frey & Gaertner, 1986; Gaertner, Dovidio, & Johnson, 1982).

Wegner and Crano (1975) found that black bystanders helped more black than white victims in a nonthreat situation, whereas white bystanders helped both races equally. They suggest that blacks may be more likely to aim their altruistic activities at other blacks when the immediate population (in their case, a university campus) is predominantly white than when it is predominantly black. West, Whitney and Schnedler (1975) found that, in locations near to a predominantly black and a predominantly white college campus, victims of the opposite race were helped faster than victims of the same race. However, in noncollege neighbourhoods, whites helped victims of the same race faster, whereas black helpers did not show a racial bias.

W. G. Stephan (1985) suggests that the inconsistent findings on interracial helping can be explained by the relative costs involved in helping. When there are few costs associated with *not* helping, whites' aversion to blacks may outweigh these costs, resulting in little helping. But when the costs involved in *not* helping are great, these may outweigh whites' aversion, leading to a helpful response towards blacks.

Group performance. Ruhe and Allen (1977) looked at the effect of racial composition on group performance. On one task that required little group interaction, no effects were found. On a second task that required member coordination and interaction, it was found that racially homogeneous groups (all black or all white) performed more effectively than racially heterogeneous groups. However, racially heterogeneous groups have been found to benefit blacks. Ruhe and Eatman (1977) studied the work attitudes and behaviors of blacks and whites in small segregated and integrated groups. Whites showed few differences in attitudes or behavior between segregated groups and integrated groups. Blacks in integrated groups performed better and had higher self-esteem than blacks in segregated groups, and had better attitudes toward self and others than whites in integrated groups. These results suggest that working in integrated groups improves the performance and attitudes of blacks without adversely affecting the performance and attitudes of whites.

Cooperating interracial groups.   A number of studies have examined ways of improving race relations in group situations. The most frequent method is to have interracial groups engage in cooperative behavior, and it has been found that such cooperation leads to greater member attraction (M. Goldman, Stockbauer, & McAuliffe, 1977; D. W. Johnson, Johnson, & Maruyama, 1983; Ryen & Kahn, 1975; G. M. Stephenson, Skinner, & Brotherton, 1976; Worchel, Andreoli, & Folger, 1977). R. H. Weigel, Wiser, and Cook (1975) found that in cooperating interracial groups of schoolchildren, white students felt greater attraction towards Mexican-American children, but Mexican-American and black children did not show increases in attraction. F. A. Blanchard and Cook (1976) found that members of cooperating interracial groups felt significantly greater satisfaction with the group and greater attraction for a less competent teammate when they were induced to help him than when help was provided by another member of the group. No differences were found as a function of race (black/white) of the less competent member, even though the subjects were from small towns and rural areas of the southern United States. S. W. Cook and Pelfrey (1983) noted that previous research has shown how cooperative activities in interracial groups can improve race relations. One factor that may offset such benefits is associated with the mutual assistance that occurs in cooperative activities. Normally, group members show increased attraction to teammates who help them. However, it has been found that decreased attraction can occur when the help cannot be reciprocated (e.g., Castro, 1974). But, S. W. Cook and Pelfrey argued that in interdependent and cooperating groups the obligation to help teammates may eliminate any resentment at not being able to return help. Cook and Pelfrey investigated the respect and liking felt for a member of an interracial work group for a teammate who provided unreciprocated help. It was found that group members liked and respected a teammate who helped voluntarily more than one who did not help. Both black and white helpers were liked as much when the group succeeded as when it failed. These findings suggest that in task-oriented interdependent groups, receiving help may relieve the discomfort felt by the recipient at handicapping the group's performance and increases liking for the helper, even under conditions of group failure and when the helper is of a different racial grouping.

Expectation states.   As with studies of sex differences, expectation-states theory has been applied to improving the lot of racial minorities in mixed-race groups. In his review, I. Katz (1970) noted that in problem-solving groups of blacks and whites, whites participated more and exerted more influence, and were believed by both blacks and whites as having greater task ability. Assertiveness training for blacks did increase their participation somewhat but it also aroused hostility and denigration of blacks by whites. In terms of expectation-states, the assertiveness training may have increased blacks' expectations about themselves, but did not increase whites' expectations of blacks. Thus ensued a status struggle or conflict (for a review of equal-status contact and interracial acceptance, see Norvell & Worchel, 1981). Entwisle and Webster (1974) examined how effective adults were in raising performance expectations of children in mixed-race groups. They found that white adults were effective at raising expectations in both black and white kids, but black adults were only effective in raising the expectations of black children.

E. G. Cohen (Cohen & Roper, 1972; Cohen, 1982) attempted to increase black boys' status by giving them special training at the task and then demonstrating their superior task ability to other group members both black and white. By adding a specific status characteristic (task ability) in this way, Cohen found that the disadvantage of low diffuse status in blacks was offset in subsequent group interactions (see also Riordan & Ruggiero, 1980). Webster and Driskell (1978) similarly found in females that status generalization occurred on the basis of race when race was the only status cue. Increasing the status of black women by tapping into the specific abilities at which black women were superior to white, offset the effects of the lower status of black women. However, K. A. Adams (1980) argued that sex-role stereotypes are different for whites and blacks; white females and black males are perceived as being passive and submissive, whereas white males and black females are perceived as being active and assertive. Therefore white males and black females are expected to be more dominant than white females and black males. White females have been found to be less likely than white males and black females to initiate verbal acts or assume positions of influence (Lockheed & Hall, 1976). K. A. Adams examined the effects of sex and race on dominance behavior, where dominance was defined as withstanding verbal challenges against one's choices by a partner on a joint-decision task. Black females were found to be more dominant than white females and black males, and white males were more dominant than black males. With a black partner, however, black males become significantly more dominant, whereas the behavior of the other three groups did not change. Contrary to expectation-states theory, all subjects withstood *fewer* challenges from females than from males. These findings indicate that sex and race cannot be considered in isolation, since their influence was found to be interactive (see also K. A. Adams, 1983).

Educational interventions. An important educational intervention designed to improve race relations, as well as school attitudes and academic performance, is the "Jigsaw Classroom" (Aronson, Blaney, Stephan, Sikes, & Snapp, 1978; Aronson & Bridgeman, 1978; Aronson & Yates, 1983). This method involves a combination of increasing cooperation and equalizing expectation-states. Students are assigned to small, mixed-race groups of five or six for about one hour each day. The learning topic for the day is split up into as many segments as there are group members, and each student is given a unique part (hence the "jigsaw"). Each student is responsible for learning their particular segment well enough to teach it to the others: teachers only act as facilitators and do not directly teach any of the material. Group members can only learn the whole lesson by pooling their knowledge; this is the cooperative or interdependent part of the method. In addition, students from different groups assigned the *same* segment meet to discuss this particular segment in "expert groups." They prepare and practise their presentations together, so that when they return to their group they can demonstrate competence: This constitutes the status equalizing element of the method. When the students return to their jigsaw group, they teach each other their particular segment, and, to reinforce cooperation rather than competition, the students are tested on the whole topic. By this jigsaw method the students learn that they cannot do well without the help of every group member and that each member makes a unique contribution. Compared with children who remain in traditional classrooms, children, including racial minorities, who spend part of their day in jigsaw groups show greater interpersonal attraction, more positive interracial attitudes, better attitudes to school, and better academic performance (Blaney, Stephan, Rosenfield, Aronson, & Sikes, 1977; Lucker, Rosenfield, Sikes, & Aronson, 1977). Peer tutoring alone — where students learn material to teach to other students — has also been successful in increasing interracial attraction and academic performance (DeVries, & Slavin, 1978; S. Rosen, Powell, & Schubot, 1975; Slavin, 1977).

For other studies on race, see: L. Davis & Burnstein, 1981; Gerard & Miller, 1975; Gray-Little, 1980; I. Katz, 1981; Lerner & Frank, 1974; McCann, Ostrom, Tyner, & Mitchell, 1985; N. Miller & Brewer, 1984; W. G. Stephan & Feagin, 1980; Tuma & Hallinan, 1979; Whitley, Schofield, & Snyder, 1984.

Other Studies of Social Characteristics

Apart from studies of race and sex, there has been little systematic study of other social characteristics and small groups. For studies of other social characteristics (such as abilities, age, birth order, culture, friendship, physical attractiveness, social class, etc.), see: Adamopoulos, 1984; G.R. Adams, 1977; G. R. Adams & Read, 1983; Ahmed, 1982; Asser, 1978; Austin, 1980; Bachtold, 1982; Bass, 1980; Belgrave & Mills, 1981; Binning & Lord, 1980; J.W. Burgess, 1984; Cappella, 1981; Carron, Ball, & Chelladurai, 1977; Chaiken, 1979; Chell, 1979; Compas, 1981; Critelli & Baldwin, 1979; K. K. Dion, 1974; Edney & Grundmann, 1979; Egerbladh, 1976; Furnham, 1983; S. J. Gill, Menlo, & Keel, 1984; Hastorf, Wildfogel, & Cassman, 1979; E. Hatfield, Roberts, & Schmidt, 1980; Higgins, 1976; Ickes & Turner, 1983; Juni & Roth, 1981; I. Katz, Glass, Lucido, & Farber, 1977; Klauss & Bass, 1974; Kleck & Strenta, 1980; Kleinke, 1977b; Kriss, Indenbaum, & Tesch,

1974; Kukita, 1984; Laughlin, 1978; Leung & Bond, 1982; Levitt & Kornhaber, 1977; Littlepage & Whiteside, 1976; Mathes, 1975; Midlarsky & Midlarsky, 1976; N. Miller & Maruyama, 1976; J. Mills, Belgrave, & Boyer, 1984; A. Nadler, Shapira, & Ben-Itzhak, 1982; Ohbuchi & Izutsu, 1984; Piché & Sachs, 1982; P. H. Powell & Dabbs, 1976; Reis, Nezlek, & Wheeler, 1980; Reis, Wheeler, Spiegel, Kernis, Nezlek, & Perri, 1982; Reisman, 1984; Scheidt & Smith, 1974; Simonton, 1985; H. W. Smith, 1977; Soble & Strickland, 1974; Tallman & Miller, 1974; Terborg, Castore, & DeNinno, 1976; Vassiliou & Vassiliou, 1974; Winstead & Derlega, 1985; Zander, 1983.

SUMMARY

Although correlations between personality traits and behavior tend to be relatively low due to the influence of situational variables, psychologists continue to search for those traits that have the greatest degree of predictability. The most common trait that is either measured directly or in combination with some other trait is dominance versus submission. Scales for assertiveness, dominance, and extraversion provide direct measures. Machiavellianism combines activity with a need to manipulate encounters for personal gain. Persons who are high on self-monitoring are concerned about their public impression and will change their behavior to suit the situation. Those high on self-esteem are less likely to be influenced by a group. The traits of anxiety and depression are both associated with low rates of interaction and negative behavior.

A second dimension of behavior that has been measured in several ways is friendly versus unfriendly. On the friendly side are measures of sociability, affiliation, and intimacy, and on the unfriendly side is a measure of loneliness. Not surprisingly, persons who are friendly are more positive in their social interaction, while those who are lonely are more inhibited.

A third dimension involves acceptance versus rejection of authority, although little relevant research has been carried out using trait measures of this dimension. Authoritarians have a respect for power and authority; when in a position of power, they act in a domineering and punitive manner, but when in a subordinate position, they act in a submissive and conformist way.

Two other variables that have received attention in the research literature are field dependence-independence (extent of autonomous self-functioning or reliance on internal versus external cues) and locus of control (the extent to which behavior is believed to be governed by internal versus external forces). Field-independent persons who have a more highly developed sense of identity are similar to persons with an internal locus of control, who tend to see their behavior as governed by internal forces such as their personality, abilities, effort, and motivation. Both field independents and those with an internal locus of control have less need to be involved in social situations.

Groups with members who have compatible personalities are likely to be happier, more efficient, and more productive than groups with incompatible members. However, a moderate amount of tension may lead to greater productivity than complete harmony.

Inequalities in participation rates develop quickly in a new group, and they seem to be the result of differences in "performance expectation states" (beliefs about the task ability of each group member). Persons who are judged to have high task ability are encouraged to contribute more. These early estimates of ability are based on social status characteristics that are external to the group, such as age, sex, race, and occupation. Once the status of a person has been determined, behavior related to that status will tend to follow. Thus, high status persons will be more dominant and low status persons will be more submissive. Positions in the hierarchy can be altered by increasing the task ability of low status persons.

In problem-solving groups, males are typically active and task-oriented, whereas females are typically positive and expressive, involving intimacy and friendliness. In nonverbal behavior, females show more involvement and immediacy in their encounters, as indicated by gaze, body posture, and gesture. Males are more likely to be concerned about maintaining their personal space, are more likely to go alone to public places, are more aggressive, and more likely to give help than to receive it. In Western society, assertiveness, competitiveness, dominance, and power are all characteristics associated with masculine behavior, as are nonconformity and leadership.

Part II

THE INFLUENCE OF OTHERS ON THE INDIVIDUAL

Chapter 3

The Presence of Others

M. Valerie Kent

When we perform a task in the presence of other people, we may both feel and behave differently from when we are alone. These differences may, of course, depend also on what sort of other people they are and how many, on whether they are an audience (friendly or otherwise) or people engaged on the same or some other task, and on the nature of the task itself. Nonetheless, the sense that in some way the presence of other people has an effect on us is a commonplace of everyday experience.

There are three main research themes in this area: Social facilitation — the effect of the presence of others upon performance; social inhibition — the suppression, in the presence of others, of behavior which would have occurred when alone; affiliation — the emotion reducing effects of the presence of others when in an anxiety-provoking situation.

Each of these broad topics can lead to paradoxical implications, both within and between them. For example, does the presence of others truly "facilitate," or does it sometimes lead to a deterioration of performance? Is the presence of others a source of arousal (socially learned or otherwise), or does it lead to the reduction of arousal? Despite the familiarity of the experience that the presence of others affects us, the research listed below does not reflect straightforward answers, but a plethora of data and conflicting explanations, in addition to which there is a body of information in which it is argued that the "classic" effects do not occur at all. In this field, nothing is sacred! Even Allport's classic 1924 study of coaction was replicated and reinterpreted as a retest effect (Granberg, Steele, & Brent, 1975).

SOCIAL FACILITATION

The most influential paper in this area was Zajonc's (1965) review of the literature on the effect of the presence of others, in which he put forward his own explanation for the diverse findings in the field. This explanation, derived from Hull-Spence Drive Theory, rested on the assumption that the presence of other people is arousing, and that this arousal enhances the performance of dominant responses. This formulation could then elegantly accommodate the apparent conflict where some studies found better performance in the presence of others, while other studies found evidence for a decline in performance. It did so by saying that well-learned or easy (hence dominant) responses would be enhanced by the presence of others, while performance of novel, poorly-learned, or complex tasks would deteriorate, since the dominant responses would be errors.

This view was the stimulus to much research, not only to test its basic predictions, but also to establish *why* the presence of others should be arousing. Still more recently, explanations have been proposed which depend much more on cognitive or attentional factors, or on symbolic interaction and the meaning of the situation for the subject. For reviews of the social facilitation literature see: C. F. Bond and Titus (1983), for a meta-analysis of 241 studies; Guerin and Innes (1984); Geen and Gange (1977); G. S. Sanders (1984).

Drive Theories

There are three main explanations as to why the presence of others should be arousing. The first, mere presence (Zajonc, 1965) or compresence (Zajonc, 1980) asserts that it is the mere presence of a conspecific which, for survival reasons, has become a trigger for an increase in arousal. The second explanation is based on arousal as a socially induced drive, learned from experience that others may reward or punish us. (See, for example, Geen & Gange, 1983.) Thirdly, it has been argued that the presence of others is arousing because others distract attention, so that arousal increases in coping with both the task and the distraction.

Mere presence.   For a review of mere presence effects, see Guerin (1986a, 1986b), in which he concludes, rather like G. S. Sanders (1983), that while there are mere presence effects, there are also effects of the presence of others due to expectations of approval or disapproval. Guerin argued that the various theories did not compete but described different levels of the same process, again, a very similar view to Sanders (see below).

One problem with testing for mere presence effects lies in establishing an "alone" situation. Markus (1978) used an "unobtrusive test" in which subjects dressed or undressed in familiar or unfamiliar clothing either alone, in the presence of a passive, inattentive other, or with an attentive onlooker.

The familiar task, dressing in own clothes, was enhanced by audience presence; dressing in unfamiliar clothes showed what she called social interference effects.

Another study, expressly designed to be similar to Markus's procedure but "modified to remove some critical ambiguities of interpretation" was carried out by

B. H. Schmitt, Gilovich, Goore, and Joseph (1986), using a difficult or easy typing task, apparently (to the subjects) before the experiment proper had started. Instead of a passive presence condition for comparison, they had one group of subjects work in the presence of a person wearing a blindfold and earmuffs. The other two experimental groups were "alone" and "evaluative experimenter." The authors claim that their data clearly show that mere presence is sufficient to produce social facilitation.

Guerin (1986a, 1986b), too, found support for mere presence effects on performance of a simple pursuit rotor task, having manipulated "mere presence" to remove any confound with competition or experimenter presence effects.

Rajecki, Ickes, Corcoran, and Lenerz (1977) found that, while mere presence affected performance, it was not sufficient to explain the differences between their alone, blindfolded companion and observing peer conditions. They invoked the "distractibility or predictability of the other" as a further aspect of presence which should be taken into account. Similarly, Guerin and Innes (1982) argued that the increase in arousal which was assumed to mediate the mere presence effect only occurred if the other person present could not be monitored. Guerin (1983), in a test of three models of social facilitation, concluded that separate effects on performance occurred as a result of perceived threat (social monitoring), social evaluation, and cognitive distraction. Forgas, Brennan, Howe, Kane, and Sweet (1980) argued, from their study of audience effects on squash players' performance, that both mere presence/arousal and more cognitive variables needed to be taken into account.

Evaluation apprehension. Some theorists have argued that the increase in drive arising from the presence of others occurs because of the socially learned expectation of evaluation by others (hence the use, in so many studies, of blindfolded "observers," originally done by Cottrell, Wack, Sekerak, & Rittle, 1968, who first proposed that social facilitation effects were due to a socially learned drive). For a review or discussion of these, see: Bray & Sugarman, 1980; Geen, 1981a; Geen & Gange, 1983.

Support for the evaluation apprehension view comes from studies by: L. H. Cohen, 1980; F. G. Miller, Hurkman, Robinson, & Feinberg, 1979; VanTuinen & McNeel, 1975.

Within the evaluation apprehension framework, some researchers have also looked at the effects of feedback on performance (see, e.g., Geen, 1981a, 1981b; H. P. Beck & Seta, 1980). The latter study used coacting subjects, that is, subjects working on at the same time on the same task, and showed not only feedback effects but also that coacting subjects responded more than those working alone. Seta (1982) having found that subjects, paired with coactors of apparently differing performance levels, argued that within the coaction situation, social comparison processes are also operating.

Meglino (1976) extended the range of responses used as an index of social facilitation, finding that highly dominant subjects became more dominant in the presence of an evaluator, while low dominants behaved less dominantly. See also Wankel (1975).

Distraction/conflict.   G. S. Sanders and Baron (1975) conducted two experiments in which distraction and task difficulty were varied and concluded that distraction has drivelike properties in its effects on task performance, facilitating simple tasks and impairing performance on complex tasks. While these studies simply used looking up from the task on hearing a signal, the presence of a coactor may also serve as a source of distraction.

G. S. Sanders, Baron, and Moore (1978) argued that the social comparison process occurring in the coaction situation leads to attentional conflict for the subject, having to concentrate both on the task in hand and to take, literally or metaphorically, a sideways look at the coactor's performance. This attentional conflict, they argue, leads to increased arousal and hence the social facilitation effect as described by Zajonc. They stated that their data ruled out both "mere presence" and "evaluation apprehension" as explanations for the changes in performance.

The presence of a coactor only affected performance in those conditions where social comparison information was both desirable and available.

Further studies supporting this view are: Groff, Baron, and Moore (1983), which also showed that choice enhances the drive-like effects of attentional conflict; Suenaga, Andow, and Ohshima (1981), where the effect of audience presence was also related to whether subjects were induced to attribute their failure to ability or to mood; Strube, Miles, and Finch (1981), where joggers were timed on a stretch of indoor track under various audience conditions—this study also found that joggers who reported more distraction were also faster, but only in the attentive audience condition.

Gastorf, Suls, and Sanders (1980) found that Type A coronary-prone subjects were facilitated on a simple task but impaired on a complex task by the presence of similar or superior coactors. Type B's showed only weak effects, and only with coactors. They interpreted this as support for the distraction/conflict view, because of the Type A's concern about evaluation, achievement, and social comparison.

G. S. Sanders (1981a, 1981b) has argued that the three explanations for the increase in drive in the presence of others are not mutually exclusive, but in fact reflect different stages of a process (see also G. S. Sanders, 1983). His view has itself been contested by Markus (1981), who amongst other criticisms suggested that Sanders "too often substituted description and labelling for explanation," made inappropriate comparisons and prematurely excluded "some of the more simple or minimal explanations of social facilitation."

Arousal.   Much of the research on social facilitation addresses itself in some way or other to the notion that the presence of other people increases drive. At this point Sanders and many other researchers were still accepting the basic tenet that social facilitation effects were mediated by enhanced drive affecting dominant responses. As in other areas of social psychology where drive or arousal are introduced as mediating or explanatory variables, it is somewhat disconcerting to note how relatively rarely, in comparison with the total number of studies, has an attempt been made to measure levels of arousal. It is, of course, the case that such measures are not always easy to administer or to interpret, and an excellent discussion of the difficulties of physiological measures in this area, as well as a review of those studies which have attempted to do so, can be found in D. L. Moore and Baron (1983). Kushnir (1981) has also reviewed the status of arousal in the literature, and criticizes the over-simplistic research models used to study social facilitation.

Even where arousal has been measured, and been found to increase in the observer plus experimenter condition, a social facilitation of performance has not necessarily been found (Laughlin & Wong-McCarthy, 1975).

It is to be hoped that future studies will be informed by the recent growing interest in social psychophysiology.

Habit strength. Even more rare than attempts to measure arousal have been recent attempts to affect habit strength, the other significant component of the Hull-Spence equation. Carron and Bennett (1976) established, during pretraining, different habit strength hierarchies for their coacting subjects. However, they found no support for the view that habit strength and coaction would interact to show the "social facilitation effect," nor, indeed, did they find any difference between coaction and alone conditions. Rajecki, Kidd, and Ivins (1976) had found in their investigation of chickens' consummatory responses that only companion but not stranger chickens were "facilitative." Furthermore, the differences between conditions were qualitative, not merely quantitative, as the Hull-Spence model would suggest. The authors proposed that any analysis of the social facilitation effect should not look merely at the Drive x Habit Strength formulation, but at the level of the stimulus situation $(S-(D \times H)-R)$. Whilst this view hardly propounds higher cognitive functioning in chickens in order to explain social facilitation findings, it was a reflection of dissatisfaction with an oversimplistic formulation, even for the behavior of domestic fowl.

Different levels of initial skill are another way of looking at habit strength, as in the Forgas, Brown, & Menyhart (1980) study of squash players and the Paulus, Shannon, Wilson, and Boone (1972) study of gymnastic skill. The latter study also introduced forewarning of an audience: Only this led to social facilitation. Again, the need to modify Zajonc's formulation was emphasized.

Kushnir and Duncan (1978) analyzed social facilitation effects in terms of signal detection theory. They argued that by focusing on response bias, researchers had not adequately considered the possibility of stimulus bias. Their research led them to conclude that subjects in the audience condition showed impaired sensitivity compared with "alone" subjects. They, too, argued that the "traditional" model was oversimplified.

Andersson and Brehmer (1977) felt that, given their failure to replicate Zajonc's findings, his theory might only apply for tasks where very simple stimulus connections are involved.

Cognitive Approaches

Glaser (1982) reviewed the literature, including a list of failures to replicate social facilitation effects. In a severely critical analysis, he argued that overenthusiasm for the Zajonc formulation, based on what he says is inappropriately applied and poorly supported Hull-Spence theory, has been a hindrance to the development of an understanding of the effects of the presence of others. He considers that the effects of other-presence should be looked at in terms of the meaning of the situation for the subject.

For failures to replicate within the time frame of this Handbook, not mentioned elsewhere in the text, see: Hitchman, 1975; Kawamura-Reynolds, 1977; A. Newman, Dickstein, & Gargan, 1978. Many of the other studies cited by Glaser are unpublished doctoral theses; he sees this partly as a reflection of the lack of "academic respectability" of positions disagreeing with the basic arousal formulation.

Manstead and Semin (1980) also reported failures to replicate; in particular, that in their own series of five studies, using video equipment, they were unable to find evidence of the "classic" social facilitation effect. However, their data did suggest that an attentional model might be appropriate for explaining social facilitation effects. Unlike the Sanders, Baron, and Moore view, where distraction of attention leads to arousal, they postulated a purely cognitive model, along the lines of the "attentional overload" research of W. Schneider and Shiffrin (1977). According to this view, the presence of others would serve to increase the focus of attention on a simple task, but lead to attentional overload for a complex or unfamiliar task. See also Abrams and Manstead (1981), for similar conclusions from a study using a musical task under mere presence, evaluation apprehension and objective self awareness conditions.

Objective self-awareness. It is, of course, possible that the presence of others may lead to a greater sense of objective self-awareness which might equally well be achieved by having solitary subjects perform in front of a mirror. This stratagem was one condition in the Manstead studies, above. For a validating study of this procedure, see Carver and Scheier (1978), who found both a mirror and an audience were each effective in heightening self-attention. A fuller discussion of their view of the role of self-directed attention in social facilitation, together with supporting evidence, is presented in Carver and Scheier (1981). They argue that self-directed attention leads to a cybernetic feedback loop, in which discrepancies between the person's current performance and a comparison level are reduced.

Innes and Gordon (1985), found both a mirror and a nonattentive person to produce negative effects on performance when compared with an "alone" condition. They found no differences in stress or motivation between conditions, and they concluded that self-directed attention theory cannot fully account for the performance of subjects in the presence of nonevaluative audiences. See also Innes and Young (1975).

Self-presentation and sex differences. There is a growing interest in the possibility that self-presentation may play a part in social facilitation (see Baumeister, 1982, for a review of research on self-presentation, and its relevance to a wide variety of social phenomena).

C. F. Bond (1982) carried out an ingenious experiment in which the lists of paired associates which subjects had to learn were not of either simple or difficult items, but contained some difficult associations in an easy list and vice versa. Were Zajonc to be correct in saying that the social facilitation effect is due to the enhancing of dominant responses, then Bond should have found differential effects of arousal on learning of items within the lists. However, he did not do so, and claimed that embarrassment was occasioned by failure on difficult items in the presence of others, which carried over to the interpolated easy items. Conversely, he said, performance of easy items in the presence of another led to a positive self-evaluation which helped performance on the difficult items within the list. He also commented on his finding, through questionnaire responses, a naturally occurring confound between the difficulty of the task and subjects' perceptions of failure.

In a study of the latency and commonness of word associations, Blank, Staff, and Shaver (1976) found that the presence of an observer did not affect latency, but was associated with more common responses. They, too, suggested that drive theory was inadequate to explain the differential performance found between words with or without a consensual association, and invoked the concept of self-presentation to account for their data.

R. S. Weinberg, Poteet, Morrow, and Jackson (1982) found sex differences in audience effects on performance of a competitive motor task, mediated by subjects' differential attributions of performance to ability, effort, task difficulty, or luck. Such differential attributions may have implications more widely for social facilitation, not merely due to sex differences, but to other sources of subjects' differential expectations.

Sex role composition of groups: For a review of the literature, see D. N. Ruble and Higgins (1976) who argue that the mere presence of certain proportions of males and females may be sufficient to affect sex-role awareness and sex-related responses from members, even where no interaction takes place.

Both self-attention and self-presentation explanations might also account for another finding in the literature, namely that the presence of others inhibits overt practice. (See: S. M. Berger, Carli, Garcia, & Brady, 1982; S. M. Berger, Hampton, Carli, Grandmaison, Sadow, Donath, & Herschlag, 1981.) Yarczower and Daruns (1982) have also noted social inhibition of facial expressions in children, and Guerin and Innes (1982) noted that subjects in their social facilitation studies talked to themselves, counted on their fingers, and engaged in other overt behaviors to help them in the task when alone, but not when they thought they were being watched. Thus, awareness of the presence of others may disrupt those activities the person might normally engage in to optimize performance.

G. S. Sanders (1984) has reviewed the literature on both the drive and the self-presentation explanations of social facilitation. From experimental evidence he describes, he concludes that both points of view are valid but that neither perspective can, alone, account for all the data. See also: Blank, Staff, & Shaver, 1976; Borden, 1975; Dua, 1977.

One problem with research on social facilitation is whether or not a subject who knowingly takes part in an experiment ever truly feels "alone." In some cases, as noted by Geen and Gange (1983), the experimenter has actually been present during the subject's task performance in a so-called "alone" condition. In any case, the subject may feel there is an implied presence or awareness of the experimenter, and this will be affected by the nature of the task and the cover story (see Orne, 1962, on the demand characteristics of experiments). Obviously, this could lead to a general sense of threat, evaluation apprehension, distraction, objective self-awareness, attempts at favorable self-presentation, attentional overload. Hartnett, Gottlieb, and Hayes (1976) argued that an experimenter who was perceived to be attractive might lead to heightened arousal and hence differential performance.

Field Studies

The essentially simple nature of the social facilitation problem — whether or not the presence of others affects behavior — lends itself to field studies, which have used a range of unobtrusive dependent measures.

Worringham and Messick (1983) looked at runners alone, encountering a confederate facing away from, or towards, them. Their data supported an evaluation apprehension explanation.

There may be more than one type of other present. For example, teams may practice together (coaction) and subsequently perform in front of an audience as well. Fielding, Murray, and Steel (1976) looked at teams' performance in a final competition after variation of audience conditions during training. No effects were found.

Krantz (1979) investigated the effect on meal size of being accompanied by others, observing obese and nonobese subjects in a cafeteria. Obese subjects ate less when accompanied, whereas nonobese subjects ate more when in the company of others. (See also: Polivy, Herman, Hackett, & Kuleshnyk, 1986; and Berry, Beatty, & Klesges, 1985, for laboratory studies of social or attentional effects on eating).

D. P. Pedersen, Keithly, and Brady (1986) found that women, after elimination in a public rest room, were more likely to wash their hands if an observer were present. They attributed this to social pressure, but at least some of the arguments for social facilitation seem pertinent.

Other Experimental Variables

Field studies, whist ingenious and often illuminating, can rarely achieve the level of control of the laboratory. As ever, there is a trade-off between internal and external validity. In the laboratory one may quite easily vary the type of task, or the nature and degree of other-presence.

It is also possible to vary the mental set of subjects: McGlynn, Gibbs, and Roberts (1982) found that cooperative versus competitive set interacted with coaction-alone conditions, but that in addition there were sex differences. See also: McGlynn, 1981; Grush, 1978.

Interpersonal distance was hypothesized to have an effect on social facilitation, through its effect on arousal. Although an effect was found, it consistently showed a significant interaction with sex (E. Elliot & Cohen, 1981).

Knowles (1983) looked at audience size and distance effects on social judgments and behavior. He found that audience size, but not distance, affected learning and cue recall.

Audience Effects

For many people, performing in front of others is indeed an arousing, even deeply distressing notion (Borden, 1980). For others, it is an elating experience, enabling them to give of their best. R. F. Weiss and Miller (1971) suggested that observation by an audience evokes an aversive drive; Sanchez and Clark (1981) found supporting evidence for this, and suggested that a relevant but not irrelevant drive paradigm could extend the traditional work on social facilitation.

The most familiar term for one's reaction to performing in front of others is "stage-fright." According to Latané (1981), who has developed a systematic theory of stage-fright known as Social Impact Theory, the effect of others on an individual will be a mathematical function of the social impact of the audience, that is, of their numbers, immediacy, and strength. Latané derived early support for his theory in a study of anticipated tension (Latané & Harkins, 1976). A fuller description of the theory is given below, in the section on social inhibition.

Knowles' (1983) study of the effect of audience size and distance revealed that his subjects, in front of the largest audience (8 people) learned more slowly, forgot less during rests, and recalled fewer peripheral aspects of the experiment. He regarded his data as broadly supporting social impact theory, and "an empirical law of interpersonal reactions:" Reactions to others increase as a square root of their number and decrease as the square root of their size.

In contrast Mullen (1982) argued that an algorithm based on the relative size of the individual's subgroup could describe the effect of the group on the individual. His argument was that this effect is mediated by the person's self-attention, which increases as relative group size decreases, making the person more concerned to match "standards of appropriate behavior."

Laughlin and Jaccard (1975) in an unusual study, found that their audiences (of one or two persons) not only affected the performance of individuals and interacting groups, but also performed differently themselves, according to the condition they had observed.

Baumeister and Steinhilber (1984) found, from looking at archival data, that supportive audiences may sometimes lead to a deterioration in performance, as the authors had predicted from the self-presentation, self-attention research.

Group Size

For other studies specifically investigating group size effects, see: McCullagh & Landers, 1976 (activation and nervousness increased with group size—but performance effects did not occur); J. M. Jackson and Latané, 1981a, 1981b; Khalique, 1980; Hillery & Fugita, 1975; Petty, Harkins, Williams, & Latané, 1977.

McKinney, Gatchel, and Paulus (1983) looked at the effects of group size on performance of a speaking task for high and low speech-anxious subjects. They measured anxiety level by self report, physiological responses (heart rate and skin conductance), and by the subjects' overt motor behavior. Given choice, highly anxious subjects preferred to speak alone; low anxious subjects preferred to address three or more people, despite the fact that both groups showed similar physiological responses before and during speaking. There are, of course, two further possibilities; that the physiological measures were not appropriate or sufficiently sensitive, or that the subjects perceived their arousal differently, attributing it to different causes. See also Steptoe & Fidler (1987). As regards audience size and status—see Latané & Harkins (1976).

For studies of the effect of being part of an audience upon laughter, see A. J. Chapman (1975b), A. J. Chapman and Chapman (1974), Chapman and Wright (1976), in which research on the social facilitation of laughter in 7–9 year old children is presented.

J. C. Moore (1974) found that in the presence of an audience subjects distorted communications where they believed the audience would disagree with the original communication (and see Chapter 4).

Individual Differences

Some studies have focused on personality variables which might be associated with the effects of the presence of others on behavior.

See: Desportes, & Dequeker, 1973-1974; Gastorf, Suls, & Sanders, 1980; R. W. Griffin, Bateman, Wayne, & Head, 1987; Meglino, 1976; Musick, Beehr, & Gilmore, 1981.

For other research on social facilitation, see also: Beatty, 1980; Desportes & Dequeker, 1973-1974; Geen, 1977, 1979, 1980; Isozaki, 1979; Lombardo & Catalano, 1978; Rittle & Bernard, 1977; Musick, Beehr, & Gilmore, 1981.

SOCIAL INHIBITION

Although one might expect social inhibition to be the opposite of social facilitation, the term is in fact used to refer to a somewhat different range of issues, although once again the independent variable in research is the presence, real or implied, of other people.

The dependent measures range from helping in emergencies to the extent to which subjects think about the quality of a poem. In the former case, interest tends to be focused on whether a particular behavior occurred or not; in the latter, the dependent measure is more likely to be cast in terms of effort or motivation. Readers who are interested in social inhibition, especially with regard to its effects on effort, should also look below and at Chapter 11 on social loafing.

Helping Behavior

Work on social inhibition really began to gather pace with Latané and Darley's (1968) studies of bystander intervention in emergencies. This section is in no way intended to cover the extensive literature on helping and prosocial behavior, but simply to present the material relevant to social inhibition or mere presence effects on bystander intervention. For reviews of the helping literature in general, the interested reader might consult: Staub, 1978, 1979; N. Eisenberg, 1982, 1986; M. V. Kent, 1983; Piliavin, Dovidio, Gaertner, & Clark, 1981; Krebs & Miller, 1985; Liktorius & Stang, 1975. For a classified bibliography, see M. V. Kent and Blumberg (1988b).

Some experimental measures of helping are more like emergencies than others. They may range from a lost contact lens (Murray & Vincenzo, 1976), dropping pencils or coins (Latané & Dabbs, 1975), lost commuters (de Guzman, 1979; Harada, 1985), to the "classic" lady-in-distress type of manipulation originally used by Latané and Darley (Abele, 1982), choking (Gottlieb & Carver, 1980), or arterial bleeding (Shotland & Heinold, 1985).

Shotland and Huston (1979) sought to identify the factors used by bystanders to define whether or nor a situation is an emergency. They also looked at whether subjects would be more likely to help in perceived emergencies rather than non-emergencies. They found that emergencies were seen as a subclass of the problem situation arising from an accident, particularly differentiated from other problem situations by the perception that threatened or actual harm would increase with time, that easy solutions were unavailable, and that the victim would need outside help to solve the problem. There was high agreement among their 1,232 undergraduate subjects on what problem situations were definitely emergencies; disagreement reflected a differing perception of increased harm over time. Bystanders were more likely to help in emergency situations, with the victim's need a particularly salient feature.

It is likely that many of the "problem situations" used in studies of bystander intervention would not be perceived by the subjects as emergencies, and it is wise to be cautious in imagining that the same process may explain all instances of bystander intervention. Broadly speaking, the explanations for bystander intervention or nonintervention are in terms of (a) the person's perception/interpretation of the event, (b) their perception of the appropriate response and whether they are competent to act appropriately, (c) the likely cost of intervention, and (d) diffusion of responsibility. Each of these explanations relates differently to the variables and issues outlined in the sections below.

Number of Bystanders

The number of bystanders present has frequently been found to be inversely related to intervention, as in Latané and Darley's original work. For reviews of this literature, see: Mishra & Das, 1983; Latané & Nida, 1981.

Social Impact Theory

The size of the group may affect helping for a range of reasons. Latané (1981) sees group size as one major variable in his Theory of Social Impact, where the impact of the group on the individual is, he argues, a multiplicative function of the strength, immediacy, and number of other people. If the individual is, with the other people, a target of forces from outside the group, the impact on the individual is divided, in such a way that the resultant impact is an inverse function of the strength, immediacy, and number of other people in the group, or rather people "standing together," since there is no assumption of interaction and hence, strictly speaking, no "group." Latané argues that this theory can be applied in the context of bystander intervention, affiliation, stage fright, conformity, and group productivity; see elsewhere in this chapter, also Chapters 4 and 11. J. M. Jackson and Latané (1981a, 1981b) argued that the "social impact" of the door-to-door solicitors for donations used in their study (number of solicitors, their "strength" in terms of seniority and dress, and their nearness to the door), provided some support for the usefulness of social impact theory in predicting "generosity and altruism."

J. M. Jackson and Latané (1981a, 1981b) found that performers at a university Greek Week talent show reported less nervousness and tension when they were part of a large act rather than a small act. They had found in an earlier part of the study that in the laboratory, performance apprehension increased with the size and status of the audience, but decreased as a power function of the number of performers. In both studies, the power functions proposed by Latané were found to be a good fit to the data. Mullen (1985) reviewed Social Impact Theory and challenged it on conceptual grounds: J. M. Jackson (1986) argued that Mullen's argument was both misleading in its exclusion of several studies reported in the literature, and the Mullen's categorization scheme for his meta-analysis was misleading. See Mullen (1986) for his reply to Jackson!

Social Impact Theory is only one model for explaining the effects of group size on helping. Group size, often used synonymously with number of persons in the immediate environment, may also enhance diffusion of responsibility (Latané & Dabbs, 1975, picking up pencils or coins; Ahmed, 1979, motorists helping on a lonely or busy road). Berkowitz (1978) found that apparent group size made a difference to how hard female subjects would work for a "needy" confederate. Subjects who believed there were two other co-workers worked less hard; the effect of a greater number of others was, according to Berkowitz, because of a reduced sense that the needy other was dependent solely on the subject.

Although studies have generally indicated a decrease in helping with increased group size (and see, for example, Grofman, 1974 for an early example of stochastic modeling to fit such data) some studies have noted an increase in helping. Yinon, Sharon, Gonen, and Adam (1982) found that when a suspicious-looking package was left in a public place in Israel, passers-by in groups were more likely to take action (such as informing the police) than passers-by alone. However, there was an interaction with whether or not the passers-by were locals or "transients;" no transient when alone took action. The authors concluded that the norm of social responsibility was stronger than the tendency to diffuse responsibility. De Guzman (1979) also found, in a field study in the Phillippines, that pairs of bystanders were more likely to intervene to help a lost passenger, and that, unlike the findings of some studies, urban subjects were no less likely to help than those in rural areas: Greatest intervention occurred for the most dependent victims. For other studies of group size and population, see: Rushton, 1978; Latané & Dabbs, 1975.

Sex Differences

For a review and meta-analysis of gender differences and helping behavior, see Eagly and Crowley (1986).

Pandey and Griffitt (1977) found that while an increase in the number of bystanders reduced helping, the group size effect interacted with sex of helper and victim's dependency to influence helping behavior; verbal measures of helping were, in addition, found to relate to the helper's need for nurturance.

Sex differences in helping were not found by Murray and Vincenzo (1976) in a "mild need" situation (searching for a lost contact lens). A female victim who verbally requested help was more likely to be helped that a female who requested help nonverbally, which did not apply to male victims. Bihm, Gaudet, and Sale (1979) using the "lost letter technique" found that females assisted females more than males assisted females, and that the presence of others did not inhibit helping. They also found that bad news was delivered more quickly than good news.

M. E. Valentine and Ehrlichman (1979) found that victim's gaze at a bystander led to increased helping of females by females, and decreased helping of males by males. They suggested that gaze may be interpreted differently by the sexes in helping encounters. In a subsequent study using only female subjects, M. E. Valentine (1980) found that gaze increased helping, whether the subject was alone or with a passive confederate. Bystander effects were noted when the victim did not look at the subject, but gaze reversed the effects. She suggested that gaze may lead to a coalition between female victim and bystander. See also Austin (1979), cited below.

If the gaze of a victim may affect helping, then some awareness of victim behavior might illuminate the subject of group size effects. K. B. Williams and Williams (1983) have, in support of social impact theory, found that the number of bystanders decreased the extent to which a victim *sought* help, as a function of the increased number and increased strength of potential help givers. That is, the presence of a larger number of bystanders increased the social inhibition of help *seeking*.

For reviews of the growing literature on help-seeking, see: B. A. Fisher, 1982; J. D. Fisher, Nadler, & Whitcher-Alagna, 1982.

Group Interaction

Rutkowski, Gruder, and Romer (1983) pointed out that most bystander intervention research had been carried out using unacquainted bystanders, thus keeping an important characteristic of groups, cohesiveness, at a very low level. In their first study, they found evidence in support of the hypothesis that group size inhibits helping in low-cohesive groups, but facilitates helping in high-cohesive groups. From the results of a second study, they concluded that the effects of cohesiveness occurred because increased cohesiveness enhanced the salience of the norm of social responsibility.

Self-focused Attention

Misavage and Richardson (1974) had similarly suggested that the notion of diffusion of responsibility as an explanation for the bystander effect only applied in noninteracting situations. Using alone, noninteracting, and interacting subjects, they found support for their claim that interacting groups who are aware of a help-demanding situation in fact focus responsibility, rather than diffusing it. Wegner and Schaefer (1978) proposed an objective self-awareness interpretation of group size effects in helping, and in a study varying both the number of helpers present and the numbers of victims, noted that their data reflected both diffusion and concentration of responsibility, since help was more likely when there were either fewer helpers or more victims. This, taken together with attentional focus ratings by the subjects, was taken as substantiation of the authors' view that group size effects in helping are mediated by the effects of the presence of others upon self-focused attention.

Anonymity and Deindividuation

Anonymity or deindividuation may be used to explain group effects on helping and indeed on aggression. See R. D. Johnson and Downing (1979) for a review of the effects of de-individuation on both pro- and anti- social behavior (Bihm, Gaudet, & Sale, 1979). Members of laboratory groups were found to be less likely to help the leader if the leader did not recognize their individuality (Weldon, 1984).

However, Becker-Haven and Lindskold (1978) using a deindividuation device, costuming, usually used in studies of aggression, found that the deindividuated subjects in pairs acted more quickly than normally dressed subjects to help a "lady-in-distress." Normally dressed subjects were more rapid in responding than deindividuated subjects in the "alone" condition. Thus, they argued that deindividuation hastens response when in pairs because anonymity lessens the subjects' feelings that they could be negatively evaluated by their peers, if the action of aiding another might be damaging to the self-image.

Bystanders' presence does not only inhibit helping others. Petty, Williams, Harkins, and Latané (1977) found that, when in the presence of others, subjects were less likely to help themselves to a leaflet entitling them to a free cheeseburger, although there was no shortage of such leaflets.

Freeman, Walker, Borden, and Latané (1975) found restaurant tipping to be inversely related to group size; for further research on this topic, see Elman (1976).

Diffusion of Responsibility

Certainly, the idea that responding in a noncmergency, or inappropriately, is one that is often mentioned when people are asked why bystanders might not respond in an emergency. Equally, however, one might have expected that the presence of others would make people ashamed if they did not respond in a putative emergency. Cacioppo, Petty, and Losch (1986) asked subjects to adopt the perspective of a helper following an accident. They found that subjects expected, with the arrival of increasing numbers of bystanders, that they would increasingly be held responsible for the victim's plight. That this expectation might have some basis in reality was given some support from the responses of other subjects asked to imagine that they had arrived at the scene of an accident. As the number of people described as already being present increased, the hypothetical onlookers described the person aiding the victim as the one to whom responsibility for the victim's harm should be attributed. Cacioppo et al. emphasize a distinction between confusion and diffusion of responsibility.

Pluralistic Ignorance

Another common line of argument is that the bystanders at the scene of an emergency are victims of pluralistic ignorance: The inaction of the others present leads each individually to conclude that either there is no emergency, or that action is inappropriate. D. T. Miller and McFarland (1987) took this point further by arguing that pluralistic ignorance arises when individuals believe that, while embarrassment is a sufficient cause for their own behavior, it does not explain the behavior of others. In a series of three experiments in which subjects had to rate themselves and others on traits related to social inhibition, finding that people attribute such traits more to themselves than others. Secondly, a study in which subjects could engage in or refrain from an act which could have both beneficial and embarrassing consequences subsequently both avoided the embarrassing course of action and overestimated the percentage of others who would take that course of action. Finally, groups of subjects were exposed to the same predicament as individuals in the second study; all subjects refrained from the embarrassing action, but assumed that their reasons for so doing were different from those of the others in the group.

Ambiguity

L. Z. Solomon, Solomon, and Stone (1978) found, in one field study and three lab studies, that the ambiguity of the event produced a more pronounced reduction in helping as group size increased. They varied ambiguity by making the emergency heard-only, or both seen and heard. In the former situation, subjects were more able to define the situation as not an emergency, were less certain that help was needed and more able to reduce situation-induced stress than those who had received an audio-visual presentation of the emergency.

In a later study, L. Z. Solomon, Solomon, and Maiorca (1982) found that anonymous subjects were less likely to help than those who could be identified, that urban dwellers were less helpful than suburban dwellers, especially for a poorly dressed victim, and that ambiguity decreased helping. They proposed that city dwellers may attempt to adapt to stimulus overload by "ignoring such low-priority inputs as low-status victims and ambiguous requests for help."

The Intervening Bystander

Some studies have tried to approach the problem of bystander effects from a different perspective. Lay, Allen, and Kassirer (1974) looked at the characteristics of real-life bystanders who did intervene. They found that males were more likely to intervene than females, and that responsive bystanders were more likely to act alone. Sex differences are not often specifically addressed in bystander studies (see above). Tice and Baumeister (1985), however, examined the effects of sex-role orientation, as measured on the Bem Sex-Role Inventory, and found that highly masculine subjects were less likely to help the victim of an apparent choking fit than were other subjects. Femininity and actual gender had no differential effect on helping. In line with the research reported above, they suggested that highly masculine subjects may fear potential embarrassment and loss of poise, which may be occasioned by intervening in an emergency.

Relationship with, and Behavior of, Bystander

In two field studies by Harada (1985), both situational ambiguity and acquaintance with the other bystander were varied. Harada argued that both normative and informational influence accounted for the finding in both studies that the effect of ambiguity on helping was most pronounced in the two acquaintance condition, being more helpful in the low-ambiguity condition, in which victims actually asked for help.

Using the "lady-in-distress" paradigm, Abele(1982) found that subjects who were dedicated to filling in their questionnaires were slower to respond than those less involved in the given task. More importantly, perhaps, she found that while the passive behavior of a confederate inhibited intervention by subjects, a startled expression by the confederate increased readiness to intervene. This was especially so if the startle were expressed nonverbally.

In a field study by Borges and Penta (1977), subjects were very much more likely to help a person lying moaning on the ground if an experimental confederate were present, saying "Do you think we should do something?" The difference between their subjects' helping when alone or in groups was not significant in the no-confederate conditions.

Gottlieb and Carver (1980) have suggested that the bystander effect would be minimized if the bystanders merely anticipated future interaction with one another. Subjects took part in a "group" discussion over an intercom, during which one member apparently had a choking fit. Subjects believed either that they were involved only with this one other person, or with five others. Help was offered more quickly among those subjects who expected future interaction; the bystander effect, although in the expected direction, was not significant for these subjects. Among those who did not expect interaction, however, the "usual" bystander effect occurred, with longer latencies for helping in 6-member rather than 2-member groups.

Costs of Helping

C. J. Morgan (1978), noting that experiments on group size and helping have produced conflicting results, tested a model (developed by Morgan and R. K. Leik) by using groups of three different sizes and testing them under two different conditions of cost of helping. Although in a baseline condition there was no effect of group size on latency of helping, latencies did increase with group size if the cost to the helper and the benefits to the noninterveners increased. D. J. Edwards (1975) also found response cost, in the form of embarrassment, reduced level of helping.

Competence

Several of the possible variables involved in the bystander effect might be modified by the person's sense of competence. Previous training or experience of emergencies might not only make it easier to define the situation, but also to clarify the appropriate action. Carrying out such action may involve less perceived and actual cost(the person sees it as within their power, and it is); indeed, there may be an awareness of the costs of *not* intervening and of the value or rewards of helping. There may be less wish to diffuse responsibility and greater acknowledgement and acceptance of responsibility. Moreover, the bystander may feel that others will disapprove if he or she does not intervene if it later transpires that they were particularly competent to do so. There are, too, various ways in which a change in intervention might be reflected; subjects may be faster, more likely to help, more effective in the help that is given. Such effects may appear to be only short-term (Pantin & Carver, 1982) or only to show up in a long-term follow-up (11 to 20 months later—S. H. Schwartz and Gottlieb, 1980a, 1980b).

For other studies on the effects of knowledge or competence, see: L. Peterson, 1984; Rayko, 1977; Shotland & Heinold, 1985.

Intervention and Risk Situations

In the studies mentioned above, the independent variables may have included ambiguity, group size, anonymity, competence, and the dependent measure has involved giving assistance to a person in need. As noted at the beginning of this section, the severity of need may vary greatly. However, despite risks and costs which subjects might have perceived, the experimental task did not on the whole involve real threat to the subjects. There are a number a studies on intervention in crime or other risk situations.

Moriarty (1975) found that subjects were more likely to intervene if a radio were stolen from a beach blanket if they had earlier committed themselves to keep an eye on it. Harrell and Goltz (1980), in a university library setting, noted that intervention to stop a thief was more likely if the victim appeared to be impoverished rather than prosperous, particularly for female subjects and for subjects themselves who had earlier been wrongly accused of theft. Rather similarly to both these studies, Austin (1979) found that bystanders' willingness to stop a theft depended, according to pretest data, upon a priori verbal commitment. Beyond that, he found a significant interaction of harm to victim, sex of bystander, and sex of victim. Sex of thief was not significant. W. Howard and Crano (1974), also in a library setting, found group size to be negatively related to intervention, while prior conversation, sex of victim, and physical location were significantly related to intervention.

Bleda, Bleda, Byrne, and White (1976) found that when faced with a confederate who lied to the experimenter to gain a cash bonus for a task, subjects were more likely to report a female than a male. Female subjects were more likely to report than males if the victim were a person rather than a corporation or the bystander; all subjects were most likely to report the deceit if they were competing with the confederate, rather than working with them or independently. Subjects were less likely to become active accomplices if they initially reported the misdeed.

Bickman and Rosenbaum (1977) found in two studies, one at a supermarket checkout and the other in the laboratory, that a few comments from a confederate designed to encourage reporting were very effective in increasing the rate of crime reporting, compared with discouraging comments or no comment. This effect was apparent even when the confederate immediately left the scene, suggesting that the reporting was not merely due to compliance. Moreover, the lab study indicated that the effect held even if the confederate had not actually witnessed the crime. Bickman and Rosenbaum, who had designed the confederate's comments so they would answer the questions in Latané and Darley's (1970) information processing model of bystander intervention, felt the their data supported this model.

S. H. Schwartz and Gottlieb (1976) exposed their subjects to a violent crime during an experiment, varying lack of reaction of other bystanders and others' awareness of the subjects' actions (evaluation apprehension). This latter condition increased helping, whilst the presence of others, especially nonresponsive others, reduced helping. In a later study (S. H. Schwartz & Gottlieb, 1980a) the effect of anonymity on intervention in either a violent assault or a seizure were examined. A further difference was introduced in the form of the speed at which the nature of the emergency became unequivocally apparent. Although anonymity from the victim had no effect, anonymity with regard to the other bystander affected helping, seemingly by reducing evaluation apprehension. However, this in itself was affected by the clarity of the emergency. When the emergency was ambiguous, evaluation apprehension delayed the decision to intervene; when unambiguous, anonymity affected the decision on whether or not the person was obliged to intervene.

Schreiber (1979) had a simulated murder staged in university classes. Only 2 of the 213 subjects directly intervened, one a football player and the other a probation officer. Fourteen other bystanders went for help once the murderer was out of sight. H. Harari, Harari, and White (1985) used a simulated rape in a naturalistic setting to test for interventions by white male undergraduates either alone or in groups. Observers were used to assess responses; intervention was more likely from groups than individuals and of the interventions, 80 percent were by direct action rather than summoning the police.

It may be that intervention, its appropriateness, and likely consequences are perceived differently in situations of violence between a man and a woman where the protagonists are seen to be strangers or a married couple. Shotland and Straw (1976) found that using a staged fight, in a series of experiments, subjects not only intervened more frequently if the fight were between "strangers," but that in the stranger condition the fight was seen as more damaging, the woman more in need of help, and the attacker more likely to run away. If the subject had little information about the participants, they were more likely to be seen as married, lovers, or dating couples than as strangers.

Huston, Ruggiero, Conner, and Geis (1981) studied 32 people who had intervened in violent crime and compared them with a matched group of noninterveners. They found that interveners had themselves been more exposed to crime, but that the intervention depended less on humanitarian impulse or indeed antisocial aggression than on the interveners' sense of capability, both from both their superior strength and their training experiences. (See also above, section on subjects' competence.)

Aggression

The effects of the presence of others on aggressive behavior have most often been construed in terms of anonymity or deindividuation. An early review of the aggression and altruism literature on group size and deindividuation was by Paloutzian (1974). Dunand, Berkowitz, and Leyens (1984) found that when viewing aggressive movies alone, or in the presence of a passive or an active confederate, the level of subsequent aggression was increased by the presence of an active confederate. Dunand et al. invoke social facilitation and social inhibition to interpret their data.

Many of the studies that deal with the effects of deindividuation on aggressive behavior concern the aggression of a small group or collection of individuals on some person who is not a member of the group or on some members of another group or category. Although these studies have implications for behavior within a group—for example, the relationships between subgroups or between a subgroup and a scapegoat who is a group member—this is not their principal focus. A sample of this research includes: Diener, 1976; Diener, Dineen, Endresen, Beaman, & Fraser, 1975; Diener, Fraser, Beaman, & Kelem, 1976; Gaebelein & Mander, 1978;

Goethals & Perlstein, 1978; Jaffe, Shapir, & Yinon, 1981; Jaffe & Yinon, 1979; Paloutzian, 1975; Propst, 1979; Prentice-Dunn & Rogers, 1980, 1982; Prentice-Dunn & Spivey, 1986; R. W. Rogers, 1980; R. W. Rogers & Prentice-Dunn, 1981; Ruben, 1984. For a classified bibliography on aggression, see M. V. Kent and Blumberg (1988a).

Social Loafing

Petty and his co-workers were interested to see if social inhibition, or social loafing — not trying so hard when others are present, or working on the same task — extends into cognitive effort with, for example, consequences for attitude change in response to persuasive communications. In some of these studies, other people are not in fact present, but subjects are told, for example, that they are part of a team and that their responses will be pooled with those of the other members of the "group."

A study of this type was carried out by Petty, Harkins, and Williams (1980) who found that where there were no implied others, there was differential attitude change in response to good or poor arguments. In the implied presence of others, attitude change was much the same for those who had heard either type of argument. Subjects who changed most were those who heard a good argument thinking they were solely responsible for judging it. (See also, Petty, Harkins, Williams, & Latané, 1977.)

Much of this work relates to Petty et al.'s research on central versus peripheral processing in attitude change (see Petty & Cacioppo, 1981). See also the section on social loafing, Chapter 11.

In this type of research it is the implication that the subject's responses are in some sense part of a group response which gives rise to the effect, due to a reduction of effort; this is different from other work on social inhibition where it is the presence of others who are *not* jointly working with the subject, but merely present, which leads to inhibition of the *behavior* which might occur if the subject were alone.

For an attempt to integrate experimental findings on social loafing and social facilitation, see J. M. Jackson and Williams (1985); note that in their study of the two paradigms, they compared alone, coaction, and working collectively.

Harkins (1987) argues that social facilitation and social loafing, treated as two separate lines of research in the past, are in fact complementary, and can be accommodated within the same paradigm.

In a further exploration of this, Szymanski and Harkins (1987) controlled for one feature of social loafing research, namely that when participants "work together," not only does the experimenter find it impossible to identify and evaluate individual output, but so do the participants. While in the first study, as in other loafing research, experimenter presence was enough to eliminate social loafing, in the second study, where the experimenter could not evaluate outputs, the opportunity for *self-evaluation* was just as effective in increasing subjects' motivation as potential evaluation by the experimenter. K. H. Price (1987) found no effect of identifiability upon cognitive loafing in group decision making, and further, that unidentifiable subjects solely responsible for the task loafed more than those who shared responsibility. Yamaguchi, Okamoto, and Oka (1985) deduced from their study that social facilitation and social loafing effects cancel each other.

AFFILIATION

Anxiety Reduction

Schachter (1959) suggested that misery loves company. He argued that the presence of another person might be preferred when a person is facing an anxiety-provoking event, such as a subject facing an electric shock. Superficially, this might appear paradoxical in the light of the assertions of those workers on social facilitation who say that the presence of others increases arousal. However, Schachter found that it was only others who faced a similar threat who were welcomed, not just any "other person"—misery loved miserable company!

Research on affiliation and the presence of others continues, but is not extensive. For a review, see Lauth (1980), who considers the literature both on affiliation while awaiting stress, and on the processes involved in stress attenuation, including the role of social interaction.

There has been some controversy as to whether people under stress do indeed seek the company of others. Wrightsman (1975) defended his earlier (1960) findings that the physical presence of others decreased self-reported anxiety against an attack from Epley (1974) on what he regarded as "methodological inadequacy." Epley (1975) still contended that Wrightsman had not fully considered all of the methodological criticisms which had been made and regarded the evidence for group-produced anxiety reduction as inconclusive.

P. E. Spector and Sistrunk (1978) found no anxiety-reducing effects of mere presence, even for first-borns, as had been claimed by Wrightsman. However a field study by Cutrona (1986), in which students kept a daily record for 14 days of stressful experiences and social interactions, found a significant relation between social interaction and stress.

If affiliation does occur in response to stress, there are two main lines of explanation. The first, exemplified by miserable company, is social comparison. That is, the other person serves as a source against which the subject can evaluate attitudes, emotions and behavior. The second is that other people may help the person to appraise the situation and thus cope with the stress (Shaver & Klinnert, 1982). This view is further supported by a study by Rofé (1984), who found that in some cases subjects preferred to be with someone who was very competent and intelligent, but in other cases a warm and supportive person was sought. Thus studies which vary the nature of the companion are important in clarifying the processes at work. In addition to these two ideas, S. Cohen and Wills (1985) suggested that other people act as a buffer, serving to reduce the impact of stress.

Companion Variables

Epley (1974) found that the presence of a calm companion reduced fear responses in a number of species, ranging from chickens to humans. Epley and Cottrell (1977) investigated whether speed of escape from a mild or aversive electric shock would be increased or decreased in the presence of a companion undergoing the same conditions. He found evidence for social facilitation, insofar as the presence of a companion was associated with an increase in speed of escape. The "company breeds comfort" hypothesis would have suggested, to the contrary, that speed would have decreased. Epley proposed a resolution of his findings with others studies of stress reduction in the presence of others, by saying that social conditions might differentially affect reactions to primary sources of noxious stimuli from responses to acquired sources.

Morris, Worchel, Bois, Pearson, Rountree, Samaha, Wachtler, and Wright (1976) found that subjects who were told they were to wait for an electric shock experiment when compared with controls who had no such expectation, interacted more with each other and spent more time discussing the impending experiment.

D. L. Moore, Byers, and Baron (1981) also considered the possible mechanisms for socially mediated fear reduction, this time in laboratory rats. They found that rats paired with an experimentally naive rat were no less fearful in an open field setting than controls. However, rats paired with a partner already exposed to the open field showed fewer fear responses than controls. Having noted that preexposed companions initiated more social interactions than naive rats, Moore et al. thought that the companion rat might induce distraction from the threatening setting. A second experiment confirmed this, in that socially deprived rats with socially deprived, preexposed companions led to both the greatest social interaction and the greatest fear-reduction, in comparison with socially sated subject or companion rat combinations. The possibility that distraction explains affiliation under stress had been suggested in Schachter's (1959) study, but ruled out because only companions facing the same situation were preferred.

P. E. Spector and Sistrunk (1979) found that anxiety was reduced in human subjects only if the companions were reassuring, but not in a "mere presence" condition. No birth order effects were found.

Task Variables

There is some evidence, then, that affiliation with some types of companions may lead to stress reduction, but that this may also depend on the origin of the stress. A suggestion as to why this might occur was made by L. Friedman (1981), who investigated the effects of the presence of calm others on arousal in fear situations and anxiety situations. In the fear situation, subjects anticipated a physically painful stimulus, whereas in the anxiety situation they were expecting to be embarrassed. Freedman found that fear was only reduced by the presence of the "calm" other if the other were looked at. In the anxiety condition, the mere presence of a calm other was stress-inducing. Stressed-fear subjects were said to have directed their attention outward and were thus able to model a calm companion, whereas the stress-anxiety subjects turned their attention inwards and thus were unaffected by the model.

Shaver and Liebling (1976) conducted two studies, the first to test for the interaction of other presence and task complexity, as predicted by Zajonc, and the second specifically to address the "apparent paradox" between Zajonc and Schachter, by manipulating fear and observer behavior as well as presence and task complexity. They argued that the conflict could be resolved by seeing social comparison and modelling as modifiers of social facilitation effects.

Fish, Karabenick, and Heath (1978) found that subjects anticipating an embarrassing act preferred to be alone, especially if they also anticipated surveillance by the experimenter. Subjects anticipating a painful act preferred affiliation, and this preference was also enhanced if surveillance was anticipated. Whether or not the potential companion was to be a "fellow subject," that is, facing a similar fate or not, was not found to affect the results.

Individual Differences

In addition to the birth order variable, for which the evidence is mixed, Taylor's Manifest Anxiety Scale was used by Fouts (1979) who found the performance of anxious subjects to be improved on a simple task in the presence of others, and by Nasu (1975) who also used the TAT and a self-image questionnaire.

Dembroski and MacDougall (1978) found that Type A coronary prone subjects preferred to wait with others before performing an experimental task, regardless of the level of threat (electric shock), compared with Type B subjects. However, the Type A subjects when under high stress preferred to perform the task itself on their own, rather than in the company of others or in a leader-directed group. See also the studies which include birth order, noted above.

SUMMARY

The effect of the presence of others on individual performance has been explored. One line of research follows Zajonc's hypothesis that, when subjects are aroused by the presence of others, well-learned or easy (hence dominant) responses would be enhanced by the presence of others, while performance on novel, poorly learned, or complex tasks would deteriorate, since the dominant responses would be errors. Arousal may be increased because of a drive based on survival, or the knowledge that others may reward or punish behavior, or because the others distract the subject's attention and it becomes necessary to deal with both the task and the distraction.

The meaning of the situation for the subject is also important. The presence of others can serve to focus attention on a simple task but lead to attentional overload on a complex or unfamiliar task. Embarrassment, when the subject fails on some part of a task, may carry over to the whole situation and depress performance. Embarrassment in turn is related to self presentation when persons act in a way that is not in accord with their desired role.

People who volunteer for experiments may never feel truly "alone" since there is an implied presence of the experimenter. This could lead in turn to a general sense of threat, evaluation apprehension, distraction, objective self-awareness, attempts at favorable self-presentation and behavioral overload.

In field studies of people performing alone or in the presence of others (on tasks such as running or eating) and in observations of the effects of an audience on "stage fright," the results are similar to those of laboratory or other contrived studies. Latané equates the strength of the effect of an audience with the social impact resulting from their numbers, immediacy, and strength.

Research on social inhibition has dealt with a somewhat different range of issues than research on social facilitation. Much of the research has focused on behavior related to helping — where bystanders are found to be more likely to help a victim in an emergency when the victim's need is a particularly salient feature. The number of bystanders present is frequently found to be inversely related to the intervention (if the persons are unacquainted), since an onlooker may feel less responsible. However, if the bystanders are part of a cohesive group, there may be an increase of the salience of the norm of social responsibility. Intervention will be less if the inaction of others or the ambiguity of the event leads the subject to believe that intervention is not necessary. If the costs and risks of helping are high or the potential helper not competent to deal with the problem, intervention is also less likely. Social loafing can affect cognitive tasks in the same way.

The presence of another person is generally preferred when a subject is facing an anxiety-provoking event, such as receiving an electric shock, especially if the other person faces a similar threat, and if the companions are reassuring. However, subjects anticipating embarrassment prefer to be alone.

Chapter 4

Conformity

M. Valerie Kent

In the last two decades, much of the research on social influence has looked at the effect of minorities upon majorities. Recently there has been debate on the difference, if any, between minority and majority influence processes. However, work continues on familiar problems, following the work of Sherif (1935), Asch (1956), and Milgram (1963). There is rather less intrinsic interest in variables such as group size, composition, task, and status as traditionally viewed than reported in earlier editions of the Handbook. New hypotheses about the nature of influence processes do still lead to the inclusion of these variables in many studies, because of their possible role in elucidating a particular theoretical stance.

The research reviewed here does not include work specifically on persuasion or attitude change, except where some aspect of group process is also involved, but for the interested reader, a comprehensive overview of the field can be found in W. J. McGuire (1985). For an excellent recent review of the persuasion literature, see Eagly and Chaiken (1984). There are several recent and good reviews of the literature on attitude change and on the vexed relationship between attitudes and behavior. See for example: Chaiken & Stangor, 1987; Fazio, 1986; Petty & Cacioppo, 1986. For applications related to social influence, see J. Edwards, Tinsdale, Heath, and Posavac, 1990.

The effects of social influence may be reflected in changes in behavior or belief; it is sadly the case that few follow-up studies are conducted to look for long-term change. However, the studies of minority influence do emphasize "conversion" rather than "compliance," and like some recent attitude research (Petty & Cacioppo, 1986, above), do reflect an interest in enduring change, and not "mere" behavioral compliance.

This introductory note already indicates the definitional minefield in the realm of social influence. There are many possible ways of responding to social influence, including compliance, conversion, and congruence. There are, of course, many ways of resisting influence, such as anticonformity or independence. For a review and analysis of the definitional issues, see Nail (1986).

These alternative modes of responding to social pressures are among the issues raised as having received too little attention, in a review of trends in conformity research (Wiesenthal, Edwards, Endler, Koza, Walton, & Emmott, 1978). The review also referred to a lack of theory construction and to the need for nonreactive techniques. Although it is still true to say that there is no adequate theory of social influence, the area is being investigated from a wide and interesting variety of theoretical perspectives. In particular, the work of Moscovici on minority influence has been challenging, and has provoked a debate whose resolution may come somewhat nearer to an understanding of social influence.

BEHAVIORAL COMPLIANCE

Face-to-Face Persuasion

Currently, there are many pragmatic studies in which subjects are asked to comply with a request. The various stratagems which serve to enhance compliance seem to be not unfamiliar to sales personnel. These include the "foot-in-the-door" (FITD), "door-in-the-face" (DITF), and "low-ball" techniques. Each will be briefly outlined below.

For a review of these strategies, see Fern, Monroe, and Avila (1986).

Foot-in-the-door. The idea here is that people are induced to comply with a large request by first being asked to grant a smaller one. There appear to be two elements in the foot-in-the-door procedure which are necessary to produce the effect. Firstly, the initial request must be large enough to provoke the subject into thinking about its implications (C. Seligman, Bush & Kirsch, 1976); secondly, the person must feel that there was freedom of choice as to whether or not to comply. See, for example: Beaman, Svanum, Manlove, & Hampton, 1974; Zuckerman, Lazzaro & Waldgeir, 1979.

The reason for the effectiveness of the foot-in-the-door (FITD) may be that subjects experience a change in self-perception; after agreeing to the initial request they perceive themselves as the sort of person who behaves in that kind of way, and hence compliance with the second, larger request is a way of confirming the changed self-image (see, for example: Dejong, 1979; Dejong & Musilli, 1982; M. Snyder & Cunningham, 1975).

An alternative view is that the initial compliance provides an opportunity for subjects to discover that helping is not as threatening or negative experience as they might have thought, and this new knowledge and confidence means that they are more willing to comply with a larger request (see Rittle, 1981). It may, of course, be the case that both processes may operate to produce this widely reported effect.

Interestingly, it does not appear that the initial request has to be about the same issue as the second request (C. Seligman, Bush, & Kirsch, 1976), although these authors did find that within the condition where similar issues were used, there was a cumulative effect of small request and similar message. If the issue does not have to be similar, then involvement in the particular issue does not seem to provide the explanation for the foot-in-the-door effect. Either, or both, of the two explanations outlined above could apply, however.

A further explanation has been proposed by B. K. Kilbourne and Kilbourne (1984), who suggested on the basis of data from a four-condition study which included justifications and excuses for compliance/noncompliance, that response to requests from strangers may be governed by social norms, which apply easily to some situations, but which people find hard to apply to FITD, because, say Kilbourne and Kilbourne, the situation may be "normatively ambiguous." Beaman, Svanum, Manlove, and Hampton (1974) found that compliance with the first request was not influenced by knowing whether or not others had agreed, but this part of their findings only refers to the initial compliance, not to the whole FITD procedure.

Cialdini and Schroeder (1976) found that donation size was not reduced, and frequency of donation was increased, if a legitimizing procedure for a very small donation were used. ("Even a penny will help").

Schwarzwald, Bizman, and Raz (1983) found that foot-in-the-door, evoked by petition-signing, enhanced donations, but donation size was also increased by asking for specific amounts rather than leaving the sum to the subject's discretion.

Importantly, FITD may produce verbal compliance rather than costly behavioral compliance. Foss and Dempsey (1979) tested the technique for its effectiveness in enhancing blood donation. Despite three experiments, each designed to produce the FITD effect, they were unable to find any increase in blood donation, and suggested that FITD may be limited to verbal compliance for fairly minimal forms of aid. See also: Baer & Goldman, 1978; Carducci & Deuser, 1984; M. Goldman, Kiyohara, & Pfannensteil, 1985; M. Goldman, Seever, & Seever, 1982; R. L. Miller & Suls, 1977; Pliner, Hart, Kohl, & Saari, 1974; E. B. Swanson, Sherman, & Sherman, 1982).

N. Eisenberg, Cialdini, McCreath, and Shell (1987) have demonstrated that the FITD appears in second graders but not kindergartners, and that in both second and fifth grade children, once it appeared, it was significantly related to the children's preference for consistency.

Those who refuse the initial request are less likely to comply with the larger one than those who did not receive the initial request (M. Snyder & Cunningham, 1975). Furthermore, FITD has not always proved effective in studies making large requests, such as for blood donation (Foss & Dempsey, 1979). It has also been found that the FITD effect appears to be inhibited where there is a considerable perceptual contrast between the two requests (Shanab & Isonio, 1982; Shanab & O'Neill, 1982).

M. Goldman, Creason and McCall (1981) looked at the effect of "two-feet-in-the-door," by testing for any effects of an intermediate request between the initial and final request. Where the intermediate request was moderate, significantly more compliance was produced when compared to the FITD procedure.

For a review and meta-analysis of 15 years of studies on the effectiveness of the "foot-in-the-door," see Beaman, Cole, Preston, Klentz, and Steblay (1983).

Door-in-the-face. This term was coined by Cialdini, Vincent, Lewis, Catalan, Wheeler, and Darby (1975). Here, the reverse procedure to foot-in-the-door applies. Subjects are confronted with a large request which they are likely to refuse. They are then asked for a smaller favor, which they are seemingly more likely to grant than control subjects exposed to no prior request. See, for example: Cialdini & Ascani, 1976; DeJong, 1979; Mowen & Cialdini, 1980.

Cann, Sherman, and Elkes (1975) compared FITD and DITF, including a further variable, the delay between first and second request. Their evidence led them to suggest that small request-no delay leads to a change in self-perception, whereas the large request-no delay condition suggested a bargaining explanation for compliance, since compliance was greater after an initial refusal. Even-Chen, Yinon, and Bizman (1978) also compared the two procedures, and concluded that the door-in-the-face only applied to situations in which the initial request was large. They argue that subjects who see no situational reason for their initial refusal make internal attributions which lead them to refuse the subsequent smaller request.

Pendleton and Batson (1979) concluded from studies of DITF that the effect could best be explained by the idea that the situation gives rise to concern about self-presentation. They conducted a study in which they compared subjects' self-ratings after refusal of a large or moderate request, finding that the latter group felt that they would be seen as less helpful, friendly, and concerned.

In a study of perhaps more practical significance to the student than most, H. Harari, Mohr, and Hosey (1980) investigated which type of approach to university professors was the most effective in eliciting help! They found door-in-the-face to be significantly more successful than FITD or a control technique: FITD was in fact even less successful than the control technique (moderate request only). Perhaps this study is not entirely typical of such situations, however, in that professors may both anticipate further interactions with students, as well as seeing it to be part of their role to assist students. They are also fairly experienced in receiving such approaches!

Fern, Monroe, and Avila, (1986) have compared effects of FITD and DITF as reported in published research. While finding support for the greater effectiveness of FITD, they note that compliance rates vary, and depend on situational factors, the type of respondent and the nature of the requests. See also: M. Goldman, McVeigh, & Richterkessing, 1984; Shanab & O'Neill, 1979.

Low ball. Here, the technique used is to change the rules about the situation after the subject has agreed to an initial request.

This is different from the foot-in-the-door approach in that, rather than following a small request with a large one, here the subject finds that the promised advantages of compliance with the request have been changed—to the subject's disadvantage, naturally! The low ball effect may depend on commitment and a negative self-view resulting form changing a decision. It may be that a sense of obligation is created (J. M. Burger & Petty, 1981). Deaux and Wrightsman (1988) have also suggested that, having dealt with the stress of making the choice in the first place, people may be reluctant to reopen the decision and begin the stressful task of making a new choice.

See also: J. M. Burger & Petty, 1981; Cialdini, 1985; Cialdini, Cacioppo, Bassett, & Miller, 1978; Pallak, Cook, & Sullivan, 1980.

That's-not-all! Recently, J. Burger (1986) has added to the list of strategies brought to social psychology from the everyday practitioners, that is, effective salespersons! The "That's-not-all" technique involves offering a product at a high price, not allowing the customer to respond for a few seconds and then offering a better deal by either adding another product or lowering the price. Having demonstrated the effectiveness of the technique in two experiments, Burger went on to test the hypothesis that it provokes the norm of reciprocity in the customer. A fifth experiment also suggested that the new price serves as an anchor, but not (from the results of another experiment) that the customer perceives it to be a bargain. Burger compared the technique with, and differentiates it from, the door-in-the-face, finding "that's not all" to be the more effective, in that it produced greater compliance.

Scripts

Abelson (1981) and Langer (1978) have argued that much behavior is scripted and people follow their "script" for a social interaction without necessarily processing the information which might be relevant Langer, Blank, and Chanowitz (1978) found that in a simple request to butt into a queue to use a photocopier, subjects would comply with a "placebic" explanation—please may I use the copier because I have to make copies—if the number of copies were small, but compliance for a large number (20) depended on the use of a realistic explanation. Thus, there is some evidence that request + explanation may induce a "compliance script," and that the information will be properly processed only if there is a demand which threatens the subject's own position. Langer refers to the subject's state as "mindless."

Langer and Imber (1980) found evidence for the application of the notion of "mindlessness" to the perception of deviance, arguing that the induction of mindfulness in subjects before viewing a videotape of a person purported to be in a statistical minority (millionaire, homosexual, ex-mental patient, divorced, a cancer victim) would lead to more accurate perception of the target's characteristics, whether associated with positive or negative "deviance." These entirely normal and typical characteristics were also more likely to be regarded as extreme by the mindful subjects than by those in (mindless) control groups.

Folkes (1985) partially replicated and extended Langer, Blank, and Chanowitz (1978), but concluded that her subjects were in fact mindful, as indicated by the fact that she found different compliance rates in the request + explanation format, depending upon the controllability of the explanation (e.g., "I feel really sick" or "I don't want to wait"). Folkes argued that her four studies pointed to cognitive processing in social interaction rather than mindlessness. Langer, Chanowitz, and Blank (1985) responded that they saw no reason to change their position, as people are sometimes mindful and sometimes not. They also clarified the notion of mindlessness, stating that it does not imply the absence of cognitive processing, but "the absence of flexible cognitive processing. Under such circumstances, individuals are neither reasoning well or reasoning badly about the significance of the environment. They are not reasoning at all" (p.605).

In a study of linguistic forms in dyads, Drake and Moberg (1986) refer to the use of certain forms which act as linguistic "palliatives and sedatives." The target may be palliated into compliance where there is no sufficient inducement for behavior, or may be sedated into automatic compliance. On the other hand, where inducements are sufficient, language that violates power or social distance expectations may undermine compliance, despite the favorable information which the message contains about social exchange considerations.

See also: Ellsworth & Langer (1976); Kleinke and Singer (1979), on the effects of gaze and social context on the compliance of males and females to male and female experimenters; and M. L. Patterson (1976) on direction of gaze and compliance.

Obedience

The best known study of behavioral compliance to an order, that is, obedience, rather than to a request as in the studies above, is Milgram's (1963) classic work. In that study, each subject was ordered to administer "electric shocks" to another "subject," in fact an experimental confederate. Several replications and extensions of Milgram's original research have been published, some cross-cultural, and many are reviewed by Eckman (1977).

S. J. Gilbert (1981) has argued that the effect may depend on the fact that the subjects delivered incremental shocks, such that the innocuous beginning led to compliance without providing a "breakpoint" at which subjects could switch from obedience to disobedience. The underlying process, in this view, is akin to the foot-in-the-door effect. Burley and McGuinness (1977) found that Social Intelligence Test scores related to the degree to which subjects were willing to comply, concluding that cognitive abilities rather than temperament might mediate obedience to make another person suffer.

Whereas Milgram himself had suggested that the situation led subjects to cast off their sense of responsibility for their actions in obeying a higher authority figure, Mantell and Panzarella (1976) disputed this, finding that compliant subjects did not disown responsibility for shocking a victim, but rather defined themselves as authority figures.

However, an ingenious study by J. Martin, Lobb, Chapman and Spillane (1976) asked secondary school boys to say what level of noxious sound (which could cause up to a 50 percent hearing loss) were they willing to administer to themselves. The experiment used a fake "sound generator" similar to Milgram's fake "shock generator," and the danger level of the stimulus was clearly displayed in front of the subjects. The results were very similar to Milgram's. This led them to suggest that the Milgram effect does not depend on injuring another, but reflects a more general human tendency to concede to authority. They draw attention to F. H. Allport's (1924) J-curve of institutional conformity—something rarely discussed in recent social psychology.

In a rather different vein, Safer (1980) showed that subjects who had viewed Milgram's 1974 film on obedience and were then given a description of Milgram's control experiment in which subjects had been free to choose the level of shock, overestimated the amount of shock, compared with naive subjects who had not seen the film. Safer argues that the Milgram study leads people to conclude that others are aggressive, rather than appreciating the situational forces acting on "obedience condition" subjects.

Geller (1978) carried out a role-playing replication of Milgram, successfully replicating both the obedience findings and the participants' experience of the situation. He discusses whether such simulations can in fact avoid the ethical issues aroused by the Milgram paradigm, since the subjects showed "realistic and stressful emotional responses" (p. 219).

Other studies: Baglioni, Nencini, & Meschieri-Belcecchi, 1974; Bonny Miranda, Bordes Caballero, Garcia Gomez, & Martin Zamorano, 1981; Gaebelein & Hay, 1974; Shanab & Yahya, 1977 (using Jordanian children as subjects).

See also: Mander and Gaebelein (1977) for a study of third party aggression in relation to noncooperation and veto power, which considered results in terms of norm-conformity, compliance, and maintenance of power.

Reactance

Sometimes people may be influenced to behave in a way that has been forbidden them, because they wish to restore their freedom of action. The psychological process underlying this is known as reactance. Since an influence attempt may well be construed as an attempt to limit freedom, the concept of reactance has obvious relevance to the study of social influence. Although on the whole the research in this area is not small group research as defined in this volume, readers interested in the implications of this theory might wish to read S. S. Brehm and Brehm (1981). Studies which have specifically looked at reactance in the small group context include: J. W. Brehm & Mann, 1975; Organ, 1974; Yarnold, Grimm, & Mueser, 1986.

Reactance may partly underlie S. M. Schmidt and Kipnis's (1987) finding that employees who "refuse to take no for an answer" are less effective than those who use other styles of influence.

Heilman (1976) interpreted subjects' compliance with petition signing in terms of reactance — whether or not the influence agent was viewed as threatening, having the power to implement the threat and whether the subject could remain anonymous.

INFLUENCE IN GROUPS

Norm Formation and Transmission

Muzafer Sherif's (1935) classic study on norm formation, taking advantage of the autokinetic effect, was extended by Jacobs and Campbell (1961) to demonstrate that confederates setting an arbitrarily high norm for naive subjects' judgements had an effect over eleven successive "generations" of naive subjects. MacNeil and Sherif (1976) followed the same procedure for replacing subjects over "generations" but differed from Jacobs and Campbell by using two arbitrary norms, each clearly distinguishable from the "natural" norm and from each other. Around each norm was a broad latitude of 7 inches (17.78 cm), in contrast to the narrow latitude of 2 inches (5.08 cm.) used by Jacobs and Campbell. MacNeil and Sherif found, in accordance with their predictions from social judgment theory, that this enlarged latitude permitted the effective "enculturation and transmission of arbitrary norms" which was more persistent through generations than found by Jacobs and Campbell. MacNeil and Sherif say that the difference between the two studies is more apparent than real, and can be reconciled by a consideration of the nature of norms in the light of social judgment theory.

R. L. Montgomery, Hinkle, and Enzie (1976) also followed the Jacobs and Campbell procedure, and also used two levels of arbitrary norms. Their subjects were formed into high- or low-authoritarian "societies," according to their scores on the California F scale. Authoritarian societies perpetuated both norms for more generations, with the high norm declining over time, but the lower norm hardly declined at all. In low-authoritarian societies, both arbitrary norms rapidly declined.

Sorrels and Kelley (1984) used the autokinetic effect on subjects either alone or with two confederates. Subjects led to believe they were with other subjects who reported no movement reported less movement than subjects who were alone. Sorrels and Kelley suggest that a distinction may be made between conformity by *commission* (emitting behavior) and conformity by *omission* (omitting behavior). See also: Bradley, 1978b; Kumar & Sharma, 1981; Otani & Dixon, 1976, discussed below; J. S. Williams, Martin, & Gray, 1975).

Majority Influence: The Asch Paradigm

More than 30 years since Asch's first publication on conformity, the basic research paradigm appears to be flourishing, although often the situation is viewed from the perspective of new theory. For example, L. G. Ross, Bierbrauer, and Hoffman (1976) consider the role of attribution theory in conformity and dissent in the Asch situation.

In a study in which subjects were faced with the Asch situation, modified so that the group always showed a consistent bias and half way through the experiment the subject was asked to reply first rather than last, J. J. Sheehan (1979) found that subjects, in his words, conformed "prior to the emergence of a group norm." That is, when answering first, they anticipated the group bias, showing a highly significant shift in that direction. Sheehan suggests that people behave in a way that they believe will lead to smooth social interaction. It seems however possible that subjects acted according to the anticipated consequences for themselves of deviating from the biased responding which they had perceived.

The extent to which subjects were involved in friendly interactions was systematically varied in a study using not the Asch paradigm but the autokinetic effect was found to have a significant effect upon conformity (Otani & Dixon, 1976). This also suggests that interaction per se plays a part in the conformity effect, even in simple (if ambiguous) perceptual judgment.

Anticipation of future interaction after a Crutchfield type conformity situation (Crutchfield, 1955, based on Asch) mediated the effect of prior group support on conformity according to a study by Hancock and Sorrentino (1980). This finding perhaps serves to underscore the importance of looking at social influence over time, which may involve different factors than a one-off meeting, even in artificially created laboratory groups. (See below: social influence and social interaction.)

Group size. Insko, Smith, Alicke, Wade, and Taylor (1985) found that the group size effect is a function of subjects' wishing both to be right and to be liked. They also found that conformity was induced in private judgements. L. B. Jennings and George (1984) deduced from their study a similar dual process, in that subjects were found simultaneously both to falsify their perceptions and to experience genuine perceptual change, with falsification having by far the greater effect. They also suggested a curvilinear relationship may exist between degree of majority distortion and degree of genuine perceptual distortion by subjects.

Y. Yasui (1985) also concluded that conformity in perceptual judgment involved an active cognitive process on the part of subjects.

Group composition.   In a rather different approach, Wilder and Allen (1977) compared unanimous group pressure, using Crutchfield apparatus, with giving subjects veridical social support or extreme support in the same direction as the correct response. Both opinion and visual tasks were used. Both types of support served to reduce conformity, with veridical support more effective on opinion items. Subjects' attributions to the supporters were dispositional, rather than based on the veridicality of their answers. See also Bragg & Allen, 1972; Perrin & Spencer, 1981 (discussed below).

T. P. Williams and Sogon (1984) found significant differences in conforming depending on whether the other members were friends or strangers.

The section on gender and social influence, below, includes several studies on gender and group composition, although not within the Asch framework.

Personality.   There is perhaps less interest in correlating personality variables with social influence than there was when the earlier Handbooks were published. The variables can largely be cast into what would be predicted from either effect dependence or information dependence. Subjects with low-self esteem or high need for social approval may be susceptible. High-conformity subjects may be less assertive than low-conformity subjects (J. M. Williams & Warchal, 1981). This study failed to find a predicted relationship with locus of control however, but a study by Larsen, Triplett, Brant and Langenberg (1979) did find a relationship between locus of control and conformity, externals conforming significantly more than internals. Froming and Cooper (1977) suggested that compliance might relate to level of moral judgment, on the basis that lower levels of moral judgment are concerned with external standards, whereas at higher levels, people are more likely to use internalized standards of behavior. They presented evidence from two studies of male college students in support of this.

Yarnold, Grimm, and Mueser (1986) found, using the Asch paradigm, that Type B (noncoronary prone) subjects conformed twice as often as Type A (coronary prone) subjects. They suggested that this might be explained in terms of reactance, in that Type A subjects might be particularly sensitive to threats to their personal control and resistant to social pressure to conform. (See *Reactance*, above).

See also: Almazov & Vostroknutov, 1977; Fenigstein, 1979; Froming & Carver, 1981; Santee & Maslach, 1982; Stamps & Teevan, 1974; Yuferova, 1975.

Female subjects high on trait-anxiety were found to conform more to a high prestige model than those low on trait-anxiety (Bauer, Schlottmann, Bates, & Masters, 1983).

Ego-identity status and adolescence: see Adams et al., under *Subjects' age*, below.

Response pattern.   J. J. Sheehan (1979) used a consistent bias in the false responses, and found that when, half-way through the experiment subjects were switched to responding last rather than first, they anticipated the group response and demonstrated the effects of social influence even prior to the statement of the group norm for a particular item.

Task.   D. Liberman and Meyerhoff (1986) found that subjects' performance in an Asch-type situation showed conformity on a perceptual task but not on a logical task.

See also Wilder and Allen (1977), who used both visual and opinion items in a Crutchfield conformity set-up.

Attractiveness/cohesiveness.   Crosbie, Stitt, & Petroni, 1974; Matsuda, 1985.

Stimulus ambiguity.   For a fuller discussion of the potential significance of stimulus ambiguity see the section on ambiguity below. Studies which have specifically used the Asch paradigm are: Radocy, 1975; Zaleska & Askevis-Leherpeux (1973–1974).

Status.   Higher conformity for high status confederates rather than peers was found by Larsen, Triplett, Brant, and Langenberg (1979). (See the more lengthy discussion of status below.)

Cultural setting.   The Asch findings have been replicated, sometimes using modified Asch procedures, in many different cultural settings. It is not normally the case, however, that they are truly cross-cultural studies as often they are simply studies carried out in cultures other than the United States. Amir, 1984 (Kuwait); Askevis-Leherpeux & Zaleska, 1975 (France); Avramov-Kiwetz & Gaffie, 1974 (France); Doms & Van Avermaet, 1980 (Belgium); Nicholson, Cole, & Rocklin, 1985 (British and American comparison); Matsuda, 1985 (Japan); Shulghina, 1974 (USSR); Vlaander & Van Rooijen, 1985 (Holland); T. P. Williams & Sogon, 1984 (Japan); Yasui, 1985 (Japan); Zaleska & Askevis-Leherpeux, 1973–1974 (France).

What is perhaps remarkable is that, although the results of these studies do vary somewhat from each other, broadly speaking they all confirm Asch's findings (although also see Lamb & Alsikafi, 1980). However, it should be noted that subjects in these "cross-cultural" studies in fact share a sort of common culture, in that all were in educational settings and all but one study used undergraduates. Larsen (1974) argued from his replication study that there were different pressures towards conformity at different points in history and pointed to the McCarthyism of America at the time of Asch's original work. The notion of historical differences, while important, does not entirely account for the seeming robustness of the Asch findings.

Perrin and Spencer (1981) took both cultural and historical points to argue that the Asch data reflected the United States of the 1950s. While the cross-cultural studies cited above might seem enough to refute this, the common educational culture has already been mentioned. Perrin and Spencer went far beyond this to look at undergraduates who were on probation, and unemployed West Indians as well as undergraduates not on probation. They found only one instance of compliance in the undergraduate nonprobation sample in 396 critical trials. However, the probation group conformed when the experimenter and confederates were probation officers and the West Indian sample when the experimenter was white. They concluded that the Asch effect occurs when the subjects perceive high personal costs in not yielding to the majority. Perrin and Spencer (1980) had already suggested that the Asch findings were subject to cultural relativity; Larsen (1982) however, contended that the studies cited in that review were nondirect replications of the Asch paradigm, and claimed that this cast doubt on Spencer and Perrin's conclusions. T. P. Williams and Sogon (1984) looked at Japanese students' responses in an Asch situation and detected no overall change in level of conforming, compared to earlier studies, comparable to that found by Perrin and Spencer (1981) in Britain.

Lamb and Alsikafi (1980) suggested that people have become more "other-directed" in modern society and should therefore be more susceptible to the influence of others. They found both significantly higher rates of conforming than Asch, and supported their underlying argument with the finding that there was a correlation between subjects' other-directedness and their conformity.

Subjects' age. Those studies which have looked at children include: Pasternack, 1973; Shulghina, 1974; Yuferova, 1975. Fujihara (1976) compared responses to conformity pressure from peer-, teacher-, and mother-pressure, in Japanese children from second grade to senior high school students.

G. R. Adams, Ryan, Hoffman, Dobson, and Nielsen (1984) used Toder and Marcia's (1973) work on identity status in late adolescence to look for a relation between the ego-identity status of both male and female undergraduates and their conformity in the Asch situation. While not replicating Toder and Marcia's findings of greater conformity on the Asch task for subjects in a state of diffusion of identity, Adams et al. did find a relation between diffusion and other measures of conformity, including peer ratings, pencil and paper tests and an experimental task.

Other studies. For other studies related to Asch's work see: Gleitman, 1981, 1984; M. I. Stein, 1984.

Other Approaches to Majority Influence

Several studies have taken concepts encountered outside the social influence literature and applied them to conformity. These include:

1. Endler, Minden, and North (1973) explained conformity in terms of social learning, and concluded, from their study of subjects with high or low need for social approval in one of three conditions of agreement, that reinforcement, a situational factor, was a more important determinant of conformity than was need for social approval.

2. Cognitive shifts/changes in meaning: V. L. Allen and Wilder (1980).
3. Attributional analysis: Goethals (1976).
4. Objective self-awareness: S. Duval (1976).
5. Information integration: N. H. Anderson and Graesser (1976) used this approach to explain attitude change effects found as a consequence of group discussion.
6. Situated identity theory, based on symbolic interaction, concerns the way in which people define a situation and its normative structure, and the theory has been used in a simulation study of social influence to predict the distribution of anticipated responses (Alexander & Lauderdale, 1977).

Status. Expectation states theory (M. M. Berger, 1958; J. Berger, Fisek, Norman, & Zelditch, 1977) has been widely used to explain the differential response to others in small groups seemingly made on the basis of such status characteristics as sex, race, or occupation. It is argued that these status characteristics operate on a "burden of proof" principle, and will affect group behavior through the expectation state process unless their relevance to task performance is challenged. That is, group members use distinguishing status characteristics to make inferences about task performance, regardless of whether the characteristics are relevant to the task in hand. Many studies of status, sex and race differences are based on, and interpreted in terms of, expectation states theory and processes of status generalization.

However, M. T. Lee and Ofshe (1981) reported a study which they felt showed social influence to be determined more by actual behavior than by status characteristics. Greenstein (1981) argued that Lee and Ofshe's study was an inadequate test of expectation states theory and could therefore not permit conclusions to be drawn about the relative validity of expectation states theory and two-process theory of social influence. Ofshe and Lee (1981) published a rebuttal of Greenstein's points. However J. Berger and Zelditch (1983) also criticize Lee and Ofshe's work, and are supported in this by Nemeth (1983). Nemeth, though, points out that the other authors have neglected the importance of the interrelationship between status and behavior. She argues that both structural characteristics of groups (status distributions) and group process (changes in patterns of verbal and nonverbal cues over time) are reflected in the influence which occurs within small groups.

For further reading on this subject, see: Webster & Driskell, 1978; Webster & Driskell, 1983. See also Chapter 2 of this volume, and the section below on gender differences.

For a review of the experimental literature on the relationship between status and conformity see R. T. Stein (1980). (See also: Mazur, 1975; Ridgeway, 1981; J. M. Williams, 1984.)

Sex differences. As in many areas of psychology, one approach to looking at the literature is to undertake a meta-analysis of available and statistically comparable studies. An early meta-analysis on the familiar "stereotype" that women are more susceptible to influence than men, was undertaken by H. M. Cooper (1979).

He argued for the superiority of the meta-analytic method over the conventional literature review, as undertaken by E. E. Maccoby and Jacklin (1974) and by Eagly (1978). The meta-analysis reaches opposite conclusions to those of the "literary" reviewers, who had concluded that sex differences, where found, were small and could often be ascribed to cultural context and aspects of the female sex role. Tuthill and Forsyth (1982) supported Eagly's analysis, arguing that in their own study, when need to manage impressions was high, females were more likely to include opinion conformity and males were more likely to include independence and dissent in their self-presentations. Eagly (1978) also felt that where social influence is found it may also be due to a tendency on the part of women to be oriented to interpersonal goals in group settings. However, Eagly, Wood, and Fishbaugh (1981) found no support for a hypothesis that women conformed more because of a concern for harmony in social relationships. Sohn (1980) roundly criticized Cooper's study for statistical flaws.

Eagly and Carli (1981) themselves conducted a meta-analysis of social influence studies, looking also at sex of researchers and sex-typed communications. They found that women are more persuasible than men and that women were more likely than men to conform in group pressure situations where they were also under the surveillance of the influencing agent. Contrary to expectations, perhaps, they did not find greater frequency of masculine rather than feminine content in the studies. They did, however, find that sex difference in researchers was a determinant of the sex differences observed. Of the influenceability studies, 79 percent were male, and men obtained larger sex differences (in the direction where women were more persuasible and conforming); women researchers did not find sex differences. In a later review, Eagly (1983) proposes that the inequalities of status in natural settings may account for the differences in influence and influenceability between men and women. However, she points out, small stereotypic sex differences have also been found in laboratory settings where ostensibly men and women should have equal status. She suggests that the expectancies about male and female social interaction, learned from unequal status encounters, affect the behaviors found in the laboratory.

Interestingly, the Eagly, Wood, and Fishbaugh (1981) study found that males were significantly less likely than females to conform when under surveillance, and conformity was also significantly less than for males or females without surveillance. This was interpreted as reflecting the independence of the male gender role and the greater likelihood that males' but not females' nonconformity will itself result in social influence. Eagly and Wood (1982) have also looked at inferred sex differences in status as an explanation of differences in yielding to influence.

In a laboratory study designed to examine expectation states theory, Pugh and Wahrman (1983) found that sex acts as a diffuse status characteristic. Unless there were experimental intervention, females in mixed-sex groups deferred to the judgement of males, and males refused to be influenced by the judgement of women. In a study similar to Wahrman and Pugh's (1972) test of Hollander's notion of idiosyncrasy credit, Ridgeway and Jacobson (1977) examined the effects on females' judgements of early or late nonconformity by a male or a female confederate on a game described either as a quasimathematical task or as a common game. There was greater conformity for a male confederate and for a quasimathematical task, without interaction effects. As in Wahrman and Pugh (1972), no support was found for Hollander's view that early conformity leads to greater influence. Wahrman and Pugh (1974) found that a female confederate in a male group was more rejected the earlier she deviated in a series of trials. Cull (1976) found, using only male subjects, that male confederates induced greater conformity on perceptual tasks than did female confederates. For a further review of the area, see Lockheed (1985).

Other experimental studies of sex differences in yielding to social influence have found evidence for the role of comprehension (Schumacker, 1981); task content (Javornisky, 1979); and the content of the measuring instruments (Peuckert, 1975).

Pasternack (1973) found that younger children yielded more than older children and girls more than boys. Until the sixth grade, however, boys rather than girls were more likely to yield publicly more than privately.

Some studies have specifically focused upon the influence strategies of males and females towards targets of either sex. Ridgeway (1982) found differential influence success by males and females according to message type "I know this to be correct" versus "I'd really like to help the group." In a self-report study, Offermann and Schrier (1985) found women claimed a greater likelihood of using Personal/Dependent and Negotiation strategies than men, while men reported a greater likelihood of using Reward/Coercion and Indirect strategies than women. In a transactional analysis of compliance-gaining behavior, deTurck (1985) focused on an instrumental learning theory approach, finding sex-differences in reward-and punishment-oriented strategies for handling noncompliance.

Marked differences between the persuasion strategies of attractive males and attractive females have been found by K. K. Dion and Stein (1978), each being successful in persuading opposite sex peers. These differences were not found between the behavior of unattractive males and females. Unattractive females were generally unsuccessful, but unattractive males were more successful than attractive males in same-sex influence attempts. This study suggests that while there may be differences between persuasion strategies of males and females, these differences may have been acquired through success in past interactions, and that differential success may have been based not on message content variables, but on the physical attractiveness of the sender.

Instone, Major, and Bunker (1983) found weak gender differences in social influence strategies, but in line with sex-role stereotypes. They argued that the gender-linked differences in influence strategy in fact reflected differences in self-confidence: females displayed lower levels of self-confidence than males.

For other studies, see: Endler, Minden, & North, 1973; Finney, 1984; Geffner & Gross, 1984; C. Goldberg, 1975; Larsen, Triplett, Brant, & Langenberg, 1979;

Lefebvre, 1973; McGovern & Holmes, 1976; Osman, 1982; Saltzstein & Ast, 1975; R. F. Weiss, Weiss, Wenninger, & Balling, 1981.

Personality.   Bauer, Schlottmann, Bates, and Masters (1983) looked at the relationship of both state and trait anxiety on subjects' imitation of a high or low status model, finding the high prestige model was imitated more, and that the high trait anxious subjects were the most likely to do so.

L. L. Davis (1984) found that the relationship between ambiguity and conformity seemed to occur primarily for those subjects who were highly self-conscious. He suggested that these individuals, in tending to focus attention on themselves, are more sensitive than others to "the subtle nuances" of the ways in which they see themselves responding to social pressure. This finding seems to relate ambiguity as a variable to effect dependence, whereas, as discussed in the section on ambiguity, it is more usually seen as giving rise to information dependence.

Assertiveness was found to be a mediating variable in the relationship between conformity and status, with high-assertive subjects being significantly less likely than low-assertive subjects to conform to low-status confederates.

Personality, or dispositional, variables do not act as single causes in a vacuum, but often interact with each other and with situational variables to affect behavior. However, for situational variables to have an impact (as is normally presumed in studies of social conformity), subjects may have to notice situational variability and respond to it accordingly.

M. Snyder and Monson (1975) made one of two reference groups salient in a group discussion and found that high self-monitoring, low neuroticism subjects conformed differently between the two contexts, whereas low-self-monitoring, high neuroticism subjects did not. In a second part of the study, Snyder and Monson looked at ratings of subjects' generosity, honesty, and hostility in nine situations, and noted that high self-monitoring subjects reported more situational variability than did low self-monitoring subjects.

For studies including other personality variables, see also: Bickman, 1974b; Bushman, 1984; Endler, Minden, & North, 1973; Howell, Lederman, Owen & Solomon, 1978; Nagata, 1980; P. B. Smith, 1976a, 1976b; Tao, 1974; Tuzlak & Moore, 1984; H. M. Weiss & Nowicki, 1981; Zimmer & Sheposh, 1975.

Race.   Ethnicity has been considered in two studies which looked at the differential response of subjects to communicators of differing race. Ramirez (1977) found Anglo and Chicano communicators to be viewed equally positively by their adult Chicano subjects, but they were more likely to comply with the Anglo communicator. Banks, Stitt, Curtis, and McQuater (1977) varied positive and negative reinforcement for blacks by a black or white evaluator, finding greater compliance for negative reinforcement from a black evaluator. There were no compliance differences for positive reinforcement. They suggest, from a second study, that the black evaluator was perceived to be more objective when making negative statements.

For a discussion of race as a status factor in interaction, see: Webster & Driskell, 1983; I. Katz, 1983.

Age. Readers should also refer to the section on age as a variable in studies using the Asch paradigm, above. Most of the studies listed here do not investigate the relationship between age and social influence, but use children or adolescents as subjects and may thus be of relevance to an overall view of developmental changes in social influence.

See: Chu, 1979; N. Eisenberg, Shell, Pasternack, Lennon, Beller, & Mathy, 1987; Gleitman, 1981, 1984; J. Guttmann, 1981; Pasternack, 1973; M. I. Stein, 1984.

Looking at the other side of the age coin, that is, age as a variable in style of exerting social influence, Finley and Humphreys (1974) examined the role of age in persuasive appeals by girls aged 5, 9, or 13 years, to their mother and best friend. They found that diplomacy increased with age, simple requests decreased, and "high pressure" tactics increased between 5 and 9 years and decreased between 9 and 13 years. The focus on how children exert and respond to influence is a very different approach from that normally adopted in small group research. However, interested readers may also wish to consult Garvey (1975), who studied the requests and responses of nursery school dyads, or even Cappella and Greene (1982) who have looked at the mutual influence of expressive behavior in adult and adult-infant dyads.

For a discussion of adolescent conformity to peers or parents, see T. Berndt (1979). For other studies see: G. R. Adams, Ryan, Hoffman, Dobson, & Nielsen, 1984; N. S. Endler, Coward, & Wiesenthal, 1975; J. Cohen, 1978.

Cross-cultural studies. Chu (1979) compared American and Chinese children on their susceptibility to social influence in a series of ambiguous perceptual tasks. Meade and Barnard (1975) followed up an earlier study comparing Chinese and American males' conformity with a comparison of group pressure effects on Chinese and American females. Sasaki (1979) has reviewed research on group norms in Japan since 1960.

See also: Cho, 1980 (Korea); Ittyerah & Modi, 1981 (Indian students, on high and low value statements); Yoshitake, 1985 (Japan). These last are not cross-cultural as such, but the information from varied cultural groups may be of use to some researchers.

Ambiguity. Increased ambiguity has long been found to increase social influence. In line with Festinger's (1954) social comparison theory, it seems that where dependence on physical reality is low, dependence on social reality is correspondingly high. Faced with uncertainty, subjects turn to one another: they are increasingly information dependent on each other. The classic study involving ambiguity was Sherif (1935), who looked at the formation of norms. The variable was also included by Asch (1956). Earlier volumes of the Handbook cite the many studies in this area.

Developing a mathematical model for social influence on perceptual judgements based on signal detection theory, Kriss, Kinchla, and Darley (1977) claimed that this model fitted their data. They suggest that the model could be used to interpret social influence on perceptual judgments in which the influence effects only arise when the subject has ambiguous sensory impressions.

In a very different vein, focusing on the dynamics of mutual influence between subjects, Lemaine (1975) argued, on the basis of two studies which he conducted, that even in the situation of "normalization" when viewing an ambiguous stimulus, the "negotiation of influence" was rarely symmetrical.

Social influence and social interaction. Discussions between same-sex adult dyads were coded using modified Bales Interaction Process Analysis categories in a study by Ziffo (1977). A tendency for social-emotional acts to increase over the interaction was not matched by an increase in task-related directives, as had been expected. It appears that there may be a two-stage influence process, firstly focusing on task-relevant cognitive changes. If this strategy is unsuccessful, the influencer may shift to the use of sanctions and rely on extrinsic rather than intrinsic persuasion.

However, the very perception of the sanctions may depend on the type of relationship in which people find themselves. Where members of dyads had common interests (correspondent relationships) threat appeared to be perceived as an indicator of the influencer's conviction and confidence that the choice of action was correct. This is further affected by the other person's relative attributions of informational power within the dyad. Where there is conflict of interest (noncorrespondent relationships), threats are not perceived as sources of information about the task but as straightforward coercion (Friedland, 1976). (See also: Thibaut, Friedland & Walker, 1974.)

Focusing on the influencer in interaction, a study by D. T. Gilbert, Jones and Pelham (1987) suggests that observers make different attributions from influencers about how and why the targets are being influenced. Observers are more aware of other concurrent sources of influence on the target's behavior, whereas inducers make deductions based on their (experimentally varied) personal power. See also Cialdini, Braver, and Lewis (1974), who found that influencers regard those influenced as more intelligent and attractive than those who resist, and Cialdini and Mirels (1976) who found that this difference between perceptions of yielding and resisting targets applied to subjects high on personal control.

For other studies of conformity or mutual influence in dyads, see: L. L. Davis,

1984; Delin & Poo Hong, 1974; Füchsle, Fröhlich, & Burger, 1982; Pace & MacNeil, 1974; C. E. Spitzer & Davis, 1978.

Group size.   Since Asch's early studies it has been clear that group size has an effect on conformity, but that the effect is nonlinear. In current research it is more likely to be construed in terms of social impact theory or minority influence, as is discussed below in the section on minority influence. A study by Wilder (1977) varied the organization of the number of persons attempting to influence subjects, so that the subjects perceived them as a single group, as several separate groups, or as an aggregate of unrelated individuals. He found that varying group size as such had little effect on conformity, but conformity did increase as the number of separate individuals and groups increased. Petty, Cacioppo, and Harkins (1983) have explored the effect of number of message sources and number of different arguments in persuasion, explaining the interaction effect they found in terms of the extent to which the subject is induced to engage in cognitive effort. Although their study was on persuasion rather than small group conformity, there seems to be room for cross-fertilization here. This is especially the case as they are suggesting that the numbers effect serves to enhance thinking about the message and genuine attitude change. This idea could have some bearing on studies of minority influence which focus on conversion. Perhaps in both cases a more general case could be made for the role of thought in social influence, and factors which serve to promote it, leading, perhaps via an induced sense of information dependence to internalization.

Task competence.   People may yield to the judgments or influence attempts of others if they believe that they are differentially competent. If this is the case, people may be particularly susceptible to informational influence. Data from a study by J. D. Campbell, Tesser, and Fairey (1986) suggest that matters are rather more complex than this. The study examined the effects of group pressure, self-doubt, norm extremity, and the order in which norm extremity was presented. One dependent variable was attention to the stimulus which they found to be low where both pressure and self-doubt were absent, moderate where both were present, and high when only one of the two variables was present. Campbell, Tesser, and Fairey believe that different psychological processes are reflected in their pattern of results. Where there are low-extremity norms, attention to the stimulus occurs when the subject wishes to resist group pressure; here yielding is due to informational influence. On the other hand, high-extremity norms seem to lead subjects to yield to normative influence, and attention to the stimulus increases as subjects search for evidence not to reject the group's judgments. The role of attention to the stimulus had been examined in an earlier study by Tesser, Campbell, and Mickler (1983), when conformity had also been found to be positively associated with self-doubt and negatively associated with attention to the stimulus. Here again social pressure increased conformity, and this was particularly related to subjects paying little attention to the stimulus. The authors stated that their findings partly supported both Asch on the one hand and Moscovici's work on minority influence on the other (see below, under Minority Influence).

The notion that a synthesis of research and theory carried out on cognitive effort and attitude change with the debate on whether or not majority influence is "merely" conforming while minority influence is "conversion" seems to be a fruitful possibility, with its base firmly in the conceptual distinction between effect and information dependence (M. Deutsch & Gerard, 1955). This general idea is raised elsewhere in this chapter, in the sections on *Group size*, above, and Minority Influence, below.

It may be that the subject is inclined to feel generally incompetent, in which case personality variables such as self-esteem or low personal control may be the proper focus of study. The section on personality in this chapter, and Chapter 2 should be consulted.

On the other hand, low self-esteem may be experimentally induced, as in Steele (1975) who found an effect on compliance of negative name calling, which was not specific to the initial task. Conversely, Endler, Coward, and Wiesenthal (1975) found that prior experience of group agreement and correctness on a task led to conformity on a different task within the same task category.

Other studies which have looked at relative task competence are: Foschi, Warriner, & Hart, 1985; Kameda, 1983; E. L. Knight, Alpert, & Witt, 1976; Kugihara, 1985; K. H. Price & Garland, 1981a, 1981b; Wiesenthal, Endler, Coward, & Edwards, 1976.

Anonymity.   From the early days of the experimental study of conformity, anonymity of response has proved to be a significant variable. Where it is effective in reducing conformity, it suggests that the underlying process of social influence is based on a concern for being liked or maximizing outcomes (gaining rewards or avoiding costs). In Deutsch and Gerard's terms, the situation gives rise to effect dependence rather than information dependence. Current studies of anonymity often use the word "deindividuation," suggesting a state in which the person does not feel accountable as an identifiable individual, and may thus feel released from the constraints of normative expectations.

Using the number of profane remarks made by subjects in group discussions as the dependent variable, M. J. White (1977) found this counternormative behavior to increase significantly in deindividuating conditions. The lack of a salient reference group was also found to affect counternormative behavior. Lindskold and Finch (1982) looked at how subjects resolved conflicting pressure from the experimenter and from peers. They drew on the deindividuation literature to explain their finding that anonymity played an important part in the resolution of conflicting social pressures, in this case between accepting ideas from a confederate peer and being harshly critical of them as directed by the experimenter. (See also deindividuation in Chapter 3 of this volume.)

Deviants in Groups

While anonymity may sometimes serve to promote nonconformity, a whole body of work on social influence specifically focuses on the study of deviance – the group's response to it, individual resistance to conformity pressure, and the problem of innovation for the group's leader who may thus be perceived to deviate from the group's norms.

A factor which may need to be taken into account for any understanding of deviance is that people may believe that their own behavior is more in accordance with group norms than is the behavior of others. This belief in one's own superiority and the effects created by opportunities for social comparison which arise in small groups is also a feature of research in group polarization (q.v.). The phenomenon has been studied by Codol (1973a, 1973b) and by Wolosin, Sherman, and Cann (1975). In addition to this, Codol (1975a) found that subjects believe their own group to conform more on values than other groups. However, it appears that while subjects may believe that they are "first among equals" within a group, they cannot adopt this view on more than one norm at a time in a situation where norms are conflictual (Codol, 1975b).

Individual resistance to conformity pressure. For a review of the literature on social support for nonconformity, see V. L. Allen (1975).

In a study by Darley, Moriarty, Darley, and Berscheid (1974) subjects found themselves in a group where all but one other person (all confederates) disagreed with the subjects' views on a variety of issues. When the deviant subjects were then paired with either a majority confederate or the confederate who had provided social support, greater conformity was found where the subject was paired with the previously supportive confederate. Although subjects also tended to like the confederate who had provided social support, conformity to that confederate was predictable from the prior experience being a "deviant," rather than from liking for the confederate.

Three studies by Boyanowsky, Allen, Bragg and Lepinski (1981) found that providing social support for a subject on one type of item did not generalize to reducing conformity on other types of item, although there was a reduction in conformity on the items directly receiving social support. (See also: R. S. Feldman, 1976.)

Morris and Miller (1975) found, contrary to their expectations, that conformity was reduced more by a confederate who responded correctly prior to the unanimous incorrect responses of other confederates (preempting consensus) than when the social support came last (consensus breaking). They speculated that this might be because early agreement served to consolidate the subject's initial opinion and hence reduce the impact of the opposing majority. This was only partially confirmed by Morris, Miller, and Spangenberg (1977) where, although conformity was least if the dissenter replied first, conformity was greater if the dissenter replied second or third rather than first or fourth. They suggest that in addition to their earlier consolidation hypothesis, a late dissenter reduces maximal uncertainty and appears attractive.

V. L. Allen and Wilder (1980) found that the conformity effects of group consensus and social support were mediated by cognitive restructuring. (See also: Kimball & Hollander, 1974.)

However, it would seem that the actual presence of a social supporter in a small group may not be necessary. If the subject believes that an absentee person would also resist social pressure when facing the same situation, conformity is reduced (V. L. Allen & Wilder, 1979). The notion of the reference group or reference person has a long history in the psychology of social influence, and resistance to it. It seems not, however, to be considered in most studies; concern is focused more on the factors which produce influence in groups, rather than on those distant drummers to whose tune the nonconformist or independent subject may perhaps be marching.

Certainly there are good reasons for understanding the variables which are effective in social influence. Perhaps, though, the time has come for a greater effort to understand resistance to influence, both because of the general importance of the issue and because of the current interest in the effect of minorities on majorities (see the section below). Minorities in such studies are generally paid to take the role; an understanding of the motivation and behavior of genuine minorities in small groups (not minority groups as such) would seem to have an important contribution to make to the study of social influence processes.

Status and deviance.   Nagata (1980) found that status affected dissent in four-person groups, such that a high status member would conform more than a low status member if the norm benefitted the group, but would dissent more if the group norm was detrimental to task achievement. J. M. Williams (1984) found that high-assertive subjects were more likely than low-assertive subjects to resist conforming to low-status confederates.

Deviants and interaction.   The verbal behavior of deviates in small-decision-making groups has been studied by Bradley (1978b), who found ego-involvement and task importance to influence verbal behavior, as well as sex differences. Over the period of discussion, deviates' statements increased in emotionality and decreased in rationality. Deviates initially increased and ultimately decreased in dominance as discussions progressed.

See also: Atkins, 1973; Dedrick, 1978; R. S. Feldman, 1976; J. M. Levine, Saxe, & Ranelli, 1975; J. M. Levine, Sroka, & Snyder, 1977; Norland, 1978.

Filter and Gross (1975) induced a sense of deviance in half their subjects by the type of feedback they were given after carrying out a battery of tests. They were then asked by a confederate to write letters for an educational campaign. Half of the subjects also believed that the confederate knew of their deviance. Furthermore, within each condition, half the subjects anticipated future meetings with the confederate making the request. Deviants complied more than nondeviants, regard less of whether future interaction was expected. However, the compliance was unrelated to the subjects' being in the "known" or "secret" deviant condition. This finding suggests that compliance is more to do with improving self-image than avoiding mistreatment. (See also: Saltzstein, 1975.)

In a multivariate study which attempted to reflect everyday life rather more closely than some conformity situations, Santee and Maslach (1982) had subjects in groups express opinions about 20 scenarios describing human relations problems. Some of the participants could hear three confederates agreeing on a solution, and the subjects could conform, dissent, or generate their own solution. Santee and Maslach predicted, taking a self-presentational perspective, that private self-consciousness, individuation, and self-esteem should relate directly to dissent and inversely with conformity. Public self-consciousness, social anxiety, shyness, and self-monitoring were predicted to be directly related to conformity and inversely to dissent. With the exception of self-monitoring, the study confirmed all the predictions. Where peer opinion was unanimous the relationship of the self-concept to dissent and conformity was stronger. Thus Santee and Maslach argue that social influence research must address itself to the characteristics of the experimental situation insofar as they provide the opportunity to conform or dissent, as well as to the effect of individual differences on the meaning of the experimental situation for the subjects.

The group's response to deviants. Groups may respond unfavorably to deviants because of the consequences for the group's decision making. C. E. Miller and Anderson (1979) had groups of four naive female subjects and a female confederate discuss a case history of a juvenile delinquent in an institution, so they could make a decision—so designed that naive subjects would recommend release, against the confederate's deviate role. There were three decision rules: majority, unanimity, or dictatorship. Under the latter two, the deviant could sometimes force her decision on the group. Under the majority rule, the deviant was only weakly rejected and the decision rules were perceived as fair. In the other two conditions, but especially under dictatorship, the deviant was strongly rejected and the decision was seen as unrepresentative, with unfair decision rules. In a later study, C. E. Miller, Jackson, Mueller, and Schersching (1987) used the same three decision rules with male undergraduates led to believe that they were working in groups with a four-person majority and a single deviate. The findings were very much in line with Miller and Anderson, with greatest dissatisfaction where the decision was seen to be unrepresentative, and the greatest rejection of the deviate when he had been able to impose his unrepresentative views on the minority.

The idea that the decision rule for the group may affect compliance was also investigated by R. S. Baron and Sanders (1975). They were studying the impact of group decision making upon individual compliance, as originally reported by Kurt Lewin (1958), and found that group consensus is less likely to favor compliance if a majority decision rule is used rather than an individual decision. The explanation they offer, based on a second study, is that subjects are less likely to comply under majority rather than individual decision rules if they perceive that compliance is against their own interests. It is perhaps possible also to cast this study into a minority influence framework, in that the continued existence of a minority view might have enduring effects. (See Minority Influence, below).

Carpenter and Hollander (1982) found an interaction effect on independence when subjects had positive feedback on their judgements and there was no requirement for a majority decision thus, the authors believed, helping the subjects to overcome some of the "impediments," such as the risk of disapproval, which independent subjects face.

A further issue in the reaction of groups to deviants may be whether or not the group is overstaffed. Arnold and Greenberg (1980) investigated R. G. Barker's (1968) hypothesis on vetoing mechanisms in groups, finding that overstaffed groups rejected the deviate confederate more often than less-staffed groups.

J. M. Levine and Ruback (1980) found that not merely deviation but the deviate's apparent reasons for it affected group reaction. In this case, the deviate was represented as neutral, out of either indifference, ignorance, or ambivalence, whereas the group consensus was at one end of a 9-point scale. Other manipulations ruled out a contrast effect explanation in favor of a rationale-for-neutrality explanation for the groups' differential rejection of deviates. (See also: Dornbusch, 1987.)

Influential deviance.   Wahrman and Pugh (1972) had found that male subjects accepted the influence of a deviate significantly more if the deviate acted differently from the beginning of a series of 15 trials. This study supported Moscovici's view of minority influence, rather than Hollander's concept of idiosyncrasy credit (see below). However, when the confederate was female in a group of male subjects (Wahrman & Pugh, 1974), she was rejected, and the more so the sooner she deviated from group expectations.

Minority Influence

Not all deviates are rejected and some deviates influence majority opinion. Indeed, R. Brown (1986) noted that in Schachter's (1951) classic study of rejection of a persistent deviate, those groups where the deviate influenced the majority opinion to their own were discounted from the analysis. Brown's chapter on social influence is a useful review.

Bradley, MacHamon, and Harris (1976) found that group members were significantly more likely than chance to use the very arguments which they had heard presented by lone deviates in earlier group discussions. They concluded that arguments by deviates do have an effect on subsequent discussions of the same topic.

However, the most thoroughgoing analysis and debate on the role of the minority in influencing the majority arises from the work of Moscovici. For a fuller statement of his earlier views on minority influence, see Moscovici (1975). A more recent book on the power of minorities is Mugny (1982).

Moscovici asserts that the traditional emphasis on norm formation and majority influence entirely fails to cope with the fact the there is social change, that innovations are accepted. He refers to these earlier approaches to conformity as "functional," in which conformity is seen as serving the group's ends and deviance is negatively valued. To the contrary, he argues that innovation and social change are vital for social groups, and that they are usually the product of minority influence. He discounts as totally inappropriate Hollander's (1958) attempt to explain innovation by the notion of "idiosyncrasy credits" accrued by leaders through conforming to group norms—if that were so, he says, then Lenin would first have had to become Tsar of all the Russias before attempting revolution (Moscovici & Paicheler, 1983).

Mugny and Papastamou (1975–1976) argued that their evidence suggested that Hollander's idiosyncrasy credit concept did not fit their data as well as did a view that acceptance of the innovation depended not only on initial agreement of group and initiator, but also on the interindividual negotiation behavior throughout the interaction. This approach is closely linked to Mugny's position on rigidity/fairness of behavioral style in minority influence.

Bray, Johnson, and Chilstrom (1982) had a confederate argue a minority position only on the last issue, in line with Hollander's view, and compared the effectiveness of this with the strategy of dissenting from the beginning, as proposed by Moscovici and Faucheux (1972). In fact both procedures showed significant influence in comparison with a baseline control. Hollander's procedure was more successful than Moscovici's for males, especially where the confederate showed high competence. Female groups were less influenced overall, and were equally influenced by either method, irrespective of confederate competence.

In Moscovici's view, it is the behavioral style of the minority which serves to convince the majority that the "deviant" position must be correct. The presence of a deviant minority generates conflict; one way of resolving the conflict is to accept that the minority is correct. In fact, any influence attempt creates conflict; whereas the majority view will generate interpersonal conflict (Guillon & Personnaz, 1983), the minority viewpoint may elicit cognitive conflict.

The effect of the behavioral style of the minority is on the attributions which the majority make about the causes of minority behavior. In many ways, Moscovici's analysis extends the points made by Kelley (1967) in his attributional analysis of social influence. Kelley argued that people would be more susceptible to informational influence if they believed that the other person's causal attributions were more stable than their own, and that no inappropriate causes for the influencer's behavior could be attributed (for example, being paid to make the dissenting statements—in fact the case in most conformity studies!) Thus, if the minority is consistent, and if there is more than one member of a minority, they also share consensus, as well as being by definition distinctive, then the conditions exist for social influence by internalization (according to Kelley's ANOVA model), or as Moscovici terms it, conversion.

In many studies of majority influence, the subjects, while publicly conforming, privately disagree with their stated judgement, as investigated in M. Deutsch and Gerard's classic study (1955). Subjects might be said to be effect-dependent, that is, concerned that the consequences of their behavior would be mediated by others, through blame or dislike, for example. This change, then, is due to normative influence. Information dependence, where the subject turns to others for valid information, as suggested by Festinger's theory of social comparison (1954), leads to internalization, that is, enduring change as a consequence of informational influence.

The effect of minority influence is often not apparent in public statements, but is shown when subjects respond privately. It also often has effects which are indirect rather than direct, that is, changes are noted on material related to the influence material but not identical to it.

The process is seen, then, as one of genuine cognitive or perceptual change; conversion rather then compliance. This has led to considerable debate in the literature as to whether majority and minority influence should be seen as distinct processes (dual process theory) or as part of essentially the same process.

For reviews, see: Maass & Clark, 1984; Moscovici & Mugny, 1983; Moscovici & Paicheler, 1983; Mugny, Papastamou, & Sherrard 1982.

Behavioral style. Moscovici, Mugny, and Van Avermaet (1985) says that behavioral style refers to a behavioral and judgmental "rhetoric": "the organization of responses, the appropriateness and intensity of their expression." They exert two kinds of pressure, because they provide both information and a meaning. Referential pressure is tied to the responses given by the source of influence, while inferential pressure stems from the manner, or behavioral style, in which the responses are given (Moscovici & Neve, 1973a).

Moscovici's basic paradigm is rather like a reverse Asch experiment, in which two dissenting confederates, in a group with four naive subjects, agree that a blue slide is "green" (Moscovici, Lage, & Naffrechoux, 1969). The influence effect was quite small in comparison with Asch majority effects (8% rather than about 33%) but significant.

Three main components of behavioral style have been investigated.

Autonomy. Nemeth and Wachtler (1974) found that the minority confederate who chose to sit at the head of the table for a group discussion was more influential than the dissenter who was assigned to that seat by the experimenter.

Consistency. Moscovici (1976) argued that it is the consistency of the confederates, not their majority, which leads to social influence. A larger but nonunanimous majority is not as effective as a unanimous group of three. Equally, a group larger than three, even if unanimous, does not have a significantly greater effect. (See also: Montmollin, 1977; Moscovici, Lage, & Naffrechoux, 1973; Mugny, 1975a; Nemeth, 1974.)

Rigidity. While the rigidity of a minority might appear to be the same as consistency, it has rather different effects. Where the minority is perceived to be rigid and unwilling to negotiate with the majority, it may be, in H. Tajfel's term, "psychologized" and dismissed as an outgroup irrelevant to the group's functioning and psychosocial identity (Mugny, 1984a, 1984b). The research on minority influence has largely developed within European social psychology, and tends to place the discussion within a wider social context, both in terms of intergroup relations and society at large. Social representations and the meaning of social behavior in context are regarded as important in a way which is not as apparent in the social psychology of North America.

See: Moscovici & Personnaz, 1986; Mugny, 1975b; Mugny, Kaiser, Papastamou, & Perez, 1984; Mugny & Papastamou, 1976–1977, 1980, 1982; Mugny, Rilliet, & Papastamou, 1981; Nemeth, 1981; Nemeth, Swedlund, & Kanki, 1974; Papastamou, 1985, 1986.

For other studies of the effects of behavioral style, see: Cramer, 1975; Moscovici, 1975; Mugny, 1975a, 1975b; Mugny, Perez, Kaiser, & Papastamou, 1984; Nemeth, 1975; Paicheler, 1976; S. Wolf, 1979. (See also, Nemeth, 1979, on intergroup relations.)

Effects on perception. Mugny (1974–1975) found, using the Muller-Lyer illusion, that majority influence affected verbal responses, while minority influence affected "perceptive standards" (also confirmed in other studies by Mugny, 1976; and Personnaz, 1979).

See also: Doms & van Avermaet, 1980; Moscovici, 1976; Moscovici & Doms, 1982; Moscovici & Lage, 1976; Personnaz, 1979; Sorrentino, King, & Leo, 1980.

Moscovici and Personnaz (1980) demonstrated that not only were perceptual effects obtained by minority influence, but in the same experiments using the blue-green paradigm, were able to show that subjects' afterimages were modified by minority influence especially in the absence of the influence source. This finding was replicated by Moscovici and Doms (1982) and by Personnaz (1981).

Creativity. Nemeth and Kwan (1985) found that after exposure to the blue-green situation, more original word associations to "blue" and "green" were given by subjects in the minority influence condition. Nemeth and Kwan (1987) confirmed, using an anagram task, the prediction made by Nemeth (1986) that exposure to minority viewpoints would lead to divergent thinking. (See also: Moscovici & Lage, 1978; Nemeth, 1985; Nemeth & Wachtler, 1983.)

Minority size. Arbuthnot and Wayner (1982) found that a minority of one was less effective than a minority of two, or a minority of one who gained a convert.

Nemeth, Wachtler, and Endicott (1977) examined the relative gains and losses of increasing minority size; it appeared from their data that with increased size, the presumed competence of the minority increases, but their presumed confidence decreases. Effective influence was predicted by a combination of the two.

Reactionary minorities.   Paicheler (1977b) found that including a reactionary minority (opposed to feminism) in a group discussion led to bipolarization of the group. Once again, this study of social influence was construed as existing in a wider society, in this case where the norms are perceived to be shifting.

Mugny (1979) has disputed the findings from her own evidence. Paicheler (1979a) rejoindered that the studies were not comparable.

Double minority status.   Maass, Clark, and Haberkorn (1982) found that double minorities were perceived to have a stronger self-interest in the minority position, and hence less influence, than those people who were in other regards like the rest of the group.

Direct or indirect influence.   Often, minority influence is manifest not on direct measures but on related items. Mugny (1984a, 1984b) found, using the Asch paradigm, found that while a majority led to direct influence, indirect influence could be produced by both a majority (if the subjects believed there was an illusion) or a minority. (See also: Mugny & Papastamou, 1976–1977; Saltzenstein & Sandberg, 1979.)

This issue obviously merges into the points made below on compliance and conversion.

Compliance or conversion.   Insofar as minority influence produces change which is apparent in private, if not always in public statements (Maass & Clark, 1983), it may be argued that it produces genuine conversion and is thus, arguably, more effective than majority influence (Moscovici, 1980). A comparison may usefully be drawn with recent work by Petty and Cacioppo (1981, 1986) on their elaboration likelihood model of persuasion, which distinguishes between enduring change via the central route and temporary and superficial change via peripheral routes. It is hard to see, however, that it should inevitably be the case that majorities can only produce transient change, or minorities effect enduring conversion. The pursuit of this false dichotomy will be fruitless unless attention is paid to the processes within any minority or majority influence attempt. For a consideration of these issues, see the section below on single versus dual processes of influence.

For a review of compliance and conversion, see Moscovici (1980).

Moscovici, Mugny, and Papastamou (1981) have reanalyzed the sleeper effect (where influence manifested itself some weeks after the influence attempt by a source of low credibility), casting it into the framework of a minority influence effect. See also: Aebischer, Hewstone, & Henderson, 1984 (who used musical preference in adolescents); Moscovici & Doms, 1982; Moscovici & Lage, 1976; Mugny, 1984a, 1984b, 1984–1985; Personnaz, 1981; Tesser, Campbell, & Mickler, 1983.

Change within the group—success/failure. See: C. A. Kiesler & Pallak, 1975; Kitayama, 1983; Kitayama, 1984.

Social Influence: Two Processes or One?

Social influence researchers disagree as to whether research on minority influence suggests that it involves a different psychological process from majority influence. Broadly speaking, support for a single process comes from those who construe influence in terms of social impact. For a general discussion of social impact theory and social influence, see Latané and Nida (1980). (See also: Wolf & Latané, 1981.)

In this view, the minority is seen as being effective if it has social impact, which is determined by the strength and immediacy of the minority, as well as their number. Thus, for example, a high-status minority or one which is perceived to be competent will have more impact, as will a minority which is very immediate (close in space or time). The very consistency of a minority is seen as adding to its strength.

Tanford and Penrod (1984a) have developed a Social Impact Model, similar to social impact theory, but explicitly extend the idea to private measures of social influence as well as public behavior.

L. Mann (1977) partially confirmed social impact theory in a study of queue-joining behavior, but maintained that it seemed only to apply above a certain size threshold. However, studies of minorities in small groups suggest that social impact theory does apply.

For further reading of the single process arguments, see: Doms & Van Avermaet, 1980; Latané & Wolf, 1981; S. Wolf, 1985.

Many of those who regard minority and majority influence as involving different mechanisms, the dual process view, come from a background of studying minority influence. For further reading on dual process theorists, see Maass & Clark, 1983, 1986; Moscovici, Mugny, & Van Avermaet, 1985; Mugny, 1985.

Other attempts at resolution: Laughlin (1988) has examined what he calls "collective induction" in an attempt to relate three areas, namely group performance, social combination processes and the mutual influence of minorities and majorities. Among his findings, using yoked four-person majority and two-person minority cooperative groups, were improved performance based on exchange of evidence rather than hypotheses, and that majority influence occurred more than minority influence, although in both cases it occurred through exchange of evidence. It is worth noting, too, that the majority performed better than the minority, which could be an important finding, not only with regard to group performance but also because people may make such assumptions when they are exposed to discrepancies.

Interestingly, too, majorities and minorities followed similar strategies, which were affected quantitatively but not qualitatively by faction size. It may well be that the subtleties of social influence will need a more complex 'real-world' model of this sort.

Mackie (1987) has looked at the systematic and nonsystematic processing of persuasive communications emanating from minorities and majorities. In a series of four experiments she used a very different exposure to group discrepancy from other studies. In the first two studies she exposed subjects to a minority with which they agreed and a majority with which they disagreed. She found that subjects showed considerably more issue-relevant processing of the majority message and long-term generalized private acceptance of the majority position. Her third study showed that the change was in fact due to a response to the majority position rather than merely a reaction to the minority, in that subjects did not receive a persuasive communication but were given consensus information about both minority and majority positions. There was significant change toward the majority position here also, but it was neither generalized nor mediated by the way in which the subjects thought about the issue. Disagreement in itself may serve as a useful cue; Mackie also found a slight shift to the minority when subjects were exposed to a minority view. This work has much in common with contemporary analysis of attitude change processes, and is, strictly speaking, not a small group study. However, this approach to an integration of social influence approaches is a very promising line of development, and Mackie's study is specifically addressing the important debate on possible differences between majority and minority influence.

SUMMARY

Research on social influence has continued to use the classic paradigms of Sherif, Asch, and Milgram, often in different cultural settings, where the traditional findings seem almost surprisingly persistent. Alongside these approaches, new issues, variables and perspectives have burgeoned, with as yet no clearly adequate integration, although some attempts are in the making.

Many studies look at mere behavioral compliance, such as foot-in-the-door (FITD) or door-in-the-face techniques. The effectiveness of these techniques may depend on their implications for the subjects' self-perceptions, although FITD may also be mediated by subjects' discovery that compliance is more pleasant and less threatening than they had feared.

People may sometimes respond with a compliance "script;" in other circumstances they may respond to an influence attempt with reactance, and resist. Sex differences may reflect perceived status differences, but it seems that males and females exert influence differently and may interpret an influence attempt differently.

Deviants in groups are often subject to group pressure, but they themselves may become sources of influence for the group. This is most likely to be the result of their behavioral style, which should be consistent but not rigid. Minority influence leads to conversion. Majority influence may be internalized but may also simply reflect social, rather than cognitive, pressure. Majorities and minorities differ in their social impact, but whether the two approaches to social influence can be subsumed under a single process is currently a matter of dispute. Recent work on attitude change might usefully inform the discussion of social influence in small groups.

Part III
GROUP STRUCTURE

Chapter 5

Roles and Relationships

A. Paul Hare

ROLES

The concept of role, as a set of rights and duties and behaviors, that are associated with a position (status) in a social group is important whether the group under consideration is small or large, or even constitutes a whole society. For this reason much is written about roles in organizations or societies that is also applicable to small groups. Indeed, to the extent that a small group represents a "microcosm" of a society, all of the roles that have been identified in small groups have their counterparts in larger social systems. Moreover the status that a person has in a larger system often carries over into a small group, even though it may not be especially relevant for the functioning of that group. Thus it is difficult to draw the line between the social-psychological literature that pertains to larger organizations and that which is especially relevant for the small group. For example, R. Thornton and Nardi (1975) describe four stages in the acquisition of a role (anticipatory, formal, informal, and personal) that would apply at any level of society. Similarly, Sieber's (1974) observation that the benefits to a person from accumulating a number of roles far outweighs any stress to which ensuing conflicts in roles might give rise, could provide a point to begin the analysis of role conflict in small groups. Adato's (1975) description of "leave-taking," that terminates the sense of occasioned presence and being together, but does not necessarily terminate focused interaction, would be useful in the analysis of the termination of a group activity. Gudykunst's (1983) review of the relationship between "host" and "stranger," with primary reference to intercultural contexts, could be applied to the introduction of the newcomer in a group.

Another difficulty in defining roles in small groups is that for some research the term "role" is used to refer to well recognized formal positions in a group, such as chairperson, secretary, or member, and for some authors "role" refers to informal positions such as the joker or the scapegoat; whereas for others "role" refers to the extent to which a relationship is "intimate" or not (Argyle, Henderson, & Furnham, 1985) or to a type of behavior that predominates, as when someone is identified as a "silent member" or a "nonconformist." P. M. Baker (1981) suggests that two types of division of labor can be distinguished: task specialization and actor specialization. Task specialization causes interdependence of group members and thus increases cohesion, while actor specialization creates isolation, and thus decreases cohesion. With regard to the general role of "member," Zander (1976) suggests that it is important to note the basis in a group for determining who will be expelled from a group and who will be initiated into the group.

In any event, the basic dimensions of behavior for roles are the same as those for behavior in general (Coyne, 1984; Stiles, 1978). Since roles always exists in reciprocal pairs, where the rights of one role are the duties of another, a person playing one role also knows the expectations for the other counter-players. Further, following social-interactionist theory, the basic form of social control arises from the ability of a person to "take the role of the other" and evaluate the performance of the self from the perspective of the other (Alexander, 1977). However, Tjosvold and Sagaria (1978) report that in an experiment in which subjects were given various degrees of power over another, those with "absolute" power were less interested in taking the other's perspective.

If an individual is prevented from playing a role that promised some satisfaction, the situation may be given a negative assessment (Zurcher & Wilson, 1981). If an individual is not clearly defined as being in a role, the counter-players may not be fully involved (Bick & Loewenthal, 1976).

Texts with a focus on roles include: Biddle, 1979; Ickes & Knowles, 1982; NATO, 1982; Wilshire, 1982; Zurcher, 1983.

Additional studies of roles and role behavior are reported by: Bixenstine, Lowenfeld, & Englehart, 1981; Golu & Bogatu, 1984; Huici, 1979; Willke, 1976.

DEVELOPMENT OF INFORMAL STRUCTURE

With the exception of very simple tasks, such as taking part in one side of a "tug of war" in which two teams pull on opposite ends of a rope, some role differentiation is necessary to take full advantage of the productive capabilities of a group. If no formal structure is provided, then an informal structure or set of role relationships will develop. Even when there is a formal structure, there is likely also to be an informal structure. Not only does the structure (or structures) have important consequences for the group task, but also it facilitates the individual's "fundamental quest for systematization" (Neimeyer & Merluzzi, 1982). Ridgeway (1978) suggests that the attainment of a status in a small group involves both conformity and nonconformity.

FLUCTUATIONS IN ORGANIZATION

The organization of a group may vary over time for at least two reasons. One, to be discussed below, is that it may take several periods of conflict before a "pecking order" can be established that is appropriate for the task of the group. The other reason is that the activities required in each phase of the development of a group may call for a different constellation of roles. Farrell, Heinemann, and Schmitt (1986) describe some of the roles associated with each phase in the development of interdisciplinary health care teams: superman or wonderwoman, clown, tyrant, and helper. Piper, Jones, Lacroix, Marrache, and Richardsen (1984) record that the leader-member interactions in the early stages of a learning group, when roles are presumably not well defined, are relatively ineffective for the purpose of retaining members. Griffith and Gray (1978) report that the greater the amount of external reinforcement of a laboratory group, the less the structural differentiation. Within a group an individual's behavior relative to other group members, for example verbal contributions, can be changed through reinforcement or the provision of role models (Robins & Wexley, 1975). Members who move in and out of a group from newcomer, to full member, to ex-member, provide an additional source of fluctuation (Moreland & Levine, 1982).

POWER AND PERFORMANCE

Two bases of status in a group that have received considerable attention are power and performance. Persons who have the power to give rewards and punishments have high status and so do those who perform well on the task. The use of reward power by a group leader increases group productivity, whereas the use of coercive power decreases productivity (Sheley & Shaw, 1979). Further, the extended use of coercive power is taken as an indication of weakness of the leader (P. M. Hall, 1985). Relative to males, females with high power in a laboratory simulation made fewer influence attempts, used a more limited range of influence strategies, and used fewer reward strategies. Being able to reward members of one's own group apparently gives one greater skill in negotiating contracts with other groups (C. N. Jackson & King, 1983). Persons who are on their own "turf" have a power advantage over outsiders (Bar-Tal & Kubzansky, 1987).

A test of the relationship between power imbalance and power use was preformed by Molm (1985) using pairs of university students as subjects who took part in the experiment to earn money in a series of exchanges with their partners. Nine different combinations of dependent relationship were tested. If the two persons were unequally dependent on one another, the less dependent person had a power advantage. A power imbalance was predicted to lead to asymmetrical exchange, with the more dependent person giving more than he or she receives. This occurs when the less dependent persons use their power advantage, giving or withholding rewards contingent on the others' behavior, to shift the ratio of exchange more in their favor. Previous studies had assumed that the greater the asymmetry in the exchange, the greater would be the power use. However, Holm's study indicated that power imbalance is not a unitary variable, and that the dependencies of the weaker and stronger persons in the relationship can have very different effects on power use. Holm found that the dependence of the weaker person had a strong and predominantly linear effect on power use, whereas the dependence of the stronger person had a weak and curvilinear effect. In addition the relations were causally mediated by the reinforcement contingencies that the powerful person established to control the other's behavior. These contingencies mediated the effects of the stronger person's dependence, but not the effects of the weaker person's dependence.

Persons who are judged to have low status in a paired relationship because of poor performance will receive less than an equal share of the payoff, especially if they are perceived as investing less effort (Schwinger, Kayser, & Muller, 1981-1982). However, partners who are perceived to have lower ability than the subject may be judged to be more cooperative, friendly, and trustworthy, especially when they enhance the subject's own estimate of ability (Bailey & Stout, 1983). Persons with low power look at a partner more when listening than when speaking (Dovidio, Ellyson, Keating, Heltman, & Brown, 1988).

Power may also "command obedience" (cf. Chapter 4), but even in modern military settings there is also an obligation to *dis*obey illegal or inhuman orders (Kelman & Hamilton, 1989).

Additional research related to power includes: Andreoli, Worchel, & Folger, 1974; L. N. Gray & Sullivan, 1978; Jamieson & Thomas, 1974; D. C. Jones, 1983; and Molm, 1981b, 1981c. Additional research on performance is given by: M. Field, 1979; Forgas, 1978; Lindow, Wilkinson, & Peterson, 1985; Roger & Reid, 1982; and Schlenker, 1975c.

DIFFERENTIATION IN HIERARCHIES

A striking feature of the initially leaderless groups of university students that were observed in small groups laboratories in the 1950s was that they regularly developed a status hierarchy within the first few minutes of interaction. Berger explained the inequality of status as the result of "performance expectation states." These expectations are ideas about the relative task ability of each member that develop during the initial phases of interaction, since other group members will want to pay attention to and reward others who have high ability (Webster & Driskell, 1983, pp. 57-58). When it is apparent that group members have a different status in other groups, based on age, sex, ethnic group, or other variables, then there may be "status inconsistencies" that will effect group performance (Crosbie, 1979b).

J. Berger, Rosenholtz, and Zelditch (1980) provide a review of the literature on "status organizing processes" that covers the period up to September 1979. They define a *status organizing process* as any process in which evaluation of and beliefs about the characteristics of actors become the basis of observable inequalities in face-to-face social interaction. A key concept in this theory is the *status characteristic*, any characteristic, such as age, sex, or ethnicity, of actors around which evaluations and beliefs about status are organized. As noted above, the phenomenon with which this theory is concerned is often observed in the study of problem-solving groups whose members differ in status characteristics that are significant in the larger society. These groups do not create a new social organization, but maintain the external status differences inside the group. These status characteristics plus judgements about future performance that arise from the task-related interaction of group members, give rise to "expectation states" concerning the relative value of the contributions of the members. (See the section on "Status characteristics and expectation states" in Chapter 2.)

Additional discussions and models of expectation states theory are given by: Bonacich & Light, 1978; Camilleri & Conner, 1976; Conner, 1977; J. Fox & Moore, 1979; Hembroff, 1982; Mazur, 1975; Ofshe & Lee, 1983; Rosa & Mazur, 1979; S. J. Sherman, 1983; Skvoretz, 1981; Tammivaara, 1982.

Examples of research not included in the review by J. Berger, Rosenholtz, and Zelditch (1980) confirm that it is easier to develop a hierarchy if the group members have different characteristics (W. A. Scott & Cohen, 1978), including differences in attractiveness (M. E. Shaw & Wagner, 1975), position in the communication network (Stolte, 1978a, 1978b), or age and performance (Knottnerus & Greenstein, 1981). From the observer's point of view, it is apparently easier to identify a hierarchy based on dominance than one based on ability. In a dyad, the dominance relationship may be clearer if a male is dominating a female (van Kreveld & Menckeberg, 1974). If there is status incongruence because the same member has a different rank on different characteristics, then group members may attempt to develop a single hierarchy (Trow, 1977), though this is less likely if the members are in competition (Van Kreveld, Willigers, Gloudemans, Rancuret, van der Wiel, & Poot, 1974).

The hierarchy that is given or developed — for example, one that is more authoritarian or more democratic — may not be consistent with the members' desire for a particular structure (Bord, 1976a; Carron & Chelladurai, 1978). In such a case productivity will be reduced (J. P. Wilson, Aronoff, & Messé, 1975).

High status members will typically prefer greater consistency between status and performance, while low status members will prefer activities in which all members are equal in their performance (Karuza & Brickman, 1981). High status persons are more likely to be presumptuous (Cansler & Stiles, 1981).

For additional research on aspects of hierarchies see: Beilin & Rabow, 1981; J. Berger & Zelditch, 1985; M. H. Bond, Wan, Leung, & Giacalone, 1985; Bradley, 1978a; W. J. Duncan, 1985; Foot & Russon, 1975; L. N. Gray & Griffith, 1984; Jablin & Sussman, 1978; Jaspars, van den Oever, & van Gils, 1974; Kimberly, 1986;

Koomen, Van de Bovenkamp, & Forma, 1980; Lamb, 1980; Parcel & Cook, 1977; Racine, 1978; Rosa & Mazur, 1979; W. A. Scott & Cohen, 1978; W. A. Scott & Scott, 1981; C. R. Snyder & Newburg, 1981; R. T. Stein, 1980; R. T. Stein, 1982; Strayer & Trudel, 1984; Webster, 1977.

PATTERNS OF ROLE DIFFERENTIATION

Probably the most common set of roles reported in the small group literature is the division of leadership functions between a "task" leader, with a primary concern for group productivity, and a "social-emotional" leader, with a concern for group morale (W. R. Morgan, 1975; Wheeless, Wheeless, & Dickson-Markman, 1982). Meeker and Weitzel-O'Neill (1977) suggest that in many groups men are more likely to be the task leaders and women the social leaders and that this is the result of status differences. Since men are thought to have higher status than women, men are expected to be more competent than women. It is expected that competitive or dominating behavior is legitimate for men but not for women. Meeker and Weitzel-O'Neill review a set of empirical studies of sex roles as related to task appropriateness, group problem solving, conflict, dominating behavior, and role expectations that support this hypothesis. (See also: M. L. Barnes & Buss, 1985; Golub & Canty, 1982.)

The sex of the participant also makes a difference when other roles are played. For example, men and women tend to discuss different topics when they are paired with someone who is either a friend, a co-worker, a sibling, or a parent (A. Haas & Sherman, 1982). (See also: N. P. Marshall, Pederson, & Weiler, 1978.)

Other roles that have received attention in the literature are the newcomer (R. Crandall, 1978; A. Jones & Crandall, 1985) and a conflict resolver (J. A. Kelly et al., 1982). As a test of the influence on a person's behavior when the person is a newcomer in a group, Moreland (1985) conducted a laboratory experiment with 20 groups of university students. Each group contained five unacquainted subjects of the same sex who met once a week to discuss topical issues. Within each group, two randomly selected subjects were told that they were "newcomers" entering a group of "oldtimers." The three remaining control subjects received no such information and instead believed (correctly) that everyone was new to the group. The experimental subjects who thought they were newcomers exhibited strong ingroup-outgroup (new-old) biases in that they behaved more favorably toward each other than toward the control subjects. However, by the third week the differences between the two sets of subjects had disappeared since the "newcomers" were fully assimilated in their groups.

Whatever the pattern of role differentiation in a group, whether informal or formal, persons are likely to experience difficulty in performing a role if the expectations for the role are ambiguous or if the expectations are in conflict with another role that they are also playing (S. E. Jackson & Schuler, 1985; Mossholder, Bedeian, & Armenakis, 1981; Schuler, 1977). (For additional perspectives, see: R. H. Turner & Colomy, 1988.)

GROUP SIZE

In field research that replicates early findings concerning the size of "natural groups," that is, casual work or play groups, most natural groups consist of only two or three members (Bakeman & Beck, 1974). However natural groups of children and adolescents are usually larger than those of adults, and larger for adult women compared with adult men (J. W. Burgess, 1984). In free-forming groups, as in a conversation lounge, individuals are more likely to leave a group as group size increases (Calsyn & Becker, 1976).

The optimum group size for many group discussion tasks is five members (Yetton & Bottger, 1983). In smaller groups individuals are forced to be too prominent and in larger groups there are fewer opportunities to speak and more control is required. Once a group exceeds size three there are no new sociometric or cognitive properties to consider (Hallinan & McFarland, 1975). There may also be no gain in the reliability of the group decision process (Felsenthal & Fuchs, 1976). The effects of having a large number of people in the same space, who are not necessarily members of the same group, are described in Chapter 1 on the physical situation.

A number of studies report changes in individual behavior or group activity that are correlated with increasing group size. As size increases individuals become less self-conscious (Diener, Lusk, DeFour, & Flax, 1980), there is less intermember interaction (G. W. Gentry, 1980) and less satisfaction (D. C. Lundgren & Bogart (1974), members use less effort (Petty, Harkins, Williams, & Latané, 1977) with lower performance (Paulus, Annis, Seta, Schkade, & Matthews, 1976), with less cooperation (Hamburger, Guyer, & Fox, 1975), and more conforming behavior when judging an ambiguous stimulus (Nordholm, 1975). In larger groups, only a few members may actually take part in decision making (especially for types of problems for which the group is given credit for solving a problem if at least one member can solve it) and there will be more subgroups and cliques (Lindsay, 1976; Mamali & Paun, 1982). Despite the fact that the average contribution per member may be less in larger brainstorming groups, the larger group may still produce more ideas (Renzulli, Owen, & Callahan, 1974). Also, in larger groups, members are more likely to use a "truth-supported wins" process of making decisions in which two correct group members are necessary and sufficient for a correct group response (Laughlin, Kerr, Davis, Halff, & Marciniak, 1975).

An example of this research is the study by Bray, Kerr, and Atkin (1978). They designed an experiment to examine the influence of group size, task difficulty, and sex of members on the relationship between actual productivity and potential productivity and also to test the predictive accuracy of "hierarchical" and "equalitarian latency" models of performance. University students worked on three intellectual problems of varying difficulty, either as individuals or as members of same-sex groups of 2, 3, 6, and 10 members. The easy problem was presented as follows:

> As a prospector you have been very successful. You must now discharge a small debt
> by paying *exactly* 27 ounces of gold dust (no more, no less) to a friend. You have

three containers which hold exactly 9 ounces, 42 ounces, and 6 ounces, respectively. How would you remove the *exact* amount from the safe, using only these containers? You must use all three containers. (Answer: Fill the 42-ounce container; from it fill the 9- and 6-ounce containers, leaving 27 ounces.)

The medium problem and difficult problem were similar, but required more filling and emptying of different sized containers. The actual performance of the individuals and groups was assessed using indexes of the proportion of solvers and the time to solution. Potential performance scores were generated from the theoretical models for the same indexes. Group performance on both indexes generally fell below potential as size and difficulty of problem increased. The sex of the group members generally made no difference. The concept of "functional size" was advanced to explain the observed pattern of group performance. As group size was increased, the number of nonparticipants also increased, resulting in a functional group that was smaller than the actual size. The groups solved the problems at the rate of the fastest member of the functional group.

Of special interest in the United States has been the comparison of six-person and twelve-person juries, since there was an interest on the part of state legislatures to reduce jury size. In one study jury size had no effect on conviction when apparent guilt of the defendant was low. But when apparent guilt was high the six-person juries were more likely to convict (Valenti & Downing, 1975), perhaps because the probability of a dissenter being present was reduced. (See discussion of juries in Chapter 8.)

M. W. Segal (1977) reports that a logarithmic model provides the best fit with the proportion of attraction choices within a subgroup as the size of the subgroup increases.

Additional studies related to group size are reported by: S. T. Allison & Messick, 1985a; Brownell & Smith, 1973; Butcher & Whissell, 1984; Emurian & Brady, 1984; J. L. Freedman, Birsky, & Cavoukian, 1980; Golubeva, 1982; Grofman, 1974; L. M. Jones & Foshay, 1984; Knowles, Kreuser, Haas, Hyde, & Schuchart, 1976; Kugihara, Misumi, & Sato, 1980; Kurokawa & Misumi, 1975; M. McGuire, 1974; Patterson & Schaeffer, 1977; Seta & Schkade, 1976; Swerts, Peeters, & d'Ydewalle, 1983.

DYAD

Early research on the dyad and the triad indicated that each type of group had special characteristics. Interaction in the dyad is characterized by a delicate balance of power and more tension between members. Over time, one member of the pair becomes more active. In the research during the period covered by this volume a number of studies refer to the dyad in the title of the research, and indeed refer to the interaction between two persons. However no comparison is made with larger groups to show that the behavior observed is especially related to the fact that only two persons are present. Since, in groups of any size, individuals primarily relate to one person at a time, all of the findings summarized under the category of "dyadic interaction" apply equally well to interaction between persons in larger groups.

The performance of dyads is better if the members like each other (Krivonos, Byrne, & Friedrich, 1976) and have the same intellectual background (M. Foddy, 1978a). Competitive pairs have different interaction patterns than cooperative pairs (B. A. Fisher, 1983), and relative power is important, especially in a competitive situation (Tjosvold, 1981), and is related to learning ability in children (Glascock, 1976). When pairs do tasks involving analogies and crossword puzzles, a division of labor is efficient, but sharing labor is more effective (Shiflett, 1976). If one member of the pair is focused on the self, it tends to trigger self focus in the other (B. Stephenson & Wicklund, 1984).

Models of dyadic behavior include a probabilistic model of dynamics (E. A. Thomas & Malone, 1979) and a balance theory model of cognition and communication (I. M. White, 1982).

Additional studies that involve dyads have been conducted by: Frandsen & Rosenfeld, 1973; Gupta, 1985, Maynard & Zimmerman, 1984; Janousek, 1973; Perju-Liiceanu, 1973; Solano & Dunnam, 1985; Stamm & Pearce, 1974.

INTIMATE RELATIONSHIPS

The study of intimate relationships comes closer to the earlier research on the dyad since one of the special characteristics of a pair is the possibility of intimacy. However, from a broader perspective, the research on intimate relations is similar to research on friendship, since friendships may include only pairs, but they may also involve larger sets of persons who meet face-to-face or in a network. Thus the findings concerning intimate relationships are essentially the same as those on friendship.

Levinger (1980) provides some models of close relations in which he addresses two questions: (a) How does one distinguish among relationships differing in closeness at any single point in time? (b) How do relationships change over either a short or long time span? The first question suggested looking inside the Person-Other "Intersection." Here he looked at three logically distinct levels of relatedness: (a) P has a unilateral awareness of O without any implication of reciprocity; examples include phenomena such as impression formation or interpersonal evaluation, where one person judges another without the second persons's awareness, (b) bilateral surface contact where there is some P-O interaction, but it is confined to casual role related matters; examples include initial interaction between strangers, and also repeated interactions among acquaintances or co-workers who limit their behavior to culturally prescribed roles, and (c) going beyond culturally prescribed roles; this refers to graduations in P-O mutuality, where interaction becomes increasingly personal and unique and interdependence deepens. The relationships of deep mutuality are marked by intimate disclosure, knowledge of each other's personal feelings, joint development of pair norms, and mutual responsibility for one another's outcome, with strong mutual attraction.

Levinger's second question led to a consideration of short-term and long-term processes. Regarding long-term pair processes he noted a five phase sequence that extended from (a) initial attraction, to (b) building a relationship, (c) continuation, (d) deterioration, and (e) ending. He has written a model in the form of a computer program, called "Relate," that has been used to simulate a variety of interpersonal encounters, including the occurrence of "altruism" in mixed-motive situations, the analysis of interpersonal disclosure, and the hypothetical development of a romantic relationship between two imaginary young people.

Kelley, Berscheid, Christensen, Harvey, Huston, Levinger, McClintock, Peplau, and Peterson (1983) also provide a framework for the analysis of close relationships and extensive reviews of related literature. They focus primarily on heterosexual couples. In their view, any social relationship can be seen as a pattern of interdependence: the ways which two people influence each other's thoughts, feelings, and actions. A relationship, whether it is cordial or conflict ridden, is "close" to the extent that people have a strong, frequent, and continuing effect on one another. Events in the relationship are multiply determined by several sets of relatively stable causal conditions: those that reside in individuals, in the fit between the two individuals, in the physical environment, and in the social environment. The causal links are causal loops: causal conditions effect patterns of interaction, and these patterns can modify the causal conditions. As causal conditions change, relationships themselves develop and change.

Additional general perspectives on interpersonal relationships are given by Argyle, 1983; Argyle & Henderson, 1985; R. A. Bell & Daly, 1984; Blumstein & Kollock, 1988; Burnett, McGhee, & Clarke, 1987; de Rivera, 1984; Duck, 1986, 1988; Duck & Gilmour, 1981; Forgas & Dobosz, 1980; R. Gilmour & Duck, 1986; Heyman & Shaw, 1978; Hinde, 1976, 1977, 1978, 1979; Hinde & Stevenson-Hinde, 1976; Kelley, 1978, 1979; Kenny & La Voie, 1984; Markus-Kaplan & Kaplan, 1984; Mikula, 1984; Morton, Alexander, & Altman, 1976; Oskamp & Spacapan, 1987; Parsons, 1973; Roloff, 1976; Zaborowski, 1977.

Relationships between persons are found to be closer if they have the same birth order (Scheidt & Smith, 1976), similar status (Argyle & Furnham, 1982), similar values and interests (Gupta, 1983; Wyant & Gardner, 1977), and if each is close to the "ideal self" of the other (Wetzel, Schwartz, & Vasu, 1979). In addition if the pair are complementary with regard to the affiliation dimension of interaction, there will be a correspondence in the relationship. In contrast, complementarity on the control dimension results in reciprocity (T. L. Wright & Ingraham, 1986). If persons are asked to associate with others who are unlikable and obnoxious, they may learn to live with them (Tyler & Sears, 1977).

If there is a positive relationship, the members will make more equal claims on resources (Mikula & Schwinger, 1973). However, if their claims on resources are incompatible there will be conflict (Kayser, 1982). Over time, positive relationships become more rewarding and less costly (Eidelson, 1981). Relationships are terminated when alternative sources of satisfaction are less costly (Holt, 1982). There may be an ebb and flow of competition (B. A. Fisher & Drecksel, 1983), as the members are more likely to express both positive and negative feelings and have physical contact (Rands & Levinger, 1979).

Intimacy increases over time (J. D. Davis, 1976), as does satisfaction (L. A. Baxter & Wilmot, 1983; Eidelson, 1980). If the partner is disagreeable, fewer and less intimate topics will be discussed (Yoder, 1981). If the intimate pair are of opposite sex, each member may use "secret tests" to discover what other relationships the partner has (L. A. Baxter & Wilmot, 1984). In military settings superiors appear to be free to approach subordinates at distances that indicate intimacy, while subordinates are not at liberty to do so (Dean, Willis, & Hewitt, 1975).

An example of research in this area is the study by J. D. Davis (1976) who conducted an acquaintance exercise to investigate the process through which members of a dyad negotiate the level of intimacy of their exchanges. Pairs of university students of the same sex were asked to take turns disclosing information from an intimacy-scaled list of topics. The main results were that intimacy increased as the encounters progressed and that the matching of levels of intimacy was achieved, not as a result of mutual reciprocity, but through a process of role differentiation whereby one partner assumed the major responsibility for prescribing levels of intimacy and the other reciprocated.

A second example is the research of Yoder (1981) who introduced a laboratory procedure for developing a positive relationship between strangers for the purpose of examining the effects of a cost, in the form of a disagreement, on the continuation of that relationship. Yoder hypothesized that after a disagreement subjects will select fewer and less intimate topics to discuss with their partner and speak for a shorter duration than subjects whose partners are in agreement. As a test, 60 female undergraduates and a female confederate exchanged information about themselves over eight trials that became increasingly more intimate. The confederate then disagreed with the subject on some issue. The subjects were again asked to select topics to discuss with the confederate. Subjects who had experienced disagreement selected fewer topics.

Additional Research on Relationships

For additional research on aspects of relationships see: Argyle, Henderson, & Furnham, 1985; Burgess & Huston, 1979; Ciminero, Graham, & Jackson, 1977; M. S. Clark, 1984; Conville, 1983; Cowan, Drinkard, & MacGavin, 1984; Dorris & Knight, 1978; Duck & Sants, 1983; Dymkowski, 1980; Enright & Lapsley, 1980; Fincham & Bradbury, 1987; Glick, 1985; S. K. Green & Sandos, 1983; Grzesiuk, Migdalska-Wierzbowska, & Makuch-Rusinowska, 1985; Hewstone, Argyle, & Furnham, 1982; Lloyd, Cate, & Henton, 1982; Neville, 1978; H. Newman, 1981;

Noller, 1980, 1982; Paczkowska & Zaborowski, 1975; Planalp & Honeycutt, 1985; Rempel, Holmes, & Zanna, 1985; Rubinstein & Timmins, 1978; Sabatelli, Buck, & Dreyer, 1982; Safilios-Rothschild, 1981; Serpe & Stryker, 1987; Sillars & Scott, 1983; Sommers, 1984; Tesser, 1980a; Vertommen, 1980; Zuber, 1977.

Additional Research on Friendship

For additional research on aspects of friendship see:

General (most of the research uses university students as informants with a focus of the relationships between couples or persons with a romantic involvement): Ashton, 1980; Bailey, Finney, & Helm, 1975; P. M. Baker, 1983; R. R. Bell, 1981; Buunk, 1983; J. F. Campbell, 1980; A. Crouch & Yetton, 1988; F. M. Deutsch & Mackesy, 1985; Duck & Allison, 1978; Duck & Craig, 1978; Grush & Yehl, 1979; Hansell, 1981; Hays, 1985; Husain & Kureshi, 1983; Huston & Levinger, 1978; Ickes & Barnes, 1978; C. W. Knapp & Harwood, 1977; Lea, 1979; Lea & Duck, 1982; Lopata, 1981; Mathes, Adams, & Davies, 1985; McAdams, Healy, & Krause, 1984; B. McCarthy, & Duck, 1976; Milardo, Johnson, & Huston, 1983; S. J. Morse & Marks, 1985; Peretti, 1980; Rawlins, 1983a, 1983b; S. M. Rose, 1985; Rusbult, Morrow, & Johnson, 1987; Schullo & Alperson, 1984; M. W. Segal, 1979; Shrivastava, 1973; Stokes & Levin, 1986; Verbrugge, 1983; R. V. Wagner, 1975; S. M. Wall, Pickert, & Paradise, 1984; Werner & Parmelee, 1979; J. G. Williams & Solano, 1983; P. H. Wright, 1974, 1978.

Children: Eder & Hallinan, 1978; Gottman, Gonso, & Rasmussen, 1975; Hallinan, 1979; Hallinan & Hutchins, 1980; S. A. Richardson, Ronald, & Kleck, 1974.

Adolescents: J. Cohen, 1979; DeVries & Edwards, 1974; Duck, 1975; Kandel, 1978a, 1978b; J. C. Wright, Giammarino, & Parad, 1986.

Elderly: E. A. Powers & Bultena, 1976; Verbrugge, 1977.

Couples, Married, dating, or with romantic involvement: M. L. Barnes & Buss, 1985; J. K. Butler, 1986; Critelli & Baldwin, 1979; Critelli & Dupre, 1978; Feingold, 1982a, 1982b; Fengler, 1974; Fletcher, Fincham, Cramer, & Heron, 1987; Folkes, 1982; Gaelick, Bodenhausen, & Wyer, 1985; S. S. Hendrick, Hendrick, & Adler, 1988; M. P. Johnson & Leslie, 1982; Krain, 1977; Kurdek & Schmitt, 1986; Michaels, Edwards, & Acock, 1984; Milardo, 1982; Morton, 1978; Parks, Stan, & Eggert, 1983; Quinn, 1977; Rusbult, 1983; Rusbult, Johnson, & Morrow, 1986a, 1986b; Rusbult & Zembrodt, 1983; Rusbult, Zembrodt, & Gunn, 1982; Schaefer & Burnett, 1987; Schroder, 1981; Stephen & Harrison, 1985; Sternberg & Barnes, 1985; Stewart & Rubin, 1976; Surra, 1985; G. L. White, 1980.

Theoretical analyses: Alessio, 1984; J. H. Berg & McQuinn, 1986; Cate, Lloyd, Henton, & Larson, 1982; Conte, 1982; Gudykunst, Yang, & Nishida, 1985; Inoue, 1985; Lujansky & Mikula, 1983; Murstein, Cerreto, & MacDonald, 1977; Rusbult, 1980; T. D. Stephen, 1984; Törnblom, Fredholm, & Jonsson, 1987; Traupmann, Hatfield, & Wexler, 1983.

TRIAD

The characteristic of a triad that is most often recorded is the division of two against one. In this respect the research on triads is similar to that on coalitions in general (see Chapter 10), to research reporting relationships between person (P), other (O), and "X," where X is an object and not a person (D. S. Hong, 1979), and to other examples of balance in triadic relations (Rodrigues & de la Coleta, 1983). Subjects also prefer balance when the triad involves other persons and only feel unpleasant in an unbalanced situation that includes themselves (M. J. White, 1977).

As with the research with "dyad" in the title, so research labeled "triad" is not necessarily limited to a situation in which only three people are present. For example, when a subject is interacting with both a male and a female in a three-person group, the sex of the other person is not found to be related to being gazed at (F. W. Schneider, Coutts, & Garrett, 1977). Similar negative results could undoubtedly be obtained in larger groups.

Additional research on triads has been reported by Emurian, Emurian, Bigelow, & Brady, 1976; Emurian, Emurian, & Brady, 1978; R. W. Peters & Torrance, 1973; Messé, Vallacher, & Phillips, 1974.

TASK AND STRESS

The finding that members of a group that is successful will be more satisfied continues to have support in current research (Borsig & Frey, 1979; Michaels & McCulloch, 1976). Individual members who are successful are more likely to think that others will be (Bowerman, Vermunt, & Van der Berg, 1982). However if a team is unsuccessful, the members are more likely to attribute the outcome to external causes (D. L. Gill & Martens, 1977), a finding that would be expected from attribution theory that predicts that favorable outcomes are more likely to be attributed to the self (see Chapter 12).

In a simulated military conflict, high information loads for group members were found to lead to tension (M. J. O'Connell, Cummings, & Huber, 1976). However, with husbands and wives compatibility was not found to be strongly related to stress management (Burke, Firth, & McGrattan, 1974). In joint faculty-student informal discussions groups, faculty were observed to give up their authority positions as a way of coping with the stressful situation (Hauser & Shapiro, 1976).

If one wishes to avoid stressful situations, note that affiliative smiling takes place in situations that involve greetings and departures, while laughter takes place in a recreational context (Lockard, Fahrenbruch, Smith, & Morgan, 1977). It may not be a surprise to learn that drinking a little alcohol while having a discussion in an experimental laboratory with a member of the opposite sex increases elation, giddiness, and happiness (R. C. Smith, Parker, & Noble, 1975).

SUMMARY

As a formal definition, a role is a set of rights and duties associated with a position in a social group. However, the term role is used not only to refer to formal positions in a group, such as chairperson, secretary, or member, but also to informal positions, such as joker or scapegoat, or to identify a person by a predominant type of behavior, such as silent member or nonconformist. Task specialization in roles increases interdependence of group members, while actor specialization creates isolation. Research on roles in larger groups concerning role conflict, leave taking, or other phenomena can also be applied to the small group.

In addition to the formal structure of a small group, an informal set of relationships usually develops to deal with aspects of group function that are not met by the formal structure. The organization of a group will vary over time, either because the appropriate structure is slow to develop or because different sets of role relationships are necessary at different phases of group growth. Persons who have the power to give rewards and punishments and those who perform well on the task are given high status in a group. Age, sex, and ethnicity are also taken by group members as indications of presumed task ability. These attributes lead to expectations, early in a group's life, concerning the potential contribution of a group member and relative status.

The most common set of roles in a group is a division of the leadership functions between a "task leader," with a primary concern for group productivity, and a "social-emotional leader," with a concern for intermember relations. Men are more likely to take the task role and women the social-emotional role.

The optimum size for many discussion groups is five members since in smaller groups individuals may feel too prominent and in larger groups there may be fewer opportunities to speak and more control may be required. As groups increase in size members may become less self-conscious, but they may also use less effort, with the result of lower performance.

Research on intimate relations is similar to early research on the dyad and on friendship. Relationships between intimate pairs include intimate disclosure, knowledge of each other's personal feelings, joint development of pair norms, and mutual responsibility for one another's outcome, with strong mutual attraction. Relationships are generally closer if the persons have similar social characteristics and compatible personality traits.

In a triad, the characteristic pattern of division is two against one. For groups of any size, success in the task with minimal stress produces more satisfied members.

Chapter 6

Leadership

A. Paul Hare and M. Valerie Kent

The study of leadership in small groups was one of the earliest interests of social psychologists as well as persons concerned with leadership in organizations and larger units of society. Although all studies of leadership at any level of the social system can help one to understand leader activities in small groups, this review is limited to studies that have focused on a small group. In some cases, as with the classic studies of leadership by Lewin, Lippitt, and White of authoritarian, democratic, and laissez-faire group atmospheres, the concern was with the impact of different leader styles on whole societies, even though the actual experiment was carried out with small groups of nine year old boys with adult leaders.

Although there is more emphasis in the recent literature on situational differences in leader style and group productivity and on women as leaders than there was in the period covered by the earlier *Handbook* (Hare, 1976, pp. 278–303), many of the themes remain the same. Therefore, as an introduction to the literature on leadership we begin with a summary of the research from the previous volume.

The general functions of the leader and the traits of the persons who typically become leaders are related to the requirements of the task and the needs of the members in the small group. Thus the effectiveness of a particular leader style is dependent upon the characteristics and status of the leader, the personalities of the members, the task in relation to the development of the group, the organization or larger unit to which the small group may belong, and the culture of the larger society.

As regards traits: Potential leaders usually have higher ratings than other group members on traits such as intelligence, enthusiasm, dominance, self-confidence, and social participation. These traits tend to be found in clusters which have been described by terms such as "authoritarian," "democratic," "Machiavellian," or "internal locus of control." The persons who emerge as leaders in leaderless group discussions tend to be of a type that includes more assertiveness, presumably because more assertive behavior is required to establish a position than to maintain one.

As regards functions: In some groups the same leader may serve the functions of pace setter and coordinator for both task and social-emotional behavior. However, when there is a division of the leadership function into two roles, the most common division is for a "task leader" who emphasizes serious behavior conforming to the group norms and a "social-emotional leader" who is concerned with the relationships between members. (See: Latham, 1987; Riedesel, 1974; Riedesel & Seem, 1976.)

In support of the "situational" theorists, autocratic task oriented leaders are usually more effective in favorable situations where the leader has high power, the group accepts the leader, and the task is highly structured, or in very unfavorable situations where the group does not accept the leader, the task is not structured, and where strong, controlling leadership is required. Relationship-oriented leaders are more effective in intermediate situations where the group may accept the leader even though the task may not be well defined. This concludes the review of leadership research covered in the previous edition of this *Handbook*.

In a subsequent analysis, Blake and Mouton (1982) concluded that a major controversy in leadership theory, research, and practice, is between two opposing positions. One is that of situational or contingency theory; the other is "one most effective style" theory. Advocates of situational or contingency theory say "No one style is more effective than another. The style you lead depends on the situation." One-most-effective-style theorists say, "There is one most effective style, and it involves applying principles of leadership behavior as these are emerging and becoming known in the behavioral sciences." Other articles discussing general theory include: Gemmill, 1986; R. W. Griffin, Skivington, & Moorhead, 1987; Holly, 1979.

Reviews of research on leadership are given by: Graumann & Moscovici, 1986; Hollander, 1985; Holly, 1980; J. B. Miner, 1982; Storm, 1978. In other comments McElroy and Shrader (1986) suggest that network analysis is useful for evaluating leader-subordinate relationships and leader behavior, and S. Kerr and Jermier (1978) conclude that certain individual, task, and organizational variables act as "substitutes for leadership," negating the hierarchical superior's ability to exert either positive or negative influence over subordinates' attitudes and effectiveness.

PEOPLE WHO BECOME LEADERS

As we have noted, and will again in the section on contingency below, the people who become leaders are those who take the initiative for the type of task and the type of other people they wish to lead. D. A. Kenny and Zaccaro (1983) suggest that rather than involving a set of personality traits, leadership may simply be based on the ability to perceive the needs and goals of a constituency and to adjust one's personal approach to group action accordingly. Leary, Robertson, Barnes, and Miller (1986) reached a similar conclusion when they found, in their research on self-presentations of potential leaders, that the leaders conveyed images of themselves to the group that were consistent with the type of leader they believed was needed for maximal effectiveness. In one experiment, when followers were pushed to lead, they led, and when pushed to follow, they increased their social-emotional activity (Beckhouse, Tanur, Weiler, & Weinstein, 1975).

Since most group research concerns groups that are relatively democratic, in contrast to groups that are very authoritarian, or rebellious, or designed for fun and games, it is not surprising that the people who become leaders in these groups have personality traits of dominance, friendliness, and task orientation. For example, in one study these variables are identified as persuasion, openness, and information (S. B. Weinberg, Smotroff, & Pecka, 1978), and in another study they are dominance, masculinity-femininity, and intelligence (Lord, deVader, & Alliger, 1986). Other studies emphasize a single variable, such as dominance (Scioli, Dyson, & Fleitas, 1974), intelligence (Fiedler, 1986; Fiedler & Leister, 1977), or self-esteem (P. H. Andrews, 1984; N. C. Hill & Ritchie, 1977), or self-monitoring ability (Garland & Beard, 1979). Additional personality traits associated with leadership are Machiavellianism (Drory & Gluskinos, 1980; Gleason, Seaman, & Hollander, 1978; Okanes & Stinson,1974) or anxiety and cognitive style (McWhirter & Frey, 1987).

Experience as a person with a particular status in a previous group will often carry over into a small group setting. For example, persons whose family status was as a first-born tend to become task-oriented leaders, while later-borns will be more relationship-oriented (Dagenais, 1979). The same is true for experience as a person of a given gender or race, where a social status is implied, as we will review in the next section.

Additional research related to personality or background characteristics of leaders is given by: Fodor, 1985; C. A. Johnson & Aderman, 1979; Nydegger, 1975a; Seeman, 1982; Strodtbeck & Lipinski, 1985.

INDIVIDUAL DIFFERENCES

Most of the research on the effect of individual differences has concerned gender and race, with gender being the primary focus, especially with the rather recent interest in the characteristics of women as leaders. (See also Chapter 2 on sex roles and leadership.)

In the typical laboratory study of discussion groups composed of male and female university students, men take the lead (Fleischer & Chertkoff, 1986; H. H. Frank & Katcher, 1977; Golub & Canty, 1982; Nyquist & Spence (1986); L. B. Rosenfeld & Fowler, 1976; Snodgrass & Rosenthal, 1984). In a study of self-presentations by leaders to followers of the same sex, Forsyth, Schlenker, Leary, and McCown (1985) found that the self-presentations of the leaders' own abilities were primarily determined by sex-role stereotypes rather than by situational factors. Male leaders emphasized their social influence and task abilities; female leaders emphasized their interpersonal, socioemotional abilities. However, both men and women who were high on "psychological androgyny" (possessing both instrumental and expressive traits) shared leadership more and were less likely to react to others according to sex type (Porter, Geis, Cooper, & Newman, 1985).

The nature of the task can shift the balance in favor of a woman as leader if she is clearly an expert or if the task calls for skills or information associated with women (Hollander & Yoder, 1980; P. A. Knight & Saal, 1984; Wentworth & Anderson, 1984).

Although on occasion male leaders may receive higher leadership ratings than female leaders or female leaders may be reacted to more negatively than males, many studies report no actual difference in leader behavior (V. Brown & Geis, 1984; Bullard & Cook, 1975; Eskilson & Wiley, 1976; Kushell & Newton, 1986; G. N. Powell & Butterfield, 1980, 1982, 1984; Reed, 1983; R. W. Rice, Bender, & Vitters, 1982; R. W. Rice, Yoder, Adams, Priest, & Prince, 1984; Schneier & Bartol, 1980; Stitt, Schmidt, Price, & Kipnis, 1983).

Additional research on gender and leadership is reported by: Alagna & Reddy, 1985; L. R. Anderson & McLenigan, 1987; Bussey & Bandura, 1984; Denmark, 1977; Dobbins, Pence, Orban, & Sgro, 1983; Dobbins, Stuart, Pence, & Sgro, 1985; Geis, Boston, & Hoffman, 1985; M. B. Jacobson & Koch, 1977; Kremer & Mack, 1983; Leary & Schlenker, 1980; Linimon, Barron, & Falbo, 1984; Offermann, 1984; R. W. Rice, Bender, & Vitters, 1980; Spillman, Spillman, & Reinking, 1981; Stake, 1981; Yerby, 1975.

So few studies deal with leadership and race that it is probably best not to generalize. Only one study reports a difference in leader style between black and white leaders (V. G. Thomas & Littig, 1985), two studies report no differences (W. A. Hill & Hughes, 1974; Holmes, Sholley, & Walker, 1980), and one study deals with the reactions of the leader to persons of different races (Garza, Romero, Cox, & Ramirez, 1982). (See also Chapter 2 on race.)

LEADERSHIP BEHAVIOR

Our readers may sense a certain amount of redundancy at this point since the traits that tend to make people become leaders will be exhibited in behavior once the leader role is assumed. Thus, compared with followers, leader behavior for the typical task-oriented group is characterized by higher participation (Knutson & Holdridge, 1975; Koomen, Ouweltjes, Wester, van Bovenkamp, & Forma, 1979; Lord & Alliger, 1985; Reynolds, 1984; Ruback, Dabbs, & Hopper, 1984; Sorrentino & Boutillier, 1975; R. T. Stein, 1975; R. T. Stein & Heller, 1979, 1983; Tyler, Rasinski, & Spodick, 1985), more consideration for and leniency toward the other group members (Schriesheim, Kinicki, & Schriesheim, 1979; R. G. Swanson & Johnson, 1975), and more contribution to the task (Gintner & Lindskold, 1975; Lonetto & Williams, 1974). In their nonverbal behavior leaders are more likely to gesture with their shoulders or arms (J. E. Baird, 1977).

If there is role differentiation between two leaders, then one will usually specialize in task behavior and the other in social-emotional behavior (Misumi & Ishida, 1972; Rees & Segal, 1984). The phase of the task, that is, beginning, middle, or end also affects the leader style (Misumi, Shinohara, & Sato, 1974) as do other conditions and situational variables (L. W. Fry, Kerr, & Lee, 1986; T. E. Hill & Schmitt, 1977; S. Kerr & Schriesheim, 1974). (See also section on Contingency Theories below.)

Additional research on leader behavior is given by: Accolla, Geffroy, Abraham, & Schutzenberger, 1982; Lord & Rowzee, 1979; Rush, Thomas, & Lord, 1977; Schultz, 1980.

PERCEPTIONS OF LEADERS

This section deals with the perceptions that both leaders and followers have of the leader's behavior and the relationship between these perceptions and the group's success or failure. Concerning causal attribution, the findings for groups are essentially the same as those for individuals. An individual who succeeds in a task is likely to attribute the success to his or her own effort, while failure is attributed to the task or the situation. The same effect is found with leaders and followers in groups. Group success is claimed by all, with the followers likely to attribute some of the success to the leader. If the group fails, the followers may blame the leader, unless the leader is an expert, in which case they may blame situational factors (J. B. Adams, Adams, Rice, & Instone, 1985; Caine & Schlenker, 1979; S. G. Green & Mitchell, 1979; Dobbins & Russell, 1986; T. R. Mitchell, Larson, & Green, 1977; Norvell & Forsyth, 1984; J. S. Phillips & Lord, 1981). (See also Chapter 12.)

In a study of discussion groups of university students, perceptions of elected leaders were compared with perceptions of leaders appointed by the experimenter. The elected leaders were seen by followers as more responsive to followers' needs, more interested in the group task, and more competent than leaders who were appointed, suggesting that a leader's source of legitimacy has distinct consequences for leader-follower relations (Ben-Yoav, Hollander, & Carnevale, 1983). A similar experiment compared the effects of internal promotion versus external appointment of a leader by someone who was presumed to be either expert or not expert at the task (P. A. Knight & Weiss, 1980). In this case, leaders chosen by a competent agent of selection were themselves seen as having greater task expertise and were better able to influence the decisions of group members than leaders selected by a less competent agent. The origin of the leader had no effect on either perceptions of the leader or the leader's influence. (See also: Daum, 1975; Pandey, 1976.)

Additional research related to perception of leaders is reported by: S. Barlow, Hansen, Fuhriman, & Finley, 1982; Cronshaw & Lord, 1987; di Marco, Kuehl, & Wims, 1975; Ilgen & Fujii, 1976; Niebuhr & Davis, 1984; Rush, Phillips, & Lord, 1981; Sakamaki, 1974; Sande, Ellard, & Ross, 1986; R. T. Stein, 1977.

FOLLOWERS

The view of group interaction from the bottom up—that is, from the point of view of the followers—is the mirror image of the reports given by leaders with regard to followers. Thus if a democratic leader, or someone observing the leader, reports that the followers seem better satisfied with the friendly approach than they do with the more negative approach of the authoritarian leader, then we shall not be surprised if, when we ask the followers, or focus on their behavior, we find them more satisfied under the same conditions. In general then, the upward (active), positive, and forward (task-oriented) behavior of the democratic leader is evaluated more positively by followers than the behavior of an authoritarian leader (Heilman, Hornstein, Cage, & Herschlag, 1984; Sinha & Sinha, 1977), and the followers are more satisfied (Fulk & Wendler, 1982). A summary of the propositions about leadership and followers included in a special issue of the *Journal of Applied Behavioral Science* is given by T. Heller and Van Til (1982).

Some research findings are related to the characteristics of the followers. For example, followers who are low in task competence will comply more with leader demands (K. H. Price & Garland, 1981a, 1981b). Followers who are high on "internal control" (in contrast to external control) favor a participatory leader and are less likely to comply with leader demands (Cravens & Worchel, 1977; Rucker & King, 1985). Followers' creativity will be enhanced by a leadership climate that supports individual initiative (Fiene, 1979; Glover & Chambers, 1978; Leana, 1985; Ruzicka, Palisi, Kelly, & Corrado, 1979).

Studies that explore the categories used by followers in describing the behavior and attitudes of leaders are reported by: Herold, 1977; Lord, Foti, & de Vader, 1984; Sims & Manz, 1984.

Additional related research includes: R. G. Field, 1982; Michener & Lawler, 1975; Morran & Hulse, 1984; Rutte & Wilke, 1984; Schultz, 1978; Solem, 1976; Watson & Michaelsen, 1984, 1985; Weed, Mitchell, & Moffitt, 1976.

POWER

The typology of bases of leader power suggested by J. R. P. French and Raven in 1959 continues to provide a framework for contemporary research. They identified five bases of power as: reward, coercive, legitimate, expert, and referent (Podsakoff & Schriescheim, 1985). Although French and Raven did not indicate that any one of these bases of power was more important than any other, they can be ordered in a "cybernetic hierarchy" from the perspective of functional analysis (Hare & Naveh, 1986). First "expert" power can be separated from the other bases since it refers to task effectiveness rather than to positive or negative behavior directed to the group members. The expert might be supplying or withholding ideas at any level of creativity, from low order facts to high order theory. On the social-emotional side, rewards (giving or taking money, for example) would be expected to have the least amount of power, coercive power (to give or refrain from punishment) would have more power, next in order would be referent power (friendly or unfriendly association with the leader), and at the top of the hierarchy, legitimate power (where the leader's position is accepted as representing the values of the group).

A few recent studies that compare two sources of power lend some support to the cybernetic hierarchy hypothesis. For example, the leader has more support if the source of power is legitimate rather than usurped (Wilke, de Boer, & Liebrand, 1986) and positional authority is given more support than personal authority (Spillane, 1983). In general, whatever the level of the basis of power, positive reinforcement can be expected to be more effective than negative (J. A. Barlow, 1984; Michener & Burt, 1975; Nydegger, 1975b; Sheley & Shaw, 1979).

Additional research on power includes: L. R. Anderson, Karuza, & Blanchard, 1977; Ashour & Johns, 1983; G. Falk & Falk, 1981; R. A. Feldman, 1973; Fodor & Farrow, 1979; L. N. Gray & Griffith, 1984; L. N. Gray, Mayhew, & Campbell, 1974; Griffith & Gray, 1978; Lawler & Thompson, 1979; Lord, 1977; Molm, 1981b, 1981c; Ng, 1977; Tjosvold, 1985; Umino, 1983.

SITUATIONAL AND TASK VARIABLES

As with so many research topics in the study of interaction in small groups, researchers who report on variations in situation or task as they are related to leadership style focus on only one type of situation or task. As a result some research focuses on differences in the communication network imposed by seating arrangement, some compares tasks requiring cooperation with those implying competition, some deals with small versus large groups, and so on. As it turns out many of the effects of these apparently different variables are similar. Large groups, groups with centralized communication networks, competitive groups, and authoritarian groups all tend to require more activity on the part of the leader, with less positive interpersonal relations between members, and higher productivity in the short run. Small groups, groups with open communication, cooperative groups, and democratic groups tend to have the opposite characteristics (cf. C. N. Greene & Schriesheim, 1980; Tjosvold, 1982). The following summary of some of the research in this area reflects these patterns. (See also the section on Contingency Theories below.)

With regard to task differences, the more the task is structured, the less it becomes necessary for the leader to take an active part in defining the situation for the followers (Jurma, 1978; Lord, 1976). Positive feedback concerning the group task tends to make the leaders more task oriented, whereas negative feedback may increase negative social-emotional behavior (R. P. Butler & Jaffee, 1974). Followers work harder if the task is judged to be important (Murnighan & Leung, 1976).

Persons in the center of a communication network, either because of some imposed limitation on channels of communication or simply because they are seated in a more central and prominent position tend to become leaders (Jolley, 1973) while physical closeness of seating encourages friendship formation (J. Greenberg, 1976). Persons who choose the central positions are likely to have prior leadership experience and are high on tests of internal control (Hiers & Heckel, 1977). For a task requiring creativity, tolerance for diverse viewpoints was found to be more important then whether or not communication was channeled through the leader (Cielecki, 1979). (See also the section in Chapter 1 on seating arrangements.)

As in the research on contingency theories, the leader is generally more effective if the followers share the same values or have similar types of personalities (Dyson, Godwin, & Hazelwood, 1976). For example, in one experiment, groups were superior in performance when both leaders and followers were high on "internal locus of control" (C. R. Anderson & Schneier, 1978).

Additional research is given by: Eakin, 1975; R. E. Kaplan, 1979; O'Brien & Kabanoff, 1981; Pagerey & Chapanis, 1983; Strickland, Guild, Barefoot, & Paterson, 1978.

CRISIS LEADERSHIP

As with so many other studies of leadership, the research on leadership behavior in a crisis could well apply to large groups, especially crowds who have gathered for some purpose or persons who have no common goal other than the fact that they happen to be in the same subway station. Indeed, some studies of panic behavior were carried out with relatively small groups partly as a model of the possible effects of a situation in which many more people were involved.

A common subject of research in this area concerns the efforts of a leader to evacuate a group of people from a dangerous place or to secure their help in a medical emergency. The group's reaction to a crisis requiring immediate action is more rapid if the leader is assertive (Firestone, Lichtman, & Colamosca, 1975). However, if there is time for group discussion to reach a decision before reacting to the crisis, then it is better if the leader uses a nondirective style that will produce more suggestions for solutions and a more considered use of available facts (Flowers, 1977).

In the panic situation it helps if the leader who gives directions for escape (A. L. Klein, 1976) is in the same room in which the group is assembled (Kugihara, Misumi, Sato, & Shigeoka, 1982). It is even better if the leader says "follow me" and leads at least one person out of the area (Sugiman & Misumi, 1984). It also helps if the leader urges the others to stay calm (Misumi & Sako, 1982). Additional research on leadership in panic situations deals with the effects of "performance" and "maintenance" leadership (Kugihara & Misumi, 1984; S. Sato, Kugihara, Misumi, & Shigeoka, 1984).

Additional findings on crisis or stress situations include: high stress may bring out more authoritarian leadership (Fodor, 1976, 1978), subjects are less likely to revolt against inequitable pay rates if the leader is not responsible (Lawler & Thompson, 1978) and is cooptive rather than threatening (Lawler, 1983), and positive leader feedback can be used to ameliorate the negative effects of failure (K. H. Price & Garland, 1978).

CONTINGENCY THEORIES

Although earlier research on situational differences in leader behavior sought to discover the best style for each type of task, most of the research during the past decade has centered on the work of Fiedler and his associates. They find that group performance is contingent upon the interaction of leadership style and situational favorableness. "Task-oriented" leaders do well in very favorable or unfavorable situations. "Relationship-oriented" leaders are more effective in intermediate situations. The "relationship-oriented" leader is one who gives favorable ratings to his "least preferred co-workers" on a scale developed by Fiedler. In style this leader tends to be permissive, passive, and accepting, while the "task-oriented" leader is managing, controlling, and more active. As a result, the task-oriented leader is more effective in favorable situations where the group accepts the leader and the task is highly structured, or in very unfavorable situations where strong controlling leadership is required.

After reviewing some 145 hypothesis tests validating Fiedler's model, as well as the 33 results on which the model is based, Strube and Garcia (1981) concluded that the model is extremely robust in predicting group performance. (See also Vecchio's comment, 1983 and Strube and Garcia's rejoinder, 1983.)

In an unpublished paper, Bales (1987) notes that the three dimensions used by Fiedler to denote situational favorableness, namely leader power, positive relationship with members, and structured task are essentially the same as the three dimensions in SYMLOG theory (Bales & Cohen, 1979). Favorable situations are those in which the group members are friendly and the task is well defined; intermediate situations are those in which there is friendliness, but the members are not motivated to work or the task is not well defined; finally, unfavorable situations have neither friendly nor task oriented group members.

Recent research that supports Fiedler's theory concerning task and relationship oriented leaders includes: Csoka, 1975; Fiedler & Chemers, 1984; Fiedler & Garcia, 1987; Garvin & Rice, 1982; Konar-Goldband, Rice, & Monkarsh, 1979; R. W. Rice,

1978; R. W. Rice & Kastenbaum, 1983; Tanaka, 1975; Vecchio, 1981; Wofford & Srinivasan, 1983.

Partial support for the theory is given in research by: Bird, 1977; Bons & Fiedler, 1976; Neuberger & Roth, 1974; M. Yoshida & Shirakashi, 1973.

In an extension of the theory, R. W. Rice, Seaman, and Garvin (1978) found that task-oriented persons not only showed a greater differentiation in their judgments about most and least preferred co-workers than did relationship-oriented persons, but they are more extreme in their attitudes toward other objects.

Some research suggests the need for additional or better measures of some of the concepts in the theory, such as potential influence (Kabanoff, 1981), supportiveness (Vecchio, 1980), and the Least Preferred Co-worker and situational control measures (Stewart & Latham, 1986).

As in the earlier period of research, some studies fail to find support for the model: R. W. Johnson & Ryan, 1976; J. K. Kennedy, 1982; Newcomer, 1985; Sarges, 1975; Schneier, 1978; Singh, 1983; Stinson & Tracy, 1974; Vecchio, 1977; Wofford, 1985.

Additional research on Fiedler's theory includes: Chemers, Rice, Sundstrom, & Butler, 1975; Hewett, O'Brien, & Hornik, 1974; Hoffman, 1984; Hoffman & Roman, 1984; Levy-Leboyer, Moser, Vedrenne, & Veyssiere, 1976; Petrovskii, 1980; R. W. Rice, 1981; Saha, 1979; Shirakashi & Yoshida, 1975; Theodory, 1982; Vecchio, 1982.

Some authors have proposed contingency theories based on a somewhat different conception of the major variables. For example, S. Kerr, Schreisheim, Murphy, and Stogdill (1974) reviewed the published literature involving the leader behavior dimensions of "consideration" and "initiating structure," to develop some situational propositions of leader effectiveness. The variables that were found to moderate the relationships between leader behavior predictors and satisfaction and performance criteria were the following: subordinate need for information, job level, subordinate expectations of leader behavior, perceived organizational independence, leader's similarity of attitudes and behavior to managerial style of higher management, leader upward influence, and characteristics of the task (including pressure and intrinsic satisfaction).

Additional studies that consider other variables related to contingency include: Justis, 1975; Kabanoff & O'Brien, 1979a; J. R. Nicholls, 1985; O'Brien & Harary, 1977.

GROUP EVOLUTION

A few studies deal with consistencies or changes in leadership during phases of group evolution. Over a series of meetings, when group membership remains constant, persons who are high on both success-oriented and affiliation-oriented needs participate more and receive high ratings on leadership initially, and continue to do so (Sorrentino & Field, 1986). In contrast, when subjects are continually removed from groups and replaced by new members, seniority plays a determining part in who will be the leader (Insko, Thibaut, Moehle, Wilson, Diamond, Gilmore, Solomon, & Lipsitz, 1980; Insko, Gilmore, Moehle, Lipsitz, Drenan, & Thibaut, 1982).

CROSS CULTURAL STUDIES

Since most of the social-psychological research on small groups uses university students in the United States, few studies are available to demonstrate the cultural differences that do exist. However, persons interested in evidence of cultural differences may wish to consider Krichevskii's (1977b) comment that some American research is based on the false ideological and philosophical notion of positivism and examine his own research on Moscow basketball, volleyball, and handball teams and other groups (Krichevskii, 1977a, 1981, 1984). Zamarripa and Krueger (1983) report research on cultural differences in groups composed of university students whose backgrounds were American, French, and Arab. They note that each group composed of members from the same background presented an internally consistent set of leadership rules prior to group interaction; however, groups composed of persons from different cultures presented internally varied rules.

ADDITIONAL RESEARCH

Additional research on leadership includes: Bugen, 1978; Bulak, 1972; Dollinger & Thelen, 1978; Gallagher & Burke, 1974; T. A. Hill, 1976; Hobson, 1986; Jesuino, 1986; Klinger & McNelly, 1976; Lippitt, 1986; Lord, Binning, Rush, & Thomas, 1978; Misumi, 1985; Nachman, Dansereau, & Naughton, 1985; Remland, 1984; Schultz, 1986; P. B. Smith & Peterson, 1988.

SUMMARY

People who become leaders are those who take the initiative for the type of task and the type of other people they wish to lead. In the typical democratic task-oriented group the people who become leaders have personality traits of dominance, friendliness, and task orientation.

Given the sex-role stereotypes in Western cultures, men are more likely to take the lead in discussion groups than women. However, the nature of the task can shift the balance in favor of a woman as leader if she is clearly a leader or if the task calls for skills or information associated with women. Once a man or woman has taken the leader role many studies report no differences in leader behavior. Regardless of gender, leaders tend to be high participators, show more consideration, and contribute more to the task than followers. If there is role differentiation between two leaders, then one will usually specialize in task-behavior and the other in social-emotional behavior.

Responsibility for group success is typically claimed by all, with the followers likely to attribute some of the success to the leader. However, if the group fails, the followers may blame the leader, unless the leader is an expert, in which case they may blame the situation. Followers evaluate a democratic leader more positively than an authoritarian leader and are more satisfied with the group experience.

Whatever the base of power used by a leader, positive reinforcement can be expected to be more effective than negative. Large groups, groups with centralized communication networks, competitive groups, and authoritarian groups all tend to require more activity on the part of the leader, with less positive interpersonal relations between members, and higher productivity in the short run. Persons in the center of the communication network, either because of imposed limitations on communication, or simply seating position, tend to become leaders. In panic situations it helps if the leader gives directions and urges others to stay calm.

Effective leader style is related to the situation. "Task-oriented" leaders do well in very favorable or unfavorable situations. "Relationship-oriented" leaders are more effective in intermediate situations.

Part IV
GROUP PROCESS

Chapter 7

Social Interaction

A. Paul Hare and Martin F. Davies

COMMUNICATION CHANNELS AND MODALITIES

A complete analysis of social interaction includes a consideration of the form of communication (the communication network and the frequency of interaction along each path in the network), the process (directed toward the task and the relationships with other group members), and the content (in terms of the function being performed or some other set of categories describing the subject of the interaction) (Hare, 1976, pp. 5–6; 1982, pp. 20–22). Recent research on these aspects of social interaction is included in the second section of this chapter. However, we begin with a focus on nonverbal interaction, an aspect of interaction that only began to receive attention in the late 1960s (Hare, 1976, pp. 83–85). Nonverbal behavior has held special interest because it is often less consciously controlled and may contradict as well as amplify verbal behavior. However, as with the early research, more recent accounts often do not distinguish between nonverbal behaviors that a subject emits unconsciously (and which may give information to others) and nonverbal signals that are used in lieu of verbal communication or to supplement it.

Most of the research on interpersonal communication is concerned with a set of individuals performing some task although, even then, some of the interaction may be directed towards gaining knowledge about the persons in the relationship (C. R. Berger, Gardner, Clatterbuck, & Schulman, 1976). In an article on "the syntaxes of bodily communication" Argyle (1973) discusses research on nonverbal communication and the problems in establishing the meanings in nonverbal signals. He identifies a number of separate systems of nonverbal communication, each with distinctive properties as communication systems. The systems vary in (a) whether there is intention to communicate, (b) hierarchial structure, (c) external reference, and (d) rule of sequence. There are different nonverbal codes, each functioning in a different way for (a) sign languages, (b) illustrations during speech, (c) synchronizing signals and feedback during speech, (d) emotions and interpersonal attitudes, (e) rituals and ceremonies, and (f) sequences of social acts. Different parts of the body act as channels in different ways. The main channels are appearance, facial expression, gestures, spatial behavior, bodily contact, gaze, and tone of voice. Communication through several channels may be combined to give a clearly understood meaning (L. M. Schwartz, Foa, & Foa, 1983).

Examples of the relationship between the expression of feelings and nonverbal behaviors are found in observations of pairs discussing intimate topics. Persons who were reluctant to disclose information nodded less, showed less facial pleasantness and animation, displayed more anxiety and tension, and leaned away more (J. K. Burgoon & Koper, 1984), while persons discussing intimate topics with good friends were relaxed (Keiser & Altman, 1976). Similarly, embarrassed persons decreased eye contact and increased body motion and speech disturbances (Edelmann & Hampson, 1979). Persons who spoke two languages were able to discuss embarrassing topics at greater length in their second language, presumably because the second language had the effect of distancing the person from the topic (M. H. Bond & Lai, 1986). In other examples, interaction with "warm" persons produced more direct eye gaze, head nods, and smiles (Ho & Mitchell, 1982), and strong emotional expression (whether positive or negative) evoked more direct gaze (Kimble, Forte, & Yoshikawa, 1981).

The primary dimensions of nonverbal behavior are the same as those for verbal behavior, namely dominance versus submission, positive versus negative, conforming to the norms of the task versus nonconforming, and being serious versus being expressive (Hare, 1976, pp. 78–80; see also, Bienvenu & Stewart, 1976; L. Miller & Bart, 1985). For many task-oriented groups the third and fourth dimensions can be combined into "forward" behavior that is serious and conforming and "backward" behavior that is nonconforming and expressive (Bales & Cohen, 1979). Dominant, assertive nonverbal behavior is evidenced in lateral opposition, precedence, erect posture, elevation, and loud voice for humans (McFall, Winnett, Bordewick, & Bornstein, 1982; Norton-Ford & Hogan, 1980; Y. J. Rose & Tryon, 1979; B. Schwartz, Tesser, & Powell, 1982) and other primates (Mazur, 1985). Men tend to exhibit more assertive nonverbal behaviors than women (Benoist & Butcher, 1977; G. Butterfield, 1977; Fine, Stitt, & Finch, 1984; Guy, 1979; Shrout & Fiske, 1981). Research with married couples reports that positive behavior is associated with smiling (Noller, 1980, 1982, 1984; Noller & Gallois, 1986) and that, whatever the nonverbal behavior, married couples that have a good relationship are better at sending and receiving unambiguous nonverbal messages (Beier, 1974; Sabatelli, Buck, & Dreyer, 1982). Friends are also more intimate and active than strangers when greeting (Riggio, Friedman, & DiMatteo, 1981) or parting (Summerfield & Lake, 1977). Forward, task-oriented behavior is facilitated by face-to-face communication compared to other modes of communication such as computers or television (Ochsman & Chapanis, 1974; Preston, 1984; Short, 1974; J. Siegel,

Dubrovsky, Kiesler, & McGuire, 1986; Siegman & Reynolds, 1983a; Stoll, Hoecker, Krueger, & Chapanis, 1976; Tartter, 1983; Turnbull, Strickland, & Shaver, 1974; Weeks & Chapanis, 1976; Wiemann, 1977).

For general models or overviews of interpersonal communication, see: Argyle, 1988; L. L. Barker, Wahlers, Watson, & Kibler, 1987; Beattie, 1983; Cicourel, 1974; S. Duncan & Fiske, 1977; Goodwin, 1981; R. G. Harper, Wiens, & Matarazzo, 1978; Henley, 1977; Heslin & Patterson, 1982; Kendon, Harris, & Key, 1975; M. L. Knapp, 1978, 1984; M. L. Knapp & Miller, 1985; McCroskey, & Daly, 1987; Metcalfe, 1981; G. R. Miller, 1975, 1976, 1978; M. L. Patterson, 1983; Potter & Wetherell, 1987; Roloff, 1981; Roloff & Miller, 1987; Siegman & Feldstein, 1979; Siegman & Pope, 1978; Sigman, 1987; Weitz, 1979; Wiemann & Harrison, 1983. The following provide reviews of research: Cragan & Wright, 1980; Edinger & Patterson, 1983; Johansen, Miller, & Vallee, 1974; E. Williams, 1975.

Additional articles on other aspects of nonverbal communication include: Beach & Sokoloff, 1974; Bohannon, Stine, & Ritzenberg, 1982; Chapanis, 1975; Felmlee, Eder, & Tsui, 1985; Gitter, Black, & Goldman, 1975; Kemp & Rutter, 1982; Lochman & Allen, 1981; Shea & Rosenfeld, 1976; and Wexley, Fugita, & Malone, 1975.

Gaze and Eye Contact

The eyes are the most important medium for interpersonal communication since they preface most new relationships, overshadowing other sensory inputs, while transmitting a variety of emotional cues, according to Grumet (1983). He notes that visual behavior may at times be decisive in assuring survival, in amorous encounters, and in clarifying interpersonal motives. Although he concludes that eye contact is a crucial factor in defining relationships and allowing reciprocal influences to be exchanged as persons relate, not everyone agrees. Some research has been designed to test a hypothesis by Rutter, Stephenson, Lazzerini, Ayling, and White (1977) that eye contact is merely a *chance* product of individual looking (Hargreaves & Fuller, 1984; Lazzerini, Stephenson, & Neave, 1978). However, the weight of evidence given in the next few paragraphs, suggests that the "eyes have it" in many important situations (M. Cook, 1977).

Some of the contradictory findings in the literature may result from the failure to differentiate between a "look" and a "stare". A "look" involves a dynamic eye presentation and a "stare" a static eye presentation (R. D. Deutsch & Auerbach, 1975). The stare is more likely to be taken as an indication of the looker's intention to attend visually to the subject (R. D. Deutsch, 1976), and may be taken as a stimulus to approach or avoidance depending on the context (Ellsworth & Langer, 1976; Ellsworth & Ross, 1975; Ellsworth, Friedman, Perlick, & Hoyt, 1978; Tobiasen & Allen, 1983).

As with nonverbal behavior in general, reviews of research on gaze and eye contact conclude that gaze can be an indicator of dominance, affection, or interest, and in addition can serve as a regulator of interaction by indicating that it is time for someone to start or stop speaking (Argyle & Cook, 1976); Kleinke, 1986; Mazur, Rosa, Faupel, Heller, Leen, & Thurman, 1980; Rime, 1977). An obvious exception is that persons without sight need to rely on other cues (Rutter & Stephenson, 1979a).

Additional research on the part played by gaze in gaining attention or controlling conversation is recorded by: Harrigan & Steffen, 1983; B. J. Hedge, Everitt, & Firth, 1978; Kalma & Van Rooij, 1982; Kleinke, 1977a; Krantz, George, & Hursh, 1983.

A dominant person tends to look more at another person while speaking (Timney & London, 1973). A less dominant person tends to look more while listening. The dominance can result from personality traits (Argyle, Lefebvre, & Cook, 1974; Dovidio & Ellyson, 1982), expertise with the task (Breed & Colaiuta, 1974; Brooks, Church, & Fraser, 1986; Cherulnik, Neely, Flanagan, & Zachau, 1978; Dovidio, Ellyson, Keating, Heltman, & Brown, 1988; Ellyson, Dovidio, & Corson, 1981), or social status (Dorch & Fontaine, 1978; Ellyson, Dovidio, Corson, & Vinicur, 1980; LaFrance & Mayo, 1976; Rall, Greenspan, & Neidich, 1984). Persons who are not ordinarily dominant may show dominant gaze patterns when they are elated and submissive patterns when they are depressed or embarrassed (Natale, 1977; Rutter, 1976, 1978).

Eye contact together with some other nonverbal indication of closeness, such as physical proximity or smiling, results in higher positive evaluations (S. E. Scherer, 1974) or greater intimacy (Walsh & Hewitt, 1985). However, levels of intimacy that are judged to be either too high or too low may produce an adverse effect (M. Goldman & Fordyce, 1983). Mutual eye contact is, of course, more likely if persons are seated opposite each other than adjacent (Muirhead & Goldman, 1979).

When working on a common task, gaze at one's partner, or at some object relevant for the task, not only indicates involvement with the task but allows the person observing to monitor the other's reactions and be more effective in cooperation (Argyle & Graham, 1976; M. H. Bond & Komai, 1976; Ehrlichman, 1981; M. Foddy, 1978b; R. Fry & Smith, 1975; Hore, 1976; Rutter & Stephenson, 1979b; G. M. Stephenson, Ayling, & Rutter, 1976; Swain, Stephenson, & Dewey, 1982).

As with other verbal and nonverbal aspects of interaction, the sex of the persons involved should be noted. Relative to males, females in one experiment were found to gaze more and were more responsive to changes in the confederate's gaze direction (F. W. Schneider & Hansvick, 1977). Additional differences depend on the situation (Gielen, Dick, Rosenberg, Kelly, & Chiafettelli, 1979; Hughes & Goldman, 1978; Juni & Hershkowitz-Friedman, 1981; F. W. Schneider, Coutts, & Garrett, 1977). For a general review of language and sex differences, as these bear on small groups, see Kramarae (1981).

Additional research on gaze and eye contact is provided by: D. E. Allen & Guy,

1977; Beattie, 1978, 1981; M. Cook & Smith, 1975; Daibo, 1980; Jellison & Ickes, 1974; Kidd, 1975; Kleinke, Meeker, & LaFong, 1974; Kleinke & Singer, 1979; Krop, Messinger, & Reiner, 1973–1974; Lesko & Schneider, 1978; Naiman & Breed, 1974; Rimé, 1982; Rimé & McCusker, 1976.

Facial Expression

Research on facial expression has tended to concentrate on the patterns of facial movement associated with particular emotions, the accuracy with which people can recognize facial expressions of emotions, and the role of facial expression in regulating emotions (Bassili, 1979; Buck, 1980; Ekman & Friesen, 1975, 1978; Ekman & Oster, 1979; Ekman, Friesen, & Ancoli, 1980; Laird, 1974, 1984; Rinn, 1984; Tourangeau & Ellsworth, 1979; Winton, 1986; Zajonc, 1985). Facial expressions can be identified that represent various combinations of dominant, positive, and forward behavior and their opposites (Bales & Cohen, 1979). Generally, only six emotions can be reliably identified from posed facial expression—happiness, surprise, fear, anger, sadness, and disgust (Ekman, 1982). *Spontaneous* facial expressions are not as easily identified (H. L. Wagner, MacDonald, & Manstead, 1986; Zuckerman, Larrance, Hall, DeFrank, & Rosenthal, 1979).

Happiness is the most accurately identified emotion, and smiling is one of the most clear-cut facial expressions (Ekman, 1982), as well as being one of the most widely researched (cf. J. A. Graham & Argyle, 1975). In addition to expressing happiness, smiling conveys friendliness and is a potent reinforcer of another person's actions, especially talking. The social nature of smiling was confirmed by Kraut and Johnston (1979) who reported a series of observations in everyday settings. In a bowling alley, bowlers often smiled when socially engaged, looking at and talking to others, but not necessarily after scoring a spare or a strike. At hockey games, fans smiled both when they were socially involved and after events favorable to their team. Pedestrians were much more likely to smile when talking but only slightly more likely to smile in good weather than in bad weather. Mackey (1976) also found that people smile more in the presence of other people than when alone. Smiling as an indication of positive behavior is also used when a subject wishes to appease or ingratiate another person (Goldenthal, Johnston, & Kraut, 1981; Lefebvre, 1975).

Lockard, Fahrenbruch, Smith, and Morgan (1977) observed the smiling and laughter of pairs of adults in social situations that included goal-oriented interactions, work breaks, chance encounters, and leisure episodes. They concluded that their data support the hypothesis that the human smile had its origin in the silent bared-teeth submissive grimace of primates and that the facial expression accompanying laughter evolved from the relaxed open-mouth display of play. Affiliative smiling occurred in greeting and departure interactions, whereas frank laughter was almost exclusively seen in a recreational context.

174   HARE AND DAVIES

Brunner (1979) noted that smiles show a strong tendency to occur at the same locations in a stream of dyadic interaction as "back channel" responses (such as "yeah," "uh-huh," and head nods). He concluded that smiles can function as a type of back channel that makes communication more efficient by providing a speaker with feedback on a number of levels simultaneously.

Smiles can apparently be interpreted differently by female subjects when they are given by women or men. Hackney (1974) examined the effects of four levels of nonverbal facial gestures on client verbal behavior in a quasi-interview setting. Nonverbal behaviors included no expression, head nod, smile, and head nod/smile combination. Each level of treatment was presented by a male and female experimenter. Treatments were videorecorded for standardized presentation to 72 female undergraduates. Subjects produced progressively and significantly greater amounts of feeling and self-reference feeling statements for head nod, smile, and head nod/smile combination when stimuli were presented by the female experimenter. The opposite effect was evident when stimuli were presented by the male experimenter.

Additional research on facial expression is provided by: Bugenthal, 1986; Craig & Patrick, 1985; H. S. Friedman, 1979; C. F. Keating, Mazur, Segall, Cysneiros, Divale, Kilbride, Komin, Leahy, Thurman, & Wirsing, 1981; Kraut, 1982; Lanzetta & Orr, 1986; Patrick, Craig, & Prkachin, 1986; Sabatelli, Buck, & Dreyer, 1980.

Posture, Gesture, and Touch

As with facial expression, posture, gesture, and touch, alone or in combination, can be used to communicate all combinations of dominant, positive, and forward behavior (Bales & Cohen, 1979). However, here also, the main focus of research has been on the positive-negative dimension of behavior. For example, M. H. Bond and Shiraishi (1973, 1974) conducted a study in Japan in which student volunteers were interviewed by confederates who leaned forward 20 degrees in half of the interviews and leaned backward 20 degrees in the other half. The forward-leaning interviewers appeared more polite and more flexible than the backward-leaners to students of both sexes.

In relation to task behavior, Lockard, Allen, Schiele, and Wiemer (1978) studied postural stance as an indication of intention to leave a dyadic social situation for several hundred human adults. They noted whether one leg was bearing more weight than the other, stance weight shifts, and stance shifts toward or away from the other member of the pair. The sex of the subjects and whether the members of the pairs left separately or together were recorded. The authors concluded that unequal weight stances and stance weight shifts are intention movements indicating imminent departure. Also, shifts toward or away from the other member of the pair just prior to departure correlated with sex and whether the members of the pair left separately or together.

Observing pairs of college students, Bull and Brown (1977) were interested in postural changes associated with the introduction of new information into the conversation. They observed that postural shifts involving at least half of the body indicated a shift in the point. Smaller movements were associated with the specific type of speech they preceded (e.g. question, answer). Persons who assume the same posture and "mirror" each other in a social setting are generally more involved in the interaction, are more likely to see each other as similar, and like one another more (LaFrance, 1979; LaFrance & Broadbent, 1976; LaFrance & Ickes, 1981; Maxwell & Cook, 1985; Navarre, 1982). In a group setting, LaFrance (1985) found greater intergroup relative to intragroup mirroring for cooperating dyads than for competing dyads.

Gestures can be "illustrators" (instantiating what is being said), or "emblems" (substituting for speech, such as the thumbs-up signal), or "batons" (emphasizing points while speaking). In fact, McNeill (1985) suggests that speech and gestures are part of the same language system, such that gestures are manifestations of inner speech just as overt speech is the usual external manifestation. Gestures are also used by listeners as "back-channel" responses, especially nodding and shaking the head (Hadar, Steiner, & Rose, 1985), and as regulators of conversation, such as turning the head away before replying to a question, or raising a hand to claim the floor (Bull, 1987; S. Duncan & Niederehe, 1974; S. Duncan & Fiske, 1977; A. P. Thomas & Bull, 1981). Originally, Condon and Ogston (1966) suggested that there is a very fine degree of *interactional synchrony* for body movements during conversation. This 'gestural dance' between speaker and listener was found to be closely linked to speech. However, a reappraisal of the phenomenon by McDowall (1978) suggested that the original results could have been due to chance and McDowall was unable to find significant degrees of synchrony in either strangers or friends.

Although the member of a pair who initiates touching is generally more dominant or of higher status (Major & Heslin, 1982) and touch may be important in securing compliance to a request (Kleinke, 1977a; Paulsell & Goldman, 1984; Willis & Hamm, 1980), most of the research on touch deals with it in reference to the positive-negative dimension of behavior. The sex of the subject is an especially important variable in the reactions to touch (Henley, 1977). The response of hands touching hands was found to be uniformly positive for females, with males more ambivalent (J. D. Fisher, Rytting, & Heslin, 1976). In intimate encounters at an airport where someone was arriving or departing, men tended to initiate touch with women more than vice versa (Heslin & Boss, 1980). In general, touching interactions are rated more positively than nontouch interactions, with cross-sex interactions rated more positively than same-sex ones (Hewitt & Lewis, 1985). Women like being touched more than men, but touch from an opposite-sex stranger is considered unpleasant by women, whereas men find touch from a same-sex stranger unpleasant (Heslin, Nguyen, & Nguyen, 1983; Stier & Hall, 1984). In a medical setting, Whitcher and Fisher (1979) found that female patients benefited from increased touching by nurses, whereas male patients were adversely affected. A sex-role explanation was adduced for these findings: Females are socialized to be comfortable with dependency and thus experience nurse-patient touch as a gesture of caring and warmth, whereas males are socialized to be uncomfortable with dependency and experience nurse-patient touch as inferiority and submission.

Additional research on touching is provided by: Crusco & Wetzel, 1984; Hoddinott & Follingstad, 1983; Nguyen, Heslin, & Nguyen, 1976; D. E. Smith, Willis, & Gier, 1980; N. M. Sussman & Rosenfeld, 1978: and D. N. Walker, 1975.

Paralanguage

Current research continues to reinforce some of the earlier findings in small group research, that paralanguage indicators such as speaking order and talking time are associated with dominance (Lamb, 1980, 1981). In order to avoid interruption, a speaker will often fill pauses with "er," "um," or other sounds (Beattie, 1977; P. Ball, 1975).

When pauses do occur between speakers, Snow and Brissett (1986) argue that such pauses should not be relegated to the status of a residual category nor should pauses be conceptualized as breaks in action or periods of inactivity. They suggest that pauses are an essential element of the social rhythm that demonstrates degrees of personal and community well-being and vitality, and that pausing may be an important, perhaps even necessary, part of the process of commitment and self-esteem. They offer a typology of pauses: (a) benchmarks for distinguishing actions, relationships, and physical place; (b) periods of taking stock; (c) respites for physical and mental rejuvenation; (d) periods of waiting; and (e) moments of temporary withdrawal. Another type of pause is the "awkward silence" that often occurs after there has been a minimal response to some statement and is followed by a series of questions and answers (McLaughlin & Cody, 1982).

Tone of voice is an indication of emotion (Zuckerman, Lipets, Koivumaki, & Rosenthal, 1975) and may be more revealing than facial expressions which are more controllable and closer to one's awareness than vocal cues (Zuckerman, Larrance, Spiegel, & Klorman, 1981; Zuckerman, Amidon, Bishop, & Pomeranz, 1982). In an experiment in which undergraduate listeners attempted to identify the emotions from content-filtered recordings, sadness was more accurately identified than anger, happiness, or surprise (Apple & Hecht, 1982).

In reviewing research on prosodic features involved in communicating emotion, Frick (1985) suggests that low speech tones are used to convey dominance or aggression, while high tones signal a lack of aggression and friendliness; a high-pitched voice occurs during sadness or fright; and a change in prosodic features occurs in anxiety or during deception. However, he suggests that specific emotions might be communicated better by particular *patterns* of pitch and loudness over time ("prosodic contours"). Due to technical difficulties insufficient research has been carried out to provide firm evidence so far.

K. R. Scherer's (1986) review of vocal affect expression analyzed the acoustic-phonetic correlates of the physiological responses associated with different emotional states and identified three major *voice types* (wide-narrow, lax-tense, and full-thin). From this analysis, specific emotional states were predicted to have particular voice-type patterns, for example, wide, relaxed, and slightly full for happiness, narrow, lax, and thin for sadness. Comparing these predictions with the empirical findings on vocal cues in emotional expression (confined mainly to the lax-tense voice type), Scherer found a high degree of convergence.

For a review of paralanguage, see Siegman (1978). Additional research on vocal aspects of speech is provided by: Apple, Streeter, & Krauss, 1979; J. A. Hall, 1980; R. J. Hart & Brown, 1974; K. R. Scherer, 1978.

Linguistic Factors

In an introduction to a special issue of the *Social Psychology Quarterly* on language and social interaction, Maynard (1987) observes that during the previous two decades sociologists and social psychologists have directed increasing attention to language and its use in social contexts. This work has come from a variety of subdisciplines including cognitive sociology, conversational analysis, discourse analysis, the ethnography of speaking, and interpretive sociolinguistics. The present chapter includes only a small fraction of this literature that is covered in *Psychological Abstracts* and *Sociological Abstracts*. A review of research on the use of cognitive-linguistic concepts in understanding everyday social interactions is given by Cicourel (1981).

Drake and Moberg (1986) demonstrate the part played by linguistic form in effecting compliance patterns in dyads. They showed how language may be used to sedate a target person from thinking about the equity implicit in an influence attempt by using semantic indirectness and cognitive script triggering. They argue that effective communication will enhance compliance over and above that predicted by exchange considerations focused solely on content. Influencers who use language that violates power or social-distance expectations may sabotage their attempts even if otherwise adequate inducements are present. In contrast, certain linguistic forms palliate the targets into compliance when inducements are insufficient, and other forms sedate them into automatic compliance responses.

On the positive-negative continuum of behavior, "verbal staring," evidenced in a constant "you" orientation, or a focus on the other person in talk, is apparently taken to be negative since it results in defensive responses (R. J. Cline & Johnson, 1976). In contrast, positive feelings and intimacy can also be conveyed in conversational style. Hornstein (1985) analyzed naturally occurring telephone conversations between pairs of female friends, acquaintances, and strangers to investigate how intimacy was indicated. She found that, in comparison with strangers, friends used more implicit openings, raised more topics, were more responsive to each other, and used more complex forms of closing.

In task-oriented behavior, persons are observed to "fine-tune" their communication patterns to different categories of listeners. For example, when an undergraduate woman was asked to teach a block design to a six-year-old child, her speech was clearer, simpler, more attention maintaining, and included longer pauses (DePaulo & Coleman, 1986). Different patterns were also observed when the listener was a retarded adult, a foreigner who was using a second language, and a peer who spoke the same language. Different patterns are observed when subjects are instructed to solve a problem using only brief communications (W. R. Ford, Weeks, & Chapanis, 1980) or not allowed to ask questions (G. G. Kent, Davis, & Shapiro, 1978, 1981). In general, the more people talk, the better they are understood (Mortensen & Arntson, 1974). Although the use of too many rhetorical interrogatives, such as "you know," "you see, " or "okay," suggests that the speaker is either anxious or believes there is a potential for interruption (W. G. Powers, 1977). People, especially university professors talking to students, will seem presumptuous if they use many forms of advisement, interpretation, confirmation, or reflection (Stiles, 1978; Stiles, Waszak, & Barton, 1979).

Tjosvold, Johnson, and Lerner (1981) investigated the way in which effective problem-solvers discuss opposing opinions and incorporate them into their ideas. In their experiment, college men and women discussed a dilemma with confederates who took an opposing view. In the affirmation condition, the confederates positively evaluated the subjects' competence. In the acceptance condition, confederates minimized evaluative comments but indicated that the subject was arguing in a reasonable manner. In the disconfirmation condition, subjects were informed that they were ineffective. Compared to the affirmation and acceptance conditions, disconfirmation resulted in uncertainty about the correctness of one's views, closed-mindedness toward opposing information, lack of interest in learning the other's position, misunderstanding of the other's reasoning, unwillingness to incorporate the other's arguments, and dislike for the other.

Additional research on linguistic factors includes: Bertacchini, Canestrari, & Umilta, 1975; Brenner & Hjelmquist, 1974b, 1974c; Ettin, 1986; Franco & Kulberg, 1975; Garvey, 1975; A. Haas & Sherman, 1982; Hogg, 1985; Holtgraves, 1986; Kuiken, 1981; Rossel, 1981; Swann, Giuliano, & Wegner, 1982; G. Wolf, 1974.

INTERACTION PATTERNS

As in the 2nd edition of the *Handbook of Small Group Research* (Hare, 1976), the type of interaction pattern revealed by research depends upon the theory and the category system of the observer. The most common division of interest is between interaction patterns that result from problem-solving behavior and those that result from the social and emotional relations of the group members. Both of these patterns are affected by variables such as the age, sex, and personalities of the group members. Some nonverbal features of these patterns have been reviewed in the first part of this chapter and research on changes in patterns over time that reflect phases in group development will be reviewed in the last part.

Forgas (1979, 1983a) takes a broad view of social interaction in the study of "social episodes" which he identifies as "shared, consensual cognitive representations about recurring interaction routines within a subculture." Examples of social episodes include having morning coffee with colleagues, eating at a restaurant with friends, or visiting a doctor. He suggests that research should provide descriptions of episode domains and subcultural, group, and individual differences in episode perceptions, as well as indications of the cognitive and affective representations of different episode representations.

Janet Bavelas (1975, 1978) argues that dyadic interaction should be studied as a formal system, with the behaviors of each individual studied separately in such a way that the whole can be constructed from the parts. She suggests that a mechanism for the interaction between individuals is their interpersonal judgements. This is illustrated in an experiment with university undergraduates acting as teachers, who were given performance scores and asked to set goals for students. Their responses were a linear function of the performance score, independent of their assigned aim or the students' task.

Discussion of theory and reviews of the literature on social interaction are given by: Abraham, 1974–1975; Boros, 1985; S. Duncan & Fiske, 1985; Forbes, 1982; Halas, 1981; Raush, 1976; Tubbs, 1984. Other general texts include: Lofland (1978);

Examples of studies that focus on task behavior include Babayeva, Vojskunskiy, Kirichenko, & Matsneva (1984) who found that the team work of dyads depended on the individual characteristics of the partners, and Hirokawa (1987) who compared the decision process in groups making "high-quality" decisions with those making "low-quality" decisions. High-quality decisions were characterized by vigilance, second-guessing, accurate information processing, and an absence of improbable fantasy chains.

Additional studies of task behavior focus on specific categories of behavior or roles. For example, M. E. Shaw and Small (1981) on skills; Callan, Chance, and Pitcairn (1973) on attention; Brent and Sykes (1979) on information transmission (1979); and K. H. Russ and Gold (1975) on the roles of task expert and bungler.

An example of a study with a focus on social-emotional behavior is that of Bolle de Bal (1981) who discusses feelings of isolation and detachment in groups. He proposes the word "reliance" as a neologism to express the desire of individuals for bonds and connections with others.

Additional studies of social-emotional behavior that focus on specific categories or events include: Apsler (1975) on embarrassment; Bakken (1977) on saying goodbye; Leary, Kowalski, and Bergen (1988), on interpersonal information acquisition; Ogilvie and Haslett (1985) and Rotheram, la Cour, and Jacobs (1982) on feedback; and Sykes (1983) on choice of partners.

Analyses and Dimensions of Social Interaction

Compared with the number of social-psychologists who use post-meeting question-naires or checklists for the analysis of social interaction, relatively few are prepared to spend time and energy on act-by-act coding of the process. Bales's 12 category system for interaction process analysis, introduced in 1950 became the most often used method through the early 1970s. More recently Bales and others have shifted to the analysis of behavior in terms of a limited number of dimensions (see the discussion of Bales & Cohen, 1979, in the Introduction of the present book). However, new category systems are still being proposed, some general and some with a specific focus on a type of group or a type of behavior.

Trujillo (1986, p. 389) offers a taxonomy of coding-scheme constituents to suggest similarities and differences in the way coding schemes are constructed and applied. The taxonomy includes six aspects:

1. Philosophical perspective: Experienced, experiencing, and experiencer views.
2. Theoretical and operational foci: Conceptual and operational foci.
3. Observer inference: Degree of inference required and frame of reference.
4. Methodological design: Exhaustiveness and mutual exclusivity of categories and level of categorization.
5. Unit of analysis: Recording, context, and enumeration units.
6. Recording device: Fixed form, still photography, audio recording, audiovisual recording, and chronograph.

Examples of category systems are given in the Appendix of the present handbook.

Additional examples of research include:

1. General: Brenner and Hjelmquist (1974a) for function and form of speech process; B. A. Fisher, Drecksel, and Werbel (1979) for information processing analysis; Hare, Kritzer, and Blumberg (1979) for functional analysis; W. F. Hill (1977) for style, content, and work; Parke and Houben (1985) and L. Kelly and Duran (1986) for the classification of group types; Poyatos (1985) for holistic analysis; Schlesinger (1974) for enumerating utterances; Strong, Hills, Kilmartin, DeVries, Lanier, Nelson, Strickland, and Meyer (1988) for 8 categories that form an "interpersonal circle"; Wish, D'Andrade, and Goodnow (1980) for speech acts; Wish and Kaplan (1977) for cooperation, intensity, dominance, formality, and task orientation; and Zlate (1985) for 12 opposing behavioral tendencies. See also: Goss, 1988; Molm, 1984.

2. Specific type of group: see Markell and Asher (1984) for patterns of influence among children; Gottman (1979) for patterns of marital interaction.

3. Specific type of behavior: Bonoma and Rosenberg (1978) for social influence ratings; Cody (1982) for disengagement strategies; B. A. Fisher and Drecksel (1983)

for relational control modes; Friedlander, Thibodeau, Nichols, Tucker, and Snyder (1985) for cohesive talk; Haskell (1978, 1982) for analogic group talk; Hawes and Foley (1978) for group decisions; Herman (1983) for group skills; Ickes, Robertson, Tooke, and Teng (1986) for naturalistic social cognition; Kavanaugh and Bollet (1983) for verbal intimacy; Marcy and Fromme (1979) for "here-and-now" versus "there-and-then" and positive versus negative affective tone; and Royce (1982) for skill ratings.

With the advent of computers with memories in the mid-1950s more social-psychologists were able to measure the correlations among all their observational variables and to carry out factor analyses to determine the minimum number of factors or dimensions necessary to describe interpersonal behavior (Hare, 1976, pp. 69–80). Recent research continues this search, with most of the variance still accounted for by two dimensions: dominance versus submission and positive versus negative behavior or similar variations (Benjamin, 1974, 1979; A. P. Bochner & Kaminski, 1974; A. P. Bochner, Kaminski, & Fitzpatrick, 1977; D. J. Kiesler, 1983; Nascimento-Schulze, 1981). As noted above, Bales and others add a third dimension of task-oriented and conforming versus expressive and nonconforming (Bales & Cohen, 1979; Lustig, 1987; M. J. Solomon, 1981).

On the methodological side, a number of articles discuss problems of reliability and validity of category schemes, raise questions concerning analysis, or compare schemes: Billings, McDowell, Gomberg, Kessler, & Weiner, 1978; Cairns, 1979; S. Duncan, Kanki, Mokros, & Fiske, 1984; Foon, 1987; Hare, 1978; Hewes, 1985; Ingraham & Wright, 1986; Orford, 1986; and Poole & Folger, 1981.

Suggestions for data analysis using the Markov chain and other models are given by: Budescu, 1984, 1985; Manderscheid, Rae, McCarrick, & Silbergeld, 1982; Mendoza & Graziano, 1982; and Warner, Kenny, & Stoto, 1979. Malone (1975) presents a model of two person interaction in the form of a computer simulation. See also the Appendix for observation techniques.

Affiliation and Participation Rates

Perhaps the earliest generalization reached by persons observing behavior in small groups is that some people talk more than others. A second conclusion was that some people are more friendly than others. Since these two dimensions of interpersonal behavior are so basic and account for so much of the variance in interaction, they continue to be of interest. Persons who have high participation rates generally make long speeches (Chell, 1979; Koomen & Sagel, 1977). A preferred rate of participation is assumed to be a personality trait (Elworth & Gray, 1982), with high participators seen as extroverted—unless they talk too much (Daley, McCroskey, & Richmond, 1977). However, persons who perceive themselves as extroverts may continue to believe this even though in a given situation they talk no more than persons who perceive themselves to be introverts (Kulik & Mahler, 1986). In general, all of the personality traits and background factors associated with dominance result in high participation (S. J. Gill, Menlo, & Keel, 1984; M. Kohn & Parnes, 1974; Ryzhov, 1981), especially factors that lead to high status in a group (Jablin & Sussman, 1978; Skvoretz, 1988). If individuals are ignored they will decrease their participation (Geller, Goodstein, Silver, & Sternberg, 1974). General silences by all group members, especially in therapy groups, are related to phases in the group process (B. F. Lewis, 1977).

Early in the life of a group a hierarchy tends to form based on participation rates, with a few persons doing most of the talking (Karp & Yoels, 1976) although there may be two or more hierarchies (Nowakowska, 1978) with one for males and another for females (Smith-Lovin, Skvoretz, & Hudson, 1986). A tendency for high participation is enhanced if one sits in a highly visible seat (P. M. Baker, 1984) where one can have more eye contact (Caproni, Levine, O'Neal, McDonald, & Garwood, 1977). With regard to the direction of the communication, women tend to address more comments to individuals, whereas men tend to address the group as a whole (Aries, 1976).

Additional research on participation is provided by: Dabbs & Ruback, 1987; Kirkwood, 1984; M. E. Shaw, Ackerman, McCown, Worsham, Haugh, Gebhardt, & Small, 1979; and Wicker, Kirmeyer, Hanson, & Alexander, 1976.

The early sociometric finding that some people are more friendly and have more friends than others continues to find support in a study of preschool children (La Freniere & Charlesworth, 1983). However, rather than consider affiliation in general, much of the recent research focuses on a particular aspect of intimate behavior (Reis, Senchak, & Solomon, 1985), such as "self-disclosure" (see summary of research below). In studies related to affiliation, as with so many aspects of social behavior, the sex of the subject is a major variable with regard to the topic of discussion (Aries & Johnson, 1983), physical attractiveness of the partner (Reis, Nezlek, & Wheeler, 1980), and decreasing need for affiliation over time among first year college students (Wheeler & Nezlek, 1977).

Communication Patterns in Groups

The earlier interest in communication networks in groups—that was sparked by Leavitt's experiment in 1951 and that was one of the major topics in the 1976 *Handbook of Small Group Research* (cf. Sievers & Langthaler, 1974)—is not evident in research during the late 1970s and early 1980s. However there are a few studies that consider patterns of communication by role, age, gender, or race and some report differences in process for effective and ineffective groups.

Leaders tend to talk more often (Reynolds, 1984) and more to the group as a whole (Goetsch & McFarland, 1980), and have messages directed upward toward them in the hierarchy of power (Bradley, 1978a). At the other end of the continuum, persons who are unsure of the content or context of the interaction will say as little as possible of substance and try to push the conversation toward safer and more certain grounds (Rumelhart, 1983).

Additional research deals with patterns related: to age (Eckerman, Whatley, & Kutz, 1975; Savin-Williams, 1982; H. W. Smith, 1977), gender (Dabbs & Ruback, 1984), race (Schofield & Sagar, 1977), effective groups (DeStephen, 1983b; Hirokawa, 1980), and other variables (Boyd & Wilson, 1974; Brownell & Smith, 1973; Caravia & Lunca, 1977; Thune, Manderschcid, & Silbergeld, 1980; Toseland, Krebs, & Vahsen, 1978; K. B. Valentine & Fisher, 1974).

Prior Beliefs

The influence of prior beliefs (expectancies) about a target individual is examined in research with regard to three phenomena: the target's behavior, the processing of the target's behavior by the perceiver, and the target's self-perception (D. T. Miller & Turnbull, 1986; see also Darley & Fazio, 1980). The most common finding is in the form of a "self-fulfilling prophecy" when the subject channels social interaction with a target in such a way that the target's behavioral response confirms the original expectancy (Fazio, Effrein, & Falender, 1981; Schul & Benbenishty, 1985; M. Snyder & Swann, 1978a; M. Snyder, Tanke, & Berscheid, 1977; Yarkin, Harvey, & Bloxom, 1981; Yarkin-Levin, 1983). One way to do this is to ask a series of questions of the target that will reveal the expected behavior (Riggs & Cantor, 1984; M. Snyder, 1984; M. Snyder & Campbell, 1980; M. Snyder & Swann, 1978b; M. Snyder & White, 1981) although some doubt has been cast on this proposition (Pennington, 1987; Semin & Strack, 1980; Trope & Bassok, 1982; Trope, Bassok, & Alon, 1984).

Individuals who are the targets of high performance-expectations may fail strategically in order to create lower and safer standards for their performances (Baumgardner & Brownlee, 1987) or in general behave in a way that conforms to their own expectations (Swann, 1987; Swann & Ely, 1984; Swann & Hill, 1982; Swann & Read, 1981a, 1981b).

Additional research on prior beliefs is given by: Ickes, Patterson, Rajecki, & Tanford, 1982; Kardes & Kimble, 1984; Koomen, 1984; Swann & Predmore, 1985.

Conversational Sequencing

Research on conversational sequences has considered both form, such as relationship of action to silence (Cappella & Planalp, 1981; Daibo, 1982) and content, such as the fact that strangers may talk more about some topics when they first meet than later on (C. R. Berger, Gardner, Clatterbuck, & Schulman, 1976). During the terminal phase of a social encounter persons are more likely to make summary statements of content and affective state; continuity, justification, and well-wishing statements; and statements of positive affect (Albert & Kessler, 1976, 1978).

Verbal as well as nonverbal signals, including head nods, direction of gaze, and pauses, are given by a speaker when it is someone else's turn to speak as a method of synchronizing conversation. Listeners also signal that they are listening or that they wish a turn to speak. Douglis (1987) describes Frederick Erickson's research on the shared rhythms and beats which synchronize conversation. Examples of research on turn-taking and synchronizing include: Beattie, 1983; Bull, 1987; Cary, 1978; Dabbs & Ruback, 1987; S. Duncan, 1974; S. Duncan, Brunner, & Fiske, 1979; S. Duncan & Fiske, 1977, 1979; S. Duncan & Niederehe, 1974; Gallois & Markel, 1975; Gatewood & Rosenwein, 1981; Harrigan & Steffen, 1983; Kendon, 1978; McDowall, 1978; Natale, 1975a, 1975b; Parker, 1988; Robbins, Devoe, & Wiener, 1978; Rutter & Stephenson, 1977; Rutter, Stephenson, Ayling, & White, 1978; M. B. Walker, 1982; T. P. Wilson, Wiemann, & Zimmerman, 1984.

Interrupting another speaker is a form of dominance that is more likely to be used by persons who are self-confident and are not afraid of negative evaluation. Women are more likely to be interrupted than men. For examples of this research, see: Ferguson, 1977; Goldband, 1981; C. W. Kennedy & Camden, 1983; Natale, 1976; and Natale, Entin, & Jaffe, 1979.

Related research includes: Heath, 1982; Kraut, Lewis, & Swezey, 1982; and Leplat & Savoyant, 1983–1984.

Intimacy Equilibrium

Early research by Argyle and Dean (1965) suggested that individuals try to maintain an equilibrium with regard to level of intimacy or involvement. For example, if they preferred to be fairly intimate, they would compensate for distance (which implied lack of intimacy) with more direct gaze (cf. P. A. Andersen & Andersen, 1984; Cappella, 1981; Firestone, 1977; M. L. Patterson, 1982; Raffagnino, 1982). However, tests of this hypothesis have led to mixed results. Some studies support the hypothesis (Amerikaner, 1980; Buchanan, Goldman, & Juhnke, 1977; Coutts, Irvine, & Schneider, 1977; Coutts & Schneider, 1976; Dietch & House, 1975; J. G. Ford, Cramer, & Owens, 1977; Fukuhara, 1977; M. Goldberg & Wellens, 1979; P. Greenbaum & Rosenfeld, 1978; C. I. Greenberg & Firestone, 1977; C. F. Johnson & Dabbs, 1976; Lesko, 1977; M. L. Patterson, 1977; R. Schulz & Barefoot, 1974; Sodikoff, Firestone, & Kaplan, 1974). Other studies provide limited support or no support (D. R. Anderson, 1976; Carr & Dabbs, 1974; A. J. Chapman, 1975a; Kleinke, Staneski, & Pipp, 1975; Lockard, McVittie, & Isaac, 1977; M. L. Patterson, 1975; Russo, 1975; F. W. Schneider & Hansvick, 1977).

Small variations in intimacy level may not be sufficient to produce disequilibrium and hence compensatory reactions (Aiello & Thompson, 1980b; J. K. Burgoon & Jones, 1976; M. L. Patterson, 1976, 1977). Conversely, extremely large changes in intimacy level may also not produce compensation because equilibrium cannot be established by sufficient changes in compensatory behaviors (Aiello, 1977a, 1977b; Aiello & Thompson, 1980a). Some studies report that the phenomenon occurs under certain conditions: for men but not women (Aiello, 1977a, 1977b; H. M. Rosenfeld, Breck, Smith, & Kehoe, 1984), for likeable but not unlikeable interviewers (K. J. Kaplan, Firestone, Klein, & Sodikoff, 1983), depending upon the subject's state of arousal (McAndrew, Gold, Lenney, & Ryckman, 1984; M. L. Patterson, 1978; M. L. Patterson, Jordan, Hogan, & Frerker, 1981; M. B. Walker & Bragg, 1981).

In attempting to account for some of the contradictory findings, M. L. Patterson (1976) devised a theory that predicts *reciprocal* as well as *compensatory* changes. Patterson argued that changes in intimacy-level produce changes in nonspecific *arousal* (Middlemist, Knowles, & Matter, 1976) that accentuates existing feelings. This arousal may be felt as a negative state (anxiety, embarrassment, discomfort) or as a positive state (attraction, comfort, warmth) depending on the setting, the other person, the relationship, and individual differences. If one person increases the intimacy of the encounter, and this produces negative feelings in the other person, the other person will compensate and try to reduce the arousal by lowering the intimacy level. But, if a positive feeling is produced, the other person will attempt to maintain or increase the intimacy level by a *reciprocal* reaction. Support for Patterson's model has come from Foot, Chapman, and Smith (1977), M. L. Patterson (1977, 1978), R. J. Smith and Knowles (1978, 1979), and Whitcher and Fisher (1979). In a related manner, Schiffenbauer and Schiavo (1976) and Storms and Thomas (1977) provide evidence that close physical distances intensify existing feelings. Recently, M. L. Patterson (1982) has altered his model to take account of the fact that the functional bases of interaction are variable. In addition to intimacy functions, included in his revised nonverbal exchange model are social-control and service-task functions.

Additional research is reported by: Coutts, Schneider, & Montgomery, 1980; Dean, Willis, & Hewitt, 1975; McAdams, Jackson, & Kirshnit, 1984.

Self-disclosure

What counts as self-disclosure? D. V. Fisher (1984) suggests that self-disclosure can be conceptually defined as "verbal behavior through which individuals truthfully, sincerely, and intentionally communicate novel, ordinarily private information about themselves to one or more addressees." Early recollections of life style are counted (D. Barrett, 1983) and accounts of sexual experience are taken as an especially good indicator of intimate self-disclosure (J. G. Allen, 1974; Petronio, Martin, & Littlefield, 1984). However, observers' perceptions of self-disclosing behavior are usually based on more than content alone. Variables such as the sex of the speaker and the amount, intimacy, rate, and affective manner of self-relevant information explain significant amounts of variance in the overall perception of disclosing behavior (Chelune, Skiffington, & Williams, 1981). For example, the same content category may be judged to be more intimate in opposite-sex conversation than in same-sex conversation (J. D. Cunningham, 1981).

Reviews of the literature on self-disclosure are presented by: Codol, 1977–1978; Enomoto, 1983; S. J. Gilbert, 1976; Krzemionka-Brozda, 1984; Pearce & Sharp, 1973. C. T. Hill and Stull (1982) comment on the extent to which the understanding of the process of disclosure exchange has been hindered by confusion about conceptualization and measurement. H. A. McAllister & Bregman (1985) and Z. Rubin (1976) also discuss methodological problems.

In terms of the three behavioral dimensions of Bales (Bales & Cohen, 1979) the intimate behavior that is the hallmark of self-disclosure would be rated as positive and backward. Positive because it is associated with behavior that is likeable and affectionate and is usually directed toward special friends. Backward because it does not place an emphasis on the task but is evident during periods of social conversation when individuals are emotionally expressive. Self-disclosure is similar to helping behavior, which is also positive and backward but involves more upward behavior since more initiative is required. Thus one should not be surprised if many of the same conditions that increase self-disclosure are the same as those for helping behavior and are the opposite of the conditions that increase behaviors, such as aggressive behavior (Upward and Negative), that are at the other end of one or more of these same dimensions.

How can self-disclosure be increased? A person being interviewed by a high status person who serves as a model will increase the amount of self-disclosure if the model either speaks first or reinforces the person for the desired behavior (Arlett, Best, & Little, 1976; DeWine, Bennett, & Medcalf, 1978; C. F. Johnson & Dabbs, 1976; D. McGuire, Thelen, & Amolsch, 1975; R. N. Morgan & Evans, 1977; Z. Rubin, 1975). The model does not have to be physically present but can be represented by a video or audio recording (Annis & Perry, 1977, 1978). More self-disclosure takes place when the individuals trade information as an equitable exchange (J. H. Berg & Archer, 1982; Gordon, 1985; S. J. Lynn, 1978; D. A. Taylor & Belgrave, 1986), and when norms exist or are developed that encourage intimate disclosures (J. D. Davis, 1977; Derlega & Chaikin, 1976; Derlega & Stepien, 1977; S. J. Lynn, 1978).

Less self-disclosure can be expected if the subject has a low self concept (A. Shapiro & Swensen, 1977). To make subjects self-aware by placing a mirror in the cubicle where they are undergoing the experiment may suppress self-disclosure (R. L. Archer, Hormuth, & Berg, 1982). Being videotaped may have a similar effect (J. M. McGuire, Graves, & Blau, 1985).

With regard to the gender of the subject, research continues to support the conclusion that females are more likely than males to engage in self-disclosure, especially to other females (Annis & Perry, 1977; Arlett, Best, & Little, 1976; S. E. Berger, Millham, Jacobson, & Anchor, 1978; R. J. Cline & Musolf, 1985; Cohn &

Strassberg, 1983; S. J. Gilbert & Whiteneck, 1976; Gitter & Black, 1976; Goodstein & Russell, 1977; J. P. Grigsby & Weatherley, 1983; Pellegrini, Hicks, Meyers-Winton, & Antal, 1978; Z. Rubin, Hill, Peplau, & Dunkel-Schetter, 1980; Stevens, Rice, & Johnson, 1986; D. A. Taylor & Hinds, 1985). However this is not always the case (Kohen, 1975a, 1975b; Stokes, Childs, & Fuehrer, 1981). Several studies report that males disclose more than females (J. M. McGuire, Graves, & Blau, 1985; O'Kelley, & Schuldt, 1981; D. R. Shaffer & Ogden, 1986). Other research suggests that the size of the group may affect the findings, with groups of two encouraging more intimacy than larger groups (R. B. Taylor, DeSoto, & Lieb, 1979). Males were found to be more likely to make disclosures in dyads than in groups of three or more (Pearson, 1981).

Does it make a difference who the other person is? In addition to differences between same and opposite sex pairs of persons of similar status noted above, it also makes a difference if the subject is speaking to a parent of the same or opposite sex (Balswick & Balkwell, 1977; Komarvosky, 1974; D. M. Pedersen, 1973)—and there is also higher disclosure to mother than to father—and more to peers than to parents. In some research, persons are found to disclose more to strangers than to friends (Derlega, Wilson, & Chaikin, 1976) or with a person one does not know in an attempt to become known (S. E. Berger & Anchor, 1978). However, in most cases disclosure is more frequent to friends than to strangers (Gaebelein, 1976; Lombardo, Franco, Wolf, & Fantasia, 1976; Z. Rubin & Shenker, 1978; L. S. Walker & Wright, 1976; Wheeless, 1976, 1978; Winum & Banikiotes, 1983). More responses are given to persons judged to be "high openers" who elicit more disclosure because of their greater receptiveness and attentiveness and use of more follow-up questions (L. C. Miller, Berg, & Archer, 1983) and more is given to persons who are physically attractive (Cash & Soloway, 1975).

Other variables have included the timing of the other's disclosure, either before or after the subject (R. L. Archer & Burleson, 1980; B. Mann & Murphy, 1975; Wortman, Adesman, Herman, & Greenberg, 1976). Changes in rates and types of disclosures over time are reported from studies of couples in a long term relationship. Generally intimacy is low at first, becomes higher, and falls off later in the relationship (D. R. Falk & Wagner, 1985; S. J. Gilbert, 1976; Tolstedt & Stokes, 1984; Won-Doornink, 1979).

Additional research on self-disclosure includes: J. H. Berg & Archer, 1980, 1983; Brewer & Mittelman, 1980; Derlega & Chaikin, 1977, 1979; Ebersole, McFall, & Brandt, 1977; S. J. Gilbert, 1977; Hick, Mitchell, Bell, & Carter, 1975; Horenstein & Gilbert, 1976; D. L. Johnson & Ridener, 1974; E. E. Jones & Archer, 1976; J. I. Lange & Grove, 1981; D. Ludwig, Franco, & Malloy, 1986; Miell, Duck, & la Gaipa, 1979; L. C. Miller & Kenny, 1986; Neimeyer & Banikiotes, 1981; Nelson-Jones & Dryden, 1979; Pellegrini, Hicks, & Meyers-Winton, 1978; Petty & Mirels, 1981; G. R. Rose & Bednar, 1980; M. Roth & Kuiken, 1975; Z. Rubin, 1976; Skotko & Langmeyer, 1977; W. G. Stephan, Lucker, & Aronson, 1976; Stokes, Fuehrer, & Childs, 1983; Strassberg, Gabel, & Anchor, 1976; S. A. Sussman, 1977; D. A.

Taylor & Altman, 1975; D. A. Taylor, Gould, & Brounstein, 1981; Tolor, Cramer, D'Amico, & O'Marra, 1975; Town & Harvey, 1981; M. N. Wilson & Rappaport, 1974.

Impression Management

Individuals generally use tactical self-presentations as a means of establishing particular relationships with others that are congruent with their preferred modes of dealing with the social world (Leary, 1979; Schlenker, Soraci, & Schlenker, 1974). For example, being liked is the goal of the ingratiator, whereas the self-promoter is concerned to appear competent (E. E. Jones & Pittman, 1982). Thus, Godfrey, Jones, and Lord (1986) found that subjects who were asked to ingratiate themselves with a partner used *reactive* verbal and nonverbal behaviors, whereas those who were asked to act as self-promoters used *proactive* behaviors.

Self-presentations can be determined by, among other things, the particular roles people play. In a group situation, leaders were led to believe that either a task-oriented or a relationship-oriented approach would be most effective in facilitating group performance. Leaders subsequently presented images of themselves to the group that were consistent with the type of leader believed to be most effective (Leary, Robertson, Barnes, & Miller, 1986; see also, Forsyth, Schlenker, Leary, & McCown, 1985; Leary & Schlenker, 1980). People's self-presentations may also be affected by sex-role concerns. In a study conducted by von Baeyer, Sherk, and Zanna (1981), female job applicants were interviewed by a male confederate whose stereotype of the ideal female applicant conformed closely either to the traditional female stereotype or its opposite. Applicants presented themselves in a traditionally "feminine" manner in their verbal and nonverbal behavior and physical appearance when they knew the interviewer held traditional views of women.

If people are induced to behave in a self-enhancing manner (such as in an interview), this can have carry-over effects in terms of boosting their self-esteem; that is, public displays of self-enhancing behavior can result in changes in private self-evaluations (E. E. Jones, Rhodewalt, Berglas, & Skelton, 1981).

For reviews of research on impression management and self-presentation, see: Baumeister, 1982; Schlenker, 1980, 1985; Tedeschi, 1981.

For additional research on impression management and self-presentation, see: Apsler, 1975; Baumeister, Cooper & Skib, 1979; Baumeister & Jones, 1978; Braver, Linder, Corwin & Cialdini, 1977; Gaes, Kalle & Tedeschi, 1978; Gurevitch, 1984; Hass & Mann, 1976; Rawlins, 1983b; Reis & Gruzen, 1976; Satow, 1975; Schlenker, 1975b, 1975c; Schlenker, Forsyth, Leary & Miller, 1980; Schlenker, Miller, & Leary, 1983; S. H. Schwartz & Gottlieb, 1976, 1980a; Sigman, 1984; Steele, 1975; Tanur, 1975.

Exchange and Reward Patterns

Throughout the 1960s and early 1970s, there was considerable interest in social psychology in exchange theory, modeled on economics. The analysis was based on the assumption that persons would enter into or maintain a social relationship if they could realize some "profit," that is if the rewards exceeded the costs. Various social commodities were used in the exchanges, such as love, status, information, or money. Researchers associated with the major contributions to this theory included Thibaut and Kelley, Homans, and Blau. Some of this interest continues during the years covered by this volume with general comments on the theory made by: Brinberg & Castell, 1982; D. F. Haas & Deseran, 1981; Lebra, 1975.

A satisfactory exchange may be no more than responsiveness to a question (D. Davis & Holtgraves, 1984; D. Davis & Perkowitz, 1979). In general, positive behavior is exchanged for positive behavior (Levenstein, Jacobs, & Cohen, 1977). An example involving both children and adults is the study by N. L. Cantor and Gelfand (1977). Their subjects were 48 female university students and 6 male and 6 female children ages 7–10 years. To assess whether children could control adult's social behavior, the children's responsiveness to their adult partners was varied. In the responsive condition, the child confederates initiated conversation, asked for evaluations of their performance on art tasks, and smiled when praised. In the unresponsive condition, the same children avoided looking at or interacting with the adult. Adults attended more to the responsive children and gave more help to responsive than unresponsive girls. The adults also rated the children as more attractive, likeable, and competent when the children behaved responsively. In another example, married couples at home and in the laboratory were found to be more positive in their interaction (emit more "pleases") when they were not distressed (Birchler, Weiss, & Vincent, 1975).

For reviews of research on social exchange, see: R. L. Burgess & Huston, 1979; Gergen, Greenberg, & Willis, 1980; H. H. Kelley & Thibaut, 1979; C. G. McClintock, Kramer, & Keil, 1984; and Roloff, 1981.

Additional research on exchange and rewards is given by: M. S. Clark, 1986; D. Davis & Brock, 1979; D. Davis, Rainey, & Brock, 1976; Dowd, 1981; Molm, 1981a; Schaible & Jacobs, 1975. See also the last section of Chapter 10.

Deceptive Communication

Studies of deceptive communication have focused on patterns of communication and nonverbal cues associated with deception. Experimenters ask observers to judge subjects who are telling the truth or lying about some other person, for example by pretending they like a person who is actually disliked. Cues that a person is engaged in deception include: messages that are ambivalent, discrepant, indifferent, and tense (DePaulo, Rosenthal, Green, & Rosenkrantz, 1982); descriptions that are spoken slowly and contain many "um's" and "er's" (DePaulo, Rosenthal, Rosenkrantz, & Green, 1982); suppressing leg and foot movements (Cody & O'Hair, 1983); and using fewer illustrative gestures while increasing voice pitch (Ekman, Friesen, & Scherer, 1976).

Facial cues may not be particularly useful in detecting deception (Littlepage &

Pineault, 1978, 1981; Manstead, Wagner, & MacDonald, 1984). For additional research involving facial cues, see: Riggio & Friedman, 1983; Zuckerman, Driver, & Koestner, 1982; Zuckerman, Koestner, & Colella, 1985; and Zuckerman, Spiegel, DePaulo, & Rosenthal, 1982.

Persons with higher social skills are better at deception (Riggio, Tucker, & Throckmorton, 1987). However, the lie is easier to detect by the subject if the subject is similar to the liar, for example with regard to physical attractiveness (DePaulo, Tang, & Stone, 1987). If a person *plans* to lie, it may be more (O'Hair, Cody, & McLaughlin, 1981) or less (Littlepage & Pineault, 1985) difficult to detect. See the Chapter 2 section of this book on Machiavellianism for further information about deception.

For a review of deceptive communication, see: Zuckerman, DePaulo, & Rosenthal, 1981.

Individual Differences

The individual differences that are most often observed are related to gender. Males (and masculine typed persons of both sexes) take more initiative and are more concerned with the task than females (or feminine typed persons) who are more concerned and responsive to interpersonal relationships (Alfgren, Aries, & Olver, 1979; S. M. Andersen & Bem, 1981; L. R. Anderson & Blanchard, 1982; W. W. Crouch, 1976; Fromme & Beam, 1974; Hacker, 1981; J. A. Hall & Braunwald, 1981; J. A. Kelly, Wildman, & Urey, 1982; Kimble, Yoshikawa, & Zehr, 1981; Lamke & Bell, 1982; Mabry, 1985; J. N. Martin & Craig, 1983; McLaughlin, Cody, Kane, & Robey, 1981; Orcutt & Harvey, 1985; M. L. Patterson & Schaeffer, 1977; W. Wood & Karten, 1986).

Another type of individual difference that has received some attention is "social competence" (and its opposite, social anxiety). Individuals with high social competence are found to take the initiative and be more responsive to the other person, especially to nonverbal cues (Cappella, 1985; D. Christensen, Farina, & Boudreau, 1980; J. C. Conger & Farrell, 1981; Dodge, Heimberg, Nyman, & O'Brien, 1987; Faraone & Hurtig, 1985; Forgas, 1983b; Glasgow & Arkowitz, 1975; Purvis, Dabbs, & Hopper, 1984; Riggio & Friedman, 1986; Steffen & Reckman, 1978; Steffen & Redden, 1977). High social competence would appear to involve high "self-monitoring" since persons who are high on self-monitoring are also found to be more facile speakers and more sensitive to positive and negative cues (Dabbs, Evans, Hopper, & Purvis, 1980; W. Douglas, 1984; Fenigstein, 1979).

A number of personality measures distinguish primarily between persons who are high interactors and those who are low and often somewhat negative. High interaction rates are associated with high scores on dominance (Roger & Schumacher, 1983), intelligence (Matarazzo, Wiens, & Manaugh, 1975), and sensation seeking (S. Williams & Ryckman, 1984). Low interaction rates are associated with anxiety or alienation (J. K. Burgoon & Burgoon, 1974; Daibo, Sugiyama, & Akama, 1973), and depression (Gotlib & Robinson, 1982; Howes & Hokanson, 1979)

High social status, either inside or outside of the group, is associated with taking more initiative and claiming more personal space. Related research includes: teachers and students (Leffler, Gillespie, & Conaty, 1982); social class of mother-child pairs (S. Greenberg & Formanek, 1974), and blacks and whites (Fugita, Wexley, & Hillery, 1974; Shuter, 1982; A. Smith, 1983).

Additional research on individual differences includes: A. S. Cohen & Melson, 1980; Leary, Rogers, Canfield, & Coe, 1986; L. D. Miller, 1977; B. M. Montgomery, 1984; Sabatelli, Buck, & Dreyer, 1983; Sternberg & Smith, 1985; and T. L. Wright & Ingraham, 1985. See also Chapter 2 of the present volume for research on individual differences in interpersonal and group behavior.

GROUP DEVELOPMENT

A detailed summary of early theories of group development is given in the *Handbook of Small Group Research* (Hare, 1976, pp. 88 112; see also Hare, 1982, pp. 68-89). A four phase sequence can be identified: First, the purpose of the group is defined and the commitment of the members secured; second, resources or skills must be acquired or provided; third, appropriate roles must be developed or learned and a sufficiently high level of morale achieved; and fourth, the group works at the task with the coordination of leadership. Eventually these four phases are followed by a fifth, terminal phase, during which the group redefines the relationships between members as the group is disbanded.

In a more fine-grain analysis, phases can be identified, in the same order, within each of the first four phases and in reverse order in the fifth phase. Some persons may drop out of the group at the end of the first phase, if they find that they are not committed to the idea of the group, or at the end of the second phase if they judge that the resources are inadequate. However the "revolution within the revolution" is most likely to occur near the end of the third phase if they are dissatisfied with the leadership or the role distribution. By this time they have become committed to the purpose of the group and the resources seem to be adequate. If change does not occur at this point, there is nothing left to do but carry on the work.

More recent research that reflects the earlier theories includes: Babad & Amir, 1978; M. A. Bell, 1982; Caple, 1978; Davies & Kuypers, 1985; Farrell, 1976; Farrell, Heinemann, & Schmitt, 1986; Hare & Naveh, 1984; Lacoursiere, 1980; B. F. Lewis, 1978; D. C. Lundgren & Knight, 1978; Mabry, 1975; Near, 1978; Palisi & Ruzicka, 1974–1975; Pedigo & Singer, 1982; Reggio, 1980–1981; Saravay, 1978; Shalinsky, 1983; Tuckman & Jensen, 1977; Ziffo, 1977. Nichol (1977) notes the developmental stages in a dyadic relationship between a child and a significant other person, and S.

Long (1984) draws parallels between the early stages of group integration and the early psychological integration of an infant.

A number of studies do not report well defined phases in group development, but rather continued growth related to some type of interpersonal behavior as the group becomes more cohesive and better able to handle the task (Adelson, 1975; Boyd, 1984; Conville, 1983; Doreian, 1986; Evensen & Bednar, 1978; Fuentes Avila, 1983; Giesen & McClaren, 1976; C. S. Green, 1975; Gustafson & Cooper, 1979; Killworth & Bernard, 1976; Kuypers, Davies, & Hazewinkel, 1986; Louche & Magnier, 1978; Neimeyer & Merluzzi, 1982; Perez Yera, 1984; Peteroy, 1980; Petrovskii, 1986; Shambaugh, 1978; Vaisman, 1977; Vraa, 1974; Ziller, 1977).

Other authors suggest that there may be no phases in group development that apply to all types of groups and that it would be better to concentrate on identifying significant differences between various types of groups and relating these to important group outcomes (Cissna, 1984; Hirokawa, 1983; Sorensen & McCroskey, 1977).

Moreland and Levine (1982) outline a model of individual socialization in a group, which is, in effect, a description of group development from the point of view of the individual member, especially if the person joins a group that is already formed. Their model has five phases, each associated with a role type:

1. Prospective member: where the primary activity is investigation, including recruitment and reconnaissance.
2. New member: where the activity involves socialization, including accommodation and assimilation.
3. Full member: involving role maintenance, including role negotiation.
4. Marginal member: where the activity focuses on the resocialization of an individual who no longer appears to be committed to the group, including accommodation and assimilation.
5. Ex-member: a final role after the individual has left the group, including remembrance on the part of the remaining members about the individual's contribution as part of the group tradition, and reminiscence on the part of the individual.

Additional studies concerned with group development include: Elstrup Rasmussen, 1978; Gouran & Geonetta, 1977; London & Walsh, 1975; G. R. Rose & Bednar; N. M. Webb, 1984b; T. L. Wright & Ingraham, 1985.

SUMMARY

The main channels of nonverbal communication are gaze and eye contact, facial expression, posture, gestures and touch, bodily contact, spatial behavior, paralinguistic and linguistic factors. Each of these channels can be used intentionally to amplify or unintentionally to contradict a verbal communication implying dominance, emotion, or interest in the task. In addition verbal behaviors can serve as regulators of interaction by indicating that a person is listening or that it is someone else's turn to start or stop talking.

Some studies of interaction patterns in groups focus on task behavior and others on the relationships between members. While earlier research used separate categories for a number of types of behavior that were assumed to be independent or important for the analysis of group process, more recent research concentrates on a few dimensions that result from the factor analysis of many variables. The two dimensions that are revealed most often are dominance versus submission and friendly versus unfriendly behavior, with some theoretical perspectives adding a third or fourth or additional dimensions. Age, sex, social class, ethnic group, and personality variables are all associated with different patterns of individual interaction, with persons of higher status in a group taking the more dominant role and persons whose background or personality has led them to value positive relations being more friendly. The extent of self-disclosure during conversations is taken as an indication of an especially friendly relationship.

Having prior beliefs about a person may result in a "self-fulfilling prophecy" if an individual channels social interaction with that person in such a way that the person's behavioral response will confirm the original expectancy. An individual who is lying may be given away by unintentional patterns of speech or nonverbal cues.

A typical pattern of development in many types of groups includes five phases: First, obtaining commitment to the goals of the group; second, supplying resources; third, developing roles and an appropriate level of morale; fourth, carrying out the task with leadership coordination; and fifth, a terminal phase as the group is disbanded. However, for some groups a continual growth with regard to group cohesion and task effectiveness may be more evident than distinct phases.

Chapter 8

Group Decision Making and Choice Shift

Herbert H. Blumberg

People's views have often been found to change following discussion in small groups. The central tendency may be altered – that is, different people's opinions may tend to change in the same direction. For example, changes can be in the direction implied by persuasive arguments or by comparison with the perceived views of others. Also, variability may increase or decrease. The group may converge onto a narrower range of opinions. (See also, Chapter 4.) Alternatively, people's views may "polarize" in the direction of their respective initially-held views – that is, becoming more extreme. These effects could result in a net shift toward risk or caution – or along other, SYMLOG-type dimensions. (See the Introduction and Appendix of this volume.)

In this chapter and the two following chapters, we report on comparatively small "areas" that have been "mined" through extensive research in an effort accurately to quantify social transactions. There is a wealth of information which may vary in generality. In particular, much of the work has been done using just a few experimental paradigms, in settings which are slightly dominant, slightly positive or neutral (but with a "negative" task in the case of juries), and clearly task-oriented. Findings might not generalize to other paradigms in other parts of SYMLOG-type space (R. F. Bales, informal communication, April 1988) – for instance, where the situation varies in activeness, (un)friendliness, or analytical-vs.-emotional.

The generalities of specific findings represent open questions. However, the resulting list of variables which may be "worth looking at" is probably itself more robust – i.e., the environmental and personal variables, effects of group composition, and so on, may often have an effect, even though the nature of that effect may vary. For example, for juries the law wants the jury's line of reasoning concealed; it requires only their verdicts. In contrast, for continuing organizations, particularly when dispersed members are counted upon to carry out the mission of the organization, participation in a group decision may need to be a public affair when enduring commitment to the decision is sought.

We may conveniently examine two traditions of research on group decision making — mock juries and choice shift — plus residual work. Decisions in mock juries can be seen as a specific instance of choice shift. These two traditions might possibly benefit from a systematic program of integration, in which the same groups were given both juridical and other decision-making tasks.

Probably the oldest tradition of research on group discussion was with laboratory groups — cf. work done by Terman, by Munsterberg, and by Riddle, in the period 1900–1925 (see Hare, 1976, p.387, for this and subsequent research).

In the 15 years or so ending in 1988 there were well over 50 published studies on simulated jurors' verdicts and well over 100 papers each, on choice shift and "residual." So when we describe the effects of group discussion within these categories, the descriptions are in particular need of further subdivision. All three sections of this chapter use adaptations of the same list of subdivisions, as follows.

Group discussion involves several components, not unlike those of the larger topic of Small Groups itself. These include effects due to physical and personal backgrounds, exposure to others' opinions, group composition and decision rules, and of course the effects of the actual discussion. Readers who wish to make inferences which follow from the *general* effects of a particular "component," such as the effects of sex or personality, may wish also to consult the appropriate parts of other chapters in the present book.

For overviews of group decision making, see J. H. Davis, Laughlin, & Komorita (1976, pp. 509–516). See also, Brandstätter, 1985; Brandstätter, Davis, & Schuler, 1978; Brandstätter, Davis, & Stocker-Kreichgauer, 1982; D. A. Graham, 1984. For group decision making in organizations, see Guzzo (1982).

G. Wright (1985) has edited a broad work on decision making in general, which does include aggregation of individual choices, group processes, and related topics.

SIMULATED JURIES

When do juries provide the fairest verdicts? Real juries cannot usually be manipulated for experimental research purposes. A well-established "tradition" of research on group discussion has used simulated juries. See, for example, the 1956 work of Strodtbeck and Mann (Hare, 1976, pp. 203–204). Contemporary jury research has been of three kinds (Tindale & Davis, 1983): gathering data indirectly such as from ex-jurors or court records, studying "mock juries" in simulated trials, and attempting to apply general research on small-group performance, either analytically or in computer simulations. Combining aspects of the last two approaches, Hastie, Penrod, and Pennington (1983) have developed a computer model (JUS) to fit a variety of findings from their mock-jury data.

Potentially, many of the effects—on verdicts—of communication, impression formation, and attitude change do not require any social interaction as such. Indeed, about half of the present studies do not entail any. Typically, a court "case" is compiled with specific variations—for example, in the sex or apparent guilt of the accused—and subjects are asked to give "verdicts" and possibly other information. In keeping with a general guideline for the present book, the studies which do not involve social interaction are not considered in detail. However, for the benefit of readers who are specifically interested in jury effects, they are listed at the end of this section on juries. Unless noted otherwise, all of the studies in this section use mock or simulated jury trials rather than real ones.

The other major sections of this chapter also bear on decision making in juries. Indeed, in the study of decision rules—and, for that matter, in experiments on choice shift—there is no obvious sharp line between simulated *juries* and other ad hoc groups.

Background Variables and Group Composition

Although much research concerns the effects of background variables on individuals' judgments, there are apparently only a few such studies specifically relating to "juries" and entailing actual social interaction among the "jury" members. In one such study, no significant differences were found between the sexes in terms of verdict or persuasiveness, despite "folklore" about female jurors and despite perceived "differences" on influence and other characteristics (Nemeth, Endicott, & Wachtler, 1976). In another study, subjects have been found less likely to find a defendant of their own sex guilty (C. Stephan, 1974). N. L. Kerr (1981b), too, has considered the sex composition of juries. After deliberation, jurors who had had a male defense attorney have been found more likely to vote "not guilty" (M. V. McGuire & Bermant, 1977).

For a review of the (conviction-prone) effects of authoritarianism and a variety of other background variables in real juries, see Moran and Comfort (1982).

Previous jury experience has little effect on conviction likelihoods, but small juries with large proportions of experienced jurors were *slightly* more likely to convict (Werner, Strube, Cole, & Kagehiro, 1985; cf. N. L. Kerr, 1981a). One's experience relative to that of others on a given jury has been found to affect a juror's impact and satisfaction (Kassin & Juhnke, 1983). Decisions have moved in the direction of an assertive confederate (Snortum, Klein, & Sherman, 1976)—a finding in which one's personality is relevant to *others'* decisions. For additional work relating background variables to decision-making or to "foreman" selection, see: Gleason & Harris 1976; M. F. Kaplan & L. E. Miller, 1978; C. J. Mills & Bohannon, 1980; D. R. Shaffer, Plummer, & Hammock, 1986; Strodtbeck & Lipinski, 1985. See S. S. Diamond and Ziesel (1974) for comparison of outcomes from real juries with those of "juries" selected randomly from a jury pool (no challenges) and with those of experimental juries composed entirely of people who had been challenged by the defense or the prosecution.

Decision Rules and Related Processes

Valenti and Downing (1974, 1975) found that jury size had no effect on conviction rate when apparent guilt was low — but when apparent guilt was high, 6-member juries were substantially more likely to convict than were 12-member juries. Not surprisingly, mock juries with a unanimous decision rule have been less likely to reach a verdict than juries assigned a majority rule; and minority members have been particularly dissatisfied with the deliberation under majority rule (N. L. Kerr, Atkin, Stasser, Meek, Holt, & Davis, 1976). In a series of studies, Davis and colleagues have found that: *individuals* gave a higher proportion of guilty verdicts in a rape case than did juries (J. H. Davis, Kerr, Atkin, Holt, & Meek, 1975); juries informed that they would be publicly accountable (queried by experts) moved faster than did "private" juries if they were moving away from a guilty consensus near the end of deliberation (J. H. Davis, Tindale, Nagao, Hinsz, & Robertson, 1984).

In a study based on computer modeling of jury decision making, Tanford and Penrod (1983) investigated the effects of a consistent uncompromising opinion under various jury sizes and decision rules. When consistent "jurors" constituted a minority, influence was much stronger in six-person "juries" than twelve-person ones. Decision rules did not influence acquittal rate, but there were fewer *hung* juries under rules requiring smaller majorities. For other work relating to (explicit or implicit) decision rules and decision alternatives, see: J. H. Davis, Kerr, Stasser, Meek, & Holt, 1977; Foss 1981; Larntz, 1975; Nemeth, 1977; Penrod & Hastie, 1980; Schönemann, 1979. For general research on decision rules, which may have implications for juries, see the last section of the present chapter and also see Chapter 12.

For effects of inadmissable evidence, see W. C. Thompson, Fong, and Rosenhan (1981).

Effects of Initial Opinions and Discussion Per Se

Jurors' preexisting biases and sentiments may have no effect on verdicts but may be associated with the severity of sentences when the verdict is guilty (Clary & Shaffer, 1985). In an experimental study of size of faction, subjects anticipated that there would be "strength in numbers" but (with increasingly large factions) became less extreme in estimating outcome than the size of their faction warranted (N. L. Kerr & Watts, 1982). M. F. Kaplan and Krupa (1986) found that real jurors were more certain of guilt and more likely to convict than were simulated jurors. In keeping with some of the choice-shift findings (see the next major section of this chapter, below), Myers and Kaplan (1976; M. F. Kaplan, 1977) found that deliberation could polarize opinions. Following deliberation, subjects became more severe—in judgment of guilt and recommendation of penalty—in apparently-high-guilt cases and more lenient in low-guilt cases.

Stasser and Davis (1977, 1981) have developed a social interaction sequence (SIS) model, in which the probabilities of changes are related to the current distributions of opinion and opinion-certainty. According to their abstract of the 1977 study, "rate and direction of opinion change was found to be relatively constant throughout deliberation and appeared to be a simple linear function of the proportion of jurors favoring the verdict in the direction of change." Fischoff (1979) has also looked at effects of verdict certainty and other variables.

"Late" Effects of Deliberation and Content

The direction of one's initial judgments may predict later shifts, which are typically "polarized" in "the same direction" as the initial judgment. That is, a later opinion is likely to be in the same direction, for or against, but to have become more extreme or polarized (M. G. Rumsey, Allgeier, & Castore, 1978). In fact, not surprisingly, the initial vote distribution is not a bad predictor of final outcomes (Tanford & Penrod, 1986). Majorities favoring "not guilty" have been found to be more influential than those favoring guilty verdicts (J. H. Davis, Holt, Spitzer, & Stasser, 1981). According to a study by N. L. Kerr (1981b), the momentary state of a jury (distribution of opinions) gives a good prediction of its future state, though the prediction is improved by including additional information, such as how long the jury has already been deliberating. Deliberation may also sometimes result in a "shift toward leniency" in criminal cases (MacCoun & Kerr, 1988).

One corollary of polarization is as follows: If group members differ in their initial judgments, perhaps because they remember different information, discussion may increase polarization *within* the group (M. F. Kaplan & C. E. Miller, 1977).

Leadership, too, can have a significant effect on decision outcome (regardless of group size), particularly if it is toward lesser compensation (Eakin, 1975, using a simulated civil case).

For other studies of the effects of deliberation, see: J. H. Davis, Stasson, Ono, & Zimmerman, 1988; Foss, 1976; Hamilton, 1978; J. Howard & Levinson, 1985; Worth, Allison, & Messick, 1987. For a simulation relevant to group processes in juries, see Seibold & Steinfatt (1979).

Jury Simulation without Social Interaction

A number of studies deal specifically with information presented to individual "jurors" (or include deliberation only incidentally or as prior experience)—for example, N. J. Barnett & Feild, 1978; Boor, 1976; Calder, Insko, & Yandell, 1974; Dowdle, Gillen, & Miller, 1974; Efran, 1974; S. G. Fox & Walters, 1986; Gleason &

Harris, 1975; A. G. Goldstein, Chance, & Gilbert, 1984; J. Greenberg, Williams, & O'Brien, 1986; Kaplan & Kemmerick, 1974; Kassin & Wrightsman, 1980; N. L. Kerr, 1978; N. L. Kerr & MacCoun, 1985a; LaKind & Hornstein, 1979; Lindsay, Lim, Marando, & Cully, 1986; K. Ludwig & Fontaine, 1978; McComas & Noll, 1974; Nagao & Davis, 1980; Rusbult, Musante, & Solomon, 1982; D. R. Shaffer, Case, & Brannen, 1979; Sue, Smith, & Pedroza, 1975; Tanford & Penrod, 1984b; B. Thornton, 1977; D. W. Wilson & Donnerstein, 1977; Worth, Allison, & Messick, 1987.

Of course, some of the studies without social interaction may nonetheless bear relevance for studying the effects of discussion. To take just one example, McMahon and Fehr (1984) conclude that inconsistent findings in mock jury studies may be attributable in part to (usually) unmanipulated factors, such as the exact case used and the specific voices used on audiotapes.

For a synthesis of more general research on communication and attitude change, see W. J. McGuire (1985). For research on impression formation see, e.g., Bootzin, Bower, Zajonc, & Hall, 1986, Chapter 26; M. Cook, 1984; Doob, 1975; D. J. Schneider, Hastorf, & Ellsworth, 1979; and see also, *Advances in Social Cognition* (from 1988, Vol. 1, onward). For work on equity and justice, see the last section of Chapter 10.

CHOICE SHIFT

In a typical study of choice shift, group members would be presented with one or more problems and asked to note their personal views (e.g., "On a scale from 1 to 10, what is the minimum estimated likelihood of success on the new job that would lead you to advise her to change jobs?"). Then each group would have an opportunity to discuss the problem(s) and perhaps agree on an answer. Finally, individuals would again note their personal views.

Many people are familiar with work done in the 1960s and early 1970s showing that, following group discussion, people's opinions may show a systematic shift in a particular direction. Since then, perhaps surprisingly, there have been well over 100 further studies on this topic. The majority of these, but by no means all of the main ones, appeared before 1980. The work appears to represent a large elaboration of a fairly narrow topic. However, it does provide a further "foothold" for studying the effects of group discussion—and indeed for the broader topics of social influence, conformity, and social interaction, treated in Chapters 3, 4, 7, and elsewhere in this book. The work on choice shift arguably does not yield a unitary theory but does provide a catalog of some of the variables that may lead to opinion shifts during social interaction—and examples of apposite conditions and settings.

In keeping with what was thought to be their typical direction, the changes were at first called "risky shift," and later simply "choice shift" or "group polarization." According to a review by Isenberg (1986), the two primary explanatory mechanisms, social comparison and persuasive argumentation processes, both occur, "although the persuasive argumentation effects tend to be larger." This difference is likely to be marked when "a decision has many factual and logical components" and is not too ego-involving. A decade earlier, but with less cumulated evidence, others (e.g., Burnstein & Vinokur, 1977; Myers & Lamm, 1975, 1976; G. S. Sanders & Baron, 1977) had reached broadly similar conclusions.

Other interesting (albeit miscellaneous) extensions of this research area include treating choice shift in terms of: social decision schemes (Crott, Zuber, & Schermer, 1986), political decision-making in groups (Kirkpatrick, Davis, & Robertson, 1976), changes over trials (G. S. Sanders, 1978) or over "time spent thinking" (Tesser & Conlee, 1975), and how subjects understand their task (Reingen, 1976). Shifts may apply to subjects acting on others' behalf as well as on their own, and may involve a conscious change or a distortion of one's memory of one's initial position.

The next two sections are concerned with "social comparison" and "persuasive arguments," respectively. According to Burnstein and Schul (1983), cognitive (informational) processes such as those based on persuasive arguments offer a more adequate explanation of polarization than do affective (normative) processes such as those based on social comparison.

> From a broader theoretical perspective, however, the relationship between cognition and affect in respect to opinion change might be conceptualized as one in which the former deals with the more immediate determinants of polarization and the latter with relatively more remote determinants. Thus, for instance, the information gained from comparisons with other group members may have influence by biasing the argument sample a person retrieves during opinion formation. (Burnstein & Schul, 1983, p. 61.)

Social comparison

What distinguishes ordinary conformity (as discussed in Chapter 4) from social comparison effects? Probably, with social comparison the emphasis may be on agreeing with some reference group, in contrast to more direct pressures to agree, that would be considered in Chapter 4 on conformity. That is, following discussion, the whole group shifts its estimates as it were, perhaps because of individuals' real or exaggerated perceptions of the values of a real or projected group norm. Sometimes individuals may "overconform," selecting options which are "in the direction of a group norm, only more so."

In one study demonstrating social comparison effects (Mackie & Cooper, 1984), "undergraduates listened to a taped discussion that advocated either the retention or the abolition of standardized testing.... the taped discussion was attributed either to a group the S was about to join or to a group with whom the S's group was to compete." Attitudes shifted toward the position advocated on the tape only when the discussion was attributed to the in-group. The effect may well have been due to subjects' paying more *attention* to the in-group's contributions (and norms) and thereby perceiving them more accurately, rather than to selective conformity as such. The magnitude of social comparison effects varies, but in this particular experiment subjects conformed (up) to a perceived norm rather than exceeding it.

One's "reference group" need not actually appear to be present. For instance, subjects have been found to conform to scripts derived from their past experiences in similar social settings (Bettenhausen & Murnighan, 1985), or to conform to an abstract norm by giving larger estimates to an autokinetic effect in those conditions where larger estimates "denoted intellectual and academic promise" (R. S. Baron & Roper, 1976).

For other examples and explanations of social comparison effects, see: Cotton & Baron, 1980; Goethals & Zanna, 1979; N. L. Kerr, Davis, Meek, & Rissman, 1975; Mackie, 1986; Myers, 1978; Paicheler, 1976, 1977a, 1977b; Singleton, 1979; Ueno & Yokogawa, 1982.

Persuasive Arguments

"Persuasive arguments theory," attributed to Vinokur and Burnstein, accounts for the largest choice-shift effects. People are found to be sensitive to the number of arguments in a particular direction as well as to the novelty and persuasiveness of these arguments. Effects are strongest when there is an overall pool of arguments in a particular direction, presented by, and discussed with, several other people. Each time a new discussant speaks in an interactive setting, subjects may "wake up" or retune or regear themselves (cf. Burnstein & Schul, 1983). Discussion may lead to choice shift, whereas "mere exposure" to arguments may not do so, or hardly does so. Moreover, the postdiscussion shift may have an impact on issues other than the one actually under discussion (D. R. Spitzer, 1975a, 1975b). For delineations of this theory or approach, see: N. H. Anderson & Graesser, 1976; Bishop & Myers, 1974; Brandstätter & Klein-Moddenborg, 1979; Burnstein & Vinokur, 1975; Burnstein, Vinokur, & Pichevin, 1974; Hinsz & Davis, 1984; Kleiven, Fraser, & Gouge, 1974; D. B. Madsen, 1978; T. W. McGuire, Kiesler, & Siegel, 1987; McLachlan, 1986a, 1986b; C. P. Morgan & Aram, 1975; Semin, 1975; Stasser & Titus, 1987; Vinokur & Burnstein, 1978a, 1978b; Vinokur, Trope, & Burnstein, 1975.

Other "Theories" and Mechanisms?

Various other possible bases for choice shifts have been studied. For instance, is there a general "cultural value for risk"? Results for these other theories have generally been negative, except under fairly specific circumstances or except when the mechanisms *underlie* effects due to persuasive arguments or social comparison. For instance, in a comparison between Chinese from Taiwan, having a Confucian ethic, and Americans: The arguments and norms for a particular (Chinese) culture appeared to be inherently cautious and to produce cautious shifts (L. K. Hong, 1978).

For examples of studies emphasizing the investigation of "other theories", see: Billig & Cochrane, 1976; Blascovich, Ginsburg, & Howe, 1974; Blascovich, Ginsburg, & Howe, 1975; Chapko & Solomon, 1974; J. H. Davis, Kerr, Sussman, & Rissman, 1974; Forgas, 1977; Kahan, 1975; Muehleman, Bruker, & Ingram, 1976; Murnighan & Castore, 1975; Sauer, 1974. For examples of studies which evaluate multiply determined effects, see: Benoit, 1982; Chlewinski, 1980; Coet & McDermott, 1979; Laughlin & Earley, 1982; Mayer, 1985; Pruitt & Cosentino, 1975; Silzer & Clark, 1977; Wilke, 1974; Yinon, Jaffe, & Feshbach, 1975; Zaleska, 1976.

Sex and Personality

There have been a number of significant findings, but they await integration. It is plausible, at least, that many of the results are special cases of persuasive-arguments and social-comparison theories. That is, various norms and arguments are sex- or personality-linked, and these links may be specific to particular contexts or tasks. When a group of males, say, or high need-achievers are exposed to each others' arguments for a given problem, a shift occurs in the direction of the group's particular arguments or norms. In a "mixed" group—whether the mix is based on background variables or simply on initial opinions (cf. G. M. Stephenson & Brotherton, 1975)—the constituent subgroups may "move" toward each other, with net overall *group* shifts being correspondingly reduced.

For general effects of sex and personality, see also Chapter 2.

Generally, male subjects have displayed more risk than females, and have been more influential in "promoting" risky alternatives (Coet & McDermott, 1979; DiBerardinis, Ramage, & Levitt, 1984; Jahan & Begum, 1977; Seeborg, Lafollette, & Belohlaw, 1980). However, some studies have found no sex differences in riskiness in particular contexts (e.g., Kelling, Zirkes, & Myerowitz, 1976) or, apparently, higher risk among females (Tuchman, 1981).

As a sample finding related to personality: Higher risk, and a greater shift toward risk, have been found among (female) subjects high in need for achievement (E. K. Goldman, 1975).

Of course, shifts can take place on dimensions other than "risky-cautious." For instance, particularly after discussion, low authoritarian "jurors" reached fewer guilty verdicts (Bray & Noble, 1978).

Among additional studies concerned with sex, age, personality, and other background variables are: LaFollette & Belohlav, 1982; Lamm & Myers, 1976; McGraw & Bloomfield, 1987; Noe, McDonald, & Hammitt, 1983; Plax & Rosenfeld, 1976; Sadava & Forsyth, 1976; Spencer, Williams, & Oldfield-Box, 1974.

Specific Processes and Output Variables

For representative studies delineating the polarizing impact of particular variables, such as the *salience* of specific arguments or the *consequences* associated with particular outcomes, see: Abramo, Lundgren, & Bogart, 1978; T. R. Cline & Cline, 1979; Fortenberry & Smith, 1981; Higbee, 1973; M. B. Jacobson, 1975, 1977; M. B. Jacobson & Uleman, 1976; N. R. Johnson & Glover, 1978; N. R. Johnson, Stemler, & Hunter, 1977; Knox & Safford, 1976; Lamm, Myers, & Ochsmann, 1976; T. W. McGuire, Kiesler, & Siegel, 1987; Moscovici & Néve, 1973b; Mugny, 1979; Myers & Bach, 1974; Paicheler, 1977a, 1979b; Rettig, 1975; Ridley, Young, & Johnson, 1981; Rule & Gareau, 1977; M. G. Rumsey & Castore, 1980; Wilke & Meertens, 1973.

For "field-related studies" showing the presence of choice shifts, see Blascovich & Ginsburg, 1974; Blascovich, Ginsburg, & Howe, 1975; M. A. Lewin & Kane, 1975; Nagel & O'Driscoll, 1978; G. S. Sanders, 1980; D. R. Spitzer, 1975a, 1975b; G. M. Stephenson & Brotherton, 1975; Vinokur, Burnstein, Sechrest, & Wortman, 1985; Winter, 1976.

For a bibliography of the early work on risky shift, see Myers, 1973.

Some additional studies which help to delineate or review the effects of choice shift are listed below. (See also the section of Chapter 11 dealing with "risky shift.") Their coverage seems truly miscellaneous, but not uninteresting. For an indication of the specific variables examined, see the titles (in the list of references) of the papers: P. H. Baron, Baron, & Roper, 1974; Bazerman, Giuliano, & Appelman, 1984; Borcherding & Kistner, 1982; Bordley, 1983; Carlston, 1977; A. W. Clark & Powell, 1984; Dickson, 1978; D. G. Fischer, McDowell, & Boulanger, 1976; Foster & Finchilescu, 1985; Glover, 1977; Gologor, 1977; Granberg & Campbell, 1977; Isozaki, 1984; Isozaki, Ueno, Amane, & Yokogawa, 1981; Jesuino, 1986; Knowles, 1975; Kostinskaya, 1976; Lamm & Myers, 1978; Lamm & Sauer, 1974; Lilienthal & Hutchison, 1979; Minix, 1982 (emphasizes political applications); Myers, 1975; Néve & Gautier, 1977-1978; Néve & Moscovici, 1982; Orive, 1984; Prabhu & Singh, 1975; Reingen, 1977; Reingen & Kernan, 1977; Romer, 1983; St. Jean, 1979; Schaffer, 1978; Schellenberg, 1974, 1976; P. E. Spector, Cohen, & Penner, 1976; Swap & Associates, 1984; J. E. Thompson & Carsrud, 1976; Verma & Sinha, 1981; Wahrman, 1977; Widmar, 1974; Yinon & Bizman, 1974; Zaleska, 1974, 1980.

OTHER TOPICS

Groupthink

Janis examined a number of "historic fiascos" — such as America's decision to escalate the war in Vietnam — made as a result of defective policy planning by political decision-making groups (Janis, 1982 [first edition, 1972], 1983). He identified a number of main symptoms of excessive "concurrence thinking" or "groupthink." These include: a shared illusion of invulnerability, fostering optimism and risk taking; rationalizations which discount warnings that might lead to reconsidering a continuation of past policy decisions; inflated faith in the group's morality; stereotyped views of opponents as being inept or as being too evil for negotiation; pressure against any dissenting "disloyal" group members; a resulting shared illusion of unanimity; and "self-appointed mindguards" "who protect the group from adverse information."

A number of "prescriptive hypotheses" are described by Janis, as follows. Group members should be aware of the causes and consequences of groupthink. Leaders should be initially impartial among options. Critical evaluation from all members should be encouraged. At each meeting one or more members should be assigned the role of devil's advocate and moreover be prepared to defend their counterarguments. Decisions should be made by two subgroups that subsequently hammer out their differences. In addition, the organization should set up two or more independent planning and evaluation groups (separately chaired) for each major policy question. All "warning signals" from rivals and elsewhere should be surveyed and analyzed. After provisional decisions are made, there should be a "second chance" meeting in which all members describe their residual doubts. A rota of outside experts within the organization should be present at meetings and "should be encouraged to challenge the views of the core members." Members should discuss decisions with trusted colleagues and report back.

In a laboratory experiment related to groupthink, Callaway & Esser (1984) confirmed that the poorest decisions were made by highly cohesive groups with inadequate decision-making procedures. The best decisions were made by groups of intermediate cohesiveness. In a subsequent study (Callaway, Marriott, & Esser, 1985), groups composed of highly dominant members made better decisions — perhaps because they also tended to make more statements of disagreement and agreement, with more resultant group influence on members.

Other researchers have also provided support or partial support for the strength of "groupthink phenomena" and in some cases suggest that the effects interact with additional factors (Castore & Murnighan, 1978; Courtright, 1978; Flowers, 1977; Leana, 1985; Manz & Sims, 1982; Moorhead, 1982; Moorhead & Montanari, 1986; Myers & Bach, 1976; Tetlock, 1979). For a general discussion of conformity in the context of group decision-making, see J. M. Levine, Saxe, and Harris (1976) and also see Chapters 3 and 4. For a review of several studies related to "groupthink," see Posner-Weber (1987).

Decision Rules (Aggregation of Individual Choices)

Can group decisions be recommended or predicted on the basis of component individual choices? Various decision rules have been proposed for such predictions. Two rough examples are consensus (in which any member can veto an action) and majority rule. The general issue is as follows: "Given a particular distribution of opinions in a group, the relevant problem is to ascertain the probability that the group will choose a given alternative." A more precise example of a rule which *maps members' preferences into a group response* could be: Any option commanding a majority over other options will win, otherwise equiprobability among popular options (Bowman & Colantoni, 1972; Tindale & Davis, 1983, pp. 15–16). In the case of mock-jury research, discussed above, two main variables have been size of group and how large a majority is required for a decision. For some general considerations, see also: D. R. Farris & Sage, 1975; Sengupta & Dutta, 1979; Stefánsson, 1974.

Randomized comparisons between the practical effects of different decision rules, particularly between majority and unanimity, have been carried out in a number of studies. Researchers have looked at both the quality of decisions and group members' satisfaction. In general, majority and unanimity usually result in the *same* decision, though the group may take deviant views into account if they have sufficient information to do so and if a varied gradation of decisions is possible (C. E. Miller, 1985b). Member satisfaction with one or another rule appears to depend on the specific context. For instance, in unequal-power groups, a unanimity rule was associated with less task conflict (G. Falk, 1982). However, if "anti-disagreement norms" are associated with consensus rules, groupthink may develop and threaten the quality of the group decision (Gero, 1985).

Relevant comparisons have been carried out by: G. Falk, 1981; Gouran & Geonetta, 1977; S. G. Green & Taber, 1980; Hare, 1980; M. F. Kaplan & Miller, 1987; C. E. Miller & Anderson, 1979; C. E. Miller, Jackson, Mueller, & Scherching, 1987; Nurmi, 1984; Packel, 1980; Straffin, 1977; L. L. Thompson, Mannix, & Bazerman, 1988; Tjosvold & Field, 1983, 1985.

Felsenthal and Fuchs (1976) compared several decision-making procedures or "organizational systems". Their work is summarized as follows:

> The study was based on a simulation using 1674 college students, who were required to compute a hypothetical person's salary according to certain instructions. Each participant was assigned randomly to a group of three or six, which used one of five redundant processes: completely independent [work alone], sequential [Asch-type consecutive answers], mixed-independent [individual decisions, then discuss, then individual answers], group [all work together], and delphi [individual rationales/ answers are distributed anonymously, then revised individual answers are again distributed, then final individual answers]. For each redundant number and process, the frequencies of four different levels of agreement were recorded (total disagreement, plurality, simple and qualified majority, unanimity) as well as the probability of obtaining the correct solution given a certain agreement level. Results indicate that (a) there is no gain in overall reliability by increasing group size beyond a triad; (b) there is a significant increase in reliability when some agreement is obtained as compared with total disagreement, but no gain in reliability as a function of the actual level of agreement; (c) completely independent and sequential processes are inferior regardless of group size and should be avoided; and (d) mixed-independent group, group, and delphi process are equally reliable in triads, while the delphi process was the most reliable in hexads — hence delphi may be the best choice among these three processes. (Felsenthal & Fuchs, 1976, *Psychological Abstracts* 57:7063)

In an experimental comparison of four decision-making formats, Erffmeyer and Lane (1984) found that "Delphi groups produced the highest quality decisions, followed by those of consensus, interacting, and NG" (nominal groups—i.e., working alone). Other studies have reached broadly similar conclusions, usually employing other tasks and comparing somewhat different sets of conditions (G. W. Fischer, 1975; see also, Grofman, Owen, & Feld, 1982; Poole, McPhee, & Seibold, 1982).

For a problem requiring high technical quality and high participant acceptance, F. C. Miner (1979) found that a PCL (problem-centered leadership) approach was more effective than nominal-group and delphi procedures. Where the cost of bringing people together physically is high, Van de Ven and Delbecq (1974) recommend the Dalkey delphi technique—respondents to a postal survey worked individually but received two rounds of "feedback reports" describing their group's ideas and solutions.

Some decision procedures—for instance those which "statistically" aggregate people's views—do not require a live, interacting group. For comparisons between individuals and groups, see Chapter 11. Even if a group does not forge a new, creative solution, social interaction—and its attendant "choice shifts"—may at least provide all members with something which approaches the *best* individual solution (Burleson, Levine, & Samter, 1984; Tindale & Davis, 1983). Shared decision-making may in any case clarify goals and available options (Maple, 1977).

The remainder of this section is concerned with studies that discuss consensus or other specific procedures, or which compare groups that spontaneously use different procedures. Consensus has been viewed as superior to majority rule in terms of decision quality, valuing of all members, and conflict resolution; however, it can increase time-consuming discussions (M. E. Gentry, 1982; cf. Hare, 1973). To foster consensus, Christopher and Dodd (1972) recommend that a group should increase members' intent to agree, give all members an opportunity to discuss the issue, practice achieving increased agreement on other issues. Stasser and Titus (1985) concluded that consensus reached through unstructured discussion may be inadequate, for example because distortions shared by an initial plurality may get perpetuated.

One does need to watch what people call "consensus." Often it is used to mean that the final decision is unanimous, rather than to describe a structured process in which a group may "unite" in a decision. Such a structured process is used by Quakers and in various experiments (see Hare, 1982, pp. 148–149, 163–166; see also, G. M. Phillips & Wood, 1984).

Several studies have compared a variety of decision-scheme models to see which ones best fit the processes used by laboratory or other groups (for instance, Godwin & Restle, 1974). Laughlin, Kerr, Munch, and Haggarty (1976) found that a "truth wins" process provided the best fit for decisions on the Remote Associates Test. That is, if any group member knows the correct answer, all will tend to agree on it. However, for the Otis Quick-Scoring Mental Ability Test, the best-fitting decision scheme was "a complex combination of a truth-supported-wins process when three or four members knew the correct answer, an increment from grouping [i.e., better than if an average or random person were selected] when two members knew the answer or no members knew the answer, and strong conformity pressures against a single correct member" (p.80). (See also, Godwin & Restle, 1974; Laughlin, Kerr, Davis, Halff, & Marciniak, 1975.)

MacKinnon and others have presented a computer program for collecting participants' judgments and synthesizing group decisions (MacKinnon & Anderson, 1976; cf. Gilmartin & MacKinnon, 1974). The effects of group size and space upon group decision-making performance was reviewed by Cummings, Huber, and Arendt (1974); see also, Chapter 1.

Gillett (1977) summarizes various difficulties with Condorcet procedures, in which (a) everyone ranks the available alternatives, (b) for every possible *pair* of alternatives, it is determined which (if any) is preferred by a majority of voters, and (c) the alternative (if there is one) which defeats all others wins.

For a discussion of various other procedures, see: S. M. Holland, Fedler, & Ditton (1986); Donohue, Hawes, & Mabee (1981); Gillett (1977, 1980); Kervin (1974); Laing & Slotznick (1987); Libby, Trotman, & Zimmer (1987).

S. L. Hart (1985) has reviewed the literature on group decision making in order to derive criteria for evaluating the quality of collective judgments. According to Hirokawa (1985) and others, the group's satisfaction with requisite conditions is a better predictor of performance than are the specific discussion procedures employed. Poole has argued that decision making often lacks an orderly uniform sequence—rather, there may be several tracks of activity and "breakpoints" to "mark changes in the development of the strands" (Poole, 1983a, 1983b; cf. Poole, Seibold, & McPhee, 1985).

A number of studies have discussed the effects of various specific factors and tasks, such as group attribution errors and divergent perceptions of disagreement. Some of these may operate only under particular conditions, such as groups with positive or negative climates, or with strong or weak power. Readers interested in particular "other effects" should consult one or more of the following (for a rough guide to the contents of these items, see their titles in the list of references): S. T. Allison & Messick, 1985a; Boje & Murnighan, 1982; Bozeman & McAlpine, 1977; Camilleri & Conner, 1976; L. G. Cooper & Thomas, 1974; L. Cooper & Gustafson, 1981; Egerbladh, 1981; Enos, 1985; G. F. Farris, 1972; Fodor & Smith, 1982; Gamble & Strain, 1977; Geist & Chandler, 1984; Gouran, Brown, & Henry, 1978; Grofman, Feld, & Owen, 1984; Guzzo & Waters, 1982; S. L. Hart, 1985; E. W. Hart & Sung, 1976; Hirokawa, 1980; Hirokawa & Pace, 1983; Hunsaker & Hunsaker, 1974; Keeney & Raiffa, 1976; G. K. Kenny, Butler, Hickson, Cray, Mallory, & Wilson, 1987; N. L. Kerr, MacCoun, Hansen, & Hymes, 1987; Kirchler & Davis, 1986, Klopfer & Moran, 1978; Kostinskaya, 1984; Lane, Mathews, Chaney, Effmeyer, Reber, & Teddlie, 1982; Lehrer, 1976; A. W. Lerner, Rundquist, & Cline, 1984; Louche, 1974–1975; McCormick, Lundgren, & Cecil, 1980; McKelvey &

Ordeshook, 1981; Mukerji, 1976; O'Connell, Cummings, & Huber, 1976; Parrillo, Stimson, & Stimson, 1985; Peay, 1980; P. B. Pedersen, 1985; Poole, 1981; Press, Ali, & Yang, 1979; Qucreshi & Strauss, 1980; Rauch, 1983; Robertson, 1980; Saaty & Vargas, 1980; T. M. Schwartz, Wullwick, & Shapiro, 1980; U. A. Segal, 1982a, 1982b; Siperstein, Bak, & Gottlieb, 1977; K. A. Smith, Petersen, Johnson, & Johnson, 1986; Snapka, 1976; Sugiman, 1977, 1979; van Asperen, 1981; Vinokur, Burnstein, Sechrest, & Wortman, 1985; D. G. Wagner & Berger, 1982; Wolosin, Sherman, & Mynatt, 1975; E. F. Wright & Wells, 1985.

SUMMARY

Following group discussion there may be a change in members' opinions in several directions. The average opinion may change as a result of persuasive arguments or because of the perceived views of other group members. Opinions may converge in a narrower range, or alternatively polarize. The result may be a shift toward risk or caution.

Research on the decision of juries has been conducted using simulations. In much of the research no actual interaction between the "jurors" occurs. Typically a court case is compiled with variations in, for example, the sex or apparent guilt of the accused. Subjects are then asked to give their verdicts. Aside from the fact that the decision is about another human being leading — for instance — to more sympathy for a defendant of one's own sex or a greater certainty of guilt and willingness to convict if the experimental subject had had actual jury experience, the gist of the results of jury deliberations is similar to that for other task groups. It is easier for a jury to reach a decision under a majority decision rule than one requiring a unanimous decision, although there may be a dissatisfied minority. After deliberation, individual opinions may become polarized. The initial distribution of opinions in a jury is a good predictor of the final outcome.

Individual choice shift as a result of group discussion is influenced by social comparison and persuasive argumentation. The process of social comparison appears to involve an exaggerated perception of the group norm on the part of individual members or a shift to a position more extreme than the group norm (overconformity). Group members are also found to be sensitive to the number of arguments in a particular direction as well as to the novelty and persuasiveness of the arguments. Some norms and arguments may be sex- or personality-linked and thus only have an effect in particular contexts or with particular tasks.

Defective policy planning by political decision making groups has been labeled "groupthink" by Janis. This phenomenon can be avoided if measures are taken to insure that all negative information is thoroughly considered and group members are given a second chance to express doubts. As a safeguard, more than one set of members and experts may be asked to reach a decision and the results compared.

A decision rule that calls for a majority agreement and one that requires unanimity (all members have, or at least agree to, the same opinion) usually result in the same decision. However, a decision made by consensus (members unite in their support of a decision) has been viewed as superior to majority rule in terms of decision quality, valuing of all members, and conflict resolution. When the cost of bringing group members together is high, a decision method that combines individual opinions statistically may produce satisfactory solutions. For problems where the solution is obvious once one member has discovered it, "truth wins," and others will easily agree.

Part V
INTERACTIVE MODES

Chapter 9

Cooperation, Competition, and Conflict Resolution

Herbert H. Blumberg

Cooperation and the resolution of conflict appear to be similar topics. One might imagine that research that deals with one is likely also to deal with the other. This is indeed the case with much of the work that uses specific experimental paradigms — for example, studies on bargaining, interdependence, and coalitions — which are covered in Chapter 10, and which compare conditions that may foster cooperative, uncooperative, or other behaviors.

However, most studies that use more diverse methods tend to focus on more specific concepts, such as cooperation *or* competition *or* conflict. These and similar concepts form the main sections of the present chapter. In general, each section begins by mentioning some general work, and in some cases giving details of a representative study. The rest of each section is arranged in a progression including, with some variations, some or all of: (a) studies which emphasize background variables, (b) effects manifest from "early rules of interaction" or other experimental conditions, (c) effects of social interaction or other group processes. Sometimes, of course, essentially the same characteristic, such as competitiveness, may be studied as either a background personality characteristic or as an experimentally-produced condition. Our classification is in some cases a bit arbitrary.

The present chapter emphasizes cooperation and competition in settings of face-to-face interaction, either within or between groups. Intergroup relations (between large social or cultural groups) are not, as such, covered here. (See, for example: Deaux & Wrightsman, 1988; Lindzey & Aronson, 1985.)

Readers may also wish to consult Chapter 4, insofar as conformity and "compliance" are akin to cooperation. In addition, Chapter 11 includes, for example, some coverage of cooperative groups solving problems too difficult for all or most of the individual members acting on their own. For a review of theory and research mainly from the 1970s, see J. H. Davis, Laughlin, & Komorita (1976).

COOPERATION

Are there effective strategies for eliciting cooperation from an adversary—strategies which might even cut across the spectrum from small-group laboratory experiments to international studies? According to the summary of Patchen's (1987) review, "a policy of general reciprocity, combined with the use of unilateral cooperative initiatives to break out of lock-ins on mutual competition" is generally effective (Patchen, 1987, p. 164).

For similar conclusions, see Axelrod (1984) and, in Chapter 10, the discussion introducing "prisoner's dilemma," which includes a brief quotation from Axelrod's work.

Looking at specific classes of *situations in which cooperation may be difficult to achieve*—for example, collective dilemmas and prisoners' dilemma (discussed later in this chapter and in Chapter 10)—W. Buckley, Burns, and Meeker (1974) concluded that the situations had a common underlying structure related to social context and social processes involved in "perceptions and evaluations, action possibilities, decision procedures, and likely interaction patterns."

For reference to the "jigsaw classroom," a cooperative learning procedure, see: Chapter 2 (under race) and Aronson, Blaney, Stephan, Sikes, & Snapp, 1978; Aronson & Bridgeman, 1978; Aronson & Yates, 1983. Sharan (1984) and Vedder (1985), too, describe the benefits of cooperative learning in the classroom. For a collection of papers with discussion of related findings in the Netherlands, Israel, and the United States, see Slavin, Sharan, Kagan, Hertz-Lazarowitz, Webb, & Schmuck (1985).

Background Variables

Possibly about half of the post-1974 studies on cooperation deal with the effects of physical situation or personal backgrounds. Chertock (1974), for instance, studied the effects of background sound on the behavior of primary-school children. Time sampling showed more cooperative behavior with "art music" or "mood music" than with no sound or with adults reading aloud. Whether one has heard a "good" or "bad" newscast can effect cooperative behavior (Hornstein, LaKind, Frankel, & Manne, 1975).

A number of studies do show significant effects of physical and personal background, but sometimes in contradictory directions. Meeker (1977) found that women tended to be more cooperative, but Rokach (1982) found male dyads to be more cooperative. Both researchers used college students carrying out (different) laboratory tasks with cooperative reward structures. More work is needed in delineating how cooperation is linked with other variables.

Perhaps something like Pruitt's goal-expectation hypothesis, described in Chapter 10, will also apply to the present diverse situations. The principle is that people are likely to cooperate when they have a *goal* of mutual cooperation and expect that the other party or parties have a similar goal. Depending on circumstance, a particular background variable — or a particular profile of background variables (Manning, Pierce-Jones, & Parelman, 1974) — could be related either positively or negatively (or not at all) to cooperation.

Indeed, a factorial experiment by Meeker (1984), described in the next section (on cooperation versus competition), essentially confirms the importance of goals and expectations (and possibly variables which underlie them) in mediating cooperation.

Variables such as ethnicity and group composition can interact with each other. Both Anglo-Americans and Hispanic undergraduates were equally cooperative when constituting the majority of a four-person group. However, as a minority of one person, the Anglo-American students were even more cooperative whereas the Hispanic students were less cooperative (Espinoza & Garza, 1985). Being in a numerical minority in a particular working group can increase the salience of one's ethnic identity. In principle, the strength of this identity, and perhaps the basic values associated with it, may differ according to the specific identity concerned (ethnicity, sex, age, etc.).

Ethnic composition need not have any significant effect on the amount of cooperative behavior (R. H. Weigel & Quinn, 1977). However, small interdependent mixed work groups can promote cross-ethnic helping behavior and positive sentiment (R. H. Weigel, Wiser, & Cook, 1975, in a study using middle- and secondary-school students). The finding supports the "contact hypothesis" that inter-group (e.g., interethnic) contact reduces prejudice under specific conditions, such as equal-status members working together with support from authority (e.g., teacher), and with rewards based on group performance (cf. S. W. Cook, 1978; Slavin, 1985). For this effect (reduced prejudice) to generalize, group members need to be perceived as being not "exceptional." Perhaps a situation could call for individuals to have occasion to work with a number of different members of a particular background. N. Miller, Brewer, and Edwards (1985) conclude that a generalized increase in outgroup acceptance depends on "(a) an interpersonal as opposed to task orientation toward team members, and (b) the assignment of persons to teams on the basis of their unique personal attributes rather than attributes that explicitly exemplify their category."

In the first phase of an experimental study of the effects of group identity (Worchel, Axsom, Ferris, Samaha, & Schweizer, 1978), subjects either competed or acted interdependently, and "wore either similar or different uniforms to distinguish the groups." In the second phase of the study, with members of the different group identities brought together on a cooperative task, "intergroup cooperation increased attraction for outgroup members except when the cooperative endeavor resulted in failure and the groups had previously competed. Wearing distinctive uniforms damped the positive effects of the cooperative phase.

For other studies relating cooperativeness to physical and personal background, see: H. Cook & Sloane, 1985; Hamburger, Guyer, & Fox, 1975; F. C. Hatfield, 1978; D. W. Johnson, 1975; Szmajke, 1984; Yamada, Tjosvold, & Draguns, 1983.

Effects of Rules or Experimental Conditions

Morton Deutsch (1973) carried out a series of laboratory experiments on conflict resolution. For example, using a "resource accumulation" procedure, he investigated various strategies which might induce cooperation. In each turn a player could choose various colored pegs, which might roughly be described as leading to: own gain, own gain (if other chooses same color), other's gain, take from other, attack, defend, disarm. Although responses to programmed strategies varied according to context, a "turn-the-other-cheek" strategy was consistently exploited except when it was preceded by a "show of strength". A "deterrent" strategy became less effective in increasingly "cooperative" contexts.

Third-grade American children achieved and retained more from a setting "in which members discussed how well their group was functioning and how they could improve its effectiveness" (cooperation combined with "group processing") than in a setting of cooperative learning without any group processing (Yager, Johnson, Johnson, & Snider, 1986). They achieved and retained least in a setting of "individualistic learning." Other studies concerned with the effects of social-interaction variables such as type of activity, availability of task and group roles, and opportunities for communication have been reported by: M. S. Clark, Mills, & Powell, 1986; Janousek, 1973; M. W. Martin & Sell, 1983; E. A. Pepitone, 1977; J. A. Schellenberg, 1985; and Yanoushek, 1982.

Group Processes

In order to help account for the rise and fall of group cooperation and solidarity, Hechter (1982) has presented a theory based on the premise of *rational individual action*, which "takes account of the free-rider problem" and provides a framework for generating testable hypotheses. Readers interested in the free-rider problem should see the discussion of social loafing in Chapter 11.

Ten studies using a classroom intervention—Teams-Games-Tournament (TGT)—have shown positive effects of TGT on achievement, mutual concern, and race relations (DeVries & Slavin, 1978). The TGT instructional process uses simulation games as part of primary and secondary school education (DeVries & Slavin, 1976). (Slavin, 1975, reviewed research on the effects of reward structure.)

Some other studies concerned with interaction or perception in the course of a cooperative task are as follows: Schmid & Hake, 1983; Seiler, 1974; Tao, 1974; and Tjosvold, Johnson, & Johnson, 1981.

Additional Research

For additional research concerned more generally with cooperation in small groups, consult: Colecchia & Aureli, 1985; R. E. Kaplan, 1978; Katovich, Weiland, & Couch, 1981; Krivohlavy & Klicperova, 1985; Marwell & Schmitt, 1975; K. A. Smith, Johnson, & Johnson, 1984.

COOPERATION VERSUS COMPETITION

In a meta-analytic review covering 122 studies, D. W. Johnson, Maruyama, Johnson, Nelson, and Skon (1981) "compared the relative effectiveness of cooperation, cooperation with intergroup competition, interpersonal competition, and individualistic goal structures in promoting achievement and productivity . . . Results . . . indicate (a) that cooperation is considerably more effective than interpersonal competition and individualistic efforts, (b) that cooperation with intergroup competition is also superior to interpersonal competition and individualistic efforts, and (c) that there is no significant difference between interpersonal competitive and individualistic efforts" (p.47). Findings may be moderated by variables such as size of group and whether a product is required of the group as a whole. For a popular description of some of the relevant research, see A. Kohn (1986). Kohn's article also describes the advantages of cooperative peer tutoring in the classroom.

However, D. R. Schmitt (1986) suggests that conclusions which stress the advantages of cooperation over competition may be premature, at least in principle, because of poor sampling of the possible variety of competitive situations. For instance, performance may be best in semicompetitive situations in which a high proportion of competitors receive at least some of a large reinforcer over an extended period of time.

In a factorial experiment, Meeker (1984) systematically varied orientation (to group vs. individual) as well as sex, amount of risk, level of cooperative feedback, and sequence of behaviors. She looked at how these variables affected one's own choices and one's expectations of other's choices. *Reciprocity tendencies* (in a prisoner's-dilemma type situation) may strongly affect behavior *independently* of self interest or of motives such as desire to communicate, need to coordinate, or attempts to influence others. Other variables may affect reciprocity "under some but not all combinations of conditions."

For other general considerations regarding cooperation versus competition see: Baumgartner, Buckley, & Burns, 1975; Bonoma, 1976; Busching & Milner, 1982; Colman, 1982a; Gustafson, Cooper, Lathrop, Ringler, Seldin, & Wright, 1981a, 1981b; G. A. King & Sorrentino, 1983. Also, see Chapter 10, which deals with prisoner's dilemma games and other specific experimental paradigms.

Background Variables

The extent of cooperation and competition may vary according to subjects' age, sex, culture, nationality, race, etc. (Georgas, 1985; M. C. Madsen & Sunin, 1975; C. G. McClintock & Moskowitz, 1976; Munroe & Munroe, 1977; B. O. Richmond & Vance, 1974; Shapira, 1976; Stingle & Cook, 1985; and D. R. Thomas (1976). The direction or magnitude of the differences may be affected by other variables, such as the reward structure (Alvarez & Pader, 1979) and whether a problem's solution is easy or complex (M. C. Madsen & Shapira, 1977). In general, more cooperation has been found among rural/traditional subjects (than among urban/industrial ones). Sex and age sometimes make a difference, but not in a consistent direction, though older children (e.g., 8-year-olds) have generally been found to be more cooperative than younger ones (e.g., 5-year-olds).

Cross-cultural competitiveness may itself be viewed as an (enduring) personality variable. Nevertheless, it has been found that competitors taking the role of cooperators in a lab experiment eventually shift to a view of others typically held by "true cooperators."

In some studies of interethnic or interracial groups, or groups composed partly of handicapped students, "cooperation versus competition" has served as an independent variable (D. W. Johnson & Johnson, 1982, 1985a, 1985b; R. T. Johnson & Johnson, 1982; R. T. Johnson, Johnson, Scott, & Ramolae, 1985). In such cases, cooperation is generally associated with more cross-group interaction and more positive cross-group attitudes.

With regard to physical arrangements: group size and proximity have been found to interact (Seta & Schkade, 1976): four-person cooperative groups outperformed two-person cooperative groups, and undergraduates in the cooperative groups performed better when seated close together. For competitive groups, better performance was associated with the smaller groups and with more distant seating. Communication mode, too, may affect problem solving (cf. Chapter 7). Modes with a voice channel, such as telephone, video, and face-to-face have been found to be superior (but more verbose) than those without one (e.g., teletype); however, the effects were largely independent of whether problems were cooperative (requiring the exchange of factual information) or "conflictive" (Weeks & Chapanis, 1976).

For other studies concerned with background, personality, and group composition, see: W. M. Becker & Miles, 1978; R. J. Brown, 1984; Concha, Garcia, & Perez, 1975; Gotay, 1981; Rabbie, Visser, & Tils, 1976; Rosenfield, Stephan, & Lucker, 1981.

Effects of Rules or Experimental Conditions

The breadth of permissible behavioral repertoire may interact with other effects. For instance, when the repertoire is narrow (and there is little or no "middle ground" for behavior) — but *not* when it is wide — subjects with a competitive orientation may expect more homogeneity amongst their opponents than subjects with a cooperative orientation, and the competitive subjects may behaviorally "dominate" the cooperative subjects (D. T. Miller & Holmes, 1975).

Some beneficial effects of cooperation may be due to the opportunities it affords for discussion rather than to the cooperative structure per se (Schick & McGlynn, 1976).

In a study of the effects of the structure and sequence of rewards (as manifest in instructions): maximum task performance among triads of third graders was found with a reward structure favoring cooperation (equal rewards to each participant on all trials) (D. C. French, Brownell, Graziano, & Hartup, 1977).

Using a simple problem-solving task, Okun and diVesta (1975) found that the *inverse* relation between differential reward structure and group efficiency was greater under conditions of high task independence among group members. Information was found to be more equally distributed when rewards were equal.

Examining the effects of (assigned) power, Tjosvold, Johnson, and Johnson (1984; cf. Tjosvold, 1981, and Tjosvold & Okun, 1979) found that "unequal power seemed to undermine negotiations within a competitive context while not detracting from working relationships within a cooperative context" (p. 141).

Whether a setting is cooperative or competitive may affect one's choice of whom to interact with. Van Blerkom and Tjosvold (1981) concluded that "persons in cooperation may test the validity of their ideas through controversy [choosing a discussant with an opposing viewpoint]; persons in competition may attempt to strengthen their opinion either by choosing a more competent discussant with the same opinion or a less competent discussant with an opposing view."

In an attempt to review the effects of "type of communication" on cooperation or conflict, D. W. Johnson (1974) concluded that progress has been impeded by the lack of a common operational definition of "communication"!

For other work concerned with how the rules of interaction may relate to cooperation/competition (and to associated results), see: Fujimori, 1985; Garibaldi, 1979; Koomen & Sagel, 1977; Kumar & Kaur, 1976; LaFrance, 1985; Olvera & Hake, 1976; D. R. Schmitt, 1976; Simmons, King, Tucker, & Wehner, 1986.

Group Processes

Examining the relationship between expectation of successful group performance and emergent cooperative or competitive behavior, Shimizu (1973) concluded that "group-oriented or cooperative behavior prevailed when the group output was perceived as lower, but not remarkably lower, than the group goal." Several other studies consider the relationship between cooperation-competition and other variables as manifest in social interaction: Hansell, Tackaberry, & Slavin, 1981; Mooij, 1980; Osato, 1983; D. R. Schmitt, 1984; C. Stephan, Burnam, & Aronson, 1979; C. Stephan, Presser, Kennedy, & Aronson, 1978; Tscherbo, 1984.

Additional Research

For other work related to cooperation versus competition see: Ames, Ames, & Felker, 1977; Brousek, 1979; Cohen, 1982; L. Cooper, Johnson, Johnson, & Wilderson, 1980; Emurian, Emurian, Bigelow, & Brady, 1976; Feldens & Rasche, 1983; Holloway, Tucker, & Hornstein, 1977; Janousek, 1979; Kitano, 1972; Knapczyk & Yoppi, 1975; B. A. Matthews, Kordonski, & Shimoff, 1983; E. A. Pepitone, 1980; Rabbie, 1974; Rabbie, Benoist, Oosterbaan, & Visser, 1974; W. E. Scott & Cherrington, 1974; Tyerman & Spencer, 1983.

COMPETITION

Perhaps *conflict* is just a particularly negative and unruly form of *competition*, but the two can in any event be distinguished in the research literature. However, occasionally authors do use the word conflict to cover a task, such as chess-playing, which we here regard as competition. The present section focuses on competition, the next one on conflict and its management, and the one after that deals with mediation and other third-party procedures for resolving conflict. The chapter concludes with a consideration of social dilemmas. Additional research relevant to competition is reviewed in Chapter 3, which includes discussion of the presence of co-acting others. Literature specifically pertaining to education or to developmental psychology has not been directly searched for the present purpose and might contain additional relevant studies.

In a series of studies drawing on stimulus-response theory, Steigleder, Weiss, Cramer, and Feinberg (1978) found that the *cessation* of competition acts like reinforcers in escape conditioning.

Background Variables

Apparently only a few background variables, as related to competition in small groups, have been studied since 1974. For instance, competition can decrease intrinsic motivation in puzzle solving. This was found to occur for both sexes but particularly for females (Deci, Betley, Kahle, Abrams, & Porac, 1981).

At least two studies of the effects of own and other's sex on competitiveness have yielded essentially negative results (Crabbe & Johnson, 1979; Valle, DeGood, & Valle, 1978). However, sex may interact with other variables even where it does not show a significant main effect (see, e.g., R. S. Weinberg, Yukelson, & Jackson, 1980). Alagna (1982) did find that men and women in androgynous and masculine groups had higher expectancies and better performance on a competitive task than did feminine groups. However, this finding would not necessarily hold true for all competitive tasks.

Increased size of group can have a deleterious effect in a competitive situation, according to Kugihara, Misumi, and Sato (1980), who used a situation—similar in principle to that used by Mintz (1951)—in which group members need to "escape" within a fixed amount of time. Also, high achievement orientation has been found to be associated with more realistic competitiveness in task selection—that is, selecting a moderately difficult task rather than a very easy or difficult one—but not in "opponent selection" (groups of high- and low-achievement orientation tended to choose opponents of equal ability) (L. H. Levy, 1976)

Effects of Rules or Experimental Conditions

The few studies in this category mainly represent extensions of earlier work. For example, does competition increase creativity? Roweton's (1982) review of six studies showed inconsistent, or at least inconclusive, results. Competition can increase creativity, but so can a mere practice task. Also, subjects in noncompetitive situations can be "more flexible in their thinking." For studies concerned with other variables, see: Conolley, Gerard, & Kline, 1978; R. Gould, Brounstein, & Sigall, 1977; B. A. Matthews, 1979; Lefebvre & Cunningham, 1974; Roweton, 1982; R. S. Weinberg, Yukelson, & Jackson, 1980.

Group Processes

In at least one controlled experiment, individual performance was not much affected by whether a subject "won" 20 percent or 80 percent of the games (or was in a noncompetitive control condition), regardless of task type (D. L. Gill & Martens, 1977). Perhaps not surprisingly, however, individuals in the 20-percent-win condition were less satisfied with their performance and were more likely to attribute the outcome to external causes. Losing is also associated with diminished motivation (Vallerand, Gauvin, & Halliwell, 1986), which might of course affect *future* performance.

Is competition between teams preferable to competition between individuals? Using a Team-Games-Tournament (TGT) instructional technique (see above, section on Cooperation, subsection on group processes) with American seventh-graders as subjects, Hulten and DeVries (1976) carried out a 2 X 2 factorial experiment with an external control group. Two kinds of reward were used (implying individual or group competition) and two kinds of practice (individual and group). Findings are summarized as follows:

(a) Team Competition subjects improved significantly more on the Stanford Achievement Test (SAT), attached more value to game success, and reported a higher level of peer group interest and pressure to do well at the game than Individual Competition Ss [subjects]. (b) Group Practice Ss did not differ from

Individual Practice Ss on their SAT performance, but they did attach less importance to game success than Ss who practised alone. (c) When compared to the external control group, the Team Competition Ss (standard TGT treatment) had significantly more improvement on the SAT, reported a higher expectancy of success at the game, attached more importance to this success, reported more peer interest in their performance, and were more satisfied with the game task. An expectancy-value motivational theory was used to interpret results. (Hulten & DeVries, 1976, *Psychological Abstracts* 56:4766.)

Competition between undergraduate opponents has been found to be aversively motivating but to have a generally energizing effect (Steigleder, Weiss, Balling, Wenninger, & Lombardo, 1980). Perhaps competition between teams (with varying team memberships) can provide the energizing advantages of competition without the motivational disadvantages.

For an additional study of the "process" effects of competition, see: Krogius (1984). For other studies related to competition in general, see: Martens & White, 1975; Mettee & Riskind, 1974; Neale & Bazerman, 1985b; J. Z. Rubin, Greller, & Roby, 1974.

CONFLICT AND ITS MANAGEMENT OR RESOLUTION

In a multistage model of dispute formation, developed by Bordessa and Cameron (1984), events (a) might or might not be interpreted similarly by each party, (b) may lead neither, either, or both parties to believe there are grounds for a grievance and, furthermore, to pursue the matter, (c) may lead one or more parties to persuade the other(s) of the legitimacy of one's grievance, (d) may or may not lead to negotiation, (e) which might or might not produce a settlement. Depending on the "path" traced through the preceding levels, an active dispute or conflict might or might not arise.

According to Abbey (1982), the early development of many small groups is marked by conflict manifest in the formation of two subgroups, one of which tries to stick to plans and the other of which "seeks novelty and spontaneity." In SYMLOG-like terms (see Introduction and Appendix), the two groups may differ in emphasizing (a) task orientation and conformity vs. (b) expressiveness and anticonformity.

In reviewing his own and others' work—spanning more than three decades—on cooperation, conflict, and justice, Morton Deutsch (1983) concludes that:

1. Few conflicts are intrinsically and inevitably win-lose conflicts. . . . There has been developing a technology of how to help people maintain an awareness of their common interests even as they deal with their opposing interests.
2. If the conflict is not by its nature a win-lose conflict, one should develop and

maintain a cooperative problem-solving orientation that focuses on the interests of the different parties (and not their positions) . . .

3. A full, open, honest, and mutually respectful communication process should be encouraged . . .
4. A creative development of a wide range of options for potentially solving the problem of the diverging interests of the conflicting parties should be fostered. . . .
5. . . . there are resources and effective procedures for dealing with many of the common problems and impasses that often cause a conflict to degenerate into a destructive process. There are potentially helpful third parties . . . (M. Deutsch, 1984, pp. 450–451)

See also, M. Deutsch (1985) for elaboration of his theoretical approaches and for further applications.

Consonant with Deutsch's conclusions, Fogg (1985) describes six variable components for categorizing "creative, peaceful approaches" for resolving conflicts: the parties, basis of conflict, location, timing, nature of involvement, and causes. The analysis is meant to be applicable at all levels, from interpersonal to international, and (as Fogg concludes) provides a useful checklist for researchers, negotiators, and the general public.

In one dynamic model for conflict resolution, parties repeatedly decide among various options: new solutions, ratings, redefining the conflict, gathering more information, and attempting influence (Levi & Benjamin, 1977). Examples relating to the model are drawn from a series of workshops. (The specific conflict issues were supplied by participants, who were Jewish and Arab students in their final year of secondary school.) For an analysis and review of problem-solving workshops — as developed by Burton, Doob, Kelman, and others — see B. J. Hill (1982). Hill concludes that workshops have very good potential for facilitating change but that better ways to assess their success are needed.

Developing what is probably a more "mechanically applicable" procedure, Hammond and Grassia (1985) review studies of cognitive aspects of disputes and give examples of applying "a specially developed interactive-graphics computer program that can assess varying cue weights and functional relations in judgments and communications among people who disagree." Examples have included acquiring land for public open spaces and selecting an "acceptable" police bullet. For a review of simulations of social conflict, see Jandt (1974).

Those who are less optimistic that conflicts can be resolved (or believe that conflict is endemic, including the Marxists) prefer the term "management" instead of "resolution." It depends on what one calls "conflict" and what is considered a "resolution."

One specific unfortunate aspect of much conflict resolution is the creation of "win-lose" situations, that is, one party's gains are another's losses. Likert and Likert (1978) suggest that a "win-win" solution is more likely if an additional step is added to the typical resolution process, after the problem is stated and before solutions are sought. The step is for group members to list the conditions or *criteria* they feel a solution must meet in order to be acceptable to them.

Although there is a substantial literature on third-party efforts at conflict resolution (discussed later in this chapter), a smaller but important literature, reviewed by K. W. Thomas & Pondy (1977), concerns the conflict-management efforts made by parties themselves. In determining the nature and outcome of such efforts, a crucial variable is the intent that each party attributes to the other. (One is at least reminded of Pruitt's goal-expectation theory that cooperation is most likely when parties wish to cooperate and expect that others will do so.)

Is external conflict associated with internal cohesiveness (the "in-group out-group hypothesis")? Not necessarily, according to A. A. Stein's (1976) literature review. One needs to consider various intervening variables such as whether the group already has some cohesivenes — and whether the external conflict entails a roughly equal threat to the entire group and invokes a feasible "group solution."

For other general issues about conflict and its management, see: J. M. Baxter, 1982; Blake & Mouton, 1984; Blalock, 1987; D. W. Cole, 1983; Druckman, 1977a, 1977b; Hegtvedt & Cook, 1987; Kayser, 1982; Lawler, 1986; Lewicki & Litterer, 1985 (labor negotiation); C. W. Moore, 1986; Oberschall, 1978; N. Perry, 1974; Steinfatt & Miller, 1974. For a taxonomy of levels of interpersonal conflict — and applications in reducing conflict — see Kelley (1987).

Background Variables

Some widespread misconceptions about human violence are addressed in a brief statement by David Adams and 19 other scientists from a variety of disciplines and countries (1987).

According to a review by Frost (1980), men and women may typically learn different strategies for dealing with conflict and may speak differently (women learning more expressive speech and men using more task-oriented language). Sex differences in the conflict strategies employed by undergraduates are reported by Fitzpatrick and Winke (1979). "With an opposite-sex other, regardless of the level of emotional involvement, one is more likely to use emotional appeals in a conflict situation than one is with a same-sex friend" (p. 9). Males favor "non-negotiation" as a conflict strategy (refuse to discuss a matter or keep repeating things) whereas females tend to use empathy (e.g., talk about "why we disagree"). Issues regarding conflict in all-women groups are discussed by Hagen (1983).

Preferred modes of conflict resolution have also been found to have some (modest) link to personality needs (as measured by the Edwards Personal Preference Schedule — EPPS) and also to actual task effectiveness (R. E. Jones & White, 1985). E. C. Bell and Blakeney (1977) tried to relate personality variables both to preferences among modes of conflict resolution (smoothing, forcing, and confronting) and (in a field study) to actual rated resolution modes. The only clear relationship was between achievement (as measured by the EPPS) and confronting. For other research on the effects of personality in conflict situations, see: Füchsle, Burger, & Trommsdorff, 1983; and Sternberg & Soriano, 1984.

Would one expect "low differentiating" people to be mutually attractive and amenable to conflict resolution? Although interpersonal attraction (and other output variables) may generally depend on degree of match mismatch of personality variables, this "rule" may vary according to situation. For example, attraction may generally follow from a match in "level of differentiation". However, in a conflict-resolving setting, given the "more accommodating quality of low-differentiation persons," dyads with either one or two "low-differentiation" parties showed more reconciliation and more attraction than did (matched) pairs composed of two "high-differentiation" members (Oltman, Goodenough, Witkin, Freedman, & Friedman, 1975).

A review of the possible biological and environmental bases of human conflict is beyond the scope and purview of the present chapter. See, for example: Nelson, 1975; and Zur, 1987.

Previous experience may affect the progress of conflict. In a "negotiable allocation situation . . . inexperienced subjects applied more threats, . . . more often broke off interaction aggressively," and were less satisfied than experienced subjects (Müller, 1981–1982). Whether a previous history of cooperation will inhibit conflict or not depends on the situation (K. Goldman, 1989).

Physical arrangements, such as whether two teams are seated opposite or intermixed, can affect the outcome of negotiations, but the nature of the effect can be complex. G. M. Stephenson and Kniveton (1978) found an interaction between seating position and strength of case. The side with a stronger case was particularly successful in the mixed-seating condition, perhaps because the "seated opposite" condition afforded greater visual access and a *decreased* salience of interparty concern.

In a study comparing face-to-face with television-mediated interaction in a simulated supervisor-worker conflict, the face-to-face groups showed more variability in discussion time and supervisor dominance; Barefoot and Strickland (1982) interpret this as indicating more intragroup conflict in the face-to-face situation because "electronic mediation serves to weaken the forces of emergent leadership."

Conflict resolution may also be affected by the structural relations between concerned parties. For example, a subordinate member of an organization may wish to remain in the organization and to be protected from arbitrary actions, and such wishes may in turn affect which strategies are selected from a "list" such as problem solving, bargaining, appeasing, competing, and withdrawing (Musser, 1982).

For sample studies on the effects of identity and culture on conflict resolution see: Deschamps & Brown, 1983; Leung, 1987; Mackie, 1980.

Effects of Rules or Experimental Conditions

When groups of undergraduates were assigned to one of three conditions — "majority rule" or a "unanimity decision rule" or no decision rule — and role-played the resolution of a task conflict, G. Falk (1982) found that, in unequal power groups, majority rule was associated with increased task conflict, perhaps because the low-power members may form a coalition. (See Chapter 8 for a discussion of decision rules as such.)

Control over choice of decision rule can matter as much as the specific decision rule used in a particular instance. In an experiment carried out by Musante, Gilbert, and Thibaut (1983), all aspects of a *trial* experience were evaluated more positively by subjects who exercised control of rule choice — regardless of their role in the dispute and regardless of "obtaining a preferred rule in the absence of actual choice."

Cosier and Ruble (1981) identified five modes for managing conflict — competing, collaborating, avoiding, accommodating, and compromising — based on a two-dimensional model (dominance/assertiveness and cooperativeness). In a study using business students, the wider availability of choices "resulted in some behaviors that would have been 'hidden' in two-choice experimental games."

If negotiators are accountable to a constitutency, they are more likely to engage in "complex thinking" and to reach integrative solutions (Carnevale, 1985).

Conflicting views can follow as much from cognitive orientation as from the "facts" of a situation. In a study by C. M. Judd (1978), pairs of undergraduates "were assigned attitude positions on how National Health Insurance should be organized." For any two positions, there were areas of agreement and of disagreement; whether the former or the latter were salient depended on whether discussion took place under competitive or cooperative contingencies.

On the whole, "cognitive conflicts," in which two persons think differently about a policy, may be easy to reduce but very difficult to resolve totally (Brehmer, 1975, 1976).

In learning groups, however, the deliberate injection of "conflict" in the sense of *controversy* can promote satisfaction, achievement, and understanding (K. Smith, Johnson, & Johnson, 1981).

Some conflict-resolution research is focused on the results of particular strategies. When will a "pacifist" strategy be successful? In a laboratory study of the effects of eight variables, Reychler (1979) found that a "pacifist strategy tends to be most effective in reducing violence and exploitative behavior when the human distance between the subject and opponent is small, the subject is well informed about the intentions of the pacifist, the subject is required to justify [own] . . . behavior post-facto, and when a partial third party [showing partiality to the subject] is present. . . . The strongest predictors of the effectiveness of the pacifist strategy were the demand characteristics and the image of the pacifist held by the opponent."

A number of studies have been concerned with aggression, sometimes using procedures which may remind one of Milgram's obedience research. Typically, subjects are given a task in which aggressive behavior is potentially elicited. The procedure may permit subjects to administer mild shocks to each other or to ask representatives to (appear to) do so. Many of these studies use only male subjects. In one study, aggression was most effectively reduced if the opponent showed *low counter-aggression* rather than a *matching* strategy (Kimble, Fitz, & Onorad, 1977). In another experiment, with kindergarten and first-grade males, all of the following were associated with lower levels of aggression: task having lower competition, task having lower levels of reward magnitude, and lower levels of rated dispositional aggression (Rocha & Rogers, 1976). The *perceived* aggressive intent of one's opponent may be more important than behavioral involvement (S. P. Taylor, Shuntich, & Greenberg, 1979). Rivera and Tedeschi (1976) reached a similar conclusion, using both male and female subjects.

For other related studies see: Bertilson, Wonderlich, & Blum, 1983, 1984; Borden & Taylor, 1976; Camino, Leyens, & Cavell, 1979; Dengerink & Bertilson, 1974; Dengerink, Schnedler, & Covey, 1978; S. Epstein & Rakosky, 1976; Gaebelein, 1977a, 1977b, 1978a, 1978b; Gaines, Kirwin, & Gentry, 1977; Hynan, Harper, Wood, & Kallas, 1980; S. D. Johnson, 1980; Kingsbury, 1978; Ohbuchi, 1982; Ohbuchi & Saito, 1986; E. O'Neal, Caldwell, & Gallup, 1977, D. G. Perry & Perry, 1976; D. Richardson, Leonard, Taylor, & Hammock, 1985.

For other studies of the effects, on conflict resolution, of various conditions, see: Brehmer, 1974b; Donohue, 1981a, 1981b; Donohue, Weider-Hatfield, Hamilton, & Diez, 1985; Haccoun & Klimoski, 1975; Maitland & Goldman, 1974; Mardellat, 1975; Müller, 1980; Pood, 1980; G. M. Stephenson, Skinner, & Brotherton, 1976; Syna & Pruitt, 1986.

A variety of conflict reducing strategies have been experimentally evaluated with the prisoner's-dilemma paradigm and other simulation procedures. For a discussion of these, see Chapter 10.

Group Processes

In a study by H. McCarthy (1977), based on Hammond's lens model, conflicts based on preexisting beliefs were reduced when subjects were simply allowed free discussion (rather than consensus being required) and when they were not evaluated by "task-accuracy feedback."

Some empirically-derived prescriptions for successful negotiation are as follows (J. Z. Rubin, 1983, *Psychological Abstract* 71:23077): "(a) be aware of the tightropes that confront both parties, (b) avoid the need to impress others, (c) maintain moderate sensitivity to the moves and gestures of the other party, (d) encourage moves that allow the other negotiator to feel competent, (e) avoid commitments to positions of intransigence, and (f) maintain sensitivity to the intensity of the conflict." For a different but similar list, emphasizing the importance of negotiators' rationality, see Bazerman (1983, 1986). See also, N. Beckmann, 1977.

Certain interaction patterns (cf. Chapter 7) have been found to distinguish couples who have sought marriage guidance counseling, compared with those who have not done so. These include, among others, more negative behaviors and more "positive things said in negative ways," higher rates of *reciprocating negative behavior*, more "counter-complaining," less readiness to agree to (legitimate) accusations, more comments on the process of communication itself, and less tendency in conflict situations for the more dominant party to be responsive to the other party's momentary shifts in mood (H. H. Blumberg, Davies, & Kent, 1986, describing work by Krokoff & Gottman, 1983).

Sillars (1980) developed a typology of conflict-resolution strategies based on undergraduate roommates' open-ended descriptions of conflicts. The main categories, "passive-indirect, distributive, and integrative," differ "in the extent to which they promote information exchange and are oriented toward individual vs. mutual goals."

Perhaps contrary to one's expectation, the relationship between number of conflict episodes and quality of subsequent decisions may be *curvalinear* (V. D. Wall, Galanes, & Love, 1987). That is, there was an optimal amount of conflict for good decision making. (However, most of the significant effects in this study were of small magnitude.) Less surprisingly, in the same study, satisfaction was negatively related to conflict; and "integrative conflict-management strategies were associated with higher quality solutions than were distributive strategies."

Conflict (among undergraduate roommates) may *increase* rather than decrease cohesiveness, if it is "communal" (the parties agree "in principle") rather than "principled" conflict (Wheaton, 1974). That is, cohesiveness may grow if there is initial agreement in principle rather than disagreement spanning opposite sides of an issue's neutral point. Alternatively, the explanation for this may be that disagreement across a "neutral point" (or any other specified point) simply tends to span a larger gap.

Interaction strategies and behaviors which lead to peaceful resolutions in some cases (e.g., police officers' typical behavior toward suspects) may, if not modified, aggravate other situations (possibly, e.g., confrontations with civil rights and antiwar demonstrators) (Brent & Sykes, 1980).

Studying conflict in the classroom, Jamieson and Thomas (1974) noted the "prevalent use of coercion" by secondary-school and college teachers, and found that coercion was "negatively related to student satisfaction, learning, and the extent to which teacher influence transcends the classroom. Despite considerable dissatisfaction, students at all levels report relative passivity in attempting to change what occurs in the classroom."

For case examples of creative problem solving – analyzed partly by using field diagrams (such as developed in Bales's SYMLOG) – see Hare and Naveh (1985). For the development of a "language" to describe the moves of parties in a conflict situation (whether nations in the cold war or players in a laboratory conflict), see Pilisuk and Uren (1975).

Other work on the interaction and decision-making processes associated with conflict and its management has been reported by: R. Bell & Coplans, 1976; S. G. Cole, Phillips, & Hartman, 1977; Donohue, 1981a, 1981b; Donohue & Diez, 1985; D. Jacobson, 1981; Knudson, Sommers, & Golding, 1980; Nilsen, 1983; Radford & Larwood, 1982; Sillars & Parry, 1982; Tjosvold, 1977a; V. D. Wall & Nolan, 1986; R. M. Weigel, 1984; Zachary, 1977.

Additional Research

For additional work related to conflict, see: Assadi, 1982; Bazerman, Mannix, & Thompson, 1988; P. D. Blanchard, 1975; H. H. Blumberg, 1990; Boehringer, Zeruolis, Bayley, & Boehringer, 1974; Brehmer & Garpebring, 1974; Földesi, 1978; Goodge, 1978; Kabanoff, 1985; T. C. Kent, 1986; Klimoski, 1978; Kranas, 1982; H. A. McAllister & Bregman, 1986; T. Mitchell & Heeler, 1981; Polozova, 1981; Rohde, 1974; G. L. Rose, Menasco, & Curry, 1982; Rothbart & Hallmark, 1988; T. L. Ruble & Thomas, 1976; Schultz & Anderson, 1984; Tjosvold, 1983.

CONFLICT AND THIRD PARTIES

Third parties can provide mediation, arbitration, and other services. As well as highlighting small-group applications, this section draws slightly on the large *general* literature concerned with third-party intervention. Partisan mediation has already been considered, in the previous section.

J. Z. Rubin's (1980) review extracts three generalizations about third-party services: "(a) Third parties facilitate concession making without loss of face, thereby promoting more rapid and effective conflict resolution . . .; (b) traditional third-party intervention techniques that are effective when conflict intensity is relatively low may prove to be ineffectual and even exacerbating when conflict intensity is high; (c) The parties to a conflict may view third-party intervention as an unwelcome and unwarranted intrusion. To the extent that the disputants can resolve conflict of their own accord, they will" (p. 379).

In reviewing studies of third-party consultation, B. A. Fisher (1983) concludes that there are useful applications in a wide variety of settings — from interpersonal to international but that the underlying theory is very incomplete: The major components include "identity, situation, role, objectives, functions, tactics, and the helping relationship."

Especially in the context of international conflict, a number of social scientists have pointed out the value of bringing disputants together in informal small-group workshops, possibly under the auspices of a prominent third party (see, e.g., J. Burton, 1979; R. J. Fisher, 1980; Hare & Naveh, 1985; B. J. Hill, 1982; C. R. Rogers, 1982; see also, R. K. White, 1986, Chapters 28–30).

Several researchers have provided general analyses. A general paradigm for reviewing a mediated negotiation system has been described by J. A. Wall (1981b). He feels it would be useful systematically to map whether various techniques (such as "clarifies situation," "threatens to quit") are differentially effective in different contexts — for example, presence or absence of constituents, or differing complexity of issues). His large table of techniques might itself be reducible, possibly to SYMLOG-like dimensions. (See the theory section in the Introduction of this book.)

Raiffa (1983) discusses judicial and business mediation, and describes approaches to evaluating the qualities of a good mediator.

According to J. Webb (1982), an arbitrator may have at least two different and contrasting roles — one is to manage a semi-judicial process and the other is to be a joint negotiator with the parties.

For a discussion of the distinctions among third-party consultation, mediation, and coercive bargaining, see Westbrook (1985). (The consultant and mediator are both generally impartial; the mediator and bargainer may both take an active and skilled part in negotiation.) For some other general considerations, see: Bercovitch, 1984; A. M. Davis & Salem, 1984; Holzworth, 1983.

Background and Experimental Variables

Much of the relevant research has been carried out using *simulated* conflicts.

The presence of a third party does not necessarily affect outcomes. Whether it is more important for a third party to focus on interpersonal relations or on "task" appears to depend on the situation and other variables (Sheppard, Saunders, & Minton, 1988; Touzard, 1974–1975). Some procedures (such as "instrumental process analysis") may have a positive effect regardless of the presence or not of a third party (Lipshitz & Sherwood, 1978) or of the attractiveness of the third party (Breaugh, Klimoski, & Shapiro, 1980); indeed third parties with high power (arbitrators) may have more deadlocks and other difficulties requiring them to impose solutions than do low-power third parties. Nevertheless, in ratings by law students and undergraduates, arbitration — entailing high third-party decision control — was the most generally preferred means of resolving disputes, and bargaining procedures were least preferred (Houlden, LaTour, Walker, & Thibaut, 1978; LaTour, Houlden, Walker, & Thibaut, 1976). It is generally an advantage if arbitration (when needed) is provided by the same third party who has attempted mediation (McGillicuddy, Welton, & Pruitt, 1987).

The preferred mode of intervention may vary with the magnitude and intensity of a conflict. At least one study has indicated that less outside intervention may be advantageous where there is *high* bargaining conflict (Bigoness, 1976).

However, in simulated conflicts which permitted concession exchange, disputants preferred procedures in which they controlled the process and partially controlled the decision; "weak-case" disputants wanted the *least* third-party involvement (Heuer & Penrod, 1986; cf. Welton & Pruitt, 1980).

In a simulated conflict resolved by third parties, subjects receiving favorable outcomes were, not surprisingly, more satisfied than those with unfavorable outcomes (Rusbult, Musante, & Solomon, 1982). Those with unfavorable outcomes were more satisfied if the decision was based on a clear decision rule. However, for those with favorable outcomes, satisfaction was greatest if the decision was based on an unclear, undefined rule!

Setting may have a marked effect on preferred methods of conflict resolution; for example, in many labor-management disputes, those procedures which avoid work stoppages but preserve collective bargaining may be preferred (Subbarao, 1978). For instance, in final-offer-selection (FOS) procedures (Chelius & Dworkin, 1980; Starke & Notz, 1981) each side provides a "final offer" and an arbitrator chooses between them.

Some dependent variables, such as deadlock frequencies, may be under the joint control of several factors, including arbitration rules (such as FOS vs. conventional) and perceived risks to negotiators (Haccoun & Turcotte, 1983).

Of course the effectiveness of a third party can vary (R. J. Fisher, 1983) — partly by analogy with the effectiveness of a doctor varying according to the state of medical knowledge. A third party can suggest or request whatever conditions have elsewhere been found (experimentally) to be advantageous — for example, ask disputants to work out a package settlement ("holistic set") rather than deal with issues one at a time (Erickson, Holmes, Frey, Walker, & Thibaut, 1974). Of course, as in R. Fisher's classic (1971) advice, a very complex dispute may benefit from being "fractionated" into fairly separate problems.

For other relevant research see: Bartunek, Benton, & Keys, 1975; Brookmire & Sistrunk, 1980; Crawford, 1982; M. A. Eisenberg & Patch, 1976; Kolb, 1983 (concerns labor mediation); Krebs & Miller, 1985; Lind, Kurtz, Musante, Walker, & Thibaut, 1980; Neale, 1984; Prein, 1984; Touzard, 1975–1976, 1977–1978; Van de Vliert, 1985.

COLLECTIVE DILEMMAS

In collective dilemmas there is usually a "conflict" between group and (in the short-term) individual interests. In a prototypical "commons dilemma" (cf. Hardin, 1968) individuals must choose how much of a "public resource" (such as public-commons grazing for their sheep) they wish to use up. An over-used resource may fail to regenerate itself, a situation in which everybody loses. The prisoner's dilemma game (PDG), discussed in Chapter 10, represents a form of collective dilemma, in that the individual is rewarded for a behavior which is ultimately not to the common good (individual gain and joint gain are *both* higher when parties implicitly cooperate with each other than when two parties both fail to do so). There does not seem to be a sharp line between PDG and other studies of social dilemmas. However, unlike PDG, much of the other research on collective dilemmas uses a "regenerating resource pool," involves more than two subjects, offers participants a spectrum of choices, and uses a variety of situations where a specific "interdependence matrix of rewards" is not necessarily or immediately evident.

In a review of social-dilemma research (including prisoner's dilemma), Dawes (1980) concludes that cooperation is encouraged by factors associated with knowledge, morality/altruism, and trust. M. Lynn and Oldenquist (1986) draw similar conclusions. R. Price (1986), too, provides a brief review of the commons dilemma and how to overcome it. And Schroeder (1983) has reviewed factors promoting prosocial behavior in "social-trap" studies. For a review of altruism and aggression, see Krebs & Miller (1985).

Stroebe and Frey (1982) reviewed several different areas—"experimental games, simulations of market transactions, group productivity, and helping [in emergencies]"—and found, in all of them, evidence of "free riding," especially as group size increases.

In Brechner's (1977) laboratory analog of the commons dilemma, undergraduates, playing in groups of three, could "harvest" points from a common pool. The pool was periodically replenished at "fixed rates" (i.e., new points added for every point remaining in the pool). "The least effective resource management occurred when the [maximum size of] pool was small and no communication allowed."

In a more recent simulation, a common grazing ground is actually represented on a minicomputer screen, and subjects decide how many sheep to graze on each trial (K.Sato, 1985).

Loss of "group motivation" may be due not only to the "social-loafing" and "free-rider" effects (see Chapter 11) but also to what N. L. Kerr (1983) calls the "sucker" effect: If group members see a capable other who is "free riding," then they too may reduce their efforts.

Social traps (Platt, 1973; Brockner & Rubin, 1985)—of which the commons dilemma is an example—refer to any (social) situations where individuals are lured by immediate rewards into an unrewarding situation. A vivid if contrived example is the "dollar auction" (devised by Martin Shubik and studied extensively by Allan Teger—as described by J. Z. Rubin, 1981) in which a one-dollar bill is sold to the highest bidder, but with the proviso that the two highest bidders *both* have to pay in their bids. The highest bids typically wind up being far in excess of a dollar, with economic motives predominating in the early stages of bidding (people hope to win the dollar cheaply) and interpersonal needs (not wanting to lose or be seen to lose) being added for those who continue to make higher bids. Using the Dollar Auction, and more realistic procedures in naturalistic settings, Rubin derives some advice on how to avoid entrapment:

Set limits on your involvement and commitment in advance.
Once you set a limit, stick to it.
Avoid looking to other people to see what you should do.
Beware of your need to impress others.
Remind yourself of the costs involved.
Remain vigilant.

Messick and McClelland (1983) experimentally separated the social and temporal aspects of traps and concluded that the main effects of both aspects were important.

The "public goods problem," where people decide how much to contribute to (rather than withdraw from) a common pool, can be psychologically and functionally different from the commons dilemma even when framed so as to be logically identical. For instance, undergraduate subjects kept more of the resource for themselves in the public-goods condition, particularly if they were in large-size groups (Brewer & Kramer, 1986; see also, Fleishman, 1988).

For some additional general implications of commons-dilemma research, see: Edney, 1980, 1983; Edney & Bell, 1987.

Background Variables

Gifford (1982a) found that even children, three to sixteen years of age, were more effective than expected at managing a commons dilemma. Effectiveness increased with age. There was no main effect of sex, but in the younger groups females were better whereas in the older groups males were better. N. L. Kerr and MacCoun (1985b)—using mixed-sex as well as same-sex dyads of undergraduates—found that both sexes were readier to free-ride on male partners than on female ones, perhaps because "interaction with women, per se, encourages greater effort."

Personality variables may interact with situational ones. For example, subjects high in social anxiety may be more susceptible to instructions (about whether or not it is wise to invest conservatively—see below), particularly if a large audience is present (Brockner, Rubin, & Lang, 1981).

Perceived similarity among group members (using bogus test scores) did not help preserve a resource pool, but a previous experience of the group actually sharing a monetary reward did help (J. S. Baird, 1982).

No differences between American and Dutch subjects were found by Liebrand and Van Run (1985). However, for both cultures, a premeasure of social motives was associated with the quantity of resources taken. Not surprisingly, competitive subjects took most, "followed by individualistic, cooperative, and altruistic" subjects.

Effects of Rules or Experimental Conditions

Some effects of experimental conditions (such as the group advantages of communication) have already been covered in the initial portion of this collective-dilemmas section, dealing with general paradigms. Others are as follows.

The threat of a fine for defectors, or providing incentives (if represented as large price differentials) for group-oriented behavior, may deter socially irresponsible behavior in a commons game (R. B. Powers & Boyle, 1983; Stern, 1976). In a laboratory commons simulating a car pool, providing detailed information about long-term consequences was also effective, but "spot messages" were not (Stern, 1976). An experiment by Komorita and Barth (1985) suggests that bonuses for cooperative choices are more effective than penalties for noncooperative ones. Promoting group welfare may, in and of itself, provide sufficient motivation for cooperative choices (Caporael, Dawes, Orbell, & van de Kragt, 1989).

In a "point-harvesting" commons (Edney & Bell, 1984), all subjects were free to "steal" points from others, which in fact occurred for most subjects and at least helped preserve the life of the common's resources. In groups where individuals earned a share of the *group*'s total score, the group scores were higher and, not surprisingly, "stealing" was less common. Stealing was *less* frequent in groups programmed to experience a "disaster" in the form of an individual (or the entire group) losing all accumulated earnings at some point.

Obviously, the structure of resources and rewards is important. More conservation is likely when rewards are based on a group's combined score than on individuals' scores (Rubenstein, Watzke, Doktor, & Dana, 1975). However, there is more defection if *penalties* (or "costs") are taken from those who harvest most, as compared with a condition in which costs are distributed equally (K. Sato, 1987). Ironically, those in the latter condition were then more likely to vote in favor of having a punishment rule, because they had experienced the consequences of over-harvesting. Also, subjects conserved a resource more if it was already "half-exhausted" at the start of a game.

Brockner and his colleagues have investigated circumstances that moderate the degree of entrapment. Witnessing a model who becomes entrapped (by making increasing commitments in a losing situation) can apparently make one *more* likely also to become entrapped (Brockner, Nathanson, Friend, Harbeck, Samuelson, Houser, Bazerman, & Rubin, 1984). This finding held for both sexes, "on measures of both process [whereby subjects come to be entrapped] and outcome," across different experimental procedures, and for viewing of the model either before or after subjects made their own decisions. However, a "reverse modeling effect" did take place if the model expressed "regret rather than pleasure" or was "unlikable and unintelligent."

Entrapment effects are also weakened if subjects make a public statement of their maximum intended investment, if a decision to *continue* to invest has to be made "actively" rather than automatically (Brockner, Shaw, & Rubin, 1979), or if, early in their interaction, subjects have a chart which makes salient the costs associated with investing (Brockner, Fine, Hamilton, & Turetsky, 1982)—or if subjects are instructed beforehand on the "virtues of investing conservatively" (rather than on the "advantages of investing a considerable amount") (Brockner, Rubin, & Lang, 1981). Perhaps not surprisingly, subjects invested less when the "importance of costs" was highly salient; however, "reward importance had no effect."

Availability of a "compromise" choice, in addition to cooperative and competitive ones, can yield significantly more cooperation (Komorita & Lapworth, 1982a).

Although the laboratory research provides useful demonstrations of collective dilemmas, individual differences in behavior in a particular (laboratory) simulation will not necessarily be significantly correlated with subjects' anticipated behavior in real-world commons dilemmas (Jorgenson, Jenks, & Reaney, 1980).

Motivation and Group Processes

Subjects who believe that others are overusing a resource may, if given the opportunity, be particularly likely to opt to turn decision-making over to an elected leader (Samuelson, Messick, Rutte, & Wilke, 1984).

Poppe and Utens (1986) found that "greed and not fear of being cheated was the major motivation behind not contributing" to a common pool. Discussion can enhance cooperation provided that, in the course of discussion, all subjects promise to cooperate (Orbell, van de Kragt, & Dawes, 1988).

In a laboratory study using undergraduates, Samuelson and Messick (1986b) concluded that harvest size is "governed by self-interest, a desire to use the common resource responsibly, and conformity to implicit group norms."

Additional Research

For other research and analyses concerned with collective dilemmas, see: Brann & Foddy, 1987; Braver & Wilson, 1986; Dawes, 1974; Dawes, McTavish, & Shaklee, 1977; Diekmann, 1985; Edney & Bell, 1987; Jerdee & Rosen, 1974; Jorgenson, 1980; Jorgenson & Papciak, 1981; Klandermans, 1984; Kline, Harrison, Bell, Edney, & Hill, 1984; Liebrand, 1984; Marwell & Ames, 1979; Messick, Wilke, Brewer, Kramer, Zemke, & Lui, 1983; Rutte & Wilke, 1985; Rutte, Wilke, & Messick, 1987a, 1987b; Samuelson & Messick, 1986a, 1986b; Schroeder & Johnson, 1982; Yamagishi, 1986a, 1986b.

SUMMARY

To elicit cooperation, a policy of general reciprocity, combined with the use of unilateral cooperative initiatives to break out of mutual competition is generally effective. Cooperation is more likely in pleasant surroundings, with persons who are perceived to have similar goals, and after some instruction in or experience with cooperative methods.

Cooperation is more effective in promoting achievement and productivity than either interpersonal competition or individual work. Background variables—such as age, sex, and nationality—will have a positive effect on cooperation if they enhance the members' ability to cooperate or make it easier for them to communicate. It helps if subjects are rewarded for their cooperative efforts.

Competition between individuals in a group can reduce performance, especially in large groups with limited equipment or resources that may constitute a "bottle-neck" in production. Competition between teams may increase motivation and performance within each team.

Some conflict and competition appears to be unavoidable and indeed may prevent groups from making decisions that do not consider all the relevant facts or the feelings of all members. Thus it is better for members to create conditions for constructive conflict—for example, by turning situations in which one party's gains are another's losses into "win-win" solutions. If the group members do not possess the necessary experience, skills, or personality traits for conflict management, they may need to seek the services of a third party. The five common modes for dealing with conflict are competing, collaborating, avoiding, accommodating, and compromising. Although compromising may provide some benefits for both sides, collaborating has the highest potential for reaching "win-win" solutions.

In collective dilemmas, in which an individual is rewarded for behavior that is ultimately not for the common good, cooperation is encouraged by knowledge, morality, and trust. In larger groups some individuals may engage in social loafing or become free riders. A threat of fine for defectors, providing incentives for group-oriented behavior, or providing information about long-term consequences may deter socially irresponsible behavior.

Chapter 10

Bargaining, Coalitions, and Games

Herbert H. Blumberg

To follow the example of Charles G. McClintock (1972) and others, much of the systematic effort to quantify social negotiations (defined broadly) can still be classified conveniently under three headings: bargaining, coalition formation, and games. The lines between these "headings" are fuzzy, and sometimes one word (such as "gaming," or "bargaining" itself) may refer to more than one of the three areas.

After the present introduction, these three areas form the main sections of this chapter. However, material on games is in fact split into two sections, the first dealing with prisoners' dilemma games and direct extensions of them; and the second dealing with other paradigms and simulations. The chapter concludes with a discussion of exchange and equity. As with the sequence of chapters in the book as a whole, the main sections of the chapter are organized, internally, so as to begin with background variables and conclude with complex effects of social interaction.

Bargaining is probably the most general of the present topics. Two or more parties may be said to be *bargaining* if they have different perspectives on a matter, and if they are interacting with an (implicit or explicit) view toward reaching an agreed decision. A "party" can often consist of more than one person or other unit. In "fluid" situations, one can study how people "join forces," or break up, thereby *forming coalitions* or dissolving them. Parties who interact under a specific "interesting" set of rules and payoffs, may be said to be playing a particular *game*. One such form, the prisoners' dilemma game (PDG), remains especially widely studied. Most of the research in this chapter is based on small-group settings, but the hope (for much of it) is also to model larger political processes.

For reviews as of the mid-1970s, see: McClintock, 1972, Chapters 9 to 11; J. H. Davis, Laughlin, & Komorita, 1976, pp. 516–525; Pruitt & Kimmel, 1977; Sauermann, 1978a, 1978b. Pruitt and Kimmel pointed out the need to extrapolate from the laboratory to real-life settings, a need which has been only partly realized.

For a bibliography of game theory, written in Russian but covering English-language and other works, see Vorob'ev (1980).

A more recent review (W. P. Smith, 1987) traces the "current concerns with the cognitive and tactical aspects of multiple issue bargaining and conflict in close personal relationships," including "the active role the parties themselves play in the structuring of their conflict" (p. 641). Smith notes that until about 1975 much of the research was atheoretical and restricted to a few paradigms, but that the imbalance has subsequently lessened.

Kahan, Coston, Helwig, Rapoport, and Wallsten (1976) developed a computer program for studying bargaining and coalition formation.

BARGAINING

For a classification scheme to compare and integrate a variety of bargaining models, see Oliva and Leap (1981a). A typology of "metamodels in collective bargaining" has also been developed by Oliva and Leap (1981b). The typology includes a table of strengths, limitations, and examples of both mathematical models—continuous and noncontinuous functions—and verbal models: process (description), forces, limits (of settlement range), and third-party interaction.

For discussion of bargaining mediated by a third party, see Chapter 9.

An explicit bargaining situation, according to Chertkoff and Esser (1976, 1983), requires that parties have at least partly divergent interests, that communication and mutual compromise are both possible, and that provisional offers must also be possible but must not fix the outcomes until an offer is accepted by all parties.

The still-frequent typical experiment:

> involves two people negotiating an economic exchange. The people are given information about the payoffs to their own side [and sometimes for the other side as well] for all possible agreements. . . . Then the two sides exchange offers. . . . the payoff schedule [may be] constant-sum or varying-sum. . . . In a varying-sum schedule, the profits of the respective bargainers do not always sum to the same amount. (Chertkoff & Esser, 1983, p.145)

In examining potential theories of bargaining, Chertkoff and Esser note the usefulness but inadequacies of mathematical utility models, equity theory, and psychological evaluations (such as face-saving, attribution, and level-of-aspiration). Their review of actual findings covers: personality (see below), social relationships, and strategies; and various aspects of the payoff system: minimum acceptable profit point, time pressure, cost of not agreeing, bonuses, the magnitudes and kinds of payoffs, and goals such as maximizing-own-gain vs. maximizing-difference.

Bargainers may typically explore successive frontiers of lower profit for self, making concessions until there is a mutually acceptable outcome. At a given self-profit, some options may be more or less preferred by the other party (or parties). As of Chertkoff and Esser's (1976) review: the form of communication may interact with performance—when communication is restricted to making offers, a competitive orientation may yield higher joint profits than a less competitive orientation. Promises and threats (if they are comparatively nonhostile signals of intentions) may have positive effects, and penalties may have negative ones. Social relationships may affect outcomes—for example: the nature of an appeal may increase concern for the interests of the opponent; bargainers representing constituencies may bargain more competitively; and (depending on extent of disagreement and complexity of issues) agreement may be facilitated by "fractionating" a conflict or, on the other hand, higher joint profit may be realized by working on more than one issue simultaneously. Regarding strategy: up to a point, being "tough (but fair)" usually gives one a more favorable outcome.

Theoretically, people might strive to be fair and would eventually agree on a solution midway between past demands and offers (cf. Bartos, 1977, drawing on Homans's work and the Nash solution to two-party bargaining problems). However, Felsenthal and Diskin (1982b) found that subjects generally failed "to stumble upon the . . . logic of theoretically-fair . . . solutions and/or adopt these solutions in practice."

A rather different paradigm, based on one's expectations of other's strategies— and on an expectation that others will base their strategies on "corresponding expectations"—has been presented by Heckathorn (1980) as potentially applicable at all levels from dyad upward, but requires empirical testing.

R. H. Wagner (1979) suggests that a general theory of two- person bargaining must allow for differences among bargaining situations—particularly, whether agreement is required and whether the bargainers are reasonably familiar with all relevant factors (including each other's utilities). A. E. Roth and Malouf (1979) concluded that some of the main differences between various theoretical predictions and empirical results are probably due to variation in what information is shared by the bargainers.

Viewing negotiation as a decision-making process can help explain the frequent failure to reach optimal solutions; this perspective complements those based on economics, structure, personality, and behavioral systems (Neale & Bazerman, 1985a).

In a review of five major works which extend bargaining research from the typical laboratory experiments, Shea (1980), among other things, tabulates several important dimensions: focus (e.g., industrial relations, interpersonal conflict), major dependent and independent variables, data bases, real-world audiences, and benefits and costs. He offers "simple but useful" advice—for example, negotiators should examine the source of conflict, and they should limit themselves to areas they can affect.

Part of D. T. Miller & Turnbull's (1986) review deals with bargaining and the marked effects of interpersonal expectations. For broader reviews and analyses of bargaining and negotiation, see, for example, Bacharach & Lawler, 1981; Morley & Stephenson, 1977; J. A. Wall, 1985; and four books recommended by Klimoski (1982): Druckman, 1977b; Pruitt, 1981; J. Z. Rubin & Brown, 1975; Zartman, 1978. For a review of bargaining studies in German-speaking countries, see Crott (1981).

Background Variables

Few sex differences have been reported (but see Kimmel, Pruitt, Magenau, Konar, Goldband, & Carnevale, 1980; Knouse, 1980). Especially in competitive cultures (Alcock, 1974; Druckman, Benton, Ali, & Bagur, 1976) female constituents and bargainers have been found to be more cooperative than males. Females may reach the same number of agreements as males but do so more quickly (J. A. Wall, 1976). Perhaps not surprisingly, mixed-sex dyads (but not same-sex dyads) reached agreement more quickly when bargaining face-to-face rather than apart (Vallacher, Callahan-Levy, & Messé, 1979; cf. Turnbull, Strickland, & Shaver, 1976). Negotiators representing female *constituents* may produce more equal outcomes than those representing male constituents (Pruitt, Carnevale, Forcey, & Van Slyck, 1986).

Face-to-face communication can also have a negative effect (S. A. Lewis & Fry, 1977). Carnevale and Isen (1986) found that "only when bargainers were face to face and not in a positive state [not asked beforehand to sort funny cartoons nor given a gift] was there heavy use of contentious tactics, reduced trade-offs, and fewer integrative solutions" (p.1).

Chertkoff and Esser's (1976) conclusions about personality appear still to hold, namely that tougher bargaining is associated with (preexisting or experimentally induced) traits related to people maintaining a perception of high personal strength (cf. Assor & O'Quin, 1982; Benton, 1975c; D. L. Ford, 1983; W. R. Fry, 1985; Huber & Neale, 1986; Tjosvold, 1977b, 1977c; J. A. Wall, 1977a, 1977b).

Perceived attitudinal similarity to one's partner may: (a) elicit bargaining which is less tough but takes longer to reach agreement (Druckman & Bonoma, 1976), and (b) increase the *variance* of bargaining toughness (some partners becoming softer than they otherwise would and some becoming harder). For a review of the concept of bargaining strength, see Komorita (1977; see also, Slusher, 1978).

Trust of others may be either a personality or attitudinal variable. Constituents' degree of distrust of their representatives may lead to more competitive bargaining and fewer agreements (J. A. Wall, 1974, 1975a, 1975b). Using a framework based on Lewin and taking into account "the impacts of personality, perception, expectation, persuasion, and their interactions," B. I. Spector (1977) concludes that "outcomes are more strongly determined by personality and perceptual predictors than by the use of mutual persuasion" (p. 607).

Professional real estate negotiators may have done better than amateurs (graduate and undergraduate students), in a laboratory-type study, but the *patterns* of results were similar (Neale & Northcraft, 1986). The implication is that laboratory findings are likely to be robust across levels of population expertise.

Cross-cultural effects on bargaining competitiveness have been found to be consistent with "cultural orientations" (Alcock, 1974, 1975; Druckman, Benton, Ali, & Bagur, 1976).

The relationships and expectations that one brings to a bargaining session can be important. Close acquaintance can be *negatively* associated with joint profit if people, being less competitive and having lower aspirations, are less concerned with exploring their various payoff options. Using dating couples and also control mixed-sex stranger dyads, W. R. Fry, Firestone, and Williams (1983) found a significant association between Love-scale scores and *de*creased profit. However, subjects who had experienced a conciliatory ("GRIT") strategy have shown higher aspirations and more effective interaction in later integrative bargaining (Lindskold & Han, 1988a).

Much of the bargaining research has focused on dyads; there have been few studies of the effects of group size. However, comparatively smaller groups (7 or 8 members) having a complete communications network were better able to limit the profits of a monopolist member than were larger groups or those with restricted communication (Murnighan & Roth, 1978).

The centrality of one's position in a bargaining exchange network may affect attitudes and attributions toward others (Stolte, 1978a, 1978b), which might in turn affect outcomes.

Merely observing earlier sessions can affect one's bargaining strategy and outcomes. For example, subjects who had previously observed their (present) opponents using a matching strategy presumably expected that the opponents would continue to do so and therefore conceded more than those subjects who had observed a tough or soft strategy (McGillicuddy, Pruitt, & Syna, 1984).

Effects of Rules or Experimental Conditions

Some variables, such as *expectations* about bargaining, can be either part of the background or experimentally induced. In any event, an expectation of future cooperation may be associated with high joint outcomes when resistance to yielding is high; however, when resistance to yielding is already low, expectation of future cooperative interaction may lessen parties' already-low aspirations, thus leading to lower joint outcomes (Ben-Yoav & Pruitt, 1984b).

Experimentally induced cooperative orientation plus unrestricted communication can interact to produce higher agreement (J. G. Greenwood, 1974; cf. D. C. King & Glidewell, 1980). Other investigators (J. W. Schulz & Pruitt, 1978) have found that a team orientation, rather than an individualistic one, produced higher joint outcomes regardless of communication conditions.

When negotiators were set easy, moderate, or difficult goals, high joint (i.e., total) profits were realized when at least one negotiator was set a moderate goal and the other a moderate or difficult one; *individual* high profit was associated with being set a difficult goal (Huber & Neale, 1986, 1987).

The presence of a third-party, even a silent one, can increase the amount of communication in bargaining (Belliveau & Stolte, 1977), perhaps by increasing drive. (See also the discussion of social facilitation in Chapter 3 and of third parties in Chapter 9; see also Grigsby & Bigoness, 1982.) For disputants in a bargaining situation, both mediation and arbitration have been found to be more effective than simple two-party bargaining (Hiltrop & Rubin, 1982); *anticipation* of third-party intervention was particularly effective in small (bargaining) disputes, whereas actual intervention was more effective in large disputes.

There may be an *optimal level* of intervention. J. A. Wall (1979) found that, compared with a control condition, there were more concessions and higher joint outcomes when a mediator *either* suggested concessions *or* rewarded concessions (but each technique was "more potent in the absence of the other").

Accountability to constituents does not necessarily lead to tougher bargaining; for instance, it can lead to increased joint profit if one's constituent expects one to behave cooperatively (Benton & Druckman, 1974; Lindskold & Han, 1988b) or if there is an expectation of cooperative future interaction with the other negotiator (Ben-Yoav & Pruitt, 1984a).

According to the "weakness as strength" paradox, a bargaining *representative* who is free to accept only certain offers ("my hands are tied") may be more likely to have such offers accepted, if they are within the adversary's acceptable range. Otherwise the ploy may "enhance the adversary's intransigence" (Friedland, 1983; see also J. Z. Rubin, Brockner, Eckenrode, Enright, & Johnson-George, 1980).

For other research on the effects of having constituents, see: Benton, 1975a; Breaugh & Klimoski, 1981; Carnevale, Pruitt, & Britton, 1979; Carnevale, Pruitt, & Seilheimer, 1981; Klimoski & Ash, 1974.

Payoff matrix and concession strategies: for studies based on these variables, usually with interesting but intuitively plausible results, see: Bateman, 1980; Dwyer, 1984; Dwyer & Walker, 1981; Felsenthal, 1977; Hamner & Harnett, 1975; Hessel, 1981; and Komorita & Leung, 1985.

To take a sample issue: reciprocating a party's concessions can elicit more concessions and moreover make agreement more likely (Esser & Komorita, 1974; J. A. Wall, 1977a, 1977b). Reciprocity of *non*concessions may lead to more concessions "if and only if concessions were also fully reciprocated" (Komorita & Esser, 1975). Violation of reciprocity may reduce concessions from competitively motivated subjects even more than from cooperative ones (Esser & Komorita, 1975). On the other hand rewarding another party's concessions may lead to one doing more *poorly* than bargainers who do not reward (Bateman, 1980). The relative effects of different strategies (such as hard, soft, or matching) may depend on the context produced by one's initial offer (Lawler & MacMurray, 1980) or on other variables (Michener, Vaske, Schleifer, Plazewski, & Chapman, 1975).

Level of aspiration, as induced by level of rewards, may lead to one obtaining a "better deal" (Crott & Müller, 1976; Crott, Simon, & Yelin, 1974).

For other studies of the effects of various experimental manipulations see:

Batchelor, 1975; Brenenstuhl & Blalack, 1978; Carnevale & Lawler, 1986; Chatterjee & Lilien, 1984; Chertkoff, Sherman, Till, & Hammerle, 1977; Duffy & Kavanagh, 1983; Komorita, Lapworth, & Tumonis, 1981; Lamm & Sauer, 1974; Roering, Slusher, & Schooler, 1975; D. Smith, Pruitt, & Carnevale, 1982; Stech & McClintock, 1981; Tjosvold & Fabrey, 1980; Yukl, Malone, Hayslip, & Pamin, 1976.

In an application of bargaining research, Cialdini, Bickman, and Cacioppo (1979) found that "a consumer could realize substantial savings on the price of a desired automobile by taking a tough bargaining stance."

Group Processes

For solutions to bargaining problems—that is, models which may successfully describe the sequence and outcome of bargaining—see, for example: J. J. Buckley & Westen (1976); Crawford (1980); England (1979); and P. Rice (1979). For an analysis of players' possible "decision rules," and their implications, see R. W. Rosenthal and Landau (1979).

Pruitt (1983b; cf. Pruitt & Lewis, 1975) compared four negotiating strategies. The abstract for the work provides a clear, concise description:

> Analyzes 4 basic negotiating strategies (problem solving, contending, yielding, and inaction); the outcomes that they encourage and the determinants of their use. Problem solving involves pursuit of a formula for reconciling the 2 parties' aspirations. Its outcome is of benefit to both parties when there is a high integrative potential and when both parties maintain moderately high aspirations. Contending involves trying to persuade the other party to accept alternatives that favor one's own interests. Yielding involves reductions in the underlying goals and values sought rather than in overt demands. The ideal is for parties to yield to a point that is compatible with the integrative potential and engage in flexible problem solving. Inaction wastes time and may contribute to a breakdown in negotiation. There are 2 theories of how negotiators choose among the four strategies. The dual concern model suggests that a negotiator encourages the other party to become concerned about the 1st negotiator's outcomes. Feasibility considerations suggest that a negotiator adopt an explicit problem-solving strategy that is clearly understood by the other party. The adoption of such a strategy should encourage the other party to do the same. (Pruitt & Lewis, 1975, *Psychological Abstracts* 55:735)

For a further analysis of concession strategies, see Saraydar (1984).

Comparisons of (in situ) "tough" and "soft" bargaining strategies may yield conflicting results, because soft initial offers may often be associated with tough concession making (because one feels there is little left to give?) and vice versa (S. H. Gray, 1977). The efficacy of one party's strategy may, at least in part, depend on the strategy of the other party and on the "match" between the parties with regard to initial (and successive) offers. J. A. Wall (1977b) confirmed that the rewarding of concessions may elicit more concessions.

Subjects in one experiment preferred to bargain against a "soft reciprocal" strategy—rather than a "tough reciprocal" strategy or a "tough" strategy—and moreover, when bargaining against a [programmed] party with a soft reciprocal strategy, achieved high joint profits "by virtue of the greater number of agreements," despite comparatively low profit per agreement (Seholm, Walker, & Esser, 1985).

O'Quin and Aronoff (1981) investigated the effects of making an influence attempt in a humorous or nonhumorous way. "Humor led to greater compliance and a more positive evaluation of the task, but did not increase liking for the partner. There were no sex differences in compliance, but females did laugh and smile more than males."

For small groups of *large* parties (such as nations), small-group bargaining principles may be "more applicable than not," but one must be very wary about the "wholesale application" of laboratory-derived principles, especially if the effects of large constituencies are not taken into account. (For an analysis of international bargaining, see, for example, Coplin, 1980, Chapter 9 and elsewhere.)

For a review and analysis of the literature on communication in bargaining, see Putnam and Jones (1982).

For other studies relevant to performance and group processes see: Church & Esser, 1980; Crott, Kayser, & Lamm, 1980; Crott, Müller, & Maus, 1978; Hamner, 1974; Hamner & Harnett, 1975; Hessel, 1984; Hiltrop & Rubin, 1981; Komorita & Kravitz, 1979; Lamm & Kayser, 1976; Leng & Walker, 1982; Neale, Huber, & Northcraft, 1987; Pruitt & Syna, 1985; Spindler, 1976; G. M. Stephenson, Kniveton, & Morley, 1977; Tjosvold, 1978a, 1978b; Tjosvold & Huston, 1978; Wadington, 1975; J. A. Wall, 1981a; Weber, 1977; Yukl, 1974, 1976.

Additional Research

For additional work related to bargaining see: Cross, 1977; C. Eiser & Eiser, 1976; Felsenthal & Diskin, 1982a, 1982b; Heckathorn, 1978; Malouf & Roth, 1981; Oliva, Peters, & Murphy, 1981; R. W. Rosenthal & Landau, 1981; Ulvila, 1983.

COALITIONS

Coalition formation has been studied from at least three different perspectives: game theory (which focuses on the different payoffs that coalitions can obtain—and in particular on "solutions, subsolutions, and the core; bargaining set models; and the Shapley value"), social psychology (mainly laboratory evaluations of theories predicting which coalitions are most likely to form and how rewards are to be divided), and political coalitions. Murnighan (1978a) has reviewed and compared all of these perspectives and pointed out the advantages of inter-area collaboration (see also Kahan & Rapoport, 1984a, 1984b). Small groups research would seem to emphasize the social psychological and also game theoretical work, but not to the exclusion of political perspectives. (See, e.g.: Komorita, 1984; Plous, 1987.)

Theories of coalition formation are discussed below, after the sections on background variables and experimental conditions. Coalition formation and dissolution may also be viewed more generally in terms of integration and differentiation processes (Wilke & Van Knippenberg, 1983).

For other general considerations see: Cobb, 1982; K. S. Cook & Gillmore, 1984; Stanfield, Jenks, & McCartney, 1975; and Stanton & Morris, 1987; Stevenson, Pearce, & Porter, 1985 (coalitions in organizations); Wilke, 1985.

Background Variables

Physical arrangements. The "isolate" among three-person roommates may feel more crowded, lonelier, and so on; thus the effects of a physical arrangement may be determined partly by one's place in a coalition structure (D. M. Reddy, Baum, Fleming, & Aiello, 1981). A less-restricted communication channel does enhance a pair's likelihood of forming a winning coalition (Pool, 1976).

Other variables. Group size, sex, personality, attitudinal match, and culture — at least as studied mainly in laboratory experiments — often have some effect on coalition behavior but typically the differences, if found, are small or occur only under certain conditions (Albers, Crott, & Murnighan, 1985; Ashour, 1975; Flaherty, 1980; Helm, Nacci, & Tedeschi, 1976; Kravitz & Iwaniszek, 1984; Lawler, 1975a, 1975b; McBride & Loo, 1978; Murnighan & Roth, 1980; Nacci & Tedeschi, 1976; Valiant-Dyckoff, 1977; Wilke, Van Knippenberg, & Bruins, 1986). The differences which do occur are generally plausible ones — for example, achievement-oriented players prefer moderate-risk strategy options (McGaffey, 1976). For a review of personality-trait approaches as of 1974, see Stanfield (1974).

"Important" (simulated ideological) interpersonal differences may provide a good prediction of coalition behavior (Nicholson, Cole, & Rocklin, 1986). Previous experience, with the experimental situation and/or with particular other players, may affect outcomes (Komorita & Kravitz, 1981; Wilke & Mulder, 1974). Liking may affect coalition formation in the absence of resource differentials; when players differed in both liking and resources, only resources had a significant effect (C. E. Miller, 1981).

Any variable, or combination of variables, which predicts interaction (see Chapter 9) may also predict enhanced "coalition" (i.e., clique) likelihood, for example, a variable such as positive self-perception plus reciprocal perception (Virk, Aggarwal, & Bhan, 1983).

Effects of Rules or Experimental Conditions

In a study varying game structure and players' resources (without confounding the two), Kravitz (1981) found that assigned resources as such had little effect on coalition frequency and reward distribution. Coalition size was negatively related to both likelihood of occurrence and size of payoff. Thus those players did best who potentially could be in the most "small winning coalitions."

Most of the experimental studies are designed to test among various theories, though some also focus on more specific effects such as (a) the power distribution of parties and (b) the payoff structure, including amount and nature of reward, division "rule" (e.g., rewards proportional to outcomes vs. winners-take-all), and (c) other variables such as time pressure and the presence or absence of a "veto" player. (A veto player is one whose presence is required in all winning coalitions – and who, it turns out, can successfully obtain a larger share of the reward than most theories would predict.) See: Folkes & Weiner, 1977; Kahan & Rapoport, 1977, 1979; Kaneko, 1972; C. E. Miller, 1979a, 1981; Murnighan, 1985; Murnighan & Szwajkowski, 1979; Oliver, 1980; A. Rapoport & Kahan, 1981; B. M. Roth, 1979; J. Segal, 1981; Simpson & Punwani, 1975; Tack, 1987.

Theories

Among the theories reviewed by Komorita and Kravitz (1983), "bargaining theory" and an "equal excess" model actually predict obtained changes in coalitions over trials – at least they do so in simple resource-irrelevant games (i.e., in which all players are included in an equal number of "possible" winning coalitions) (but see C. E. Miller & Komorita, 1986). "The bargaining theory assumes that coalition members who are above average in resources will expect and demand a share of the reward based on the proportionality norm [rewards proportional to the resources one contributes], whereas those who are below average will expect and demand an equal share. On the initial trial an outcome midway between proportionality and equality is predicted. . . . after an indefinite number of trials . . . the bargainers will base their demands on their maximum expectations in alternative coalitions . . ., and the reward will be divided proportionally to these alternatives" (Komorita & Kravitz, 1983, pp. 191–192).

The equal excess model is particularly applicable to parties engaged in multiple rounds of coalition bargaining, in *multi-valued* (rather than *simple*) games – that is, different theoretically-possible coalitions have different total rewards for their members. "At the asymptote the model predicts an equilibrium solution in which none of the players in any of the coalitions is tempted to defect" (Komorita & Kravitz, 1983, p.193; see also, Komorita, 1979).

No theory appears to fit all approaches. For instance, there was little support for either an equal excess or a "weighted probability" model in a study by Komorita and Miller (1986; cf. Funk, Rapoport, & Kahan, 1980), which did show that a party's coalition outcomes are separately affected both by the number of alternative coalitions (which modifies payoff shares) and their size (which influences frequencies of coalitions)—and also (on the basis of previous research) their value or profit.

Komorita and Kravitz conclude that there has been little (relative) support for two other theories which predict coalition likelihood and reward division: (a) minimum power theory, which predicts an inverse relation between coalition frequency and the sum of its members' pivotal power indices; and (b) minimum resource theory, predicting rewards to be in proportion to players' resources, and the most likely winning coalitions to be those which have minimum (but sufficient) resources. Support for minimum resource theory occurs only for "resource-irrelevant" games.

Which theories are best may depend partly on "alternative outcomes"—that is, what happens to parties if no agreement can be reached (Komorita, Hamilton, & Kravitz, 1984). Wide variability of outcomes is not well predicted by existing theories but seems best explained by differences in subjects' aspiration levels (Komorita & Ellis, 1988).

In a field study—interviewing members of four-person families—Bonacich, Grusky, and Peyrot (1985) confirmed a hypothesis that coalitions may form to maintain existing status systems.

For a variety of additional experimental comparisons of theories of coalition formation see: Balkwell, 1976; H. Becker & Körner, 1974; Cassidy & Mangold, 1975; Chertkoff & Esser, 1977; Crott & Albers, 1981; Day, 1974–1975, 1975; Flaherty & Arenson, 1978; K. E. Friend, Laing, & Morrison, 1974, 1977; Kahan & Rapoport, 1984b; Komorita, 1974, 1978; Komorita & Brinberg, 1977; Komorita & Meek, 1978; Komorita & Moore, 1976; Komorita & Nagao, 1983; Komorita & Tumonis, 1980; Laing & Morrison, 1973; Lawler & Youngs, 1975; Lawler, Youngs, & Lesh, 1978; Messé, Vallacher, & Phillips, 1975; Michener, Fleishman, & Vaske, 1976; Michener, Fleishman, Vaske, & Statza, 1975; C. E. Miller, 1979b, 1980a, 1980b, 1980c, 1985a; C. E. Miller & Wong, 1986; R. J. Morrison, 1974; Müller & Autenrieth, 1985; Murnighan, 1978b, 1982; Murnighan, Komorita, & Szwajkowski, 1977; Nail & Cole, 1985a, 1985b; A. L. Nichols, 1977; Nitz, 1976; A. Rapoport, 1984; A. Rapoport & Kahan, 1976; H. D. Schneider, 1977, 1978; J. Segal, 1979; Shindelman, 1980; Urruti & Miller, 1984; Webster & Smith, 1978; Wilke, Pruyn, & de Vries, 1978; G. Wolf & Shubik, 1977; Zerschling & Palisi, 1975; Zwick & Rapoport, 1985.

Group Processes

Some of the studies cited above are relevant to group *processes*, but those with a more specific pertinence are considered here.

The variables affecting coalition formation in natural settings appear similar to those studied in the laboratory, but with a different distribution of emphasis (Chertkoff, 1975). For a study of payoffs to political parties in government cabinet coalitions, see Browne & Feste (1975).

In a simulated business setting, S. C. Freedman (1981) found that threat capability produced less compliance than promises, and that threats were sometimes used gratuitously.

Anzai (1977) has developed a computer program which plays as a participant in Chinese checkers and, after the game, decides whether a coalition was formed among the players! Another program, SIMCO, can simulate two of the three players in carrying out investigations of coalitions among triads (Flaherty, 1976).

For other coalition studies bearing on group processes see: Bonacich, 1979; Brams & Garriga Pico, 1975; Brams & Heilman, 1974; Cassidy & Neave, 1977; Coe & Prendergast, 1985; K. E. Friend & Laing, 1978; Kahan & Bonacich, 1980; Kushner & de Maio, 1977; Lawler, 1975a, 1975b; Lawler & Thompson, 1979; Medlin, 1976; Murnighan, 1981; Norton, 1979; Nydegger & Owen, 1977; Thurman, 1979; Van de Vliert, 1981.

PRISONER'S DILEMMA GAMES (PDG)

Pruitt (1983a) has used the phrase *experimental gaming* to refer to a variety of prespecified situations involving interdependent parties; the five most common situations relate to: negotiation, coalitions, matrix games, social traps (reviewed in Chapter 9), and locomotion games. The first three are reviewed in the present chapter as bargaining, coalitions, and games, respectively. Locomotion games have been the subject of little recent research and are covered under Other Games, below.

In a typical Prisoner's Dilemma Game (PDG), two parties must each choose between two options, which are sometimes called C (for Cooperate) and D (for Defect). If both cooperate, then both receive moderate rewards. If one defects, then that party receives a high reward but the other receives nothing. If both defect, then both receive low rewards. Unless the parties can trust each other to cooperate, the temptation for both is to defect and thereby receive only low rewards. The dilemma may be framed in terms of either penalties or rewards.

The goal/expectation hypothesis, developed by Pruitt and Kimmel (1977), fits a variety of findings from studies based on the prisoner's dilemma paradigm (PDG). It predicts that parties are most likely to cooperate if they have a *goal* of achieving mutual cooperation and an *expectation* that the other party or parties are also likely to cooperate.

To test the potential effectiveness of different strategies, Axelrod (1980a) carried out a "computer tournament," where (for any given round) each "party" in an iterated (multiply repeated) PDG was a programmed rendition of one of the "decision procedures" submitted by experts from various disciplines. "The results . . . demonstrate that there are subtle reasons . . . to cooperate as long as the other side does, to be somewhat forgiving, and to be optimistic about the other side's responsiveness" (Axelrod, 1980a, p.3; see also, Bonacich, 1985); being "provocable" is also important (Axelrod, 1980b).

In a study testing for various effects and interactions, Murnighan and Roth (1983) found that cooperation increased with the "probability that the game would continue"—though this finding varied with different payoff structures. These variables were among those included in an "equilibrium model" for predicting PDG interactions.

According to Sommer (1982), PDG research might have more impact if applied to a wider range of issues, including studies of increased relevance to the criminal justice system.

For general considerations of PDG and other paradigms see: Brams & Kilgour, 1987; Downing, 1975; N. Howard, 1976; Krivohlavy, 1976; Tyszka & Grzelak, 1976.

Background Variables

Spatial arrangement. As with bargaining studies in general, the effects of playing a PDG face-to-face (vs. in separate cubicles) may interact with other variables: for instance, subjects who were "concrete" information processors (but not those who were "abstract") cooperated most when face-to-face (Nydegger, 1980). The effects of face-to-face playing can also interact with how the task is framed (whether the matrix contains minus scores as well as plus ones; Yamauchi, 1982). When one is playing with a person (as distinct from a programmed automaton), ease of communication can of course facilitate cooperation (Enzle & Morrison, 1974), or can also, in PDG, hinder cooperation (Grandberg, Stevens, & Katz, 1975). A. H. Patterson and Boles (1974) found that body orientation and seating distance did not influence cooperation although they affected postgame interpersonal attitudes.

Sex. Sex, too, interacts with other variables—and the effects may be specific to particular populations. Males (but not females) have been found to be more cooperative if partner is described as being of low status (M. L. Clark, 1983). Of course, an *interaction* effect of sex in one study may be consistent with a *main* sex effect (or lack of it) in another study which happens not to vary a particular other relevant dimension. In a Polish study, females were more cooperative than males (Steuden, 1979). In an American study, if subjects were given the opportunity to communicate, females were less likely to discuss strategic matters and in consequence were *less* cooperative than males (Hottes & Kahn, 1974). Sex of the *experimenter* was found to be relevant in a study by Skotko, Langmeyer, and Lundgren (1974): female subjects (but not male ones) showed more competitiveness when the experimenter was male. Sometimes little or no sex difference is found (Grandberg, Stevens, & Katz, 1975; E. A. Hartman, 1974). Complex effects of sex have been found by: Baefsky & Berger, 1974; Beckman & Bishop, 1973; Lacy, 1978; N. S. Smith, Vernon, & Tarte, 1975. See also: G. P. Knight, 1980.

Personality.   Again one finds interaction effects. For instance dissimilar pairs (cooperatively vs. competitively motivated) became more cooperative over time if initially given veridical information about their dissimilarity, but became less cooperative if misinformed that they were in similar pairs (Garner & Deutsch, 1974). In a study using female undergraduates, Tedeschi (1979) found that subjects with prior frustration would establish more credible threats against a defiant partner in PDGs; however, if the frustrated subjects had had an opportunity to "express their aggression in fantasy" by composing a TAT story, they were less likely to use their coercive power. Pincus & Bixenstine (1979) concluded that general *cognitive* abilities were positively associated with cooperative resolution of the PDG. For other studies bearing on personality and motivational effects see: Bennett & Carbonari, 1976; Dornette, 1975; Haley & Strickland, 1986; T. R. Kane, Monteverde, & Tedeschi, 1976; Kuhlman & Marshello, 1975; Misra & Kalro, 1979; A. Pines, 1976; Schlenker & Goldman, 1978; Stix, 1974; Terhune, 1974.

Other variables.   Outcome differences have been found as a function of culture (Bethlehem, 1975), group size (Bonacich, Shure, Kahan, & Meeker, 1976), impression of partner (e.g., more cooperation if one believes that other prefers to cooperate—Braver & Rohrer, 1975—or if subjects believe that they are playing against a real person rather than a computer, Fitting et al., 1976); previous experience (e.g., more cooperative if one *observes* a competitive PDG than if one has actually played in one—Braver & Rohrer, 1978). See also: Apfelbaum & Personnaz, 1974; Braver, 1975; Braver & Barnett, 1976; J. R. Eiser & Bhavnani, 1974; Furnham & Quilley, 1989; Mack, 1976; Pulkowski-Rebellius, 1973).

Effects of Rules or Experimental Conditions

"Opportunity for communication" could depend both on spatial arrangement, discussed above or on other controlled experimental conditions (covered here). However, for convenience, the topic is covered under *spatial arrangement*, above.

J. Fox and Guyer (1978) found more cooperation if each subject's choices were made "public" to others in a 4-person PDG, than if subjects were simply told "how many" of the others cooperated on each round (see also Stults & Messé, 1985).

In general, cooperation seems likely to decrease both with the number of parties in a PDG and with the number of people composing each party (each party can consist of more than one person; a party could, for instance, consist of a predetermined coalition) (Komorita & Lapworth, 1982b; Komorita, Sweeney, & Kravitz, 1980; D. M. McCallum, Harring, Gilmore, Drenan, Chase, Insko, & Thibaut, 1985; cf. J. Fox & Guyer, 1977). Komorita (1976) has suggested that an

N-person dilemma-type game (not unlike the social dilemmas discussed in Chapter 9) has more applicability to the real world than does the more commonly studied two-party PDG.

How a payoff matrix and other aspects of PDG are "framed" can affect outcomes. One example has been given above under *spatial arrangements*. Another example relates to presentation of information in a decomposed matrix rather than a traditional one; the decomposed matrix may be mathematically identical to a traditional one but may make some of the implications of PDG clearer (Pinous & Bixenstine, 1977). More cooperation might be elicited by punishing competition than by rewarding cooperation (J. I. Shaw, 1975).

Playing for real money (rather than just points) was associated with greater consistency within dyads with respect to matched cooperation, but more variability across dyads (J. I. Shaw, 1975, 1976). Competition might sometimes be partly due to "boredom" (J. I. Shaw & Thorslund, 1973, 1975).

Slusher, Rose, and Roering (1978) found a statistical interaction among commitment to future interaction, relative power, and the structure of interdependence (PDG vs. other patterns). For PDG, subjects were more cooperative when committed to future interaction than when uncommitted.

Even being told to "sound angry" can depress cooperative choices (Summerfield, 1975).

For other studies relating to experimental conditions see: Armstrong & Roback, 1977; Bonacich, 1976; Caldwell, 1976; Hama, 1980; Insko, Pinkley, Hoyle, Dalton, Hong, Slim, Landry, Holton, Ruffin, & Thibaut, 1987.

Group Processes

Much of the PDG research concerns how parties are likely to respond to various (programmed) choices made by other parties.

Particularly if the environment is "noisy" (imperfect information between players), one strategy for maintaining cooperation is tit-for-tat but leaning toward cooperation (Mueller, 1987). See also, the general introduction to PDG, above, for a description of Axelrod's "computer tournament."

Laboratory confirmation of the effectiveness of Osgood's GRIT proposals (graduated reciprocated initiatives for tension-reduction) has been provided by Lindskold, both in reviewing others' research (Lindskold, 1978) and in his own experiments (Lindskold, 1979; Lindskold & Collins, 1978; Lindskold & Finch, 1981; Lindskold, Han, & Betz, 1986a; Lindskold, Walters, & Koutsourais, 1983).

For discussion of "spirals of retaliatory exchanges" as a function of frequency and size of threats and punishments, see Youngs (1986; see also: Tedeschi, Schlenker, & Bonoma, 1975). For the development of trust—found to be highest if the other party is perceived as "impotent and good"—see Quigley-Fernandez, Malkis, & Tedeschi (1985). Other effects of experimentally varied strategies are described by: Behr, 1981; Bonoma & Tedeschi, 1974; Braver, 1975; Goehring & Kahan, 1976; Horai & Tedeschi, 1975; G. P. Knight, 1980; Lindskold & Aronoff, 1980; Lindskold, Betz, & Walters, 1986; Lindskold, Han, & Betz, 1986b; McNeel, & Reid, 1975; Michelini, 1975; N. S. Smith, Vernon, & Tarte, 1975; F. Yoshida, 1984; F. Yoshida & Ohmoto, 1985.

Not all of the experiments on strategy make use of a pre-programmed "player." For studies of attributions and strategies, and general considerations, see: Bartholdi, Butler, & Trick, 1986; Downing & Ritter, 1976; Grofman & Pool, 1977; Kuhlman & Wimberley, 1976; Hussy, 1979a, 1979b; Lindskold, McElwain, & Wayner, 1977; Messé & Sivacek, 1979; Murata, 1982; Myers & Bach, 1976; Okuda, 1985; U. Schulz & Hesse, 1978; Srivastava, 1985; Tedeschi, Riordan, Gaes, & Kane, 1983.

Additional Research

For other considerations and research see: Brams, 1975; Brickman, Becker, & Castle, 1979; Henss & Ostmann, 1985; Mikula & Mueller, 1983; Orkin, 1987.

OTHER GAMES AND SIMULATIONS

Much (but not all!) of this section represents a catalogue of references.

The systematic study of people in interdependent situations has been covered by Kelley and Thibaut's interdependence theory, which is concerned with the properties of outcome matrices for various situations and the properties of transition lists for progressions among situations (Kelley, 1984a, 1984b, 1984c; Kelley & Thibaut, 1978; see also, W. Harrison & McCallum, 1983).

Crawford (1985) has reviewed "recent developments in static and dynamic noncooperative game theory and dynamic contract theory," with some emphasis on internal and external implicit contracts and ways of enforcing them. Enforcement methods included incentives derived from investments, legal enforcement, threats to end cooperation forever if the agreement is violated, and maintaining a reputation for quality and honesty.

In a review of the use of games to study conflict, Schlenker & Bonoma (1978) conclude that various criticisms mainly raise questions about theories of conflict rather than about the games which are used to explore the theories.

The metaphor of drama can help to explain the meaning and course of much social interaction (Hare & Blumberg, 1988). (In a similar context the phrase "games people play" was brought to some prominence by Eric Berne's book with that title.)

The Teams-Games-Tournament (TGT) classroom intervention was briefly discussed in Chapter 9, near the end of the section on Cooperation. For a review of earlier research on simulation games in education, see Reiser and Gerlach (1977).

Simulated jury research was covered in Chapter 8.

Social dilemma games were described in Chapter 9, but for a broader discussion of game settings relevant to social dilemmas see Liebrand (1983a, 1983b). A 3x2x2x2 cross-game experiment by Liebrand, Wilke, Vogel, and Wolters (1986) used three types of social-dilemma game (PDG, Chicken, and Trust Dilemma), two classes of subjects (cooperators and defectors), pre- and post- games (before and after bogus feedback), and two kinds of feedback (defecting vs. cooperative majority). In PDG and trust games, defecting feedback was especially effective with defector-inclined subjects.

In a replication of the Deutsch-Krauss trucking (locomotion) game, Pruitt & Gleason (1978) confirmed that the presence of capability of using gates, to block the other party, interferes with cooperation; however, defensive threat capacity (to fine the other for gate use) did increase cooperation. See also: Matsumoto, 1980.

For a bibliography on experimental games, see Guyer & Perkel (1973). For comments on the (quasibiological) evolution of cooperation, see A[natol] Rapoport (1985).

For other general considerations of game research see: Bludszuweit, 1975; Brams & Hessel, 1982; Breckheimer & Nelson, 1976; Cabell, 1974; Chamberlin, 1978; Colman, 1982a; Czwartosz, 1985; Diskin & Felsenthal, 1978; Greenblat, 1980; Greenblat & Gagnon, 1979; Harding, 1986; Kahan & Rapoport, 1981; Katz, 1974; T. D. Lundgren & Loar, 1978; Michener & Potter, 1981; Rijsman & Poppe, 1977; Seibold & Steinfatt, 1979; L. Walker, LaTour, Lind, & Thibaut, 1974; Young, 1977.

Background variables

For developmental, sex, personality, and cross-cultural effects in Maximizing Difference and other games, see: Banerjee & Pareek, 1974; Carment, 1974a, 1974b; Carment & Alcock, 1984; Czwartosz, 1976; M. D. Harvey & Enzle, 1977; Kremer & Mack, 1983; J. C. Levy, 1978; Liebrand, Jansen, Rijken, & Suhre, 1986; Meeker & Hornung, 1976; Pareek & Banerjee, 1974, 1976; Sakamoto, 1980; W. G. Stephan & Kennedy, 1975; Van Egeren, 1979; J. H. White, 1974; Wilke, Liebrand, Lotgerink, & Buurma, 1986.

Experimental Variations

A number of studies by Michener and others have varied the payoff matrix or other variables in order to test the predictive power of various solution concepts: Michener, Macheel, Depies, & Bowen, 1986; Michener, Ginsberg, & Yuen, 1979; Michener, Potter, Macheel, & Depies, 1984; Michener, Sakurai, Yuen, & Kasen, 1979; Michener & Yuen, 1983; Michener, Yuen, & Geisheker, 1980; Michener, Yuen, & Ginsberg, 1977; A[natol] Rapoport, Frenkel, & Perner, 1977; Westen & Buckley, 1974.

One's expectations or comparison level ("CL") may be more important than the absolute magnitude of rewards in determining the frequency of noncompetitive behavior (Friedland, Arnold, & Thibaut, 1974). This finding reminds one of Komorita's conclusion, with regard to coalition formation, that level of aspiration seems to be a key determinant of individual differences. It is also consistent with J. C. Turner's (1987) reminder that social norms and personal identification can have a crucial effect on one's expectations and behavior.

Other experiments have examined the effects of: power (Earle, Giuliano, & Archer, 1983); conflicts of interest and of ideology (Love, Rozelle, & Druckman, 1983); incentives and perceived goal (Braver & Barnett, 1974); communication (Santi & Wells, 1975); interaction of communication and threat availability (W. P. Smith & Anderson, 1975); and additional variables (Enzle, Hansen, & Lowe, 1975; M. Foddy, 1978a; Grzelak & Tyszka, 1974; Kahan & Rapoport, 1975; Kaplowitz, 1977; Shubik, Wolf, & Poon, 1974; Takigawa, 1985; B. Thornton & Ryckman, 1979; R. H. Williams, McCandless, Hobb, & Williams, 1986).

Group Processes

Perception of others' choices can of course affect one's own choices. In a study of whether accuracy of perception would differ for subjects with different value orientations (as measured in an initial series of games), Maki and McClintock (1983) concluded that "Cooperative and individualistic subjects demonstrated comparatively high levels of accuracy . . ., whereas altruistic and competitive subjects' predictive accuracy varied" as a function of the (pre-programmed) other's orientation.

Several studies have been concerned with the effects of another party's using various (programmed) strategies: Enzle & Hansen, 1976; Fürntratt & Weimann, 1980; Huggard, 1975; J. C. Levy, 1978; Matsumoto, 1981; Nishikawa, 1985; Oliver, 1984; Plous, 1987; D. C. Williams & Mueller, 1975; Van Egeren, 1979.

A series of 17 experiments "support the Core [set of all undominated points] as a solution concept when it exists" (Berl, McKelvey, Ordeshook, Winer, 1976).

For a revision of SIMSOC, a game which simulated social interaction, see Gamson & Stambaugh (1978).

For descriptions of the processes involved in various games and simulations see: Brams & Zagare, 1977; Glover, Romero, Romero, & Petersen, 1978; Lendenmann & Rapoport, 1980; Schwanenberg & Huth, 1977; Stech, McClintock, & Moss, 1984; Uray, 1976.

Additional Research

Additional studies and analyses relating to games include: Bernhardt, 1978; Bierschenk, 1978a, 1978b; Bridges & Schoeninger, 1977; Chen, 1975; Codol, 1975a, 1975b; S. Fox, 1976; Grzelak, 1976; Michener, Dettman, & Choi, 1984; Noesjirwan & Freestone, 1979; Seidner & Dukes, 1976; Selten, 1978.

EXCHANGE AND EQUITY

One of the themes in much of the research reported in this chapter has to do with whether rewards get distributed equitably and whether parties make fair exchanges, in the context of bargaining, coalitions, and games. In this last section of the chapter, the theme of equity is reviewed more generally.

For a comprehensive examination of theories of social exchange, see Gergen, Greenberg, and Willis (1980) (cf. W. E. Solomon, 1982). For "incremental exchange theory" – a computer model for the development of social interaction – see Huesmann & Levinger (1976).

Exchanges can differ in their formality (explicit contracts, conventions, etc.); Hardin (1982) suggests that, with narrowly defined issues, social exchange involving rational collective action may be more prevalent in the small group than at societal levels.

In a series of experiments on resource exchange, R. L. Burgess and Nielsen (1974) concluded that the likelihood of an exchange taking place – and the extent to which the exchanger is seen as equitable – are determined by the relative values not only of the resources being exchanged but also of the relative value of any alternative(s) to making the exchange.

A factorial experiment by Michener, Cohen, and Sørensen (1975, 1977) confirms the power of J. S. Coleman's paradigm which uses information on interest and initial control to predict the value of events, the resources of persons, and the eventual pattern of control.

For a category system for coding social exchange in small group interaction, see Hare & Mueller (1979). Fichten (1982) discusses possible predictions (based on social exchange theory) of small-group performance. Social exchange theory has also been applied to family crisis intervention (A. H. Brown, 1975).

Piaget's views, including communicative and intellectual exchanges, are discussed by M. Chapman (1986). Symbolic aspects of exchanges are considered by D. F. Haas and Deseran (1981).

For additional general considerations regarding social exchange, see: Castelfranchi & Parisi, 1984; Conte & Miceli, 1984; Shumaker & Brownell, 1984. See also the section on "exchange and reward patterns" toward the end of Chapter 7.

Equity

A substantial body of research concerns the extent to which rewards are distributed equitably, the extent to which people feel the need for equitable distributions, and the meaning of equitable. (When does equitable mean equal, proportional to need, or proportional to effort or other inputs?) Only some of the research relates directly to small groups, but for an overview of equity theory, see E. Hatfield (1983).

Many of the experiments on coalitions (see above) relate to equity, particularly those which are concerned partly with how the rewards of a winning coalition are to be distributed.

An additional body of literature, following from the work of Tajfel (1970, 1983), deals with the "minimal group." How are rewards to be distributed among a group of hypothetical other people? Typically, some of the others are said to belong to an in-group — or to one's own "group" — and some (to whom subjects may be likely to "allocate" lesser rewards) to an out group.

Some similar research deals not with hypothetical groups but with real ones. In an experiment which varied both group membership and participation in a competition, Ancok and Chertkoff (1983) found that high-performers actually received larger allocations from low-performers than from non-performers or from themselves. A harmful distribution of rewards may occur if, in a particular situation, group members fail to recognize the group-wide benefits of coupling large contributions with proportional rewards (Yamagishi, 1984). Other studies concerned with criteria for reward division, cross-cultural differences, and other factors, are reported by: Carles & Carver, 1979; J. Greenberg, 1978a, 1978b; R. J. Harris & Joyce, 1980; Hayakaya, 1972; Hirose, 1977; Kayser & Schwinger, 1982; Nishikawa & Hirata, 1978; O'Malley & Davies, 1984; Reis & Gruzen, 1976; Shubik, 1986; Surazska, 1986; von Grumbkow & Wilke, 1978.

Background variables. Moessinger (1974) examined developmental changes in making exchanges. Mathes & Edwards (1978) confirmed that physical attractiveness has exchange value in heterosexual interaction. (They hypothesized that attractiveness is associated with erotic pleasure, and one of their experiments confirmed that, predictably, slides of attractive men and women were rated, by the opposite sex, as being more erotic than unattractive slides.) A personality-like scale of propensity to make exchanges has been developed by Murstein, Wadlin, and Bond (1987).

Experimental variables. For a systematic investigation of the "exchange rules" used by subjects to maintain equality in a particular laboratory setting, see Meeker (1979). Subjects used "a variety of strategies, including short- and long-term alternating patterns." For experimental investigations of the effects of different reward structures and other variables see: K. Baker, 1974; Enzle & Lowe, 1976; Greenstein, 1985; Michaels & Wiggins, 1976; Mølm, 1979a, 1979b, 1980, 1981a, 1983; Mølm & Wiggins, 1979; Teichman & Foa, 1975.

Group processes. In predicting satisfaction with a dating relationship, level of reward may be more important than equity as such (Cate, LLoyd, Henton, & Larson, 1982). Nevertheless, in a longitudinal study of dating couples, J. H. Berg and McQuinn (1986) found that satisfaction and relationship longevity could be accurately predicted on the basis of social exchange and other behaviors. For other relevant studies see: Alessio, 1984; B. A. Matthews & Shimoff, 1979; Stolte, 1983.

Additional research. R. L. Burgess and Huston (1979) edited a review of social exchange in close relationships. Eckhoff (1974) has considered exchange and related topics (such as restitution) in terms of principles of justice. For additional research related to exchange and equity see: R. L. Burgess & Huston, 1979; K. S. Cook & Hegtvedt, 1983; Coombs, 1973; Crott & Albers, 1981; Eisenstadt & Roniger, 1980; Garrabé, 1976; Mar & Wright, 1978; Organ, 1974; Reason, 1980. See also several of the papers in Lawler (1985).

SUMMARY

Bargaining involves two or more parties who have different goals or priorities and are trying to reach agreement. Coalitions are formed when some of the parties join forces to seek an advantage. Parties who follow an explicit set of rules and payoffs are playing "games." The most widely studied game is the prisoner's dilemma in which the outcome for a "prisoner" (who must decide whether to "confess" or not) is partly dependent on the decision of *another* "prisoner" to confess or not.

The typical bargaining task is some form of economic exchange in which the final agreed amount is somewhere between the highest and lowest amounts suggested. Total joint profits are often enhanced by increased communication between parties who are tough but fair, though this depends on the particular situation. Tougher bargaining is associated with maintaining a perception of high personal strength. Trust in the other(s) leads to more cooperation and more agreements. In competitive cultures, female bargainers have been found to be more cooperative than males. Persons who are friends may be less concerned with exploring their payoff options, and thus make less profitable decisions.

The presence of a third party, either as mediator or arbitrator, leads to a more satisfactory result. The common negotiating strengths of problem solving, contending, yielding, and inaction are similar to those identified for dealing with conflict in general. Problem solving, that provides a formula for reconciling the aspirations of the two parties, is most effective.

Research on coalitions in small groups has been concerned with predicting which coalitions are most likely to form and how rewards will be divided in the context of a game. In a typical experiment, subjects have an opportunity to form and reform coalitions over a series of trials to maximize their gains. One theory suggests that coalition members bargain to obtain a reward proportional to the resources they contribute. Another theory predicts that eventually coalition members will reach a state of equilibrium in which none will be tempted to defect from the coalitions existing at that time.

In a prisoner's dilemma type game the parties are most likely to cooperate if they have a goal of achieving mutual cooperation and an expectation that the other party or parties are also likely to cooperate. As with other tasks, variations in the setting that facilitate communication — or background or personalities that increase compatibility — will increase cooperation. Similar results are found in research using other types of games.

Part VI

GROUP PERFORMANCE CHARACTERISTICS

Chapter 11

Individual Versus Group

A. Paul Hare

The earliest experimental studies in social psychology in the years 1898 through 1905 were concerned with the behavior of an individual working alone or when others were nearby working on the same task. Recent research of this type is reviewed in Chapter 3 on the effect of the presence of others. In this chapter we review research comparing individual performance with that of a group working on the same task.

For research comparing the productivity of the individual versus that of a group, the task has to be one that is capable of being performed by an individual. There would be no contest if the task required a set of actions to be performed simultaneously that would be impossible for an individual. Although on occasion an individual may choose to simulate a "one person band," the number of instruments that can be played simultaneously is limited. Thus we should not be surprised to find that an individual can be just as effective as a group in many problem-solving situations.

When an individual is performing as part of a group it is not enough to have a good idea, but the individual must also be able to put it across to the other members of the group. Further, if the group is to be involved in the enactment of the idea, the group must be organized to this end. Although task behavior and social-emotional behavior can be analyzed in a number of ways, we introduce two perspectives at this point that may be useful in understanding some of the research that compares individual with group performance in this chapter and groups with groups in the chapter that follows. The first perspective provides a category system for the analysis of levels of creativity and the second a set of dimensions for the analysis of interpersonal behavior. Creativity is a significant element in task behavior while most of the variance in social-emotional behavior can be explained in terms of three principal dimensions.

CREATIVITY

The categories for the analysis of creativity are based on those of I. A. Taylor (1975) and have been developed through several applications (Hare, 1982, 1985, 1986; Hare & Naveh, 1986). Each of the five levels of creativity, listed from lowest to highest, is represented by three examples. The name of the category and the example listed as "a" is taken from Taylor's definition of the category, where Taylor was concerned with major innovations for a whole society. His example for the C1 category was children's drawings, of C2, Stradiavari's violin, of C3, Edison's light and Bell's telephone, of C4, Jung and Adler elaborating on the theory of Freud, and of C5, the ideas of Einstein, Freud, and Picasso. The example given as "b" is based on Stock and Thelen's (1958) observation of small discussion groups. The example give as "c" is derived from the literature on negotiation and analyses of the negotiation process.

- C1 *Expressive*: (a) spontaneous contributions that indicate that a person is warming up for the task, (b) work that is personally need oriented and unrelated to group work, and (c) suggestions that allow a group to bypass a problem without actually solving it.
- C2 *Technical*: (a) contributions or solutions that involve skill and a new level of proficiency, (b) work that is maintaining and routine in character, and (c) providing standard or "textbook" solutions to a problem.
- C3 *Inventive*: (a) ingenuity with materials, providing combinations to solve old problems in new ways, (b) suggesting alternative methods for solving a problem or clarifying already established plans, and (c) providing solutions that involve "trade-offs," so that each party receives some gain.
- C4 *Innovative*: (a) basic principles are understood so that older theories can be extended to cover new areas, (b) active problem solving by introducing new points of view, and (c) "extending the margins" of concepts to fit new situations.
- C5 *Emergentive*: (a) involves the most abstract ideational principles or assumptions underlying a body of art or science, (b) work that is highly insightful and integrative. It often interprets what has been going on in the group and brings together in a meaningful way a series of experiences, and (c) suggestions that allow the group to reach consensus through a new definition of the situation.

The assumption is that the level of creativity of a task will influence the motivation of the individual or group member and be related to the individual's or group's ability to carry out the task effectively. For example, tasks requiring low levels of creativity, such as shouting or clapping hands, should lead to low motivation to perform well and more incidents of social loafing. For tasks that require a high level of creativity, the apparent superiority of a group may simply be the fact that more individuals are involved which increases the probability that at least one person of high ability will be present.

Some systems for classifying tasks combine tasks requiring different levels of creativity in the same category. Once this has been done it becomes difficult to sort out the effects of level of creativity on performance. For example, McGrath classifies task in four general types (McGrath, 1984; McGrath & Kravitz, 1982): I. To Generate, II. To choose, III. To resolve, and IV. To execute. Each type includes several subtypes. Type I, to generate, includes "plans" (that probably require creativity at levels 2 or 3) and "creative ideas" (that would seem to require creativity at levels 4 or 5). In contrast, his Type III, to resolve, includes negotiation, bargaining, dilemmas, coalition formation, and allocation. All of these tasks are usually solved by some "trade off," or creativity at level 3. Type IV, to execute, includes contests, competitive sports, wars, and physical tasks. These tasks require creativity at level 2, skill. Over all, McGrath's types seem to be listed according to the level of creativity involved, with Type I requiring the highest levels of creativity, on the average, and Type IV requiring the lowest levels of creativity. Additional examples of the effect of the level of creativity required by the task will be cited throughout this chapter and the following chapter on group versus group productivity.

DIMENSIONS OF INTERPERSONAL BEHAVIOR

From the mid-1950s when the advent of electronic computers with memories made it possible for social psychologists to intercorrelate a large number of variables representing different types of interpersonal behavior, there has been a search for the limited number of factors (dimensions) that would summarize the major part of the variance in the observations. Time and again a similar set of dimensions was derived whether the observations were of behavior, attitudes, values, or personality traits. Bales (Bales, 1985; Bales & Cohen, 1979; Polley, Hare, & Stone, 1988) places his analysis of three basic dimensions of behavior in the context of a *field theory* that considers every act of behavior as taking place in a larger context that is part of an interactive field of influence. The approach assumes that one needs to understand the larger context (personal, interpersonal, group, and situation) in order to understand the patterns of behavior. The dimensions of the field are represented by three bipolar behavioral characteristics:

1. Dominance versus Submissiveness
2. Friendliness versus Unfriendliness
3. Acceptance versus Non-acceptance of Authority

Dominant members of a group may be high participators, probably extroverts; they may also show a tendency to impose their views on the group. The more submissive members are typically seen as quiet, passive, or introverted. Friendliness is associated with behavior and values perceived as egalitarian, cooperative, or protective of others. Unfriendliness is associated with self-interest and self-protection. The term "authority" refers to a group environment of more or less organized restraints and constraints, widely recognized to have some kind of "legitimacy." Some restraints that have a quality of "authority" are widely accepted, some are not. Those restraints that are accepted by an individual are felt as part of the "conscience." (See also the section on theories in the Introduction.)

Research with a variety of groups indicates that the most effective style of interpersonal behavior for problem solving groups is to be active (dominant), friendly, and accepting of authority (Polley, Hare, & Stone, 1988). The three dimensions of behavior will be used in the analysis of some of the examples of research cited in this and the following chapter.

EFFICIENCY OF THE INDIVIDUAL VERSUS THE GROUP

Since before the turn of the century social psychologists have been interested in the comparison of individuals and groups for the solution of the same types of problems. In the simplest case the task is an individual one and other persons are present also working as individuals. In this condition the effect on the individual is similar to that of the individual working in the presence of others. This literature has been reviewed under the heading of "social facilitation" in Chapter 3. In some cases the individual is stimulated to be more productive (Egerbladh, 1976; Egerbladh & Sjodin, 1981), in some cases less, and in some cases it makes no difference. For example, it may help to have someone to talk to while solving problems (Durling & Schick, 1976), but having others present may not effect the enjoyment of watching television (Sapolsky & Zillmann, 1978). If a second person provides a high-performing role model, then an individual will improve performance (Earley & Kanfer, 1985; D. Gould & Weiss, 1981). In any event, working with others may be more enjoyable than working alone (Garibaldi, 1979).

G. W. Hill's (1982) extensive review of research compares the efficiency of groups and individuals in various types of problem solving. Generally groups are found to be better than the average individual, but seldom better than the best. On tasks that require judgements, groups report fewer but more accurate facts. Group productivity tends to be less than that of individuals if no division of labor is required, if there are major problems of control, or if there is a group norm for lower productivity. Hill concludes that much of the research supports the concept of "process loss" in groups, where potential productivity is defined as the maximum level of productivity that can occur when an individual or group employs its fund of resources to meet the task demands of the work situation. Actual productivity is defined as potential productivity minus loss due to faulty process. Both levels of productivity vary as a function of task demands, member resources, and group process. However there can also be process gain if group members have the capacity to learn or if they receive cognitive stimulation.

Part of the group effect is simply that of having a larger number of persons to remember facts, identify objects, or produce ideas. Thus groups are more productive on tasks of this type, especially for those that require only the lowest levels of creativity (Kanekar, 1982; Morrissette, Hornseth, & Shellar, 1975; G. M. Stephenson, Brandstatter, & Wagner, 1983; Warnick & Sanders, 1980). However, on a decision task, the group may be no better that the best individual member (F. C. Miner, 1984; Zaleska, 1978).

Another group effect is largely statistical, since the average of a number of judgments is usually more accurate than a single judgment. Thus groups are found to be more accurate than the average individual (Laughlin & Barth, 1981). G. M. Stephenson, Clark, and Wade (1986) provide an example of this averaging effect, in this case by requiring that group members agree on their joint judgment. University students, as individuals or in two or four person groups, heard an audio recording of a simulated police interrogation of a woman alleging rape. They were then asked to recall details and answer questions about the interrogation. Group members were required to agree on all responses. A macropropositional analysis of the interrogation was used to classify propositions in each recall protocol in terms of their correspondence to those of the original. The total number of recall propositions and reconstructive and confusional errors did not vary between conditions; however groups produced twice as many "correct" propositions as did individuals. Individuals were more inclined to make evaluative comments, since they gave five times as many "metastatements" as did groups. Recalled propositions were classified as "metastatements" if they made a comment on (a) the content or organization of the text, (b) the subject's own attitudes toward the text, or (c) the motives of characters that were not explicitly stated in the text.

Groups have been found to be more efficient with difficult and complex tasks, such as designing computer programs, that require relatively high levels of creativity (Margulis, 1981, 1984). This effect may result from the fact that a group may contain one excellent problem-solver (Laughlin & Futoran, 1985; M. L. Nichols & Day, 1982), who has more influence on the group decision (Bottger, 1984; Daszkowski, 1981; Kernaghan & Cooke, 1987). If more than one member discovers the correct answer, the group is even more likely to accept the solution (Laughlin & Shippy, 1983). Yetton and Bottger (1982) recognize this fact and suggest that groups would improve performance by adopting a "best-member strategy," and simply endorse the decisions of their best member. It is even better if the "truth" is supported by one additional member (Laughlin & Adamopoulos, 1980).

Groups are less effective if members have difficulty reaching agreement (Kawasaki, 1974), or if members experience anxiety and stress (Kanekar, Neelakantan, & Lalkaka, 1975). Groups may also have difficulty if the task is complicated so that members have difficulty learning from group experience. This is demonstrated in an experiment by S. T. Allison and Messick (1985b) using a "replenishable resource trap" as a task. (See also discussion of social dilemmas in Chapter 9.) When university students arrived in the laboratory they were randomly seated at six computer booths. Subjects were told that they were either working alone or in a group of three or six subjects. They were then informed of the nature of the regenerating resource pool. Each pool initially contained 100 points per subject. Students were then told that they could make withdrawals from their pools using their computer keyboards. After each person had withdrawn points from the pool, it would replenish itself by 20 percent. If the replenished amount exceeded the amount with which each group (or individual) started, subjects were informed that the pool would be truncated back to that initial amount. They were then told that they were to continue making withdrawals until their resource pool was exhausted or until the experimenter terminated the study. Subjects were given experience with the task prior to managing resources in groups. As predicted, individual experience improved subsequent performance more than did group experience.

Individuals will have higher motivation if they are paid directly for their own work rather than for a group incentive plan (London & Oldham, 1977). High achievers prefer to work alone (Ginste, 1976). Zander (1974) suggests that individuals with low motivation may become more highly motivated in situations fostering group motivation for success.

The difference between the average judgment of a set of persons who are not members of a group and a group decision may result from a plurality/majority decision rule used in groups (Tindale & Davis, 1985). A majority decision would not include deviant opinions that would be included in an average. A model to test this and the probability that the best member of a group will be more likely to be correct than the majority is presented by Grofman (1978).

As a side effect, after participating in a group problem-solving discussion, individuals generally do better. Presumably part is due to learning from more highly skilled members and part from experience with the task (Gabbert, Johnson, & Johnson, 1986; F. W. Goldman & Goldman, 1981; Laughlin & Adamopoulos, 1980). The orientation of the group a student lives with at university can also effect individual performance (Moos, Van Dort, Smail, & DeYoung, 1975). For additional studies of the effects of group participation on individual learning or attitude change see: O'Neill & Levings, 1979; N. M. Webb, 1984b.

Some research reports no differences between individuals and groups (G. M. Griffin & Edwards, 1983; T. G. Walker, 1974), and other research suggests that other variables may determine the direction and extent of the differences (Argote, Seabright, & Dyer, 1986; Casey, Gettys, Pliske, & Mehle, 1984; Chalos & Pickard, 1985; Doise & Mugny, 1975; Doise, Mugny, & Perret-Clermont, 1975; Gorman, Gorman, Latta, & Cunningham, 1984; Mesch, Lew, Johnson, & Johnson, 1985; Remus & Jenner, 1979; Tholey, 1973).

SOCIAL LOAFING

In some group situations individuals may put in less effort than they would in doing a task on their own. This phenomenon has been referred to in the literature as "social loafing" (Harkins, Latané, & Williams, 1980; J. M. Jackson & Williams, 1985; Kravitz & Martin, 1986; Messick & McClelland, 1983). Individuals will exert less effort if there is a shared responsibility for the outcome (Weldon & Gargano, 1985) or if they believe their efforts are dispensable (Kerr & Bruun, 1983), especially with tasks requiring a low level of creativity.

For example, the effect of shared responsibility was observed when subjects in an experiment in the United States were asked to shout or clap their hands (Latané, Williams, & Harkins, 1979a, 1979b). University student either performed alone, or in groups of 2, 4, or 6 persons. Although some subjects seemed embarrassed at making noise in public, as was expected, the more people cheering or clapping together, the more intense the noise and the more sound pressure produced. However the amount of sound did not grow in proportion to the number of people, leading the authors to conclude that "many hands make light the work." (See also K. Williams, Harkins, & Latané, 1981.) This same effect was not observed in Japan (Shirakashi, 1984). For another test of the hypothesis, 162 Lennon-McCartney songs were compared according to their popularity. Jointly authored songs were found to be lower in quality than identifiable individually authored songs (J. M. Jackson & Padgett, 1982).

Harkins and Petty (1982), in a series of experiments, find that social loafing can be eliminated by telling subjects that their individual outputs can be identified even when they perform in groups (or by suggesting that there would be an opportunity for participants to evaluate themselves (Szymanski & Harkins, 1987)). Loafing can also be reduced by either increasing the difficulty of the task, for example asking subjects to brainstorm ideas for uses of a knife (easy) or a detached doorknob (difficult), or by giving each subject a different task to perform, for example recoding dots that appear on one fourth of a TV screen. The authors conclude that when subjects perceive that they can make a unique contribution to the group effort, social loafing is reduced even if individual contributions remain unidentifiable. (However, in the long run, it could be counterproductive to tell subjects that individual output is identifiable unless it actually is identifiable.)

For additional research on the relationship between individual contribution and group product see Chapter 3 and: Berkowitz, 1978; Gabrenya, Latané, & Wang, 1983; Gabrenya, Wang, & Latané, 1985; Harkins, 1987; Harkins & Jackson, 1985; J. M. Jackson & Harkins, 1985; Kerr & Bruun, 1983; Petty, Harkins, & Williams, 1980; K. H. Price, 1987; M[elvin] L. Snyder, 1976; Yamaguchi, Okamoto, & Oka, 1985; Zaccaro, 1984.

BRAINSTORMING

As a method of enhancing creativity in groups, members are asked to suggest as many new ideas on a given subject as they can, usually without criticizing the ideas of others. At a later point in the group process the ideas are usually evaluated.

However much of the research on "brainstorming" deals only with the first phase by contrasting the number of new ideas generated by groups with the number produced by individuals. Research with tasks such as suggesting new uses for paper clips, corks, or newspapers tend to replicate earlier findings. Sets of individuals working alone produce more ideas than the same number of persons working as a group (Chatterjea & Mitra, 1976; Jablin, 1981; Lamm & Trommsdorff, 1973; D. B. Madsen & Finger, 1978; Maginn & Harris, 1980; Philipsen, Mulac, & Dietrich, 1979; Street, 1974), although some research reports no difference in productivity (Pape & Bolle, 1984).

One reason for the lower productivity of groups may be a "production block," since group members use valuable time as they take turns talking (Diehl & Stroebe, 1987), and group leaders may consume more than their share of the talking time (Ruback, Dabbs, & Hopper, 1984). More ideas are generated by individuals and groups if the problem is unrealistic or irrelevant. O. Harari and Graham (1975) suggest that the effect of knowing that the ideas might actually be used by a familiar organization depresses brainstorming effectiveness. They conclude that the ability to brainstorm is impaired when the task is one that the subjects are genuinely interested in and care about.

Additional research relevant to brainstorming is given by: Andre, Schumer, & Whitaker, 1979; Casey, Mehle, & Gettys, 1981; O. Harari & Graham, 1975. For additional work on creative problem solving, see: Silver, Cohen, & Rainwater, 1988.

STATISTICAL POOLING

Given some of the problems of having subjects actually work in groups, various systems have been suggested to take advantage of the problem solving abilities of a number of individuals without actually having them interact in a group (Boje & Murnighan, 1982), such as "social judgment analysis," "nominal group technique," and "Delphi technique" (Brightman, Lewis, & Verhoeven, 1983; G. E. Burton, 1987; Hegedus & Rasmussen, 1986; Rohrbaugh, 1979, 1981; Vroman, 1975). The sets of individuals who are not group members but whose products are combined by some method are sometimes called "nominal" groups. In one experiment the nominal groups made more errors than real groups (Kanekar, Libby, Engels, & Jahn, 1978). Presumably this occurs because of the possibility that someone in a group may catch errors. In many cases a group decision can be simulated simply by averaging the individual opinions of the members before discussion. For example, McLaughlin and Jordan (1975) asked groups of three university students to evaluate persons with affectively consistent personality traits. The group impression was accurately predicted from a simple averaging of each individual's initial impression. However, group impressions of persons with affectively incongruent personality profiles were best predicted by a weighted averaging model, with the weights derived from each individual member's proportion of total utterances having to do with task control.

RISKY SHIFT

During the 1960s and 1970s a rash of experiments were performed to test the hypothesis that an individual would shift to a more risky position when taking part in a group judgment. After a considerable amount of research it was concluded that judgments might become more risky or more conservative, depending upon the situation, so the research was then labeled "choice shift." The same factors appeared to influence group decisions involving risk as any other type of group decision, including the facts involved, the extent to which the group members felt responsible for the decision, the influence of the majority, and social approval of the type of decision. The literature on the "risky" or "choice" shift is reviewed in detail in Chapter 8. As examples of the findings in the period covered by this review, some research continues to report greater risk taking in groups (Chlewinski, 1975; Forgas, 1981; Hashiguchi, 1974; Yinon, Jaffe, & Feshbach, 1975), and some reports no difference (Felsenthal, 1979). Some research reports that judgments, as a result of group discussion, become more extreme, leading to polarization (J. Greenberg, 1979; Forgas, O'Connor, & Morris, 1983).

Some research reports variables that increase risk taking for both individuals and groups. Familiarity with a gambling game increases the likelihood of taking risks (Ladouceur, Tourigny, & Mayrand, 1986) as do task instructions emphasizing rewards for risk taking (Dickson, 1978). Personality variables have also been found to be related to risk taking in groups (Plax & Rosenfeld, 1976; Roberts, 1974).

ADDITIONAL RESEARCH

Additional research comparing individuals with groups includes: Bazerman, Giuliano, & Appelman, 1984; Chlewinski, 1984; Damos, 1984; Emurian, Emurian, Bigelow, & Brady, 1976; Janssens & Nuttin, 1976; Henry, Nelson, & Duncombe, 1984; Mathes & Guest, 1976; K. Smith, Johnson, & Johnson, 1981; Weldon & Gargano, 1985.

SUMMARY

For the comparison of individuals with groups and groups with groups in their task performance, five levels of creativity in task performance and three dimensions of interpersonal behavior can be identified. The five levels of creativity range from individual activities that do not contribute to the group goal at the lowest level, to insights that provide a new perspective on a problem or redefine the situation for the group at the highest level. The three dimensions of behavior that define the social field are: dominance versus submissiveness, friendliness versus unfriendliness, and acceptance versus nonacceptance of authority.

A person performing an individual task in the presence of others may do less well, as well, or better than when performing alone. Performance is lower if the other persons interfere with the activity and higher if the others provide high performance roles models.

When groups are compared with individuals on the same task, groups are generally found to be better than the average individual, but seldom better than the best. The productivity of the group tends to be less than that of the same number of individuals if no division of labor is required, if there are problems of control, or if the group develops a norm against high productivity. When groups do appear to be better than individuals, part of the group effect — especially for tasks requiring low levels of creativity — is simply having a larger number of persons to remember facts, identify objects, or produce ideas. The average of a number of judgments is also usually more accurate than that of a single individual. In addition, the result of a group decision by majority opinion may be more accurate than that of the average of the same number of individuals since the majority decision will not include deviant opinions that would be included in the average.

The fact that groups do better than individuals on difficult and complex tasks, requiring high levels of creativity, may result from having at least one skilled problem solver in the group. This is especially true for puzzles for which the correct answer is obvious once one person discovers it. Thus truth wins the group decision. Groups may do less well if the type of feedback they are given makes it difficult to locate the nature of their errors.

Individuals' productivity in groups may be lower if they engage in "social loafing" and put in less effort than they would doing the same task on their own. This is more likely to happen if there is shared responsibility for the outcome, if the individuals believe their efforts are dispensable or cannot be identified, or if their motivation is low. These effects are more likely to result with tasks requiring low levels of creativity.

The group process called "brainstorming" was developed as a method of enhancing creativity in a group by having individuals generate ideas without criticism from other group members. However, as with other tasks, sets of individuals working alone produce more ideas than the same number of persons working in a group. Part of the problem in groups is a "production block" as group members use valuable time as they take turns talking. For both individuals and groups it is easier to produce ideas if there is no limit on their practical usefulness.

Several systems have been suggested to take advantage of the problem-solving abilities of a number of individuals without having them participate in group discussion. In these "nominal" groups individual judgments are combined by some system of averaging.

Some researchers continue to explore the possibility that individuals will make more "risky" decisions when they participate in group discussion. However, the body of research indicates that the factors that influence "choice" in a group are the same as those that influence any other type of behavior, namely attributes of the situation, the group, and the individual.

Chapter 12

Group Versus Group

A. Paul Hare

In this final chapter we summarize the literature on small groups from the point of view of productivity. Given all the variables that can affect social interaction that have been described in the preceding chapters, how do these affect group productivity. How is it that some groups are more productive than others? The most productive groups solve both task and social-emotional problems for the individual members and for the group as a whole. For these purposes the group members must have commitment to a clear goal, and they need a combination of members' personalities and skills, type of group structure, role assignment, morale, and problem solving experience that are appropriate for the task.

MODELS OF GROUP PERFORMANCE

McGrath (1984) presents a general model that links: (a) properties of individual group members, (b) properties of group structure, (c) properties of the surrounding environment, (d) properties of the task/situation, (e) the behavior setting (defined as patterned relations of the standing group and task/situation, and (f) the group interaction process. The group interaction process consists of: form, content, and consequences. Form refers to the communication process and involves modalities and channels of communication and participation patterns. Content refers to the task and interpersonal components of what is being communicated. Consequences refers to the effects of communication, task performance and interpersonal relationship patterns on one another and on the group members.

General discussions of group characteristics and productivity and models are given by: Blake & Mouton, 1981; J. H. Davis & Stasson, 1988; Foushee, 1984; W. M. Fox, 1987; Hoffman, 1979a, 1979b; Humphrys & O'Brien, 1985; Liptak, 1980;

Napier & Gershenfeld, 1983; Ridgeway, 1984; Shiflett, 1979b; Singer, Astrachan, Gould, & Klein, 1975; Sipek, 1974; Sorrels & Myers, 1983; R. T. Stein, 1975; Wisdom, 1985; Zander, 1982.

SATISFACTION AND PRODUCTIVITY

Although competition between members of a group may result in higher total output, high productivity may be purchased at the cost of low satisfaction for the average group member, even though the leader may be satisfied. Usually groups in which members are in competition have lower productivity and lower satisfaction than groups in which the members cooperate (Kitano, 1972). In terms of the three dimensions of interpersonal behavior described in Chapter 11, the members of a competitive group are operating on the unfriendly side of the interaction field, while those in a cooperative group are operating on the friendly side. Both types of groups are task oriented and accepting of authority. Satisfaction with a group experience is positively associated with the friendliness of the group and also the extent to which an individual has been dominant, as is the case with the leader of a group.

M. E. Rosenbaum, Moore, Cotton, Cook, Hieser, Shovar, and Gray (1980) performed two related experiments to demonstrate the relationship between group productivity and interpersonal attraction with pure and mixed reward structures and task interdependence. Groups of three university students were given 15 seconds to construct towers from wooden blocks. In the first experiment, the task was executed either interdependently in the form of a single tower or individually in the form of three separate towers. Reward points were distributed equally (cooperative condition), in relation to contribution (independent condition), or only to the most productive group member (competitive condition). Results indicated that cooperative and independent conditions were associated with greater productivity than the competitive condition only under conditions of high task interdependence, but there was no relation between reward system and productivity for the individualistic task. The competitive condition also impaired taking turns, that would facilitate the process, and led to less efficient, poorer quality products than the cooperative condition. In the second experiment, independent and competitive rewards were combined in different proportions to examine the effects of mixed reward systems on productivity and process. The results of the second study showed that even a small percentage of competitive reward led to lower efficiency and productivity. In both experiments subjects reported higher levels of interpersonal attractiveness in the cooperative condition than in the competitive condition.

As one might expect, if a group is successful, the members may become satisfied as a result (Hagen & Burch, 1985), especially if they receive higher pay (Michaels & McCulloch, 1976).

For additional research on mood and performance, see: Biersner, McHugh, & Bennett, 1977; and Wheeless, Wheeless, & Dickson-Markman, 1982.

MEMBERS' PERSONALITIES

Some personality characteristics are associated with high productivity if all members of a group are similar. These characteristics include being field independent (as opposed to field dependent) (G. Simon, Langmeyer, & Boyer, 1974) and having an abstract orientation (as opposed to a concrete orientation) (H. W. Hendrick, 1979).

For the personality characteristic of dominance (as opposed to submissiveness), creativity was found to be higher for pairs who were both dominant (or both submissive), than for pairs composed of one dominant member and one submissive member (Hlavsa & Podrabsky, 1973). However, a study correlating group member compatibility on three dimensions of inclusion, control, and affection with learning in peer groups did not produce significant results (M. E. Shaw & Webb, 1982). In this case the "learning" was an individual, not a group task.

In mock-jury studies authoritarian persons were more likely to convict defendants and recommend more severe punishments (Bray & Noble, 1978; R. M. Friend & Vinson, 1974; Werner, Kagehiro, & Strube, 1982). High and low authoritarians also differ in the extent to which they are influenced by the sex and moral character of the defendant (Siegel & Mitchell, 1979), defendant-juror attitude dissimilarity (H. E. Mitchell & Byrne, 1973), and testimony of prosecution and defense (Sue, Smith, & Pedroza, 1975).

In a management simulation game (R. E. Jones & White, 1983), groups composed of persons who tend to manipulate interpersonal encounters (Machiavellians), were more successful that groups composed of persons low on Machiavellianism. They made better strategic and operating decisions.

Schlenker, Soraci, and McCarthy (1976) gave subjects bogus feedback after they had completed a group problem-solving task. Subjects who had high self-esteem felt that their solutions to the problems had not been influenced by other group members in success conditions, but that their solutions were influenced by other group members in failure conditions. Subjects low in self-esteem felt equally influenced in all conditions.

Although groups whose members have compatible personality traits may be more productive (Hewett, O'Brien, & Hornik, 1974), it is also possible that a moderate amount of tension within a group results in greater productivity (R. E. Hill, 1975). (See Chapter 2 on personality characteristics.)

When personality variables and group structure are compatible, productivity will be higher. For example, J. P. Wilson, Aronoff, and Messé (1975) investigated the interactive effects of group structure and members' psychological motivation on productivity. They had noted that two of the motives described by Maslow, safety and esteem needs, had a direct influence on the emergent social structure in groups. Safety-oriented individuals developed groups with authoritarian leadership and hierarchically organized social structures. Esteem-oriented individuals developed groups with democratically shared leadership and egalitarian social structures. The authors predicted that neither motive nor structure alone would control task productivity. Instead there would be lower productivity when the predominant motivational orientation of the group members was incongruent with an imposed groups structure.

Wilson, Aronoff, and Messé used three-person groups of male university students for their experiment. Three hundred students were given a sentence completion test to identify safety and esteem needs. From these, 36 students were selected who had high scores on safety orientation and low on esteem orientation, and 36 with the opposite characteristics. Three-person groups were formed whose members all had either a strong safety orientation or a strong esteem orientation. The task was to construct a model of a building, using small interlocking pieces of plastic blocks, doors, windows, etc. Group structure was manipulated through instructions to each group. Half of the groups (the hierarchical condition) were told that one of them (chosen at random) should take control of the group. The other half of the groups (the egalitarian condition) were told that it was best to share the leadership equally. The total number of plastic pieces used by each group in the construction of the model was used as a measure of output. The average output for groups with hierarchical structures was higher than that for egalitarian structures. However, as predicted, members were less productive when member motivation and group structure were incompatible.

In a similar experiment conducted by Ruble (1976), also with three person groups, groups with members who were high on "internal" control performed better when provided with an opportunity to plan their own procedures. Groups with members who were high on "external" control performed better when a manager planned for them. However, both internals and externals were most satisfied with the self-planning condition.

Friedlander and Green (1977) assumed that group members would develop a group structure that was compatible with their life styles. Undergraduate students in a group oriented course were divided into three sets of groups and given problem-solving tasks. Some groups were composed of persons who placed a heavy reliance on higher authority, some composed of persons who were more "personalistic," wanting to "do their own thing," and some composed of persons who placed a high value on close, intimate relations. The groups in which members valued authority created a bureaucratic structure and were the most effective on the task. The groups with members who were personalistic created an anarchistic structure and were the least effective. Groups whose members valued intimate relations created a collaborative structure and scored in the mid-range.

High or low levels of trust were found to alter the incidence of positive and negative social-emotional behaviors, but not communication effectiveness (Ratajczak & Jagoda, 1984).

Response to frustration (being extrapunitive, intropunitive, or impunitive) was also found to be related to problem-solving behavior in groups (Khatschenko, 1982). However, whether group members were oriented toward themselves, others, or the task did not seem to make a difference in one experiment, possibly because high task orientation was required of everyone (Quirk & DiMarco, 1979).

Pollio and Bainum (1983) wondered if funny people would make funny groups that would be better in task performance. They concluded that joking and laughing did not seem to hurt, but did not clearly help either.

Perhaps not surprisingly, groups will perform better if members are high on individual ability (D. L. Gill, 1979; M. E. Shaw & Ashton, 1976; Shiflett, 1979a). Other studies of ability include: M. B. Jones, 1974; Mugny & Doise, 1978; Shiflett, 1976; Shiota et al., 1974. See also Chapter 2.

MEMBERS' SOCIAL CHARACTERISTICS

M. E. Shaw (1981) suggests that groups composed of both men and women may be more effective that same-sex groups when the task requires the different skills and perspectives that are traditionally associated with male and female roles. However mix-sex groups can be less efficient if the presence of members of the opposite sex distracts from task performance. (See also Chapter 2 on sex and group perfor- mance.)

COHESIVENESS

High group cohesiveness, usually measured by the members' willingness to belong to the group, is associated with high productivity (Dailey, 1977; Krivonos, Byrne, & Friedrich, 1976). Identification with a "collective" is especially important in Russia (Dontsov, 1975; Petrovskii, 1976, 1983).

Members of cohesive groups are found to take fewer risks (Yinon & Bizman, 1974), gain new information more efficiently (O'Keefe, Kernaghan, & Rubenstein, 1975), and have better recall of interrupted group tasks (Sheikh & Koch, 1977). In military units under combat conditions, individuals who had been appropriately led developed bonds of identification with one another that were strong and functional in overcoming and escaping danger (C. W. Greenbaum, 1979).

Group cohesiveness has been of special concern in sports groups. Usually friendly interpersonal relations have a positive effect on team performance through increased cooperation (Nixon, 1976; Slepicka, 1975), and increased success leads to a further increase in cohesiveness (Carron & Ball, 1977; Nixon, 1977).

For additional research on cohesiveness, see: J. D. Anderson, 1975; Bagarozzi, 1982; J. R. Ball & Carron, 1976; Dailey, 1978; Hogg & Turner, 1985a, 1985b; Kirshner, Dies, & Brown, 1978; E. McClintock & Sonquist, 1976; M. J. Melnick & Chemers, 1974; Mickelson & Campbell, 1975; Narayanan & Nath, 1984; Nemov & Shestakov, 1981; Pluckham, 1973; W. A. Scott & Scott, 1981; Steck & Sundermann,

1978; Stokes, 1983; Stokes, Fuehrer, & Childs, 1983; W. F. Straub, 1975; D. M. Taylor, Doria, & Tyler, 1983; J. C. Turner, Hogg, Turner, & Smith, 1984; Tziner, 1982a, 1982b.

GROUP SIZE

The number of members in a group considered in relation to the number needed for the task, has been referred to as "manning" or staffing. Tasks may be "understaffed" or "overstaffed." Having more members than necessary is found to produce weaker and more variable feelings of involvement (Wicker, Kirmeyer, Hanson, & Alexander, 1976). In a situation where there are less than the required number of persons, members work harder (Perkins, 1982). Overstaffed groups are more likely to reject a deviant member (Arnold & Greenberg, 1980). In a simple task, such as rope pulling, that requires a low level of creativity, individual performance declines significantly with the addition of one or two coworkers, but does not increase with the addition of members up to size six (Ingham, Levinger, Graves, & Peckham, 1974).

See also Chapter 5 — and C. I. Greenberg, Wang, and Dossett (1982).

TASK

In relation to the type of task, individual performance in a group is better if each member has an opportunity to participate in setting the group goal (Erez, Earley, & Hulin, 1985). It is better if all members have the same information (London, 1975), since they may base their decision only on the information they have in common (Stasser & Titus, 1987), and adequate time is allowed for the completion of the task (J. R. Kelly & McGrath, 1985), although time pressure may increase the influence of the leader (Isenberg, 1981).

For additional research on task, see: Kabanoff & O'Brien, 1979b; and Nakanishi, 1988.

COMMUNICATION NETWORK

Groups are more efficient if there is active communication between members (Voicu, 1973). This is more easily done by voice in face-to-face situations rather than by telephone or other methods of communication (Chapanis & Overbey, 1974; Krueger, 1977). It is best if members are seated close to each other (Seta & Schkade, 1976) and can communicate directly with everyone in the group (Shane, 1979). Within groups, the members who participate most are usually the most satisfied (Vanderslice, Rice, & Julian, 1987).

LEADERSHIP

It usually helps to have a leader to coordinate group activity (Babayeva, Voiskunskiy, Kirichenko, & Matsneva, 1983; Eakin, 1975; G. F. Farris, 1972; Harper & Askling, 1980; Solem, 1976; Valentinova & Myedvyedyev, 1973). However, in a comparison of university undergraduate tutorial meetings, with and without a tutor present, students participated more and felt they learned more when the tutor was absent (J. P. Powell, 1974)!

Individuals who attempt to provide leadership are rewarded (J. S. Williams, Gray, & von Broembsen, 1976). If the group members seem especially passive, Gustafson (1976) suggests that the source of the problem may lie in intergroup difficulties, patterns of shared magical thinking, or negative judgements about the safety of the situation for individual contributions.

DECISION RULES

Various decision rules were noted, in the previous chapter and in Chapter 8, to combine individual decisions in "nominal" groups so that the result would approximate group decisions without having the individuals actually meet. When a group does meet, almost any decision rule is likely to be better than having no rule at all since it leads members to be more systematic in their consideration of the facts and the members' abilities. For example, a simple rule is "truth wins" in which a group is given credit for solving a problem if any member solves the problem (Egerbladh, 1981).

Even without a conscious decision rule, if the correct answer to a problem is clear, group members will adopt it after it has been suggested by one of the members. This effect is evident in an experiment by Laughlin and Bitz (1975) comparing individuals and cooperative pairs in their ability to discover "remote associations." University students first took a test consisting of 30 sets of three words which could be related in some way by a common remote association. For example, the three words *cookies*, *sixteen*, and *heart* can be related by the common association *sweet*. By definition, the items in the test are postulated to be "insight" or "eureka" tasks in which the correct answer is immediately evident and accepted once it is proposed. Thus the authors expected that pairs of individuals should be able to perform at least as well as their best member, and should exceed their individual performance to the extent that each member knows items not known in common by both members. For the experiment, six types of pairs were formed from combinations of students whose performance on the first test was either high, medium, or low. The same test was given again to the pairs, who were instructed to agree on a common response for each item. As predicted, regardless of the combination of abilities, a pair was more likely to choose the correct answer, if it occurred to one of them, than to choose an incorrect answer.

A variety of decision processes have been suggested with different emphases, some including computers: Social Participation Allocation Network (SPAN) (Gilmartin & MacKinnon, 1974), Program Planning Model (PPM) (Van de Ven, 1980), Explicit Norm-Structuring Procedure (ENSP) (Spich & Keleman, 1985), Group Decision Support System (GDSS) (Jessup, 1987), and Brainstorming (Comadena, 1984; Sappington & Farrar, 1982).

Gaenslen (1980) suggests that the most effective group decision process would be to combine trust, desire for unanimity, and "advocacy." The method of "consensus" does this except that the goal is "unity" in which members unite in their commitment to the group decision, in contrast to sharing the same point of view in "unanimity." Nemiroff and King (1975) and Hare (1980) provide experimental evidence.

TRAINING AND FEEDBACK

Training for the group task, feedback about the performance, or previous experience with the same task, all result in improved performance. Research on these topics includes the following:

1. Training: Elman & Rupple, 1978; L. N. Gray, von Broembsen, Kowalczyk, & Williams, 1976; D. W. Johnson, 1977; Kurecka, Austin, Johnson, & Mendoza, 1982; Pyke & Neely, 1975.
2. Feedback: Amir-Elkerbout, 1983; Bleda, 1976; DeNisi, Randolph, & Blencoe, 1983; Garvill & Garvill, 1983; Gear, Marsh, & Sergent, 1985; C. R. Greenwood, Hops, Delquadri, & Guild, 1974; D. A. Nadler, 1979; Harackiewicz & Larson, 1986; Turovskaya, 1976; Wiewiorowski, 1975.
3. Video feedback: DiBerardinis, 1978; Walter, 1975b, 1975c.
4. Rewards as reinforcement for good performance: Emurian, Emurian, & Brady, 1985; T. M. Sherman & Smith, 1976.

ALLOCATION OF REWARD

The allocation of reward by members within a group has the effect of giving feedback. When group members distribute rewards to each other within a group, performance, friendship, and level of need determine whether there will be equity or equality (Aikawa, 1981; Benton, 1975b; Elliott & Meeker, 1986; Kayser, 1980; Lamm & Kayser, 1978; Mikula, 1974).

Kahn, Nelson, Gaeddert, and Hearn (1982) examined the process by which the allocation of rewards under equity and equality are achieved. They analyzed videotaped discussions of 24 triads. The choice of a norm for allocation of rewards appeared to be determined by who spoke first, who spoke most, and what norm the person suggested. The evidence suggested that a norm of equity was favored by persons who contributed least to the discussion and equality favored by person who contributed most. In each case the subjects appeared to be interested in maximizing the social rewards in the situation and making a positive impression on other group members, since the subjects suggested a an allocation of norms that deprived themselves of monetary rewards but enhanced the monetary rewards of others.

Related research has been conducted by L. N. Gray, Griffith, von Broembsen, & Sullivan, 1982; J. Greenberg, 1983; W. R. Morgan & Sawyer, 1979; Ogunladc, 1977; Streater & Chertkoff, 1976; Wilke, de Boer, & Liebrand, 1986. See also the last section of Chapter 10.

ATTRIBUTION OF RESPONSIBILITY

The attributions concerning the causes of success or failure for groups are similar to those of individuals (see, e.g., Deaux & Wrightsman, 1988). Group members and their leaders attribute success to skill and effort of the members (Iso-Ahola, 1976b, 1977; Lefebvre & Cunningham, 1977; Schlenker, 1975a). Opposing teams may be blamed for failures (Dorfman & Stephan, 1984; D. L. Gill, 1980). If the leader of a failing group was supposed to be an expert on the task, the members are likely to seek external explanations for their failure (Norvell & Forsyth, 1984).

C. R. Snyder, Lassegard, and Ford (1986) report the results of an experiment on distancing after group success and failure. They tested two image-maintenance processes by which people manipulate their association with others: the tendency to bask in reflected glory as a means of increasing one's association with others who are successful and the tendency to cut off reflected failure as a means of decreasing one's association with others who are unsuccessful. As an experiment, 102 university students were initially involved in a group task and were then assigned to one of three group-performance feedback conditions: failure, no information, or success. Distancing was measured by self report and whether or not the subjects took team badges and wore them. Subjects in the failure group manifested less association with their group than did the subjects in the no-information or success groups. There was also a tendency on the behavioral but not the self-report measures for the subjects in the success group to manifest more association with their group than for the subjects in the no-information feedback group. Thus, more support was found for the "cutting-off-reflected-failure" process than for the "basking-in-reflected-glory" process as an image-maintenance tactic.

Additional research on attribution in groups has been conducted by: Downey, Chacko, & McElroy, 1979; Dustin & East-Trou, 1974; Forsyth & Mitchell, 1979; Forsyth & Schlenker, 1977; Ho & Lloyd, 1983; Howe, 1987; Iso-Ahola, 1976a; R. S. Miller, Goldman, & Schlenker, 1978; R. S. Miller & Schlenker, 1985; Mynatt & Sherman, 1975; Schlenker & Miller, 1977; D. M. Taylor & Doria, 1981; Zaccaro, Peterson, & Walker, 1987.

ADDITIONAL RESEARCH

Additional research on group performance includes: Apfelbaum & Personnaz, 1977–1978; Amabile, 1983; Boalt-Boëthius, 1983; Bouchard, Barsalou, & Drauden, 1974; Brehmer, 1974a; Destephen, 1983a; Dontsov & Sarkisyan, 1980; Doreian, 1979; Emurian & Brady, 1979; Emurian, Bigelow, Brady, & Emurian, 1975; D. L. Ford, Nemiroff, & Pasmore, 1977; Glover, 1979; Godwin & Restle, 1974; J. A. Graham, Argyle, & Furnham, 1980; Graziano, French, Brownell, & Hartup, 1976; Griffith & Gray, 1985; Halmiova & Potasova, 1985; Jablin, Sorenson, & Siebold, 1978; Janssens & Nuttin, 1976; Kronik, 1981; Lynch, 1985; Mallinger, 1981; Materska, 1982; R. C. Mathews, Lane, Reber, Buco, Chaney, & Erffmeyer, 1982; M. V. McGuire & Bermant, 1977; S. A. Miller & Brownell, 1976; C. M. Moore, 1987; M. J. O'Connell, Cummings, & Huber, 1976; Payne, 1981; Pearce & Ravlin, 1987; Pridham, 1975; Putnam, 1983; W. B. Reddy, 1975; Simkin, Lederer, & Seligman, 1983; Tindall, Houtz, Hausler, & Heimowitz, 1982; and Vance & Biddle, 1985; Walter, 1975a.

SUMMARY

Productive groups have a commitment to a clear goal and a combination of members' personalities and skills, type of group structure, role assignment, morale, and problem solving experience that are appropriate for the task. Although competition between members may result in higher total output, there is usually a cost in terms of low member satisfaction. However if the group members are interdependent and some cooperation is necessary, then competition will lower efficiency.

Groups composed of individuals whose personality traits enable them to take initiative, act independently, and act compatibly with other members will be more productive. When possible, group members will develop a group structure that is compatible with their personalities. For example, members who value authority will create a bureaucratic structure and those who value intimate relations will create a collaborative structure. When a structure is imposed on a group, productivity will be higher when the structure fits the personality characteristics.

High cohesiveness, measured by members' desire to belong to the group, is associated with high productivity. In sports groups, group success leads to a further increase in cohesiveness.

For a discussion task, a five member group is optimal. Groups will be less efficient if they have either fewer or more members than those actually required for the task.

Productivity is increased if group members have appropriate information, adequate time for task completion, and a communication network that allows for maximum communication. It usually helps to have a leader designated to coordinate group activity, unless group members are accustomed to sharing the coordination functions. Training for the group task, feedback about the performance, or previous experience with the same task, all result in improved performance.

A variety of decision rules have been suggested to increase group efficiency. All have the effect of leading members to a more systematic consideration of the facts and members' abilities. Even without a conscious decision rule, when the answer to a problem is immediately evident, once it has been proposed by one member, the answer will be accepted by the group.

Group success tends to be attributed to the skill and effort of the members. Opposing teams or other external features are likely to be blamed for failure.

Appendix

Research Methods and Special Types of Groups

A. Paul Hare

RESEARCH METHODS

Reviews of methods applicable to the study of small groups are given in Lindzey and Aronson's *Handbook of Social Psychology* (1985). (See also Cairns, 1979.) In addition, the articles that deal primarily with methodological questions are summarized in the following paragraphs under some of the same headings that were used in the appendix on research methods in the 1976 edition of the *Handbook of Small Group Research*.

Research Design and Experimental Method

Several authors note methodological and design problems in small group research. R. G. Weigel and Corazzini (1978) list a number of problems such as the use of anecdotal evidence, the lack of control groups, and the lack of replication. Ruzicka, Palisi, Kelly, and Corrado, (1979) suggest that many problems could be solved if researchers would use Cattell's Three Panel Model (involving syntality, characteristics of internal structure, and population traits). Bullivant (1978) recommends a move towards a neo-ethnographic approach that includes: (a) a logical inclusion of theory, together with methodology and techniques, (b) a participant-observation approach supplemented by quasi-statistical measures developed ad hoc as required in the field, (c) a concern with studying the influence of context on behaviors in interaction settings, and (d) the use of dialectic questioning as a basic interview strategy. J. D. Greenwood (1983) argues that role playing could be used as an alternative to the traditional laboratory groups to achieve experimental realism. Maier (1975) also uses role playing. Kaul and Bednar (1978) note that independent variables should be specific to the group under study. Mossholder and Bedeian (1983) report that the use of data collected at an individual level to make inferences concerning the effects of group-level processes on individual behavior and attitudes often results in unrecognized inaccuracies. They recommend a multilevel approach. Kenny and LaVoie (1985) propose a model that includes both individual and group effects.

Some of the researchers using the experimental method have proposed innovations. Kano (1973) has designed a laboratory for experimental work, the "group structure analyzer," Petrovskii (1985) offers a "group sensorimotor integrator" for the experimental study of active group emotional identification, and Blakar (1973) recommends the creation of an interaction setting in which subjects are give a false belief that they are sharing the same psychological frame. Laughlin and McGlynn (1986) suggest that an inductive task and yoking methodology will be useful for research on majority and minority influence.

Additional comments on approach and design include: Kaul & Bednar, 1978; Myers, Di Cecco, & Lorch, 1981; R. G. Weigel & Corazzini, 1978.

Observational Techniques and Category Systems

In the years since category systems were introduced for the observation of interpersonal behavior in the 1920s a few researchers have developed comprehensive schemes, but most have concentrated on a particular group role, usually the leader, a special observation instrument, or a particular type of behavior. Tresemer (1976) reviews some of the methods of observation used in both laboratory and field. As examples of these trends Accolla, Geffroy, Abraham, and Schutzenberger (1982) describe a leadership observation grid for objective clinical observation of individuals exercising one or more leadership functions in a group. McCorcle (1982) presents a Group Observation Scoring System designed to be used with a theory that incorporates distinctive features of interdisciplinary task teams, with emphasis on the scoring of seating position.

Albrecht (1985) recommends the use of a video camera for field work, Peery (1978) advocates frame-by-frame analysis of filmed interaction, and Abraham, Geffroy, and Ancelin-Schutzenberger (1980) analyze videotaped segments of group sessions with an observational rating grid. Wicker (1975) uses multiple observers with multiple behavior samples. Ickes and Trued (1985) present a computer program that can be used to summarize dyadic interaction data. Natale (1975a) is concerned with correspondences in vocal level and Sievers and Langthaler (1974) with the frequencies of transitions from one speaker to another.

As a general purpose category system the method of Interaction Process Analysis proposed by Bales (1950) is still in use. Scapinello and Sibbald (1976) compare the results of using Bales's IPA system with Leary's Interpersonal System of Personality Diagnosis.

In the theory section (of this Handbook's introductory chapter), the SYMLOG theory was identified as the most comprehensive system to date. The methods associated with SYMLOG include both questionnaires and categories for the direct observation of interaction at several system levels. Computer programs for data analysis have been prepared by Bales and his colleagues. The SYMLOG Consulting Group can supply a list of available materials (18580 Polvera Drive, San Diego, CA 92128, USA).

Basic categories for use with functional theory, four dimensions of interaction, dramaturgical theory, and exchange analysis are given by Hare (1982).

Several category systems are proposed with emphasis on some particular aspect of group dynamics. Bonoma and Rosenberg (1978) are concerned with social influence, Halliday (1982) with group reinforcement of the individual, Zlate (1984) with perceptions of individual personality, Hartmann (1981) with "conflict of experience" when different interpretations of the "same" reality confront each person, Hirschhorn and Krantz (1982) with unconscious group planning to solve a developmental problem, R. D. Conger and McLeod (1977) with verbal and physical contacts, especially emotional affect, commands, and compliancies, and Lindholm and Lundquist (1973) with independence and cooperation. Elworth and Gray (1982) and O'Brien and Gross (1981) suggest ways to measure the extent to which a individual can be expected to participate in a group task.

Some authors report negative results when category systems are used. C. L. Williams (1981) did not find observations helpful in a study of social conversation. O'Keefe, Delia, and O'Keefe (1980) conclude that standard interaction analysis techniques are unlikely to recover the natural organization of human interaction when the focus in only on the temporal ordering of behavioral acts and sequences.

For statistical analysis of observational data L. R. Anderson and Ager (1978) discuss an ANOVA (analysis of variance) design appropriate for small group research in which dependent variables are derived from individual member responses. P. D. Allison and Liker (1982) present procedures for the analysis of time-series data on behavior in two person groups. Hewes (1985) discusses some of the problems associated with the reliability of observational categories. See also Chapter 7 on scoring systems.

Sociometry

Sociometry, which deals primarily with the measurement of social choice and interpersonal attractiveness, has represented a major emphasis in social research from the late 1930s when Moreno first introduced the approach. It has become an established method for depicting interpersonal choice in a "sociogram." However some current researchers may have lost sight of the fact that the discovery that a person is "overchosen" or "underchosen" in a group does not reveal the type of personality of the individual. Moreno (1953) used "spontaneity tests" for his more detailed analysis. Thus sociometry should be combined with some form of personality or value assessment for a more complete analysis of interpersonal relations. Holban (1972) has done this by developing a sociometric test that identifies dominant personality traits. Kuethe (1975) uses a "blank sociogram" in which, in one version, names are associated with personality descriptions.

Noma and Smith (1978) have developed a computer program to sort out and count the dyads and triads in a matrix of sociometric choices. M. L. Levin (1976) describes computer programs that display sociometric graphs as well as provide for some types of analysis. For statistical analysis of choices, Kolominskii (1974) proposes a "mutuality coefficient" to describe the internal structure of small groups composed of individuals of different ages. Kafer (1976) discusses the problems in using factor analysis of sociometric choices to identify group boundaries and P. W. Holland and Leinhardt (1973) discuss the problems of measurement error. Additional statistical techniques for the analysis of sociometric data are proposed by Alba (1973), Kafer (1976), Kano (1985), Paniotto (1976), and Sherwin (1975).

O. Heller and Krüger (1974) suggest that sociometric data can be obtained by direct scaling of concrete interaction (speaking and feeling angry) between group members. MacNeil, Davis, and Pace (1975) have developed a "sociogame" for use with teenage boys to give a highly unobtrusive measure of status rank.

Additional articles discussing sociometric analysis include: Czapinski, 1982; J. A. Davis, 1977; W. J. Duncan & Beeland, 1980; Doreian, 1986; Eaton, Bonney, & Gazda, 1978; Grove & Hays, 1978; Hunter, 1978; Killworth & Bernard, 1974; Kolominskii, 1974; and Larzelere & Huston, 1980.

Questionnaires

Over the years researchers have used various types of questionnaires for data collection, some involving direct questions, some "Q" Sorts, and some projective. Guzzo, Wagner, Maguire, Herr, and Hawley (1986) suggest that it is better if questions depend on recognition rather than recall of group activity. J. E. Crandall (1977) reports findings on the construct validity of his Social Interest Scale as a measure of attraction of new acquaintances. C. E. King and Christensen (1983) offer the Relationship Events Scale, a Guttman scale that reflects the increasing intimacy, interdependence, and commitment in dating relationships. Bryson (1977) indicates that multidimensional scaling techniques can be used to discover how judged similarity and perceptual similarity are related to interpersonal attraction. Knowles (1978a) and Love and Aiello (1980) caution against the use of figure placement procedures (such as placing dolls on a felt board) as a projective device for measuring spatial behavior. Several authors propose measures of group cohesiveness (N. J. Evans & Jarvis, 1980, 1986; Lawlis & Klein, 1973; Piper, Marrache, Lacroix, Richardsen, & Jones, 1983; van Nieuwenhuizen, 1983). L. K. White and Brinkerhoff (1978) suggest combining husband and wife reports for a composite measure of marital adjustment. N. W. Brown and Sullivan (1979) report on the use of an interpersonal relationship rating scale. B. M. Montgomery (1986) indicates that, under certain procedural conditions, peer assessments are highly reliable and valid.

Models and Simulations

Models and simulations for aspects of interaction include group decisions (MacKinnon & Anderson, 1976), bargaining and coalition formation (Kahan, Coston, Helwig, Rapoport, & Wallsten, 1976; A. Rapoport & Kahan, 1974), asymmetries in team play (P. Gould & Greenawalt, 1981), strategies of interactive behavior (Bierschenk, 1978a, 1978b), and attitude change (J. L. Smith, 1975). Models that are more general are based on Markov chains (Conlisk, 1976), cybernetics (Meile, 1975), and a cognitive group map (O'Connor, 1980). In addition, small groups are used to simulate behavior in large organizations (J. S. Williams, Singh, Gray, & Von Broembsen, 1974)

Mathematical models for identifying communication structures and sociometric structures are described by: Freeman, 1977; Killworth & Bernard, 1976; Klaua, 1975a, 1975b.

Problems with Laboratory Experiments

There is a continuing interest in the ethics of laboratory experiments, especially if subjects suffer pain or humiliation (D. Archer, 1974; B. McCarthy & Duck, 1979; Zimbardo, 1973). Experimenters have also been interested in whether or not all behavior can be "faked" by confederates (Mixon, 1976) and the effect on the experiment if the subjects know someone is faking (J. D. Martin, 1979; P. W. Sheehan & Marsh, 1974).

McNamara and Blumer (1982) are concerned that role playing may only have a modest correspondence with behavior in naturalistic settings. In particular, Polozova (1980) suggests that instead of studying interpersonal conflict by means of the Prisoner's Dilemma game, it would be better to have members of real groups fill out questionnaires about friction and conflict within the group. F. D. Miller (1976) notes that individuals who have had an intensive experience in a laboratory group may have difficulty in transferring the learning to a home situation. Carlston and Cohen (1980) report that subjects with different role-play motivations differed significantly in their attention to various facets of the instructions and in their behavioral responses in an experimental task.

Koppelaar (1983) reports that observers who are empathetic with the subjects make different judgments than those who are neutral. Others have noted that persons who volunteer for experiments may have special psychological or social characteristics (C. T. Hill, Rubin, Peplau, & Willard, 1979; Kuiken, Rasmussen, & Cullen, 1974) and those who have already had experience with similar experiments will behave differently than those who are not strangers to the procedures (Lamb,

1986). M. L. Barnes and Rosenthal (1985) urge researchers to take gender, physical attractiveness, and attire of the experimenter into account.

Additional suggestions concerning methodology are given by: L. N. Gray & von Broembsen, 1976; Friedlander, 1982; Hendrickx, 1982; Huston & Robins, 1982; C. J. Couch, 1987.

SPECIAL TYPES OF GROUPS

Most of the research literature covered in this volume refers to studies of laboratory groups. However some is based on observations of groups in natural settings and some on special types of groups such as sensitivity training groups, therapy groups, or sports groups. Where the conclusions of research on one of the special types of groups seems to have general application, we have usually included the findings under the appropriate content heading. However, in the course of our search of the literature we have identified a number of articles that seem to apply especially to one type of group. These articles are listed below as an introduction to this type of research. (See also, the journal *Group and Organization Studies*.) It is only a small sample of the literature since we made no systematic search of the literature under these group headings. Observations made on special types of groups have often yielded perspectives that have wide-spread application. For example Bion's analysis of work and group cultures in therapy groups stimulated considerable research in other types of groups. Observations of interaction in "self-analytic" groups provided much of the basis for Bales's theory of SYMLOG. Minuchin's (1974) family research has introduced the idea of a "dominant triangle." In the following lists, most of the items pertain to sensitivity training (group dynamics, T-groups) since research on this type of groups appears more frequently in the journals we have searched and the categories of abstracts that we have examined.

Sensitivity Training Groups

Reviews and general comment. Alderfer & Cooper, 1980; J. D. Anderson, 1975, 1978; Bednar & Kaul, 1979; Braaten, 1974; C. L. Cooper, 1973; Dies, 1978; Ganzarain, 1974–1975; Goldbart & Cooper, 1976; Heider, 1974; Hirsch, 1987; Kissen, 1976; Krege, 1974; A. Levy, 1983; Lundberg & Lundberg, 1974; Mangham, 1977; J. Melnick & Woods, 1976; Nau, 1983; Ninane, 1980; W. E. O'Connell, 1975; Oomkes & Bakker, 1984; Ritvo & Sargent, 1983; M. Rosenbaum & Snadowsky, 1976; Rudestam, 1982; Scheidlinger, 1974; Sevigny, 1977; *Small Group Behavior*, 1987; P. B. Smith, 1975, 1980; Stockton, 1978.

As a social movement. Laschinsky & Koch, 1975.

Contributing to personal growth. N. E. Adler & Goleman, 1975; J. D. Andrews, 1974; A. Blumberg & Golembiewski, 1976; C. L. Cooper, 1977; C. L.

Cooper & Kobayashi, 1976; D'Augelli, 1974; Finkelstein, Wenegrat, & Yalom, 1982; J. J. Hartman, 1979; V. Harvey, DiLuzio, & Hunter, 1975; Höper et al., 1975/1976; Klingberg, 1973; Lennung & Ahlberg, 1975; E. M. Levin & Kurtz, 1974; P. Lewis, Dawes, & Cheney, 1974; Lieberman, 1976; W. B. Reddy, 1973; P. B. Smith, 1976a, 1976b, 1983; Sundel, Glasser, Sarri, & Vinter, 1985; Watkins, Noll, & Breed, 1975; T. L. Wright & Duncan, 1986.

Attitude change. Jasiecki & Necki, 1983; S. Miller, Nunnally, & Wackman, 1976; J. D. White & White, 1974; K. R. White, 1974.

Marathon groups. Foulds, Guinan, & Warehime, 1974; D. S. Jones & Medvene, 1975; Marks & Vestre, 1974; Seldman, McBrearty, & Seldman, 1974.

Special applications. Babad, Birnbaum, & Benne, 1978; Carnes & Laube, 1975; D'Augelli & Chinsky, 1974; di Marco, 1973; Holleran & Holleran, 1976; Pfister, 1975.

Trainers and training skills. L. F. Anderson & Robertson, 1985; Bertcher, 1979; Hurley, 1975, 1976; W. L. Kelly, 1974; Lennung, 1974–1975; T. J. Long & Bosshart, 1974; T. J. Long & Schultz, 1973; D. C. Lundgren, 1974; D. C. Lundgren & Knight, 1974, 1977; Miles, 1980; R. J. Shapiro & Klein, 1975; Shinohara & Misumi, 1977; H. H. Straub, 1975; Weinstein & Hanson, 1975; Vidal, 1978.

Problems and ethical issues. C. L. Cooper, 1975a; Hogan, 1974; J. J. Peters, 1973.

Research methods. Rae, Vathally, Manderscheid, & Silbergeld, 1976; Wagner P., 1972.

Additional research. J. D. Anderson, 1978; Bednar & Battersby, 1976; Conyne & Rapin, 1977; D'Augelli, Chinsky, & Getter, 1974; T. B. Davis, Frye, & Joure, 1975; DeJulio, Bentley, & Cockayne, 1979; Gruenfeld & Lin, 1984; Handlin, Breed, Noll, & Watkins, 1974; Kuypers, Davies, & Hazewinkel, 1986; Lawlis & Klein, 1973; D. C. Lundgren, 1977; D. C. Lundgren & Knight, 1978; D. C. Lundgren & Schaeffer, 1976; L. Martin & Jacobs, 1980; McLeish & Martin, 1975; T. L. Morrison, Greene, & Tischler, 1979; Mumford, 1974; D. L. Patterson & Smits, 1974; Pfeiffer & Jones, 1974; Plutchik & Landau, 1973; Ratner & Hathaway, 1984; Rugel & Meyer, 1984; P. B. Smith, 1974; Tindall, 1979; Wimer & Derlega, 1983.

Group Therapy

Agazarian & Peters, 1981; Authier & Fix, 1977; Bunker, 1974; Butkovich, Carlisle, Duncan, & Moss, 1975; Desmond & Seligman, 1977; Dies, 1978, 1979; Durkin,

1981; Feder & Ronall, 1980; Gruen, 1979; M. N. Hendricks, 1984; Horwitz, 1977; Kaseman, 1976; Kreeger, 1975; Lieberman, 1976; McCanne, 1977; Meeks, 1973; Milman & Goldman, 1974; Naar, 1982; M. Pines, 1983; Scheidlinger, 1980; Warehime, 1981; Wogan, Getter, Amdur, Nichols, & Okman, 1977.

Education

I. H. Berkovitz, 1975; E. W. Christensen, 1983; Hauser & Shapiro, 1976; Heisterkanp, 1974; Hieden, 1974; Moos, Van Dort, Smail, & DeYoung, 1975; P. L. Peterson & Swing, 1985; Vicino, Krusell, Bass, Deci, & Landy, 1973.

Family

Bockus, 1975; W. Cook & Dreyer, 1984; Craddock, 1985; de la Haye, 1983; Kratcoski, 1984; McCubbin & Figley, 1983, P. C. Miller, Lefcourt, Holmes, Ware, & Saleh, 1986; Neal, Ivoska, & Groat, 1976; R. Rapoport, Rapoport, & Thiessen, 1974; Schafer & Keith, 1985; Sorrels & Myers, 1983; Tallman & Miller, 1974; Tyrell, 1983; Wild, Shapiro, & Abelin, 1977.

Counseling

Bonney, 1974; Horejsi, 1974; F. Lee & Bednar, 1977; Mace, 1975; Merbaum & Osarchuk, 1975.

Attitude Change

Breckheimer & Nelson, 1976.

Interviewing

Arlett, Best, & Little, 1976; Bitti, Giovannini, & Palmonari, 1974; J. D. Davis & Sloan, 1974; Dietch & House, 1975; N. Judd, Bull, & Gahagan, 1975; Kleinke, 1975; Kleinke, Staneski, & Berger, 1975; Koomen & Dijkstra, 1975; Matarazzo, Wiens, & Manaugh, 1975; A. McAllister & Kiesler, 1975; Podmore, Chaney, & Golder, 1975; Rand & Wexley, 1975; Siegman, 1976; Siegman & Reynolds, 1984; Sodikoff, Firestone, & Kaplan, 1974; Weight, 1974.

Group Work and Other Applications

Babad, Tzur, Oppenheimer, & Shaltiel, 1977; Barbara, Usher, & Barnes, 1978; A. Brown, 1986; P. Gould & Gatrell, 1980; F. B. Green, 1978; Harzem & Damon, 1975; Haskell, 1975; Hayano, 1978; T. Heller, 1978; Jaques & Patterson, 1974; I. H. Kaplan, 1967; L. H. Levy, 1976; Lieberman & Bond, 1978; Lippitt, 1986; Manninen, 1977; Payne & Cooper, 1981; Reed & Garvin, 1983; M. Robinson, 1984; Short & Strodtbeck, 1974; Swinth, 1981; Whitaker, 1975, 1985.

References

No attempt has been made to locate all of the articles and books listed here in *Psychological Abstracts* (PA) or *Sociological Abstracts* (SA), but abstract numbers have been included in many citations as aids to the reader who may wish further details. PA numbers begin with a volume number. However, as is customary with SA numbers, these begin with (the last two digits of) the SA year rather than with the SA volume number.

Because of the comparatively large number of duplicate surnames, authors' full first names have been given wherever possible, if these appeared in the original work. Occasionally, an initial has been expanded in brackets (e.g., R[obert]), if an original work gave only an initial, but the fuller name was needed to keep a particular author's works in their appropriate temporal/alphabetical sequence.

In the few cases where the names of multiple authors are not known, citations including *et al.* appear at the end of the first author's list of works. Issue number is given (in parentheses) after volume number, if the pagination for a particular journal restarts at page 1 for each issue in a volume *or* if it was not known whether a journal used a single sequence of continuous pagination throughout the volume.

Aamodt, Michael G.; & Kimbrough, Wilson W. (1982). Effect of group heterogeneity on quality of task solutions. *Psychological Reports, 50,* 171–174. PA 68:8091.

Abbey, David S. (1982). Conflict in unstructured groups: An explanation from control-theory. *Psychological Reports, 51,* 177–178. PA 69:7867.

Abdel-Halim, Ahmed A. (1981). Personality and task moderators of subordinate responses to perceived leader behavior. *Human Relations, 34,* 73–88.

Abele, Andrea. (1982). Hilfsbereitschaft in Abhangigkeit von Aufgaben- und sozialer Struktur der Situation. Ein Experiment zum Interventionsverhalten [Readiness to help in relation to the problem and social structure of the situation: An experiment on intervention behavior]. *Zeitschrift fur Experimentelle und Angewandte Psychologie, 29,* 1–23. PA 68:5754.

Abelson, Robert P. (1976). Script processing in attitude formation and decision making. In J. S. Carroll and J. W. Payne (Eds.), *Cognition and social behavior* [Symposium on Cognition, 11th, Carnegie-Mellon University] (pp.33–45 [plus references at end of book]). Hillsdale, NJ: Erlbaum.

Abelson, Robert P. (1981). Psychological status of the script concept. *American Psychologist, 36,* 715–729.

Abraham, Ada. (1974–1975). Processes in groups. *Bulletin de Psychologie, 28,* 746–758. PA 55:02316.

Abraham, Ada; Geffroy, Yannick; & Ancelin-Schutzenberger, Anne. (1980). A method for analyzing group interaction: Development and application of a video observation grid. *Connexions,* No. 31, 145–166. PA 66:5729.

Abramo, Joseph L.; Lundgren, David C.; & Bogart, Dodd H. (1978). Status threat and group dogmatism. *Human Relations, 31,* 745–752. PA 63:966. SA 79K2621.

Abrams, Dominic; & Manstead, A. S. (1981). A test of theories of social facilitation using a musical task. *British Journal of Social Psychology, 20,* 271–278. PA 67:12058.

Accolla, Patrick; Geffroy, Yannick; Abraham, Ada; & Schutzenberger, Anne. (1982). Observation et notation des comportements de leader dans les petits groupes [Observation and re-

cording of leader behavior in small groups]. *Recherches de Psychologie Sociale, 4,* 93–109. PA 70:12626.

Adamopoulos, John. (1984). The differentiation of social behavior: Toward an explanation of universal interpersonal structures. *Journal of Cross Cultural Psychology, 15,* 487–508. PA 72:28019.

Adams, David; Barnett, S. A.; Bechtereva, N. P.; Carter, Bonnie Frank; Delgado, José M. Rodriguez; Diaz, José Luis; Eliasz, Andrzej; Genovés, Santiago; Ginsburg, Benson E.; Groebel, Jo; Ghosh, Samir-Kumar; Hinde, Robert; Leakey, Richard E.; Malasi, Taha H.; Martin Ramìrez, J.; Mayor Zaragoza, Federico; Mendoza, Diana L.; Nandy, Ashis; Scott, John Paul; & Wahlström, Riita. (1987). Statement on violence. *Medicine and War, 3,* 191–193.

Adams, Gerald R. (1977). Physical attractiveness research: Toward a developmental social psychology of beauty. *Human Development, 20,* 217–239. PA 60:7412.

Adams, Gerald R.; & Read, Doris. (1983). Personality and social influence styles of attractive and unattractive college women. *Journal of Psychology, 114,* 151–157. PA 71:9473.

Adams, Gerald R.; Ryan, John H.; Hoffman, Joseph J.; Dobson, William R.; & Nielsen, Elwin C. (1984). Ego identity status, conformity behavior, and personality in late adolescence. *Journal of Personality and Social Psychology, 47,* 1091–1104. PA 72:14532.

Adams, Jeffrey B.; Adams, Jerome; Rice, Robert W.; & Instone, Debra. (1985). Effects of perceived group effectiveness and group role on attributions of group performance. *Journal of Applied Social Psychology, 15,* 387–398. PA 72:30762.

Adams, Kathrynn A. (1980). Who has the final word? Sex, race, and dominance behavior. *Journal of Personality and Social Psychology, 38,* 1–8. PA 65:5375.

Adams, Kathrynn A. (1983). Aspects of social context as determinants of Black women's resistance to challenges. *Journal of Social Issues, 39*(3), 69–78. PA 71:12138.

Adams, Kathrynn, A.; & Landers, Audrey D. (1978). Sex differences in dominance behavior. *Sex Roles, 4,* 215–223. PA 63:3184.

Adato, Albert. (1975). Leave-taking: A study of

commonsense knowledge of social structure. *Anthropological Quarterly, 48*, 255-271. SA 76H9439.

Adelson, Joseph P. (1975). Feedback and group development. *Small Group Behavior, 6*, 389-401. SA 7718724.

Adler, Leonore L.; & Iverson, Marvin A. (1974). Interpersonal distance as a function of task difficulty, praise, status orientation, and sex of partner. *Perceptual and Motor Skills, 39*, 683-692. PA 53:9460.

Adler, Leonore L.; & Iverson, Marvin A. (1975). Projected social distance as a function of praise conditions and status orientation: Comparison with physical interpersonal spacing in the laboratory. *Perceptual and Motor Skills, 41*, 659-664. PA 55:7106.

Adler, Nancy E.; & Goleman, Daniel. (1975). Goal setting, T-group participation, and self-rated change: An experimental study. *Journal of Applied Behavioral Science, 11*, 197-208. PA 54:7439. SA 7714642.

Aebischer, Verena; Hewstone, Miles; & Henderson, Monika. (1984). Minority influence and musical preference: Innovation by conversion not coercion. *European Journal of Social Psychology, 14*, 23-33.

Agazarian, Yvonne; & Peters, Richard. (1981). *The visible and invisible group: Two perspectives on group psychotherapy and group process.* London: Routledge.

Ahlgren, Andrew; & Walberg, Herbert J. (1978). Basic dimensions in characteristics of classroom groups. *Alberta Journal of Educational Research, 24*(4), 244-256. SA 81L6522.

Ahmed, S. M. (1979). Invasion of personal space: A study of departure time as affected by sex of the intruder and saliency condition. *Perceptual and Motor Skills, 49*, 85-86. PA 65:3237.

Ahmed, S. M. (1980). Reactions to crowding in different settings. *Psychological Reports, 46*, 1279-1284. PA 66:3597.

Ahmed, S. M. (1982). Factors affecting frustrating and aggression relationships. *Journal of Social Psychology, 116*, 173-177. PA 68:10312.

Ahrentzen, Sherry; & Evans, Gary W. (1984). Distraction, privacy, and classroom design. *Environment and Behavior, 16*, 437-454. PA 71:32711.

Ahrentzen, Sherry; Jue, Gregory M.; Skorpanich, Mary Anne; & Evans, Gary W. (1982). School

environments and stress. In G. W. Evans (Ed.), *Environmental stress* (pp. 224-255). New York: Cambridge University Press.

Aiello, John R. (1977a). A further look at equilibrium theory: Visual interaction as a function of interpersonal distance. *Environmental Psychology and Nonverbal Behavior, 1*, 122-140. PA 60:3025.

Aiello, John R. (1977b). Visual interaction at extended distances. *Personality and Social Psychology Bulletin, 3*, 83-86. PA 58:7421.

Aiello, John R.; & Baum, Andrew E. (Eds.). (1979). *Residential Crowding and Design*. New York: Plenum.

Aiello, John R.; DeRisi, Donna T.; Epstein, Yakov M.; & Karlin, Robert A. (1977). Crowding and the role of interpersonal distance preference. *Social Psychology Quarterly, 40*, 271-282. PA 60:5219.

Aiello, John R.; Epstein, Yakov; & Karlin, Robert A. (1975). Effects of crowding on electrodermal activity. *Sociological Symposium, 14*, 43-57.

Aiello, John R.; Nicosia, Gregory; & Thompson, Donna E. (1979). Psychological, social, and behavioral consequences of crowding in children and adolescents. *Child Development, 50*, 195-202. PA 62:5752.

Aiello, John R.; & Thompson, Donna E. (1980a). Personal space, crowding, and spatial behavior in a cultural context. In I. Altman, A. Rapoport, & J. Wohlwill (Eds.), *Human Behavior and environment: Advances in theory and research: Vol. 4, Environment and culture* (pp. 107-178). New York: Plenum Press.

Aiello, John R.; & Thompson, Donna E. (1980b). When compensation fails: Mediating effects of sex and locus of control at extended interaction distances. *Basic and Applied Social Psychology, 1*, 65-82. PA 64:12438.

Aiello, John R.; Thompson, Donna E.; & Brodzinsky, David M. (1983). How funny is crowding anyway? Effects of room size, group size, and the introduction of humor. *Basic and Applied Social Psychology, 4*, 193-207. PA 71:23047.

Aikawa, Atsushi. (1981). [Individual vs. group decisions on reward allocation.] *Japanese Journal of Psychology, 52*(2), 113-119. PA 68:3516.

Alagna, Sheryle Whitcher. (1982). Sex role identity, peer evaluation of competition, and the responses of women and men in a competitive situation. *Journal of Personality and Social Psychology*, *43*, 546–554.

Alagna, Sheryle W.; & Reddy, Diane M. (1985). Self and peer ratings and evaluations of group process in mixed-sex and male medical training groups. *Journal of Applied Social Psychology*, *15*, 31–45. PA 72:29009.

Alaphilippe, Daniel. (1981). L'influence sociale: Modalites d'une production de connaissance au sein d'une structure d'emprise [Social influence: Modalities of a production of knowledge in the context of a task structure]. *Psychologie Francaise*, *26*, 49–56. PA 67:9757.

Alba, Richard D. (1973). A graph-theoretic definition of a sociometric clique. *Journal of Mathematical Sociology*, *3*, 113–126. SA 75H5808.

Albers, Wulf; Crott, Helmut; & Murnighan, J. Keith. (1985). The formation of blocs in an experimental study of coalition formation. *Journal of Occupational Behaviour*, *6*(1), 33–48. PA 72:17307.

Albert, Stuart; & Kessler, Suzanne. (1976). Processes for ending social encounters: The conceptual archaeology of a temporal place. *Journal for the Theory of Social Behaviour*, *6*, 147–170. PA 60:1007.

Albert, Stuart; & Kessler, Suzanne. (1978). Ending social encounters. *Journal of Experimental Social Psychology*, *14*, 541–553. PA 63:9620.

Alblas, Gert. (1983). *Groepsprocessen: Het functioneren in taakgerichte groepen*. Deventer, Netherlands: Van Loghum Slaterus.

Albrecht, Gary L. (1985). Videotape safaris: Entering the field with a camera. Special Issue: Innovative sources and uses of qualitative data. *Qualitative Sociology*, *8*, 325–344. PA 74:3982.

Alcock, James E. (1974). Cooperation, competition, and the effects of time pressure in Canada and India. *Journal of Conflict Resolution*, *18*, 171–197. PA 53:5153.

Alcock, James E. (1975). Motivation in an asymmetric bargaining situation: A cross-cultural study. *International Journal of Psychology*, *10*, 69–81. PA 55:4534.

Alcock, James E.; & Mansell, Diana. (1977). Predisposition and behaviour in a collective dilemma. *Journal of Conflict Resolution*, *21*, 443–457. PA 60:3001.

Alden, Lynn E.; & Cappe, Robin. (1981). Nonassertiveness: Skill deficit or selective self-evaluation? *Behavior Therapy*, *12*, 107–114. PA 65:7984.

Alderfer, Clayton P.; & Cooper, Cary L. (Eds.). (1980). *Advances in experiential social processes* (Vol. 2). Chichester: Wiley.

Alessio, John C. (1984). Exchange, perceived alternatives, and reinforcement schedule: Cohesiveness among unmarried couples. *Journal of Psychology*, *118*, 89–98. PA 72:25389.

Alexander, C. Norman. (1977). Role-taking in constructing social realities. *Personality and Social Psychology Bulletin*, *3*, 654–657. PA 60:11709.

Alexander, C. Norman; & Lauderdale, Pat. (1977). Situated identities and social influence. *Social Psychology Quarterly*, *40*, 225–233. PA 60:5191.

Alfgren, Scott H.; Aries, Elizabeth J.; & Olver, Rose R. (1979). Sex differences in the interaction of adults and preschool children. *Psychological Reports*, *44*, 115–118. PA 64:3239.

Allen, Donald E.; Guy, Rebecca F. (1977). Ocular breaks and verbal output. *Sociometry*, *40*, 90–96. PA 58:9464.

Allen, Jon G. (1974). When does exchanging personal information constitute self-disclosure? *Psychological Reports*, *35*, 195–198. PA 56:7851.

Allen, Vernon L. (1975). Social support for nonconformity. *Advances in Experimental Social Psychology*, *8*, 1–43.

Allen, Vernon L.; & Wilder, David A. (1979). Social support in absentia: The effect of an absentee partner on conformity. *Human Relations*, *32*, 103–111. PA 64:3240.

Allen, Vernon L.; & Wilder, David A. (1980). Impact of group consensus and social support on stimulus meaning: Mediation of conformity by cognitive restructuring. *Journal of Personality and Social Psychology*, *39*, 1116–1124. PA 66:5781.

Allison, Paul D.; & Liker, Jeffrey K. (1982). Analyzing sequential categorical data on dyadic interaction: A comment on Gottman. *Psychological Bulletin*, *91*, 393–403. PA 67:12033.

Allison, Scott T.; & Messick, David M. (1985a). Effects of experience on performance in a replenishable resource trap. *Journal of Personality and Social Psychology*, *49*, 943–948. PA 73:3663.

Allison, Scott T.; & Messick, David M. (1985b).

The group attribution error. *Journal of Experimental Social Psychology*, *21*, 563–579. PA 74:1046.

Allport, Floyd H. (1924). *Social Psychology*. Boston: Houghton Mifflin.

Almazov, B. N.; & Vostroknutov, N. V. (1977). [A comparative investigation of affiliative behavior of mentally healthy and ill persons.] *Voprosy Psikhologii*, No. 2, 142–144. PA 60:11679.

Altman, Irwin. (1975). *The environment and social behavior*. Monterey, CA: Brooks/Cole.

Altman, Irwin. (1976). Privacy: a conceptual analysis. *Environment and Behavior*, *8*, 7–29.

Altman, Irwin. (1977). Privacy regulation: Culturally universal or culturally specific? *Journal of Social Issues*, *33*(3), 66–84.

Altman, Irwin; & Chemers, Martin M. (1980). *Culture and environment*. Monterey, CA: Brooks/Cole.

Altman, Irwin; Lawton, M. Powell; & Wohlwill, Joachim F. (Eds.). (1984). *Human behavior and environment: Elderly people and the environment* (Vol. 7). New York: Plenum.

Altman, Irwin; Rapoport, A.; & Wohlwill, Joachim F. (Eds.). (1980). *Human behavior and environment: Environment and culture* (Vol. 4). New York: Plenum.

Altman, Irwin; & Vinsel, Anne M. (1977). Personal space: an analysis of E. T. Hall's proxemics framework. In I. Altman & J. F. Wohlwill (Eds.), *Human behavior and environment: Advances in theory and research* (Vol. 2, pp. 181–259). New York: Plenum Press.

Altman, Irwin; Vinsel, Anne; & Brown, Barbara B. (1981). Dialectic conceptions in social psychology: An application to social penetration and privacy regulation. *Advances in Experimental Social Psychology*, *14*, 107–160.

Altman, Irwin; & Wandersman, Abraham. (Eds.). (1987). *Human behavior and environment: Neighborhood and community* (Vol. 9). New York: Plenum.

Altman, Irwin; & Werner, Carol M. (Eds.). (1985). *Human behavior and environment: Home environment* (Vol. 8). New York: Plenum.

Altman, Irwin; & Wohlwill, Joachim F. (Eds.). (1976). *Human behavior and environment: Advances in theory and research* (Vol. 1). New York: Plenum.

Altman, Irwin; & Wohlwill, Joachim F. (Eds.). (1977). *Human behavior and environment: Advances in theory and research* (Vol. 2). New York: Plenum.

Altman, Irwin; & Wohlwill, Joachim F. (Eds.). (1978). *Human behavior and environment: Children and the environment* (Vol. 3). New York: Plenum.

Altman, Irwin; & Wohlwill, Joachim F. (Eds.). (1983). *Human behavior and environment: Behavior and the natural environment* (Vol. 6). New York: Plenum.

Altman, Irwin; Wohlwill, Joachim F.; & Everett, Peter B. (Eds.). (1982). *Human behavior and environment: Transportation and behavior* (Vol. 5). New York: Plenum.

Alvarez, Carlos M.; & Pader, Olga F. (1979). Cooperative and competitive behavior of Cuban-American and Anglo-American children. *Journal of Social Psychology*, *101*, 265–271. PA 64:3077.

Amabile, Teresa M. (1983). *The social psychology of creativity*. New York: Springer-Verlag.

Amato, Paul R. (1980). City size, sidewalk density, and friendliness toward strangers. *Journal of Social Psychology*, *111*, 151–152. PA 66:1217.

Amato, Paul R. (1981a). The effects of environmental complexity and pleasantness on prosocial behaviour: A field study. *Australian Journal of Psychology*, *33*, 285–295.

Amato, Paul R. (1981b). The impact of the built environment on prosocial and affiliative behaviour: A field study of the Townsville City Mall. *Australian Journal of Psychology*, *33*, 297–303.

Amato, Paul R. (1983a). The helpfulness of urbanites and small town dwellers: A test between two broad theoretical positions. *Australian Journal of Psychology*, *35*, 233–243. PA 71:28633.

Amato, Paul R. (1983b). Helping behavior in urban and rural environments: Field studies based on a taxonomic organization of helping episodes. *Journal of Personality and Social Psychology*, *45*, 571–586. PA 71:12230.

Amerikaner, Martin. (1980). Self-disclosure: A study of verbal and coverbal intimacy. *Journal of Psychology*, *104*, 221–231. PA 65:7936.

Ames, Carole; Ames, Russell; & Felker, Donald W. (1977). Effects of competitive reward structure and valence of outcome on children's achievement attributions. *Journal of Educational Psychology*, *69*, 1-8. PA 58:3310.

Amir, Taha. (1984). The Asch conformity effect: A study in Kuwait. *Social Behavior and Personality*, *12*, 187-198. PA 73:11719.

Amir-Elkerbout, M. (1983). Aanvaarding van feedback in groepen [Acceptance of feedback in groups]. *Gedrag Tijdschrift voor Psychologie*, *11*(4), 182-189. PA 71:14957.

Ancok, Djamaludin; & Chertkoff, Jerome M. (1983). Effects of group membership, relative performance, and self-interest on the division of outcomes. *Journal of Personality and Social Psychology*, *45*, 1256-1262. PA 71:14958.

Andersen, Peter A.; & Andersen, Janis F. (1984). The exchange of nonverbal intimacy: A critical review of dyadic models [Special Issue: Nonverbal intimacy and exchange]. *Journal of Nonverbal Behavior*, *8*, 327-349. PA 74:3986.

Andersen, Susan M.; & Bem, Sandra L. (1981). Sex typing and androgyny in dyadic interaction: Individual differences in responsiveness to physical attractiveness. *Journal of Personality and Social Psychology*, *41*, 74-86. PA 67:5687.

Anderson, Alonzo B. (1975). Combined effects of interpersonal attraction and goal-path clarity on the cohesiveness of task oriented groups. *Journal of Personality and Social Psychology*, *31*, 68-75. PA 53:9461.

Anderson, Carl R.; & Schneier, Craig E. (1978). Locus of control, leader behavior and leader performance among management students. *Academy of Management Journal*, *21*, 690-698. PA 63:11936.

Anderson, Craig A.; & Anderson, Dona, C. (1984). Ambient temperature and violent crime: Tests of the linear and curvilinear hypotheses. *Journal of Personality and Social Psychology*, *46*, 91-97. PA 71:28938.

Anderson, David R. (1976). Eye contact, topic intimacy, and equilibrium theory. *Journal of Social Psychology*, *100*, 313-314. PA 58:1074.

Anderson, Joseph D. (1975). Human relations training and group work. *Social Work*, *20*(3), 195-199. SA 77I4643.

Anderson, Joseph D. (1978). Growth groups and alienation: A comparative study of Rogerian encounter, self-directed encounter, and gestalt. *Group and Organization Studies*, *3*, 85-107. SA 78J4679.

Anderson, L. Frances; & Robertson, Sharon E.

(1985). Group facilitation: Functions and skills. *Small Group Behavior*, *16*, 139-156.

Anderson, Lynn R. (1978). Groups would do better without humans. *Personality and Social Psychology Bulletin*, *4*, 557-558. PA 64:5538.

Anderson, Lynn R.; & Ager, Joel W. (1978). Analysis of variance in small group research. *Personality and Social Psychology Bulletin*, *4*, 341-345. PA 64:5514.

Anderson, Lynn R.; & Blanchard, P. Nick. (1982). Sex differences in task and social-emotional behavior. *Basic and Applied Social Psychology*, *3*, 109-139. PA 69:1006.

Anderson, Lynn R.; Karuza, Jurgis; & Blanchard, P. Nick. (1977). Enhancement of leader power after election or appointment to undesirable leader roles. *Journal of Psychology*, *97*, 59-70. PA 59:12314.

Anderson, Lynn R.; & McLenigan, Margaret. (1987). Sex differences in the relationship between self-monitoring and leader behavior. *Small Group Behavior*, *18*, 147-167.

Anderson, Norman H.; & Graesser, Cheryl C. (1976). An information integration analysis of attitude change in group discussion. *Journal of Personality and Social Psychology*, *34*, 210-222. PA 56:7887.

Andersson, Hakan; & Brehmer, Berndt. (1977). Social facilitation and inhibition in the social judgment theory paradigm. *Umea Psychological Reports*, No. 132, 11 pages. PA 60:7425.

Andre, Thomas; Schumer, Harry; & Whitaker, Patricia. (1979). Group discussion and individual creativity. *Journal of General Psychology*, *100*, 111-123. PA 65:12732.

Andreoli, Virginia A.; Worchel, Stephen; & Folger, Robert. (1974). Implied threat to behavioral freedom. *Journal of Personality and Social Psychology*, *30*, 765-771. PA 53:9462.

Andrews, John D. (1974). Interpersonal challenge workshop. *Interpersonal Development*, *5*(1), 26-36. PA 54:7441.

Andrews, Patricia Hayes. (1984). Performance-self-esteem and perceptions of leadership emergence: A comparative study of men and women. *Western Journal of Speech Communication*, *48*, 1-13. SA 85O6167.

Annis, Lawrence V.; & Perry, Donald F. (1977). Self-disclosure modeling in same-sex and mixed-sex unsupervised groups. *Journal of Counseling Psychology*, *24*, 370-372. PA 59:5619.

Annis, Lawrence V.; & Perry, Donald F. (1978). Self-disclosure in unsupervised groups: Effects of videotaped models. *Small Group Behavior, 9*, 102–108. SA 79K1075.

Anzai, Yuichiro. (1977). Recognition of coalition by computer in a three-person game. *Behavioral Science, 22*, 403–422. PA 60:10698. SA 78J4690.

Aono, Atsuko [1981]. The effects of sex and dominance upon personal space. *Japanese Journal of Psychology, 52*, 124–127. PA 68:3517.

Apfelbaum, Erika; & Personnaz, Bernard. (1974). [Inequality, conflict, and negotiation: An experience "pour voir"]. *Bulletin de Psychologie, 28*, 778–783. PA 55:2339.

Apfelbaum, Erika; & Personnaz, Bernard. (1977-1978). [Resistance in subordinate groups: Opposition behavior and breach of contract]. *Bulletin de Psychologie, 31*, 270–276. PA 63:968.

Apple, William; Streeter, Lynn A.; & Krauss, Robert M. (1979). Effects of pitch and speech rate on personal attributions. *Journal of Personality and Social Psychology, 37*, 715–727. PA 64:7958.

Apple, William; & Hecht, Kenneth. (1982). Speaking emotionally: The relation between verbal and vocal communication of affect. *Journal of Personality and Social Psychology, 42*, 864–875. PA 68:12630.

Apsler, Robert. (1975). Effects of embarrassment on behavior toward others. *Journal of Personality and Social Psychology, 32*, 145–153. PA 54:5226.

Arbuthnot, Jack; & Wayner, Marc. (1982). Minority influence: Effects of size, conversion, and sex. *Journal of Psychology, 111*, 285–295. PA 69:5566. SA 83N2338.

Archea, John. (1977). The place of architectural factors in behavioral theories of privacy. *Journal of Social Issues, 33*(3), 116–137. PA 62:859.

Archer, Dane. (1974). Ethical problems in small group observation. *Small Group Behavior, 5*, 222–243. PA 53:7281.

Archer, John; & Westeman, Karin. (1981). Sex differences in the aggressive behaviour of schoolchildren. *British Journal of Social Psychology, 20*, 31–36. PA 66:13617.

Archer, Richard L.; & Burleson, Joseph A. (1980). The effects of timing of self-disclosure on attraction and reciprocity. *Journal of Personality and Social Psychology, 38*, 120–130. PA 65:5376.

Archer, Richard L.; Hormuth, Stefan E.; & Berg, John H. (1982). Avoidance of self-disclosure: An experiment under conditions of self-awareness. *Personality and Social Psychology Bulletin, 8*, 122–128. PA 68:10339.

Arenson, Sidney J. (1977). Reactions to invasions of marked seats at a racetrack. *Social Behavior and Personality, 5*, 225–228. PA 62:3589.

Argote, Linda; Seabright, Mark A.; & Dyer, Linda. (1986). Individual versus group use of base-rate and individuating information. *Organizational Behavior and Human Decision Processes, 38*, 65–75. PA 73:29936.

Argyle, Michael. (1973). The syntaxes of bodily communication. *International Journal of Psycholinguistics*, No. 2, 71–91. PA 54:1062.

Argyle, Michael. (1983). *Psychology of interpersonal behavior* (4th ed.). Harmondsworth, England: Penguin.

Argyle, Michael. (1988). *Bodily communication* (2nd ed.). London and New York: Methuen.

Argyle, Michael; & Cook, Mark (1976). *Gaze and mutual gaze*. Cambridge, England: Cambridge University Press.

Argyle, Michael; & Dean, Janet. (1965). Eye-contact, distance, and affiliation. *Sociometry, 28*, 289–304.

Argyle, Michael; & Furnham, Adrian. (1982). The ecology of relationships: Choice of situations as a function of relationship. *British Journal of Social Psychology, 21*, 259–262. PA 69:10388.

Argyle, Michael; Furnham, Adrian; & Graham, Jean Ann. (1981). *Social situations*. Cambridge, England: Cambridge University Press.

Argyle, Michael; & Graham, Jean A. (1976). The central Europe experiment: Looking at persons and looking at objects. *Environmental Psychology and Nonverbal Behavior, 1*, 6–16. PA 60:3002.

Argyle, Michael; & Henderson, Monika. (1985). *Anatomy of relationships: And the rules and skills needed to manage them successfully.* Harmondsworth, England: Penguin.

Argyle, Michael; Henderson, M.; & Furnham, A. (1985). The rules of social relationships. *British Journal of Social Psychology, 24*, 125–139. PA 73:14423.

Argyle, Michael; Lefebvre, Luc; & Cook, Mark. (1974). The meaning of five patterns of gaze.

European Journal of Social Psychology, 4, 125-136. PA 54:5227.

Aries, Elizabeth J. (1976). Interaction patterns and themes of male, female and mixed groups. *Small Group Behavior, 7*, 7-18. SA 7718725.

Aries, Elizabeth J.; Gold, Conrad; & Weigel, Russell H. (1983). Dispositional and situational influences on dominance behavior in small groups. *Journal of Personality and Social Psychology, 44*, 779-786. PA 70:12628.

Aries, Elizabeth J.; & Johnson, Fern L. (1983). Close friendship in adulthood: Conversational content between same-sex friends. *Sex Roles, 9*, 1183-1196. SA 84N9144.

Arlett, Christine; Best, J. Allan; & Little, Brian R. (1976). The influence of interviewer self-disclosure and verbal reinforcement on personality tests. *Journal of Clinical Psychology, 32*, 770-775. PA 58:3356.

Armstrong, Stephen; & Roback, Howard. (1977). An empirical test of Schutz' three-dimensional theory of group process in adolescent dyads. *Small Group Behavior, 8*, 443-456. PA 64:989. SA 79K1076.

Arnold, David W.; & Greenberg, Carl I. (1980). Deviate rejection within differentially manned groups. *Social Psychology Quarterly, 43*, 419-424. PA 66:10310. SA 83M7338.

Aronoff, Joel; & Wilson, John P. (1985). *Personality in the social process.* Hillsdale, NJ: Erlbaum.

Aronson, Elliot; Blaney, Nancy; Stephan, Cookie; Sikes, Jev; & Snapp, Matthew. (1978). *The Jigsaw Classroom.* Beverly Hills: Sage.

Aronson, Elliot; & Bridgeman, Diane. (1978). Jigsaw groups and the desegregated classroom: In pursuit of common goals. *Personality and Social Psychology Bulletin, 5*, 438-446.

Aronson, Elliot; & Yates, Suzanne. (1983). Cooperation in the classroom: The impact of the Jigsaw method on inter-ethnic relations, classroom performance, and self-esteem. In H. H. Blumberg, A. P. Hare, V. Kent, & M. F. Davies (Eds.), *Small groups and social interaction* (Vol. 1, pp. 119-130). New York: Wiley & Sons.

Asch, Solomon E. (1956). Studies of independence and conformity: A minority of one against a unanimous majority. *Psychological Monographs, 70* (9, Whole No. 416).

Asch, S[olomon] E. (1958). Effects of group pressure upon the modification and distortion of judgments. In E. E. Maccoby, T. M. Newcomb & E. L. Hartley (Eds.), *Readings in social psychology* (3rd ed., pp. 174-183). New York: Holt.

Ashour, Ahmed S. (1975). Individual differences in coalitional behavior. *Journal of Personality and Social Psychology, 31*, 1-6. PA 53:9463.

Ashour, Ahmed S.; & Johns, Gary. (1983). Leader influence through operant principles: A theoretical and methodological framework. *Human Relations, 36*, 603-626. PA 70:12629.

Ashton, Nancy L. (1980). Exploratory investigation of perceptions of influences on best-friend relationships. *Perceptual and Motor Skills, 50*, 379-386. PA 66:1211.

Ashton, Nancy L.; & Shaw, Marvin E. (1980). Empirical investigations of a reconceptualized personal space. *Bulletin of the Psychonomic Society, 15*, 309-312. PA 66:1219.

Ashton, Nancy L.; Shaw, Marvin E.; & Worsham, Annette P. (1980). Affective reactions to interpersonal distances by friends and strangers. *Bulletin of the Psychonomic Society, 15*, 306-308. PA 66:1218.

Askevis-Leherpeux, F.; & Zaleska, M. (1975). [An experimental approach to certain aspects of conformity and innovation in small groups]. *Psychologie Francaise, 20*, 105-112. PA 58:5324.

Assadi, Reza. (1982). Conflict and its management: Iranian style. *Anthropological Linguistics, 24*(2), 201-205. SA: 85Q1236.

Asser, Eliot S. (1978). Social class and help-seeking behavior. *American Journal of Community Psychology, 6*, 465-475. PA 63:7552.

Assor, Avi; & O'Quin, Karen. (1982). The intangibles of bargaining: Power and competence versus deference and approval. *Journal of Social Psychology, 116*, 119-126. PA 68:8092.

Atkins, Burton M. (1973). Judicial behavior and tendencies towards conformity in a three member small group: A case study of dissent behavior on the U.S. Court of Appeals. *Social Science Quarterly, 54*(1), 41-53. SA 74G9766.

Atkinson, Rita L.; Atkinson, Richard C.; Smith, Edward E.; & Hilgard, Ernest R. (1987). *Introduction to psychology* (9th ed.). San Diego: Harcourt Brace Jovanovich.

Auerbach, Stephen M.; Kilmann, Peter R.; Gackenbach, Jayne I.; & Julian, Alexander, III. (1980). Profeminist group experience: Effects of group composition on males' attitudinal and affective response. *Small Group Behavior*, *11*, 50–65.

Austin, William. (1979). Sex differences in bystander intervention in a theft. *Journal of Personality and Social Psychology*, *37*, 2110–2120. PA 65:5403.

Austin, William. (1980). Friendship and fairness: Effects of type of relationship and task performance on choice of distribution rules. *Personality and Social Psychology Bulletin*, *6*, 402–408. PA 66:5730.

Austin, William; & McGinn, Neil C. (1977). Sex differences in choice of distribution rules. *Journal of Personality*, *45*, 379–394. PA 60:3026.

Authier, Jerry; & Fix, A. James. (1977). A step-group therapy program based on levels of interpersonal communication. *Small Group Behavior*, *8*, 101–107. PA 60:7826.

Averill, James. (1973). Personal control over aversive stimuli and its relationship to stress. *Psychological Bulletin*, *80*, 286–303. PA 51:4306.

Avramov-Kiwetz, Myriam; & Gaffie, Bernard. (1974). [Social pressure in small group dynamics]. *Psychologie Francaise*, *19*, 23–40. PA 54:9551.

Avron, Ophelia. (1980). Influencer et etre influence [To influence and to be influenced]. *Bulletin de Psychologie*, *34* (349), 259–269. PA 70:3376.

Axelrod, Robert. (1980a). Effective choice in the prisoner's dilemma. *Journal of Conflict Resolution*, *24*, 3–25.

Axelrod, Robert. (1980b). More effective choice in the Prisoner's Dilemma. *Journal of Conflict Resolution*, *24*, 379–403. PA 64:12440.

Axelrod, Robert M. (1984). *The evolution of cooperation*. New York: Basic Books.

Babad, Elisha Y.; Amir, Liora. (1978). Bennis and Shepard's theory of group development: An empirical examination. *Small Group Behavior*, *9*, 477–492. SA 80K5513.

Babad, Elisha Y.; Birnbaum, Max; & Benne, Kenneth D. (1978). The C-group approach to laboratory learning. *Group and Organization Studies*, *3*, 168–184. SA 78J5896.

Babad, Elisha Y.; Tzur, Amos; Oppenheimer, Bruce T.; & Shaltiel, Amnon. (1977). An all-purpose model for group work. *Human Relations*, *30*, 489–401.

Babayeva, Yu. D.; Voiskunskiy, A. Ye.;

Kirichenko, T. N.; & Matsneva, N. V. (1983). [Goal structure in collaborative problem solving]. *Novye Issledovaniya v Psikhologii*, *29*, 53–57. PA 73:6320.

Babayeva, Yu. D.; Vojskunskiy, A. Ye.; Kirichenko, T. N.; & Matsneva, N. V. (1984). [Purposeful structure in the group solution of cognitive problems: II. Methods of realizing communicational goals during the group solution of cognitive problems]. *Novye Issledovaniya v Psikhologii*, *30*, 61–65. PA 74:10179.

Babinec, Carol S. (1978). Sex, communication structures and role specification. *Sociological Focus*, *11*(3), 199–210. SA 79K1077.

Bacharach, Samuel B.; & Lawler, Edward J. (1981). *Bargaining: Power, tactics, and outcomes*. San Francisco: Jossey-Bass.

Bachtold, Louise M. (1982). Children's social interaction and parental attitudes among Hupa indians and anglo-Americans. *Journal of Social Psychology*, *116*, 9–17.

Back, Kurt W. (1974). Intervention techniques: Small groups. *Annual Review of Psychology*, *25*, 367–387. PA 52:5171.

Back, Kurt W. (1979). The small group-tightrope between sociology and personality. *Journal of Applied Behavioral Science*, *15*, 283–294. SA 80K7120.

Baefsky, Pauline M.; & Berger, Stephen E. (1974). Self-sacrifice, cooperation and aggression in women of varying sex-role orientations. *Personality and Social Psychology Bulletin*, *1*, 296–298. PA 56:2297.

Baer, Robert; & Goldman, Morton. (1978). Compliance as a function of prior compliance, familiarization, effort and benefits: The foot-in-the-door technique extended. *Psychological Reports*, *43*, 887–893. PA 64:7907.

Bagarozzi, Dennis A. (1982). The effects of cohesiveness on distributive justice. *Journal of Psychology*, *110*, 267–273. PA 68:8093.

Baglioni, L.; Nencini, R.; & Meschieri Belcecchi, M. V. (1974). [Group influence on the phenomenon of destructive obedience: A study with hypothetical subjects]. *Archivio di Psicologia, Neurologia e Psichiatria*, *35*(1), 26–35. PA 53:5187.

Bailey, Roger C.; Finney, Phillip; & Helm, Bob. (1975). Self-concept support and friendship duration. *Journal of Social Psychology*, *96*, 237–243. PA 55:742.

Bailey, Roger C.; & Stout, Constance. (1983). Congruency of ability attributions and interpersonal evaluation. *Journal of Social Psychology*, *121*, 151-152. PA 71:17764.

Baird, John E. (1976). Sex differences in group communication: A review of relevant research. *Quarterly Journal of Speech*, *62*, 179-192. PA 58:1075.

Baird, John E. (1977). Some nonverbal elements of leadership emergence. *Southern Speech Communication Journal*, *42*, 352-361. SA 81L3445.

Baird, John S. (1982). Conservation of the commons: Effects of group cohesiveness and prior sharing. *Journal of Community Psychology*, *10*, 210-215. PA 69:7868.

Bakeman, Roger; & Beck, Stephen. (1974). The size of informal groups in public. *Environment and Behavior*, *6*, 378-390. PA 53:12582. SA 75H5809.

Baker, Ellen; & Shaw, Marvin E. (1980). Reactions to interperson distance and topic intimacy: A comparison of strangers and friends. *Journal of Nonverbal Behavior*, *5*, 80-91. PA 67:1207.

Baker, Keith. (1974). Experimental analysis of third-party behavior. *Journal of Personality and Social Psychology*, *30*, 307-316.

Baker, Larry D.; & Reitz, H. Joseph. (1978). Altruism toward the blind: Effects of sex of helper and dependency of victim. *Journal of Social Psychology*, *104*, 19-28. PA 61:13404.

Baker, Paul M. (1981). The division of labor: Interdependence, isolation, and cohesion in small groups. *Small Group Behavior*, *12*, 93-106. SA 82M4020.

Baker, Paul M. (1983). The development of mutuality in natural small groups. *Small Group Behavior*, *14*, 301-311. PA 71:17742. SA 84O0826.

Baker, Paul M. (1984). Seeing is behaving: Visibility and participation in small groups. *Environment and Behavior*, *16*, 159-184. PA 71:20441. SA 85Q1237.

Bakken, David. (1977). Saying goodbye: An observational study of parting rituals. *Man-Environment Systems*, *7*(2), 95-100. SA 81L4922.

Baldassare, Mark. (1978). Human spatial behavior. *Annual Review of Sociology*, *4*, 29-56.

Bales, Robert F. (1950). *Interaction process analysis: A method for the study of small groups*. Reading, MA: Addison-Wesley.

Bales, Robert F. (1970). *Personality and interpersonal behavior*. New York: Holt, Rinehart, & Winston.

Bales, Robert F. (1984). The integration of social psychology. *Social Psychology Quarterly*, *47*, 98-101.

Bales, Robert F. (1985). The new field theory in social psychology. *International Journal of Small Group Research*, *1*, 1-18.

Bales, Robert F. (c. 1987). *SYMLOG and leadership theories*. Unpublished manuscript.

Bales, Robert F.; & Cohen, Stephen P. (1979). *SYMLOG: A system for the multiple level observation of groups*. New York: Free Press.

Bales, Robert F.; Koenigs, Robert J.; & Roman, Paul D. (1987). Criteria of adaptation of SYMLOG rating items to particular populations and cultural contexts. *International Journal of Small Group Research*, *3*, 161-179.

Balgooyen, Theodore J. (1984). A group exercise in personal space. *Small Group Behavior*, *15*, 553-563.

Balkwell, James W. (1976). Social decision making behavior: An empirical test of two models. *Sociometry*, *39*, 19-30. PA 56:639.

Ball, James R.; & Carron, Albert V. (1976). The influence of team cohesion and participation motivation upon performance success in intercollegiate ice hockey. *Canadian Journal of Applied Sport Sciences*, *1*, 271-275. PA 63:948.

Ball, Peter. (1975). Listeners' responses to filled pauses in relation to floor apportionment. *British Journal of Social and Clinical Psychology*, *14*, 423-424. PA 56:461.

Balls, Pamela; & Eisenberg, Nancy. (1986). Sex differences in recipients' reactions to aid. *Sex Roles*, *14*, 69-79. PA 74:10207.

Balswick, Jack O.; & Balkwell, James W. (1977). Self-disclosure to same- and opposite-sex parents: An empirical test of insights from role theory. *Social Psychology Quarterly*, *40*, 282-286. PA 60:5192.

Banerjee, Debadatta; & Pareek, Udai. (1974). Development of co-operative and competitive behaviour in children of some sub-cultures. *Indian Journal of Psychology*, *49*, 237-256. PA 58:881.

Banks, W. Curtis; Stitt, Kenneth R.; Curtis, Harriet A.; & McQuater, Gregory V. (1977). Perceived objectivity and the effects of evaluative reinforcement upon compliance and self-evaluation in Blacks. *Journal of Experimental Social Psychology*, *13*, 452-463. PA 60:1044.

Banziger, George; & Simmons, Renee. (1984).

Emotion, attractiveness, and interpersonal space. *Journal of Social Psychology, 124*, 255-256. PA 73:3664.

Barbara, F.; Usher, J.; & Barnes, N. (1978). The rules of "shouting" in drinking groups in Sydney public bars. *Australian Journal of Social Issues, 13*(2), 119-128.

Barchas, Patricia R. (1986). A sociophysiological orientation to small groups. *Advances in Group Processes, 3*, 209-246.

Barefoot, John C.; & Strickland, Lloyd H. (1982). Conflict and dominance in television-mediated interactions. *Human Relations, 35*, 559-566. PA 68:10314. SA 83N4031.

Barker, Larry L.; Wahlers, Kathy J.; Watson, Kittie, W.; & Kibler, Robert J. (Eds). (1987). *Groups in process: An introduction to small group communication* (3rd ed.). Englewood Cliffs, NJ: Prentice-Hall.

Barker, Roger G. (1968). *Ecological Psychology: Concepts and methods for studying the environment of human behavior.* Stanford, CA: Stanford University Press.

Barker, Roger G.; & Associates. (1978). *Habitats, environments, and human behavior.* San Francisco: Jossey-Bass.

Barkowski, Dieter; Lamm, Helmut; & Schwinger, Thomas. (1982). Einfallsproduktion von Individuen und Dyaden unter "Brainstorming"-Bedingungen [Brainstorming in group (dyadic) and individual conditions]. *Psychologische Beitrage, 24*, 39-46. PA 69:12654.

Barlow, John A. (1984). Using each other: An analysis of leadership as operant conditioning. *Behavior Analysis and Social Action, 4*(2), 20-23. PA 74:7157.

Barlow, Sally; Hansen, William D.; Fuhriman, Addie J.; & Finley, Robert. (1982). Leader communication style: Effects on members of small groups. *Small Group Behavior, 13*, 518-531. PA 70:5618.

Barnes, Michael L.; & Buss, David M. (1985). Sex differences in the interpersonal behavior of married couples. *Journal of Personality and Social Psychology, 48*, 654-661.

Barnes, Michael L.; & Rosenthal, Robert. (1985). Interpersonal effects of experimenter attractiveness, attire, and gender. *Journal of Personality and Social Psychology, 48*, 435-446.

Barnes, Richard D.; Ickes, William; & Kidd, Robert F. (1979). Effects of the perceived intentionality and stability of another's dependency on helping behavior. *Personality and Social Psychology Bulletin, 5*, 367-372. PA 64:10353.

Barnett, Mark A.; & Andrews, Judy A. (1977). Sex differences in children's reward allocation under competitive and cooperative instructional sets. *Developmental Psychology, 13*, 85-86. PA 58:5345.

Barnett, Nona J.; & Feild, Hubert S. (1978). Character of the defendant and length of sentence in rape and burglary crimes. *Journal of Social Psychology, 104*, 271-277. PA 61:13405.

Baron, Penny H.; Baron, Robert Steven; & Roper, Gard. (1974). External validity and the risky shift: Empirical limits and theoretical implications. *Journal of Personality and Social Psychology, 30*, 95-103.

Baron, Reuben M. (1979). Ecological approaches to understanding human crowding. *Journal of Population, 2*, 235-258.

Baron, Reuben M.; Mandel, David R.; Adams, Claire A.; & Griffen, Lynne M. (1976). Effects of social density in university residential environments. *Journal of Personality and Social Psychology, 34*, 434-446. PA 57:10274.

Baron, Reuben M.; & Needel, Stephen P. (1980). Toward an understanding of the differences in the responses of humans and other animals to density. *Psychological Review, 87*, 320-326. PA 64:5338.

Baron, Reuben M.; & Rodin, Judith. (1978). Personal control as a mediator of crowding. In A. Baum, J. E. Singer, & S. Valins (Eds.), *Advances in environmental psychology* (Vol. 1, pp. 145-190). Hillsdale, NJ: Erlbaum.

Baron, Robert A. (1976). The reduction of human aggression: A field study of the influence of incompatible reactions. *Journal of Applied Social Psychology, 6*, 260-274. PA 57:8169.

Baron, Robert A. (1978a). Aggression and heat: The "long hot summer" revisited. In A. Baum, J. E. Singer, and S. Valins (Eds.), *Advances in environmental psychology* (Vol. 1, pp. 57-84). Hillsdale, N.J.: Erlbaum.

Baron, Robert A. (1978b). Invasions of personal space and helping: Mediating effects of invader's apparent need. *Journal of Experimental Social Psychology, 14*, 304-312. PA 61:10897.

Baron, Robert A. (1979). Effects of victim's pain cues, victim's race, and level of prior instigation upon physical aggression. *Journal of Applied Social Psychology, 9*, 103-114. PA 66:5712.

Baron, Robert A.; & Bell, Paul A. (1975). Aggression and heat: Mediating effects of prior provocation and exposure to an aggressive model. *Journal of Personality and Social Psychology*, *31*, 825–832. PA 54:4612.

Baron, Robert A.; & Bell, Paul A. (1976a). Aggression and heat: The influence of ambient temperature, negative affect, and a cooling drink on physical aggression. *Journal of Personality and Social Psychology*, *33*, 245–255. PA 56:2279.

Baron, Robert A.; & Bell, Paul A. (1976b). Physical distance and helping: Some unexpected benefits of "crowding in" on others. *Journal of Applied Social Psychology*, *6*, 95–104.

Baron, Robert· A.; & Ransberger, Victoria M. (1978). Ambient temperature and the occurrence of collective violence: The "long, hot summer" revisited. *Journal of Personality and Social Psychology*, *36*, 351–360. PA 61:5912.

Baron, Robert S.; & Roper, Gard. (1976). Reaffirmation of social comparison views of choice shifts: Averaging and extremity effects in an autokinetic situation. *Journal of Personality and Social Psychology*, *33*, 521–530. PA 56:6021.

Baron, Robert S.; & Sanders, Glenn. (1975). Group decision as a technique for obtaining compliance: Some added considerations concerning how altruism leads to callousness. *Journal of Applied Social Psychology*, *5*, 281–295. PA 57:1145.

Barrett, David E. (1979). A naturalistic study of sex differences in children's aggression. *Merrill-Palmer Quarterly*, *25*, 193–203. SA 80K7121.

Barrett, Deirdre. (1983). Early recollections as predictors of self-disclosure and interpersonal style. *Individual Psychology Journal of Adlerian Theory, Research and Practice*, *39*(1), 92–98. PA 71:20442.

Barrios, Billy; & Giesen, Martin. (1977). Getting what you expect: Effects of expectations on intragroup attraction and interpersonal distance. *Personality and Social Psychology Bulletin*, *3*, 87–90. PA 58:7423.

Bartel, Helmut W.; Bartel, Nettie R.; & Grill, J. Jeffrey. (1973). Sociometric view of some integrated open classrooms. *Journal of Social Issues*, *29*(4), 159–173. SA 75H1329.

Bartholdi, John J.; Butler, C. Allen; & Trick, Michael A. (1986). More on the evolution of cooperation. *Journal of Conflict Resolution*, *30*, 129–140. PA 73:24464.

Bar-Tal, Yoram; & Kubzansky, Philip E. (1987). Resident advantage as social role performance.

British Journal of Social Psychology, *26*, 147–154.

Bartol, Kathryn M. (1974). Male versus female leaders: The effect of leader need for dominance on follower satisfaction. *Academy of Management Journal*, *17*, 225–233.

Bartol, Kathryn M. (1978). The sex structuring of organizations: A search for possible causes. *Academy of Management Review*, *3*, 805–815.

Bartol, Kathryn M.; & Butterfield, D. Anthony. (1976). Sex effects in evaluating leaders. *Journal of Applied Psychology*, *61*, 446–454. PA 56:10864.

Bartol, Kathryn M.; & Wortman, Max S., Jr. (1979). Sex of leader and subordinate role stress: A field study. *Sex Roles*, *5*, 513–518. SA 81L8266.

Bartos, Otomar J. (1977). Simple model of negotiation: A sociological point of view. *Journal of Conflict Resolution*, *21*, 565–579. PA 61:3519.

Bartunek, Jean M.; Benton, Alan A.; & Keys, Christopher B. (1975). Third party intervention and the bargaining behavior of group representatives. *Journal of Conflict Resolution*, *19*, 532–557. PA 55:4493.

Bass, Bernard M. (1980). Team productivity and individual member competence. *Small Group Behavior*, *11*, 431–504. SA 82M1448.

Bassili, John N. (1979). Emotion recognition: The role of facial movement and the relative importance of upper and lower areas of the face. *Journal of Personality and Social Psychology*, *37*, 2049–2058. PA 65:5404.

Batchelor, Thomas R. (1975). An application of the variable perspective model in interpersonal conflict resolution. *Journal of Experimental Social Psychology*, *11*, 389–400. PA 55:711.

Bateman, Thomas S. (1980). Contingent concession strategies in dyadic bargaining. *Organizational Behavior and Human Performance*, *26*, 212–221.

Batson, C. Daniel; O'Quin, Karen; Fultz, Jim; Vanderplas, Mary; & Isen, Alice M. (1983). Influence of self-reported distress and empathy on egoistic versus altruistic motivation to help. *Journal of Personality and Social Psychology*, *45*, 706–718. PA 71:12185.

Battegay, R. (1977). Group models, group dynamics, sociological and psychological aspects of group formation and evaluation. *Acta Psychiatrica Scandinavica*, *55*, 330–344. SA 80K8680.

Bauer, Gregory P.; Schlottmann, Robert S.; Bates, J. Vance; & Masters, Mark A. (1983). Effect of state and trait anxiety and prestige of model on imitation. *Psychological Reports, 52*, 375-382. PA 71:1306.

Baum, Andrew; Aiello, John R.; & Calesnick, Lisa E. (1978). Crowding and personal control: Social density and the development of learned helplessness. *Journal of Personality and Social Psychology, 36*, 1000-1011. PA 63:5412.

Baum, Andrew; Calesnick, Lisa E.; Davis, Glenn E.; & Gatchel, Robert J. (1982). Individual differences in coping with crowding: Stimulus screening and social overload. *Journal of Personality and Social Psychology, 43*, 821-830. PA 69:10423.

Baum, Andrew; & Davis, Glenn E. (1980). Reducing the stress of high density living; an architectural intervention. *Journal of Personality and Social Psychology, 38*, 471-481. PA 65:11391.

Baum, Andrew; & Epstein, Yakov M. (Eds.). (1978). *Human response to crowding.* Hillsdale, NJ: Erlbaum.

Baum, Andrew; Fisher, Jeffrey D.; & Solomon, Susan K. (1981). Type of information, familiarity, and the reduction of crowding stress. *Journal of Personality and Social Psychology, 40*, 11-23. PA 66:12756.

Baum, Andrew; Fleming, Raymond; & Davidson, Laura M. (1983). Natural disaster and technological catastrophe. *Environment and Behavior, 15*, 333-354.

Baum, Andrew; & Gatchel, Robert J. (1981). Cognitive determinants of reaction to uncontrollable events: Development of reactance and learned helplessness. *Journal of Personality and Social Psychology, 40*, 1078-1089. PA 67:5785.

Baum, Andrew; Gatchel, Robert J.; & Schaeffer, Marc A. (1983). Emotional, behavioral, and physiological effects of chromic disaster at Three Mile Island. *Journal of Consulting and Clinical Psychology, 51*, 565-572. PA 70:13797.

Baum, Andrew; & Greenberg, Carl I. (1975). Waiting for a crowd: The behavioral and perceptual effects of anticipated crowding. *Journal of Personality and Social Psychology, 32*, 671-679. PA 56:02328.

Baum, Andrew; Harpin, R. Edward; & Valins, Stuart. (1975). The role of group phenomena in the experience of crowding. *Environment and Behavior, 7*, 185-198. PA 55:01691.

Baum, Andrew; & Koman, Stuart. (1976). Differential response to anticipated crowding: Psychological effects of social and spatial density. *Journal of Personality and Social Psychology, 34*, 526-536.

Baum, Andrew; Shapiro, Anne; Murray, Darlene; & Wideman, Margaret V. (1979). Interpersonal mediation of perceived crowding and control in residential dyads and triads. *Journal of Applied Social Psychology, 9*, 491-507. PA 66:5731.

Baum, Andrew; & Singer, Jerome E. (Eds.). (1982). *Advances in environmental psychology* (Vol. 4). Hillsdale, NJ: Erlbaum.

Baum, Andrew; Singer, Jerome E; & Baum, Carlene S. (1981). Stress and the environment. *Journal of Social Issues, 37*(1), 4-35.

Baum, Andrew; Singer, Jerome E.; & Valins, Stuart. (Eds.). (1978 [and onward]). *Advances in environmental psychology.* Hillsdale, NJ: Erlbaum.

Baum, Andrew; & Valins, Stuart. (1977). *Architecture and social behavior: Psychological studies of social density.* Hillsdale, NJ: Erlbaum.

Baum, Andrew; & Valins, Stuart. (1979). Architectural mediation of residential density and control: Crowding and the regulation of social contact. *Advances in Experimental Social Psychology, 12*, 131-175.

Baumeister, Roy F. (1982). A self-presentational view of social phenomena. *Psychological Bulletin, 91*, 3-26.

Baumeister, Roy F.; Cooper, Joel; & Skib, Bryan A. (1979). Inferior performance as a selective response to expectancy: Taking a dive to make a point. *Journal of Personality and Social Psychology, 37*, 424-432.

Baumeister, Roy F.; & Jones, Edward E. (1978). When self-presentation is constrained by the target's prior knowledge: Consistency and compensation. *Journal of Personality and Social Psychology, 36*, 608-618.

Baumeister, Roy F.; & Steinhilber, Andrew. (1984). Paradoxical effects of supportive audiences on performance under pressure: The home field disadvantage in sports championships. *Journal of Personality and Social Psychology, 47*, 85-93. PA 71:31312.

Baumgardner, Ann H.; & Brownlee, Elizabeth A. (1987). Strategic failure in social interaction: Evidence for expectancy disconfirmation processes. *Journal of Personality and Social Psychology, 52*, 525-535. PA 74:21928.

Baumgartner, T.; Buckley, W.; & Burns, T. (1975). Relational control: The human structuring of cooperation and conflict. *Journal of Conflict Resolution, 19*, 417–440. PA 55:4494.

Bavelas, Janet B. (1975). Systems analysis of dyadic interaction: The role of interpersonal judgment. *Behavioral Science, 20*, 213–222. PA 55:4495.

Bavelas, Janet Beavin. (1978). Systems analysis of dyadic interaction: Prediction from individual parameters. *Behavioral Science, 23*, 177–186. SA 79K1078.

Baxter, James C.; & Rozelle, Richard M. (1975). Nonverbal expression as a function of crowding during a simulated police-citizen encounter. *Journal of Personality and Social Psychology, 32*, 40–54. PA 54:7443.

Baxter, Jan M. (1982). Solving problems through cooperation. *Exceptional Children, 48*, 400–407. PA 67:10483.

Baxter, Leslie A.; & Wilmot, William W. (1983). Communication characteristics of relationships with differential growth rates. *Communication Monographs, 50*, 264–272. PA 71:12143.

Baxter, Leslie A.; & Wilmot, William W. (1984). "Secret tests": Social strategies for acquiring information about the state of the relationship. *Human Communication Research, 11*, 171–201. PA 72:28020.

Bazerman, Max H. (1983). Negotiator judgment: A critical look at the rationality assumption. *American Behavioral Scientist, 27*, 211–228. PA 71:23048.

Bazerman, Max H. (1986). Why negotiations go wrong. *Psychology Today, 20*(6), 54–58. PA 73:27134.

Bazerman, Max H.; Giuliano, Toni; & Appelman, Alan. (1984). Escalation of commitment in individual and group decision making. *Organizational Behavior and Human Performance, 33*, 141–152. PA 71:20443.

Bazerman, Max H.; Mannix, Elizabeth A.; & Thompson, Leigh L. (1988). Groups as mixed-motive negotiations. *Advances in Group Processes, 5*, 195–216.

Beach, David R.; & Sokoloff, Mark J. (1974). Spatially dominated nonverbal communication of children: A methodological study. *Perceptual and Motor Skills, 38*, 1303–1310. PA 53:915.

Beaman, Arthur L.; Cole, C. Maureen; Preston, Marilyn; Klentz, Bonnel; & Steblay, Nancy

Mehrkens. (1983). Fifteen years of foot-in-the-door research: A meta-analysis. *Personality and Social Psychology Bulletin, 9*, 181–196, PA 71:5685.

Beaman, Arthur L.; Svanum, Soren; Manlove, Spencer; Hampton, Charlotte. (1974). An attribution theory explanation of the foot-in-the-door effects. *Personality and Social Psychology Bulletin, 1*, 122–123. PA 56:4019.

Bean, Bruce W.; & Houston, B. Kent. (1978). Self-concept and self-disclosure in encounter groups. *Small Group Behavior, 9*, 549–554. SA 80K4169.

Beattie, Geoffrey [W]. (1977). The dynamics of interruption and the filled pause. *British Journal of Social and Clinical Psychology, 16*, 283–284. PA 60:1008.

Beattie, Geoffrey W. (1978). Floor apportionment and gaze in conversational dyads. *British Journal of Social and Clinical Psychology, 17*, 7–15. PA 61:5915. SA 79K1079.

Beattie, Geoffrey W. (1981). A further investigation of the cognitive interference hypothesis of gaze patterns during conversation. *British Journal of Social Psychology, 20*, 243–248. PA 67:12035.

Beattie, Geoffrey W. (1983). *Talk: An analysis of speech and non-verbal behaviour in conversation.* Milton Keynes, UK: Open University Press.

Beatty, Michael J. (1980). Social facilitation and listening comprehension. *Perceptual and Motor Skills, 51*, 1222. PA 67:1208.

Beck, Hall P.; & Seta, John J. (1980). The effects of frequency of feedback on a simple coaction task. *Journal of Personality and Social Psychology, 38*, 75–80. PA 65:5378.

Beck, Steven J.; & Ollendick, Thomas H. (1976). Personal space, sex of experimenter, and locus of control in normal and delinquent adolescents. *Psychological Reports, 38*, 383–387. PA 56:3994.

Becker, Franklin D. (1973). Study of spatial markers. *Journal of Personality and Social Psychology, 26*, 439–445.

Becker, Franklin D.; Gield, Beverly; Gaylin, Kenneth; & Sayer, Susan. (1983). Office design in a community college: Effect on work and communication patterns. *Environment and behavior, 15*, 699–726. PA 71:10972.

Becker, Henrik; & Körner, Wolfgang. (1974). [Cognitive balance and clique formation: A critique and modification of balance theory]. *Zeitschrift fur Sozialpsychologie, 5,* 189–200. PA 53:11565.

Becker, W. Michael; & Miles, Carrie. (1978). Interpersonal competition and cooperation as a function of sex of subject and sex of counterpart. *Journal of Social Psychology, 104,* 303–304. PA 61:13376.

Becker-Haven, Jane F.; & Lindskold, Svenn. (1978). Deindividuation manipulations, self-consciousness, and bystander intervention. *Journal of Social Psychology, 105,* 113–121. PA 62:10959.

Beckhouse, Lawrence; Tanur, Judith; Weiler, John; & Weinstein, Eugene. (1975). . . . And some men have leadership thrust upon them. *Journal of Personality and Social Psychology, 31,* 557–566. PA 54:1013.

Beckman, Linda; & Bishop, Barbara R. (1973). Cooperation of acting-out adolescents: Reactions to the "lapsed saint" and "reformed sinner" strategies. *Journal of Clinical Psychology, 29,* 322–325. PA 55:12459.

Beckmann, Neal W. (1977). *Negotiations: Principles and techniques.* Lexington, MA: Lexington Books.

Bednar, Richard L.; & Battersby, Charles P. (1976). The effects of specific cognitive structure on early group development. *Journal of Applied Behavioral Science, 12,* 513–522. PA 58:3788.

Bednar, Richard L.; & Kaul, Theodore J. (1979). Experiential group research: What never happened! *Journal of Applied Behavioral Science, 15,* 311–319. SA 80K7122.

Begin, Guy. (1978). Sex makes a difference: 1. Evidence from a modeling study conducted in a natural setting. *Psychological Reports, 43,* 103–109. PA 63:7554.

Behr, Roy L. (1981). Nice guys finish last — sometimes. *Journal of Conflict Resolution, 25,* 289–300. PA 66:8006.

Beier, Ernst G. (1974). Nonverbal communication: How we send emotional messages. *Psychology Today, 8*(5), 52–56. PA 53:7282.

Beilin, Robert; & Rabow, Jerome. (1981). Status value, group learning, and minority achievement in college. *Small Group Behavior, 12,* 495–508.

Belgrave, Faye Z.; & Mills, Judson. (1981). Effect upon desire for social interaction with a physically disabled person of mentioning the disability in different contexts. *Journal of Applied Social Psychology, 11,* 44–57.

Bell, Eugene C.; Blakeney, Roger N. (1977). Personality correlates of conflict resolution modes. *Human Relations, 30,* 849–857. PA 60:7427.

Bell, Mae A. (1982). Phases in group problem-solving. *Small Group Behavior, 13,* 475–503. PA 70:5619.

Bell, Paul A. (1980). Effects of heat, noise, and provocation on retaliatory evaluative behavior. *Journal of Social Psychology, 110,* 97–100. PA 65:10417.

Bell, Paul A.; & Baron, Robert A. (1974). Environmental influences on attraction: Effects of heat, attitude similarity, and personal evaluations. *Bulletin of the Psychonomic Society, 4,* 479–481. PA 53:9497.

Bell, Paul A.; & Baron, Robert A. (1976). Aggression and heat: The mediating role of negative affect. *Journal of Applied Social Psychology, 6,* 18–30. PA 56:7853.

Bell, Paul A.; & Baron, Robert A. (1977). Aggression and ambient temperature: The facilitating and inhibiting effects of hot and cold environments. *Bulletin of the Psychonomic Society, 9,* 443–445. PA 59:7864.

Bell, Paul A.; Garnand, Douglas B.; & Heath, Diane. (1984). Effects of ambient temperature and seating arrangement of personal and environmental evaluations. *Journal of General Psychology, 110,* 197–200. PA 72:6624.

Bell, Robert; & Coplans, John. (1976). *Decisions, decisions: Game theory and you.* New York: Norton.

Bell, Robert A.; & Daly, John A. (1984). The affinity-seeking function of communication. *Communication Monographs, 51,* 91–115. PA 72:17308.

Bell, Robert R. (1981). Friendships of women and of men. *Psychology of Women Quarterly, 5,* 402–417. PA 67:3515.

Belliveau, Lorraine M.; & Stolte, John F. (1977). The structure of third party intervention. *Journal of Social Psychology, 103,* 243–250. PA 60:9285. SA 82M1449.

Bem, Daryl J.; & Allen, Andrea. (1974). On predicting some of the people some of the time: The search for cross-situational consistencies. *Psychological Review, 81,* 506–520. PA 53:4252.

Bem, Daryl J.; & Funder, David C. (1978). Predicting more of the people more of the time:

Assessing the personality of situations. *Psychological Review, 85*, 485–501. PA 62:8632.

Benfari, Robert C. (1976). Type A-B behavior and outcomes of group process. *Psychological Reports, 38*, 415–419. PA 56:3995.

Benjamin, Lorna Smith. (1974). Structural analysis of social behavior. *Psychological Review, 81*, 392–425. PA 53:2991.

Benjamin, Lorna Smith. (1979). Use of structural analysis of social behavior (SASB) and Markov chains to study dyadic interactions. *Journal of Abnormal Psychology, 88*, 303–319. PA 62:5025.

Bennett, Richard P.; & Carbonari, Joseph P. (1976). Personality patterns related to own-, joint-, and relative-gain maximizing behaviors. *Journal of Personality and Social Psychology, 34*, 1127–1134. PA 60:11680.

Benoist, Irving R.; & Butcher, James N. (1977). Nonverbal cues to sex-role attitudes. *Journal of Research in Personality, 11*, 431–442. PA 60:9323.

Benoit, John H. (1982). The application of expectation states theory to the "risky shift". *Canadian Journal of Sociology/Cahiers canadiens de sociologie, 7*(2), 167–179. SA 83M7339.

Benson, Peter L.; Karabenick, Stuart A.; & Lerner, Richard M. (1976). Pretty pleases: The effects of physical attractiveness, race, and sex on receiving help. *Journal of Experimental Social Psychology, 12*, 409–415. PA 56:9851.

Benton, Alan A. (1975a). Bargaining visibility and the attitudes and negotiation behavior of male and female group representatives. *Journal of Personality, 43*, 661–677. PA 59:12317.

Benton, Alan A. (1975b). Distributive justice within unsuccessful groups. *Representative Research in Social Psychology, 6*, 29–36. PA 54:5229.

Benton, Alan A. (1975c). Test anxiety and the bargaining behavior of preadolescent males. *Journal of Social Psychology, 96*, 209–219. PA 55:712.

Benton, Alan A.; & Druckman, Daniel. (1974). Constituent's bargaining orientation and intergroup negotiations. *Journal of Applied Social Psychology, 4*, 141–150. PA 53:2980.

Ben-Yoav, Orly; Hollander, Edwin P.; & Carnevale, Peter J. (1983). Leader legitimacy, leader-follower interaction, and followers' ratings of the leader. *Journal of Social Psychology, 121*, 111–115. PA 71:17765. SA 85O6168.

Ben-Yoav, Orly; & Pruitt, Dean G. (1984a). Accountability to constituents: A two-edged sword. *Organizational Behavior and Human Performance, 34*, 283–295.

Ben-Yoav, Orly; & Pruitt, Dean G. (1984b). Resistance to yielding and the expectation of cooperative future interaction in negotiation. *Journal of Experimental Social Psychology, 20*, 323–335. PA 72:11997.

Bercovitch, Jacob. (1984). *Social conflicts and third parties: Strategies of conflict resolution.* Boulder, CO: Westview.

Berg, John H.; & Archer, Richard L. (1980). Disclosure or concern: A second look at liking for the norm breaker. *Journal of Personality, 48*, 245–257. PA 66:1220.

Berg, John H.; & Archer, Richard L. (1982). Responses to self-disclosure and interaction goals. *Journal of Experimental Social Psychology, 18*, 501–512. PA 70:1048.

Berg, John H.; & Archer, Richard L. (1983). The disclosure-liking relationship: Effects of self-perception, order of disclosure, and topical similarity. *Human Communication Research, 10*, 269–281. PA 71:31313.

Berg, John H.; & McQuinn, Ronald D. (1986). Attraction and exchange in continuing and noncontinuing dating relationships. *Journal of Personality and Social Psychology, 50*, 942–952. PA 73:21902.

Berg, Kathleen S.; & Vidmar, Neil. (1975). Authoritarianism and recall of evidence about criminal behavior. *Journal of Research in Personality, 9*, 147–157. PA 54:8871.

Berger, Charles R.; Gardner, Royce R.; Clatterbuck, Glen W.; & Schulman, Linda S. (1976). Perceptions of information sequencing in relationship development. *Human Communication Research, 3*, 29–46. PA 60:5250.

Berger, Charles R.; Gardner, Royce R.; Parks, Malcolm R.; Schulman, Linda; & Miller, Gerald R. (1976). Interpersonal epistemology and interpersonal communication. In G. R. Miller (Ed.), *Explorations in interpersonal communication* (pp. 149–171). Beverly Hills, CA: Sage. PA 58:11641.

Berger, Joseph; Cohen, Bernard P.; & Zelditch, Morris. (1966). Status characteristics and expectation states. In J. Berger, M. Zelditch, & B. Anderson (Eds.), *Sociological theories in progress* (Vol. 1, pp. 29–46). Boston: Houghton Mifflin.

Berger, Joseph; Fisek, M. H.; Norman, R. Z.; & Zelditch, M. (1977). *Status characteristics and social interaction: An expectation states approach.* New York: Elsevier.

Berger, Joseph; Rosenholtz, Susan J.; & Zelditch, Morris. (1980). Status organizing processes. *Annual Review of Sociology, 6,* 479–508. PA 66:3598.

Berger, Joseph; Webster, Murray, Jr.; Ridgeway, Cecilia; & Rosenholtz, Susan J. (1986). Status cues, expectations, and behavior. *Advances in Group Processes, 3,* 1–22.

Berger, Joseph; & Zelditch, Morris. (1983). Artifacts and challenges: A comment on Lee and Ofshe. *Social Psychology Quarterly, 46,* 59–62. PA 70:10235. SA 83N2339.

Berger, Joseph; & Zelditch, Morris, Jr. (Eds.). (1985). *Status, rewards, and influence: How expectations organize behavior.* San Francisco: Jossey-Bass.

Berger, Milton Miles. (1958). Nonverbal communications in group psychotherapy. *International Journal of Group Psychotherapy, 8,* 161–178.

Berger, Seymour M.; Carli, Linda C.; Garcia, Ricardo; & Brady, James J. (1982). Audience effects in anticipatory learning: A comparison of drive and practice-inhibition analyses. *Journal of Personality and Social Psychology, 42,* 478–486.

Berger, Seymour M.; Hampton, Katherine L.; Carli, Linda L.; Grandmaison, Paul S.; Sadow, Janice S.; Donath, Clifford H.; & Herschlag, Laura R. (1981). Audience-induced inhibition of overt practice during learning. *Journal of Personality and Social Psychology, 40,* 479–491.

Berger, Stephen E.; & Anchor, Kenneth N. (1978). The disclosure process in group interaction. *Small Group Behavior, 9,* 59–63. SA 79K1080.

Berger, Stephen E.; Millham, Jim; Jacobson, Leonard I.; & Anchor, Kenneth N. (1978). Prior self-disclosure, sex differences, and actual confiding in an interpersonal encounter. *Small Group Behavior, 9,* 555–562. SA 80K5514.

Berkovitz, Irving H. (Ed.). (1975). *When schools care: Creative use of groups in secondary schools.* New York: Brunner/Mazel. PA 54:10419.

Berkowitz, Leonard. (1978). Decreased helpfulness with increased group size through lessening the effects of the needy individual's dependency. *Journal of Personality, 46,* 299–310. PA 62:8612.

Berkowitz, Leonard. (Ed). (1984, 1986). *Advances in experimental social psychology* (Vols. 18, 19). Orlando, FL: Academic Press.

Berl, Janet E.; McKelvey, Richard D.; Ordeshook, Peter C.; & Winer, Mark D. (1976). An experimental test of the core in a simple n-person cooperative nonsidepayment game. *Journal of Conflict Resolution, 20,* 453–479.

Berman, John J.; Murphy-Berman, Virginia; & Pachauri, Anju. (1988). Sex differences in friendship patterns in India and in the United States. *Basic and Applied Social Psychology, 9,* 61–71.

Berman, Phyllis W. (1976). Social context as a determinant of sex differences in adults' attraction to infants. *Developmental Psychology, 12,* 365–366. PA 60:970.

Berndt, Thomas J. (1979). Developmental changes in conformity to peers and parents. *Developmental Psychology, 15,* 608–616. PA 63:3054.

Bernhardt, Regis G. (1978). Four Way Decision Making. *Simulation and Games, 9,* 227–233. PA 63:970.

Berry, Sharon L.; Beatty, William W.; & Klesges, Robert C. (1985). Sensory and social influences on ice cream consumption by males and females in a laboratory setting. *Appetite, 6,* 41–45. PA 73:6321.

Bertacchini, Piero A.; Canestrari, Renzo; & Umilta, Carlo. (1975). An analysis of verbal behavior in socially isolated groups. *Giornale Italiano di Psicologia, 2*(1), 89–98. PA 54:11660.

Bertcher, Harvey J. (1979). *Group participation techniques for leaders or members.* Beverly Hills: Sage.

Bertilson, Hal S.; Wonderlich, S. A.; & Blum, M. W. (1983). Withdrawal, matching, withdrawal-matching, and variable-matching strategies in reducing attack-instigated aggression. *Aggressive Behavior, 9*(1), 1–11. PA 71:1307.

Bertilson, Hal S.; Wonderlich, S. A.; & Blum, M. W. (1984). Withdrawal and matching strategies in reducing attack-instigated aggression. *Psychological Reports, 55,* 823–828. PA 72:25417.

Bethlehem, Douglas W. (1975). The effect of westernization on cooperative behaviour in Central Africa. *International Journal of Psychology, 10,* 219–224. PA 58:7329.

Bettenhausen, Kenneth; & Murnighan, J. Keith. (1985). The emergence of norms in competitive decision-making groups. *Administrative Science Quarterly, 30,* 350–372. PA 73:9088. SA 86Q4825.

Bharucha-Reid, Rodabe; & Kiyak, H. Asuman. (1979). The concept of dissonance and too much personal space. *Journal of Nonverbal Behavior*, *4*, 123-125. PA 66:1221.

Bick, Peter; & Loewenthal, Kate. (1976). Silence and role uncertainty. *Journal of Social Psychology*, *99*, 151. PA 56:7937.

Bickman, Leonard. (1974a). Sex and helping behavior. *Journal of Social Psychology*, *93*, 43-53.

Bickman, Leonard. (1974b). The social power of a uniform. *Journal of Applied Social Psychology*, *4*, 47-61. PA 53:3009.

Bickman, Leonard; & Rosenbaum, Dennis P. (1977). Crime reporting as a function of bystander encouragement, surveillance, and credibility. *Journal of Personality and Social Psychology*, *35*, 577-586. PA 62:10994.

Biddle, Bruce J. (1979). *Role theory: Expectations, identities, and behaviors*. New York: Academic Press.

Bienvenu, Millard J.; & Stewart, David W. (1976). Dimensions of interpersonal communication. *Journal of Psychology*, *93*, 105-111. PA 56:3207.

Bierhoff, Hans W.; & Osselmann, Jorn. (1975). [Illegitimate use of pre-information: Effects of altruism and self-punishment in relation to internal-external control, the experimenter, and the sequence of measurement]. *Zeitschrift fur Sozialpsychologie*, *6*, 333-347. PA 58:3314.

Bierschenk, Bernhard. (1978a). [Simulating interactive behaviour: A model and a system in development]. *Zeitschrift fur Empirische Padagogik*, *2*(4), 268-304. PA 64:3244.

Bierschenk, Bernhard. (1978b). A system for interactive behaviour simulation. *Educational and Psychological Interactions*, No. 65, 24 pages. PA 62:10960.

Biersner, Robert J.; McHugh, William B.; & Bennett, Linda K. (1977). Cognitive and emotional factors representative of reinforcement patterns among an amateur softball team. *Human Factors*, *19*, 595-599. PA 60:9360.

Bigoness, William J. (1976). The impact of initial bargaining position and alternative modes of third party intervention in resolving bargaining impasses. *Organizational Behavior and Human Performance*, *17*, 185-198.

Bihm, Elson; Gaudet, Irby; & Sale, Owen. (1979). Altruistic responses under conditions of anonymity. *Journal of Social Psychology*, *109*, 25-30. PA 65:3266.

Billig, Michael; & Cochrane, Raymond. (1976). Judgements of values and group polarization: Tests of the value-for-risk hypothesis. *European Journal of Social Psychology*, *6*, 495-501. PA 59:5622. SA 78J0169.

Billings, Andrew G.; McDowell, Samuel W.; Gomberg, Christopher A.; Kessler, Marc; & Weiner, Sheldon. (1978). The validity of time-sampling in group interactions. *Journal of Social Psychology*, *104*, 223-230. PA 61:12264.

Binning, John F.; & Lord, Robert G. (1980). Boundary conditions for performance cue effects on group process ratings: Familiarity versus type of feedback. *Organizational Behavior and Human Performance*, *26*, 115-130.

Birchler, Gary R.; Weiss, Robert L.; & Vincent, John P. (1975). Multimethod analysis of social reinforcement exchange between maritally distressed and nondistressed spouse and stranger dyads. *Journal of Personality and Social Psychology*, *31*, 349-360. PA 53:11572.

Bird, Anne M. (1977). Team structure and success as related to cohesiveness and leadership. *Journal of Social Psychology*, *103*, 217-223.

Bishop, George D.; & Myers, David G. (1974). Informational influence in group discussion. *Organizational Behavior and Human Performance*, *12*, 92-104. PA 53:2992.

Bitti, Pio R.; Giovannini, Dino; & Palmonari, Augusto. (1974). A study of the interviewer effect in two person interaction. *Giornale Italiano di Psicologia*, *1*, 305-315. PA 55:714.

Bixenstine, V. Edwin; & Abascal, Juan. (1985). Another test of the effect of group composition on member behavior change. *Journal of Clinical Psychology*, *41*, 620-628. PA 73:6322.

Bixenstine, V. Edwin; Lowenfeld, Beverly; & Englehart, Charles E. (1981). Role enactment versus typology: Another test of the triangle hypothesis. *Journal of Personality and Social Psychology*, *41*, 776-788.

Bixenstine, V. Edwin; & Rivera, Enrique. (1981). Clinical observations on group composition tested by simulated groups in the laboratory. *Journal of Clinical Psychology*, *37*, 108-110. PA 65:10363.

Black, Harvey K. (1974). Physical attractiveness and similarity of attitude in interpersonal attraction. *Psychological Reports*, *35*, 403-406. PA 53:7305.

Blackwell, P. L.; & Gessner, J. C. (1983). Fear and trembling: an inquiry into adolescent perceptions of living in the nuclear era. *Youth and Society*, *15*, 237-255.

Blakar, Rolf M. (1973). An experimental method for inquiring into communication. *European Journal of Social Psychology, 3,* 415-425. PA 53:9464.

Blake, Robert R.; & Mouton, Jane Srygley. (1981). *Productivity, the human side: A social dynamics approach.* New York: AMACOM.

Blake, Robert R.; & Mouton, Jane Srygley. (1982). Theory and research for developing a science of leadership. *Journal of Applied Behavioral Science, 18,* 275-291. PA 69:2185.

Blake, Robert R.; & Mouton, Jane Srygley. (1984). *Solving costly organizational conflicts.* San Francisco: Jossey-Bass.

Blalock, Hubert M., Jr. (1987). A power analysis of conflict processes. *Advances in Group Processes, 4,* 1-40.

Blanchard, Fletcher A.; Adelman, Leonard; & Cook, Stuart W. (1975). Effect of group success and failure upon interpersonal attraction in cooperating interracial groups. *Journal of Personality and Social Psychology, 31,* 1020-1030. PA 54:9586.

Blanchard, Fletcher A.; & Cook, Stuart W. (1976). Effects of helping a less competent member of a cooperating interracial group on the development of interpersonal attraction. *Journal of Personality and Social Psychology, 34,* 1245-1255. PA 60:11682.

Blanchard, Fletcher A.; Weigel, Russell H.; & Cook, Stuart W. (1975). The effect of relative competence of group members upon interpersonal attraction in cooperating interracial groups. *Journal of Personality and Social Psychology, 32,* 519-530. PA 54:11692.

Blanchard, Paul D. (1975). Small group analysis and the study of school board conflict: An interdisciplinary approach. *Small Group Behavior, 6,* 229-237. PA 55:2320.

Blaney, Nancy T.; Stephan, Cookie; Rosenfield, David; Aronson, Elliot; & Sikes, Jev. (1977). Interdependence in the classroom: A field study. *Journal of Educational Psychology, 69,* 121-128. PA 58:12477.

Blank, Thomas O.; Staff, Ilene; & Shaver, Philip. (1976). Social facilitation of word associations: Further questions. *Journal of Personality and Social Psychology, 34,* 725-733. PA 58:1077.

Blascovich, Jim; & Ginsburg, Gerald P. (1974). Risky shifts and gambling: What's at stake? *Personality and Social Psychology Bulletin, 1,* 246-248. PA 56:2280.

Blascovich, Jim; Ginsburg, Gerald P.; & Howe, Rene C. (1975). Blackjack and the risky shift: II. Monetary stakes. *Journal of Experimental Social Psychology, 11,* 224-232. PA 54:7495.

Blascovich, Jim; Ginsburg, Gerald P.; & Veach, Tracy L. (1975). A pluralistic explanation of choice shifts on the risk dimension. *Journal of Personality and Social Psychology, 31,* 422-429. PA 54:1014.

Bleda, Paul R. (1976). Conditioning and discrimination of affect and attraction. *Journal of Personality and Social Psychology, 34,* 1106-1115. PA 60:11683.

Bleda, Paul R.; & Bleda, Sharon E. (1978). Effects of sex and smoking on reactions to spatial invasion at a shopping mall. *Journal of Social Psychology, 104,* 311-312. PA 61:13378.

Bleda, Paul R.; Bleda, Sharon E.; Byrne, Donn; & White, Leonard A. (1976). When a bystander becomes an accomplice: Situational determinants of reactions to dishonesty. *Journal of Experimental Social Psychology, 12,* 9-25. PA 56:07938.

Bleda, Paul R.; & Sandman, Paul H. (1977). In smoke's way: Socioemotional reactions to another's smoking. *Journal of Applied Psychology, 62,* 452-458. PA 59:9850.

Blesse, W.; Hlavsa, J.; & Thormannova, Ch. (1979). [Status of the creative personality in the group]. *Ceskoslovenska Psychologie, 23*(3), 180-188.

Bludszuweit, Helmut. (1975). [Presentation form and strategy in game research]. *Zeitschrift fur Psychologie, 183*(3), 269-277. PA 56:7854.

Blumberg, Arthur; & Golembiewski, Robert T. (1976). *Learning and change in groups.* Harmondsworth, England: Penguin.

Blumberg, Herbert H. (1990). Attitude formation and international conflict. *International and Intercultural Communication Annual, 14,* 56-74. [Volume title: F. Korzenny & S. Ting-Toomey (Eds.), *Communicating for peace: Diplomacy and negotiation.* Newbury Park, CA: Sage].

Blumberg, Herbert H.; Davies, Martin F.; & Kent, Valerie. (1986). Interacting in groups. In O. Hargie (Ed.), *Handbook of communication skills* (pp. 269-287). London: Croom Helm.

Blumberg, Herbert H.; Hare, A. Paul; Kent, Valerie; & Davies, Martin F. (Eds.). (1983). *Small groups and social interaction* (2 vols.). Chichester: John Wiley.

Blumberg, Stephen R.; & Hokanson, Jack E. (1983). The effects of another person's response style on interpersonal behavior in depression. *Journal of Abnormal Psychology, 92,* 196–209. PA 70:5620.

Blumstein, Philip; & Kollock, Peter. (1988). Personal relationships. *Annual Review of Sociology, 14,* 467–490.

Boalt Boëthius, Siv. (1983). *Autonomy, coping and defense in small work groups: An analysis of psychological processes within and between individual group members.* Stockholm, Sweden: Almqvist & Wiksell [for University of Stockholm]. [*Ntional Union Catalog,* register no. a-697–451]

Bochner, Arthur P.; di Salvo, Vincent; & Jonas, Thomas. (1975). A computer-assisted analysis of small group process: An investigation of two Machiavellian groups. *Small Group Behavior, 6,* 187–203. PA 55:2321.

Bochner, Arthur P.; & Kaminski, Edmund P. (1974). Modes of interpersonal behavior: A replication. *Psychological Reports, 35,* 1079–1083. PA 53:11573.

Bochner, Arthur P.; Kaminski, Edmund P.; & Fitzpatrick, Mary A. (1977). The conceptual domain of interpersonal communication behavior: A factor-analytic study. *Human Communication Research, 3,* 291–302. PA 60:5193.

Bochner, Stephen; Duncan, Robert; Kennedy, Elizabeth; & Orr, Fred. (1976). Acquaintance links between residents of a high rise building: An application of the "small world" method. *Journal of Social Psychology, 100,* 277–284. PA 58:1078.

Bochner, Stephen; & Orr, Fred E. (1979). Race and academic status as determinants of friendship formation: A field study. *International Journal of Psychology, 14,* 37–46. PA 64:7910.

Bockus, Frank. (1975). A systems approach to marital process. *Journal of Marriage and Family Counseling, 1*(3), 251–258. PA 54:9376.

Boehringer, G. H.; Zeruolis, V.; Bayley, J.; & Boehringer, K. (1974). Stirling: The destructive application of group techniques to a conflict. *Journal of Conflict Resolution, 18,* 257–275. PA 53:5157.

Bohannon, John N.; Stine, Elizabeth L.; & Ritzenberg, Deborah. (1982). The "fine-tuning" hypothesis of adult speech to children: Effects of experience and feedback. *Bulletin of the Psychonomic Society, 19,* 201–204. PA 69:10389.

Boje, David M.; & Murnighan, J. Keith. (1982).

Management Science, 28, 1187–1196. SA 84O0827.

Boldt, Menno. (1980). Canadian Native Indian leadership: Context and composition. *Canadian Ethnic Studies/Etudes Ethniques au Canada, 12*(1), 15–33. SA 82L9866.

Boles, William E.; & Hayward, Scott C. (1978). Effects of urban noise and sidewalk density upon pedestrian cooperation and trust. *Journal of Social Psychology, 104,* 29–35.

Bolle de Bal, Marcel. (1981). La reliance: connexions et sens [Reliance: Connections and meaning]. *Connexions, 33,* 9–36. PA 73:3665.

Bonacich, Phillip. (1976). Secrecy and solidarity. *Sociometry, 39,* 200–208. SA 77I4645.

Bonacich, Phillip. (1979). A single measure for point and interval predictions of coalition theories. *Behavioral Science, 24,* 85–93. PA 64:3245. SA 80K8681.

Bonacich, Phillip. (1985). Cooperation without friendship or foresight. *Contemporary Sociology, 14,* 9–10. SA 85O4343.

Bonacich, Philip; Grusky, Oscar; & Peyrot, Mark. (1985). Family coalitions: A new approach and method. *Social Psychology Quarterly, 48,* 42–50.

Bonacich, Phillip; & Light, John M. (1978). Laboratory experimentation in sociology. *Annual Review of Sociology, 4,* 145–170. PA 63:950.

Bonacich, Phillip; Shure, Gerald H.; Kahan, James P.; & Meeker, Robert J. (1976). Cooperation and group size in the N-person Prisoner's Dilemma. *Journal of Conflict Resolution, 20,* 687–706. PA 58:3288.

Bond, Charles F. (1982). Social facilitation: A self-presentational view. *Journal of Personality and Social Psychology, 42,* 1042–1050. PA 69:1033.

Bond, Charles F.; & Titus, Linda J. (1983). Social facilitation: A meta-analysis of 241 studies. *Psychological Bulletin, 94,* 265–292. PA 71:1336.

Bond, Michael H.; & Komai, Hiroshi. (1976). Targets of gazing and eye contact during interviews: Effect on Japanese nonverbal behavior. *Journal of Personality and Social Psychology, 34,* 1276–1284. PA 60:11684.

Bond, Michael H.; & Lai, Tat ming. (1986). Embarrassment and code-switching into a second language. *Journal of Social Psychology, 126,* 179–186. PA 74:25041.

Bond, Michael H.; & Shiraishi, Daisuke. (1973). [The effect of interviewers' body lean and status on the non-verbal behavior of interviewees]. *Japanese Journal of Experimental Social Psychology, 13,* 11–21. PA 54:2963.

Bond, Michael H.; & Shiraishi, Daisuke. (1974). The effect of body lean and status of an interviewer on the non-verbal behavior of Japanese interviewees. *International Journal of Psychology, 9*, 117–128. PA 53:9466.

Bond, Michael H.; Wan, Kwok-Choi; Leung, Kwok; & Giacalone, Robert A. (1985). How are responses to verbal insult related to cultural collectivism and power distance? *Journal of Cross-Cultural Psychology, 16*, 111–127. SA 8509446.

Bonney, Warren C. (1974). The maturation of groups. *Small Group Behavior, 5*, 445–461. PA 54:10267.

Bonny Miranda, Francisca S.; Bordes Caballero, Rosa; Garcia Gomez, Maria N.; & Martin Zamorano, Maria A. (1981). Obediencia a la autoridad [Obedience to authority]. *Psiquis Revista de Psiquiatria, Psicologia y Psicosomatica, 2*(6), 212–221. PA 68:3519.

Bonoma, Thomas V. (1976). Conflict, cooperation and trust in three power systems. *Behavioral Science, 21*, 499–514. PA 58:1040.

Bonoma, Thomas V.; & Rosenberg, Helen. (1978). Theory-based content analysis: A social influence perspective for evaluating group process. *Social Science Research, 7*, 213–256. PA 63:9623. SA 80K5515.

Bonoma, Thomas V.; & Tedeschi, James T. (1974). The relative efficacies of escalation and deescalation for compliance-gaining in two-party conflicts. *Social Behavior and Personality, 2*, 212–218. PA 54:992.

Bons, Paul M.; & Fiedler, Fred E. (1976). Changes in organizational leadership and the behavior of relationship- and task-motivated leaders. *Administrative Science Quarterly, 21*, 453–473. PA 57:7051.

Boor, Myron. (1976). Effects of victim injury, victim competence, and defendant opportunism on the decisions of simulated jurors. *Journal of Social Psychology, 100*, 315–316. PA 58:1131.

Booraem, Curtis D.; Flowers, John V.; Bodner, Gary E.; & Satterfield, Deborah A. (1977). Personal space variations as a function of criminal behavior. *Psychological Reports, 41*, 1115–1121. PA 61:3819.

Booth-Butterfield, Melanie; & Butterfield, Steven. (1986). Effects of evaluation, task structure, trait-CA, and reticence on state-CA and behavioral disruption in dyadic settings. *Communication Monographs, 53*, 144–159. PA 74:21863.

Bootzin, Richard R.; Bower, Gordon H.; Zajonc,

Robert B.; & Hall, Elizabeth. (1986). *Psychology today: An introduction* (6th ed.). New York: Random House.

Borcherding, Katrin; & Kistner, Karlheinz. (1982). Entwicklung und Uberprufung eines Modells zur Gruppeneinigung in Choice-Dilemma-Situationen [Development and testing of a model of group consensus in choice dilemma situations]. *Zeitschrift fur Sozialpsychologie, 13*, 323–332. PA 70:7954.

Bord, Richard J. (1976a). Impact of dogmatism on reactions to unvalidated authority and antiauthority. *Psychological Reports, 38*, 1219–1222. PA 56:7892.

Bord, Richard J. (1976b). The impact of imputed deviant identities in structuring evaluations and reactions. *Sociometry, 39*, 108–116. PA 56:06024.

Borden, Richard J. (1975). Witnessed aggression: Influence of an observer's sex and values on aggressive responding. *Journal of Personality & Social Psychology, 31*, 567–573. PA 54:01015.

Borden, Richard J. (1980). Audience influence. In P. B. Paulus (Ed.), *Psychology of group influence* (pp. 99–131). Hillsdale, NJ: Erlbaum.

Borden, Richard J.; & Taylor, Stuart P. (1976). Pennies for pain: A note on instrumental aggression toward a pacifist by vanquished, victorious, and evenly-matched opponents. *Victimology, 1*, 154–157. PA 60:1046.

Bordessa, Ronald; & Cameron, James M. (1984). A contingency model of the dispute formation process. *Human Organization, 43*, 357–361.

Bordley, Robert F. (1983). A Bayesian model of group polarization. *Organizational Behavior and Human Performance, 32*, 262–274. PA 71:3964.

Borgatta, Edgar F. (1981). The small groups movement: Historical notes. *American Behavioral Scientist, 24*, 607–618.

Borges, Marilyn A.; & Penta, James M. (1977). Effects of third party intercession on bystander intervention. *Journal of Social Psychology, 103*, 27–32. PA 60:5251.

Boros, Julius. (1985). On some problems of social interactions in Soviet psychology. *Studia Psychologica, 27*, 219–224. PA 74:1035.

Borsig, Clemens A.; & Frey, Dieter. (1979). Satisfaction with group process and group decision as a function of group structure. *Psychological Reports, 44*, 699–705. PA 64:10323.

Borucki, Zenon. (1981). Osobowosciowe determinanty efektywnosci przystosowawcej w malej izolowanej grupie zadaniowej [Personality determinants of effective adjustment in a small isolated task group]. *Przeglad Psychologiczny*, *24*, 733-753. PA 71:6687.

Bossley, M. I. (1976). Privacy and crowding: A multidisciplinary analysis. *Man-Environment Systems*, *6*(1), 8-19. PA 58:1041.

Bottger, Preston C. (1984). Expertise and air time as bases of actual and perceived influence in problem-solving groups. *Journal of Applied Psychology*, *69*, 214-221. PA 71:23050.

Bouchard, Timothy J.; Barsaloux, Jean; & Drauden, Garl. (1974). Brainstorming procedure, group size, and sex as determinants of the problem-solving effectiveness of groups and individuals. *Journal of Applied Psychology*, *59*, 135-138.

Bouska, Marvin L.; & Beatty, Patricia A. (1978). Clothing as a symbol of status: Its effect on control of interaction territory. *Bulletin of the Psychonomic Society*, *11*, 235-238. PA 61:13379.

Bowerman, W. R.; Vermunt, R.; & Van den Berg, G. (1982). A new look at social comparison: An exploration of cognitive and personality antecedents of social comparison choices following performance feedback. *Gedrag: Tijdschrift voor Psychologie*, *10*, 397-410. PA 70:7972.

Bowman, V. J.; & Colantoni, C. S. (1972). The extended condorcet condition: A necessary and sufficient condition for the transitivity of majority decision. *Journal of Mathematical Sociology*, *2*, 267-283. SA 75H1330.

Boyanowsky, Ehor O.; Allen, Vernon L.; Bragg, Barry W.; & Lepinski, John. (1981). Generalization of independence created by social support. *Psychological Record*, *31*, 475-488. PA 68:3520. SA 84N7282.

Boyce, P. (1974). Users' assessments of a landscaped office. *Journal of Architectural Research*, *3*(3), 44-62.

Boyd, Robert D. (1983). A matrix model of the small group. *Small Group Behavior*, *14*, 405-418. PA 71:23051.

Boyd, Robert D. (1984). A matrix model of the small group: II. *Small Group Behavior*, *15*, 233-250. PA 72:1223.

Boyd, Robert D.; & Wilson, John P. (1974). Three channel theory of communication in small groups. *Adult Education*, *24*, 167-183. PA 52:10009.

Bozeman, Barry; & McAlpine, William E. (1977). Goals and bureaucratic decision-making: An

experiment. *Human Relations*, *30*, 417-429. PA 59:7842.

Braaten, Leif J. (1974). Developmental phases of encounter groups and related intensive groups. *Interpersonal Development*, *5*(2), 112-129. PA 55:2659.

Bradac, James J.; Courtright, John A.; Schmidt, Gregson; & Davies, Robert A. (1976). The effects of perceived status and linguistic diversity upon judgments of speaker attributes and message effectiveness. *Journal of Psychology*, *93*, 213-220. PA 56:9853.

Bradley, Patricia H. (1978a). Power, status, and upward communication in small decision-making groups. *Communication Monographs*, *45*, 33-43. PA 61:13380. SA 81L4923.

Bradley, Patricia H. (1978b). Pressure for uniformity: An experimental study of deviate responses in group discussions of policy. *Small Group Behavior*, *9*, 149-160. SA 79K1082.

Bradley, Patricia H. (1980). Sex, competence and opinion deviation: An expectation states approach. *Communication Monographs*, *47*, 101-110. PA 66:3599.

Bradley, Patricia H.; MacHamon, C.; & Harris, Alan M. (1976). Dissent in small groups. *Journal of Communication*, *26*, 155-159. PA 61:8438.

Brady, Adele T.; & Walker, Michael B. (1978). Interpersonal distance as a function of situationally induced anxiety. *British Journal of Social and Clinical Psychology*, *17*, 127-133. PA 62:5966.

Bragg, Barry W.; & Allen, Vernon. (1972). The role of public and private support in reducing conformity. *Psychonomic Science*, *29*, 81-82. PA 53:5190.

Brams, Steven J. (1975). Newcomb's problem and Prisoner's Dilemma. *Journal of Conflict Resolution*, *19*, 596-612. PA 56:7855.

Brams, Steven J.; & Garriga-Pico, Jose E. (1975). Bandwagons in coalition formation: the 2/3's rule. *American Behavioral Scientist*, *18*, 472-496. SA 76H7086.

Brams, Steven J.; & Heilman, John G. (1974). When to join a coalition, and with how many others, depends on what you expect the outcome to be. *Public Choice*, *17*, 11-25. SA 77I6189.

Brams, Steven J.; & Hessel, Marek P. (1982). Absorbing outcomes in 2 times 2 games. *Behavioral Science*, *27*, 393-401. SA 83N4032.

Brams, Steven J.; & Kilgour, D. Marc. (1987).

Winding down if preemption or escalation occurs: A game-theoretic analysis. *Journal of Conflict Resolution, 31*, 547–572.

Brams, Steven J.; & Zagare, Frank C. (1977). Deception in simple voting games. *Social Science Research, 6*, 257–272. PA 60:03027.

Brandstätter, Hermann. (1985). Social emotions in controversial discussions and in group decision making. *Advances in Group Processes, 2*, 249–281.

Brandstätter, Hermann; Davis, James H.; & Schuler, Heinz. (Eds.). (1978). *Dynamics of group decisions*. Beverly Hills, CA: Sage.

Brandstätter, Hermann; Davis, James H.; & Stocker-Kreichgauer, Gisela. (Eds.). (1982). *Group decision making*. London: Academic Press.

Brandstätter, Hermann; & Klein-Moddenborg, Volker. (1979). A modified proportional change model of attitude change by group discussion. *European Journal of Social Psychology, 9*, 363–380. PA 65:3239.

Brann, Peter; & Foddy, Margaret. (1987). Trust and the consumption of a deteriorating common resource. *Journal of Conflict Resolution, 31*, 615–630.

Braver, Sanford L. (1975). Reciprocity, cohesiveness and cooperation in two-person games. *Psychological Reports, 36*, 371–378. PA 54:7446. SA 78J4681.

Braver, Sanford L.; & Barnett, Bruce. (1974). Perception of opponent's motives and cooperation in a mixed-motive game. *Journal of Conflict Resolution, 18*, 686–699. PA 53:9498.

Braver, Sanford L.; & Barnett, Bruce. (1976). Effects of modeling on cooperation in a Prisoner's Dilemma game. *Journal of Personality and Social Psychology, 33*, 161–169. PA 56:661.

Braver, Sanford; Linder, Darwin; Corwin, T.; & Cialdini, Robert B. (1977). Some conditions that affect admission of attitude change. *Journal of Experimental Social Psychology, 13*, 56–71.

Braver, Sanford L.; & Rohrer, Van. (1975). When martyrdom pays: The effects of information concerning the opponents' past game behavior. *Journal of Conflict Resolution, 19*, 652–662. PA 56:7940.

Braver, Sanford L.; & Rohrer, Van. (1978). Superiority of vicarious over direct experience in interpersonal conflict resolution. *Journal of Conflict Resolution, 22*, 143–155. PA 61:10898.

Braver, Sanford L.; & Wilson, L. A. (1986). Choices in social dilemmas: Effects of communication within subgroups. *Journal of Conflict Resolution, 30*, 51–62. PA 73:24465.

Bray, Robert M.; Johnson, Dennis; & Chilstrom, John T. (1982). Social influence by group members with minority opinions: A comparison of Hollander and Moscovici. *Journal of Personality and Social Psychology, 43*, 78–88. PA 69:3383.

Bray, Robert M.; Kerr, Norbert L.; & Atkin, Robert S. (1978). Effects of group size, problem difficulty, and sex on group performance and member reactions. *Journal of Personality and Social Psychology, 36*, 1224–1240. PA 63:9625.

Bray, Robert M.; & Noble, Audrey M. (1978). Authoritarianism and decisions of mock juries: Evidence of jury bias and group polarization. *Journal of Personality and Social Psychology, 36*, 1424–1430. PA 63:9624.

Bray, Robert M.; & Sugarman, Roger. (1980). Social facilitation among interacting groups: Evidence for the evaluation-apprehension hypothesis. *Personality and Social Psychology Bulletin, 6*, 137–142. PA 65:10364.

Breaugh, James A.; & Klimoski, Richard J. (1981). Social forces in negotiation simulations. *Personality and Social Psychology Bulletin, 7*, 290–295. PA 67:5698.

Breaugh, James A.; Klimoski, Richard J; & Shapiro, Mitchell B. (1980). Third-party characteristics and intergroup conflict resolution. *Psychological Reports, 47*, 447–451.

Brechner, Kevin C. (1977). An experimental analysis of social traps. *Journal of Experimental Social Psychology, 13*, 552–564. PA 61:5916.

Breckheimer, Steven E.; & Nelson, Rosemery O. (1976). Group methods for reducing racial prejudice and discrimination. *Psychological Reports, 39*, 1259–1268. PA 58:7411.

Breed, George; & Colaiuta, Victoria. (1974). Looking, blinking, and sitting: Nonverbal dynamics in the classroom. *Journal of Communication, 24*, 75–81. PA 52:10105.

Brehm, Jack W.; & Mann, Milard. (1975). Effect of importance of freedom and attraction to group members on influence produced by group pressure. *Journal of Personality and Social Psychology, 31*, 816–824. PA 54:5184.

Brehm, Sharon S.; & Brehm, Jack W. (1981). *Psychological reactance: A theory of freedom and control*. New York: Academic Press.

Brehmer, Berndt. (1974a). Effects of cue validity

and task predictability on interpersonal learning of linear inference tasks. *Organizational Behavior and Human Performance, 12,* 17–29. PA 53:2319.

Brehmer, Berndt. (1974b). Policy conflict, policy consistency, and interpersonal understanding. *Scandinavian Journal of Psychology, 15,* 273–276. PA 54:993.

Brehmer, Berndt. (1975). Social judgment theory and the analysis of interpersonal conflict. *Umea Psychological Reports,* No. 87, 41 pages. PA 55:715.

Brehmer, Berndt. (1976). Social judgment theory and the analysis of interpersonal conflict. *Psychological Bulletin, 83,* 985–1003. PA 58:1080.

Brehmer, Berndt; & Garpebring, Staffan. (1974). Social pressure and policy change in the "lens model" interpersonal conflict paradigm. *Scandinavian Journal of Psychology, 15,* 191–196. PA 53:7283.

Brenenstuhl, Daniel C.; & Blalack, Richard O. (1978). Role preference and vested interest in a bargaining environment. *Simulation and Games, 9,* 53–65. PA 62:8585.

Brenner, Sten Olaf; & Hjelmquist, Erland. (1974a). Verbal interaction in dyads I: Intensive process analysis of interactions. *Göteborg Psychological Reports, 4*(24), 28. PA 55:716.

Brenner, Sten Olof; & Hjelmquist, Erland. (1974b). Verbal interactions in dyads II: Process analysis of interactions. *Göteborg Psychological Reports, 4*(25), 31. PA 55:717.

Brenner, Sten Olof; & Hjelmquist, Erland. (1974c). Verbal interaction in dyads III: The effects of the interactions. *Göteborg Psychological Reports, 4*(26), 11. PA 55:718.

Brent, Edward E.; & Sykes, Richard E. (1979). A mathematical model of symbolic interaction between police and suspects. *Behavioral Science, 24,* 388–402. PA 65:01228.

Brent, Edward E., Jr; & Sykes, Richard E. (1980). The Interactive Bases of Police-Suspect Confrontation: An Empirically Based Simulation of a Markov Process. *Simulation and Games, 11,* 347–363. SA 8504344.

Brewer, Marilynn B.; & Kramer, Roderick M. (1986). Choice behavior in social dilemmas: Effects of social identity, group size, and decision framing. *Journal of Personality and Social Psychology, 50,* 543–549. PA 73:19789.

Brewer, Marilynn B.; & Mittelman, John. (1980). Effects of normative control of self-disclosure

on reciprocity. *Journal of Personality, 48,* 89–102. PA 65:10366.

Brickman, Philip; Becker, Lawrence J.; & Castle, Sidney. (1979). Making trust easier and harder through two forms of sequential interaction. *Journal of Personality and Social Psychology, 37,* 515–521. PA 64:7913.

Bridges, Judith S.; & Schoeninger, Douglas W. (1977). Interpersonal trust behavior as related to subjective certainty and outcome value. *Psychological Reports, 41,* 677–678. PA 60:7428.

Brightman, Harvey J.; Lewis, Danny J.; & Verhoeven, Penny. (1983). Nominal and interacting groups as Bayesian information processors. *Psychological Reports, 53,* 101–102. PA 71:9475. SA 8400829.

Brinberg, David; & Castell, Pat. (1982). A resource exchange theory approach to interpersonal interactions: A test of Foa's theory. *Journal of Personality and Social Psychology, 43,* 260–269. PA 69:5568.

Brinkerhoff, David B.; & Booth, Alan. (1984). Gender, dominance and stress. *Journal of Social and Biological Structures, 7,* 159–177. PA 72:17309.

Brockner, Joel; & Adsit, Laury. (1986). The moderating impact of sex on the equity-satisfaction relationship: A field study. *Journal of Applied Psychology, 71,* 585–590. PA 74:10180.

Brockner, Joel; Fine, Judy; Hamilton, Thomas P.; Thomas, Barbara; & Turetsky, Beth. (1982). Factors affecting entrapment in escalating conflicts: The importance of timing. *Journal of Research in Personality, 16,* 247–266. PA 69:1034.

Brockner, Joel; Nathanson, Sinaia; Friend, Alan; Harbeck, John; Samuelson, Charles; Houser, Robert; Bazerman, Max H.; & Rubin, Jeffrey Z. (1984). The role of modeling processes in the "Knee Deep in the Big Muddy" phenomenon. *Organizational Behavior and Human Performance, 33,* 77–99. PA 71:12146.

Brockner, Joel; O'Malley, Michael N.; Hite, Terrian; & Davies, Daniel K. (1987). Reward allocation and self-esteem: The roles of modeling and equity restoration. *Journal of Personality and Social Psychology, 52,* 844–850. PA 74:21900.

Brockner, Joel; & Rubin, Jeffrey Z. (1985). *Entrapment in escalating conflicts: A social psychological analysis.* New York: Springer-Verlag.

Brockner, Joel; Rubin, Jeffrey Z.; & Lang, Elaine. (1981). Face-saving and entrapment. *Journal of Experimental Social Psychology, 17*, 68–79. PA 67:3576.

Brockner, Joel; Shaw, Myril C.; & Rubin, Jeffrey Z. (1979). Factors affecting withdrawal from an escalating conflict: Quitting before it's too late. *Journal of Experimental Social Psychology, 15*, 492–503.

Brodt, Susan E.; & Zimbardo, Philip G. (1981). Modifying shyness related social behavior through symptom misattribution. *Journal of Personality and Social Psychology, 41*, 437–449.

Brookmire, David A.; & Sistrunk, Frank. (1980). The effects of perceived ability and impartiality of mediators and time pressure on negotiation. *Journal of Conflict Resolution, 24*, 311–327. PA 64:12480.

Brooks, Charles I.; Church, Michael A.; & Fraser, Lance. (1986). Effects of duration of eye contact on judgments of personality characteristics. *Journal of Social Psychology, 126*, 71–78. PA 74:25066.

Brousek, Jan. (1979). [An instrument to measure interaction]. *Psychologia u Patopsychologia Dietata, 14*(5), 467–475. PA 65:10367.

Brower, Sidney; Dockett, Kathleen; & Taylor, Ralph B. (1983). Residents' perception of territorial features and perceived local threat. *Environment and Behavior, 15*, 419–437. PA 70:13798.

Brown, Allan. (1986). *Groupwork* (2nd ed.). Aldershot, England: Gower.

Brown, Arthur H. (1975). A use of social exchange theory in family crisis intervention. *Journal of Marriage and Family Counseling, 1*(3), 259–267. PA 54:9463.

Brown, Barbara B. (1987). Territoriality. In D. Stokols and I. Altman (Eds.), *Handbook of environmental psychology* (Vol. 1, pp. 505–531). New York: Wiley

Brown, Barbara B.; & Altman, Irwin. (1983). Territoriality, defensible space, and residential burglary: An environmental analysis. *Journal of Environmental Psychology, 3*, 203–220. PA 71:19196.

Brown, Clifford E. (1981). Shared space invasion and race. *Personality and Social Psychology Bulletin, 7*, 103–108.

Brown, David; Reschly, Daniel; & Sabers, Darrell. (1974). Using group contingencies with punishment and positive reinforcement to modify aggressive behaviors in a Head Start classroom. *Psychological Record, 24*, 491–496. PA 53:10418.

Brown, Nina W.; & Sullivan, James. (1979). Validation of the interpersonal relationship rating scale. *Group and Organization Studies, 4*, 220–228. SA 80K4171.

Brown, Robert S.; & Sanders, Glenn. (1975). Group decision as a technique for obtaining compliance: Some added considerations concerning how altruism leads to callousness. *Journal of Applied Social Psychology, 5*, 281–295. PA 57:1145.

Brown, Roger. (1986). *Social psychology: The second edition.* New York: Free Press.

Brown, Rupert J. (1984). The effects of intergroup similarity and cooperative vs. Competitive Orientation on Intergroup Discrimination. *British Journal of Social Psychology, 23*, 21–33. SA 8402579.

Brown, Rupert [J.]. (1988). *Group processes: Dynamics within and between groups.* Oxford, UK: B. Blackwell.

Brown, Sandra A. (1985). Expectancies versus background in the prediction of college drinking patterns. *Journal of Consulting and Clinical Psychology, 53*, 123–130. PA 55:07156.

Brown, Virginia; & Geis, Florence L. (1984). Turning lead into gold: Evaluations of men and women leaders and the alchemy of social consensus. *Journal of Personality and Social Psychology, 46*, 811–824. PA 71:23087.

Browne, Eric C.; & Feste, Karen Ann. (1975). Qualitative dimensions of coalition payoffs. *American Behavioral Scientist, 18*, 530–556. SA 76H7087.

Brownell, Winifred; & Smith, Dennis R. (1973). Communication patterns, sex, and length of verbalization in speech of four-year-old children. *Speech Monographs, 40*, 310–316. PA 53:2993.

Brunner, Lawrence J. (1979). Smiles can be back channels. *Journal of Personality and Social Psychology, 37*, 728–734. PA 64:7914.

Bryson, R. B. (1977). The application of individual differences multidimensional scaling techniques to the study of interpersonal attraction. *Multivariate Experimental Clinical Research, 3*, 123–131. PA 61:1011.

Buchanan, Douglas R.; Goldman, Morton; & Juhnke, Ralph. (1977). Eye contact, sex, and the violation of personal space. *Journal of Social Psychology, 103,* 19–25. PA 60:5223.

Buchanan, Douglas R.; Juhnke, Ralph; & Goldman, Morton. (1976). Violation of personal space as a function of sex. *Journal of Social Psychology, 99,* 187–192.

Buck, Ross. (1980). Nonverbal behavior and the theory of emotion: The facial feedback hypothesis. *Journal of Personality and Social Psychology, 38,* 811–824. PA 65:12788.

Buckley, James J.; & Westen, T. Edward. (1976). Bargaining set theory and majority rule. *Journal of Conflict Resolution, 20,* 481–496.

Buckley, W.; Burns, T.; & Meeker, L. D. (1974). Structural resolutions of collective action problems. *Behavioral Science, 19,* 277–297. PA 53:5160.

Budescu, David V. (1984). Tests of lagged dominance in sequential dyadic interaction. *Psychological Bulletin, 96,* 402–414. PA 71:30481.

Budescu, David V. (1985). Analysis of dichotomous variables in the presence of serial dependence. *Psychological Bulletin, 97,* 547–561. PA 72:21787.

Bugen, Larry A. (1978). Expectation profiles: Members expect more than they get while leaders give more than they expect. *Small Group Behavior, 9,* 115–123. SA 79K1083.

Bugenthal, Daphne Blunt. (1986). Unmasking the "polite smile": Situational and personal determinants of managed affect in adult-child interaction. *Personality and Social Psychology Bulletin, 12,* 7–16. PA 74:12926.

Bulak, Jozef. (1972). [Interpersonal relationships and work behavior in small work groups]. *Synteza, 5*(4), 132–139. PA 53:12687.

Bull, Peter E. (1987). *Posture and gesture.* Oxford: Pergamon.

Bull, Peter E.; & Brown, R. (1977). The role of postural change in dyadic conversations. *British Journal of Social and Clinical Psychology, 16,* 29–33. PA 58:9469.

Bullard, Peter D.; & Cook, Paul E. (1975). Sex and workstyle of leaders and followers: Determinants of productivity. *Psychological Reports, 36,* 545–546. PA 55:12204.

Bullivant, Brian M. (1978). Towards a neo-ethnographic method for small-group research. *Australian and New Zealand Journal of Sociology, 14,* [Part Oct.] 239–249. SA 80K4172.

Bunker, Barbara B. (1974). The Tavistock approach to the study of group process: Reactions

of a private investigator. In D. S. Milman & G. D. Goldman (Eds.), *Group process today: Evaluation and perspective* (pp. 63–77). Springfield, IL: Charles C. Thomas. PA 53:12183.

Burch, Mark A.; & Walker, James L. (1978). Effects of population density and information overload on state anxiety and crowding perception. *Psychological Record, 28,* 207–214. PA 62:1023.

Burger, Jerry. (1986). Increasing compliance by improving the deal: The that's-not-all technique. *Journal of Personality and Social Psychology, 31,* 277–283.

Burger, Jerry M. (1987). Desire for control and conformity to a perceived norm. *Journal of Personality and Social Psychology, 53,* 355–360.

Burger, Jerry M.; Oakman, Julie A.; & Bullard, N. Garrell. (1983). Desire for control and the perception of crowding. *Personality and Social Psychology Bulletin, 9,* 475–479.

Burger, Jerry M.; & Petty, Richard E. (1981). The low-ball compliance technique: Task or person commitment? *Journal of Personality and Social Psychology, 40,* 492–500. PA 66:12788.

Burgess, J. Wesley. (1983). Interpersonal spacing behavior between surrounding nearest neighbors reflects both familiarity and environmental density. *Ethology and Sociobiology, 4,* 11–17. PA 71:1308.

Burgess, J. Wesley. (1984). Do humans show a "species-typical" group size? Age, sex, and environmental differences in the size and composition of naturally-occurring casual groups. *Ethology and Sociobiology, 5,* 51–57. PA 72:3989. SA 84O0830.

Burgess, Robert L.; & Huston, Ted L. (Eds.). (1979). *Social exchange in developing relationships.* New York & London: Academic Press.

Burgess, Robert L.; & Nielsen, Joyce McCarl. (1974). An experimental analysis of some structural determinants of equitable and inequitable exchange relations. *American Sociological Review, 39,* 427–443.

Burgoon, Judee K. (1978). A communication model of personal space violations: Explication and an initial test. *Human Communication Research, 4*(2), 129–142. PA 61:5917.

Burgoon, Judee K.; & Aho, Lynn. (1982). Three field experiments on the effects of violations of conversational distance. *Communication Monographs, 49*(2), 71–88. PA 69:3384.

Burgoon, Judee K.; & Burgoon, Michael. (1974). Unwillingness to communicate, anomia alienation, and communication apprehension as predictors of small group communication. *Journal of Psychology, 88*, 31-38. PA 53:5161.

Burgoon, Judee K.; & Jones, Stephen B. (1976). Toward a theory of personal space expectations and their violations. *Human Communication Research, 2*(2), 131-146. PA 60:972.

Burgoon, Judee K.; & Koper, Randall J. (1984). Nonverbal and relational communication associated with reticence. *Human Communication Research, 10*(4), 601-626. PA 72:14479.

Burgoon, Michael; Dillard, James P.; & Doran, Noel E. (1983). Friendly or unfriendly persuasion: The effects of violations of expectations by males and females. *Human Communication Research, 10*(2), 283-294. PA 71:31314.

Burke, Ronald J.; Firth, John; & McGrattan, Cheryl. (1974). Husband-wife compatibility and the management of stress. *Journal of Social Psychology, 94*, 243-252. PA 53:9459.

Burleson, Brant R.; Levine, Barbara J.; & Samter, Wendy. (1984). Decision-making procedure and decision quality. *Human Communication Research, 10*(4), 557-574. PA 72:14480.

Burley, Peter M.; & McGuinness, John. (1977). Effects of social intelligence on the Milgram paradigm. *Psychological Reports, 40*, 767-770. PA 59:9883.

Burlingame, Gary; Fuhriman, Addie; & Drescher, Stuart. (1984). Scientific inquiry into small group process: A multidimensional approach. *Small Group Behavior, 15*, 441-470. PA 72:14481.

Burnett, Rosalie; McGhee, Patrick; & Clarke, David. (Eds.). (1987). *Accounting for relationships: Explanation, representation and knowledge.* London: Methuen.

Burnstein, Eugene; & Schul, Yaacov. (1983). Group polarization. In H. H. Blumberg, A. P. Hare, V. Kent, & M. F. Davies (Eds.), *Small groups and social interaction* (Vol. 2, pp. 57-64). Chichester: John Wiley.

Burnstein, Eugene; & Vinokur, Amiram. (1975). What a person thinks upon learning he has chosen differently from others: Nice evidence for the persuasive-arguments explanation of choice shifts. *Journal of Experimental Social Psychology, 11*, 412-426. PA 55:4541.

Burnstein, Eugene; & Vinokur, Amiram. (1977). Persuasive argumentation and social comparison as determinants of attitude polarization. *Journal of Experimental Social Psychology, 13*, 315-332. PA 59:9884.

Burnstein, Eugene; Vinokur, Amiram; & Pichevin, Marie-France. (1974). What do differences between own, admired, and attributed choices have to do with group induced shifts in choice? *Journal of Experimental Social Psychology, 10*, 428-443.

Burton, Gene E. (1987). The "clustering effect:" An idea-generation phenomenon during nominal grouping. *Small Group Behavior, 18*, 224-238.

Burton, Ian; & Kates, Robert W. (1978). *The environment as hazard.* New York: Oxford University Press.

Burton, J. (1979). *Deviance, terrorism and war: The process of solving unsolved social and political problems.* Oxford: Robertson.

Busching, Bruce; & Milner, Murray. (1982). Limiting case models in the behavioral sciences: Perfect competition, perfect benevolence, and perfect malevolence. *Human Relations, 35*, 857-869. PA 69:7863.

Bushman, Brad J. (1984). Perceived symbols of authority and their influence on compliance. *Journal of Applied Social Psychology, 14*, 501-508. PA 72:25418.

Buss, Arnold H. (1986). *Social Behavior and Personality.* Hillsdale, NJ: Erlbaum.

Buss, Arnold H.; & Briggs, Stephen R. (1984). Drama and the self in social interaction. *Journal of Personality and Social Psychology, 47*, 1310-1324. PA 72:11998.

Bussey, Kay; & Bandura, Albert. (1984). Influence of gender constancy and social power on sex-linked modeling. *Journal of Personality and Social Psychology, 47*, 1292-1302. PA 72:11790.

Butcher, Jennifer; & Whissell, Cynthia. (1984). Laughter as a function of audience size, sex of the audience, and segments of the short film Duck Soup. *Perceptual and Motor Skills, 59*, 949-950. PA 73:19815.

Butkovich, Paul; Carlisle, Jim; Duncan, Robert; & Moss, Mervin. (1975). Social system and psychoanalytic approaches to group dynamics: Complementary or contradictory? *International Journal of Group Psychotherapy, 25*, 3-31. PA 54:11662.

Butler, John K. (1986). Reciprocity of dyadic trust

in close male-female relationships. *Journal of Social Psychology*, *126*, 579–591. PA 75:7382.

Butler, Richard P.; & Jaffee, Cabot L. (1974). Effects of incentive, feedback, and manner of presenting the feedback on leader behavior. *Journal of Applied Psychology*, *59*, 332–336.

Butterfield, D. Anthony; & Powell, Gary N. (1981). Effect of group performance, leader sex, and rater sex on ratings of leader behavior. *Organizational Behavior and Human Performance*, *28*, 129–141. PA 66:10314.

Butterfield, Gary. (1977). Analysis of interaction in observation of nonverbal behavior. *Perceptual and Motor Skills*, *45*, 235–238. PA 60:5194.

Buunk, Bram. (1983). Sekseverschillen in vriendschap [Sex differences in friendship]. *Gedrag Tijdschrift voor Psychologie*, *11*(2–3), 111–121. PA 71:6688.

Buunk, Bram. (1984). Sociale psychologie en intieme relaties [Social psychology and personal relationships]. *Nederlands Tijdschrift voor de Psychologie en haar Grensgebieden*, *39*, 369–375. PA 72:25392.

Buys, Christian J. (1978a). Humans would do better without groups. *Personality and Social Psychology Bulletin*, *4*, 123–125. PA 61:5918.

Buys, Christian J. (1978b). On humans would do better without groups: A final note. *Personality and Social Psychology Bulletin*, *4*, 568.

Bynum, Timothy S.; & Purri, Dan M. (1984). Crime and architectural style: an examination of the environmental design hypothesis. *Criminal Justice and Behavior*, *11*, 179–196. PA 72:18883.

Cabell, David E. (1974). The relevance of a management game. *Simulation and Games*, *5*, 201–211. PA 53:8490.

Cacioppo, John T.; & Lowell, Charlotte A. (1981). Sex differences in the aspects of team sport participation viewed as enjoyable. *Journal of Sport Psychology*, *3*, 190–195. PA 67:3518.

Cacioppo, John T.; Petty, Richard E.; & Losch, Mary E. (1986). Attributions of responsibility for helping and doing harm: Evidence for confusion of responsibility. *Journal of Personality and Social Psychology*, *50*, 100–105. PA 73:17223.

Caine, Bruce T.; & Schlenker, Barry R. (1979). Role position and group performance as determinants of egotistical perceptions in coopera-

tive groups. *Journal of Psychology*, *101*, 149–156. PA 64:3229.

Cairns, Robert B. (Ed.). (1979). *The analysis of social interaction: Methods, issues, and illustrations*. Hillsdale, NJ: Erlbaum.

Calder, Bobby J.; Insko, Chester A.; & Yandell, Ben. (1974). The relation of cognitive and memorial processes to persuasion in a simulated jury trial. *Journal of Applied Social Psychology*, *4*, 62–93. PA 53:3011.

Caldwell, Michael D. (1976). Communication and sex effects in a five-person Prisoner's Dilemma Game. *Journal of Personality and Social Psychology*, *33*, 273–280. PA 56:2298.

Calhoun, John B. (1962). Population density and social pathology. *Scientific American*, *206*, 139–148.

Callahan-Levy, Charlene; & Messé, Lawrence A. (1979). Sex differences in the allocation of pay. *Journal of Personality and Social Psychology*, *37*, 433–446. PA 64:3229.

Callan, Hilary M. W.; Chance, Michael R. A.; & Pitcairn, Thomas K. (1973). Attention and advertence in human groups. *Social Science Information/Information sur les Sciences Sociales*, *12*(2), 27–41. SA 75H1331.

Callaway, Michael R.; & Esser, James K. (1984). Groupthink: Effects of cohesiveness and problem-solving procedures on group decision making. *Social Behavior and Personality*, *12*, 157–164. PA 73:11721.

Callaway, Michael R.; Marriott, Richard G.; & Esser, James K. (1985). Effects of dominance on group decision making: Toward a stress-reduction explanation of groupthink. *Journal of Personality and Social Psychology*, *49*, 949–952. PA 73:3666.

Callero, Peter L.; & Piliavin, Jane A. (1983). Developing a commitment to blood donation: The impact of one's first experience. *Journal of Applied Social Psychology*, *13*, 1–16. PA 70:10264.

Calsyn, Robert J. (1976). Group responses to territorial intrusion. *Journal of Social Psychology*, *100*, 51–58.

Calsyn, Robert [J.]; & Becker, Lawrence J. (1976). Group size and population density in the probability of joining or leaving free-forming groups. *Psychological Reports*, *39*, 199–202. PA 57:3185.

Calvert-Boyanowski, J; Boyanowski, E. O.; Atkinson, M.; Gaduto, D.; & Reeves, J. (1976).

Patterns of passion: temperature and human emotion. In D. Krebs (Ed.), *Readings in social psychology*. New York: Harper & Row.

Camilleri, Santo F.; & Conner, Thomas L. (1976). Decision-making and social influence: A revised model and further experimental evidence. *Sociometry*, *39*, 30–38. PA 56:00666.

Camino, Leoncio; Leyens, Jacques Philippe; & Cavell, Barry. (1979). Les reactions agressives de groupes minoritaires: I. Etudes preliminaires. L'attribution de responsabilite, le sentiment de competence et le controle strategique [The aggressive reactions of minority groups: I. The attribution of responsibility, the feeling of competence and strategic control]. *Recherches de Psychologie Sociale*, *1*, 83–97. PA 67:1210.

Campbell, Anne; & Rushton, J. Philippe. (1978). Bodily communication and personality. *British Journal of Social and Clinical Psychology*, *17*, 31–36.

Campbell, David E. (1979). Interior office design and visitor response. *Journal of Applied Psychology*, *64*, 648–653. PA 65:2281.

Campbell, David E.; & Beets J. L. (1977). Meteorological variables and behavior: An annotated bibliography. *JSAS Catalog of Selected Documents in Psychology*, *7*(1): [MS 1403].

Campbell, David E.; & Lancioni, Giulio E. (1979). The effects of staring and pew invasion in church settings. *Journal of Social Psychology*, *108*, 19–24. PA 64:7915.

Campbell, Jennifer D.; Tesser, Abraham; & Fairey, Patricia J. (1986). Conformity and attention to the stimulus: Some temporal and contextual dynamics. *Journal of Personality and Social Psychology*, *51*, 315–324. PA 73:29938.

Campbell, Jennifer F. (1980). Complementarity and attraction: A reconceptualization in terms of dyadic behavior. *Representative Research in Social Psychology*, *11*, 74–95. PA 69:3385.

Campbell, Joan M. (1983). Ambient stressors. *Environment and Behavior*, *15*, 355–380. PA 70:9191.

Campbell, Michael D. (1974). A controlled investigation of altruistic behavior: Helping the hitchhiker. *Personality and Social Psychology Bulletin*, *1*, 174–176. PA 56:2331.

Cann, Arnie; Sherman, Steven J.; & Elkes, Roy. (1975). Effects of initial request size and timing of a second request on compliance: The foot in

the door and the door in the face. *Journal of Personality and Social Psychology*, *32*, 774–782. PA 55:7116.

Cansler, David C.; & Stiles, William B. (1981). Relative status and interpersonal presumptuousness. *Journal of Experimental Social Psychology*, *17*, 459–471. PA 67:5699.

Canter, David V.; & Craik, Kenneth H. (1981). Environmental psychology. *Journal of Environmental Psychology*, *1*, 1–11. PA 67:6641.

Cantor, Nancy; Mackie, Diane; & Lord, Charles. (1984). Choosing partners and activities: The social perceiver decides to mix it up. *Social Cognition*, *2*, 256–272. PA 72:12676.

Cantor, Nancy L.; & Gelfand, Donna M. (1977). Effects of responsiveness and sex of children on adults' behavior. *Child Development*, *48*, 232–238. PA 58:7430.

Caplan, Marc E.; & Goldman, Morton. (1981). Personal space violations as a function of height. *Journal of Social Psychology*, *114*, 167–171.

Caple, Richard B. (1978). The sequential stages of group development. *Small Group Behavior*, *9*, 470–476. SA 80K4173.

Caporael, Linnda R.; Dawes, Robyn M.; Orbell, John M.; & van de Kragt, Alphons J. C. (1989). Selfishness examined: Cooperation in the absence of egoistic motives. *Behavioral and Brain Sciences*, *12*, 683–739.

Cappella, Joseph N. (1981). Mutual influence in expressive behavior: Adult-adult and infant-adult dyadic interaction. *Psychological Bulletin*, *89*, 101–132. PA 65:5379.

Cappella, Joseph N. (1985). Production principles for turn-taking rules in social interaction: Socially anxious vs. socially secure persons. (Special Issue: Cognition in social interaction: Production principles.) *Journal of Language & Social Psychology*, *4*, 193–212. PA 74:18720.

Cappella, Joseph N.; & Greene, John O. (1982). A discrepancy-arousal explanation of mutual influence in expressive behavior for adult and infant-adult interaction. *Communication Monographs*, *49*, 89–114. PA 69:3386.

Cappella, Joseph N.; & Planalp, Sally. (1981). Talk and silence sequences in informal conversations: III. Interspeaker influence. *Human Communication Research*, *7*, 117–132. PA 67:1212.

Caproni, Valerie; Levine, Douglas; O'Neal, Edgar; McDonald, Peter; & Garwood, Gray.

(1977). Seating position, instructor's eye contact availability, and student participation in a small seminar. *Journal of Social Psychology, 103*, 315–316. PA 60:10375.

Caravia, Paul; & Lunca, Marilena. (1977). Variability in the communication network under different group conditions. *Revista de Psihologie, 23*, 429–446. PA 63:5413.

Carducci, Bernardo J.; & Deuser, Pamela S. (1984). The foot-in-the *donor* technique: Initial request and organ donation. *Basic and Applied Social Psychology, 5*, 75–81.

Carles, Elena M.; & Carver, Charles S. (1979). Effects of person salience versus role salience on reward allocation in a dyad. *Journal of Personality and Social Psychology, 37*, 2071–2080. PA 65:5367.

Carli, Linda L. (1989). Gender differences in interaction style and influence. *Journal of Personality and Social Psychology, 56*, 565–576.

Carli, Renzo; & Guerra, Giovanni. (1974). [Cognitive style and interpersonal perception]. *Archivio di Psicologia, Neurologia e Psichiatria, 35*(1), 7–25. PA 53:3012.

Carlsmith, J. Merrill; & Anderson, Craig A. (1979). Ambient temperature and the occurrence of collective violence: A new analysis. *Journal of Personality and Social Psychology, 37*, 337–344. PA 64:3246.

Carlsmith, J. Merrill; Lepper, Mark; & Landauer, T. K. (1974). Children's obedience to adult requests: Interactive effects of anxiety arousal and apparent punitiveness of the adult. *Journal of Personality and Social Psychology, 30*, 822–828. PA 53:9467.

Carlston, Donal E. (1977). Effects of polling order on social influence in decision-making groups. *Social Psychology Quarterly, 40*, 115–123. PA 59:9851. SA 78J1733.

Carlston, Donal E.; & Cohen, Jerry L. (1980). A closer examination of subject roles. *Journal of Personality and Social Psychology, 38*, 857–870.

Carment, D[avid] W. (1974a). Effects of sex role in a maximizing difference game. *Journal of Conflict Resolution, 18*, 461–472. PA 53:7286.

Carment, David W. (1974b). Indian and Canadian choice behaviour in a maximizing difference game and in a game of chicken. *International Journal of Psychology, 9*, 213–221. PA 54:7299.

Carment, D[avid] W.; & Alcock, J. E. (1984). Indian and Canadian behavior in two-person power games. *Journal of Conflict Resolution, 28*, 507–521. PA 72:6625.

Carnes, Patrick J.; & Laube, Herbert. (1975). Becoming us: An experiment in family learning and teaching. *Small Group Behavior, 6*, 106–120. PA 54:7449.

Carnevale, Peter J. (1985). Accountability of group representations and intergroup relations. *Advances in Group Processes, 2*, 227–248.

Carnevale, Peter J.; & Isen, Alice M. (1986). The influence of positive affect and visual access on the discovery of integrative solutions in bilateral negotiation. *Organizational Behavior and Human Decision Processes, 37*, 1–13. PA 73:21904.

Carnevale, Peter J.; & Lawler, Edward J. (1986). Time pressure and the development of integrative agreements in bilateral negotiations. *Journal of Conflict Resolution, 30*, 636–659. PA 74:15519.

Carnevale, Peter J.; Pruitt, Dean G.; & Britton, Scott D. (1979). Looking tough: The negotiator under constituent surveillance. *Personality and Social Psychology Bulletin, 5*, 118–121. PA 64:3275.

Carnevale, Peter J.; Pruitt, Dean G.; & Seilheimer, Steven D. (1981). Looking and competing: Accountability and visual access in integrative bargaining. *Journal of Personality and Social Psychology, 40*, 111–120. PA 66:12757.

Carpenter, William A.; & Hollander, Edwin P. (1982). Overcoming hurdles to independence in groups. *Journal of Social Psychology, 117*, 237–241. PA 69:5569.

Carr, Suzanne J.; & Dabbs, James M. (1974). The effects of lighting, distance and intimacy of topic on verbal and visual behavior. *Sociometry, 37*, 592–600. PA 53:9468.

Carron, Albert V.; & Ball, James R. (1977). An analysis of the cause-effect characteristics of cohesiveness and participation motivation in intercollegiate hockey. *International Review of Sport Sociology, 12*, 49–60. SA 78J4683.

Carron, Albert V.; Ball, James R.; & Chelladurai, P. (1977). Motivation for participation, success in performance and their relationship to individual and group satisfaction. *Perceptual and Motor Skills, 45*, 835–841. PA 60:11685.

Carron, Albert V.; & Bennett, Bonnie. (1976). The effects of initial habit strength differences upon performance in a coaction situation. *Journal of Motor Behavior, 8,* 297-304. PA 58:228.

Carron, Albert V.; & Chelladurai, P. (1978). Psychological factors and athletic success: An analysis of coach-athlete interpersonal behaviour. *Canadian Journal of Applied Sport Sciences, 3,* 43-50. PA 64:990.

Cartwright, Desmond S.; Howard, Kenneth I.; & Reuterman, Nicholas A. (1980). Multivariate analysis of gang delinquency: IV. Personality factors in gangs and clubs. *Multivariate Behavioral Research, 15,* 3 22. PA 65.5440. SA 82M1450.

Carver, Charles S. (1975). Physical aggression as a function of objective self-awareness and attitudes toward punishment. *Journal of Experimental Social Psychology, 11,* 510-519. PA 55:9765.

Carver, Charles S.; & Scheier, Michael F. (1978). Self-focussing effects of dispositional self-consciousness, mirror presence, and audience presence. *Journal of Personality and Social Psychology, 36,* 324-332.

Carver, Charles S.; & Scheier, Michael F. (1981). The self-attention-induced feedback loop and social facilitation. *Journal of Experimental Social Psychology, 17,* 545-568. PA 67:12036.

Cary, Mark S. (1978). The role of gaze in the initiation of conversation. *Social Psychology Quarterly, 41,* 269-271. PA 63:3239.

Casey, Jeff T.; Gettys, Charles F.; Pliske, Rebecca M.; & Mehle, Tom. (1984). A partition of small group predecision performance into informational and social components. *Organizational Behavior and Human Performance, 34,* 112-139. PA 71:31316.

Casey, Jeff T.; Mehle, Thomas; & Gettys, Charles F. (1981). A partition of group performance into informational and social components in a hypothesis generation task. *Catalog of Selected Documents in Psychology, 11,* 9. [MS. 2189.] PA 66:8007.

Cash, Thomas F.; & Soloway, Deborah. (1975). Self-disclosure correlates of physical attractiveness: An exploratory study. *Psychological Reports, 36,* 579-586. PA 54:7450.

Cassidy, R. Gordon; & Mangold, J. (1975). Coalition behaviour in n-person conflicts. *Journal of Mathematical Sociology, 4,* 61-82. PA 56:9823.

Cassidy, R. Gordon; & Neave, Edwin H. (1977). Dynamics of coalition formation: Prescription

vs. reality. *Theory and Decision, 8,* 159-171. PA 60:5224. SA 79J6845.

Castelfranchi, Cristiano; & Parisi, Domenico. (1984). Mente e scambio sociale [Mind and social exchange]. *Rassegna Italiana di Sociologia, 25,* 45-72. PA 72:17310.

Castore, Carl H.; Murnighan, J. Keith. (1978). Determinants of support for group decisions. *Organizational Behavior and Human Performance, 22,* 75-92. PA 63:3240.

Castro, Maria A. (1974). Reactions to receiving aid as a function of cost to donor and opportunity to aid. *Journal of Applied Social Psychology, 4,* 194-209. PA 54:2999.

Cate, Rodney M.; Lloyd, Sally A.; Henton, June M.; & Larson, Jeffry H. (1982). Fairness and reward level as predictors of relationship satisfaction. *Social Psychology Quarterly, 45,* 177-181. PA 69:10390.

Catt, Viola; & Benson, Peter L. (1977). Effect of verbal modeling on contributions to charity. *Journal of Applied Psychology, 62,* 81-85. PA 58:1044.

Cattell, Raymond B. (1947). Confirmation and clarification of primary personality factors. *Psychometrika, 12,* 197-220.

Cegala, Donald J. (1984). Affective and cognitive manifestations of interaction involvement during unstructured and competitive interactions. *Communication Monographs, 51,* 320-338. PA 72:30766.

Chaiken, Shelly. (1979). Communicator physical attractiveness and persuasion. *Journal of Personality and Social Psychology, 37,* 1387-1397. PA 64:12482.

Chaiken, Shelley; & Stangor, Charles. (1987). Attitudes and attitude change. *Annual Review of Psychology, 38,* 575-630.

Chalos, Peter; & Pickard, Sue. (1985). Information choice and cue uses: An experiment in group information processing. *Journal of Applied Psychology, 70,* 634-641. PA 73:9090.

Chamberlin, John R. (1978). The logic of collective action: Some experimental results . *Behavioral Science, 23,* 441-445. SA 80K5516.

Chapanis, Alphonse. (1975). Interactive human communication. *Scientific American, 232,* 36-42. PA 55:12205.

Chapanis, Alphonse; & Overbey, Charles M. (1974). Studies in interactive communication: III. Effects of similar and dissimilar communication channels and two interchange options on team problem solving. *Perceptual and Motor Skills*, 38, 343–374. PA 53:307.

Chapko, Michael K.; & Solomon, Henry. (1974). The cross-situational validity of risk as a value. *Memory and Cognition*, 2, 497–500. PA 53:3013.

Chapman, Antony J. (1975a). Eye contact, physical proximity and laughter: A re-examination of the equilibrium model of social intimacy. *Social Behavior and Personality*, 3, 143–155. PA 56:3998.

Chapman, Antony J. (1975b). Humorous laughter in children. *Journal of Personality and Social Psychology*, 31, 42–49. PA 53:9469.

Chapman, Anthony J.; & Chapman, Wendy A. (1974). Responsiveness to humor: Its dependency upon a companion's humorous smiling and laughter. *Journal of Psychology*, 88, 245–252. PA 54:994.

Chapman, Antony J.; & Wright, Derek S. (1976). Social enhancement of laughter: An experimental analysis of some companion variables. *Journal of Experimental Child Psychology*, 21, 201–218. PA 56:3997.

Chapman, J. Brad. (1975). Comparison of male and female leadership styles. *Academy of Management Journal*, 18, 645–650.

Chapman, Michael. (1986). The structure of exchange: Piaget's sociological theory. *Human Development*, 29, 181–194. PA 73:29940.

Charlton, Michael; Liebelt, Elsa; Sultz, Jutta; & Tausch, Anne M. (1974). [Influence of models in a TV Western on group work and aggression latency of 3rd graders]. *Psychologie in Erziehung und Unterricht*, 21(3), 164–175. PA 55:2128.

Chatterjea, R. G.; & Mitra, A. (1976). A study of brainstorming. *Manas*, 23(1), 23–28. PA 59:7866.

Chatterjee, Amitava. (1972). The organizational variables of group cohesiveness. *Indian Journal of Psychometry and Education*, 3(2), 43–52. PA 53:4210.

Chatterjee, Kalyan; & Lilien, Gary L. (1984). Efficiency of alternative bargaining procedures: An experimental study. *Journal of Conflict Resolution*, 28, 270–295. PA 71:28596.

Chelius, James R.; & Dworkin, James B. (1980). An economic analysis of final-offer arbitration as a conflict resolution device. *Journal of Conflict Resolution*, 24, 293–310. PA 64:12407.

Chell, E. (1979). Organizational factors and participation in committees. *British Journal of Social and Clinical Psychology*, 18, 53–57. PA 64:991. SA 80K7124.

Chelune, Gordon J.; Skiffington, Stephen; & Williams, Connie. (1981). Multidimensional analysis of observers' perceptions of self-disclosing behavior. *Journal of Personality and Social Psychology*, 41, 599–606. PA 67:7718.

Chemers, Martin M.; Rice, Robert W.; Sundstrom, Eric; & Butler, William M. (1975). Leader esteem for the least preferred co-worker score, training, and effectiveness: An experimental examination. *Journal of Personality and Social Psychology*, 31, 401–409. PA 54:995.

Chen, Kan. (1975). Value of information in conflictual situations: Two simple examples. *IEEE Transactions on Systems, Man, and Cybernetics*, 5(4), 466–470. PA 54:9557.

Chertkoff, Jerome M. (1975). Sociopsychological views on sequential effects in coalition formation. *American Behavioral Scientist*, 18, 451–471. PA 54:9558. SA 76H 7088.

Chertkoff, Jerome M.; & Esser, James K. (1976). A review of experiments in explicit bargaining. *Journal of Experimental Social Psychology*, 12, 464–486. PA 56:9825.

Chertkoff, Jerome M.; & Esser, James K. (1977). A test of three theories of coalition formation when agreements can be short-term or long-term. *Journal of Personality and Social Psychology*, 35, 237–249. PA 62:3554.

Chertkoff, Jerome M.; & Esser, James K. (1983). A review of experiments in explicit bargaining. In H. H. Blumberg, A. P. Hare, V. Kent, & M. F. Davies (Eds.), *Small groups and social interaction* (Vol. 2, pp. 145–161). Chichester: John Wiley. [Abridged by the authors from Chertkoff and Esser, 1976.]

Chertkoff, Jerome M.; Sherman, Steven J.; Till, Amnon; & Hammerle, Gordon. (1977). Reactions when the honesty or dishonesty of the other bargainer is discovered. *Social Behavior and Personality*, 5, 21–31. PA 60:9288.

Chertock, Sanford L. (1974). Effect of music on cooperative problem solving by children. *Perceptual and Motor Skills*, 39, 986. PA 53:9470.

Cherulnik, Paul D.; Neely, William T.; Flanagan, Martha; & Zachau, Max. (1978). Social skill and visual interaction. *Journal of Social Psychology*, 104, 263–270. PA 61:13382.

Cherulnik, Paul D.; & Souders, Susan B. (1984). The social contents of place schemata: People are judged by the places where they live and work. *Population and Environment Behavioral and Social Issues, 7,* 211-233. PA 73:29976.

Chiauzzi, Emil; & Heimberg, Richard G. (1986). Legitimacy of request and social problem solving: A study of assertive and nonassertive subjects. *Behavior Modification, 10,* 3-18. PA 74:4038.

Child, John. (1976). Participation, organization, and social cohesion. *Human Relations, 29,* 429-451. PA 57:9232.

Chlewinski, Zdzislaw. (1975). Cognitive conservatism and radicalism in individual and group decisions. *Polish Psychological Bulletin, 6,* 139-146. PA 55:7057.

Chlewinski, Zdzislaw. (1980). Zjawisko polaryzacji ostroznosc—ryzyko w sytuacjach grupowego podejmowania decyzji [Polarization risk-caution in group decision-making]. *Roczniki Filozoficzne Psychologia, 28*(4), 5-26. PA 71:14960 [Also, PA 70:12630].

Chlewinski, Zdzislaw. (1984). Zmiana decyzji indywidualnych i grupowych [Characteristics of individual and group decisions]. *Przeglad Psychologiczny, 27,* 577-590. PA 73:21905.

Cho, Geung ho. (1980). The differential effects of group pressure on favorableness impression and likableness impression]. *Korean Journal of Psychology, 3*(1), 1-18. PA 67:12061.

Christensen, Dana; Farina, Amerigo; & Boudreau, Louis. (1980). Sensitivity to nonverbal cues as a function of social competence. *Journal of Nonverbal Behavior, 4,* 146-156. PA 66:1223.

Christensen, Dana; & Rosenthal, Robert. (1982). Gender and nonverbal decoding skill as determinants of interpersonal expectancy effects. *Journal of Personality and Social Psychology, 42,* 75-87. PA 68:3521.

Christensen, E. W. (1983). Study circles: Learning in small groups. *Journal for Specialists in Group Work, 8*(4), 211-217. PA 71:17744.

Christopher, Stefan C.; & Dodd, Stuart C. (1972). Three causes of achieved consensus, controlled in two person groups. *International Review of Modern Sociology, 2,* 240-254. SA 74G7443.

Chu, Lily. (1979). The sensitivity of Chinese and American children to social influences. *Journal of Social Psychology, 109,* 175-186. PA 65:5185.

Church, Robert J.; & Esser, James K. (1980).

Effects of information on level of aspiration in bargaining. *Representative Research in Social Psychology, 11,* 38-43. PA 66:12793.

Churchman, Arza; & Ginsberg, Yona. (1984). The image and experience of high-rise housing in Israel. *Journal of Environmental Psychology, 4,* 27-41. PA 73:8253.

Cialdini, Robert B. (1985). *Influence: Science and practice.* Glenview, IL: Scott, Foresman.

Cialdini, Robert B.; & Ascani, Karen. (1976). Test of a concession procedure for inducing verbal, behavioral, and further compliance with a request to give blood. *Journal of Applied Psychology, 61,* 295-300. PA 56:668.

Cialdini, Robert B.; Bickman, Leonard; & Cacioppo, John T. (1979). An example of consumeristic social psychology: Bargaining tough in the new car showroom. *Journal of Applied Social Psychology, 9,* 115-126.

Cialdini, Robert B.; Braver, Sanford L.; & Lewis, Stephen K. (1974). Attributional bias and the easily persuaded other. *Journal of Personality and Social Psychology, 30,* 631-637. PA 53:7307.

Cialdini, Robert B.; Cacioppo, John T.; Bassett, Rodney; & Miller, John A. (1978). Low-ball procedure for producing compliance: Commitment then cost. *Journal of Personality and Social Psychology, 36,* 463-476. PA 61:13366.

Cialdini, Robert B.; Kenrick, Douglas T.; & Hoerig, James H. (1976). Victim derogation in the Lerner paradigm: Just world or just justification? *Journal of Personality and Social Psychology, 33,* 719-724. PA 56:6028.

Cialdini, Robert B.; & Mirels, Herbert L. (1976). Sense of personal control and attributions about yielding and resisting persuasion targets. *Journal of Personality and Social Psychology, 33,* 395-402. PA 56:7856.

Cialdini, Robert B.; & Schroeder, David A. (1976). Increasing compliance by legitimizing paltry contributions: When even a penny helps. *Journal of Personality and Social Psychology, 34,* 599-604. PA 58:1135.

Cialdini, Robert B.; Vincent, Joyce E.; Lewis, Stephen K.; Catalon, José; Wheeler, Diane; & Darby, Betty Lee. (1975). Reciprocal concessions procedure for inducing compliance: The door-in-the-face technique. *Journal of Personality and Social Psychology, 31,* 206-215. PA 53:11600.

Cicourel, Aaron V. (1974). *Cognitive sociology:*

Language and meaning in social interaction. New York: Free Press.

Cicourel, Aaron V. (1981). The role of cognitive-linguistic concepts in understanding everyday social interactions. *Annual Review of Sociology, 7,* 87–106. PA 68:1077.

Cielecki, Marek. (1979). [Some group attributes and creative task resolution]. *Psychologia Wychowawcza, 22,* 53–67. PA 64:12446.

Ciminero, Anthony R.; Graham, Lewis E.; & Jackson, Joan L. (1977). Reciprocal reactivity: Response-specific changes in independent observers. *Behavior Therapy, 8,* 48–56. PA 58:3290.

Ciolek, T. Matthew. (1978). Spatial arrangements in social encounters: An attempt at a taxonomy. *Man-Environment Systems, 8*(2), 52–59. PA 63:9628.

Ciolek, T. Matthew. (1982). Zones of co-presence in face-to-face interaction: Some observational data. *Man-Environment Systems, 12*(6), 223–242. PA 70:12631.

Ciolek, T. Matthew. (1983). The proxemics lexicon: A first approximation. *Journal of Nonverbal Behavior, 8,* 55–79. PA 72:11992.

Ciolek, T. Matthew; & Furnham, Adrian F. (1980). Subjective interpersonal distance in a public setting: Effect of situation and ecology. *Man-Environment Systems, 10*(2), 107–116. PA 65:7954.

Ciolek, T. Matthew; & Kendon, Adam. (1980). Environment and the spatial arrangement of conversational encounters. *Sociological Inquiry, 5,* 237–271. SA 82M3120.

Cissna, Kenneth N. (1984). Phases in group development: The negative evidence. *Small Group Behavior, 15,* 3–32. PA 71:28597.

Clark, Alfred W.; & Powell, Robert J. (1984). Changing drivers' attitudes through peer group decision. *Human Relations, 37,* 155–162. SA 8400831.

Clark, Joanne V.; & Arkowitz, Hal. (1975). Social anxiety and self-evaluation of interpersonal performance. *Psychological Reports, 36,* 211–221. PA 54:7451.

Clark, Lawrence P.; & Arenson, Sidney J. (1980). Effects of social and spatial density on group performance of an interactive motor task. *Journal of Social Psychology, 111,* 205–210. PA 66:5736.

Clark, M. L. (1983). Effect of confederate sex and status on competitive behavior of male and female college students. *Journal of Psychology, 113,* 191–198. PA 70:12632.

Clark, Margaret S. (1984). Record keeping in two types of relationships. *Journal of Personality and Social Psychology, 47,* 549–557.

Clark, Margaret S. (1986). Evidence for the effectiveness of manipulations of communal and exchange relationships. *Personality and Social Psychology Bulletin, 12,* 414–425.

Clark, Margaret S.; Gotay, Carolyn C.; & Mills, Judson. (1974). Acceptance of help as a function of similarity of the potential helper and opportunity to repay. *Journal of Applied Social Psychology, 4,* 224–229. PA 54:3000.

Clark, Margaret S.; Mills, Judson; & Powell, Martha C. (1986). Keeping track of needs in communal and exchange relationships. *Journal of Personality and Social Psychology, 51,* 333–338. PA 73:29941.

Clark, Margaret S.; & Waddell, Barbara A. (1983). Effects of moods on thoughts about helping, attraction and information acquisition. *Social Psychology Quarterly, 46,* 31–35. PA 70:10266.

Clark, Russell D. (1974). Effects of sex and race on helping behavior in a nonreactive setting. *Representative Research in Social Psychology, 5,* 1–6.

Clark, Russell D. (1976). On the Piliavin & Piliavin model of helping behavior: Costs are in the eye of the beholder. *Journal of Applied Social Psychology, 6,* 322–328. PA 58:1136.

Clarke, John; Gannon, Marjorie; Hughes, Ian; Keogh, Clare; Singer, George; & Wallace, Meredith. (1977). Adjunctive behavior in humans in a group gambling situation. *Physiology and Behavior, 18,* 159–161. PA 58:9443.

Clary, E. Gil; & Shaffer, David R. (1985). Another look at the impact of juror sentiments toward defendants on juridic decisions. *Journal of Social Psychology, 125,* 637–651. PA 74:10209.

Cline, Rebecca J.; & Johnson, Bonnie M. (1976). The verbal stare: Focus on attention in conversation. *Speech Monographs, 43,* 1–10. PA 56:5987.

Cline, Rebecca J.; & Musolf, Karen E. (1985). Disclosure as social exchange: Anticipated length of relationship, sex roles, and disclosure intimacy. *Western Journal of Speech Communication, 49,* 43–56. SA 85O7795.

Cline, Timothy R.; & Cline, Rebecca J. (1979). Risky and cautious decision shifts in small groups. *Southern Speech Communication Journal, 44*(3), 252–263. SA 82M4022.

Cobb, Anthony T. (1982). A social psychological approach to coalition membership: An expectancy model of individual choice. *Group and Organization Studies, 7*, 295–319. PA 69:1008.

Cochart, Dominique. (1982). Les foules et la Commune. Analyse des premiers ecrits de psychologie des foules [The crowds and the Commune: For an analysis of the first social psychological documents concerning the crowds]. *Recherches de Psychologie Sociale, 4*, 49–60. PA 70:12623.

Cochran, C. D.; Hale, W. Daniel; & Hissam, Christine P. (1984). Personal space requirements in indoor versus outdoor locations. *Journal of Psychology, 117*, 121–123. PA 72:9491.

Cochran, C. D.; & Urbanczyk, Sally. (1982). The effect of availability of vertical space on personal space. *Journal of Psychology, 111*, 137–140. PA 69:1009.

Codol, Jean Paul. (1973a). [Concept of superior conformity of one's own group to accepted norms–Does such a phenomenon exist?]. *Cahiers de Psychologie, 16*(1), 25–30. PA 53:7309.

Codol, Jean Paul. (1973b). [The phenomenon of superior conformity of one's self to group norms in a situation requiring perceptual estimation of physical stimuli]. *Cahiers de Psychologie, 16*(1), 11–23. PA 53:7399.

Codol, Jean Paul. (1975a). [The "PIP effect": Anticipation of the behavior of one's self and others in a game situation]. *Revue de Psychologie Appliquee, 25*, 1–14. PA 54:7452.

Codol, Jean Paul. (1975b). [The PIP effect (Primus Inter Pares, first among equals) and norm conflict]. *Annee Psychologique, 75*, 127–145. PA 55:4544.

Codol, Jean Paul. (1976). [Against the triangle hypothesis]. *Cahiers de Psychologie, 19*(1), 15–38. PA 62:1083.

Codol, Jean Paul. (1977–1978). Self-disclosure and climate of confidence. *Bulletin de Psychologie, 31*, 298–303. PA 63:971.

Codol, Jean Paul. (1978a). Espace personnel, distance interindividuelle et densité sociale [Personal space, interpersonal distance and social

density]. *Revue de Psychologie Appliqueé, 28*, 43–68. PA 70:5621.

Codol, J[ean]-P[aul] (1978b). Espace personnel, distance interindividuelle et densité sociale [Personal space, interindividual distance, and social density]. *Revue de Psychologie Appliqueé, 28*, 129–147. PA 71:3965.

Cody, Michael J. (1982). A typology of disengagement strategies and an examination of the role intimacy, reactions to inequity and relational problems play in strategy selection. *Communication Monographs, 49*, 148–170. PA 69:7872.

Cody, Michael J.; & O'Hair, H. Dan. (1983). Nonverbal communication and deception: Differences in deception cues due to gender and communicator dominance. *Communication Monographs, 50*, 175–192. PA 71:12147.

Coe, Rodney M.; & Prendergast, Christine G. (1985). The formation of coalitions: Interaction strategies in triads. *Sociology of Health and Illness, 7*, 236–247. SA 85Q1239.

Coet, Larry J.; & McDermott, Patrick J. (1979). Sex, instructional set, and group make-up: Organismic and situational factors influencing risk-taking. *Psychological Reports, 44*, 1283–1294. PA 64:10326.

Cohen, Allan S.; & Melson, Gail F. (1980). The influence of friendship on children's communication. *Journal of Social Psychology, 112*, 207–213. PA 66:5548.

Cohen, Elizabeth G. (1982). Expectation states and interracial interaction in school settings. *Annual Review Of Sociology, 8*, 209 235.

Cohen, Elizabeth G.; & Roper, Susan S. (1972). Modification of interracial interaction disability: An application of status characteristic theory. *American Sociological Review, 37*, 643–657.

Cohen, Jere. (1978). Conformity and norm formation in small groups. *Pacific Sociological Review, 21*, 441–466. SA 79K1084.

Cohen, Jere. (1979). Socio-economic status and high-school friendship choice: Elmtown's youth revisited. *Social Networks, 2*, 65–74. SA 81L3325.

Cohen, Jerry L. (1980). Social facilitation: Audience versus evaluation apprehension effects. *Motivation and Emotion, 4*, 21–34. PA 66:1257.

Cohen, Jerry L.; Sladen, Bernard; & Bennett, Barbara. (1975). The effects of situational variables on judgments of crowding. *Sociometry, 38*, 273–281. PA 54:11693. SA76H9417.

Cohen, Jiska. (1982). Cooperative and competitive styles – the construct and its relevance. *Human Relations, 35*, 621–633.

Cohen, Peter A.; & Sheposh, John P. (1977). Audience and level of esteem as determinants of risk taking. *Personality and Social Psychology Bulletin, 3*, 119–122. PA 58:7432.

Cohen, Sheldon. (1978). Environmental load and the allocation of attention. In A. Baum, J. E. Singer, & S. Valins (Eds.), *Advances in environmental psychology* (Vol. 1, pp. 1–29). Hillsdale, NJ: Erlbaum.

Cohen, Sheldon. (1980). The aftereffects of stress on human performance: A review of research and theory. *Psychological Bulletin, 88*, 82–108. PA 64:6969.

Cohen, Sheldon; Evans, Gary W; Stokols, Daniel; & Krantz, David S. (Eds.). (1986). *Behavior, health, and environmental stress.* New York: Plenum.

Cohen, Sheldon; & Lezak, Anne. (1977). Noise and attentiveness to social cues. *Environment and Behavior, 9*, 559–572. PA 60:10938.

Cohen, Sheldon; & Spacapan, Shirlynn. (1984). The social psychology of noise. In D. M. Jones & A. J. Chapman (Eds.), *Noise and society* (pp. 221–245). New York: Wiley.

Cohen, Sheldon; & Weinstein, Neil D. (1981). Nonauditory effects of noise on behavior and health. *Journal of Social Issues, 37*(1), 36–70. PA 65:11396.

Cohen, Sheldon; & Wills, Thomas A. (1985). Stress, social support, and the buffering hypothesis. *Psychological Bulletin, 98*, 310–357. PA 73:1119.

Cohen, Stephen L.; Bunker, Kerry A.; Burton, Amy L.; & McManus, Philip D. (1978). Reactions of male subordinates to the sex-role congruency of immediate supervision. *Sex Roles, 4*, 297–311. PA 63:3188. SA 80K5517.

Cohn, Nancy B.; & Strassberg, Donald S. (1983). Self-disclosure reciprocity among preadolescents. *Personality and Social Psychology Bulletin, 9*, 97–102. PA 70:12469.

Colaizzi, Antoinette; Williams, Kim J.; & Kayson, Wesley A. (1984). When will people help? The effects of gender, urgency, and location on altruism. *Psychological Reports, 55*, 139–142. PA 72:11999.

Cole, David; & Cole, Shirley. (1974). Locus of control and cultural conformity: On going against the norm. *Personality and Social Psychology Bulletin, 1*, 351–353.

Cole, Donald W. (1983). *Conflict resolution technology.* Cleveland, OH: Organization Development Institute.

Cole, Steven G.; Phillips, James L.; & Hartman, E. Alan. (1977). Test of a model of decision processes in an intense conflict situation. *Behavioral Science, 22*, 186–196.

Colecchia, Nicola; & Aureli, Tiziana. (1985). Cooperazione versus coesione: due funzioni dell'interzione [Cooperation vs. cohesiveness: Two functions of interaction]. *Eta evolutiva,* No. 20, 110–116. PA 72:30767.

Collett, Peter. (Ed.). (1977). *Social rules and social behaviour.* Totowa, NJ: Rowman and Littlefield.

Collett, Peter; & Marsh, Peter. (1980). Seat choice in an airport lounge. *Man-Environment Systems, 10*(2), 83–106. PA 65:7929.

Colman, Andrew M. (Ed.). (1982a). *Cooperation and competition in humans and animals.* Berkshire, England: Van Nostrand Reinhold.

Colman, Andrew M. (1982b). *Game theory and experimental games: The study of strategic interaction.* Oxford, England: Pergamon.

Comadena, Mark E. (1984). Brainstorming groups: Ambiguity tolerance, communication apprehension, task attraction, and individual productivity. *Small Group Behavior, 15*, 251–264. PA 72:1226.

Compas, Bruce E. (1981). Psychological sense of community among treatment analogue group members. *Journal of Applied Social Psychology, 11*, 151–165. PA 67:3519.

Concha, Pat; Garcia, Lourdes; & Perez, Ana. (1975). Cooperation versus competition: A comparison of Anglo-American and Cuban-American youngsters in Miami. *Journal of Social Psychology, 95*, 273–274. PA 54:2817.

Condon, W. S.; & Ogston, W. D. (1966). Sound film analysis of normal and pathological behavior patterns. *Journal of Nervous and Mental Disease, 143*, 338–347.

Conger, Judith C.; & Farrell, Albert D. (1981). Behavioral components of heterosocial skills. *Behavior Therapy, 12*, 41–55. PA 65:7937.

Conger, Rand D.; & McLeod, Doug. (1977). Describing behavior in small groups with the datamyte event recorder. *Behavior Research Methods and Instrumentation, 9*, 418–424. SA 80K8682.

Conlisk, John. (1976). Interactive Markov chains. *Journal of Mathematical Sociology, 4*, 157–185. PA 57:7254.

Conner, Thomas L. (1977). Performance expectations and the initiation of problem solving attempts. *Journal of Mathematical Sociology, 5*, 187–198. SA 78J3217.

Conolley, Edward S.; Gerard, Harold B.; & Kline, Teresa (1978). Competitive behavior. A manifestation of motivation for ability comparison. *Journal of Experimental Social Psychology, 14*, 123–131. PA 60:9326.

Conroy, Joseph; & Sundstrom, Eric. (1977). Territorial dominance in a dyadic conversation as a function of similarity of opinion. *Journal of Personality and Social Psychology, 35*, 570–576. PA 62:10965.

Conte, Rosaria. (1982). Le relazioni personali all'esame delle teorie dello scambio [Personal relationships as studied through exchange theory]. *Giornale Italiano di Psicologia, 9*(1), 75–106. PA 69:05570.

Conte, Rosaria; & Miceli, Maria. (1984). Teorie dello scambio in psicologia sociale: Necessità di un approccio mentalista [Exchange theories in social psychology: A mentalistic approach]. *Rassegna Italiana di Sociologia, 25*, 73–98. PA 72:17298.

Conville, Richard L. (1975). Linguistic nonimmediacy and self-presentation. *Journal of Psychology, 90*, 219–227. PA 54:9588.

Conville, Richard L. (1983). Second-order development in interpersonal communication. *Human Communication Research, 9*, 195–207. PA 70:10236.

Conyne, Robert K.; & Rapin, Lynn S. (1977). Programmed groups: A process analysis of facilitator- and self-directed treatments. *Small Group Behavior, 8*, 403–414. PA 64:992. SA 79K1085.

Cook, Harold; & Sloane, Julie. (1985). Locus of control and cooperative behavior in 10-year-old children. *Journal of Social Psychology, 125*, 619–630.

Cook, Karen S.; & Gillmore, Mary R. (1984). Power dependence and coalitions. *Advances in Group Processes, 1*, 27–58.

Cook, Karen S.; & Hegtvedt, Karen A. (1983). Distributive justice, equity, and equality. *Annual Review of Sociology, 9*, 217–241.

Cook, Mark. (1977). Gaze and mutual gaze in social encounters. *American Scientist, 65*, 328–333. PA 59:9837.

Cook, Mark. (Ed.). (1984). *Issues in person perception.* New York: Methuen.

Cook, Mark; & Smith, Jacqueline M. (1975). The role of gaze in impression formation. *British Journal of Social and Clinical Psychology, 14*, 19–25. PA 54:1020.

Cook, Stuart W. (1978). Interpersonal and attitudinal outcomes in cooperating interracial groups. *Journal of Research and Development in Education, 12*(1), 97–113. PA 64:5545.

Cook, Stuart W.; & Pelfrey, Michael. (1985). Reactions to being helped in cooperating interracial groups: A context effect. *Journal of Personality and Social Psychology, 49*, 1231–1245.

Cook, William; & Dreyer, Albert. (1984). The social relations model: A new approach to the analysis of family-dyadic interaction. *Journal of Marriage and the Family, 46*, 679–687. SA 85O7796.

Coombs, Gary. (1973). Networks and exchange: The role of social relationships in a small voluntary association. *Journal of Anthropological Research, 29*, 96–112. SA 77I4646.

Cooper, Cary L. (1973). A bibliography of current encounter and T-group research: 1971–1973. *Interpersonal Development, 4*(1), 65–68. PA 53:1036.

Cooper, Cary L. (1975a). How psychologically dangerous are T-groups and encounter groups? *Human Relations, 28*, 249–260. PA 54:11654.

Cooper, Cary L. (Ed.). (1975b). *Theories of group processes.* London: Wiley.

Cooper, Cary L. (1977). Adverse and growthful effects of experiential learning groups: The role of the trainer, participant, and group characteristics. *Human Relations, 30*, 1103–1129.

Cooper, Cary L.; & Kobayashi, Koichiro. (1976). Changes in self-actualization as a result of sensitivity training in England and Japan. *Small Group Behavior, 7*, 387–396. SA 78J0170.

Cooper, Clare. (1974). The house as symbol of the self. In J. Lang, C. Burnette, W. Moleski, & D. Vachon (Eds.), *Designing for human behavior: Architecture and the behavioral sciences* (pp. 130–146). Stroudsberg, PA: Dowden, Hutchinson & Ross.

Cooper, Harris M. (1979). Statistically combining independent studies: A meta-analysis of sex differences in conformity research. *Journal of Personality and Social Psychology*, *37*, 131–146. PA 64:979.

Cooper, Lee G.; & Thomas, Kenneth W. (1974). Divergent perceptions of disagreement. *Behavioral Science*, *19*, 336–343. PA 53:5162. SA 7610641.

Cooper, Lowell; & Gustafson, James P. (1981). Family-group development: Planning in organizations. *Human Relations*, *34*, 705–730. PA 67:1213.

Cooper, Lucille; Johnson, David W.; Johnson, Roger T.; & Wilderson, Frank. (1980). The effects of cooperative, competitive, and individualistic experiences of interpersonal attraction among heterogeneous peers. *Journal of Social Psychology*, *111*, 243–252. PA 66:5737.

Cooper, Sloan; & Peterson, Christopher. (1980). Machiavellianism and spontaneous cheating in competition. *Journal of Research in Personality*, *14*, 70–75. PA 65:10368.

Coplin, William D. (1980). *Introduction to international politics* (3rd ed.). Englewood Cliffs, NJ: Prentice-Hall.

Corrigan, John D. (1978). Salient attributes of two types of helpers: Friends and mental health professionals. *Journal of Counseling Psychology*, *25*, 588–590. PA 62:8615.

Cosier, Richard A.; & Ruble, Thomas L. (1981). Research on conflict-handling behavior: An experimental approach. *Academy of Management Journal*, *24*, 816–831. PA 67:7690.

Costin, Frank. (1985). Beliefs about rape and women's social roles. *Archives of Sexual Behavior*, *14*, 319–325. SA 86Q4856.

Cota, Albert A.; & Dion, Kenneth L. (1986). Salience of gender and sex composition of ad hoc groups: An experimental test of distinctiveness theory. *Journal of Personality and Social Psychology*, *50*, 770–776. PA 73:21906.

Cotton, John L.; & Baron, Robert S. (1980). Anonymity, persuasive arguments, and choice shifts. *Social Psychology Quarterly*, *43*, 391–404. PA 66:10347.

Cottrell, Nickolas B.; Wack, Dennis L.; Sekerak, Gary J.; & Rittle, Robert H. (1968). Social facilitation of dominant responses by the presence of an audience and the mere presence of others. *Journal of Personality and Social Psychology*, *9*, 245–250.

Couch, Arthur S. (1960). *Psychological determinants of interpersonal behavior*. Unpublished doctoral dissertation, Harvard University.

Couch, Carl J. (1987). *Researching social processes in the laboratory*. Greenwich, CT: JAI.

Courtright, John A. (1978). A laboratory investigation of groupthink. *Communication Monographs*, *45*, 229–246. PA 63:972.

Courtright, John A.; Millar, Frank E.; & Rogers-Millar, L. Edna. (1979). Domineeringness and dominance: Replication and expansion. *Communication Monographs*, *46*, 179–192.

Coutts, Larry M.; Irvine, Michael; & Schneider, Frank W. (1977). Nonverbal adjustments to changes in gaze and orientation. *Psychology*, *14*(2), 28–32. PA 59:9854.

Coutts, Larry M.; & Ledden, Maribeth. (1977). Nonverbal compensatory reactions to changes in interpersonal proximity. *Journal of Social Psychology*, *102*, 283–290. PA 60:3029.

Coutts, Larry M.; & Schneider, Frank W. (1975). Visual behavior in an unfocused interaction as a function of sex and distance. *Journal of Experimental Social Psychology*, *11*, 64–77. PA 53:11576.

Coutts, Larry M.; & Schneider, Frank W. (1976). Affiliative conflict theory: An investigation of the intimacy equilibrium and compensation hypothesis. *Journal of Personality and Social Psychology*, *34*, 1135–1142. PA 60:11687.

Coutts, Larry M.; Schneider, Frank W.; & Montgomery, Scott. (1980). An investigation of the arousal model of interpersonal intimacy. *Journal of Experimental Social Psychology*, *16*, 545–561. PA 66:12758.

Cowan, Gloria; Drinkard, Joan; & MacGavin, Laurie. (1984). The effects of target, age, and gender on use of power strategies. *Journal of Personality and Social Psychology*, *47*, 1391–1398.

Cowan, Gloria; & Inskeep, Robert. (1978). Commitments to help among the disabled-disadvantaged. *Personality and Social Psychology Bulletin*, *4*, 92–96. PA 61:5956.

Cox, Verne C.; Paulus, Paul B.; & McCain, Garvin. (1984). Prison crowding research. *American Psychologist*, *39*, 1148–1160.

Coyne, Margaret U. (1984). Role and rational action. *Journal for the Theory of Social Behaviour*, *14*, 259–275. PA 72:14467.

Crabbe, James M.; & Johnson, Glen O. (1979). Age group male and female choice reaction time performance during face to face competition. *International Journal of Sport Psychology, 10,* 231–238. PA 64:10359.

Craddock, Alan E. (1985). Centralized authority as a factor in small group and family problem solving: A reassessment of Tallman's propositions. *Small Group Behavior, 16,* 59–73. SA 86Q4836.

Cragan, John F.; & Wright, David W. (1980). Small group communication research of the 1970's: A synthesis and critique. *Central States Speech Journal, 31*(3), 197–213. SA 84N7283.

Craig, Kenneth D.; & Patrick, Christopher J. (1985). Facial expression during induced pain. *Journal of Personality and Social Psychology, 48,* 1080–1091. PA 72:19559.

Craik, Kenneth H. (1973). Environmental psychology. *Annual Review of Psychology, 24,* 403–422.

Cramer, Duncan. (1975). A critical note on two studies of minority influence. *European Journal of Social Psychology, 5,* 257–260. PA 55:7120.

Cramer, Robert E.; McMaster, M. Rosalie; Lutz, David J.; & Ford, J. Guthrie. (1986). Sport fan generosity: A test of mood, similarity, and equity hypotheses. *Journal of Sport Behavior, 9*(1), 31–37. PA 74:10181.

Cramer, Robert E.; Weiss, Robert F.; Steigleder, Michele K.; & Balling, Susan S. (1985). Attraction in context: Acquisition and blocking of person-directed action. *Journal of Personality & Social Psychology, 49,* 1221–1230. PA 73:11756.

Crandall, James E. (1977). Further validation of the Social Interest Scale: Peer ratings and interpersonal attraction. *Journal of Clinical Psychology, 33,* 140–142. PA 58:4617.

Crandall, Rick. (1978). The assimilation of newcomers into groups. *Small Group Behavior, 9,* 331–336. SA 79K2622.

Cravens, Richard W.; & Worchel, Philip. (1977). The differential effects of rewarding and coercive leaders on group members differing in locus of control. *Journal of Personality, 45,* 150–168. PA 59:1025. SA 80K7125.

Crawford, Vincent P. (1980). A note on the Zeuthen-Harsanyi theory of bargaining. *Journal of Conflict Resolution, 24,* 525–535. PA 64:12448.

Crawford, Vincent P. (1982). A comment on Farber's analysis of final-offer arbitration. *Journal of Conflict Resolution, 26,* 157–160. PA 68:1080.

Crawford, Vincent P. (1985). Dynamic games and dynamic contract theory. *Journal of Conflict Resolution, 29,* 195–224. PA 72:30768.

Critelli, Joseph W.; & Baldwin, Amy C. (1979). Birth order: Complementarity vs homogamy as determinants of attraction in dating relationships. *Perceptual and Motor Skills, 49,* 467–471. PA 65:5380.

Critelli, Joseph W.; & Dupre, Kathleen M. (1978). Self-disclosure and romantic attraction. *Journal of Social Psychology, 106,* 127–128. PA 63:7559.

Crittenden, Kathleen S. (1983). Sociological aspects of attribution. *Annual Review of Sociology, 9,* 425–446.

Crocker, Jennifer; & McGraw, Kathleen M. (1984). What's good for the goose is not good for the gander: Solo status as an obstacle to occupational achievement for males and females. *American Behavioral Scientist, 27,* 357–369. PA 71:23090.

Crocker, Jennifer; & Schwartz, Ian. (1985). Prejudice and ingroup favoritism in a minimal intergroup situation: Effects of self-esteem. *Personality and Social Psychology Bulletin, 11,* 379–386. PA 74:3993.

Cronshaw, Steven F.; & Lord, Robert G. (1987). Effects of categorization, attribution, and encoding processes on leadership perceptions. *Journal of Applied Psychology, 72,* 97–106. PA 74:15540.

Crosbie, Paul V. (1979a). The effects of sex and size on status ranking. *Social Psychology Quarterly, 42,* 340–354. PA 65:10369.

Crosbie, Paul V. (1979b). Effects of status inconsistency: Negative evidence from small groups. *Social Psychology Quarterly, 42,* 110–125. PA 64:7916. SA 81L1663.

Crosbie, Paul V.; Stitt, B. Grant; & Petroni, Frank A. (1974). Relevance in the small groups laboratory. *Humboldt Journal of Social Relations, 1*(2), 83–88. PA 55:12206. SA 75H3571.

Crosby, Faye; Bromley, Stephanie; & Saxe, Leonard. (1980). Recent unobtrusive studies of black and white discrimination and prejudice: A literature review. *Psychological Bulletin, 87,* 546–563. PA 64:3133.

Cross, John G. (1977). Negotiation as a learning

process. *Journal of Conflict Resolution, 21,* 581–606. PA 61:3526.

Crott, Helmut W. (1981). Two- and more-party bargaining: A review of recent literature devoting special attention to studies conducted in German-speaking countries. *German Journal of Psychology, 5,* 307–332. PA 68:5755.

Crott, Helmut W.; & Albers, Wulf. (1981). The equal division kernel: An equity approach to coalition formation and payoff distribution in N-person games. *European Journal of Social Psychology, 11,* 285–305. PA 67:12026. SA 83M9099.

Crott, Helmut W; Kayser, Egon; & Lamm, Helmut. (1980). The effects of information exchange and communication in an asymmetrical negotiation situation. *European Journal of Social Psychology, 10,* 149–163. PA 65:10370.

Crott, Helmut W.; & Muller, Gunter F. (1976). [The effect of level of aspiration and experience upon the decision process and the outcome in dyadic bargaining situations when complete information about probabilities of win and loss are available]. *Zeitschrift fur Experimentelle und Angewandte Psychologie, 23,* 548–568. PA 59:1026.

Crott, Helmut W; Muller, Gunter F.; & Maus, Eugen. (1978). [The influence of a partner's strategy on punishment behavior within dyadic bargaining situations]. *Archiv fur Psychologie, 131,* 39–47. PA 65:12734.

Crott, Helmut W.; Simon, Karla; & Yelin, Marianne. (1974). [The influence of level of aspiration on the course and results of negotiations]. *Zeitschrift fur Sozialpsychologie, 5,* 300–314. PA 54:5189.

Crott, Helmut W.; Zuber, Johannes A.; & Schermer, Thomas. (1986). Social decision schemes and choice shift: An analysis of group decisions among bets. *Journal of Experimental Social Psychology, 22,* 1–21. PA 74:13089.

Crouch, Andrew; & Yetton, Philip. (1988). Manager-subordinate dyads: Relationships among task and social contact, manager friendliness and subordinate performance in management groups. *Organizational Behavior and Human Performance, 41,* 65–82. PA 75:18706.

Crouch, Wayne W. (1976). Dominant direction of conjugate lateral eye movements and responsiveness to facial and verbal cues. *Perceptual and Motor Skills, 42,* 167–174. PA 56:9826.

Crusco, April H.; & Wetzel, Christopher G.

(1984). The Midas Touch: The effects of interpersonal touch on restaurant tipping. *Personality and Social Psychology Bulletin, 10,* 512–517. PA 72:30769.

Crutchfield, R. S. (1955). Conformity and character. *American Psychologist, 10,* 191–198.

Csoka, Louis S. (1975). Relationship between organizational climate and the situational favorableness dimension of Fiedler's contingency model. *Journal of Applied Psychology, 60,* 273–277. PA 54:2098.

Cull, John G. (1976). The relationship between sex role and modification of judgments. *Journal of Psychology, 93,* 313–317. PA 56:9827.

Cummings, L. L.; Huber, George P.; & Arendt, Eugene. (1974). Effects of size and spatial arrangements on group decision making. *Academy of Management Journal, 17,* 460–475. PA 53:6360.

Cunningham, Jean A.; & Strassberg, Donald S. (1981). Neuroticism and disclosure reciprocity. *Journal of Counseling Psychology, 28,* 455–458. PA 67:1214.

Cunningham, John D. (1981). Self-disclosure intimacy: Sex, sex-of-target, cross-national, and "generational" differences. *Personality and Social Psychology Bulletin, 7,* 314–319. PA 67:5701.

Cunningham, Michael R. (1979). Weather, mood, and helping behavior: Quasi experiments with the sunshine samaritan. *Journal of Personality and Social Psychology, 37,* 1947–1956. PA 65:5406.

Currant, Elaine F.; Dickson, Andrew L.; Anderson, Howard N.; & Faulkender, Patricia J. (1979). Sex-role stereotyping and assertive behavior. *Journal of Psychology, 101,* 223–228.

Cutrona, Carolyn E. (1986). Behavioral manifestations of social support: A microanalytic investigation. *Journal of Personality and Social Psychology, 51,* 201–208.

Czapinski, Janusz. (1976). Prosocial behavior as affected by the structure of the cognitive representation of others. *Polish Psychological Bulletin, 7,* 155–162. PA 58:1137.

Czapinski, Janusz. (1982). Zjawisko pozytywno-negatywnej asymetrii na poziomie grupowym i indywidualnym [Positive-negative asymmetry at the group and individual level]. *Psychologia Wychowawcza, 25,* 215–226. PA 71:28598.

Czwartosz, Zbigniew. (1976). How previous experience may affect behavior in a conflict situation. *Polish Psychological Bulletin*, 7, 187–195. PA 58:1085.

Czwartosz, Zbigniew. (1985). Refleksje nad zastosowaniem teorii gier w psychologii spolecznej [Remarks on game theory application to social psychology]. *Studia Psychologiczne*, 23, 171–189. PA 73:29929.

Dabbs, James M. Jr. (1977). Does reaction to crowding depend upon sex of subject or sex of subject's partners? *Journal of Personality and Social Psychology*, 35, 343–344. PA 62:3556.

Dabbs, James M. Jr.; Evans, Mark S.; Hopper, Charles H.; & Purvis, James A. (1980). Self-monitors in conversation: What do they monitor? *Journal of Personality and Social Psychology*, 39, 278–284. PA 66:3600.

Dabbs, James M. Jr.; & Ruback, R. Barry. (1984). Vocal patterns in male and female groups. *Personality and Social Psychology Bulletin*, 10, 518–525. PA 72:30770.

Dabbs, James M. Jr.; & Ruback, R. Barry. (1987). Dimensions of group process: Amount and structure of vocal interaction. *Advances in Experimental Social Psychology*, 20, 123–169.

Dagenais, Fred. (1979). Birth order and leadership style. *Journal of Social Psychology*, 109, 151–152. PA 65:3291.

da Gloria, Jorge; & de Ridder, Richard. (1979). Sex differences in aggression: Are current notions misleading? *European Journal of Social Psychology*, 9, 49–66. PA 64:993.

Daibo, Ikuo. (1980). The effect of the perceived interpersonal proximity on the dyadic speech behavior. *Japanese Journal of Experimental Social Psychology*, 20, 9–21. PA 66:10315.

Daibo, Ikuo. (1982). [Temporal structure of utterance and looking patterns in dyadic interaction]. *Japanese Journal of Experimental Social Psychology*, 22(1), 11–26. PA 69:12656.

Daibo, Ikuo; Sugiyama, Yoshio; & Akama, Midori. (1973). [The process of verbal activity in dyadic communication and manifest anxiety]. *Japanese Journal of Experimental Social Psychology*, 13, 86–98. PA 54:5191.

Daibo, Ikuo; Sugiyama, Yoshio; & Yoshimura, Tomoko. (1975). [The effects of manifest anxiety on the verbal activity in dyadic communication: The function of extreme high and low anxiety level on MAS]. *Japanese Journal of Experimental Social Psychology*, 15, 1–11. PA 58:1086.

Dailey, Robert C. (1977). The effects of cohesive-ness and collaboration on work groups: A theoretical model. *Group and Organization Studies*, 2, 461–469. PA 60:12835. SA 78J3218.

Dailey, Robert C. (1978). Perceived group variables as moderators of the task characteristics-individual performance relationship. *Journal of Management*, 4(2), 69–80. PA 64:3247.

Daley, John A.; McCroskey, James C.; & Richmond, Virginia P. (1977). Relationships between vocal activity and perception of communicators in small group interaction. *Western Journal of Speech Communication*, 41, 175–187. SA 80K8683.

Dalton, John E. (1983). Sex differences in communication skills as measured by a modified Relationship Inventory. *Sex Roles*, 9, 195–204. PA 70:12634.

Daly, Sandra. (1978). Behavioral correlates of social anxiety. *British Journal of Social & Clinical Psychology*, 17, 117–120.

Damos, Diane L. (1984). Individual differences in multiple-task performance and subjective estimates of workload. *Perceptual and Motor Skills*, 59, 567–580. PA 72:20076.

Danheiser, Priscilla R.; & Graziano, William G. (1982). Self-monitoring and cooperation as a self-presentational strategy. *Journal of Personality and Social Psychology*, 42, 497–505. PA 68:8095.

Darley, John M.; & Fazio, Russell H. (1980). Expectancy confirmation processes arising in the interaction sequence. *American Psychologist*, 35, 867–881. PA 66:5846.

Darley, John M.; & Gilbert, Daniel T. (1985). Social psychological aspects of environmental psychology. In G. Lindzey & E. Aronson (Eds.), *Handbook of Social Psychology* (3rd ed., Vol. 2, pp. 949–992). New York: Random House.

Darley, J[ohn] M.; Moriarty, T.; Darley, Susan; & Berscheid, Ellen. (1974). Increased conformity to a deviant as a function of prior deviation? *Journal of Experimental Social Psychology*, 10, 211–223.

Daszkowski, Julian. (1981). Teoretyczne i metodologiczne problemy psychologicznych porownan indywidualnego i grupowego wykonywania zadan [Theoretical and methodological problems of psychological comparisons in individual and group task performance]. *Przeglad Psychologiczny*, 24, 15–32. PA 68:3522.

D'Atri, David A. (1975). Psychophysiological responses to crowding. *Environment and behavior*, *7*, 237-252. PA 55:1180.

D'Augelli, Anthony R. (1974). Changes in self-reported anxiety during a small group experience. *Journal of Counseling Psychology*, *21*, 202-205. PA 52:09997.

D'Augelli, Anthony R.; & Chinsky, Jack M. (1974). Interpersonal skills and pretraining: Implications for the use of group procedures for interpersonal learning and for the selection of nonprofessional mental health workers. *Journal of Consulting and Clinical Psychology*, *42*, 65-72. PA 52:5174.

D'Augelli, Anthony R.; Chinsky, Jack M.; & Getter, Herbert. (1974). The effect of group composition and duration on sensitivity training. *Small Group Behavior*, *5*, 56-64. PA 52:10014.

Daum, Jeffrey W. (1975). Internal promotion: A psychological asset or debit? A study of the effects of leader origin. *Organizational Behavior and Human Performance*, *13*, 404-413. PA 54:7453.

Davies, Don; & Kuypers, Bart C. (1985). Group development and interpersonal feedback. *Group and Organization Studies*, *10*, 184-208. PA 72:30771.

Davies, Martin F.; & Blumberg, Herbert H. (1988 [released 1990]). Attraction, friendship, and relationships: A classified bibliography 1974-1988. *Social and Behavioral Sciences Documents*, *18*(1), 15 [Ms. No.2850].

Davis, Albie M.; & Salem, Richard A. (1984). Dealing with power imbalances in the mediation of interpersonal disputes. *Mediation Quarterly*, No. 6, 17-26. PA 72:17311.

Davis, Deborah; & Brock, Timothy C. (1979). Effects of the recipient's status and responsiveness on physical pleasuring between heterosexual strangers. *Journal of Experimental Social Psychology*, *15*, 217-228. PA 64:7967.

Davis, Deborah; & Holtgraves, Thomas. (1984). Perceptions of unresponsive others: Attributions, attraction, understandability, and memory of their utterances. *Journal of Experimental Social Psychology*, *20*, 383-408. PA 72:22599.

Davis, Deborah; & Perkowitz, William T. (1979). Consequences of responsiveness in dyadic interaction: Effects of probability of response and proportion of content-related responses on interpersonal attraction. *Journal of Personality and Social Psychology*, *37*, 534-550. PA 64:7918.

Davis, Deborah; Rainey, Hal G.; & Brock, Timothy C. (1976). Interpersonal physical pleasuring: Effects of sex combinations, recipient attributes, and anticipated future interaction. *Journal of Personality and Social Psychology*, *33*, 89-106. PA 55:7058.

Davis, James A. (1977). Sociometric triads as multi-variate systems. *Journal of Mathematical Sociology*, *5*, 41-59. SA 78J3219.

Davis, James H.; Holt, Robert W.; Spitzer, Craig E.; & Stasser, Garold. (1981). The effects of consensus requirements and multiple decisions on mock juror verdict preferences. *Journal of Experimental Social Psychology*, *17*, 1-15. PA 67:3580.

Davis, James H.; Kerr, Norbert L.; Atkin, Robert S.; Holt, Robin; & Meek, David. (1975). The decision processes of 6- and 12-person mock juries assigned unanimous and two-thirds majority rules. *Journal of Personality and Social Psychology*, *32*, 1-14. PA 54:7501.

Davis, James H.; Kerr, Norbert L.; Stasser, Garold; Meek, David; & Holt, Robert. (1977). Victim consequences, sentence severity, and decision processes in mock juries. *Organizational Behavior and Human Performance*, *18*, 346-365.

Davis, James H.; Kerr, Norbert; Sussman, Mario; & Rissmann, A. Kent. (1974). Social decision schemes under risk. *Journal of Personality and Social Psychology*, *30*, 248-271.

Davis, James H.; Laughlin, Patrick R.; & Komorita, Samuel S. (1976). The social psychology of small groups: Cooperative and mixed-motive interaction. *Annual Review of Psychology*, *27*, 501-541. PA 57:1152.

Davis, James H.; Stasser, Garold; Spitzer, Craig E.; & Holt, Robert W. (1976). Changes in group members' decision preferences during discussion: An illustration with mock juries. *Journal of Personality and Social Psychology*, *34*, 1177-1187. PA 60:11688.

Davis, James H.; & Stasson, Mark F. (1988). Small group performance: Past and present research trends. *Advances in Group Processes*, *5*, 245-277.

Davis, James H.; Stasson, Mark [F.]; Ono, Kaoru; & Zimmerman, Suzi. (1988). Effects of straw polls on group decision making: Sequential voting pattern, timing, and local majorities. *Journal of Personality and Social Psychology*, *55*, 918-926.

Davis, James H.; Tindale, R. Scott; Nagao,

Dennis H.; Hinsz, Verlin B.; & Robertson, Bret. (1984). Order effects in multiple decisions by groups: A demonstration with mock juries and trial procedures. *Journal of Personality and Social Psychology, 47,* 1003–1012. PA 72:14507.

Davis, John D. (1976). Self-disclosure in an acquaintance exercise: Responsibility for level of intimacy. *Journal of Personality and Social Psychology, 33,* 787–792. PA 56:5988.

Davis, John D. (1977). Effects of communication about interpersonal process on the evolution of self-disclosure in dyads. *Journal of Personality and Social Psychology, 35,* 31–37. PA 58:5327.

Davis, John D.; & Sloan, Margaret L. (1974). The basis of interviewee matching of interviewer self disclosure. *British Journal of Social and Clinical Psychology, 13,* 359–367. PA 53:7287.

Davis, Larry; & Burnstein, Eugene. (1981). Preference for racial composition of groups. *Journal of Psychology, 109,* 293–301. PA 68:1081. SA 83N2343.

Davis, Leslie L. (1984). Judgment ambiguity, self-consciousness, and conformity in judgments of fashionability. *Psychological Reports, 54,* 671–675. PA 72:1227.

Davis, Terry B.; Frye, Roland L.; & Joure, Sylvia. (1975). Perceptions and behaviors of dogmatic subjects in a T-group setting. *Perceptual and Motor Skills, 41,* 375–381. SA 78J1735.

Dawes, Robyn M. (1974). Formal models of dilemmas in social decision-making. *Bulletin* [Oregon Research Institute], *14*(12).

Dawes, Robyn M. (1980). Social dilemmas. *Annual Review of Psychology, 31,* 169–193. PA 64:10361. SA 84N7284.

Dawes, Robyn M.; McTavish, Jeanne; & Shaklee, Harriet. (1977). Behavior, communication, and assumptions about other people's behavior in a commons dilemma situation. *Journal of Personality and Social Psychology, 35,* 1–11. PA 58:5298.

Day, Harry R. (1974–1975). The resource comparison model of coalition formation. *Philippine Journal of Psychology, 7–8,* 52–60. PA 60:3005.

Day, Harry R. (1975). The resource comparison model of coalition formation. *Cornell Journal of Social Relations, 10*(2), 209–221. SA 76I1692.

Dean, Larry M.; Pugh, William; & Gunderson, Elizabeth K. (1978). The behavioral effects of crowding: Definitions and methods. *Environment and behavior, 10,* 419–431. PA 64:2203.

Dean, Larry M.; Willis, Frank N.; & Hewitt, Jay. (1975). Initial interaction distance among individuals equal and unequal in military rank. *Journal of Personality and Social Psychology, 32,* 294–299. PA 57:3190.

Dean, Larry M.; Willis, Frank N.; & la Rocco, James M. (1976). Invasion of personal space as a function of age, sex, and race. *Psychological Reports, 38,* 959–965. PA 61:3527.

Deaux, Kay. (1978, May). *Sex-related patterns of social interaction.* Paper presented at the meeting of the Midwestern Psychological Association, Chicago.

Deaux, Kay. (1979). Self-evaluations of male and female managers. *Sex Roles, 5,* 571–580.

Deaux, Kay. (1985). Sex and gender. *Annual Review of Psychology, 36,* 49–81. PA 72:17251.

Deaux, Kay; & Wrightsman, Lawrence S. (1988). *Social psychology* (5th ed.). Pacific Grove, CA: Brooks/Cole.

DeBeer-Keston, Kate; Mellon, Lorraine; & Solomon, Linda Zener. (1986). Helping behavior as a function of personal space invasion. *Journal of Social Psychology, 126,* 407–409.

DeBiasio, Alan R. (1986). Problem solving in triads composed of varying numbers of field-dependent and field-independent subjects. *Journal of Personality and Social Psychology, 51,* 749–754. PA 74:3994.

Deci, Edward L.; Betley, Gregory; Kahle, James; Abrams, Linda; Porac, Joseph. (1981). When trying to win: Competition and intrinsic motivation. *Personality and Social Psychology Bulletin, 7,* 79–83. PA 67:3581.

Dedrick, Dennis K. (1978). Deviance and sanctioning within small groups. *Social Psychology, 41,* 94–105. SA 79J6846.

DeFronzo, J. (1984). Climate and crime: Tests of an FBI assumption. *Environment and Behavior, 16,* 185–210. PA 71:20718.

de Guzman, Jose. (1979). Helping a lost passenger: An analysis of the number of bystanders and dependency of the victim in an urban and a rural community. *Philippine Journal of Psychology, 12,* 10–16. PA 72:17337.

DeJong, William. (1979). An examination of self-perception mediation of the foot-in-the-door effect. *Journal of Personality and Social Psychology, 37,* 2221–2239.

DeJong, William; & Musilli, Lisa. (1982). External pressure to comply: Handicapped versus nonhandicapped requesters and the foot-in-the-door phenomenon. *Personality and Social Psychology Bulletin, 8*, 522–527. PA 69:11573.

DeJulio, Steven; Bentley, Joseph; & Cockayne, Thomas. (1979). Pregroup norm setting: Effects on encounter group interaction. *Small Group Behavior, 10*, 368–388. SA 80K8684.

de la Haye, Anne Marie. (1983). Reciprocite et non-reciprocite presumee des relations dans la famille [Perceived reciprocity and non-reciprocity in family relationships]. *Annee Psychologique, 83*, 135–151. PA 71:9502.

DeLamater, John. (1974). A definition of "group." *Small Group Behavior, 5*, 30–44. PA 52:10016.

Delamater, Ronald J.; & McNamara, J. Regis. (1986). The social impact of assertiveness: Research findings and clinical implications. *Behavior Modification, 10*, 139–158. PA 74:10182.

Delin, Peter S.; & Poo-Kong, Kee. (1974). The measurement of mutual conformity in a dyadic situation. *British Journal of Social and Clinical Psychology, 13*, 211–213. SA 7717499.

Dembroski, Theodore M.; & MacDougall, James M. (1978). Stress effects on affiliation preferences among subjects possessing the Type A coronary-prone behavior pattern. *Journal of Personality and Social Psychology, 36*, 23–33.

Dengerink, H. A.; & Bertilson, H. S. (1974). The reduction of attack instigated aggression. *Journal of Research in Personality, 8*, 254–262. PA 53:7310.

Dengerink, H. A.; Schnedler, R. W.; & Covey, M. K. (1978). Role of avoidance in aggressive responses to attack and no attack. *Journal of Personality and Social Psychology, 36*, 1044–1053. PA 63:5415.

DeNisi, Angelo S.; Randolph, W. Alan; & Blencoe, Allyn G. (1983). Potential problems with peer ratings. *Academy of Management Journal, 26*, 457–464. PA 71:1309.

Denmark, Florence L. (1977). Styles of leadership. *Psychology of Women Quarterly, 2*, 99–113. PA 60:9290.

Denzin, Norman K. (Ed.). (1984). *Studies in symbolic interaction: A research annual* (Vol. 5). Greenwich, CT: JAI.

DePaulo, Bella M.; & Coleman, Lerita M. (1986). Talking to children, foreigners, and retarded adults. *Journal of Personality and Social Psychology, 51*, 945–959. PA 74:6757.

DePaulo, Bella M.; & Fisher, Jeffrey D. (1980). The costs of asking for help. *Basic and Applied Social Psychology, 1*, 23–35.

DePaulo, Bella M.; & Rosenthal Robert. (1979). Telling lies. *Journal of Personality and Social Psychology, 37*, 1713–1722. PA 65:1261.

DePaulo, Bella M.; Rosenthal, Robert; Green, Carolyn R.; & Rosenkrantz, Judith. (1982). Diagnosing deceptive and mixed messages from verbal and nonverbal cues. *Journal of Experimental Social Psychology, 18*, 433–446. PA 69:7898.

DePaulo, Bella M.; Rosenthal, Robert; Rosenkrantz, Judith; & Green, Carolyn R. (1982). Actual and perceived cues to deception: A closer look at speech. *Basic and Applied Social Psychology, 3*, 291–312. PA 70:5623.

DePaulo, Bella M.; Tang, John; & Stone, Julie I. (1987). Physical attractiveness and skill at detecting deception. *Personality and Social Psychology Bulletin, 13*, 177–187.

deRivera, Joseph. (1984). The structure of emotional relationships. *Review of Personality and Social Psychology*, No. 5, 116–145. PA 73:17198.

Derlega, Valerian J.; & Chaikin, Alan L. (1976). Norms affecting self-disclosure in men and women. *Journal of Consulting and Clinical Psychology, 44*, 376–380. PA 56:672.

Derlega, Valerian J.; & Chaikin, Alan L. (1977). Privacy and self-disclosure in social relationships. *Journal of Social Issues, 33*(3), 102–115. PA 62:1044.

Derlega, Valerian J.; & Chaikin, Alan L. (1979). [Intimacy and self-disclosure in interpersonal relationships]. *Przeglad Psychologiczny, 22*, 257–271. PA 65:3241.

Derlega, Valerian J.; & Stepien, Ewa G. (1977). Norms regulating self-disclosure among Polish university students. *Journal of Cross Cultural Psychology, 8*, 369–376. PA 60:3030.

Derlega, Valerian J.; Wilson, Midge; & Chaikin, Alan L. (1976). Friendship and disclosure reciprocity. *Journal of Personality and Social Psychology, 34*, 578–582. PA 58:1087.

Dertke, Max C.; Penner, Louis A.; & Ulrich, Kathleen. (1974). Observer's reporting of shoplifting as a function of thief's race and sex. *Journal of Social Psychology, 94*, 213–221. PA 53:9500.

Deschamps, Jean Claude; & Brown, Rupert. (1983). Superordinate goals and intergroup conflict. *British Journal of Social Psychology*, 22, 189–195. PA 71:14961.

Desmond, Richard E.; & Seligman, Milton. (1977). A review of research on leaderless groups. *Small Group Behavior*, 8, 3–24. PA 60:7832.

Desportes, Jean-Pierre; & Dequeker, Annie. (1973–1974). [Effects of the presence of the experimenter: Social facilitation and inhibition of performance]. *Bulletin du C.E.R.P.*, 22, 241–245. PA 58:1049.

DeStephen, Rolayne S. (1983a). Group interaction differences between high and low consensus groups. *Western Journal of Speech Communication*, 47, 340–363. SA 85O6019.

DeStephen, RoLayne S. (1983b). High and low consensus groups: A content and relational interaction analysis. *Small Group Behavior*, 14, 143–162. PA 71:12150.

DeTurck, Mark A. (1985). A transactional analysis of compliance-gaining behavior: Effects of noncompliance, relational contexts, and actors' gender. *Human Communication Research*, 12, 54–78. PA 73:21908.

Deutsch, Francine M.; & Mackesy, Mary E. (1985). Friendship and the development of self-schemas: The effects of talking about others. *Personality and Social Psychology Bulletin*, 11, 399–408. PA 74:3996.

Deutsch, Morton. (1973). *The resolution of conflict: Constructive and destructive processes*. New Haven: Yale University Press

Deutsch, Morton. (1979). A critical review of "equity theory": An alternative perspective on the social psychology of justice. *International Journal of Group Tensions*, 9, 20–49. PA 69:3377.

Deutsch, Morton. (1983). Conflict resolution: Theory and practice. *Political Psychology*, 4, 431–453. PA 72:11993.

Deutsch, Morton (1985). *Distributive justice: A social-psychological perspective*. New Haven, CT: Yale University Press.

Deutsch, Morton; & Gerard, Harold B. (1955). A study of normative and informational social influences upon individual judgment. *Journal of Abnormal and Social Psychology*, 51, 629–636.

Deutsch, Robert D. (1976). An empirical investigation into the grammar of visual interaction: Looks and stares. *Man Environment Systems*, 6(3), 163–173. PA 58:11650.

Deutsch, Robert D; & Auerbach, Carl. (1975). Eye movement in perception of another person's looking behavior. *Perceptual and Motor Skills*, 40, 475–481. PA 54:9591.

DeVries, David L.; & Edwards, Keith J. (1974). Student teams and learning games: Their effects on cross-race and cross-sex interaction. *Journal of Educational Psychology*, 66, 741–749.

DeVries, David L.; & Slavin, Robert E. (1976). Teams-Games-Tournament: A final report on the research. Center for Social Organization of Schools Report, Johns Hopkins U., No. 217, 76 pages. PA 58:8240.

DeVries, David L.; & Slavin, Robert E. (1978). Teams-games-tournaments (tgt): Review of ten classroom experiments. *Journal of Research and Development in Education*, 12(1), 28–38. SA 81L8137.

De Waal, Frans. (1983). *Chimpanzee politics: Power and sex among apes*. New York: Harper-Row.

DeWine, Sue; Bennett, Diane Tobin; & Medcalf, Lawrence Donald. (1978). Modeling and self-disclosure in the classroom. *Small Group Behavior*, 9, 563–578. SA 80K4174.

Diamond, Michael A.; & Allcorn, Seth. (1987). The psychodynamics of regression in work groups. *Human Relations*, 40, 525–543.

Diamond, Shari S.; & Zeisel, Hans. (1974). A courtroom experiment on juror selection and decision-making. *Personality and Social Psychology Bulletin*, 1, 276–277. PA 56:2244.

DiBerardinis, James P. (1978). The effects of videotape feedback on group and self-satisfaction. *Group and Organization Studies*, 3, 108–114. PA 61:8464. SA 78J4685.

DiBerardinis, James P.; Ramage, Kathy; & Levitt, Steve. (1984). Risky shift and gender of the advocate: Information theory versus normative theory. *Group and Organization Studies*, 9, 189–200. PA 72:30773.

Dickson, John W. (1978). The effect of normative models on individual and group choice. *European Journal of Social Psychology*, 8, 91–107. PA 63:7560. SA 79J9633.

Diehl, Michael; & Stroebe, Wolfgang. (1987). Productivity loss in brainstorming groups: Toward the solution of a riddle. *Journal of Personality and Social Psychology*, 53, 497–509.

Diekmann, Andreas. (1985). Volunteer's dilemma. *Journal of Conflict Resolution*, 29, 605–610. PA 73:14426.

Diener, Edward. (1976). Effects of prior destructive behavior, anonymity, and group presence on deindividuation and aggression. *Journal of Personality and Social Psychology, 33,* 497–507. PA 56:5989.

Diener, Edward; Dineen, John; Endresen, Karen; Beaman, Arthur L.; & Fraser, Scott C. (1975). Effects of altered responsibility, cognitive set, and modeling on physical aggression and deindividuation. *Journal of Personality and Social Psychology, 31,* 328–337. PA 53:11566.

Diener, Edward; Fraser, Scott C.; Beaman, Arthur L.; & Kelem, Roger T. (1976). Effects of deindividuation variables on stealing among Halloween trick-or-treaters. *Journal of Personality and Social Psychology, 33,* 178–183. PA 56:842.

Diener, Edward; Lusk, Rob; DeFour, Darlene; & Flax, Robert. (1980). Deindividuation: Effects of group size, density, number of observers, and group member similarity on self-consciousness and disinhibited behavior. *Journal of Personality and Social Psychology, 39,* 449–459. PA 66:5739.

Dies, Robert R. (Ed.). (1978). Symposium on: Therapy and encounter group research: Issues and answers [Special issue]. *Small Group Behavior, 9*(2).

Dies, Robert R. (1979). Group psychotherapy: Reflections on three decades of research, *Journal of Applied Behavioral Science, 15,* 361–373.

Dies, Robert R. (1985). A multidimensional model for group process research: Elaboration and critique. *Small Group Behavior, 16,* 427–446.

Dietch, James; & House, James. (1975). Affiliative conflict and individual differences in self-disclosure. *Representative Research in Social Psychology, 6,* 69–75. PA 55:9719.

di Marco, Nicholas. (1973). T-Group and workgroup climates and participants' thoughts about transfer. *Journal of Applied Behavioral Science, 9,* 757–764. PA 52:5175.

di Marco, Nicholas; Kuehl, Charles; & Wims, Earl. (1975). Leadership style and interpersonal need orientation as moderators of changes in leadership dimension scores. *Personnel Psychology, 28,* 207–213. PA 55:11141.

Dimock, Hedley G. (1987). *Groups: Leadership and group development.* San Diego: University Associates.

Dion, Karen K. (1974). Children's physical attractiveness and sex as determinants of adult punitiveness. *Developmental Psychology, 10,* 772–778. PA 53:3015.

Dion, Karen K.; & Stein, Steven. (1978). Physical attractiveness and interpersonal influence. *Journal of Experimental Social Psychology, 14,* 97–108. PA 60:9291.

Dion, Kenneth L. (1979). Status equity, sex composition of group, and intergroup bias. *Personality and Social Psychology Bulletin, 5,* 240–244. PA 64:5547.

Diskin, Abraham; & Felsenthal, Dan S. (1978). Decision making in mixed situations in which both chance and a rival player are confronted simultaneously. *Behavioral Science, 23,* 256–263. PA 63:7561.

Ditton, Jason. (Ed.). (1980). *View from Goffman.* New York: St. Martins Press.

Ditton, Robert B.; Fedler, Anthony J.; & Graefe, Alan R. (1983). Factors contributing to perceptions of recreational crowding. *Leisure Sciences, 5,* 273–288. PA 71:6728.

Dobbins, Gregory H.; Pence, Earl C.; Orban, Joseph A.; & Sgro, Joseph A. (1983). The effects of sex of the leader and sex of the subordinate on the use of organizational control policy. *Organizational Behavior and Human Performance, 32,* 325–343. PA 71:10919.

Dobbins, Gregory H.; & Platz, Stephanie J. (1986). Sex differences in leadership: How real are they? *Academy of Management Review, 11,* 118–127.

Dobbins, Gregory H.; & Russell, Jeanne M. (1986). Self-serving biases in leadership: A laboratory experiment. *Journal of Management, 12,* 475–483. PA 74:18750.

Dobbins, Gregory H.; Stuart, Cecile; Pence, Earl C.; & Sgro, Joseph A. (1985). Cognitive mechanisms mediating the biasing effects of leader sex on ratings of leader behavior. *Sex Roles, 12,* 549–560. PA 73:9091.

Dodge, Cynthia S.; Heimberg, Richard G.; Nyman, David; & O'Brien, Gerald T. (1987). Daily heterosocial interactions of high and low socially anxious college students: A diary study. *Behavior Therapy, 18,* 90–96. PA 74:15520.

Doise, Willem; & Mugny, Gabriel. (1975). [Sociogenetic research on the coordination of interdependent actions]. *Psychologie Schweizerische Zeitschrift fur Psychologie und ihre Anwendungen, 34,* 160–174. PA 55:2198.

Doise, Willem; Mugny, Gabriel; & Perret-Clermont, Anne Nelly. (1975). Social interaction and the development of cognitive operations. *European Journal of Social Psychology*, *5*, 367–383. PA 58:3093.

Dollinger, Stephen J.; & Thelen, Mark H. (1978). Leadership and imitation in children. *Personality and Social Psychology Bulletin*, *4*, 487–490. PA 64:2979.

Domachowski, Waldemar. (1980). Functions of interpersonal space. *Przeglad Psychologiczny*, *23*, 47–64. PA 66:12759.

Doms, Machteld; & Van Avermaet, Eddy. (1980). Majority influence, minority influence and conversion behavior: A replication. *Journal of Experimental Social Psychology*, *16*, 283–292. PA 65:12719.

Donnerstein, Edward; & Donnerstein, Marcia. (1972). White rewarding behavior as a function of the potential for Black retaliation. *Journal of Personality and Social Psychology*, *24*, 327–333.

Donnerstein, Edward; & Donnerstein, Marcia. (1973). Variables in interracial aggression: Potential in-group censure. *Journal of Personality and Social Psychology*, *27*, 143–150.

Donnerstein, Edward; & Donnerstein, Marcia. (1975). The effect of attitudinal similarity on interracial aggression. *Journal of Personality*, *43*, 485–502. PA 55:7125.

Donnerstein, Edward; & Wilson, David, W. (1976). Effects of noise and perceived control on ongoing and subsequent aggressive behavior. *Journal of Personality and Social Psychology*, *34*, 774–781. PA 57:12768.

Donnerstein, Marcia; & Donnerstein, Edward. (1977). Modeling in the control of interracial aggression: The problem of generality. *Journal of Personality*, *45*, 100–116. PA 59:1062.

Donnerstein, Marcia; & Donnerstein, Edward. (1978). Direct and vicarious censure in the control of interracial aggression. *Journal of Personality*, *46*, 162–175. PA 61:10939.

Donoghue, Eileen E.; McCarrey, Michael W.; & Clement, Richard. (1983). Humour appreciation as a function of canned laughter, a mirthful companion, and field dependence: Facilitation and inhibitory effects. *Canadian Journal of Behavioural Science*, *15*, 150–162. PA 71:3987.

Donohue, William A. (1978). An empirical framework for examining negotiation processes and outcomes. *Communication Monographs*, *45*, 247–257. PA 63:973.

Donohue, William A. (1981a). Analyzing negotiation tactics: Development of a negotiation interact system. *Human Communication Research*, *7*, 273–287. PA 67:3522.

Donohue, William A. (1981b). Development of a model of rule use in negotiation interaction. *Communication Monographs*, *48*, 106–120. PA 67:9758.

Donohue, William A.; & Diez, Mary E. (1985). Directive use in negotiation interaction. *Communication Monographs*, *52*, 305–318. PA 73:29944.

Donohue, William A.; Hawes, Leonard C.; & Mabee, Timothy. (1981). Testing a structural-functional model of group decision making using Markov analysis. *Human Communication Research*, *7*, 133–146. PA 67:1215. SA 82M5646.

Donohue, William A.; Weider-Hatfield, Deborah; Hamilton, Mark; & Diez, Mary E. (1985). Relational distance in managing conflict. *Human Communication Research*, *11*, 387–405. PA 73:6326.

Dontsov, Aleksandr Ivanovich. (1975). Metodologicheskie problemy issledovaniia gruppovoi splochennosti [Methodological Problems of the Study of Group Cohesion]. *Sotsiologicheskie Issledovaniya*, *2*(2), 42–52. SA 80K8685.

Dontsov, A[leksandr] I[vanovich].; & Sarkisyan, S. V. (1980). [Joint activity as a factor in interpersonal perception in a group]. *Voprosy Psikhologii*, No. 4, 38–49. PA 66:1212.

Doob, Leonard W. (1975). *Pathways to people*. New Haven: Yale University Press.

Dooley, Braddie B. (1978). Effects of social density on men with "close" or "far" personal space. *Journal of Population*, *1*, 251–265.

Dorch, Edwina; & Fontaine, Gary. (1978). Rate of judges' gaze at different types of witnesses. *Perceptual and Motor Skills*, *46*, 1103–1106. SA 81L4924.

Doreian, Patrick. (1979). On the "social law of effect" for task-oriented groups. *Social Psychology Quarterly*, *42*, 222–231. PA 65:10371.

Doreian, Patrick. (1986). Measuring relative standing in small groups and bounded social networks. *Social Psychology Quarterly*, *49*, 247–259.

Dorfman, Peter W.; & Stephan, Walter G. (1984). The effects of group performance on cognitions, satisfaction, and behavior: A process model. *Journal of Management*, *10*, 173–192. PA 71:31308.

Dornbusch, Sanford M. (1987). Individual moral choices and social evaluations: A research odyssey. *Advances in Group Processes*, *4*, 271-307.

Dornette, Wolfgang. (1975). [Decisional behavior of schizophrenic patients under varied conditions regarding partner and communication within a two-persons-non-zero-sum-game]. *Archiv fur Psychologie*, *127*, 251-270. PA 57:10434.

Dorris, William; & Knight, R. Christopher. (1978). Research on intimate relationships: An ecological perspective. *Catalog of Selected Documents in Psychology*, *8*, 61. (Ms. No. 1719) PA 62:10966.

Dor Shav, Netta K.; Friedman, Bruria; & Tcherbonogura, Rachel. (1978). Identification, prejudice, and aggression. *Journal of Social Psychology*, *104*, 217-222. PA 61:13409.

Douglas, Jack D.; Adler, Patricia A.; Adler, Peter; Fontana, Andrea; Freeman, C. Robert; & Kotarba, Joseph A. (1980). *Introduction to the sociologies of everyday life*. Boston: Allyn & Bacon.

Douglas, Tom. (1983). *Groups: Understanding people gathered together*. London: Tavistock.

Douglas, William. (1984). Initial interaction scripts: When knowing is behaving. *Human Communication Research*, *11*(2), 203-219.

Douglis, Carole. (1987, November). The beat goes on. *Psychology Today*, *21*(11), 36-39, 42.

Dovidio, John F. (1982). Sex, costs, and helping behavior. *Journal of Psychology*, *112*, 231-236. PA 70:1068.

Dovidio, John F.; & Ellyson, Steve L. (1982). Decoding visual dominance: Attributions of power based on relative percentages of looking while speaking and looking while listening. *Social Psychology Quarterly*, *45*, 106-113. PA 68:11607.

Dovidio, John F.; Ellyson, Steve L.; Keating, Caroline F.; Heltman, Karen; & Brown, Clifford E. (1988). The relationship of social power to visual displays of dominance between men and women. *Journal of Personality and Social Psychology*, *54*, 233-242.

Dovidio, John F.; & Gaertner, Samuel L. (1981). The effects of race, status and ability on helping behavior. *Social Psychology Quarterly*, *44*, 192-203.

Dowd, James J. (1981). Conversation and social exchange: Managing identities in old age. *Human Relations*, *34*, 541-553. PA 67:1216.

Dowdle, Michael D.; Gillen, H. Barry; & Miller,

Arthur G. (1974). Integration and attribution theories as predictors of sentencing by a simulated jury. *Personality and Social Psychology Bulletin*, *1*, 270-272. PA 56:2245.

Downey, H. Kirk; Chacko, Thomas I.; & McElroy, James C. (1979). Attribution of the "causes" of performance: A constructive, quasi-longitudinal replication of the Staw. (1975) study. *Organizational Behavior and Human Performance*, *24*, 287-299. PA 65:3243.

Downing, Leslie L. (1975). The Prisoner's Dilemma game as a problem-solving phenomenon: An outcome maximization interpretation. *Simulation and Games*, *6*, 366-391. PA 56:7895.

Downing, Leslie L.; & Ritter, Edward H. (1976). Effects of contingencies on cooperative responding in a prisoner's dilemma game with anticipated shock outcomes. *Personality and Social Psychology Bulletin*, *2*, 51-54. PA 56:4025.

Drake, Bruce H.; & Moberg, Dennis J. (1986). Communicating influence attempts in dyads: Linguistic sedatives and palliatives. *Academy of Management Review*, *11*, 567-584. PA 73:27136.

Drory, Amos; & Gluskinos, Uri M. (1980). Machiavellianism and leadership. *Journal of Applied Psychology*, *65*, 81-86. PA 65:5382.

Druckman, Daniel. (1977a). Boundary role conflict: Negotiation as dual responsiveness. *Journal of Conflict Resolution*, *21*, 639-662. PA 61:3529.

Druckman, Daniel. (Ed.). (1977b). *Negotiations, Social-psychological perspectives*. Beverly Hills, CA: Sage.

Druckman, Daniel; Benton, Alan A.; Ali, Faizunisa; & Bagur, J. Susana. (1976). Cultural differences in bargaining behavior: India, Argentina, and the United States. *Journal of Conflict Resolution*, *20*, 413-452. PA 57:5654.

Druckman, Daniel; & Bonoma, Thomas V. (1976). Determinants of bargaining behavior in a bilateral monopoly situation ii: opponent's concession rate and similarity. *Behavioral Science*, *21*, 252-262. SA 7714647.

Dua, J. K. (1977). Effects of audience on the acquisition and extinction of avoidance. *British Journal of Social and Clinical Psychology*, *16*, 207-212.

Duck, Steven W. (1975). Personality similarity and friendship choices by adolescents. *European*

Journal of Social Psychology, 5, 351–365. PA 58:3291.

Duck, Steve. (1986). *Human relationships: An introduction to social psychology*. London: Sage.

Duck, Steve. (Ed.). (1988). *Handbook of personal relationships: Theory, research and interventions*. Chichester, England: Wiley.

Duck, Steven W.; & Allison, Davina. (1978). I liked you but I can't live with you: A study of lapsed friendships. *Social Behavior and Personality, 6*, 43–47. PA 63:5416.

Duck, Steven W.; & Craig, Gordon. (1978). Personality similarity and the development of friendship: A longitudinal study. *British Journal of Social and Clinical Psychology, 17*, 237–242. PA 63:974.

Duck, Steve; & Gilmour, Robin. (Eds.). (1981). *Personal relationships* (2 vols.). [Volume 1 is subtitled *Studying personal relationships*; Volume 2 is subtitled *Developing personal relationships*]. London: Academic Press.

Duck, Steven W.; & Sants, Harriet. (1983). On the origin of the specious: Are personal relationships really interpersonal states? *Journal of Social and Clinical Psychology, 1*, 27–41. PA 71:17746.

Duckitt, John H. (1983). Household crowding and psychological well-being in a South African Coloured community. *Journal of Social Psychology, 121*, 231–238. PA 71:21976.

Duffy, John F.; & Kavanagh, Michael J. (1983). Confounding the creation of social forces: Laboratory studies of negotiation behavior. *Journal of Conflict Resolution, 27*, 635–647. PA 71:12152.

Duke, Marshall P. (1977). Talavage's *P*-model: A translation of Rotter's social learning theory of behavior and its application to a conceptualization of interpersonal distance behavior. *Journal of Research in Personality, 11*, 261–272. PA 60:3031.

Dunand, Muriel; Berkowitz, Leonard; & Leyens, Jacques Philippe. (1984). Audience effects when viewing aggressive movies. *British Journal of Social Psychology, 21*, 69–76. PA 71:28599.

Duncan, Starkey. (1974). On the structure of speaker-auditor interaction during speaking turns. *Language in Society, 3*(2), 161–180. PA 53:11652.

Duncan, Starkey; Brunner, Lawrence J.; & Fiske,

Donald W. (1979). Strategy signals in face-to-face interaction. *Journal of Personality and Social Psychology, 37*, 301–313. PA 64:5548.

Duncan, Starkey; & Fiske, Donald W. (1977). *Face-to-face interaction: Research, methods, and theory*. Hillsdale, NJ: Erlbaum.

Duncan, Starkey; & Fiske, Donald W. (1979). Dynamic patterning in conversation. *American Scientist, 67*, 90–98. PA 63:11942.

Duncan, Starkey; & Fiske, Donald W. (1985). *Interaction structure and strategy*. New York: Cambridge University Press.

Duncan, Starkey; Kanki, Barbara G.; Mokros, Hartmut; & Fiske, Donald W. (1984). Pseudounilaterality, simple-rate variables, and other ills to which interaction research is heir. *Journal of Personality and Social Psychology, 46*, 1335–1348. PA 71:28600.

Duncan, Starkey, Jr.; & Niederehe, George. (1974). On signalling that it's your turn to speak. *Journal of Experimental Social Psychology, 10*, 234–247.

Duncan, W. Jack. (1985). The superiority theory of humor at work: Joking relationships as indicators of formal and informal status patterns in small, task-oriented groups. *Small Group Behavior, 16*, 556–564. PA 73:29945. SA 86Q4837.

Duncan, W. Jack; & Beeland, James L. (1980). Choice consistency of interpersonal relations: Diversified task-oriented groups. *Small Group Behavior, 11*, 209–228. SA 82M1452.

Durkin, James E. (Ed.). (1981). *Living groups: Group psychotherapy and general system theory*. New York: Brunner/Mazel.

Durling, Rich; & Schick, Connie. (1976). Concept attainment by pairs and individuals as a function of vocalization. *Journal of Educational Psychology, 68*, 83–91. PA 55:6150 [PsycLIT no. 55–06149].

Dustin, David S.; & East-Trou, Henry J. (1974). Evaluative bias as a social norm. *Personality and Social Psychology Bulletin, 1*, 256–258.

Dutton, Donald G.; & Lennox, Vicki L. (1974). Effect of prior "token" compliance on subsequent interracial behavior. *Journal of Personality and Social Psychology, 29*, 65–71.

Duval, Shelley. (1976). Conformity on a visual task as a function of personal novelty on attitudinal dimensions and being reminded of the object status of self. *Journal of Experimental Social Psychology, 12*, 87–98.

Dwyer, F. Robert. (1984). Are two better than one? Bargaining behavior and outcomes in an asymmetrical power relationship. *Journal of Consumer Research, 11*, 680–693. SA 85O7797.

Dwyer, F. Robert; & Walker, Orville C. (1981). Bargaining in an asymmetrical power structure. *Journal of Marketing, 45*(1), 104–115. PA 65:12735.

Dymkowski, Maciej. (1980). Obraz siebie a atrakcyjnosc zrodla informacji osobistych [Self-concept and attractiveness of source of personal information]. *Przeglad Psychologiczny, 23*, 485–498. PA 68:5756.

Dyson, James W.; Godwin, Paul H. B.; & Hazelwood, Leo A. (1976). Group composition, leadership orientation, and decisional outcomes. *Small Group Behavior, 7*, 114–128. SA 7718823.

Eagly, Alice H. (1978). Sex differences in influenceability. *Psychological Bulletin, 85*, 86–116.

Eagly, Alice H. (1983). Gender and social influence: A social psychological analysis. *American Psychologist, 38*, 971–981. PA 71:9441.

Eagly, Alice H.; & Carli, Linda L. (1981). Sex of researchers and sex-typed communications as determinants of sex differences in influenceability: A meta-analysis of social influence studies. *Psychological Bulletin, 90*, 1–20. PA 66:8008.

Eagly, Alice H.; & Chaiken, Shelly. (1984). Cognitive theories of persuasion. *Advances in Experimental Social Psychology, 17*, 267–359.

Eagly, Alice H; & Crowley, Maureen. (1986). Gender and helping behavior: A meta-analytic review of the social psychological literature. *Psychological Bulletin, 100*, 283–308. PA 74:10139.

Eagly, Alice H; & Steffen, Valerie J. (1986). Gender and aggressive behavior: A meta-analytic review of the social psychological literature. *Psychological Bulletin, 100*, 309–330. PA 74:10140.

Eagly, Alice H.; & Wood, Wendy. (1982). Inferred sex differences in status as a determinant of gender stereotypes about social influence. *Journal of Personality and Social Psychology, 43*, 915–928.

Eagly, Alice H.; Wood, Wendy; & Fishbaugh, Lisa. (1981). Sex differences in conformity: Surveillance by the group as a determinant of male nonconformity. *Journal of Personality and Social Psychology, 40*, 384–394. PA 66:12797.

Eakin, Beth A. (1975). An empirical study of the effect of leadership influence on decision outcomes in different sized jury panels. *Kansas Journal of Sociology, 11*(1), 109–126. PA 56:6030. SA 7611805.

Earle, Walter B.; Giuliano, Toni; & Archer, Richard L. (1983). Lonely at the top: The effect of power on information flow in the dyad. *Personality and Social Psychology Bulletin, 9*, 629–637. PA 71:25823.

Earley, P. Christopher; & Kanfer, Ruth. (1985). The influence of component participation and role models on goal acceptance, goal satisfaction, and performance. *Organizational Behavior and Human Decision Processes, 36*, 378–390. PA 73:9104.

Eaton, Marc; Bonney, Warren C.; & Gazda, G. M. (1978). Teacher predictions of sociometric choices. *Group Psychotherapy, Psychodrama and Sociometry, 31*, 33–40. SA 79J9634.

Ebbesen, Ebbe B.; Kjos, Glenn L.; & Konecni, Vladimir J. (1976). Spatial ecology: Its effects on the choice of friends and enemies. *Journal of Experimental Social Psychology, 12*, 505–518.

Ebersole, Peter; McFall, Miles; & Brandt, Cindi. (1977). Imitation and prior classroom contact as determinants of reciprocal self-disclosure. *Psychological Reports, 41*, 87–91. PA 60:5226.

Eberts, E. H.; & Lepper, Mark R. (1975). Individual consistency in the proxemic behavior of preschool children. *Journal of Personality and Social Psychology, 32*, 841–849. PA 55:6825.

Eckerman, Carol O.; Whatley, Judith L.; & Kutz, Stuart L. (1975). Growth of social play with peers during the second year of life. *Developmental Psychology, 11*, 42–49. PA 53:7092.

Eckhoff, Torstein. (1974). *Justice: Its determinants in social interaction*. Rotterdam, Netherlands: Rotterdam University Press.

Eckman, Bruce K. (1977). Stanley Milgram's obedience studies. *Etc., 34*, 88–99. PA 60:1056.

Edelmann, Robert J.; & Hampson, Sarah E. (1979). Changes in non-verbal behaviour during embarrassment. *British Journal of Social and Clinical Psychology, 18*, 385–390. PA 66:5054.

Eder, Donna; & Hallinan, Maureen T. (1978). Sex differences in children's friendships. *American Sociological Review, 43*, 237–250. SA 78J5899.

Edinger, Joyce A.; & Patterson, Miles L. (1983). Nonverbal involvement and social control. *Psychological Bulletin*, *93*, 30–56. PA 69:10382.

Edney, Julian J. (1974). Human territoriality. *Psychological Bulletin*, *81*, 959–975. PA 53:7276.

Edney, Julian J. (1975). Territoriality and control: A field experiment. *Journal of Personality and Social Psychology*, *31*, 1108–1115. PA 54:9592.

Edney, Julian J. (1980). The commons problem: Alternative perspectives. *American Psychologist*, *35*, 131–150.

Edney, Julian J. (1983). The commons dilemma: A cautionary tale. In H. H. Blumberg, A. P. Hare, V. Kent, & M. F. Davies (Eds.), *Small groups and social interaction* (Vol. 2., pp. 89–94). Chichester: John Wiley.

Edney, Julian J.; & Bell, Paul A. (1984). Sharing scarce resources: Group-outcome orientation, external disaster, and stealing in a simulated commons. *Small Group Behavior*, *15*, 87–108. PA 71:28601. SA 85O6020.

Edney, Julian J.; & Bell, Paul A. (1987). Freedom and equality in a simulated commons. *Political Psychology*, *8*, 229–243.

Edney, Julian J.; & Grundmann, Michael J. (1979). Friendship, group size and boundary size: Small group spaces. *Small Group Behavior*, *10*, 124–135. SA 80K5518.

Edney, Julian J.; & Jordan-Edney, Nancy L. (1974). Territorial spacing on a beach. *Sociometry*, *37*, 92–104. PA 52:10065.

Edney, Julian J.; & Uhlig, Susan R. (1977). Individual and small group territories. *Small Group Behavior*, *8*, 457–468. PA 64:994. SA 79K1086.

Edney, Julian J.; Walker, Carol A.; & Jordan, Nancy L. (1976). Is there reactance in personal space? *Journal of Social Psychology*, *100*, 207–217. PA 58:1141.

Edwards, David J. (1975). The effect of perceived anxiety or confidence on social orientation and distance schemata. *South African Journal of Psychology*, *5*, 1–9. PA 56:4026.

Edwards, David J. (1980a). On the validity of projective measures of interpersonal distance. *Perceptual and Motor Skills*, *50*, 43–50. PA 65:9226.

Edwards, David J. (1980b). Perception of crowding and tolerance for interpersonal proximity and separation in South Africa. *Journal of Social Psychology*, *110*, 19–28. PA 65:10270.

Edwards, John; Tinsdale, R. Scott; Heath, Linda; & Posavac, Emil J. (Eds.). (1990). *Social influences processes and prevention*. New York: Plenum. [Vol. 1 in Social Psychological Applications to Social Issues.]

Efran, Michael G. (1974). The effect of physical appearance on the judgment of guilt, interpersonal attraction, and severity of recommended punishment in a simulated jury task. *Journal of Research in Personality*, *8*, 45–54. PA 53:1055.

Egerbladh, Thor. (1976). The function of group size and ability level on solving a multidimensional complementary task. *Journal of Personality and Social Psychology*, *34*, 805–808. PA 57:12743.

Egerbladh, Thor. (1981). A social decision scheme approach on group size, task difficulty and ability level. *European Journal of Social Psychology*, *11*, 161–171. SA 83M9100.

Egerbladh, Thor; & Sjodin, Sture. (1981). Group problem solving: Ability level, group size, and subsequent individual performance. *Journal of General Psychology*, *105*, 3–12. SA 82M1454.

Ehrlichman, Howard. (1981). From gaze aversion to eye-movement suppression: An investigation of the cognitive interference explanation of gaze patterns during conversation. *British Journal of Social Psychology*, *20*, 233–241. PA 67:12037.

Eidelson, Roy J. (1980). Interpersonal satisfaction and level of involvement: A curvilinear relationship. *Journal of Personality and Social Psychology*, *39*, 460–470. PA 66:5740.

Eidelson, Roy J. (1981). Affiliative rewards and restrictive costs in developing relationships. *British Journal of Social Psychology*, *20*, 197–204. PA 68:1083.

Eisenberg, Melvin A.; & Patch, Michael E. (1976). Prominence as a determinant of bargaining outcomes. *Journal of Conflict Resolution*, *20*, 523–538. PA 57:5786.

Eisenberg, Nancy (Ed.). (1982). *The development of prosocial behavior*. New York: Academic Press.

Eisenberg, Nancy. (1986). *Altruistic emotion, cognition, and behavior*. Hillsdale, NJ: Lawrence Erlbaum.

Eisenberg, Nancy; Cialdini, Robert B.; McCreath, Heather; & Shell, Rita. (1987). Consistency-based compliance: When and why do children become vulnerable? *Journal of Personality and Social Psychology*, *52*, 1174–1181.

Eisenberg, Nancy; & Miller, Paul A. (1987). The relation of empathy to prosocial and related behaviors. *Psychological Bulletin, 101,* 91–119. PA 74:15523.

Eisenberg Nancy; Shell, Rita; Pasternack, Jeanette; Lennon, Randy; Beller, Rob; & Mathy, Robin M. (1987). Prosocial development in middle childhood: A longitudinal study. *Developmental Psychology, 23,* 712–718.

Eisenstadt, S. N.; & Roniger, Louis. (1980). Patron-client relations as a model of structuring social exchange. *Comparative Studies in Society and History, 22,* 42–77. SA 81L6525.

Eiser, Christine; & Eiser, J. Richard. (1976). Acquisition of information in children's bargaining. *Journal of Personality and Social Psychology, 34,* 796–804.

Eiser, J. Richard; & Bhavnani, Kum Kum. (1974). The effect of situational meaning on the behaviour of subjects in the Prisoner's Dilemma Game. *European Journal of Social Psychology, 4,* 93–97. PA 54:2968.

Ekman, Paul. (Ed.). (1982). *Emotion in the human face.* 2nd Ed. Cambridge, England: Cambridge University Press.

Ekman, Paul; & Friesen, Wallace V. (1975). *Unmasking the face: A guide to recognizing emotions from facial cues.* Englewood Cliffs, NJ: Prentice-Hall.

Ekman, Paul; & Friesen, Wallace V. (1978). *Facial action coding system (FACS): A technique for the measurement of facial action.* Palo Alto, CA: Consulting Psychologists Press.

Ekman, Paul; Friesen, Wallace V.; & Ancoli, Sonia. (1980). Facial signs of emotional experience. *Journal of Personality and Social Psychology, 39,* 1125–1134. PA 66:5797.

Ekman, Paul; Friesen, Wallace V.; & Scherer, Klaus R. (1976). Body movement and voice pitch in deceptive interaction. *Semiotica, 16*(1), 23–27. PA 58:3292.

Ekman, Paul; & Oster, Harriet. (1979). Facial expressions of emotion. *Annual Review of Psychology, 30,* 527–554. PA 62:8644.

Elliot, Elaine S.; & Cohen, Jerry L. (1981). Social facilitation effects via interpersonal distance. *Journal of Social Psychology, 114,* 237–249. PA 67:7692.

Elliott, Gregory C.; & Meeker, Barbara F. (1986). Achieving fairness in the face of competing concerns: The different effects of individual and group characteristics. *Journal of Personality and Social Psychology, 50,* 754–760. PA 73:21909.

Ellis, Barbara B.; & Penner, Louis A. (1983). Individual differences in reactions to inequitable exchanges. *Journal of Psychology, 114,* 91–98.

Ellis, Donald G.; Werbel, Wayne S.; & Fisher, B. Aubrey. (1978). Toward a systemic organization of groups. *Small Group Behavior, 9,* 451–469. SA 80K4175.

Ellsworth, Phoebe C.; Friedman, Howard S.; Perlick, Deborah; & Hoyt, Michael E. (1978). Some effects of gaze on subjects motivated to seek or avoid social comparison. *Journal of Experimental Social Psychology, 14,* 69–87. PA 60:9270.

Ellsworth, Phoebe C.; & Langer, Ellen J. (1976). Staring and approach: An interpretation of the stare as a nonspecific activator. *Journal of Personality and Social Psychology, 33,* 117–122. PA 55:7061.

Ellsworth, Phoebe C.; & Ross, Lee. (1975). Intimacy in response to direct gaze. *Journal of Experimental Social Psychology, 11,* 592–613. PA 55:12210.

Ellyson, Steve L.; Dovidio, John F.; & Corson, Randi L. (1981). Visual behavior differences in females as a function of self-perceived expertise. *Journal of Nonverbal Behavior, 5,* 164–171. PA 67:1217.

Ellyson, Steve L.; Dovidio, John F.; Corson, Randi L.; & Vinicur, Debbie L. (1980). Visual dominance behavior in female dyads: Situational and personality factors. *Social Psychology Quarterly, 43,* 328–336. PA 66:5741.

Elman, Donald. (1976). Why is tipping "cheaper by the bunch": Diffusion or just deserts? *Personality and Social Psychology Bulletin, 2,* 307.

Elman, Donald; & Rupple, Dale. (1978). Group discussion members' reactions to a structured opening exercise. *Small Group Behavior, 9,* 363–371. SA 79K2625.

Elstrup Rasmussen, Ole. (1978). Gruppe og personlighed: En analyse af det indre forhold mellem gruppens og personlighedens udvikling [Group and personality: An analysis of the interrelationship between the development of the group and the development of the personality]. *Psykologisk Skriftserie,* No. 16, 215 pages. PA 70:3381.

Elworth, Julie T.; & Gray, Louis N. (1982). Self-reinforcement: Effects on monads and noninteractive dyads. *Social Psychology Quarterly, 45,* 129–135. PA 69:10393.

Emiley, Stephen F. (1975). The effects of crowding and interpersonal attraction on affective responses, task performance, and verbal behavior. *Journal of Social Psychology, 97,* 267–278. PA 55:9720.

Emurian, Henry H.; Bigelow, George E.; Brady, Joseph V.; & Emurian, Cleeve S. (1975). Small-group performance maintenance in a continuously programmed environment. *Catalog of Selected Documents in Psychology, 5,* 187. PA 53:11577.

Emurian, Henry H.; & Brady, Joseph V. (1979). Small group performance and the effects of contingency management in a programmed environment: A progress report. *Catalog of Selected Documents in Psychology, 9,* 58. [MS. 1891]. PA 64:7919.

Emurian, Henry H.; & Brady, Joseph V. (1984). Behavioral and biological effects of changes in group size and membership (Technical Report TR-ONR-10). *Psychological Documents, 14,* 25. MS. 2649. PA 72:28023.

Emurian, Henry H.; Brady, Joseph V.; Meyerhoff, James L.; & Mougey, Edward H. (1983). Small groups in programmed environments: Behavioral and biological interactions. *Pavlovian Journal of Biological Science, 18,* 199–210. PA 71:23054.

Emurian, Henry H.; Emurian, Cleeve S.; Bigelow, George E.; & Brady, Joseph V. (1976). The effects of a cooperation contingency on behavior in a continuous three-person environment. *Journal of the Experimental Analysis of Behavior, 25,* 293–302. PA 56:5991.

Emurian, Henry H.; Emurian, Cleeve S.; & Brady, Joseph V. (1978). Effects of a pairing contingency on behavior in a three-person programmed environment. *Journal of the Experimental Analysis of Behavior, 29,* 319–329. PA 61:13386.

Emurian, Henry H.; Emurian, Cleeve S.; & Brady, Joseph V. (1985). Positive and negative reinforcement effects on behavior in a three-person microsociety. *Journal of the Experimental Analysis of Behavior, 44,* 157–174. PA 73:27137.

Endler, Norman S.; Coward, Teresa R.; &

Wiesenthal, David L. (1975). The effects of prior experience with a task on subsequent conformity to a different task. *Journal of Social Psychology, 95,* 207–219. PA 54:3005.

Endler, Norman S.; & Magnusson, David. (1976). Toward an interactional psychology of personality. *Psychological Bulletin, 83,* 956–974. PA 57:8283.

Endler, Norman S.; Minden, Harold A.; & North, Corileen. (1973). The effects of reinforcement and social approval on conforming behaviour. *European Journal of Social Psychology, 3,* 297–310. PA 53:7313.

England, J. Lynn. (1979). Two bargaining automata: Linear and nonlinear models. *Journal of Conflict Resolution, 23,* 296–325.

Enomoto, Hiroaki. (1983). [A review of studies on self-disclosure as an interpersonal exchange]. *Japanese Psychological Review, 26,* 148–164. PA 71:31318.

Enos, Richard L. (1985). Classical rhetoric and group decision making: A relationship warranting further inquiry. *Small Group Behavior, 16,* 235–244. PA 73:11723.

Enright, Robert D.; & Lapsley, Daniel K. (1980). Social role-taking: A review of the constructs, measures, and measurement properties. *Review of Educational Research, 50,* 647–674. PA 66:10349.

Entwisle, Doris R.; & Webster, Murray, Jr. (1974). Expectations in mixed racial groups. *Sociology of Education, 47,* 301–318. SA 75H1334.

Enzle, Michael E.; & Hansen, Ranald D. (1976). Effects of video-mediated visual contact on observers' attributions of causality and reciprocal game behavior. *Simulation and Games, 7,* 281–294. PA 58:1142.

Enzle, Michael E.; Hansen, Ranald D.; & Lowe, Charles A. (1975). Causal attribution in the mixed-motive game: Effects of facilitory and inhibitory environmental forces. *Journal of Personality and Social Psychology, 31,* 50–54. PA 53:9507.

Enzle, Michael E.; & Lowe, Charles A. (1976). Helping behavior and social exchange. *Social Behavior and Personality, 4,* 261–266. PA 58:7494.

Enzle, Michael E.; & Morrison, Bruce J. (1974). Communication of intentions and requests, and the availability of punitive power in a mixed motive situation. *Psychological Reports, 34,* 899-905. PA 52:10017.

Eoyang, Carson K. (1974). Effects of group size and privacy in residential crowding. *Journal of Personality and Social Psychology, 30,* 389-392. PA 53:1038.

Epley, Stephen W. (1974). Reduction of the behavioral effects of aversive stimulation by the presence of companions. *Psychological Bulletin, 81,* 271-283. PA 52:9273.

Epley, Stephen W. (1975). The presence of others may reduce anxiety: The evidence is not conclusive. *Psychological Bulletin, 82,* 886. PA 55:7062.

Epley, Stephen W.; & Cottrell, Nickolas B. (1977). Effect of presence of a companion on speed of escape from electric shock. *Psychological Reports, 40,* 1299-1308. PA 59:9855.

Epstein, Seymour. (1979). The stability of behavior: I. On predicting most of the people much of the time. *Journal of Personality and Social Psychology, 37,* 1097-1126. PA 64:12524.

Epstein, Seymour; & Rakosky, Jack. (1976). The effect of witnessing an admirable versus an unadmirable aggressor upon subsequent aggression. *Journal of Personality, 44,* 560-576. PA 58:3319.

Epstein, Yakov M. (1981). Crowding stress and human behavior. *Journal of Social Issues, 37*(1), 126-144. PA 65:11398.

Epstein, Yakov M.; & Karlin, Robert A. (1975). Effects of acute experimental crowding. *Journal of Applied Social Psychology, 5,* 34-53. PA 54:5193.

Epstein, Yakov M.; Woolfolk, Robert L.; & Lehrer, Paul M. (1981). Physiological, cognitive, and nonverbal responses to repeated exposure to crowding. *Journal of Applied Social Psychology, 11,* 1-13. PA 66:10318.

Erez, Miriam; Earley, P. Christopher; & Hulin, Charles L. (1985). The impact of participation on goal acceptance and performance: A two-step model. *Academy of Management Journal, 28,* 50-66. PA 72:20077.

Erffmeyer, Robert C.; & Lane, Irving M. (1984). Quality and acceptance of an evaluative task: The effects of four group decision-making formats. *Group and Organization Studies, 9,* 509-529. PA 72:30774.

Erickson, Bonnie; Holmes, John G.; Frey, Robert; Walker, Laurens; & Thibaut, John.

(1974). Functions of a third party in the resolution of conflict: The role of a judge in pretrial conferences. *Journal of Personality and Social Psychology, 30,* 293-306.

Ernest, Robert C.; & Cooper, Ralph E. (1974). "Hey mister, do you have any change?": Two real world studies of proxemic effects on compliance with a mundane request. *Personality and Social Psychology Bulletin, 1,* 158-159. PA 56:4027.

Escalona, Sibylle K. (1982). Growing up with the threat of nuclear war. *American Journal of Orthopsychiatry, 52,* 600-607. PA 69:3200.

Eskilson, Arlene; & Wiley, Mary Glenn. (1976). Sex composition and leadership in small groups. *Sociometry, 39,* 183-194. PA 57:5788. SA 7714648.

Espinoza, Julio A.; & Garza, Raymond T. (1985). Social group salience and interethnic cooperation. *Journal of Experimental Social Psychology, 21,* 380-392. PA 73:19791.

Esser, James K.; & Komorita, Samuel S. (1974). Reciprocal and non-reciprocal concession strategies in bargaining. *Personality and Social Psychology Bulletin, 1,* 231-233. PA 56:2300.

Esser, James K.; & Komorita, S[amuel] S. (1975). Reciprocity and concession making in bargaining. *Journal of Personality and Social Psychology, 31,* 864-872. PA 54:5194.

Ettin, Mark F. (1986). Within the group's view: Clarifying dynamics through metaphoric and symbolic imagery. *Small Group Behavior, 17,* 407-426.

Evans, Gary W. (1978). Human spatial behavior: The arousal model. In A. Baum and Y. M. Epstein (Eds.), *Human response to crowding* (pp. 283-302). Hillsdale, NJ: Erlbaum.

Evans, Gary W. (1979). Behavioral and physiological consequences of crowding in humans. *Journal of Applied Social Psychology, 9,* 27-46. PA 64:4964.

Evans, Gary W. (Ed.). (1981). Environmental stress. *Journal of Social Issues, 37*(1), 1-204.

Evans, Gary W. (Ed.). (1982). *Environmental stress.* Cambridge, U.K.: Cambridge University Press.

Evans, Gary W.; & Jacobs, Stephen V. (1981). Air pollution and human behavior. *Journal of Social Issues, 37*(1), 95-125. PA 65:11399.

Evans, Gary W.; Jacobs, Stephen V.; & Frager, Neal B. (1982). Behavioral responses to air pollution. In A. Baum & J. E. Singer (Eds.), *Advances in environmental psychology* (Vol. 4, pp. 237-269). Hillsdale, NJ: Erlbaum.

Evans, Nancy J.; & Jarvis, Paul A. (1980). Group cohesion: A review and reevaluation. *Small Group Behavior, 11,* 359-370. SA 82M1455.

Evans, Nancy J.; & Jarvis, Paul A. (1986). The group attitude scale: A measure of attraction to group. *Small Group Behavior, 17,* 203-216.

Even-Chen, Moshe; Yinon, Yoel; & Bizman, Aharon. (1978). The door in the face technique: Effects of the size of the initial request. *European Journal of Social Psychology, 8,* 135-140. PA 63:7562.

Evensen, E. Paul; & Bednar, Richard L. (1978). Effects of specific cognitive and behavioral structure on early group behavior and atmosphere. *Journal of Counseling Psychology, 25,* 66-75. PA 60:11689.

Fagot, Beverly I. (1977). Variations in density: Effect on task and social behaviors of preschool children. *Developmental Psychology, 13,* 166-167. PA 58:8331.

Falbo, Toni. (1977). Multidimensional scaling of power strategies. *Journal of Personality and Social Psychology, 35,* 537-548.

Falbo, Toni; & Peplau, Letitia Anne. (1980). Power strategies in intimate relationships. *Journal of Personality and Social Psychology, 38,* 618-628.

Falk, Dennis R.; & Wagner, Pat N. (1985). Intimacy of self-disclosure and response processes as factors affecting the development of interpersonal relationships. *Journal of Social Psychology, 125,* 557-570. PA 74:10184.

Falk, Gideon (1981). Unanimity versus majority rule in problem-solving groups: A challenge to the superiority of unanimity. *Small Group Behavior, 12,* 379-399.

Falk, Gideon. (1982). An empirical study measuring conflict in problem-solving groups which are assigned different decision rules. *Human Relations, 35,* 1123-1138. PA 69:10395.

Falk, Gideon; & Falk, Shoshana. (1981). The impact of decision rules on the distribution of power in problem-solving teams with unequal power. *Group and Organization Studies, 6,* 211-223. PA 66:10319.

Faraone, Stephen V.; & Hurtig, Richard R. (1985). An examination of social skill, verbal productivity, and Gottman's model of interaction using observational methods and sequential analyses. *Behavioral Assessment, 7,* 349-366. PA 73:29946.

Farrell, Michael P. (1976). Patterns in the development of self-analytic groups. *Journal of Applied Behavioral Science, 12,* 523-542. PA 58:3790. SA 78J0171.

Farrell, Michael P.; Heinemann, Gloria D.; & Schmitt, Madeline H. (1986). Informal roles, rituals, and styles of humor in interdisciplinary health care teams: Their relationship to stages of group development. *International Journal of Small Group Research, 2,* 143-162.

Farris, Donald R.; & Sage, Andrew P. (1975). Introduction and survey of group decision making with applications to worth assessment. *IEEE Transactions on Systems, Man, and Cybernetics, 5,* 346-358. PA 54:7455.

Farris, George F. (1972). The effect of individual roles on performance in innovative groups. *R and D Management, 3(1),* 23-28. PA 54:12743.

Fazio, Russell H. (1986). How do attitudes guide behavior? In R. M. Sorrentino and E. T. Higgins (Eds.), *Handbook of motivation and cognition: Foundations of social behavior* (pp. 204-243). New York: Wiley.

Fazio, Russell H.; Effrein, Edwin A.; & Falender, Victoria J. (1981). Self-perceptions following social interaction. *Journal of Personality and Social Psychology, 41,* 232-242. PA 67:7682.

Feder, Bud; & Ronall, Ruth. (Eds.). (1980). *Beyond the hot seat: Gestalt approaches to group.* New York: Brunner/Mazel.

Fedler, Fred. (1984). Studies show people still willing to help a stranger, but especially a woman. *Psychological Reports, 54,* 365-366. PA 72:1229.

Feimer, Nickolaus R.; & Geller, E. Scott. (Eds.). (1983). *Environmental psychology: Directions and perspectives.* New York: Praeger.

Feingold, Alan. (1982a). Do taller men have prettier girlfriends? *Psychological Reports, 50,* 810. PA 69:1012.

Feingold, Alan. (1982b). Physical attractiveness and romantic evolvement. *Psychological Reports, 50,* 802. PA 69:1011.

Feinman, Saul. (1978). When does sex affect altruistic response? *Psychological Reports, 43,* 1218. PA 64:10364.

Feldens, Maria D.; & Rasche, Vania M. (1983). Os efeitos de ambientes coompetitivos e cooperativos na realizacao de uma tarefa cognitiva [The effects of competitive and cooperative settings on a cognitive task]. *Arquivos Brasileiros de Psicologia, 35*(3), 143–150. PA 71:17748.

Feldman, Ronald A. (1973). Power distribution, integration, and conformity in small groups. *American Journal of Sociology, 79*, 639–664. SA 74G9768.

Feldman, Robert H.; & Rezmovic, Victor. (1979). A field study on the relationship of environmental factors to helping behavior. *Journal of Social Psychology, 108*, 283–284. PA 65:1230.

Feldman, Robert S. (1976). An experimental examination of behavioral dissent. *Psychological Reports, 38*, 683–690. PA 61:3497.

Felmlee, Diane; Eder, Donna; & Tsui, Wai-Ying. (1985). Peer influence on classroom attention. *Social Psychology Quarterly, 48*, 215–226. SA: 86Q3070.

Felsenthal, Dan S. (1977). Bargaining behavior when profits are unequal and losses are equal. *Behavioral Science, 22*, 334–340. PA 60:9297.

Felsenthal, Dan S. (1979). Group versus individual gambling behavior: Reexamination and limitation. *Behavioral Science, 24*, 334–345. PA 64:12450.

Felsenthal, Dan S.; & Diskin, Abraham. (1982a). The bargaining problem revisited: Minimum utility point, restricted monotonicity axiom, and the mean as an estimate of expected utility. *Journal of Conflict Resolution, 26*, 664–691. PA 69:10396.

Felsenthal, Dan S.; & Diskin, Abraham. (1982b). Two bargaining solutions: An experimental reevaluation. *Simulation & Games, 13*, 179–197. PA 69:03387.

Felsenthal, Dan S.; & Fuchs, Eliezer. (1976). Experimental evaluation of five designs of redundant organizational systems. *Administrative Science Quarterly, 21*, 474–488. PA 57:7063.

Fengler, Alfred P. (1974). Romantic love in courtship: Divergent paths of male and female students. *Journal of Comparative Family Studies, 5*, 134–139. PA 54:2969.

Fenigstein, Allan. (1979). Self-consciousness, self-attention, and social interaction. *Journal of Personality and Social Psychology, 37*, 75–86. PA 64:980.

Fennell, Mary L.; Barchas, P. R.; Cohen, E. G.; McMahon, A. M.; & Hildebrand, P. (1978). An alternative perspective on sex differences in organizational settings: The process of legitimization. *Sex Roles, 4*, 589–604. PA 63:4305.

Ferber, Marianne; Huber, Joan; & Spitze, Glenna D. (1979). Preference for men as bosses and professionals. *Social Forces, 58*, 466–476.

Ferguson, Nicola. (1977). Simultaneous speech, interruptions, and dominance. *British Journal of Social and Clinical Psychology, 16*, 295–302. PA 60:7432.

Fern, Edward F.; Monroe, Kent B.; & Avila, Ramon A. (1986). Effectiveness of multiple request strategies: A synthesis of research results. *Journal of Marketing Research, 23*(2), 144–152. PA 73:24471.

Festinger, Leon. (1954). A theory of social comparison processes. *Human Relations, 7*, 117–140.

Fichten, Catherine. (1982). Social exchange principles applied to small group discussions: Practising what we preach. *Tires A Part, 3*, 20–24. PA 74:7158.

Fiedler, Fred E. (1986). The contribution of cognitive resources and leader behavior to organizational performance. *Journal of Applied Social Psychology, 16*, 532–548. PA 74:12147.

Fiedler, Fred E.; & Chemers, Martin M. (1984). *Improving leadership effectiveness: The leader match concept* (2nd ed.). New York: Wiley

Fiedler, Fred E.; & Garcia, Joseph E. (1987). *New approaches to effective leadership: Cognitive resources and organizational performance.* New York: Wiley.

Fiedler, Fred E.; & Leister, Albert F. (1977). Leader intelligence and task performance: A test of a multiple screen model. *Organizational Behavior and Human Performance, 20*, 1–14. PA 60:6325.

Field, Mildred. (1979). Status-liking-power: An analysis of two models. *Social Science Research, 8*, 159–171. SA 80L0082.

Field, R. George. (1982). A test of the Vroom-Yetton normative model of leadership. *Journal of Applied Psychology, 67*, 523–532. PA 69:03388.

Fielding, L.; Murray, J.; & Steel, D. H. (1976). The influence of spectator reaction and presence during training on performance. *International Journal of Sport Psychology, 7*, 73–81. PA 58:5300.

Fiene, Jack F. (1979). Elements of leadership which impede creativity. *Creative Child and Adult Quarterly*, *4*, 30–39. PA 64:10330.

Filter, Terrance A.; & Gross, Alan E. (1975). Effects of public and private deviancy on compliance with a request. *Journal of Experimental Social Psychology*, *11*, 553–559. PA 55:9778.

Fincham, Frank D.; & Bradbury, Thomas N. (1987). Cognitive processes and conflict in close relationships: An attribution-efficacy model. *Journal of Personality and Social Psychology*, *53*, 1106–1118.

Finchilescu, G. (1986). Effects of incompatibility between internal and external group membership criteria on intergroup behaviour. *European Journal of Social Psychology*, *16*, 83–87. PA 74:7159.

Fine, Gary A. (1979). Small groups and culture creation: the idioculture of little league baseball teams. *American Sociological Review*, *44*, 733–745. SA 80K7126.

Fine, Gary Alan. (1986). Behavioral change in group space: A reintegration of Lewinian theory in small group research. *Advances in Group Processes*, *3*, 23–50.

Fine, Gary A[lan]; Stitt, Jeffrey L.; & Finch, Michael. (1984). Couple tie-signs and interpersonal threat: A field experiment. *Social Psychology Quarterly*, *47*, 282–286. PA 72:25394. SA 8504347.

Finigan, Michael. (1982). The effects of token representation on participation in small decision-making groups. *Economic and Industrial Democracy*, *3*, 531–550. SA 8506021.

Fink, Edward L.; Rey, Lucy D.; Johnson, Katrina W.; Spenner, Kenneth I.; Morton, Donald R.; & Flores, Estevan. (1975). The effects of family occupational type, sex, and appeal style on helping behavior. *Journal of Experimental Social Psychology*, *11*, 43–52. PA 53:11602.

Finkelstein, Peter; Wenegrat, Brant; & Yalom, Irvin. (1982). Large group awareness training. *Annual Review of Psychology*, *33*, 515–539.

Finley, Gordon E.; & Humphreys, Carolyn A. (1974). Naive psychology and the development of persuasive appeals in girls. *Canadian Journal of Behavioural Science*, *6*, 75–80. PA 52:5178.

Finney, Phillip D. (1984). Coparticipant effects on subjects' decisions to consent for risk-involving research. *Journal of Social Psychology*, *124*, 35–41. PA 72:30775.

Firestone, Ira J. (1977). Reconciling verbal and nonverbal models of dyadic communication. *Environmental Psychology and Nonverbal Behavior*, *2*, 30–44. PA 60:11690.

Firestone, Ira J.; Lichtman, Cary M.; & Colamosca, John V. (1975). Leader effectiveness and leadership conferral as determinants of helping in a medical emergency. *Journal of Personality and Social Psychology*, *31*, 343–348. PA 53:11578.

Firth, Elizabeth A.; Conger, Judith C.; Kuhlenschmidt, Sally; & Dorcey, Tim. (1986). Social competence and social perceptivity. *Journal of Social and Clinical Psychology*, *4*, 85–100. PA 74:10212.

Fischer, Donald G.; McDowell, Kenneth; & Boulanger, Fabian. (1976). Initial position, ratio of arguments, and individual shifts in decision. *Journal of Social Psychology*, *99*, 145–146. PA 56:7897.

Fischer, Gregory W. (1975). An experimental study of four procedures for aggregating subjective probability assessments. *ONR Technical Reports*, No. 197-029.

Fischoff, Stuart. (1979). "Recipe for a jury" revisited: A balance theory prediction. *Journal of Applied Social Psychology*, *9*, 335–349. PA 66:5743.

Fish, Barry; Karabenick, Stuart A.; & Heath, Myron. (1978). The effects of observation on emotional arousal and affiliation. *Journal of Experimental Social Psychology*, *14*, 256–265. PA 61:10903.

Fisher, B. Aubrey. (1983). Differential effects of sexual composition and interactional context on interaction patterns in dyads. *Human Communication Research*, *9*, 225–238. PA 70:10237.

Fisher, B. Aubrey; & Drecksel, G. Lloyd. (1983). A cyclical model of developing relationships: A study of relational control interaction. *Communication Monographs*, *50*, 66–78. PA 70:10238.

Fisher, B. Aubrey; Drecksel, G. Lloyd; & Werbel, Wayne S. (1979). Social information processing analysis (SPA): Coding ongoing human communication. *Small Group Behavior*, *10*, 3–21.

Fisher, D. V. (1984). A conceptual analysis of self-disclosure. *Journal for the Theory of Social Behaviour*, *14*, 277–296. PA 72:14469.

Fisher, Jeffrey D. (1974). Situation-specific variables as determinants of perceived environmental aesthetic quality and perceived crowdedness. *Journal of Research in Personality*, *8*, 177–188. PA 53:5196.

Fisher, Jeffrey D.; & Baum, Andrew. (1980). Situational and arousal-based messages and the reduction of crowding stress. *Journal of Applied Social Psychology*, *10*, 191–201. PA 65:3272.

Fisher, Jeffrey D.; Bell, Paul A.; & Baum, Andrew. (1984). *Environmental psychology* (2nd ed.). New York: Holt, Rinehart, & Winston.

Fisher, Jeffrey D.; & Byrne, Donn. (1975). Too close for comfort: Sex differences in response to invasions of personal space. *Journal of Personality and Social Psychology*, *32*, 15–21. PA 54:7456.

Fisher, Jeffrey D.; Nadler, Arie; & DePaulo, Bella M. (Eds.). (1983). *New directions in helping* (3 vols.). New York: Academic Press.

Fisher, Jeffrey D.; Nadler, Arie; & Whitcher-Alagna, Sheryle. (1982). Recipient reactions to aid. *Psychological Bulletin*, *91*, 27–54. PA 67:7693.

Fisher, Jeffrey D.; Rytting, Marvin; & Heslin, Richard. (1976). Hands touching hands: Affective and evaluative effects of an interpersonal touch. *Sociometry*, *39*, 416–421. PA 57:12773.

Fisher, Roger. (1971). Fractionating conflict. In C. G. Smith (Ed.), *Conflict resolution: Contributions of the behavioral sciences* (pp. 157–169). Notre Dame, Indiana: University of Notre Dame Press. [Reprinted from Roger Fisher (Ed.), 1964, *International conflict and behavioral science: The Craigville papers* (pp. 91–109), New York: Basic Books.]

Fisher, Ronald J. (1980). A third-party consultation workshop on the India-Pakistan conflict. *Journal of Social Psychology*, *112*, 191–206. PA 66:5744.

Fisher, Ronald J. (1983). Third party consultation as a method of intergroup conflict resolution: A review of studies. *Journal of Conflict Resolution*, *27*, 301–334. PA 70:10230.

Fiske, Susan T.; Fischhoff, Baruch; & Milburn, Michael A. (Eds.). (1983). Images of nuclear war [Special issue]. *Journal of Social Issues*, *39*(1).

Fitting, Ullrich; et al. (1976). [Computer simulation of opponents and different game situations in a non-zero-sum game]. *Zeitschrift fur Experimentelle und Angewandte Psychologie*, *23*, 396–412. PA 58:7440.

Fitzpatrick, Mary Anne; & Winke, Jeff. (1979). You always hurt the one you love: Strategies and tactics in interpersonal conflict. *Communication Quarterly*, *27*(1), 3–11. SA: 82L9790.

Flaherty, John F. (1976). SIMCOL: A FORTRAN IV simulation program for use in the study of coalitional behavior. *Behavior Research Methods and Instrumentation*, *8*, 468. PA 57:11736.

Flaherty, John F. (1980). The role of sex and personality in the prenegotiation stage of coalition formation. *Journal of Research in Personality*, *14*, 49–59. PA 65:10375.

Flaherty, John F.; & Arenson, Sidney J. (1978). A test of two theories in the initial process stage of coalition formation. *Social Behavior and Personality*, *6*, 141–146. PA 63:5417. SA 79K1088.

Fleischer, Robin A.; & Chertkoff, Jerome M. (1986). Effects of dominance and sex on leader selection in dyadic work groups. *Journal of Personality and Social Psychology*, *50*, 94–99. PA 73:17201.

Fleishman, John A. (1988). The effects of decision framing and others' behavior on cooperation in a social dilemma. *Journal of Conflict Resolution*, *32*, 162–180.

Fleming, Raymond J.; Baum, Andrew; Singer, Jerome E. (1984). Toward an integrative approach to the study of stress. *Journal of Personality and Social Psychology*, *46*, 939–949. PA 71:22089.

Fletcher, Garth J. O.; Fincham, Frank D.; Cramer, Lori; & Heron, Nancy. (1987). The role of attributions in the development of dating relationships. *Journal of Personality and Social Psychology*, *53*, 481–489.

Flowers, Matie L. (1977). A laboratory test of some implications of Janis's Groupthink hypothesis. *Journal of Personality and Social Psychology*, *35*, 888–896. PA 62:8591.

Foddy, Margaret. (1978a). Patterns of gaze in cooperative and competitive negotiation. *Human Relations*, *31*, 925–938. PA 63:11943. SA 80K8686.

Foddy, Margaret. (1978b). Role-taking in a communication task. *Personality and Social Psychology Bulletin*, *4*, 388–392. PA 64:3230.

Foddy, W. H. (1984). A critical evaluation of Altman's definition of privacy as a dialectical process. *Journal for the Theory of Social Behaviour*, *14*, 297–307. PA 72:14470.

Fodor, Eugene M. (1976). Group stress, authoritarian style of control, and use of power.

Journal of Applied Psychology, 61, 313–318. PA 56:1542.

Fodor, Eugene M. (1978). Simulated work climate as an influence on choice of leadership style. *Personality and Social Psychology Bulletin, 4*, 111–114. PA 61:7465.

Fodor, Eugene M. (1984). The power motive and reactivity to power stresses. *Journal of Personality and Social Psychology, 47*, 853–859. PA 72:12000.

Fodor, Eugene M. (1985). The power motive, group conflict, and physiological arousal. *Journal of Personality and Social Psychology, 49*, 1408–1415. PA 72:12000.

Fodor, Eugene M.; & Farrow, Dana L. (1979). The power motive as an influence on use of power. *Journal of Personality and Social Psychology, 37*, 2091–2097. PA 65:5408.

Fodor, Eugene M.; & Smith, Terry. (1982). The power motive as an influence on group decision making. *Journal of Personality and Social Psychology, 42*, 178–185. PA 68:3523.

Fogg, Richard W. (1985). Dealing with conflict: A repertoire of creative, peaceful approaches. *Journal of Conflict Resolution, 29*, 330–358. PA 72:30776.

Foldesi, Tamasne. (1978). Investigation for the objective measurement of cooperative ability among the members of rowing teams. *International Review of Sport Sociology, 13*, 49–69. SA 79K1089.

Folkes, Valerie S. (1982). Forming relationships and the matching hypothesis. *Personality and Social Psychology Bulletin, 8*, 631–636. PA 70:3383.

Folkes, Valerie S. (1985). Mindlessness or mindfulness: A partial replication and extension of Langer, Blank, and Chanowitz. *Journal of Personality and Social Psychology, 48*, 600–604.

Folkes, Valerie S.; & Weiner, Bernard. (1977). Motivational determinants of coalition formation. *Journal of Experimental Social Psychology, 13*, 536–542. PA 61:5959.

Foon, Anne E. (1987). The interpretive conception of social interaction and the logic of deductive explanation. *Social Psychology Quarterly, 50*, 1–6.

Foot, Hugh C.; Chapman, Anthony J.; & Smith, Jean R. (1977). Friendship and social responsiveness in boys and girls. *Journal of Personality and Social Psychology, 35*, 401–411. PA 62:5774.

Foot, Hugh C.; & Russon, J. M. (1975). The reciprocation of unfavorable evaluations of performance in a two-person inspection task. *European Journal of Social Psychology, 5*, 289–296. PA 58:3320.

Forbes, David. (1982). Issues in the development of social interaction models: A commentary on Walton and Sedlak. *Merrill Palmer Quarterly, 28*, 533–539. PA 69:7874.

Ford, David L. (1983). Effects of personal control beliefs: An explanatory analysis of bargaining outcomes in intergroup negotiations. *Group and Organization Studies, 8*, 113–125. PA 70:3384.

Ford, David L.; Nemiroff, Paul M.; & Pasmore, William A. (1977). Group decision-making performance as influenced by group tradition. *Small Group Behavior, 8*, 223–228. PA 62:3557. SA 78J4687.

Ford, J. Guthrie; Cramer, Robert E.; & Owens, Gayle. (1977). A paralinguistic consideration of proxemic behavior. *Perceptual and Motor Skills, 45*, 487–493. PA 60:7433.

Ford, J. Guthrie; & Hoebeke, Sara. (1980). Distant interpersonal spacing and psychological distance. *Psychological Reports, 46*, 1299–1303. PA 66:3604.

Ford, J. Guthrie; Knight, Martha; & Cramer, Robert. (1977). The phenomenological experience of interpersonal spacing. *Social Psychology Quarterly, 40*, 387–396. PA 61:8429.

Ford, J. Guthrie; & Maloney, Marynell. (1982). Further considerations of the phenomenology of proxemics. *Psychological Reports, 50*, 943–952. PA 69:1013.

Ford, W. Randolph; Weeks, Gerald D.; & Chapanis, Alphonse. (1980). The effect of self-imposed brevity on the structure of dyadic communication. *Journal of Psychology, 104*, 87–103. PA 65:7586.

Forgas, Joseph P. (1977). Polarization and moderation of person perception judgements as a function of group interaction style. *European Journal of Social Psychology, 7*, 175–187. PA 60:5201.

Forgas, Joseph P. (1978). Social episodes and social structure in an academic setting: The social environment of an intact group. *Journal of Experimental Social Psychology, 14*, 434–448. PA 63:3224.

Forgas, Joseph P. (1979). *Social episodes: The study of interaction routines. European Mono-*

graphs in Social Psychology 17. London: Academic Press.

Forgas, Joseph P. (1981). Responsibility attribution by groups and individuals: The effects of the interaction episode. *European Journal of Social Psychology, 11,* 87–99. PA 67:1257.

Forgas, Joseph P. (1983a). Cognitive representations of interaction episodes. *Australian Journal of Psychology, 35,* 145–162. PA 71:27826.

Forgas, Joseph P. (1983b). Social skills and the perception of interaction episodes. *British Journal of Clinical Psychology, 22,* 195–207. PA 71:3989.

Forgas, Joseph P. (1985). *Interpersonal behaviour: The psychology of social interaction.* Sydney: Pergamon.

Forgas, Joseph P.; Brennan, Greg; Howe, Susan; Kane, John; & Sweet, Shirley. (1980). Audience effects on squash players' performance. *Journal of Social Psychology, 111,* 41–47.

Forgas, Joseph P.; & Brown, L. B. (1977). Environmental and behavioral cues in the perception of social encounters: An exploratory study. *American Journal of Psychology, 90,* 635–644. PA 61:10943. SA 80K7127.

Forgas, Joseph P.; Brown, L. B.; & Menyhart, John. (1980). Dimensions of aggression: The perception of aggressive episodes. *British Journal of Social and Clinical Psychology, 19,* 215–227. PA 66:5799.

Forgas, Joseph P.; & Dobosz, Barbara. (1980). Dimensions of romantic involvement: Towards a taxonomy of heterosexual relationships. *Social Psychology Quarterly, 43,* 290–300. PA 66:5745.

Forgas, Joseph P.; O'Connor, Kathleen V.; & Morris, Susan L. (1983). Smile and punishment: The effects of facial expression on responsibility attribution by groups and individuals. *Personality and Social Psychology Bulletin, 9,* 587–596. PA 71:25821.

Forsyth, Donelson R. (1983). *An introduction to group dynamics.* Monterey, CA: Brooks/Cole.

Forsyth, Donelson R.; & Mitchell, Tom. (1979). Reactions to others' egocentric claims of responsibility. *Journal of Psychology, 103,* 281–285. PA 65:1232.

Forsyth, Donelson R.; & Schlenker, Barry R. (1977). Attributing the causes of group performance: Effects of performance quality, task importance, and future testing. *Journal of Personality, 45,* 220–236. PA 59:9839.

Forsyth, Donelson R.; Schlenker, Barry R.; Leary, Mark R.; & McCown, Nancy E. (1985). Self-presentational determinants of sex differences in leadership behavior. *Small Group Behavior, 16,* 197–210. PA 73:11759.

Fortenberry, Jessie C.; & Smith, Leo A. (1981). A comparison of risk selections. *Human Factors, 23,* 693–700. PA 67:9761.

Foschi, Martha; Warriner, G. Keith; & Hart, Stephen D. (1985). Standards, expectations, and interpersonal influence. *Social Psychology Quarterly, 48,* 108–117. PA 73:14427. SA 85Q1240.

Foss, Robert D. (1976). Group decision processes in the simulated trial jury. *Sociometry, 39,* 305–316. PA 58:1094.

Foss, Robert D. (1981). Structural effects in simulated jury decision making. *Journal of Personality and Social Psychology, 40,* 1055–1062. PA 67:5703.

Foss, Robert D.; & Dempsey, Carolyn B. (1979). Blood donation and the foot-in-the-door technique: A limiting case. *Journal of Personality and Social Psychology, 37,* 580–590. PA 64:7972.

Foster, D. H.; & Finchilescu, G. (1985). Group-induced decision polarization: Further generalizations. *South African Journal of Psychology, 15,* 47–54. PA 73:19793.

Foulds, Melvin L.; Guinan, James F.; & Warehime, Robert G. (1974). Marathon group: Changes in a measure of dogmatism. *Small Group Behavior, 5,* 387–392. PA 54:9542.

Foushee, H. Clayton. (1984). Dyads and triads at 35,000 feet: Factors affecting group process and aircrew performance. *American Psychologist, 39,* 885–893. PA 73:9092.

Fouts, Gregory T. (1979). Social anxiety and social facilitation. *Psychological Reports, 44,* 1065–1066. PA 64:10331.

Fox, John; & Guyer, Melvin. (1977). Group size and others' strategy in an n-person game. *Journal of Conflict Resolution, 21,* 323–338.

Fox, John; & Guyer, Melvin. (1978). Public choice and cooperation in n-person Prisoner's Dilemma. *Journal of Conflict Resolution, 22,* 469–481. PA 64:995.

Fox, John; & Moore, James C. (1979). Status characteristics and expectation states: Fitting and testing a recent model. *Social Psychology Quarterly, 42,* 126–134. PA 64:7920. SA 81L1644.

Fox, Shaul. (1976). Analysis of the individualistic, competitive and cooperative motives in non-zero-sum games. *Psychological Reports*, *39*, 55–61. PA 57:2487.

Fox, Steven G.; & Walters, H. A. (1986). The impact of general versus specific expert testimony and eyewitness confidence upon mock juror judgment. *Law and Human Behavior*, *10*, 215–228. PA 74:1079.

Fox, William M. (1987). *Effective group problem solving*. London: Jossey-Bass.

Frances, Susan J. (1979). Sex differences in nonverbal behavior. *Sex Roles*, *5*, 519–535. PA 64:12451.

Franco, Edward A.; & Kulberg, Gordon E. (1975). Content analysis of the natural language of A and B males in a dyadic interaction. *Journal of Consulting and Clinical Psychology*, *43*, 345–349. PA 54:5195.

Frandsen, Kenneth D.; & Rosenfeld, Lawrence B. (1973). Fundamental interpersonal relations orientations in dyads: An empirical analysis of Schutz's FIRO-B as an index of compatibility. *Speech Monographs*, *40*, 113–122. PA 53:11579.

Frank, Harold H.; & Katcher, Aaron H. (1977). The qualities of leadership: How male medical students evaluate their female peers. *Human Relations*, *30*, 403–416. PA 59:7871.

Frank, Jerome D. (1980). The nuclear arms race: Socio-psychological aspects. *American Journal of Public Health*, *70*, 950–952.

Freedman, Jonathan L. (1975). *Crowding and behavior*. San Francisco: Freeman.

Freedman, Jonathan L. (1979). Reconciling apparent differences between the responses of humans and other animals to crowding. *Psychological Review*, *86*, 80–85.

Freedman, Jonathan L. (1980). Responses of humans and other animals to variations in density. *Psychological Review*, *87*, 327–328. PA 64:5396.

Freedman, Jonathan L.; Birsky, Joanna; & Cavoukian, Ann. (1980). Environmental determinants of behavioral contagion: Density and number. *Basic and Applied Social Psychology*, *1*, 155–161. PA 64:12452.

Freedman, Jonathan L.; Heshka, Stanley; & Levy, Alan. (1975). Population density and pathology: Is there a relationship? *Journal of Experimental Social Psychology*, *11*, 539–552. PA 55:9911.

Freedman, Jonathan L.; & Perlick, Deborah. (1979). Crowding, contagion, and laughter.

Journal of Experimental Social Psychology, *15*, 295–303. PA 64:7921.

Freedman, Stuart C. (1981). Threats, promises, and coalitions: A study of compliance and retaliation in a simulated organizational setting. *Journal of Applied Social Psychology*, *11*, 114–136. PA 67:3524.

Freeman, Linton C. (1977). A set of measures of centrality based on betweenness. *Sociometry*, *40*, 35–41. SA 77I7502.

Freeman, Stephen; Walker, Marcus R.; Borden, Richard; & Latané, Bibb. (1975). Diffusion of responsibility and restaurant tipping: Cheaper by the bunch. *Personality and Social Psychology Bulletin*, *1*, 584–587. PA 56:4031.

French, Doran C.; Brownell, Celia A.; Graziano, William G.; & Hartup, Willard W. (1977). Effects of cooperative, competitive, and individualistic sets on performance in children's groups. *Journal of Experimental Child Psychology*, *24*, 1–10. PA 59:9858.

French, John R. P., Jr.; & Raven, Bertram. (1959). The bases of social power. In D. Cartwright (Ed.), *Studies in social power* (pp. 150–167). Ann Arbor, MI: Univ. of Michigan.

Frey, David L; & Gaertner, Samuel L. (1986). Helping and the avoidance of inappropriate interracial behavior: A strategy that perpetuates a nonprejudiced self-image. *Journal of Personality and Social Psychology*, *50*, 1083–1090.

Frick, Robert W. (1985). Communicating emotion: The role of prosodic features. *Psychological Bulletin*, *97*, 412–429. PA 72:22244.

Friedland, Nehemia. (1976). Social influence via threats. *Journal of Experimental Social Psychology*, *12*, 552–563. PA 57:12774.

Friedland, Nehemia. (1983). Weakness as strength: The use and misuse of a "my hands are tied" ploy in bargaining. *Journal of Applied Social Psychology*, *13*, 422–426. PA 71:12154.

Friedland, Nehemia; Arnold, Susan E.; & Thibaut, John. (1974). Motivational bases in mixed-motive interactions: The effects of comparison levels. *Journal of Experimental Social Psychology*, *10*, 188–199.

Friedlander, Frank. (1982). Alternative modes of inquiry. *Small Group Behavior*, *13*, 428–440.

Friedlander, Frank; & Green, P. Toni. (1977). Life styles and conflict-coping structures. *Group and Organization Studies*, *2*, 101–112. PA 58:9476.

Friedlander, Myrna L.; Thibodeau, John R.; Nichols, Michael P.; Tucker, Cheryl; & Snyder,

Jilisa. (1985). Introducing semantic cohesion analysis: A study of group talk. *Small Group Behavior*, *16*, 285–302. PA 73:17921.

Friedman, Howard S. (1979). The interactive effects of facial expressions of emotion and verbal messages on perceptions of affective meaning. *Journal of Experimental Social Psychology*, *15*, 453–469. PA 64:12487.

Friedman, Lee. (1981). How affiliation affects stress in fear and anxiety situations. *Journal of Personality and Social Psychology*, *40*, 1102–1117. PA 67:5704.

Friend, Kenneth E.; & Laing, James D. (1978). Contending signals in coalition choice. *Journal of Mathematical Sociology*, *6*, 23–46. PA 64:996. SA 79J9636.

Friend, Kenneth E.; Laing, James D.; & Morrison, Richard J. (1974). Bargaining processes and coalition outcomes. *Personality and Social Psychology Bulletin*, *1*, 222–224. PA 56:2302.

Friend, Kenneth E.; Laing, James D.; & Morrison, Richard J. (1977). Bargaining processes and coalition outcomes: An integration. *Journal of Conflict Resolution*, *21*, 267–298.

Friend, Ronald M.; & Vinson, Michael. (1974). Leaning over backwards: Jurors' responses to defendants' attractiveness. *Journal of Communication*, *24*, 124–129. PA 53:3018.

Frieze, Irene H.; & Ramsey, Sheila. (1976). Nonverbal maintenance of traditional sex roles. *Journal of Social Issues*, *32*(3), 133–141. PA 57:5724.

Frodi, Ann. (1978). Experiential and physiological responses associated with anger and aggression in women and men. *Journal of Research in Personality*, *12*, 335–349. PA 63:2593.

Frodi, Ann; Macaulay, Jacqueline; & Thome, Pauline R. (1977). Are women always less aggressive than men? A review of the experimental literature. *Psychological Bulletin*, *84*, 634–660. PA 59:7938.

Froming, William J.; & Carver, Charles S. (1981). Divergent influences of private and public self-consciousness in a compliance paradigm. *Journal of Research in Personality*, *15*, 159–171. PA 67:3651.

Froming, William J.; & Cooper, Robert G. (1977). Predicting compliance behavior from moral judgment scales. *Journal of Research in Personality*, *11*, 368–379. PA 60:3068.

Fromme, Donald K.; & Beam, Donna C. (1974). Dominance and sex differences in nonverbal responses to differential eye contact. *Journal of Research in Personality*, *8*, 76–87. PA 53:1058.

Fromme, Donald K.; & Close, Stephen R. (1976). Group compatibility and the modification of affective verbalizations. *British Journal of Social & Clinical Psychology*, *15*, 189–197.

Frost, Joyce H. (1980). The influence of female and male communication styles on conflict strategies: Problem areas. *Communication Research and Broadcasting*, No. 3, 126–136. PA 68:10319.

Fry, Louis W.; Kerr, Steven; & Lee, Cynthia. (1986). Effects of different leader behaviors under different levels of task interdependence. *Human Relations*, *39*, 1067–1082. PA 74:13090.

Fry, P. S. (1976). Sex differences in reward and punishment of confederates perceived to be similar or dissimilar. *Perceptual and Motor Skills*, *42*, 523–529. PA 58:5349.

Fry, Rick; & Smith, Gene F. (1975). The effects of feedback and eye contact on performance of a digit-coding task. *Journal of Social Psychology*, *96*, 145–146. PA 54:7507.

Fry, William R. (1985). The effect of dyad machiavellianism and visual access on integrative bargaining outcomes. *Personality and Social Psychology Bulletin*, *11*, 51–62. PA 73:6327.

Fry, William R.; Firestone, Ira J.; & Williams, David L. (1983). Negotiation process and outcome of stranger dyads and dating couples: Do lovers lose? *Basic and Applied Social Psychology*, *4*, 1–16. PA 71:20447.

Frydman, Marcel; & Foucart, Pascal. (1983–1984). Le comportement d'aide dans une situation critique. Intentions exprimees et conduites adoptees en milieu urbain [Helping behavior in a critical situation: Intentions expressed and conduct adopted in an urban milieu]. *Bulletin de Psychologie*, *37*, 376–384. PA 72:17340.

Füchsle, Traudl; Burger, Christine; & Trommsdorff, Gisela. (1983). Partnerschaftsbezogene Zukunftsperspektive und Interaktionsmuster in Konfliktsituationen [Partnership-related future time perspectives and interaction patterns in conflict situations]. *Zeitschrift fur Experimentelle und Angewandte Psychologie*, *30*, 215–231. PA 71:3966.

Füchsle, Traudl; Fröhlich, Gabriele; & Burger, Christine. (1982). Nachgebeentscheidungen als Reaktion auf Unausge-   wogenheit in dyadischen Beziehungen: Der Einfluß von Künftig erwarteter Interaktion und Art de Dyadenzugehörigkeit [Compliance decisions as reactions in inequitable dyadic relationships: The effects of future interaction expectations and type of dyadic membership]. *Zeitschrift für Sozialpsychologie*, *13*, 312–322. PA 70:7957.

Fuentes Avila, Mara. (1983). Nivel de desarrollo del grupo, cohesion grupal y la actitud hacia la actividad conjunta. Su influencia en el rendimiento grupal [Group development, group cohesiveness and attitude toward the group's activity: Its influence in the group performance]. *Revista del Hospital Psiquiatrico de La Habana*, *24*(1), 121–125. PA 71:17749.

Fugita, Stephen S.; Wexley, Kenneth N.; & Hillery, Joseph M. (1974). Black-white differences in nonverbal behavior in an interview setting. *Journal of Applied Social Psychology*, *4*, 343–350. PA 54:2970.

Fuhriman, Addie; Drescher, Stuart; & Burlingame, Gary. (1984). Conceptualizing small group process. *Small Group Behavior*, *15*, 427–440. PA 72:14483.

Fujihara, Masamitsu. (1976). [An experimental study of developmental trend in conformity: The effect of group pressure from peer-, teacher-, and mother-groups on conformity]. *Japanese Journal of Psychology*, *47*, 193–201. PA 57:10011.

Fujimori, Tatsuo. (1985). The determinants of co-operative behaviour in case of conflict between individual and common interests. *Journal of Human Development*, *21*, 38–47. PA 73:17227.

Fukuhara, Shozo. (1977). An experimental study of visual behavior in social interaction: Eye contact in a dyad as affected by interaction distance and the affiliation need. *Japanese Journal of Experimental Social Psychology*, *17*, 30–38. PA 64:10332.

Fulk, Janet; & Wendler, Eric R. (1982). Dimensionality of leader-subordinate interactions: A path-goal investigation. *Organizational Behavior and Human Performance*, *30*, 241–264. PA 69:2495.

Funk, Sandra G.; Rapoport, Amnon; & Kahan, James P. (1980). Quota vs positional power in four-person apex games. *Journal of Experimental Social Psychology*, *16*, 77–93. PA 65:7938.

Furnham, Adrian. (1981). Self-monitoring and social perception. *Perceptual and Motor Skills*, *52*, 3–10. PA 67:3525.

Furnham, Adrian. (1983). Social difficulty in three cultures. *International Journal of Psychology*, *18*, 215–228. PA 71:12155.

Furnham, Adrian; & Capon, Mark. (1983). Social skills and self-monitoring processes. *Personality and Individual Differences*, *4*, 171–178. PA 70:7023.

Furnham, Adrian; & Quilley, Ruth. (1989). The Protestant work ethic and the Prisoner's Dilemma Game. *British Journal of Social Psychology*, *28*, 79–87.

Fürntratt, Ernst; & Weimann, Franz. (1980). [Effectiveness of some behavior strategies based on learning theory in a two-person game]. *Zeitschrift für Experimentelle und Angewandte Psychologie*, *27*, 72–83. PA 65:10376.

Gabbert, Barbara; Johnson, David W.; & Johnson, Roger T. (1986). Cooperative learning, group-to-individual transfer, process gain, and the acquisition of cognitive reasoning strategies. *Journal of Psychology*, *120*, 265–278.

Gabrenya, William K., Jr.; Latané, Bibb; & Wang, Yue-Eng. (1983). Social loafing in cross-cultural perspective: Chinese on Taiwan. *Journal of Cross-Cultural Psychology*, *14*, 368–384. SA 84N9145.

Gabrenya, William K., Jr.; Wang, Yue-eng; & Latané, Bibb. (1985). Social loafing on an optimizing task: Cross-cultural differences among Chinese and Americans. *Journal of Cross-Cultural Psychology*, *16*, 223–242. SA 86Q4838.

Gaebelein, Jacquelyn W. (1976). Self-disclosure among friends, acquaintances, and strangers. *Psychological Reports*, *38*, 967–970. PA 61:3532.

Gaebelein, Jacquelyn W. (1977a). The relationship between instigative aggression in females and sex of the target of instigation. *Personality and Social Psychology Bulletin*, *3*, 79–82. PA 58:7441.

Gaebelein, Jacquelyn W. (1977b). Sex differences in instigative aggression. *Journal of Research in Personality*, *11*, 466–474. PA 60:9272.

Gaebelein, Jacquelyn W. (1978a). The consequences of noncooperation for the target of third party instigated aggression. *Journal of Research in Personality*, *12*, 297–305. PA 63:3277.

Gaebelein, Jacquelyn W. (1978b). Third party instigated aggression as a function of attack pattern and a nonaggressive response option. *Journal of Research in Personality, 12,* 274–283. PA 63:3276.

Gaebelein, Jacquelyn W.; & Hay, William M. (1974). The effects of verbal and motor noncooperation on instigative aggression. *Personality and Social Psychology Bulletin, 1,* 200–202. PA 56:2303.

Gaebelein, Jacquelyn W.; & Hay, William M. (1975). The effects of verbal and behavioral noncompliance on third party instigation of aggression. *Journal of Research in Personality, 9,* 113–121. PA 54:9562.

Gaebelein, Jacquelyn W.; & Mander, Anthony. (1978). Consequences for targets of aggression as a function of aggressor and instigator roles: Three experiments. *Personality and Social Psychology Bulletin, 4,* 465–468. PA 64:3284.

Gaelick, Lisa; Bodenhausen, Galen V.; & Wyer, Robert S. (1985). Emotional communication in close relationships. *Journal of Personality and Social Psychology, 49,* 1246–1265. PA 73:11725.

Gaenslen, Fritz. (1980). Democracy vs. efficiency: Some arguments from the small group. *Political Psychology, 2,* 15–29. PA 66:12762.

Gaertner, Samuel L. (1973). Helping behavior and racial discrimination among liberals and conservatives. *Journal of Personality and Social Psychology, 25,* 335–341.

Gaertner, Samuel L. (1975). The role of racial attitudes in helping behavior. *Journal of Social Psychology, 97,* 95–101. PA 55:6913.

Gaertner, Samuel L.; & Dovidio, John F. (1977). The subtlety of white racism, arousal, and helping behavior. *Journal of Personality and Social Psychology, 35,* 691–707. PA 62:8620.

Gaertner, Samuel L.; Dovidio, John F.; & Johnson, Gary. (1982). Race of victim, nonresponsive bystanders, and helping behavior. *Journal of Social Psychology, 117,* 69–77.

Gaes, Geald G.; Kalle, Robert J.; & Tedeschi, James T. (1978). Impression management in the forced compliance situation: Two studies using the bogus pipeline. *Journal of Experimental Social Psychology, 14,* 493–510.

Gaines, Thomas; Kirwin, Paul M.; & Gentry, W. Doyle. (1977). The effect of descriptive anger expression, insult, and no feedback on interpersonal aggression, hostility, and empathy motivation. *Genetic Psychology Monographs, 95,* 349–367. PA 59:5671.

Gallagher, James; & Burke, Peter J. (1974).

Scapegoating and leader behavior. *Social Forces, 52,* 481–488. SA 75H1429.

Galle, Omer R.; & Gove, Walter R. (1979). Crowding and behavior in Chicago, 1940–1970. In J. R. Aiello & A. Baum (Eds.), *Residential crowding and design* (pp. 23–39). New York, NY: Plenum.

Gallois, Cynthia; & Markel, Norman N. (1975). Turn taking: Social personality and conversational style. *Journal of Personality and Social Psychology, 31,* 1134–1140. PA 54:9563.

Gamble, Arlene; & Strain, Phillip S. (1977). The effects of group-administered reinforcement on group consensual decisions. *Education, 98,* 47–52. PA 60:7414. SA 78J5960.

Gamson, William A.; & Stambaugh, Russell J. (1978). The model underlying SIMSOC. *Simulation and Games, 9,* 131–157. PA 63:955.

Ganzarain, Ramon. (1974–1975). A psychoanalytic study of sensitivity training. *Interpersonal Development, 5*(1), 60–70. PA 54:7458.

Garibaldi, Antoine M. (1979). Affective contributions of cooperative and group goal structures. *Journal of Educational Psychology, 71,* 788–794.

Garland, Howard; & Beard, James F. (1979). Relationship between self-monitoring and leader emergence across two task situations. *Journal of Applied Psychology, 64,* 77–81. PA 63:11944.

Garner, Katherine; & Deutsch, Morton. (1974). Cooperative behavior in dyads: Effects of dissimilar goal orientations and differing expectations about the partner. *Journal of Conflict Resolution, 18,* 634–645. PA 53:9474.

Garrabé, Michel. (1976). [A note on the praxiological division process for four individuals with probabilistic behavior]. *Mathematiques et Sciences Humaines,* No. 55, 61–67. PA 58:6725.

Garvey, Catherine. (1975). Requests and responses in children's speech. *Journal of Child Language, 2,* 41–63. PA 54:9340.

Garvill, Jorgen; & Garvill, Helena. (1983). Effects of distribution of cue validities and of feedback on multiple-cue probability judgment in groups. *Umea Psychological Reports,* No. 165, 16 pages. PA 71:28603.

Garvin, Deborah; & Rice, Robert W. (1982). Subjective meaning of the LPC scale: The view of respondents. *Basic and Applied Social Psychology, 3,* 203–218.

Garza, Raymond T.; Romero, Gloria J.; Cox,

Barbara G.; & Ramirez, Manuel. (1982). Biculturalism, locus of control, and leader behavior in ethnically mixed small groups. *Journal of Applied Social Psychology, 12*, 237–253. PA 69:7875.

Gastorf, John W.; Suls, Jerry; & Sanders, Glenn S. (1980). Type A coronary-prone behavior pattern and social facilitation. *Journal of Personality and Social Psychology, 38*, 773–780. PA 65:12720.

Gatewood, John B.; & Rosenwein, Robert. (1981). Interactional synchrony: Genuine or spurious? A critique of recent research. *Journal of Nonverbal Behavior, 6*, 12–29. PA 67:9762.

Gear, Tony E.; Marsh, Nicholas R.; & Sergent, Peter. (1985). Semi-automated feedback and team behavior. *Human Relations, 38*, 707–721. PA 73:3669.

Geen, Russell G. (1977). Effects of anticipation of positive and negative outcomes on audience anxiety. *Journal of Consulting and Clinical Psychology, 45*, 715–716. PA 59:7220.

Geen, Russell G. (1978). Effects of attack and uncontrollable noise on aggression. *Journal of Research in Personality, 12*, 15–29. PA 61:8466.

Geen, R[ussell] G. (1979). Effects of being observed on learning following success and failure experiences. *Motivation and Emotion, 3*, 355–371.

Geen, Russell G. (1980). The effects of being observed on performance. In P. B. Paulus (Ed.), *Psychology of group influence* (pp. 61–97). Hillsdale, NJ: Erlbaum.

Geen, Russell G. (1981a). Effects of being observed on persistence at an insoluble task. *British Journal of Social Psychology, 20*, 211–216. PA 68:1086.

Geen, Russell G. (1981b). Evaluation apprehension and social facilitation: A reply to Sanders. *Journal of Experimental Social Psychology, 17*, 252–256.

Geen, Russell G.; & Gange, James J. (1977). Drive theory of social facilitation: Twelve years of theory and research. *Psychological Bulletin, 84*, 1267–1288. PA 60:5202.

Geen, Russell G.; & Gange, J. J. (1983). Social facilitation: drive theory and beyond. In H. H. Blumberg, A. P. Hare, V. Kent, & M. F. Davies (Eds.), *Small groups and social interaction* (Vol. 1, pp. 141–153), Chichester: John Wiley & Sons.

Geffner, Robert; & Gross, Madeleine M. (1984). Sex-role behavior and obedience to authority: A field study. *Sex Roles, 10*, 973–985. PA 72:14484.

Geis, Florence L.; Boston, Martha B.; & Hoffman, Nadine. (1985). Sex of authority role models and achievement by men and women: Leadership performance and recognition. *Journal of Personality and Social Psychology, 49*, 636–653. PA 73:3700.

Geis, F[lorence] L.; & Moon, Tae Hyun. (1981). Machiavellianism and deception. *Journal of Personality and Social Psychology, 41*, 766–775.

Geist, Patricia; & Chandler, Teresa. (1984). Account analysis of influence in group decision-making. *Communication Monographs, 51*, 67–78. PA 72:6627.

Geller, Daniel M. (1978). Involvement in role-playing simulations: A demonstration with studies on obedience. *Journal of Personality and Social Psychology, 36*, 219–235.

Geller, Daniel M.; Goodstein, Lynne; Silver, Maury; & Sternberg, Wendy C. (1974). On being ignored: The effects of the violation of implicit rules of social interaction. *Sociometry, 37*, 541–556. PA 53:9475.

Geller, Daniel M.; & Malia, Gregory P. (1981). The effects of noise on helping behavior reconsidered. *Basic and Applied Social Psychology, 2*, 11–25. PA 66:12763.

Gemmill, Gary. (1986). The mythology of the leader role in small groups. *Small Group Behavior, 17*, 41–50. PA 74:28116.

Gentry, James W. (1980). Group size and attitudes toward the simulation experience. *Simulation and Games, 11*, 451–460. PA 66:10324.

Gentry, Martha E. (1982). Consensus as a form of decision making. *Journal of Sociology and Social Welfare, 9*(2), 233–244. PA 71:14962.

Georgas, James (1985). Cooperative, competitive and individual problem-solving in sixth grade Greek children. *European Journal of Social psychology, 15*, 67–77.

Gerard, Harold, B.; & Miller, Norman. (1975). *School Desegregation: A long-term study*. New York: Plenum.

Gergen, Kenneth J.; Greenberg, Martin S.; & Willis, Richard H. (Eds.). (1980). *Social exchange: Advances in theory and research*. New York: Plenum.

Gero, Anne. (1985). Conflict avoidance in consensual decision processes. *Small Group Behavior, 16*, 487–499. PA 73:29947.

Giddens, Anthony. (1984). Corpo, riflessivita, riproduzione sociale: Erving Goffman e la teoria sociale [The body, reflexivity, social reproduction: Erving Goffman and social theory] [Special Issue: Studies on Erving Goffman]. *Rassegna Italiana di Sociologia, 25,* 369-400 PA 72:25397.

Gielen, Uwe; Dick, Stuart; Rosenberg, Sidney; Kelly, Donna M.; & Chiafettelli, Frank. (1979). Naturalistic observation of sex and race differences in visual interactions. *International Journal of Group Tensions, 9,* 211-222. PA 69:3390.

Giesen, Martin; & Hendrick, Clyde. (1974). Effects of seating distance and room illumination on the affective outcomes of small group interaction. *Social Behavior and Personality, 2,* 87-96. PA 56:7900. SA 76I1693.

Giesen, Martin; & Hendrick, Clyde. (1977). Physical distance and sex in moderated groups: Neglected factors in small group interaction. *Memory and Cognition, 5,* 79-83. PA 58:5329. SA 81L1666.

Giesen, Martin; & McClaren, Harry A. (1976). Discussion, distance and sex: Changes in impressions and attraction during small group interaction. *Sociometry, 39,* 60-70. PA 56:677.

Gifford, Robert. (1981). Sociability: Traits, settings, and interactions. *Journal of Personality and Social Psychology, 41,* 340-347. PA 67:7695.

Gifford, Robert. (1982a). Children and the commons dilemma. *Journal of Applied Social Psychology, 12,* 269-280. PA 69:5572.

Gifford, Robert. (1982b). Projected interpersonal distance and orientation choices: Personality, sex, and social situation. *Social Psychology Quarterly, 45,* 145-152. PA 69:10400.

Gifford, Robert. (1983). The experience of personal space: Perception of interpersonal distance. *Journal of Nonverbal Behavior, 7,* 170-178. PA 71:20435.

Gifford, Robert; & Gallagher, Timothy M. B. (1985). Sociability: Personality, social context, and physical setting. *Journal of Personality and Social Psychology, 48,* 1015-1023.

Gilbert, Daniel T.; Jones, Edward E.; & Pelham, Brett W. (1987). Influence and inference: What the active perceiver overlooks. *Journal of Personality and Social Psychology, 52,* 861-870. PA 74:25072.

Gilbert, Shirley J. (1976). Self disclosure, intimacy and communication in families. *Family Coordinator, 25,* 221-231. PA 57:3094.

Gilbert, Shirley J. (1977). Effects of unanticipated self-disclosure on recipients of varying levels of self-esteem: A research note. *Human Communication Research, 3,* 368-371. PA 60:5254.

Gilbert, Shirley J.; & Whiteneck, Gale G. (1976). Toward a multidimensional approach to the study of self-disclosure. *Human Communication Research, 2,* 347-355. PA 61:10888.

Gilbert, Steven J. (1981). Another look at the Milgram obedience studies: The role of the gradated series of shocks. *Personality and Social Psychology Bulletin, 7,* 690-695. PA 68:3542.

Gill, Diane L. (1979). The prediction of group motor performance from individual member abilities. *Journal of Motor Behavior, 11,* 113-122. PA 65:10377.

Gill, Diane L. (1980). Success-failure attributions in competitive groups: An exception to egocentrism. *Journal of Sport Psychology, 2,* 106-114. PA 64:12488.

Gill, Diane L.; & Martens, Raine. (1977). The role of task type and success-failure in group competition. *International Journal of Sport Psychology, 8,* 160-177. PA 61:13388.

Gill, Stephen J.; Menlo, Allen; & Keel, Linda P. (1984). Antecedents to member participation within small groups: A review of theory and research. *Journal for Specialists in Group Work, 9*(2), 68-76. PA 72:9495.

Gillett, Raphael. (1977). Collective indecision. *Behavioral Science, 22,* 383-390. PA 60:11693. SA 78J4688.

Gillett, Raphael. (1980). The asymptotic likelihood of agreement between plurality and condorcet outcomes. *Behavioral Science, 25,* 23-32. SA 81L3326.

Gilmartin, Kevin M.; & MacKinnon, William J. (1974). The effects of staff retraining and SPAN decision making on group problem solving. *Newsletter for Research in Mental Health and Behavioral Sciences, 16*(2), 9-11. PA 53:9681.

Gilmour, D. Ross; & Walkey, Frank H. (1981). Identifying violent offenders using a video measure of interpersonal distance. *Journal of Consulting & Clinical Psychology, 49,* 287-291.

Gilmour, Robin; & Duck, Steve. (Eds.). (1986). *The emerging field of personal relationships.* Hillsdale, NJ: L. Erlbaum.

Ginste, Maric Dominique. (1976). Choice of a working partner and test outcome. *Psychologie Francaise, 21*, 73–82. PA 60:3032.

Gintner, Gary; & Lindskold, Svenn. (1975). Rate of participation and expertise as factors influencing leader choice. *Journal of Personality and Social Psychology, 32*, 1085–1089. PA 55:7132.

Gitter, A. George; & Black, Harvey. (1976). Is self-disclosure self-revealing? *Journal of Counseling Psychology, 23*, 327–332. PA 56:05992.

Gitter, A. George; Black, Harvey; & Goldman, Arthur. (1975). Role of nonverbal communication in the perception of leadership. *Perceptual and Motor Skills, 40*, 463–466. PA 54:9594.

Glascock, Anthony P. (1976). Dominance interaction in a first grade ILP class. *Journal of Research and Development in Education, 9*(4), 61–68. PA 58:4336.

Glaser, Anthony N. (1982). Drive theory of social facilitation: A critical reappraisal. *British Journal of Social Psychology, 21*, 265–282. PA 70:1045.

Glasgow, Russell E.; & Arkowitz, Hal. (1975). The behavioral assessment of male and female social competence in dyadic heterosexual interactions. *Behavior Therapy, 6*, 488–498. PA 55:791.

Glassman, Joel B.; Burkhart, Barry R.; Grant, Richard D.; & Vallery, Georgia G. (1978). Density, expectation, and extended task performance: An experiment in the natural environment. *Environment and Behavior, 10*, 299–315. PA 64:981.

Gleason, James M.; & Harris, Victor A. (1975). Race, socio-economic status, and perceived similarity as determinants of judgments by simulated jurors. *Social Behavior and Personality, 3*, 175–180. PA 56:6036.

Gleason, James M.; & Harris, Victor A. (1976). Group discussion and defendant's socio-economic status as determinants of judgments by simulated jurors. *Journal of Applied Social Psychology, 6*, 186–191.

Gleason, James M.; Seaman, F. James; & Hollander, Edwin P. (1978). Emergent leadership processes as a function of task structure and Machiavellianism. *Social Behavior and Personality, 6*, 33–36. PA 63:5418. SA 79K1228.

Gleitman, Henry. (1981). *Psychology*. New York: Norton.

Gleitman, Henry. (1984). Some comments on Dr. Stein's critique of my account of Asch's social-

pressure studies. *Perceptual and Motor Skills, 59*, 1003–1006. PA 73:19796.

Glick, Peter. (1985). Orientations toward relationships: Choosing a situation in which to begin a relationship. *Journal of Experimental Social Psychology, 21*, 544–562. PA 74:1050.

Glover, John A. (1977). Risky shift and creativity. *Social Behavior and Personality, 5*, 317–320. SA 79K1090.

Glover, John A. (1979). Group structure and creative responding. *Small Group Behavior, 10*, 62–72.

Glover, John A.; & Chambers, Terry. (1978). The creative production of the group: effects of small group structure. *Small Group Behavior, 9*, 387–392. SA 79K2626.

Glover, John A.; Romero, Dan; Romero, Pat; & Petersen, Chris. (1978). Effects of a simulation game upon tolerance for ambiguity, dogmatism, and risk taking. *Journal of Social Psychology, 105*, 291–296.

Gochman, Ilene R.; & Keating, John P. (1980). Misattributions to crowding: Blaming crowding for nondensity-caused events. *Journal of Nonverbal Behavior, 4*, 157–175. PA 66:1263.

Godfrey, Debra K.; Jones, Edward E.; & Lord, Charles G. (1986). Self-promotion is not ingratiating. *Journal of Personality and Social Psychology, 50*, 106–115. PA 73:17228.

Godwin, William F.; & Restle, Frank. (1974). The road to agreement: Subgroup pressures in small group consensus processes. *Journal of Personality and Social Psychology, 30*, 500–509.

Goehring, Dwight J.; & Kahan, James P. (1976). The uniform N-person Prisoner's Dilemma game. *Journal of Conflict Resolution, 20*, 111–128. PA 57:98.

Goethals, George R. (1976). An attributional analysis of some social influence phenomena. In J. H. Harvey, W. J. Ickes, & R. F. Kidd (Eds.), *New directions in attribution research* (Vol. 1, pp. 291–310). Hillsdale, NJ: Erlbaum.

Goethals, George R.; & Perlstein, Arnold L. (1978). Level of instigation and model similarity as determinants of aggressive behavior. *Aggressive Behavior, 4*(2), 115–124. PA 62:10968.

Goethals, George R.; & Zanna, Mark P. (1979). The role of social comparison in choice shifts. *Journal of Personality and Social Psychology, 37*, 1469–1476. PA 65:1234.

Goetsch, Gerald G.; & McFarland, David D. (1980). Models of the distribution of acts in small discussion groups. *Social Psychology Quarterly*, *43*, 173–183. PA 66:1225. SA 83M7341.

Goffman, Erving. (1959). *The presentation of self in everyday life*. Garden City, NY: Doubleday Anchor Books.

Goffman, Erving. (1974). *Frame analysis: An essay on the organization of experience*. New York: Harper.

Goffman, Erving. (1981). *Forms of talk*. Philadelphia: University of Pennsylvania Press.

Goffman, Erving. (1982). *Interaction ritual: Essays on face-to-face behavior*. New York: Pantheon.

Goldband, Steve. (1981). Imposed latencies, interruptions and dyadic interaction: Physiological response and interpersonal attraction. *Journal of Research in Personality*, *15*, 221–232. PA 67:3528.

Goldbart, Stephen; & Cooper, Lowell. (1976). Safety in groups: An existential analysis. *Small Group Behavior*, *7*, 237–256. PA 58:9479.

Goldberg, Carlos. (1975). Conformity to majority type as a function of task and acceptance of sex-related stereotypes. *Journal of Psychology*, *89*, 25–37.

Goldberg, Myron; & Wellens, A. Rodney. (1979). A comparison of nonverbal compensatory behaviors within direct face to face and television-mediated interviews. *Journal of Applied Social Psychology*, *9*, 250–260. PA 66:5747.

Goldenthal, Peter; Johnston, Robert E.; & Kraut, Robert E. (1981). Smiling, appeasement, and the silent bared-teeth display. *Ethology and Sociobiology*, *2*, 127–133. SA 82M1459.

Golding, Stephen L.; & Knudson, Roger M. (1975). Multivariable-multimethod convergence in the domain of interpersonal behavior. *Multivariate Behavioral Research*, *10*, 425–448. PA 55:7066.

Goldman, Ethel K. (1975). Need achievement as a motivational basis for the risky shift. *Journal of Personality*, *43*, 346–356. PA 54:11793.

Goldman, Florence W.; & Goldman, Morton. (1981). The effects of dyadic group experience in subsequent individual performance. *Journal of Social Psychology*, *115*, 83–88.

Goldman, Morton; Creason, Christopher R.; & McCall, Cynthia G. (1981). Compliance employing a two-feet-in-the-door procedure. *Journal of Social Psychology*, *114*, 259–265.

Goldman, Morton; & Fordyce, Jerry. (1983). Prosocial behavior as affected by eye contact,

touch, and voice expression. *Journal of Social Psychology*, *121*, 125–129. PA 71:17750.

Goldman, Morton; Kiyohara, Odette; & Pfannensteil, Dorothy A. (1985). Interpersonal touch, social labeling, and the foot-in-the-door effect. *Journal of Social Psychology*, *125*, 143–147. PA 73:24473.

Goldman, Morton; Lewandowski, Helen E.; & Carrill, Richard E. (1982). Altruistic behavior in rural and urban, residential and business areas. *Basic and Applied Social Psychology*, *3*, 155–160. PA 69:1015.

Goldman, Morton; McVeigh, James F.; & Richterkessing, Joy L. (1984). Door-in-the-face procedure: Reciprocal concession, perceptual contrast, or worthy person. *Journal of Social Psychology*, *123*, 245–251. PA 72:25424.

Goldman, Morton; Seever, Mark; & Seever, Margaret. (1982). Social labelling and the foot-in-the-door effect. *Journal of Social Psychology*, *117*, 19–23.

Goldman, Morton; Stockbauer, Joseph W.; & McAuliffe, Timothy G. (1977). Intergroup and intragroup competition and cooperation. *Journal of Experimental Social Psychology*, *13*, 81–88. PA 58:3293.

Goldmann, Kjell. (1989, March). *Does cooperation inhibit conflict?* Paper presented at the meeting of the International Studies Association, London, England.

Goldstein, Alvin G.; Chance, June E.; & Gilbert, Barbara. (1984). Facial stereotypes of good guys and bad guys: A replication and extension. *Bulletin of the Psychonomic Society*, *22*, 549–552. PA 73:1145.

Goldstein, Arnold P.; & Segall, Marshall H. (Eds.). (1983). *Aggression in global perspective*. Elmsford, NY: Pergamon.

Golin, Sanford; & Romanowski, Michael A. (1977). Verbal aggression as a function of sex of subject and sex of target. *Journal of Psychology*, *97*, 141–150. PA 59:12324.

Gologor, Ethan. (1977). Group polarization in a non-risk-taking culture. *Journal of Cross Cultural Psychology*, *8*, 331–346. PA 60:3071. SA 79J6847.

Golu, Pantelimon; & Bogatu, Nicolae. (1984). Dimensiuni tipologice ale conduitei de rol (II) [Typological dimensions of role behavior: II]. (Romanian). *Revista de Psihologie*, *30*, 283–295. PA 73:1123.

Golub, Sharon; & Canty, Eileen M. (1982). Sex-role expectations and the assumption of leadership by college women. *Journal of Social Psychology, 116*, 83–90. PA 68:8099.

Golubeva, Nina V. (1982). [The size of a group as a factor of group dynamics]. *Psikologicheskii Zhurnal, 3*(4), 78–83. PA 69:7877.

Goodge, Peter. (1978). Intergroup conflict: A rethink. *Human Relations, 31*, 475–487. PA 62:10969.

Goodstein, Leonard D.; & Dovico, Michelle. (1979). The decline and fall of the small group. *Journal of Applied Behavioral Science, 15*, 320–328. SA 80K7128.

Goodstein, Leonard D.; & Russell, Scot W. (1977). Self-disclosure: A comparative study of reports by self and others. *Journal of Counseling Psychology, 24*, 365–369. PA 59:5629.

Goodwin, Charles. (1981). *Conversational organization: Interaction between speakers and hearers.* New York: Academic Press.

Gordon, Ronald D. (1985). The self-disclosure of interpersonal feedback: The "dyadic effect" in a group context. *Small Group Behavior, 16*, 411–413. PA 73:17984.

Gormally, Jim. (1982). Evaluation of assertiveness: Effects of gender, rater involvement, and level of assertiveness. *Behavior Therapy, 13*, 219–225. PA 68:1124.

Gorman, Michael E.; Gorman, Margaret E.; Latta, R. Michael; & Cunningham, Guy. (1984). How disconfirmatory, confirmatory and combined strategies affect group problem solving. *British Journal of Psychology, 75*, 65–79. PA 72:1231.

Gormley, Frances P.; & Aiello, John R. (1982). Social density, interpersonal relationships, and residential crowding stress. *Journal of Applied Social Psychology, 12*, 222–236.

Goss, Blaine. (1988). *Communicating in interpersonal relationships.* New York: Macmillan.

Gotay, Carolyn Cook (1981). Cooperation and competition as a function of Type A behavior. *Personality and Social Psychology Bulletin, 7*, 386–392.

Gotlib, Ian H.; & Robinson, L. Anne. (1982). Responses to depressed individuals: Discrepancies between self-report and observer-rated behavior. *Journal of Abnormal Psychology, 91*, 231–240. PA 68:10321.

Gottlieb, Jody; & Carver, Charles S. (1980). Anticipation of future interaction and the bystander effect. *Journal of Experimental Social Psychology, 16*, 253–260. PA 65:12722.

Gottman, John M. (1979). *Marital interaction: Experimental investigations.* New York: Academic Press.

Gottman, John; Gonso, Jonni; & Rasmussen, Brian. (1975). Social interaction, social competence, and friendship in children. *Child Development, 46*, 709–718. PA 57:9099.

Gould, Daniel; & Weiss, Maureen. (1981). The effects of model similarity and model talk on self-efficacy and muscular endurance. *Journal of Sport Psychology, 3*, 17–29. PA 66:3635.

Gould, Peter; & Gatrell, Anthony. (1980). A structural analysis of a game: The Liverpool v Manchester United Cup Final of 1977. *Social Networks, 2*, 253–273. SA 81L4926.

Gould, Peter; & Greenawalt, Nancy J. (1981). Some methodological perspectives on the analysis of team games. *Journal of Sport Psychology, 3*, 283–304. PA 68:1087.

Gould, Robert; Brounstein, Paul J.; & Sigall, Harold. (1977). Attributing ability to an opponent: Public aggrandizement and private denigration. *Social Psychology Quarterly, 40*, 254–261. PA 60:5256.

Gouran, Dennis S.; Brown, Candace; & Henry, David R. (1978). Behavioral correlates of perceptions of quality in decision-making discussions. *Communication Monographs, 45*, 51–63. PA 61:13389.

Gouran, Dennis S.; & Geonetta, Sam C. (1977). Patterns of interaction in discussion groups at varying distance from consensus. *Small Group Behavior, 8*, 511–524. PA 64:998.

Gove, Walter R.; Hughes, Michael; & Galle, Omer R. (1979). Overcrowding in the home: An empirical investigation of its possible pathological consequences. *American Sociological Review, 44*, 59–80. PA 64:857.

Graebner, William. (1986). The small group and democratic social engineering, 1900–1950. *Journal of Social Issues, 42*(1), 137–154. PA 73:29948.

Graham, Deana Atchison. (1984). *Trust and decision making in small groups.* Doctoral thesis, University of Texas at Austin. [*National Union Catalog*, register no. b-836-160].

Graham, Jean A.; & Argyle, Michael. (1975). The effects of different patterns of gaze combined with different facial expressions, on impression formation. *Journal of Human Movement Studies, 1*, 178–182. PA 56:2345.

Graham, Jean A; Argyle, Michael; & Furnham, Adrian. (1980). The goal structure of situations.

European Journal of Social Psychology, 10, 345–366. SA 82M1460.

Gramann, James H. (1982). Toward a behavioral theory of crowding in outdoor recreation: An evaluation and synthesis of research. *Leisure Sciences, 5,* 109–126. PA 71:6693.

Granberg, Donald; & Campbell, Keith E. (1977). Effect of communication discrepancy and ambiguity on placement and opinion shift. *European Journal of Social Psychology, 7,* 137–150. PA 60:5257.

Granberg, Donald; Steele, Lee; & Brent, Edward E. (1975). Leveling effect of coaction on judgment or retest effect? *Journal of Social Psychology, 96,* 45–51. PA 54:7460.

Grandberg, Donald; Stevens, J. Scott; & Katz, Sandra. (1975). Effect of communication on cooperation in expanded Prisoner's Dilemma and Chicken games. *Simulation and Games, 6,* 166–187. PA 55:2324.

Graumann, Carl F.; & Moscovici, Serge. (Eds.). (1986). *Changing conceptions of leadership.* New York: Springer-Verlag.

Gray, L[ouis] N.; & Griffith, W. I. (1984). On differentiation in small-group power relations. *Social Psychology Quarterly, 47,* 391–396. PA 72:30779. SA 85O6022.

Gray, Louis N.; Griffith, Wanda I.; von Broembsen, Maxmilian H.; & Sullivan, Michael J. (1982). Group differentiation: Temporal effects of reinforcement. *Social Psychology Quarterly, 45,* 44–49. PA 68:8100. SA 83N2346.

Gray, Louis N.; Mayhew, Bruce H.; & Campbell, Richard. (1974). Communication and three dimensions of power: An experiment and a simulation. *Small Group Behavior, 5,* 289–320. PA 54:2971.

Gray, Louis N.; & Sullivan, Michael J. (1978). Can you create structural differentiation in social power relations in the laboratory?. *Social Psychology, 41,* 328–337. SA 79K1092.

Gray, L[ouis] N.; & Von Broembsen, M. H. (1976). On the generalizability of the Law of Effect: Social psychological measurement of group structures and process. *Sociometry, 39,* 175–183.

Gray, Louis N.; von Broembsen, Maximilian H.; Kowalczyk, Mary A.; & Williams, J. Sherwood. (1976). On the social law of effect. *Journal of Social Psychology, 99,* 221–231.

Gray, Susan H. (1977). Model predictability in bargaining. *Journal of Psychology, 97,* 171–178. PA 60:7415.

Gray-Little, Bernadette. (1980). Race and inequity. *Journal of Applied Social Psychology, 10,* 468–481. PA 66:5557.

Graziano, William G.; Feldesman, Alice Bernstein; & Rahe, Donald F. (1985). Extraversion, social cognition, and the salience of aversiveness in social encounters. *Journal of Personality and Social Psychology, 49,* 971–980.

Graziano, William; French, Doran; Brownell, Celia A.; & Hartup, Willard W. (1976). Peer interaction in same- and mixed-age triads in relation to chronological age and incentive condition. *Child Development, 47,* 707–714. PA 57:10013.

Green, Charles S. (1975). The ecology of committees. *Environment and Behavior, 7,* 411–427. PA 56:643. SA 7713062.

Green, F. Brentwood. (1978). Mainlining Synanon: Notes from the game. *Wisconsin Sociologist, 15*(1), 27–42. SA 79K1093.

Green, Richard B.; & Mack, Jonathan. (1978). Would groups do better without social psychologists? A response to Buys. *Personality and Social Psychology Bulletin, 4,* 561–563. PA 64:5552.

Green, Stephen G.; & Mitchell, Terence R. (1979). Attributional processes of leaders in leader-member interactions. *Organizational Behavior and Human Performance, 23,* 429–458. PA 64:5596.

Green, Stephen G.; & Taber, Thomas D. (1980). The effects of three social decision schemes on decision group process. *Organizational Behavior and Human Performance, 25,* 97–106. PA 65:7939.

Green, Susan K.; & Sandos, Philip. (1983). Perceptions of male and female initiators of relationships. *Sex Roles, 9,* 849–852. PA 71:12196.

Greenbaum, Charles W. (1979). The small group under the gun: Uses of small groups in battle conditions. *Journal of Applied Behavioral Science, 15,* 392–405. SA 80K7129.

Greenbaum, Paul; & Rosenfeld, Howard M. (1978). Patterns of avoidance in response to interpersonal staring and proximity: Effects of bystanders on drivers at a traffic intersection. *Journal of Personality and Social Psychology, 36,* 575–587. PA 62:5971.

Greenberg, Carl I.; & Baum, Andrew. (1979).

Compensatory response to anticipated densities. *Journal of Applied Social Psychology, 9,* 1–12. PA 64:5553.

Greenberg, Carl I.; & Firestone, Ira J. (1977). Compensatory responses to crowding: Effects of personal space intrusion and privacy reduction. *Journal of Personality and Social Psychology, 35,* 637–644. PA 62:5972.

Greenberg, Carl I.; Wang, Yau-de; & Dossett, Dennis I. (1982). Effects of work group size and task size on observers' job characteristics ratings. *Basic and Applied Social Psychology, 3,* 53–66.

Greenberg, Jeff; Williams, Kipling D.; & O'Brien, Mary K. (1986). Considering the harshest verdict first: Biasing effects on mock juror verdicts. *Personality and Social Psychology Bulletin, 12,* 41–50. PA 74:13109.

Greenberg, Jerald. (1976). The role of seating position in group interaction: A review, with applications for group trainers. *Group and Organization Studies, 1,* 310–327. PA 58:1096.

Greenberg, Jerald. (1978a). Effects of reward value and retaliative power on allocation decisions: Justice, generosity, or greed? *Journal of Personality and Social Psychology, 36,* 367–379. PA 61:5908.

Greenberg, Jerald. (1978b). Equity, equality, and the Protestant Ethic: Allocating rewards following fair and unfair competition. *Journal of Experimental Social Psychology, 14,* 217–226.

Greenberg, Jerald. (1979). Group vs individual equity judgments: Is there a polarization effect? *Journal of Experimental Social Psychology, 15,* 504–512. PA 64:12453.

Greenberg, Jerald. (1983). Self-image versus impressional management in adherence to distributive justice standards: The influence of self-awareness and self-consciousness. *Journal of Personality and Social Psychology, 44,* 5–19. PA 70:3368.

Greenberg, S.; & Formanek, R. (1974). Social class differences in spontaneous verbal interactions. *Child Study Journal, 4,* 145–153. PA 53:2995.

Greenblat, Cathy Stein. (1980). Group dynamics and game design: Some reflections. *Simulation and Games, 11,* 35–58. SA 81L4927.

Greenblat, Cathy S[tein]; & Gagnon, John H. (1979). Further explorations on the multiple reality game. *Simulation and Games, 10,* 41–59. PA 65:1223. SA 80K4176.

Greene, Charles N.; & Schriesheim, Chester A. (1980). Leader-group interactions: A longitudinal field investigation. *Journal of Applied Psychology, 65,* 50–59. PA 65:5384.

Greene, Les R. (1976). Body image boundaries and small group seating arrangements. *Journal of Consulting and Clinical Psychology, 44,* 244–249. PA 56:9830.

Greene, Les R. (1979). Psychological differentiation and social structure. *Journal of Social Psychology, 109,* 79–85. PA 65:3245.

Greene, Les R.; Morrison, Thomas L.; & Tischler, Nancy G. (1981). Gender and authority: effects on perceptions of small group co-leaders. *Small Group Behavior, 12,* 401–413. SA 83M7480.

Greenstein, Theodore N. (1981). Scope conditions and crucial tests: Comment on Lee and Ofshe. *Social Psychology Quarterly, 44,* 381–383. PA 68:1088.

Greenstein, Theodore N. (1985). Conditions for power structures embodying local exchange imbalance. *Social Science Journal, 22*(3), 15–28. PA 73:24474.

Greenstein, Theodore N.; & Knottnerus, J. David. (1980). The effects of differential evaluations on status generalization. *Social Psychology Quarterly, 43,* 147–154. PA 66:1266.

Greenwood, Charles R.; Hops, Hyman; Delquadri, Joseph; & Guild, Jacqueline. (1974). Group contingencies for group consequences in classroom management: A further analysis. *Journal of Applied Behavior Analysis, 7,* 413–425. PA 53:6104.

Greenwood, James G. (1974). Opportunity to communicate and social orientation in imaginary-reward bargaining. *Speech Monographs, 41,* 79–81. PA 53:5166.

Greenwood, John D. (1983). Role-playing as an experimental strategy in social psychology. *European Journal of Social Psychology, 13,* 235–254. PA 71:9470.

Griffin, Gregory M.; & Edwards, Ward. (1983). Individuals versus pairs in hierarchical inferences. *Organizational Behavior and Human Performance, 32,* 249–261. PA 71:3971.

Griffin, Ricky W.; Bateman, Thomas S.; Wayne, Sandy J.; & Head, Thomas C. (1987). Objective and social factors as determinants of task perceptions and responses: An integrated perspective and empirical investigation. *Academy of Management Journal, 30,* 501–523. PA 75:1376.

Griffin, Ricky W.; Skivington, Kristen D.; & Moorhead, Gregory. (1987). Symbolic and international perspectives on leadership: An integrative framework. *Human Relations, 40,* 199-218. PA 74:25047.

Griffith, Wanda I.; & Gray, Louis N. (1978). The effects of external reinforcement on power structure in task oriented groups. *Social Forces, 57,* 222-235. PA 64:999.

Griffith, W[anda] I.; & Gray, L[ouis] N. (1985). A note on the "social law of effect": Expanding the model. *Social Forces, 63,* 1030-1037. PA 73:1124.

Griffitt, William. (1970). Environmental effects on interpersonal affective behavior: Ambient effective temperature and attraction. *Journal of Personality and Social Psychology, 15,* 240-244.

Griffitt, William; & Veitch, Russell. (1971). Hot and crowded: Influences of population density and temperature on interpersonal affective behavior. *Journal of Personality and Social Psychology, 17,* 92-98.

Grigsby, David W.; & Bigoness, William J. (1982). Effects of mediation and alternative forms of arbitration on bargaining behavior: A laboratory study. *Journal of Applied Psychology, 67,* 549-554. PA 69:3392.

Grigsby, James P.; Weatherley, Donald. (1983). Gender and sex-role differences in intimacy of self-disclosure. *Psychological Reports, 53,* 891-897. PA 71:17751.

Groff, Bradford D.; Baron, Robert S.; & Moore, Danny L. (1983). Distraction, attentional conflict, and drivelike behavior. *Journal of Experimental Social Psychology, 19,* 359-380.

Grofman, Bernard. (1974). Helping behavior and group size: Some exploratory stochastic models. *Behavioral Science, 19,* 210-224. PA 53:1061.

Grofman, Bernard. (1978). Judgmental competence of individuals and groups in a dichotomous choice situation: Is a majority of heads better than one? *Journal of Mathematical Sociology, 6,* 47-60. PA 64:1000. SA 79J9638.

Grofman, Bernard; Feld, Scott L.; & Owen, Guillermo. (1984). Group size and the performance of a composite group majority: Statistical truths and empirical results. *Organizational Behavior and Human Performance, 33,* 350-359.

Grofman, Bernard; Owen, Guillermo; & Feld, Scott L. (1982). Average competence, variability in individual competence, and accuracy of statistically pooled group decisions. *Psychological Reports, 50,* 683-688. PA 69:1016.

Grofman, Bernard; & Pool, Jonathan. (1977). How to make cooperation the optimizing strategy in a two-person game. *Journal of Mathematical Sociology, 5,* 173-186. SA 78J3221.

Grossnickle, William F.; Lao, Rosina C.; Martoccia, C. T.; Range, Donna C.; & Walters, Frances C. (1975). Complexity of effects of personal space. *Psychological Reports, 36,* 237-238. PA 54:7510.

Grove, Theodore G.; & Hays, James. (1978). Ipalion: A FORTRAN IV program for comparing interpersonal perceptions in dyads. *Behavior Research Methods and Instrumentation, 10,* 747-749. SA 80K8687.

Gruen, Walter. (1979). Energy in group therapy: Implications for the therapist of energy transformation and generation as a negentropic system. *Small Group Behavior, 10,* 23-39. SA 80K5520.

Gruenfeld, Leopold W.; & Lin, Thung rung. (1984). Social behavior of field independents and dependents in an organic group. *Human Relations, 37,* 721-741. PA 72:1233.

Grumet, Gerald W. (1983). Eye contact: The core of interpersonal relatedness. *Psychiatry, 46,* 172-180. PA 71:1311.

Grush, Joseph E. (1978). Audiences can inhibit or facilitate competitive behavior. *Personality and Social Psychology Bulletin, 4,* 119-122. PA 61:5927.

Grush, Joseph E.; & Yehl, Janet G. (1979). Marital roles, sex differences, and interpersonal attraction. *Journal of Personality and Social Psychology, 37,* 116-123.

Grzelak, Janusz. (1976). Game theory and its applicability to the description of prosocial behavior. *Polish Psychological Bulletin, 7,* 197-205. PA 58:1097.

Grzelak, Janusz; & Tyszka, Tadeusz. (1974). Some preliminary experiments on cooperation in N-person games. *Polish Psychological Bulletin, 5,* 81-91. PA 53:5167.

Grzesiuk, Lidia; Migdalska-Wierzbowska, Hanna; & Makuch-Rusinowska, Ewa. (1985). Wplyw rol spolecznych i rodzaju zadania na zwiazek miedzy efektywnoscia grup zadaniowych a stylem komunikowania sie czlonkow tych grup

[The influence of social roles and type of task upon the relationship between the efficiency of task teams and styles of communication of the group members]. *Studia Psychologiczne*, *22*, 77-95. PA 74:1055.

Guardo, Carol J. (1976). Personal space, sex differences, and interpersonal attraction. *Journal of Psychology*, *92*, 9-14. PA 56:531.

Gudykunst, William B. (1983). Toward a typology of stranger-host relationships. *International Journal of Intercultural Relations*, *7*, 401-413. PA 71:23056.

Gudykunst, William B.; Yang, Seung mock; & Nishida, Tsukasa. (1985). A cross-cultural test of uncertainty reduction theory: Comparisons of acquaintances, friends, and dating relationships in Japan, Korea, and the United States. *Human Communication Research*, *11*, 407-455. PA 73:6332.

Guerin, Bernard. (1983). Social facilitation and social monitoring: A test of three models. *British Journal of Social Psychology*, *22*, 203-214. PA 71:14997.

Guerin, Bernard. (1986a). The effects of mere presence on a motor task. *Journal of Social Psychology*, *126*, 399-401.

Guerin, Bernard. (1986b). Mere presence effects in humans: A review. *Journal of Experimental Social Psychology*, *22*, 38-77. PA 74:13091.

Guerin, Bernard; & Innes, J. M. (1982). Social facilitation and social monitoring: A new look at Zajonc's mere presence hypothesis. *British Journal of Social Psychology*, *21*, 7-18. PA 68:5783.

Guerin, Bernard; & Innes, J. M. (1984). Explanations of social facilitation: A review. *Current Psychological Research and Reviews*, *3*, 32-52. PA 72:22578.

Guillon, Michel; & Personnaz, Bernard. (1983). Analyse de la dynamique des représentations des conflits minoritaire et majoritaire [Dynamic of representation of majority and minority conflicts]. *Cahiers de Psychologie Cognitive*, *3*, 65-87. PA 71:3972.

Gupta, Mahesh. (1983). A basis for friendly dyadic interpersonal relationships. *Small Group Behavior*, *14*, 15-33. PA 71:1313.

Gupta, Mahesh. (1985). Interpersonal tension: A two-factor approach to the POX situation. *Small Group Behavior*, *16*, 303-323. PA 73:17206. SA 86Q4839.

Gurevitch, Z. D. (1984). Impression formation during tactical self-presentation. *Social Psychology Quarterly*, *47*, 262-270. PA 72:25425.

Gustafson, James P. (1976). The passive small group: Working concepts. *Human Relations*, *29*, 793-803. PA 57:3872.

Gustafson, James P.; & Cooper, Lowell. (1979). Unconscious planning in small groups. *Human Relations*, *32*, 1039-1064. SA 82M1461.

Gustafson, James P.; Cooper, Lowell; Lathrop, Nancy Coalter; Ringler, Karin ; Seldin, Fredric A.; & Wright, Marcia Kahn. (1981a). Cooperative and clashing interests in small groups: Part 1. Theory. *Human Relations*, *34*, 315-339. SA 83N2348.

Gustafson, James P.; Cooper, Lowell; Lathrop, Nancy Coalter; Ringler, Karin ; Seldin, Fredric A.; & Wright, Marcia Kahn. (1981b). Cooperative and clashing interests in small groups: Part II. Group narratives. *Human Relations*, *34*, 367-378. PA 66:10326. SA 83N2349.

Guttmann, Joseph. (1981). Various measures of moral judgment as a function of social pressure. *Journal of Psychology*, *108*, 165-171. SA 83N2350.

Guy, Rebecca F. (1979). Verbal flux in dyadic conversation. *Free Inquiry in Creative Sociology*, *7*, 52-56. SA 80K5521.

Guyer, Melvin; & Perkel, Barbara. (1973). Experimental games: A bibliography. (1945-1971). *Catalog of Selected Documents in Psychology*, *3*, 47-48. PA 52-5180.

Guyot, Gary W.; Byrd, Gary R.; & Caudle, Richard. (1980). Classroom seating: An expression of situational territoriality in humans. *Small Group Behavior*, *11*, 120-128. SA 80L0083.

Guzzo, Richard A. (Ed.) (1982). *Improving group decision making in organizations: Approaches from theory and research*. New York: Academic Press.

Guzzo, Richard A.; Wagner, David B.; Maguire, Eamonn L.; Herr, Barbara; & Hawley, Charles. (1986). Implicit theories and the evaluation of group process and performance. *Organizational Behavior and Human Decision Processes*, *37*, 279-295. PA 73:19797.

Guzzo, Richard A.; & Waters, James A. (1982). The expression of affect and the performance of decision-making groups. *Journal of Applied Psychology*, *67*, 67-74. PA 67:9764.

Haas, Adelaide; & Sherman, Mark A. (1982). Conversational topic as a function of role and gender. *Psychological Reports, 51*, 453-454. PA 69:12657.

Haas, David F.; & Deseran, Forrest A. (1981). Trust and symbolic exchange. *Social Psychology Quarterly, 44*, 3-13. PA 67:1222. SA 82M1462.

Haber, Gilda M. (1980). Territorial invasion in the classroom: Invadee response. *Environment and Behavior, 12*, 17-31. PA 65:10379. SA 84O0833.

Haber, Gilda M. (1982). Spatial relations between dominants and marginals. *Social Psychology Quarterly, 45*, 219-228. SA 83N2351.

Haccoun, Robert R.; & Klimoski, Richard J. (1975). Negotiator status and accountability source: A study of negotiator behavior. *Organizational Behavior and Human Performance, 14*, 342-359. PA 55:9728.

Haccoun, Robert R.; & Turcotte, Rejean. (1983). The moderating effect of risk on the outcomes of negotiations anticipating two forms of arbitration. *Canadian Journal of Behavioural Science, 15*, 93-105. PA 71:3973.

Hacker, Helen M. (1981). Blabbermouths and clams: Sex differences in self-disclosure in same-sex and cross-sex friendship dyads. *Psychology of Women Quarterly, 5*, 385-401. PA 67:3529. SA 82M4023.

Hackney, Harold. (1974). Facial gestures and subject expression of feelings. *Journal of Counseling Psychology, 21*, 173-178. PA 52:10021.

Hadar, Uri; Steiner, T. J.; & Rose, F. Clifford. (1985). Head movement during listening turns in conversation. *Journal of Nonverbal Behavior, 9*, 214-228. PA 72:19963.

Hagen, Beverly H. (1983). Managing conflict in all-women groups. *Social Work with Groups, 6*(3-4), 95-104. PA 71:20448.

Hagen, Beverly H.; & Burch, Genevieve. (1985). The relationship of group process and group task accomplishment to group member satisfaction. *Small Group Behavior, 16*, 211-233. PA 73:11726.

Halas, Elzbieta. (1981). Symboliczny interakcjonizm — wielosc orientacji a podstawy jednosci perspektywy [Symbolic interactions: Multiplicity of orientations foundations of unity of perspective]. *Studia Socjologiczne*, No. 4 (83), 103-114. PA 72:17312.

Haley, William E.; & Strickland, Bonnie R. (1986). Interpersonal betrayal and cooperation: Effects on self-evaluation in depression.

Journal of Personality and Social Psychology, 50, 386-391. PA 73:14428.

Halford, Kim; & Foddy, M. (1982). Cognitive and social skills correlates of social anxiety. *British Journal of Clinical Psychology, 21*, 17-28. PA 68:5784.

Hall, Edward T. (1959). *The silent language*. New York: Doubleday.

Hall, Edward T. (1966). *The hidden dimension*. New York: Doubleday.

Hall, Judith A. (1980). Voice tone and persuasion. *Journal of Personality and Social Psychology, 38*, 924-934. PA 65:12738.

Hall, Judith A. (1984). *Nonverbal sex differences*. Baltimore: Johns Hopkins University Press.

Hall, Judith A.; & Braunwald, Karen G. (1981). Gender cues in conversations. *Journal of Personality and Social Psychology, 40*, 99-110. PA 66:12765.

Hall, Peter M. (1985). Asymmetric relationships and processes of power. *Studies in Symbolic Interaction*, Suppl. 1, 309-344. PA 73:19798. SA 86Q3071.

Halliday, Kirk W. (1982). Group power and social reinforcement. *Psychological Reports, 51*, 618. PA 69:12658.

Hallinan, Maureen T. (1979). Structural effects on children's friendships and cliques. *Social Psychology Quarterly, 42*, 43-54. SA 80K4177.

Hallinan, Maureen T.; & Hutchins, Edwin E. (1980). Structural effects on dyadic change. *Social Forces, 59*, 225-245. SA 81L6526.

Hallinan, Maureen T.; & McFarland, David D. (1975). Higher order stability conditions in mathematical models of sociometric or cognitive structure. *Journal of Mathematical Sociology, 4*, 131-148. PA 56:9831.

Halmiova, O.; & Potasova, A. (1985). [Binary stimulus classification: Regulation by communication]. *Studia Psychologica, 27*, 125-131. PA 73:17207.

Hama, Yasuhisa. (1980). The effect of goal setting on cooperative responding in social interaction using the PD game. *Japanese Journal of Experimental Social Psychology, 19*, 137-145. PA 65:12724.

Hamburger, Henry; Guyer, Melvin; & Fox, John. (1975). Group size and cooperation. *Journal of Conflict Resolution, 19*, 503-531. PA 55:4503.

Hamby, Russell R. (1978a). Effects of gender and sex-role on tension and satisfaction in small groups. *Psychological Reports, 42*, 403-410.

PA 62:1047. SA 81L6527.

Hamby, Russell R. (1978b). Gender and sex-role behavior in problem solving groups. *Sociological Focus, 11*(3), 211-219. SA 79K1096.

Hamid, Paul N. (1974). Actual and schematic interaction distances in children. *New Zealand Journal of Educational Studies, 9*(2), 127-133. PA 54:11456.

Hamilton, V. Lee. (1978). Obedience and responsibility: A jury simulation. *Journal of Personality and Social Psychology, 36*, 126-146.

Hammitt, William E. (1983). Toward an ecological approach to perceived crowding in outdoor recreation. *Leisure Sciences, 5*, 309-320. PA 71:6736.

Hammond, Kenneth R.; & Grassia, Janet. (1985). The cognitive side of conflict: From theory to resolution of policy disputes. *Applied Social Psychology Annual, 6*, 233-254. PA 73:9093.

Hamner, W. Clay. (1974). Effects of bargaining strategy and pressure to reach agreement in a stalemated negotiation. *Journal of Personality and Social Psychology, 30*, 458-467.

Hamner, W. Clay; & Harnett, Donald L. (1974). Goal setting, performance and satisfaction in an interdependent task. *Organizational Behavior and Human Performance, 12*, 217-230. PA 53:5199.

Hamner, W. Clay; & Harnett, Donald L. (1975). The effects of information and aspiration level on bargaining behavior. *Journal of Experimental Social Psychology, 11*, 329-342. PA 54:9565.

Hancock, Rodney D.; & Sorrentino, Richard M. (1980). The effects of expected future interaction and prior group support on the conformity process. *Journal of Experimental Social Psychology, 16*, 261-269. PA 65:12739.

Handlin, Velma; Breed, George; Noll, Gary; & Watkins, John. (1974). Encounter groups process as a function of group length: The race toward confrontation, support, and living in the here and now. *Small Group Behavior, 5*, 259-273. PA 54:2972.

Hanley-Dunn, Patricia; Maxwell, Scott E.; & Santos, John F. (1985). Interpretation of interpersonal interactions: The influence of loneliness. *Personality and Social Psychology Bulletin, 11*, 445-456. PA 74:4000.

Hansell, Stephen. (1981). Ego development and peer friendship networks. *Sociology of Education, 54*, 51-63. SA 81L4928.

Hansell, Stephen; Tackaberry, Sara N.; & Slavin, Robert E. (1981). Cooperation, competition, and the structure of student peer groups. *Representative Research in Social Psychology, 12*, 46-62.

Hansen, William B.; & Altman, Irwin. (1976). Decorating personal places: A descriptive analysis. *Environment and Behavior, 8*, 491-504. PA 58:6307.

Hansson, Robert O.; & Jones, Warren H. (1981). Loneliness, cooperation, and conformity among American undergraduates. *Journal of Social Psychology, 115*, 103-108.

Hansson, Robert O.; Slade, Kenneth M.; & Slade, Pamela S. (1978). Urban-rural differences in responsiveness to an altruistic model. *Journal of Social Psychology, 105*, 99-105. PA 62:10970.

Harackiewicz, Judith M.; & Larson, James R. (1986). Managing motivation: The impact of supervisor feedback on subordinate task interest. *Journal of Personality and Social Psychology, 51*, 547-556. PA 74:1084.

Harada, Junji. (1985). Bystander intervention: The effect of ambiguity of the helping situation and the interpersonal relationship between bystanders. *Japanese Psychological Research, 27*, 177-184. PA 74:10188.

Harari, Herbert; Harari, Oren; & White, Robert V. (1985). The reaction to rape by American male bystanders. *Journal of Social Psychology, 125*, 653-658. PA 74:10216.

Harari, Herbert; Mohr, Deborah; & Hosey, Karen R. (1980). Faculty helpfulness to students: A comparison of compliance techniques. *Personality and Social Psychology Bulletin, 6*, 373-377. PA 66:5749.

Harari, Oren; & Graham, William K. (1975). Tasks and task consequences as factors in individual and group brainstorming. *Journal of Social Psychology, 95*, 61-65. PA 54:3013.

Hardin, Garrett. (1968). The tragedy of the commons. *Science, 162*, 1243-1248.

Hardin, Russell. (1982). Exchange theory on strategic bases. *Social Science Information, 21*(2), 251-272. PA 71:20449.

Harding, D. E. (1986). "Confrontation": The game people play. *Transactional Analysis Journal, 16*(2), 99-109. PA 74:15525.

Hardy, Charles J.; Hall, Evelyn G.; & Prestholdt, Perry H. (1986). The mediational role of social influence in the perception of exertion. *Journal of Sport Psychology, 8*, 88-104. PA 74:25074.

Hare, A. Paul. (1973). Group decision by consensus: Reaching unity in the Society of Friends. *Sociological Inquiry, 43*, 75–84.

Hare, A. Paul. (1976). *Handbook of small group research* (2nd ed.). New York: Free Press.

Hare, A. Paul. (1978). A comparison of Bales' IPA and Parsons' AGIL category systems. *Journal of Social Psychology, 105*, 309–310. PA 63:5114.

Hare, A. Paul. (1980). Consensus versus majority vote: A laboratory experiment. *Small Group Behavior, 11*, 131–143. SA 82M1463.

Hare, A. Paul. (1982). *Creativity in small groups.* Beverly Hills, CA: Sage.

Hare, · A. Paul. (1985). *Social interaction as drama: Applications from conflict resolution.* Beverly Hills, CA: Sage.

Hare, A. P[aul]. (1986). Conformity and creativity in negotiations: Israeli-Egyptian examples. *Israel Social Science Research, 4*(2), 21–33.

Hare, A. Paul. (1989). New field theory: SYMLOG research 1960–1988. *Advances in Group Processes, 6*, 229–257.

Hare, A. Paul; & Blumberg, Herbert H. (1988). *Dramaturgical analysis of social interaction.* New York: Praeger.

Hare, A. Paul; Kritzer, Herbert M.; & Blumberg, Herbert H. (1979). Functional analysis of persuasive interaction in a role-playing experiment. *Journal of Social Psychology, 107*, 77–88. PA 64:3250.

Hare, A. Paul; & Mueller, John. (1979). Categories for exchange analysis in small groups: With an illustration from group psychotherapy. *Sociological Inquiry, 49*, 57–64. SA 80K8689.

Hare, A. Paul; & Naveh, David. (1984). Group development at Camp David summit, 1978. *Small Group Behavior, 15*, 299–318. SA 85O6023.

Hare, A. Paul; & Naveh, David. (1985). Creative problem solving: Camp David Summit, 1978. *Small Group Behavior, 16*, 123–138. PA 73:11729. SA 86Q4840.

Hare, A. Paul; & Naveh, David. (1986). Conformity and creativity: Camp David, 1978. *Small Group Behavior, 17*, 243–268.

Hargreaves, C. P.; & Fuller, M. F. (1984). Some analyses of data from eye-contact studies. *British Journal of Social Psychology, 21*, 77–82. PA 71:28605.

Haring, Vojto. (1976). [Psychoterritorial competence feeling and behavior]. *Ceskoslovenska Psychologie, 20*, 405–410. PA 65:3246.

Harkins, Stephen G. (1987). Social loafing and social facilitation. *Journal of Experimental Social Psychology, 23*, 1–18.

Harkins, Stephen G.; & Jackson, Jeffrey M. (1985). The role of evaluation in eliminating social loafing. *Personality and Social Psychology Bulletin, 11*, 457–465. PA 74:4001.

Harkins, Stephen G.; Latané, Bibb; & Williams, Kipling. (1980). Social loafing: Allocating effort or taking it easy? *Journal of Experimental Social Psychology, 16*, 457–465. PA 66:5750.

Harkins, Stephen G.; & Petty, Richard E. (1982). Effects of task difficulty and task uniqueness on social loafing. *Journal of Personality and Social Psychology, 43*, 1214–1229. PA 70:1049.

Harper, Nancy L.; & Askling, Lawrence R. (1980). Group communication and quality of task solution in a media production organization. *Communication Monographs, 47*, 77–100. PA 66:3605. SA 84O2585.

Harper, Robert G.; Wiens, Arthur N.; & Matarazzo, Joseph D. (1978) *Nonverbal communication: The state of the art.* New York: Wiley.

Harré, Rom. (1979). *Social being: A theory for social psychology.* Totowa, NJ: Rowman, Littlefield.

Harrell, W. Andrew. (1980). Retaliatory aggression by high and low Machiavellians against remorseful and non-remorseful wrongdoers. *Social Behavior and Personality, 8*, 217–220. PA 66:10327.

Harrell, W. Andrew; & Goltz, J. Walter. (1980). Effect of victim's need and previous accusation of theft upon bystander's reaction to theft. *Journal of Social Psychology, 112*, 41–49. PA 60:8042.

Harrell, W. Andrew; & Hartnagel, Timothy. (1976). The impact of Machiavellianism and the trustfulness of the victim on laboratory theft. *Sociometry, 39*, 157–165. PA 56:7902.

Harries, Keith D.; & Stadler, Stephen J. (1983). Determinism revisited: Assault and heat stress in Dallas, 1980. *Environment and Behavior, 15*, 235–256. PA 70:4569.

Harrigan, Jinni A.; & Steffen, John J. (1983). Gaze as a turn-exchange signal in group conversations. *British Journal of Social Psychology, 22*, 167–168. PA 71:6694.

Harris, Bruce; Luginbuhl, James E.; & Fishbein, Jill E. (1978). Density and personal space in a field setting. *Social Psychology, 41*, 350–353.

Harris, Mary B. (1977). Sex-role stereotypes, models' race, and imitation. *Psychological Reports*, *41*, 875-885. PA 60:11662.

Harris, Mary B.; & Bays, Gail. (1973). Altruism and sex roles. *Psychological Reports*, *32*, 1002. PA 56:681.

Harris, Mary B.; & Ho, Junghwan. (1984). Effects of degree, locus, and controllability of dependency, and sex of subject on anticipated and actual helping. *Journal of Social Psychology*, *122*, 245-255. PA 72:6629.

Harris, Richard J.; & Joyce, Mark A. (1980). What's fair? It depends on how you phrase the question. *Journal of Personality and Social Psychology*, *38*, 165-179. PA 65:5385.

Harrison, Albert A.; & Connors, Mary M. (1984). Groups in exotic environments. *Advances in Experimental Social Psychology*, *18*, 49-87.

Harrison, Wayne; & McCallum, J. Richard. (1983). Interdependence theory. In H. H. Blumberg, A. P. Hare, V. Kent, & M. F. Davies (Eds.), *Small groups and social interaction* (Vol. 2, pp. 413-428). Chichester: John Wiley.

Hart, Edward W.; & Sung, Yong H. (1976). Computer and experimental simulation of triad decision making. *Behavioral Science*, *21*, 532-547. PA 58:1098.

Hart, Roland J.; & Brown, Bruce L. (1974). Interpersonal information conveyed by the content and vocal aspects of speech. *Speech Monographs*, *41*, 371-380. PA 54:9595.

Hart, Stuart L. (1985). Toward quality criteria for collective judgments. *Organizational Behavior and Human Decision Processes*, *36*, 209-228. PA 73:3670.

Hartman, E. Alan. (1974). Degree of cooperation in a prisoner's dilemma as a function of sex roles, responsiveness, and the exploitativeness of the simulated other. *Personality and Social Psychology Bulletin*, *1*, 287-289. PA 56:2306.

Hartman, E. Alan. (1980). Motivational bases of sex differences in choice behavior. *Journal of Conflict Resolution*, *24*, 455-475. PA 64:12491.

Hartman, John J. (1979). Small group methods of personal change. *Annual Review of Psychology*, *30*, 453-476.

Hartmann, Terje. (1981). Conflict of experience: A categorization model for studying verbal interaction. *Scandinavian Journal of Psychology*, *22*, 207-213. PA 68:1089.

Hartnett, John J.; Bailey, Kent G.; & Hartley, Craig S. (1974). Body height, position, and sex as determinants of personal space. *Journal of Psychology*, *87*, 129-136 . PA 52:10072.

Hartnett, John J.; Gottlieb, J.; & Hayes, R. L. (1976). Social facilitation theory and experimenter attractiveness. *Journal of Social Psychology*, *99*, 293-294.

Harvey, John H. (Ed.). (1981). *Cognition, social behavior, and the environment*. Hillsdale, NJ: Erlbaum.

Harvey, Michael D.; & Enzle, Michael E. (1977). Effects of a dependent other's psychological need on subjects' use of power in a simulation game. *Simulation and Games*, *8*, 405-418. PA 60:11716.

Harvey, Virginia; DiLuzio, Geneva; & Hunter, William J. (1975). A comparison of verbal and nonverbal groups. *Small Group Behavior*, *6*, 210-219. PA 55:2325.

Harzem, Peter; & Damon, S. G. (1975). Social interactions of a group of severely retarded people with staff and peers in a ward setting. *Psychological Reports*, *36*, 959-966. SA 78J4689.

Hashiguchi, Katsuhisa. (1974). [The number of decision makers and the level of risk taking within a group]. *Japanese Journal of Experimental Social Psychology*, *14*(2), 121-131. PA 54:11664.

Haskell, Robert E. (1975). Presumptions of group work: A value analysis. *Small Group Behavior*, *6*, 469-486. SA 77I8729.

Haskell, Robert E. (1978). An analogic model of small group behavior. *International Journal of Group Psychotherapy*, *28*, 27-54. SA 80L0084.

Haskell, Robert E. (1982). The matrix of group talk: An empirical method of analysis and validation. *Small Group Behavior*, *13*, 165-191. SA 83M7342.

Hass, R. Glen; & Mann, Robert W. (1976). Anticipatory belief change: Persuasion or impression management? *Journal of Personality and Social Psychology*, *34*, 105-111.

Hastie, Reid; Penrod, Steven D.; & Pennington, Nancy. (1983). *Inside the jury*. Cambridge, MA: Harvard University Press.

Hastorf, Albert H.; Wildfogel, Jeffrey; & Cassman, Ted. (1979). Acknowledgement of handicap as a tactic in social interaction. *Journal of Personality and Social Psychology*, *37*, 1790-1797. PA 65:1269.

Hatfield, Elaine. (1983). Equity theory and research: An overview. In H. H. Blumberg, A. P.

Hare, V. Kent, & M. F. Davies (Eds.), *Small groups and social interaction* (Vol. 2, pp. 401–411). Chichester: John Wiley.

Hatfield, Elaine; Roberts, Daniel; & Schmidt, Lynn. (1980). The impact of sex and physical attractiveness on an initial social encounter. *Recherches de Psychologie Sociale*, No. 2, 27–40. PA 68:1090.

Hatfield, Frederick C. (1978). Effects of interpersonal attraction and tolerance-intolerance of ambiguity on athletic team productivity. *International Journal of Sport Psychology*, 9, 214–226. PA 63:986.

Hauser, Stuart T.; & Shapiro, Roger L. (1976). An approach to the analysis of faculty-student interactions in small groups. *Human Relations*, 29, 819–832. PA 57:6645.

Hawes, Leonard C.; & Foley, Joseph M. (1978). Stationarity of group discussion. *Small Group Behavior*, 9, 518–528. SA 80K4178.

Hayakaya, Tsuguyo. (1972). [The effect of inequity upon distributing behavior of children]. *Japanese Journal of Educational Psychology*, 20, 162–169. PA 53:3024.

Hayano, David M. (1978). Strategies for the management of luck and action in an urban poker parlor. *Urban Life*, 6(4), 475–488. SA 79K2628.

Hayduk, Leslie A. (1978). Personal space: An evaluative and orienting overview. *Psychological Bulletin*, 85, 117–134. PA 62:3561.

Hayduk, Leslie A. (1981a). The permeability of personal space. *Canadian Journal of Behavioural Science*, 13, 274–287. PA 68:1091.

Hayduk, Leslie A. (1981b). The shape of personal space: An experimental investigation. *Canadian Journal of Behavioural Science*, 13, 87–93. PA 67:5708.

Hayduk, Leslie A. (1983). Personal space: Where we now stand. *Psychological Bulletin*, 94, 293–335. PA 71:1314.

Hayduk, Leslie A.; & Mainprize, Steven. (1980). Personal space of the blind. *Social Psychology Quarterly*, 43, 216–223. PA 66:1586.

Hays, Robert B. (1985). A longitudinal study of friendship development. *Journal of Personality and Social Psychology*, 48, 909–924.

Heath, Christian C. (1982). The display of recipiency: An instance of a sequential relationship in speech and body movement. *Semiotica*, 42(2–4), 147–167. SA 84N7286.

Hechter, Michael. (1982). A theory of group solidarity. *Research in Marketing*, Suppl. 1, 285–324. PA 70:5625.

Heckathorn, Douglas. (1978). A paradigm for bargaining and a test of two bargaining models. *Behavioral Science*, 23, 73–85. PA 62:13625. SA 79J9639.

Heckathorn, Douglas. (1980). A unified model for bargaining and conflict. *Behavioral Science*, 25, 261–284. PA 66:1227.

Hedge, Alan. (1982). The open plan office: A systematic investigation of employee reactions to their work environment. *Environment and Behavior*, 14, 519–542. PA 69:4582.

Hedge, B. J.; Everitt, B. S.; & Frith, Christopher D. (1978). The role of gaze in dialogue. *Acta Psychologica*, 42, 453–475. PA 63:9631.

Hegedus, D. M.; & Rasmussen, R. V. (1986). Task effectiveness and interaction process of modified nominal group technique in solving an evaluation problem. *Journal of Management*, 12, 545–560. PA 74:18728.

Hegtvedt, Karen A.; & Cook, Karen S. (1987). The role of justice in conflict situations. *Advances in Group Processes*, 4, 109–136.

Heider, John. (1974). Catharsis in human potential encounter. *Journal of Humanistic Psychology*, 14(4), 27–47. PA 54:2973.

Heilman, Madeline E. (1976). Oppositional behavior as a function of influence attempt intensity and retaliation threat. *Journal of Personality and Social Psychology*, 33, 574–578. PA 56:7952.

Heilman, Madeline E.; Hornstein, Harvey A.; Cage, Jack H.; & Herschlag, Judith K. (1984). Reactions to prescribed leader behavior as a function of role perspective: The case of the Vroom-Yetton model. *Journal of Applied Psychology*, 69, 50–60. PA 71:12197.

Heimstra, Norman W.; & McFarling, Leslie H. (1974). *Environmental psychology*. Monterey, CA: Brooks/Cole.

Heisterkanp, Gunter. (1974). [Group dialogue in the classroom]. *Gruppendynamik Forschung und Praxis*, 5, 410–420. PA 55:13395.

Heller, Jack F.; Groff, Bradford D.; & Solomon, Sheldon H. (1977). Toward an understanding of crowding: The role of physical interaction. *Journal of Personality and Social Psychology*, 35, 183–190. PA 62:3563.

Heller, Otto; & Kruger, Hans Peter. (1974). [Direct scaling in sociometry]. *Psychologische Beitrage*, 16, 203–226. PA 54:7462.

Heller, Tamar. (1978). Group decision-making by mentally retarded adults. *American Journal of Mental Deficiency*, 82, 480–486. SA 80K5522.

Heller, Trudy; & Van Til, Jon. (1982). Leadership and followership: Some summary propositions. *Journal of Applied Behavioral Science, 18,* 405–414. PA 69:999.

Helm, Bob; Nacci, Peter; & Tedeschi, James T. (1976). Attraction, expertise, and coalition choices. *Journal of Psychology, 92,* 39–44. PA 56:682.

Ilelson, Ravenna; & Mitchell, Valory. (1978). Personality. *Annual Review of Psychology, 29,* 179–221. PA 62:11048.

Hembroff, Larry A. (1982). Resolving status inconsistency: An expectation states theory and test. *Social Forces, 61,* 183–205. PA 69:7880.

Hembroff, Larry A.; & Myers, David E. (1984). Status characteristics: Degrees of task relevance and decision processes. *Social Psychology Quarterly, 47,* 337–346. PA 72:30782. SA 8506024.

Hendrick, Clyde (Ed.). (1987a). *Group Processes.* Newbury Park, CA: Sage. [Other title: *Review of Personality and Social Psychology, 8*].

Hendrick, Clyde (Ed.). (1987b). *Group Processes and Intergroup Relations.* Newbury Park, CA: Sage. [Other title: *Review of Personality and Social Psychology, 9*].

Hendrick, Hal W. (1979). Differences in group problem-solving behavior and effectiveness as a function of abstractness. *Journal of Applied Psychology, 64,* 518–525. PA 65:1235.

Hendrick, Susan S.; Hendrick, Clyde; & Adler, Nancy L. (1988). Romantic relationships: Love, satisfaction, and staying together. *Journal of Personality and Social Psychology, 54,* 980–988.

Hendricks, Marion N. (1984). A focusing group: Model for a new kind of group process. *Small Group Behavior, 15,* 155–171.

Hendricks, Michael; & Bootzin, Richard. (1976). Race and sex as stimuli for negative affect and physical avoidance. *Journal of Social Psychology, 98,* 111–120. PA 56:2354.

Hendrickx, Mark. (1982). *Evaluatietechnieken.* Leuven, Belgium: Infodok.

Henley, Nancy M. (1977). *Body politics: Power, sex, and nonverbal communication.* Englewood Cliffs, NJ: Prentice-Hall.

Henry, Alexis D.; Nelson, David L.; & Duncombe, Linda W. (1984). Choice making in group and individual activity. *American Journal of Occupational Therapy, 38*(4), 245–251. PA 72:06630.

Henss, Ronald; & Ostmann, Axel. (1985).

Verhandlungsergebnisse und Koalitionsbildung in einem kooperativen Normalformspiel — Empirische Befunde [Negotiation results and coalition formation in a cooperative normal form: Empirical findings]. *Zeitschrift fur Sozialpsychologie, 16,* 116–127. PA 73:14429.

Heretick, Donna M. (1984). Trust-suspicion and gender differences in interpersonal functioning. *Journal of Research in Personality, 18,* 27–40. PA 72:6631.

Herman, Reg. (1983). Intervening in groups: A repertoire and language of group skills for self-directed learning in decision-making groups. *Small Group Behavior, 14,* 445–464. PA 71:23058.

Herold, David M. (1977). Two-way influence processes in leader-follower dyads. *Academy of Management Journal, 20,* 224–237. PA 59:5633.

Herskin, Bjarne K. (1979). *Grupper og gruppeprocesser.* [Copenhagen]: Samfundslitteratur. [*National Union Catalog,* register no. a-043–453].

Heslin, Richard; & Boss, Diane. (1980). Nonverbal intimacy in airport arrival and departure. *Personality and Social Psychology Bulletin, 6,* 248–252. PA 66:1228.

Heslin, Richard; Nguyen, Tuan D.; & Nguyen, Michele L. (1983). Meaning of touch: The case of touch from a stranger or same sex person. *Journal of Nonverbal Behavior, 7,* 147–157. PA 71:20480.

Heslin, Richard; & Patterson, Miles L. (1982). *Nonverbal behavior and social psychology.* New York: Plenum.

Hessel, Marek. (1981). Bargaining costs and rational behavior: A simple model. *Journal of Conflict Resolution, 25,* 535–558. PA 67:03530.

Hessel, Marek. (1984). Mutual perceptions in bargaining: A quantitative approach. *Behavioral Science, 29,* 221–232.

Heuer, Larry B.; Penrod, Steven. (1986). Procedural preference as a function of conflict intensity. *Journal of Personality and Social Psychology, 51,* 700–710. PA 74:4002.

Hewes, Dean E. (1985). Systematic biases in coded social interaction data. *Human Communication Research, 11,* 554–574. PA 73:14430.

Hewett, Thomas T.; O'Brien, Gordon E.; & Hornik, John. (1974). The effects of work organization, leadership style, and member compatibility upon the productivity of small groups working on a manipulative task. *Orga-*

nizational Behavior and Human Performance, *11*, 283–301.

Hewitt, Jay; & Lewis, Gregory. (1985). Observers' reaction to touchers. *Perceptual and Motor Skills,* *60*, 452–454. PA 73:14431.

Hewstone, Miles. (Ed.). (1984). *Attribution theory: Social and functional extensions.* Oxford, England: Basil Blackwell.

Hewstone, Miles; Argyle, Michael; & Furnham, Adrian. (1982). Favouritism, fairness and joint profit in long-term relationships. *European Journal of Social Psychology,* *12*, 283–295.

Heyman, Bob; & Shaw, Monica. (1978). Constructs of relationship. *Journal for the Theory of Social Behaviour,* *8*, 231–262. PA 68:1092.

Hick, Kenneth W.; Mitchell, Terence R.; Bell, Cecil H.; & Carter, William B. (1975). Determinants of interpersonal disclosure: Some competitive tests. *Personality and Social Psychology Bulletin,* *1*, 620–623. PA 56:4002.

Hieden, Josef. (1974). [The problem of pedagogical institutions in the pedagogy of groups, based on selected literature]. *Gruppendynamik Forschung und Praxis,* *5*, 455–460. PA 55:12951.

Hiers, J. Manning; & Heckel, Robert V. (1977). Seating choice, leadership, and locus of control. *Journal of Social Psychology,* *103*, 313–314. PA 60:9302.

Higbee, Kenneth L. (1973). Group influence on self-disclosure. *Psychological Reports,* *32*, 903–909. PA 56:644.

Higgins, E. Tory. (1976). Social class differences in verbal communicative accuracy: A question of which question? *Psychological Bulletin,* *83*, 695–714. PA 56:5970.

Hill, Barbara J. (1982) An analysis of conflict resolution techniques: from problem-solving workshops to theory. *Journal of Conflict Resolution,* *26*, 109–138.

Hill, Charles T.; Rubin, Zick; Peplau, Letitia A.; & Willard, Susan G. (1979). The volunteer couple: Sex differences, couple commitment, and participation in research on interpersonal relationships. *Social Psychology Quarterly,* *42*, 415–420. PA 65:10380.

Hill, Charles T.; & Stull, Donald E. (1982). Disclosure reciprocity: Conceptual and measurement issues. *Social Psychology Quarterly,* *45*, 238–244. PA 70:3386.

Hill, Gayle W. (1982). Group versus individual performance: Are N + 1 heads better than one?

Psychological Bulletin, *91*, 517–539. PA 68:3527.

Hill, Norman C.; & Ritchie, J. B. (1977). The effect of self-esteem on leadership and achievement: A paradigm and a review. *Group and Organization Studies,* *2*, 491–503. PA 60:12838. SA 78J3318.

Hill, R. D.; Blackham, R. E.; & Crane, D. Russell. (1982). The effect of the marital relationship on personal space orientation in married couples. *Journal of Social Psychology,* *118*, 23–28. PA 69:12660.

Hill, Raymond E. (1975). Interpersonal compatibility and workgroup performance. *Journal of Applied Behavioral Science,* *11*, 210–219. PA 54:7463.

Hill, Thomas E.; & Schmitt, Neal. (1977). Individual differences in leadership decision making. *Organizational Behavior and Human Performance,* *19*, 353–367. PA 60:2023.

Hill, Timothy A. (1976). An experimental study of the relationship between opinionated leadership and small group consensus. *Communication Monographs,* *43*, 246–257. PA 59:7873. SA 78J1862.

Hill, Walter A.; & Hughes, David. (1974). Variations in leader behavior as a function of task type. *Organizational Behavior and Human Performance,* *11*, 83–96.

Hill, William Fawcett. (1977). Hill Interaction Matrix (HIM): The conceptual framework, derived rating scales, and an updated bibliography. *Small Group Behavior,* *8*, 251–268. SA 78J5901.

Hillery, Joseph M.; & Fugita, Stephen S. (1975). Group size effects in employment testing. *Educational and Psychological Measurement,* *35*, 745–750. PA 55:11092.

Hiltrop, Jean M.; & Rubin, Jeffrey Z. (1981). Position loss and image loss in bargaining. *Journal of Conflict Resolution,* *25*, 521–534. PA 67:3532.

Hiltrop, Jean M.; & Rubin, Jeffrey Z. (1982). Effects of intervention mode and conflict of interest on dispute resolution. *Journal of Personality and Social Psychology,* *42*, 665–672. PA 68:12614.

Hinde, Robert A. (1976). On describing relationships. *Journal of Child Psychology and Psychiatry and Allied Disciplines,* *17*, 1–19. PA 56:9833.

Hinde, Robert A. (1977). On assessing the bases of

partner preferences. *Behaviour, 62*, 1–9. PA 60:5230.

Hinde, Robert A. (1978). Interpersonal relationships: In quest of a science. *Psychological Medicine, 8*, 373–386. PA 63:3245.

Hinde, Robert A. (1979). *Towards understanding relationships*. London: Academic Press.

Hinde, Robert A. (Ed.). (1983). *Primate social relationships: An integrated approach*. Boston: Blackwell.

Hinde, R[obert] A.; & Stevenson-Hinde, Joan. (1976). Towards understanding relationships: Dynamic stability. In P. P. Bates & R. A. Hinde (Eds.), *Growing points in ethology* (pp. 451–479). Cambridge, England: Cambridge Univ. Press.

Hinsz, Verlin B.; & Davis, James H. (1984). Persuasive arguments theory, group polarization, and choice shifts. *Personality and Social Psychology Bulletin, 10*, 260–268. PA 72:17313.

Hirokawa, Randy Y. (1980). A comparative analysis of communication patterns within effective and ineffective decision-making groups. *Communication Monographs, 47*, 312–321. PA 67:1226.

Hirokawa, Randy Y. (1983). Group communication and problem-solving effectiveness: An investigation of group phases. *Human Communication Research, 9*, 291–305. PA 71:9483.

Hirokawa, Randy Y. (1985). Discussion procedures and decision-making performance: A test of a functional perspective. *Human Communication Research, 12*, 203–224. PA 74:4003.

Hirokawa, Randy Y. (1987). Why informed groups make faulty decisions: An investigation of possible interaction-based explanations. *Small Group Behavior, 18*, 3–29.

Hirokawa, Randy Y.; & Pace, Roger. (1983). A descriptive investigation of the possible communication-based reasons for effective and ineffective group decision making. *Communication Monographs, 50*, 363–379. PA 71:28607.

Hirose, Yukio. (1977). [Effects of group goal attainment upon status distribution and reward allocation]. *Japanese Journal of Experimental Social Psychology, 17*, 14–21. PA 64:10333.

Hirsch, Jerrold I. (1987). *The history of the National Training Laboratories, 1947–1986: Social equality through education and training*. New York: P. Lang.

Hirschhorn, Larry; & Krantz, James. (1982). Unconscious planning in a natural work group: A case study in process consultation. *Human Relations, 35*, 805–843. PA 69:7881.

Hitchman, M. G. (1975). The learning-performance dichotomy of social facilitation. In D. M. Landers (Ed.), *Psychology of sport and motor behavior: II*. University Park, PA: Penn State [HPER Series No. 10].

Hlavsa, Jaroslav; & Podrabsky, Jaroslav. (1973). The influence of dominance and submissiveness of creative productivity in dyads. *Studia Psychologica, 15*, 321–327. PA 52:5182.

Ho, Robert; & Lloyd, Jacqueline I. (1983). Intergroup attribution: The role of social categories in causal attribution for behaviour. *Australian Journal of Psychology, 35*, 49–59. PA 71:6696.

Ho, Robert; & Mitchell, Sandra. (1982). Students' nonverbal reaction to tutors' warm/cold nonverbal behavior. *Journal of Social Psychology, 118*, 121–130. PA 69:12661.

Hobson, Charles J. (1986). Factors affecting the frequency, timing, and sign of informal supervisory feedback to subordinates in a simulated work setting. *Multivariate Behavioral Research, 21*, 187–200. PA 73:27140.

Hoddinott, Elizabeth; Follingstad, Diane R. (1983). Effects of instructional set and personality variables on the use of touching. *Perceptual and Motor Skills, 56*, 299–309. PA 70:12638.

Hoffman, Eric. (1984). An internal dimensional analysis of the Least Preferred Co-worker measure. *Journal of Social Psychology, 123*, 35–42. PA 72:24194.

Hoffman, Eric; & Roman, Paul M. (1984). Criterion-related validity of the Least Preferred Co-worker measure. *Journal of Social Psychology, 122*, 79–84. PA 71:27659.

Hoffman, L. Richard. (1965). Group problem solving. *Advances in Experimental Social Psychology, 2*, 99–132.

Hoffman, L. Richard. (1979a). Applying experimental research on group problem solving to organizations. *Journal of Applied Behavioral Science, 15*, 375–391. SA 80K7130.

Hoffman, L. Richard. (Ed.). (1979b). *The group problem solving process: Studies of a valence model*. New York: Praeger.

Hogan, Daniel B. (1974). Encounter groups and human relations training: The case against applying traditional forms of statutory regulation.

Harvard Journal on Legislation, 11, 659–701. PA 53:5169.

Hogg, Michael A. (1985). Masculine and feminine speech in dyads and groups: A study of speech style and gender salience. *Journal of Language and Social Psychology, 4,* 99–112. PA 74:10189.

Hogg, Michael A.; & Turner, John C. (1985a). Interpersonal attraction, social identification and psychological group formation. *European Journal of Social Psychology, 15,* 51–66. PA 73:1126.

Hogg, Michael A.; & Turner, John C. (1985b). When liking begets solidarity: An experiment on the role of interpersonal attraction in psychological group formation. *British Journal of Social Psychology, 24,* 267–281. SA 86Q4841.

Hokanson, Jack E.; Loewenstein, David A.; Hedeen, Carla; & Howes, Mary J. (1986). Dysphoric college students and roommates: A study of social behaviors over a three-month period. *Personality and Social Psychology Bulletin, 12,* 311–324.

Holahan, Charles J. (1974). Experimental investigations of environment-behavior relationships in psychiatric facilities. *Man-Environment Systems, 4*(2), 109–113. PA 56:10435.

Holahan, Charles J. (1976). Environmental effects on outdoor social behavior in a low-income urban neighborhood: A naturalistic investigation. *Journal of Applied Social Psychology, 6,* 48–63. PA 56:7866.

Holahan, Charles J. (1977). Effects of urban size and heterogeneity on judged appropriateness of altruistic responses: Situational vs. subject variables. *Sociometry, 40,* 378–382.

Holahan, Charles J. (1986). Environmental psychology. *Annual Review of Psychology, 37,* 381–407.

Holban, Ion. (1972). [The sociometric test of personality]. *Revue de Pedagogie,* No. 6, 107–119. PA 52:5183.

Holland, Paul W.; & Leinhardt, Samuel. (1973). The structural implications of measurement error in sociometry. *Journal of Mathematical Sociology, 3,* 85–111. SA 75H5812.

Holland, Stephen M.; Fedler, Anthony J.; & Ditton, Robert B. (1986). The group representative bias: Another look. *Leisure Sciences, 8,* 79–91. PA 74:18730.

Hollander, Edwin P. (1958). Conformity, status, and idiosyncrasy credit. *Psychological Review, 65,* 117–127.

Hollander, Edwin P. (1983). Women and leadership. In H. H. Blumberg, A. P. Hare, V. Kent, & M. F. Davies. (Eds.), *Small groups and social interaction* (Vol. 1, pp. 423–436). Chichester, England: Wiley.

Hollander, Edwin P. (1985). Leadership and power. In G. Lindzey (Eds.), *Handbook of social psychology* (3rd ed., Vol. 2, pp. 485–538). New York: Random House.

Hollander, Edwin P.; & Yoder, Jan D. (1980). Some issues in comparing women and men as leaders. *Basic and Applied Social Psychology, 1,* 267–280. PA 65:10381.

Holleran, Brian P.; & Holleran, Paula R. (1976). Creativity revisited: A new role for group dynamics. *Journal of Creative Behavior, 10,* 130–137. PA 63:9632.

Holloway, Stephen; Tucker, Lyle; & Hornstein, Harvey A. (1977). The effects of social and nonsocial information on interpersonal behavior of males: The news makes news. *Journal of Personality and Social Psychology, 35,* 514–522.

Holly, Romuald. (1979). [Studies on informal leadership in small groups]. *Przeglad Psychologiczny, 22,* 457–478. PA 65:7940.

Holly, Romuald. (1980). Koncepcje przywodztwa nieformalnego w malych grupach spolecznych [Concepts of informal leadership in small social groups]. *Studia Socjologiczne,* No. 2 (77), 79–106. PA 70:5626.

Holmes, Catherine M.; Sholley, Barbara K.; & Walker, William E. (1980). Leader, follower, and isolate personality patterns in Black and White emergent leadership groups. *Journal of Psychology, 105,* 41–46. PA 66:1213. SA 82M1464.

Holt, Robert W. (1982). Perceptions of the equity and exchange processes in dyadic social relationships. *Perceptual and Motor Skills, 54,* 303–320. PA 68:8101.

Holtgraves, Thomas. (1986). Language structure in social interaction: Perceptions of direct and indirect speech acts and interactants who use them. *Journal of Personality and Social Psychology, 51,* 305–314. PA 73:29951.

Holzworth, James. (1983). Intervention in a cognitive conflict. *Organizational Behavior and Human Performance, 32,* 216–231. PA 71:3974.

Hong, Dae shik. (1979). The effects of concreteness, balance, and sex on the ratings of pleasantness and willingness to change relationship in triadic social relations. *Korean Journal of Psychology*, *2*(4), 217–232. PA 65:12740.

Hong, Lawrence K. (1978). Risky shift and cautious shift: Some direct evidence on the culture-value theory. *Social Psychology*, *41*, 342–346.

Höper, Claus-Jurgen; et al. (1976). *Awareness games: Personal growth through group interaction* (H. Davies, Trans.). New York: St. Martin's Press. (Original work published 1975)

Hoppe, Christiane M. (1979). Interpersonal aggression as a function of subject's sex, subject's sex role identification, opponent's sex, and degree of provocation. *Journal of Personality*, *47*, 317–329. PA 64:7925.

Horai, Joann; & Tedeschi, James T. (1975). Compliance and the use of threats and promises after a power reversal. *Behavioral Science*, *20*, 117–124. PA 54:11702. SA 76H7091.

Hore, Terry. (1976). Visual behavior in teacher-pupil dyads. *American Educational Research Journal*, *13*, 267–275. SA 80L0085.

Horejsi, Charles R. (1974). Small-group sex education for engaged couples. *Journal of Family Counseling*, *2*(2), 23–27. PA 53:10249.

Horenstein, David; & Gilbert, Shirley J. (1976). Anxiety, likeability, and avoidance as responses to self-disclosing communication. *Small Group Behavior*, *7*, 423–432. PA 61:1023.

Hornstein, Gail A. (1985). Intimacy in conversational style as a function of the degree of closeness between members of a dyad. *Journal of Personality and Social Psychology*, *49*, 671–681. PA 73:3674.

Hornstein, Harvey A.; LaKind, Elizabeth; Frankel, Gladys; & Manne, Stella. (1975). Effects of knowledge about remote social events on prosocial behavior, social conception, and mood. *Journal of Personality and Social Psychology*, *32*, 1038–1046.

Horwitz, Leonard. (1977). A group-centered approach to group psychotherapy. *International Journal of Group Psychotherapy*, *27*, 423–439. SA 80L0086.

Hottes, Joseph H.; & Kahn, Arnold. (1974). Sex differences in a mixed-motive conflict situation. *Journal of Personality*, *42*, 260–275. PA 53:1092.

Houlden, Pauline; LaTour, Stephen; Walker, Laurens; & Thibaut, John. (1978). Preference for modes of dispute resolution as a function of process and decision control. *Journal of Experimental Social Psychology*, *14*, 13–30. PA 60:9303.

House, James S.; & Wolf, Sharon. (1978). Effects of urban residence on interpersonal trust and helping behavior. *Journal of Personality and Social Psychology*, *36*, 1029–1043. PA 63:5422.

Howard, Judith A.; & Levinson, Randy. (1985). The overdue courtship of attribution and labeling. *Social Psychology Quarterly*, *48*, 191–202. PA 73:24476.

Howard, Nigel. (1976). Prisoner's Dilemma: The solution by general metagames. *Behavioral Science*, *21*, 524–531. PA 58:1054.

Howard, William; & Crano, William D. (1974). Effects of sex, conversation, location, and size of observer group on bystander intervention in a high risk situation. *Sociometry*, *37*, 491–507. PA 53:9479.

Howe, George W. (1987). Attributions of complex cause and the perception of marital conflict. *Journal of Personality and Social Psychology*, *53*, 1119–1128.

Howell, Sandy; Lederman, Carol; Owen, Victoria; & Solomon, Linda Z. (1978). Compliance as a function of status. *Journal of Social Psychology*, *106*, 291–292. PA 64:6565.

Howes, Mary J.; & Hokanson, Jack E. (1979). Conversational and social responses to depressive interpersonal behavior. *Journal of Abnormal Psychology*, *88*, 625–634. PA 63:5423.

Howes, Mary J.; Hokanson, Jack E.; & Loewenstein, David A. (1985). Induction of depressive affect after prolonged exposure to a mildly depressed individual. *Journal of Personality and Social Psychology*, *49*, 1110–1113. PA 73:3675.

Hrycenko, Igor; & Minton, Henry L. (1974). Internal-external control, power position, and satisfaction in task-oriented groups. *Journal of Personality and Social Psychology*, *30*, 871–878. PA 53:11580.

Huber, Vandra L.; & Neale, Margaret A. (1986). Effects of cognitive heuristics and goals on negotiator performance and subsequent goal setting. *Organizational Behavior and Human Decision Processes*, *38*, 342–365. PA 74:7163.

Huber, Vandra L.; & Neale, Margaret A. (1987). Effects of self- and competitor goals on performance in an interdependent bargaining task. *Journal of Applied Psychology*, *72*, 197–203. PA 74:25049.

Huesmann, L. Rowell; & Levinger, George. (1976). Incremental exchange theory: a formal model for progression in dyadic social interaction. *Advances in Experimental Social Psychology*, *9*, 191–229.

Huggard, Daniel C. (1975). Behavior and person perception in mixed motive games. *Journal of Social Psychology*, *96*, 143–144. PA 54:7513.

Hughes, Jeff; & Goldman, Morton. (1978). Eye contact, facial expression, sex, and the violation of personal space. *Perceptual and Motor Skills*, *46*, 579–584. PA 62:1055.

Huici, C. C. (1979). El estudio de los roles in grupos experimentales [The study of roles in experimental groups]. *Revista de Psicologia General y Aplicada*, *34*(158), 497–504. PA 67:7698.

Hull, Debra B.; & Schroeder, Harold E. (1979). Some interpersonal effects of assertion, nonassertion, and aggression. *Behavior Therapy*, *10*, 20–28. PA 62:5977.

Hulten, Burma H.; & DeVries, David L. (1976). Team competition and group practice: Effects on student achievement and attitudes. *Center for Social Organization of Schools Report, Johns Hopkins U.*, No. 212, 26 pages. PA 56:4766.

Humphreys, Paul; & Berger, Joseph. (1981). Theoretical consequences of the status characteristics formulation. *American Journal of Sociology*, *86*, 953–983.

Humphrys, Peter; & O'Brien, Gordon E. (1985). The proposal and evaluation of two models of small group productivity. *Australian Journal of Psychology*, *37*, 175–184. PA 74:13092.

Hunsaker, Phillip L.; & Hunsaker, David M. (1974). Luna I moon colony: An adapted format for analysis of group decision-making in a competitive setting. *Psychological Reports*, *35*, 411–414. PA 53:7292.

Hunter, John E. (1978). Dynamic sociometry. *Journal of Mathematical Sociology*, *6*, 87–138. SA 79J9641.

Hunter, John E.; Gerbing, David W.; & Boster, Franklin J. (1982). Machiavellian beliefs and personality: Construct invalidity of the Machiavellianism dimension. *Journal of Personality and Social Psychology*, *43*, 1293–1305.

Hurley, John R. (1975). "Some effects of trainers on their T groups" reconsidered. *Journal of Applied Behavioral Science*, *11*, 190–196. PA 54:7464.

Hurley, John R. (1976). Two prepotent interpersonal dimensions and the effects of trainers on T-groups. *Small Group Behavior*, *7*, 77–98. SA 77I8731.

Husain, Akbar; & Kureshi, Afzal. (1983). Value similarity and friendship: A study of interpersonal attraction. *Psychologia An International Journal of Psychology in the Orient*, *26*, 167–174. PA 71:23059.

Hussy, Walter. (1979a). Game behavior depending on kind of information and degree of risk in an alternating-sequential 2 * 2 game. *Archiv fur Psychologie*, *131*, 233–248. PA 64:12455.

Hussy, Walter. (1979b). [Game behavior depending on kind of information and degree of risk in an alternating-sequential 2 * 2 game]. *Archiv fur Psychologie*, *132*, 49–62. PA 64:12456.

Huston, Ted L.; & Levinger, George. (1978). Interpersonal attraction and relationships. *Annual Review of Psychology*, *29*, 115–156. PA 62:10971.

Huston, Ted L.; & Robins, Elliot. (1982). Conceptual and methodological issues in studying close relationships. *Journal of Marriage and the Family*, *44*, 901–925. PA 70:1050.

Huston, Ted L.; Ruggiero, Mary; Conner, Ross; & Geis, Gilbert. (1981). Bystander intervention into crime: A study based on naturally-occurring episodes. *Social Psychology Quarterly*, *44*, 14–23. PA 67:1227.

Hyde, J. S. (1984). How large are gender differences in aggression? A developmental meta-analysis. *Developmental Psychology*, *20*, 722–736. PA 71:25608.

Hyde, J. S. (1986). Gender differences in aggression. In J. S. Hyde & M. C. Linn (Eds.), *The psychology of gender: Advances through meta-analysis* (pp. 51–66). Baltimore: MD; Johns Hopkins University Press.

Hynan, Michael T.; & Esselman, Judith A. (1981). Victims and aggression. *Bulletin of the Psychonomic Society*, *18*, 169–172. PA 68:1125.

Hynan, Michael T.; Harper, Suzanne; Wood, Cynthia; & Kallas, Carol. (1980). Parametric effects of blocking and winning in a competition paradigm of human aggression. *Bulletin of the Psychonomic Society*, *16*, 295–298.

Ickes, William. (1984). Compositions in Black and White: Determinants of interaction in interracial dyads. *Journal of Personality and Social Psychology*, *47*, 330–341. PA 72:1234.

Ickes, William; & Barnes, Richard D. (1977). The role of sex and self-monitoring in unstructured dyadic interactions. *Journal of Personality and Social Psychology*, *35*, 315–330. PA 62:3566.

Ickes, William; & Barnes, Richard D. (1978). Boys

and girls together — and alienated: On enacting stereotyped sex roles in mixed-sex dyads. *Journal of Personality and Social Psychology, 36,* 669–683.

Ickes, William; & Knowles, Eric S. (Eds.). (1982). *Personality, roles, and social behavior.* New York: Springer-Verlag.

Ickes, William; Patterson, Miles L.; Rajecki, D. W.; & Tanford, Sarah. (1982). Behavioral and cognitive consequences of reciprocal versus compensatory responses to preinteraction expectancies. *Social Cognition, 1,* 160–190. PA 69:12662.

Ickes, William; Robertson, Eric; Tooke, William; & Teng, Gary. (1986). Naturalistic social cognition: Methodology, assessment, and validation. *Journal of Personality and Social Psychology, 51,* 66–82. PA 73:27142.

Ickes, William J.; Schermer, Brian; & Steeno, Jeff. (1979). Sex and sex-role influences in same-sex dyads. *Social Psychology Quarterly, 42,* 373–385. PA 65:10382.

Ickes, William; & Trued, Stephen. (1985). A system for collecting dyadic interaction data on the Apple II. *Electronic Social Psychology, 1*(1), Article No. 8501012. PA 74:18731.

Ickes, William; & Turner, Marilyn. (1983). On the social advantages of having an older, opposite-sex sibling: Birth order influences in mixed-sex dyads. *Journal of Personality and Social Psychology, 45,* 210–222. PA 71:6698.

Ilgen, Daniel R.; & Fujii, Donald S. (1976). An investigation of the validity of leader behavior descriptions obtained from subordinates. *Journal of Applied Psychology, 61,* 642–651. PA 57:4682.

Inderlied, Sheila D.; & Powell, Gary. (1979). Sex-role identity and leadership style: Different labels for the same concept? *Sex Roles, 5,* 613–625. PA 65:4258.

Ingham, Alan G.; Levinger, George; Graves, James; & Peckham, Vaughn. (1974). The Ringelmann effect: Studies of group size and group performance. *Journal of Experimental Social Psychology, 10,* 371–384.

Ingham, Roger. (1974). Preferences for seating arrangements in two countries. *International Journal of Psychology, 9,* 105–115. PA 53:9480.

Ingraham, Loring J.; & Wright, Thomas L. (1986). A cautionary note on the interpretation of relationship effects in the social relations model. *Social Psychology Quarterly, 49,* 93–97. PA 74:18732.

Innes, John M.; & Gordon, Margaret I. (1985). The effects of mere presence and a mirror on performance of a motor task. *Journal of Social Psychology, 125,* 479–484. PA 74:4004.

Innes, John M.; & Young, Roger F. (1975). The effect of presence of an audience, evaluation apprehension and objective self-awareness on learning. *Journal of Experimental Social Psychology, 11,* 35–42. PA 53:11607.

Inoue, Kazuko. (1985). [An examination of equity theory in dating couples' intimate romantic relationships]. *Japanese Journal of Experimental Social Psychology, 24,* 127–134. PA 73:11730.

Insko, Chester A.; Gilmore, Robert; Moehle, Debra; Lipsitz, Angela; Drenan, Sarah; & Thibaut, John W. (1982). Seniority in the generational transition of laboratory groups: The effects of social familiarity and task experience. *Journal of Experimental Social Psychology, 18,* 557–580. PA 70:1051.

Insko, Chester A.; Pinkley, Robin L.; Hoyle, Rick H.; Dalton, Bret; Hong, Guiyoung; Slim, Randa M.; Landry, Pat; Holton, Brynda; Ruffin, Paulette F.; & Thibaut, John. (1987). Individual versus group discontinuity: The role of intergroup contact. *Journal of Experimental Social Psychology, 23,* 250–267.

Insko, Chester A.; Smith, R. H.; Alicke, Mark D.; Wade Joel; & Taylor, Sylvester. (1985). Conformity and group size: The concern with being right and the concern with being liked. *Personality and Social Psychology Bulletin, 11,* 41–50. PA 73:6334.

Insko, Chester A.; Thibaut, John W.; Moehle, Debra; Wilson, Midge; Diamond, William D.; Gilmore, Robert; Solomon, Michael R.; & Lipsitz, Angela. (1980). Social evolution and the emergence of leadership. *Journal of Personality and Social Psychology, 39,* 431–448. PA 66:5714.

Instone, Debra; Major, Brenda; & Bunker, Barbara B. (1983). Gender, self confidence, and social influence strategies: An organizational simulation. *Journal of Personality and Social Psychology, 44,* 322–333. PA 70:5627.

Isenberg, Daniel J. (1981). Some effects of time-pressure on vertical structure and decision-making accuracy in small groups. *Organizational Behavior and Human Performance, 27,* 119–134. PA 65:10383.

Isenberg, Daniel J. (1986). Group polarization: A critical review and meta-analysis. *Journal of Personality and Social Psychology, 50,* 1141-1151. PA 73:24477.

Isenberg, Daniel J.; & Ennis, James G. (1981). Perceiving group members: A comparison of derived and imposed dimensions. *Journal of Personality and Social Psychology, 41,* 293-305.

Iso-Ahola, Seppo. (1976a). Determinants of evaluation of team performance. *Scandinavian Journal of Psychology, 17,* 292-296. PA 58:3324. SA 81L8138.

Iso-Ahola, Seppo. (1976b). Evaluation of self and team performance and feelings of satisfaction after success and failure. *International Review of Sport Sociology, 11,* 33-46. SA 78J1737.

Iso-Ahola, Seppo. (1977). Immediate attributional effects of success and failure in the field: Testing some laboratory hypotheses. *European Journal of Social Psychology, 7,* 275-296. SA 79J6848.

Isozaki, Mikitoshi. (1979). An experimental study of the determinants of social facilitation. *Japanese Journal of Experimental Social Psychology, 19,* 49-60. PA 65:5386.

Isozaki, Mikitoshi. (1984). The effect of discussion on polarization of judgments. *Japanese Psychological Research, 26,* 187-193. PA 73:1127.

Isozaki, Mikitoshi; Ueno, Tokumi; Amane, Tetsuji; & Yokogawa, Kazuaki. (1981). [A study on group polarization phenomenon]. *Japanese Journal of Psychology, 52,* 248-251. PA 68:1126.

Ittyerah, Miriam; & Modi, Madhu. (1981). Effect of group pressure on value conformity. *Personality Study and Group Behaviour, 1*(2), 71-82. PA 68:3510.

Iwata, Osamu. (1974a). Empirical examination of the perception of density and crowding. *Japanese Psychological Research, 16,* 117-125. PA 54:1030.

Iwata, Osamu. (1974b). Factors in the perception of crowding. *Japanese Psychological Research, 16,* 65-70. PA 54:1029.

Iwata, Osamu. (1980). Territoriality orientation, privacy orientation and locus of control as determinants of the perception of crowding. *Japanese Psychological Research, 22,* 13-21. SA 85O9449.

Izraeli, Dafna N. (1983). Sex effects or structural effects? An empirical test of Kanter's theory of proportions. *Social Forces, 62,* 153-165. SA 83N4033.

Jablin, Fredric M. (1981). Cultivating imagination: Factors that enhance and inhibit creativity in brainstorming groups. *Human Communication Research, 7,* 245-258. PA 67:3533. SA 82M5648.

Jablin, Fredric M.; Sorenson, Ritch L.; & Siebold, David R. (1978). Interpersonal perception and group brainstorming performance. *Communication Quarterly, 26*(4), 36-44. SA 82L9791.

Jablin, Fredric M.; & Sussman, Lyle. (1978). An exploration of communication and productivity in real brainstorming groups. *Human Communication Research, 4,* 329-337. PA 63:7588.

Jackson, Conrad N.; & King, Donald C. (1983). The effects of representatives' power within their own organizations on the outcome of a negotiation. *Academy of Management Journal, 26,* 178-185. PA 70:3387.

Jackson, Jeffrey M. (1986). In defense of Social Impact theory: Comment on Mullen. *Journal of Personality and Social Psychology, 50,* 511-513.

Jackson, Jeffrey M.; & Harkins, Stephen G. (1985). Equity in effort: An explanation of the social loafing effect. *Journal of Personality and Social Psychology, 49,* 1199-1206. PA 73:11731.

Jackson, Jeffrey M.; & Latané, Bibb. (1981a). All alone in front of all those people: Stage fright as a function of number and type of co-performers and audience. *Journal of Personality and Social Psychology, 40,* 73-85. PA 66:12802.

Jackson, Jeffrey M.; & Latané, Bibb. (1981b). Strength and number of solicitors and the urge towards altruism. *Personality and Social Psychology Bulletin, 7,* 415-422.

Jackson, Jeffrey M.; & Padgett, Vernon R. (1982). With a little help from my friend: Social loafing and the Lennon-McCartney songs. *Personality and Social Psychology Bulletin, 8,* 672-677. PA 70:3388.

Jackson, Jeffrey M.; & Williams, Kipling D. (1985). Social loafing on difficult tasks: Working collectively can improve performance. *Journal of Personality and Social Psychology, 49,* 937-942. PA 73:3676.

Jackson, Susan E.; & Schuler, Randall S. (1985). A meta-analysis and conceptual critique of research on role ambiguity and role conflict in work settings. *Organizational Behavior and Human Decision Processes, 36,* 16-78.

Jacobs, Robert C.; & Campbell, Donald T. (1961). The perpetuation of an arbitrary tradition through several generations of a laboratory microculture. *Journal of Abnormal and Social Psychology, 62,* 649–658.

Jacobson, Dan. (1981). Intraparty dissensus and interparty conflict resolution: A laboratory experiment in the context of the Middle East conflict. *Journal of Conflict Resolution, 25,* 471–494. PA 67:3534.

Jacobson, Marsha B. (1975). Dichotomous choices on life-dilemma problems, subjective expected utility, and the group shift effect. *Social Behavior and Personality, 3,* 71–80. PA 55:723.

Jacobson, Marsha B. (1977). Effect of reinstating initial response on the shift to risk. *Psychological Reports, 40,* 631–634. PA 59:5636.

Jacobson, Marsha B.; & Effertz, Joan. (1974). Sex Roles and leadership: Perceptions of the leader and the led. *Organizational Behavior and Human Performance, 1,* 383–396. PA 57:10227.

Jacobson, Marsha B.; & Koch, Walter. (1977). Women as leaders: Performance evaluation as a function of method of leader selection. *Organizational Behavior and Human Performance, 20,* 149–157. PA 60:8417.

Jacobson, Marsha B.; & Uleman, James S. (1976). Recall of initial response, probability scale meaning, and the group-shift effect. *Psychological Reports, 39,* 1271–1278. PA 58:7447.

Jaffe, Yoram; Shapir, Nahum; & Yinon, Yoel. (1981). Aggression and its escalation. *Journal of Cross-Cultural Psychology, 12,* 21–36. SA 83N2353.

Jaffe, Yoram; & Yinon, Yoel. (1979). Retaliatory aggression in individuals and groups. *European Journal of Social Psychology, 9,* 177–186. PA 64:7928. SA 80K8691.

Jahan, Rowshan; & Begum, Hamida A. (1977). Individual and group risk-taking as a function of sex of subjects. *Asian Journal of Psychology and Education, 2*(1), 1–9. PA 61:5928.

Jamieson, David W.; Lydon, John E.; & Zanna, Mark P. (1987). Attitude and activity preference similarity: Differential bases of interpersonal attraction for low and high self-monitors. *Journal of Personality and Social Psychology, 53,* 1052–1060.

Jamieson, David W.; & Thomas, Kenneth W. (1974). Power and conflict in the student-teacher relationship. *Journal of Applied Behavioral Science, 10,* 321–336.

Jandt, Fred E. (1974). Communication and the simulation of social conflict. In G. R. Miller & H. W. Simons (Eds.), *Perspectives on communication in social conflict* (pp. 76–89). Englewood Cliffs, NJ: Prentice-Hall.

Janis, Irving L. (1982). *Groupthink: Psychological studies of policy decisions and fiascoes.* Boston: Houghton Mifflin. [Rev. Ed. of *Victims of groupthink,* 1972.]

Janis, Irving L. (1983). Groupthink. In H. H. Blumberg, A. P. Hare, V. Kent, & M. F. Davies (Eds.), *Small groups and social interaction* (Vol. 2., pp. 39–46). Chichester: John Wiley.

Janousek, Jaromir. (1973). [Task-directed dialogue of cooperating persons possessing different initial information]. *Ceskoslovenska Psychologie, 17,* 107–124. PA 52:10026.

Janousek, Jaromir. (1979). [Comparison of cooperation and competition under conditions of joint remembering]. *Ceskoslovenska Psychologie, 23,* 463–473. PA 65:3247.

Janssens, Ludo; & Nuttin, Joseph R. (1976). Frequency perception of individual and group successes as a function of competition, coaction, and isolation. *Journal of Personality and Social Psychology, 34,* 830–836.

Jaques, Marceline E.; & Patterson, Kathleen M. (1974). The self-help group model: A review. *Rehabilitation Counseling Bulletin, 18,* 48–58. PA 53:6034.

Jasiecki, Maciej; & Necki, Zbigniew (1983). Zmiana postaw interpersonalnych w grupach treningowych [Changes of interpersonal attitudes in training groups]. *Przeglad Psychologiczny, 26,* 367–381. PA 72:3996.

Jason, Leonard A.; Reichler, Arnold; & Rucker, Walter. (1981). Territorial behavior on beaches. *Journal of Social Psychology, 114,* 43–50. SA 84O0834.

Jaspars, Joseph M.; van den Oever, Ton; & van Gils, Jacques A. (1974). Cognitive balance and visual interaction. *Nederlands Tijdschrift voor de Psychologie en haar Grensgebieden, 29,* 557–568. PA 53:7294.

Javornisky, Gregory. (1979). Task content and sex differences in conformity. *Journal of Social Psychology, 108,* 213–220. PA 65:1272.

Jellison, Jerold M.; & Ickes, William J. (1974). The power of the glance: Desire to see and be seen in cooperative and competitive situations. *Journal of Experimental Social Psychology, 10,* 444–450. PA 53:3026.

Jennings, Luther B.; & George, Stephen G. (1984). Group-induced distortion of visually perceived extent: The Asch effect revisited. *Psychological Record, 34*, 133–148. PA 71:28608.

Jerdee, Thomas H.; & Rosen, Benson. (1974). Effects of opportunity to communicate and visibility of individual decisions on behavior in the common interest. *Journal of Applied Psychology, 59*, 712–716. PA 53:7315.

Jessup, Leonard M. (1987). Group decision support systems: A need for behavioral research. *International Journal of Small Group Research, 3*, 139–158.

Jesuino, Jorge Correia. (1986). Influence of leadership processes on group polarization. *European Journal of Social Psychology, 16*, 413–423.

Johansen, Robert; Miller, Richard H.; & Vallee, Jacques. (1974). Group communication through electronic media: Fundamental choices and social effects. *Educational Technology, 14*, 7–20. PA 54:2974.

Johnson, Carl F.; & Dabbs, James M. Jr. (1976). Self-disclosure in dyads as a function of distance and the subject-experimenter relationship. *Sociometry, 39*, 257–263. PA 57:5794.

Johnson, Carol A.; & Aderman, Morris. (1979). Leadership style and personal history information. *Journal of Psychology, 102*, 243–251.

Johnson, David L.; & Ridener, Larry R. (1974). Self-disclosure, participation, and perceived cohesiveness in small group interaction. *Psychological Reports, 35*, 361–362. PA 53:7316.

Johnson, David W. (1974). Communication and the inducement of cooperative behavior in conflicts: A critical review. *Speech Monographs, 41*, 64–78. PA 53:5170.

Johnson, David W. (1975). Cooperativeness and social perspective taking. *Journal of Personality and Social Psychology, 31*, 241–244. PA 53:11609.

Johnson, David W. (1977). The distribution and exchange of information in problem-solving dyads. *Communication Research, 4*, 283–298. PA 59:9862.

Johnson, David W.; & Johnson, Roger T. (1982). Effects of cooperative, competitive, and individualistic learning experiences on cross-ethnic interaction and friendships. *Journal of Social Psychology, 118*, 47–58.

Johnson, David W.; & Johnson, Roger T. (1985a). Mainstreaming hearing-impaired students: The effect of effort in communicating on coopera-tion and interpersonal attraction. *Journal of Psychology, 119*, 31–44. PA 73:7713.

Johnson, David W.; & Johnson, Roger T. (1985b). Relationships between Black and White students in intergroup cooperation and competition. *Journal of Social Psychology, 125*, 421–428. PA 74:3750.

Johnson, David W.; Johnson, Roger T.; & Maruyama, Geoffrey M. (1983). Interdependence and interpersonal attraction among heterogeneous and homogeneous individuals: A theoretical formulation and a meta-analysis of the research. *Review of Educational Research, 53*, 5–54. PA 70:12640.

Johnson, David W.; Johnson, Roger T.; Roy, Patricia; & Zaidman, Brian. (1986). Oral interaction in cooperative learning groups: Speaking, listening, and the nature of statements made by high-, medium-, and low-achieving students. *Journal of Psychology, 119*, 303–321.

Johnson, David W.; Maruyama, Geoffrey; Johnson, Roger; Nelson, Deborah; & Skon, Linda. (1981). Effects of cooperative, competitive, and individualistic goal structures on achievement: A meta-analysis. *Psychological Bulletin, 89*, 47–62. PA 65:5387.

Johnson, Jean E. (1984). Psychological interventions and coping with surgery. In A. Baum, S. E. Taylor, & J. E. Singer (Eds.), *The handbook of psychology and health: Vol. 4. Social psychological aspects of health* (pp. 167–187). Hillsdale, NJ: Erlbaum.

Johnson, Michael P.; & Leslie, Leigh. (1982). Couple involvement and network structure: A test of the dyadic withdrawal hypothesis. *Social Psychology Quarterly, 45*, 34–43. PA 68:08102.

Johnson, Norris R.; & Glover, Maryline. (1978). Individual and group shifts to extreme: Laboratory experiment on crowd polarization. *Sociological Focus, 11*(4), 247–254.

Johnson, Norris R.; Stemler, James G.; & Hunter, Deborah. (1977). Crowd behavior as risky shift: A laboratory experiment. *Social Psychology Quarterly, 40*, 183–187. PA 59:9863. SA 78J1738.

Johnson, Paula. (1976). Women and power: Toward a theory of effectiveness. *Journal of Social Issues, 32*(3), 99–110. PA 57:5732.

Johnson, Robert D.; & Downing, Leslie L. (1979). Deindividuation and valence of cues: Effects on prosocial and antisocial behavior. *Journal of Personality and Social Psychology, 37*, 1532–1538. PA 65:1225.

Johnson, Roger T.; & Johnson, David W. (1982). Effects of cooperative and competitive learning experiences on interpersonal attraction between handicapped and nonhandicapped students. *Journal of Social Psychology, 116,* 211–219.

Johnson, Roger T.; Johnson, David W.; Scott, Linda E.; & Ramolae, Beverly A. (1985). Effects of single-sex and mixed-sex cooperative interaction on science achievement and attitudes and cross-handicap and cross-sex relationships. *Journal of Research in Science Teaching, 22*(3), 207–220. PA 73:4851.

Johnson, Ronald W.; & Ryan, Brenda J. (1976). A test of the contingency model of leadership effectiveness. *Journal of Applied Social Psychology, 6,* 177–183. PA 57:5795.

Johnson, Stephen D. (1980). Reverse discrimination and aggressive behavior. *Journal of Psychology, 104,* 11–19. PA 65:7932.

Johnson, Thomas E.; & Rule, Brendan G. (1986). Mitigating circumstance information, censure, and aggression. *Journal of Personality & Social Psychology, 50,* 537–542. PA 73:19819.

Johnstad, Trygve. (Ed.). (1980). *Group dynamics and society: A multinational approach.* Cambridge, MA: Oelgeschlager, Gunn & Hain.

Jolley, Jerry C. (1973). Leadership and task completion in wheel and circle configurations: A small groups experiment. *Utah State University Journal of Sociology, 4*(1), 35–44. SA 78J1739.

Jones, Alvin; & Crandall, Rick. (1985). Preparing newcomers to enhance assimilation into groups: A group therapy example. *Small Group Behavior, 16,* 31–57.

Jones, Dean C. (1975). Spatial proximity, interpersonal conflict, and friendship formation in the intermediate-care facility. *Gerontologist, 15*(2), 150–154. PA 54:3948.

Jones, Diane Carlson. (1983). Power structure and perceptions of power holders in same-sex groups of young children. *Women & Politics, 3*(2-3), 147–164. SA 84N9146.

Jones, Dorothy S.; & Medvene, Arnold M. (1975). Self-actualization effects of a marathon growth group. *Journal of Counseling Psychology, 22,* 39–43. PA 53:7295.

Jones, Edward E.; & Archer, Richard L. (1976). Are there special effects of personalistic self-disclosure? *Journal of Experimental Social Psychology, 12,* 180–193. PA 56:04048.

Jones, Edward E.; & Pittman, Thane S. (1982). Toward a general theory of strategic self-presentation. In J. Suls (Ed.), *Psychological*

perspectives on the self (Vol. 1, pp. 231–262). Hillsdale, NJ: Erlbaum.

Jones, Edward E.; Rhodewalt, Frederick; Berglas, Steven; & Skelton, James A. (1981). Effects of strategic self-presentation on subsequent self-esteem. *Journal of Personality and Social Psychology, 41,* 407–421.

Jones, John W.; & Bogat, Anne G. (1978). Air pollution and human aggression. *Psychological Reports, 43,* 721–722. PA 64:7196.

Jones, Linda M.; & Foshay, Natalie N. (1984). Diffusion of responsibility in a nonemergency situation: Response to a greeting from a stranger. *Journal of Social Psychology, 123,* 155–158. PA 72:25402.

Jones, Marshall B. (1974). Regressing group on individual effectiveness. *Organizational Behavior and Human Performance, 11,* 426–451.

Jones, Robert E.; & White, Charles S. (1983). Relationships between Machiavellianism, task orientation and team effectiveness. *Psychological Reports, 53,* 859–866. PA 71:17753.

Jones, Robert E.; & White, Charles S. (1985). Relationships among personality, conflict resolution styles, and task effectiveness. *Group and Organization Studies, 10,* 152–167. PA 72:30783.

Jones, Warren H.; Hobbs, Steven A.; & Hockenbury, Don. (1982). Loneliness and social skill deficits. *Journal of Personality and Social Psychology, 42,* 682–689. PA 68:12615.

Jones, Warren H.; Nickel, Ted W.; & Schmidt, Alan. (1979). Machiavellianism and self-disclosure. *Journal of Psychology, 102,* 33–41.

Jorgenson, Dale O. (1975). Field study of the relationship between status discrepancy and proxemic behavior. *Journal of Social Psychology, 97,* 173–179. PA 55:9786.

Jorgenson, Dale O. (1980). Identifiability and behavior in a simulated commons dilemma. *Catalog of Selected Documents in Psychology, 10,* 64. (Ms. No. 2099) PA 66:5752.

Jorgenson, Dale O.; & Dukes, Fred O. (1976). Deindividuation as a function of density and group membership. *Journal of Personality and Social Psychology, 34,* 24–29. PA 56:7904.

Jorgenson, Dale O.; Jenks, John A.; & Reaney, Douglas. (1980). Consistency of response to a simulated commons dilemma and behavior in an actual commons. *Journal of Social Psychology, 111,* 297–298. PA 66:5751.

Jorgenson, Dale O.; & Papciak, Anthony S.

(1981). The effects of communication, resource feedback, and identifiability on behavior in a simulated commons. *Journal of Experimental Social Psychology*, *17*, 373–385. PA 67:7699.

José, Paul E.; & McCarthy, William J. (1988) Perceived agentic and communal behavior in mixed-sex group interactions. *Personality and Social Psychology Bulletin*, *14*, 57–67.

Jourard, Sidney M. (1971). *Self-disclosure: An experimental analysis of the transparent self*. New York: Wiley.

Judd, Charles M. (1978). Cognitive effects of attitude conflict resolution. *Journal of Conflict Resolution*, *22*, 483–498. PA 64:1045.

Judd, N.; Bull, R. H.; & Gahagan, D. (1975). The effects of clothing style upon the reactions of a stranger. *Social Behavior and Personality*, *3*, 225–227. PA 56:6040.

Jungk, Robert; & Müllert, Norbert R. (1981). *Zukunftswerkstätten*. Hamburg: Hoffmann und Campe.

Juni, Samuel; & Hershkowitz-Friedman, Tobi. (1981). Interpersonal looking as a function of status, self-esteem, and sex. *Psychological Reports*, *48*, 273–274. PA 67:3537.

Juni, Samuel; & Roth, Michelle M. (1981). Sexism and handicapism in interpersonal helping. *Journal of Social Psychology*, *115*, 175–181. PA 68:1127.

Jurma, William E. (1978). Leadership structuring style, task ambiguity, and group member satisfaction. *Small Group Behavior*, *9*, 124–134. SA 79K1097.

Justis, Robert T. (1975). Leadership effectiveness: A contingency approach. *Academy of Management Journal*, *18*(1), 160–167. PA 54:2088.

Kabanoff, Boris. (1981). The potential influence index as a measure of situational favourability in the contingency model of leadership. *Australian Journal of Psychology*, *33*, 47–59. SA 85O9557.

Kabanoff, Boris. (1985). Potential influence structures as sources of interpersonal conflict in groups and organizations. *Organizational Behavior and Human Decision Processes*, *36*, 113–141.

Kabanoff, Boris; & O'Brien, Gordon E. (1979a). Cooperation structure and the relationship of leader and member ability to group performance. *Journal of Applied Psychology*, *64*, 526–532. PA 65:1236.

Kabanoff, Boris; & O'Brien, Gordon E. (1979b).

The effects of task type and cooperation upon group products and performance. *Organizational Behavior and Human Performance*, *23*, 163–181. PA 64:5557.

Kafer, Norman F. (1976). A sociometric method for identifying group boundaries. *Journal of Experimental Education*, *45*(1), 71–74. PA 57:11768.

Kahan, James P. (1975). A subjective probability interpretation of risky shift. *Journal of Personality and Social Psychology*, *31*, 977–982.

Kahan, James P.; & Bonacich, Phillip. (1980). Palette: A resource-free experimental paradigm for studying coalition formation. *Simulation and Games*, *11*, 259–278. SA 85O4350.

Kahan, James P.; Coston, Arthur W.; Helwig, Richard A.; Rapoport, Amnon; & Wallsten, Thomas S. (1976). A PDP-11/45 program for playing n-person characteristic function games. *Behavior Research Methods and Instrumentation*, *8*, 165–169. PA 56:5129.

Kahan, James P.; & Rapoport, Amnon. (1975). Decisions of timing in conflict situations of unequal power between opponents. *Journal of Conflict Resolution*, *19*, 250–270. PA 55:724.

Kahan, James P.; & Rapoport, Amnon. (1977). When you don't need to join: The effects of guaranteed payoffs on bargaining in three-person cooperative games. *Theory and Decision*, *8*(2), 97–126. PA 60:5231. SA 79J6849.

Kahan, James P.; & Rapoport, Amnon. (1979). The influence of structural relationships on coalition formation in four-person apex games. *European Journal of Social Psychology*, *9*, 339–361. PA 65:3248. SA 81L6528.

Kahan, James P.; & Rapoport, Amnon. (1981). Matrix experiments and theories of n-person games. *Journal of Conflict Resolution*, *25*, 725–732.

Kahan, James P.; & Rapoport, Amnon. (1984a). Social psychology and the theory of games: A mixed-motive relationship. *Representative Research in Social Psychology*, *14*, 65–71. PA 73:21912.

Kahan, James P.; & Rapoport, Amnon. (1984b). *Theories of coalition formation*. Hillsdale, NJ: LEA.

Kahn, Arnold; & McGaughey, Timothy A. (1977). Distance and liking: When moving closer produces increased liking. *Sociometry*, *40*, 138–144. PA 59:9891.

Kahn, Arnold; Nelson, Robin E.; & Gaeddert,

William P. (1980). Sex of subject and sex composition of the group as determinants of reward allocations. *Journal of Personality and Social Psychology*, *38*, 737–750. PA 65:12741.

Kahn, Arnold; Nelson, Robin E.; Gaeddert, William P.; & Hearn, June L. (1982). The justice process: Deciding upon equity or equality. *Social Psychology Quarterly*, *45*, 3–8. PA 68:8103. SA 83N2355.

Kahn, Arnold; O'Leary, Virginia E.; Krulewitz, Judith E.; & Lamm, Helmut. (1980). Equity and equality: Male and female means to a just end. *Basic and Applied Social Psychology*, *1*(2), 173–197. PA 64:12498.

Kalma, Akko; & Van Rooij, Jan. (1982). Dominantie en interactieregulering: het kijkgedrag van invloedrijke personen [Dominance and regulation of interaction: Looking behavior of influential persons]. *Nederlands Tijdschrift voor de Psychologie en haar Grensgebieden*, *37*(7), 431–443. PA 70:1052.

Kameda, Tatsuya. (1983). [Informational social influence by a similar or dissimilar other]. *Japanese Journal of Experimental Social Psychology*, *23*, 1–8. PA 71:23095.

Kanaga, Kim R.; & Flynn, Mark. (1981). The relationship between invasion of personal space and stress. *Human Relations*, *34*, 239–248. PA 66:1231.

Kandel, Denise B. (1978a). Homophily, selection, and socialization in adolescent friendships. *American Journal of Sociology*, *84*, 427–436. PA 64:1002.

Kandel, Denise B. (1978b). Similarity in real-life adolescent friendship pairs. *Journal of Personality and Social Psychology*, *36*, 306–312. PA 61:991.

Kane, Rosalie A. (1975). The interprofessional team as a small group. *Social Work in Health Care*, *1*(1), 19–32. SA 7716193.

Kane, Thomas R.; Monteverde, Frank J.; & Tedeschi, James T. (1976). Trust and the use of promises. *Perceptual and Motor Skills*, *42*, 439–443. PA 58:5332.

Kanekar, Suresh. (1982). Individual and group performance on an anagrams task. *Australian Journal of Psychology*, *34*, 337–344. PA 71:1317.

Kanekar, Suresh; Libby, Cynthia; Engels, Jeff; & Jahn, Gretchen. (1978). Group performance as a function of group type, task condition and scholastic level. *European Journal of Social Psychology*, *8*, 439–451. PA 63:7565. SA 80K4179.

Kanekar, Suresh; Neelakantan, Priya; & Lalkaka, Pareen K. (1975). Nominal and real group performance in relation to manifest anxiety and induced stress. *Social Behavior and Personality*, *3*(2), 197–204. PA 56:5994.

Kaneko, Satoru. (1972). [Bargaining behavior in coalition formation: I.] *Japanese Journal of Experimental Social Psychology*, *11*, 109–126. PA 53:1064.

Kano, S[oro]. (1973). [A development of the "group structure analyzer"]. *Japanese Journal of Experimental Social Psychology*, *13*, 55–61. PA 54:2975.

Kano, Soro. (1985). [A condensation model for macroscopic group structure analysis] *Japanese Journal of Experimental Social Psychology*, *24*, 111–119. PA 73:11732.

Kanter, Rosabeth Moss. (1977). *Men and women of the corporation*. New York: Basic Books.

Kaplan, Irving H. (1967). Fantasies, fables and facts about groups. *Journal of the Fort Logan Mental Health Center*, *4*(4), 149–162. SA 76H9421.

Kaplan, Kalman J. (1977). Structure and process in interpersonal distancing. *Environmental Psychology and Nonverbal Behavior*, *1*(2), 104–121. PA 60:3036.

Kaplan, Kalman J.; Firestone, Ira J.; Klein, Katherine W.; & Sodikoff, Charles. (1983). Distancing in dyads: A comparison of four models. *Social Psychology Quarterly*, *46*, 108–115. PA 71:3975. SA 83N2356.

Kaplan, Martin F. (1977). Discussion polarization effects in a modified jury decision paradigm: Informational influences. *Sociometry*, *40*, 262–271. PA 60:5205. SA 78J4690.

Kaplan, Martin F.; & Kemmerick, Gwen D. (1974). Juror judgment as information integration: Combining evidential and nonevidential information. *Journal of Personality and Social Psychology*, *30*, 493–499. PA 53:3028.

Kaplan, Martin F.; & Krupa, Sharon. (1986). Severe penalties under the control of others can reduce guilt verdicts. *Law and Psychology Review*, *10*, 1–18. PA 74:13114.

Kaplan, Martin F.; & Miller, Charles E. (1977). Judgments and group discussion: Effect of presentation and memory factors on polarization. *Social Psychology Quarterly*, *40*, 337–343. PA 61:8468.

Kaplan, Martin F.; & Miller, Charles E. (1987). Group decision making and normative versus informational influence: Effects of type of issue and assigned decision rule. *Journal of Personality and Social Psychology, 53,* 306–313.

Kaplan, Martin F.; & Miller, Lynn E. (1978). Replacing the effects of juror bias. *Journal of Personality and Social Psychology, 36,* 1443–1455.

Kaplan, Robert E. (1978). Maintaining relationships openly: Case study of "total openness" in a communal organization. *Human Relations, 31,* 375–393. PA 62:5980.

Kaplan, Robert E. (1979). The utility of maintaining work relationships openly: An experimental study. *Journal of Applied Behavioral Science, 15,* 41–59. PA 63:11948.

Kaplowitz, Stan A. (1977). The influence of moral considerations on the perceived consequences of an action. *Journal of Conflict Resolution, 21*(3), 475–500. PA 60:3075.

Karabenick, Stuart A. (1977). Fear of success, achievement and affiliation dispositions, and the performance of men and women under individual and competitive conditions. *Journal of Personality, 45,* 117–149. PA 59:1072.

Kardes, Frank R.; & Kimble, Charles E. (1984). Strategic self-presentation as a function of message valence and the prospect of future interaction. *Representative Research in Social Psychology, 14,* 2–11. PA 73:6335.

Karlin, Robert A.; McFarland, Dianne; Aiello, John R.; & Epstein, Yakov M. (1976). Normative mediation of reactions to crowding. *Environmental Psychology and Nonverbal Behavior, 1*(1), 30–40. PA 60:3037.

Karlin, Robert A.; Rosen, Leslie S.; & Epstein, Yakov M. (1979). Three into two doesn't go: A follow-up study on the effects of overcrowded dormitory rooms. *Personality and Social Psychology Bulletin, 5,* 391–395.

Karp, David A.; & Yoels, William C. (1976). The college classroom: Some observations on the meanings of student participation. *Sociology and Social Research, 60*(4), 421–439. SA 7716194.

Karuza, Jurgis; & Brickman, Philip. (1981). Preference for similarity in higher and lower status others. *Personality and Social Psychology Bulletin, 7,* 504–508. PA 67:9768.

Kaseman, Betty M. (1976). An experimental use of

structured techniques in group psychotherapy. *Group Psychotherapy, Psychodrama and Sociometry* (29), 33–39. SA 79J9643.

Kassin, Saul M.; & Juhnke, Ralph. (1983). Juror experience and decision making. *Journal of Personality & Social Psychology, 44,* 1182–1191. PA 71:01346.

Kassin, Saul M.; & Wrightsman, Lawrence S. (1980). Prior confessions and mock juror verdicts. *Journal of Applied Social Psychology, 10,* 133–146.

Katovich, Michael A. (1984). Symbolic interactionism and experimentation: The laboratory as a provocative stage. *Studies in Symbolic Interaction, 5,* 49–67. PA 72:2817.

Katovich, Michael [A.]; Weiland, Marion W.; & Couch, Carl J. (1981). Access to information and internal structures of partisan groups: Some notes on the iron law of oligarchy. *Sociological Quarterly, 22*(3), 431–445. SA 82M1465.

Katz, Irwin. (1970). Experimental studies of Negro-White relationships. *Advances in Experimental Social Psychology, 5,* 71–117.

Katz, Irwin. (1981). *Stigma: A Social Psychological Analysis.* Hillsdale, NJ: Erlbaum.

Katz, Irwin. (1983). The process of stigmatization. In H. H. Blumberg, A. P. Hare, V. Kent, & M. F. Davies (Eds.), *Small groups and social interaction* (Vol. 1, pp. 99–108). Chichester: John Wiley & Sons.

Katz, Irwin; Cohen, Sheldon; & Glass, David. (1975). Some determinants of cross-racial helping behavior. *Journal of Personality and Social Psychology, 32,* 964–970. PA 55:7140.

Katz, Irwin; Glass, David C.; Lucido, David J.; & Farber, Joan. (1977). Ambivalence, guilt, and the denigration of a physically handicapped victim. *Journal of Personality, 45,* 419–429. PA 60:3076.

Katz, Irwin; Glass, David C.; Lucido, David; & Farber, Joan. (1979). Harm-doing and victim's racial or orthopedic stigma as determinants of helping behavior. *Journal of Personality, 47,* 340–364. PA 64:7930.

Katz, Marsha. (1974). Trivial games as predictors of a mixed-motive game. *Journal of Conflict Resolution, 18,* 700–706. PA 53:9520.

Kaul, Theodore J.; & Bednar, Richard L. (1978). Conceptualizing group research: A preliminary analysis. *Small Group Behavior, 9,* 173–191. SA 79K2631.

Kavanaugh, Raphael R. Jr.; & Bollet, Robert M.

(1983). Levels of verbal intimacy technique (LOVIT): An initial measurement of verbal intimacy in groups. *Small Group Behavior, 14*, 35–49. PA 71:187.

Kawamura-Reynolds, Mio. (1977). Motivational effects of an audience in the content of imaginative thought. *Journal of Personality and Social Psychology, 35*, 912–919. PA 62:8625.

Kawasaki, Michio. (1974). [Functional utilization of speech in group problem solving]. *Japanese Journal of Educational Psychology, 22*, 80–90. PA 53:11581.

Kayser, Egon. (1980). [Distributing justice: Rationality in hypothetical and actual situations]. *Zeitschrift für Sozialpsychologie, 11*(2), 112–123. PA 66:3642.

Kayser, Egon. (1982). Alltagskonflikte zwischen zwei Personen: Vorschlag eines Analysemodells [Everyday conflicts between two persons: An analytic model proposal]. *Zeitschrift für Sozialpsychologie, 13*, 278–286. PA 70:7959.

Kayser, Egon; & Schwinger, Thomas. (1982). A theoretical analysis of the relationship among individual justice concept, layman's psychology, and distribution decision. *Journal for the Theory of Social Behaviour, 12*, 47–51. PA 68:8105.

Keating, Caroline F.; & Keating, E. Gregory. (1980). Distance between pairs of acquaintances and strangers on public benches in Nairobi, Kenya. *Journal of Social Psychology, 110*, 285–286. PA 65:10384.

Keating, Caroline F.; Mazur, Allan; Segall, Marshall H.; Cysneiros, Paulo G.; Divale, William T.; Kilbride, Janet E.; Komin, Suntaree; Leahy, Peter; Thurman, Blake; & Wirsing, Rolf. (1981). Culture and the perception of social dominance from facial expression. *Journal of Personality and Social Psychology, 40*, 615–626. PA 67:5756.

Keating, John P.; & Snowball, Halina. (1977). Effects of crowding and depersonalization on perception of group atmosphere. *Perceptual and Motor Skills, 44*, 431–435. PA 59:3316. SA 79J8024.

Keeley, Rosalie M.; & Edney, Julian J. (1983). Model house designs for privacy, security, and social interaction. *Journal of Social Psychology, 119*, 219–228.

Keeney, Ralph L.; & Raiffa, Howard. (1976). *Decisions with multiple objectives: Preferences and value tradeoffs.* New York: Wiley.

Keiser, George J.; & Altman, Irwin. (1976). Relationship of nonverbal behavior to the social penetration process. *Human Communication Research, 2*(2), 147–161. PA 60:1021.

Kellerman, Henry; Buirski, Peter; & Plutchik, Robert. (1974). Group behavior in a baboon troop: Implications for human process. In L. R. Wolberg & M. L. Aronson (Eds.), *Group therapy 1974: An overview.* New York: Stratton Intercontinental Medical. PA 54:743.

Kelley, Harold H. (1967). Attribution theory in social psychology. In D. Levine (Ed.), *Nebraska symposium on motivation* (Vol. 15, pp. 192–240). Lincoln: University of Nebraska Press.

Kelley, Harold H. (1979). *Personal relationships: Their structures and processes.* Hillsdale, NJ: Lawrence Erlbaum.

Kelley, Harold H. (1984a). Affect in interpersonal relations. *Review of Personality and Social Psychology*, No. 5, 89–115. PA 73:17208.

Kelley, Harold H. (1984b). Interdependence theory and its future. *Representative Research in Social Psychology, 14*, 2–15. PA 73:21913.

Kelley, Harold H. (1984c). The theoretical description of interdependence by means of transition lists. *Journal of Personality and Social Psychology, 47*, 956–982. PA 72:14489.

Kelley, Harold H. (1987). Toward a taxonomy of interpersonal conflict processes. In S. Oskamp & S. Spacapan (Eds.), *Interpersonal processes* [The third Claremont Symposium on Applied Social Psychology] (pp. 122–147), Newbury Park, CA: Sage.

Kelley, Harold H; Berscheid, Ellen; Christensen, Andrew; Harvey, John H.; Huston, Ted L.; Levinger, George; McClintock, Evie; Peplau, Letitia Anne; & Peterson, Donald R. (1983). *Close relationships.* New York: Freeman.

Kelley, Harold H.; & Thibaut, John W. (1978). *Interpersonal relations: A theory of interdependence.* New York: Wiley.

Kelling, George W.; Zirkes, Rhea; & Myerowitz, Deena. (1976). Risk as value: A switch of set hypothesis. *Psychological Reports, 38*, 655–658. PA 56:6042.

Kello, Alexandra; & Ruisel, Imrich. (1979). Effect of personality traits on group status in sportsmen. *Studia Psychologica, 21*, 155–159. PA 64:12457.

Kelly, Janice R.; & McGrath, Joseph E. (1985). Effects of time limits and task types on task performance and interaction of four-person groups. *Journal of Personality and Social Psychology, 49*, 395–407. PA 73:1128.

Kelly, Jeffrey A.; Wildman, Hal E.; & Urey, Jon R. (1982). Gender and sex role differences in group decision-making social interactions: A behavioral analysis. *Journal of Applied Social Psychology, 12*, 112–127. PA 70:10242.

Kelly, Jeffrey A.; et al. (1982). Interpersonal reactions to assertive and unassertive styles when handling social conflict situations. *Journal of Behavior Therapy & Experimental Psychiatry, 13*(1), 33–40. PA 68:10348.

Kelly, Lynne; & Duran, Robert L. (1986). A replication of Parke and Houben's study of group types. *International Journal of Small Group Research, 2*(2), 186–196.

Kelly, William L. (1974). Group-training: Perspectives of professional trainees on group dynamics. *Small Group Behavior*, 427–444. PA 54:09772.

Kelman, Herbert C.; & Hamilton, V. Lee. (1989). *Crimes of obedience: Toward a social psychology of authority and responsibility*. New Haven: Yale Univ. Press.

Kelvin, Peter. (1973). A social-psychological examination of privacy. *British Journal of Social and Clinical Psychology, 12*, 248–261.

Kemp, N. J.; & Rutter, D. R. (1982). Cuelessness and the content and style of conversation. *British Journal of Social Psychology, 21*, 43–49. PA 68:05758.

Kendon, Adam. (1976). The F-formation system: The spatial organization of social encounters. *Man-Environment Systems, 6*(5), 291–296. SA 80K8692.

Kendon, Adam. (1978). Looking in conversation and the regulation of turns at talk: A comment on the papers of G. Beattie and D. R. Rutter et al. *British Journal of Social and Clinical Psychology, 17*, 23–24. PA 61:5930.

Kendon, Adam; Harris, Richard M.; & Key, Mary R. (Eds.). (1975). *Organization of behavior in face-to-face interaction*. Hague, Netherlands: Mouton.

Kennedy, Carol W.; & Camden, Carl. (1983). Interruptions and nonverbal gender differences. *Journal of Nonverbal Behavior, 8*(2), 91–108. PA 72:22582.

Kennedy, John K. Jr. (1982). Middle LPC leaders and the contingency model of leadership effectiveness. *Organizational Behavior and Human Performance, 30*, 1–14. PA 68:11472.

Kenny, David A.; & la Voie, Lawrence. (1982). Reciprocity of interpersonal attraction: A confirmed hypothesis. *Social Psychology Quarterly, 45*, 54–58. PA 68:8106.

Kenny, David A.; & La Voie, Lawrence. (1984). The social relations model. *Advances in Experimental Social Psychology, 18*, 142–182.

Kenny, David A.; & La Voie, Lawrence. (1985). Separating individual and group effects. *Journal of Personality and Social Psychology, 48*, 339–348.

Kenny, David A.; & Zaccaro, Stephen J. (1983). An estimate of variance due to traits in leadership. *Journal of Applied Psychology, 68*, 678–685. PA 71:3977.

Kenny, Graham K.; Butler, Richard J.; Hickson, David J.; Cray, David; Mallory, Geoffrey R.; & Wilson, David C. (1987). Strategic decision making: Influence patterns in public and private sector organizations. *Human Relations, 40*, 613–632.

Kenrick, Douglas T.; & Cialdini, Robert B. (1977). Romantic attraction: Misattribution versus reinforcement explanations. *Journal of Personality and Social Psychology, 35*, 381–391. PA 62:5957.

Kenrick, Douglas T.; & Johnson, Gregory A. (1979). Interpersonal attraction in aversive environments: A problem for the classical conditioning paradigm? *Journal of Personality and Social Psychology, 37*, 572–579. PA 64:7991.

Kenrick, Douglas T.; & MacFarlane, Steven W. (1986). Ambient temperature and horn honking: A field study of the heat/aggression relationship. *Environment and Behavior, 18*, 179–191. PA 73:26042.

Kent, Gerald G.; Davis, John D.; & Shapiro, David A. (1981). Effect of mutual acquaintance on the construction of conversation. *Journal of Experimental Social Psychology, 17*, 197–209. PA 67:01229.

Kent, Gerald G.; Davis, John D.; & Shapiro, David A. (1978). Resources required in the construction and reconstruction of conversation. *Journal of Personality & Social Psychology, 36*, 13–22. PA 62:05981.

Kent, [M.] Valerie. (1983). Prosocial behaviour and small group processes. In H. H. Blumberg, A. P. Hare, V. Kent, & M. F. Davies (Eds.), *Small groups and social interaction* (Vol. 1, pp. 227–241). Chichester: John Wiley & Sons.

Kent, M. Valerie; & Blumberg, Herbert H. (1988a [released 1991]). Aggression and social interaction: A classified bibliography 1974-1990. *Social and Behavioral Sciences Documents*. [Also, *1988b* is a bibliography on prosocial behavior.]

Kent, Theodore C. (1986). *Conflict resolution: A study of applied psychophilosophy*. Woodbridge, CT: Ox Bow.

Kernaghan, John A.; & Cooke, Robert A. (1987). The relationship of group process factors to the quality and acceptance of group output. *International Journal of Small Group Research*, *3*, 39-60.

Kernis, Michael H.; & Reis, Harry T. (1984). Self-consciousness, self-awareness, and justice in reward allocation. *Journal of Personality*, *52*, 58-70. PA 72:14472.

Kerr, Norbert L. (1978). Beautiful and blameless: Effects of victim attractiveness and responsibility on mock jurors' verdicts. *Personality and Social Psychology Bulletin*, *4*, 479 482.

Kerr, Norbert L. (1981a). Effects of prior juror experience on juror behavior. *Basic and Applied Social Psychology*, *2*, 175-193.

Kerr, Norbert L. (1981b). Social transition schemes: Charting the group's road to agreement. *Journal of Personality & Social Psychology*, *41*, 684-702. PA 67:09769.

Kerr, Norbert L. (1983). Motivation losses in small groups: A social dilemma analysis. *Journal of Personality and Social Psychology*, *45*, 819 828. PA 71:12158.

Kerr, Norbert L.; Atkin, Robert S.; Stasser, Garold; Meek, David; Holt, Robert W.; & Davis, James H. (1976). Guilt beyond a reasonable doubt: Effects of concept definition and assigned decision rule on the judgments of mock jurors. *Journal of Personality and Social Psychology*, *34*, 282-294. PA 56:7906.

Kerr, Norbert L.; & Bruun, Steven E. (1981). Ringelmann revisited: Alternative explanations for the social loafing effect. *Personality & Social Psychology Bulletin*, *7*, 224-231. PA 67:05710.

Kerr, Norbert L.; & Bruun, Steven E. (1983). Dispensability of member effort and group motivation losses: Free-rider effects. *Journal of Personality and Social Psychology*, *44*, 78-94. PA 70:3389.

Kerr, Norbert L.; Davis, James H.; Meek, David; & Rissman, A. Kent. (1975). Group position as a function of member attitudes: Choice shift effects from the perspective of social decision scheme theory. *Journal of Personality & Social Psychology*, *31*, 574-593. PA 54:01031.

Kerr, Norbert L.; & MacCoun, Robert J. (1985a). The effects of jury size and polling method on the process and product of jury deliberation. *Journal of Personality and Social Psychology*, *48*, 349-363.

Kerr, Norbert L.; & MacCoun, Robert J. (1985b). Role expectations in social dilemmas: Sex roles and task motivation in groups. *Journal of Personality and Social Psychology*, *49*, 1547-1556. PA 73:11733.

Kerr, Norbert L.; MacCoun, Robert J.; Hansen, Christine H.; & Hymes, Janet A. (1987). Gaining and losing social support: Momentum in decision-making groups. *Journal of Experimental Social Psychology*, *23*, 119-145.

Kerr, Norbert L.; & Sullaway, Megan E. (1983). Group sex composition and member task motivation. *Sex Roles*, *9*, 403-417. PA 71:1319.

Kerr, Norbert L.; & Watts, Barbara L. (1982). After division, before decision: Group faction size and predeliberation thinking. *Social Psychology Quarterly*, *45*, 198-205. PA 70:3390. SA 83N2357.

Kerr, Steven; & Jermier, John M. (1978). Substitutes for leadership: Their meaning and measurement. *Organizational Behavior and Human Performance*, *22*, 375-403. PA 63:10792.

Kerr, Steven; & Schriesheim, Chester. (1974). Consideration, initiating structure, and organizational criteria: An update of Korman's 1966 review. *Personnel Psychology*, *27*, 555-568. PA 55:01673.

Kerr, Steven; Schreisheim, Chester A.; Murphy, Charles J.; & Stogdill, Ralph M. (1974). Toward a contingency theory of leadership based upon the consideration and initiating structure literature. *Organizational Behavior & Human Performance*, *12*, 62-82. PA 53:04230.

Kervin, John B. (1974). Extending expectation states theory: A quantitative model. *Sociometry*, *37*, 349-362. PA 53:05172.

Khalique, Nazre. (1980). Effect of increasing number of passive spectators on the speed of verbal learning. *Psychologia: An International Journal of Psychology in the Orient*, *23*(1), 47-49. PA 66:01271.

Khatschenko, T. G. (1982). [The role of frustration and partner's gender in cooperative solutions of thinking problems]. *Voprosy Psikhologii*, No. 5, 118-122. PA 70:7960.

Kidd, Robert F. (1975). Pupil size, eye contact, and instrumental aggression. *Perceptual & Motor Skills*, *41*, 538. PA 55:07141.

Kidder, Louise H.; Bellettirie, Gerald; & Cohn, Ellen S. (1977). Secret ambitions and public performances: The effects of anonymity on reward allocations made by men and women. *Journal of Experimental Social Psychology, 13*, 70–80. PA 58:03295.

Kiesler, Charles A.; & Pallak, Michael S. (1975). Minority influence: The effect of majority reactionaries and defectors, and minority and majority compromisers, upon majority opinion and attraction. *European Journal of Social Psychology, 5*, 237–256. PA 55:07142.

Kiesler, Donald J. (1983). The 1982 Interpersonal Circle: A taxonomy for complementarity in human transactions. *Psychological Review, 90*, 185–214. PA 70:10243.

Kilbourne, Brock K.; & Kilbourne, Maria T. (1984). Norms of social conduct and the foot-in-the-door. *Journal of Social Psychology, 123*, 13–20. PA 72:25428.

Killworth, Peter [D.]; & Bernard, H. Russell. (1974). Catij: A new sociometric and its application to a prison living unit. *Human Organization, 33*(4), 335–350. SA 7714651.

Killworth, Peter D.; & Bernard, H. Russell. (1976). A model of human group dynamics. *Social Science Research, 5*(2), 173–224. PA 56:07907.

Kimball, Richard K.; & Hollander, Edwin P. (1974). Independence in the presence of an experienced but deviate group member. *Journal of Social Psychology, 93*, 281–292. PA 53:5211.

Kimberly, James C. (1984). Cognitive balance, inequality and consensus: Interrelations among fundamental processes in groups. *Advances in Group Processes, 1*, 95–126.

Kimberly, James C. (1986). Instrumental and expressive structures in small groups: The stabilization of injustice in groups in organizational settings. *Small Group Behavior, 17*, 395–406.

Kimble, Charles E.; Fitz, Don; & Onorad, James R. (1977). Effectiveness of counteraggression strategies in reducing interactive aggression by males. *Journal of Personality & Social Psychology, 35*, 272–278. PA 62:03610.

Kimble, Charles E.; Forte, Robert A.; & Yoshikawa, Joyce C. (1981). Nonverbal concomitants of enacted emotional intensity and positivity: Visual and vocal behavior. *Journal of Personality, 49*, 271–283. PA 67:09770.

Kimble, Charles E.; Yoshikawa, Joyce C.; & Zehr, H. David. (1981). Vocal and verbal assertiveness in same-sex and mixed sex groups. *Journal of Personality & Social Psychology, 40*, 1047–1054. PA 67:05712.

Kimmel, Melvin J.; Pruitt, Dean G.; Magenau, John M.; Konar-Goldband, Ellen; & Carnevale, Peter J. D. (1980). Effects of trust, aspiration, and gender on negotiation tactics. *Journal of Personality & Social Psychology, 38*, 9–22. PA 65:05389.

King, Charles E.; & Christensen, Andrew. (1983). The Relationship Events Scale: A Guttman scaling of progress in courtship. *Journal of Marriage and the Family, 45*, 671–678. PA 71:9484.

King, Dennis C.; & Glidewell, John C. (1980). Dyadic bargaining outcomes under individualistic and competitive orientations. *Human Relations, 33*, 781–803.

King, Gillian A.; & Sorrentino, Richard M. (1983). Psychological dimensions of goal-oriented interpersonal situations. *Journal of Personality and Social Psychology, 44*, 140–162. PA 70:3391.

Kingsbury, Steven J. (1978). Self-esteem of victim and the intent of third-party aggression in the reduction of hostile aggression. *Motivation & Emotion, 2*, 177–189. PA 64:03289.

Kinzel, Augustus F. (1970). Body-buffer zone in violent prisoners. *American Journal of Psychiatry, 127*, 59–64.

Kirchler, Erich; & Davis, James H. (1986). The influence of member status differences and task type on group consensus and member position change. *Journal of Personality and Social Psychology, 51*, 83–91. PA 73:27143.

Kirkpatrick, Samuel A.; Davis, Dwight F.; & Robertson, Roby D. (1976). The process of political decision-making in groups: Search behavior and choice shifts. *American Behavioral Scientist, 20*, 33–64. PA 57:10161.

Kirkwood, William G. (1984). Effects of incubation sequences on communication and problem solving in small groups. *Journal of Creative Behavior, 18*, 45–61. PA 72:1237.

Kirmeyer, Sandra. (1978). Urban density and pathology: A review of research. *Environment and Behavior, 10*, 247–270. PA 63:823.

Kirshner, Barry J.; Dies, Robert R.; & Brown, Robert A. (1978). Effects of experimental manipulation of self-disclosure on group cohesiveness. *Journal of Consulting and Clinical Psychology, 46*, 1171–1177. PA 62:5982.

Kissen, Morton. (Ed.). (1976). *From group dynamics to group psychoanalysis: Therapeutic application of group dynamic understanding.* Washington: Hemisphere.

Kitano, Eimasa. (1972). [Effect of group competition and cooperation on recall]. *Japanese Journal of Educational Psychology, 20,* 226-235. PA 53:2998.

Kitayama, Shinobu. (1983). Majority-minority relations in a changing context. *Japanese Psychological Research, 25,* 164-169. PA 71:25826. SA 8509450.

Kitayama, Shinobu. (1984). The influence of a minority within a group. *Japanese Journal of Experimental Social Psychology, 23,* 97-105. PA 71:28610.

Klandermans, Beit. (1984). Het aantal verwachte participanten, de effectiviteit van collectieve acties en de bereidheid om te participeren: het zwart-rijders dilemma heroverwogen [The number of expected participants, the effectiveness of collective action and the readiness to participate: The free-rider dilemma reconsidered]. *Nederlands Tijdschrift voor de Psychologie en huur Grensgebieden, 39*(6), 319-334. PA 72:22583.

Klaua, D[ieter]. (1975a). [Basic concepts of graph theory in the coherence and application of social structures]. *Zeitschrift für Psychologie, 183*(2), 141-162. PA 58:8692.

Klaua, Dieter. (1975b). [Length of network structures in communication processes]. *Zeitschrift für Psychologie, 183*(3), 295-305. PA 56:7908.

Klauss, Rudi; & Bass, Bernard M. (1974). Group influence on individual behavior across cultures. *Journal of Cross Cultural Psychology, 5,* 236-246. PA 53:5036.

Kleck, Robert E.; & Strenta, Angelo. (1980). Perceptions of the impact of negatively valued physical characteristics on social interaction. *Journal of Personality and Social Psychology, 39,* 861-873. PA 66:8014.

Klein, Andrew L. (1976). Changes in leadership appraisal as a function of the stress of a simulated panic situation. *Journal of Personality and Social Psychology, 34,* 1143-1154. PA 60:11666.

Klein, Kitty; & Harris, Bruce. (1979). Disruptive effects of disconfirmed expectancies about crowding. *Journal of Personality and Social Psychology, 37,* 769-777. PA 64:7992.

Kleinke, Chris L. (1975). Effects of false feedback about response lengths on subjects' perception of an interview. *Journal of Social psychology, 95,* 99-104. PA 54:3021.

Kleinke, Chris L. (1977a). Compliance to requests made by gazing and touching experimenters in field settings. *Journal of Experimental Social Psychology, 13,* 218-223. PA 59:3335.

Kleinke, Chris L. (1977b). Effects of dress on compliance to requests in a field setting. *Journal of Social Psychology, 101,* 223-224. PA 59:3334.

Kleinke, Chris L. (1986). Gaze and eye contact: A research review. *Psychological Bulletin, 100,* 78-100. PA 73:27160.

Kleinke, Chris L.; MacIntire, Susan C.; & Riddle, Diane M. (1978). Sex differences in compliance with legitimate and illegitimate requests. *Journal of Social Psychology, 105,* 153-154. PA 62:10972.

Kleinke, Chris L.; Meeker, Frederick B.; & La Fong, Carl. (1974). Effects of gaze, touch, and use of name on evaluation of engaged couples. *Journal of Research in Personality, 7,* 368-373. PA 56:7909.

Kleinke, Chris L.; & Singer, David A. (1979). Influence of gaze on compliance with demanding and conciliatory requests in a field setting. *Personality and Social Psychology Bulletin, 5,* 386-390. PA 64:10381.

Kleinke, Chris L.; Staneski, Richard A.; & Berger, Dale E. (1975). Evaluation of an interviewer as a function of interviewer gaze, reinforcement of subject gaze, and interviewer attractiveness. *Journal of Personality and Social Psychology, 31,* 115-122. PA 53:9522.

Kleinke, Chris L.; Staneski, Richard A.; & Pipp, Sandra L. (1975). Effects of gaze, distance, and attractiveness on males' first impressions of females. *Representative Research in Social Psychology, 6,* 7-12. PA 54:5245.

Kleiven, Jo; Fraser, Colin; & Gouge, Celia. (1974). Are individual and group decisions dependent on available information? *Scandinavian Journal of Psychology, 15,* 178-184. PA 53:7296.

Klimoski, Richard J. (1978). Simulation methodologies in experimental research on negotiations by representatives. *Journal of Conflict Resolution, 22,* 61-77. PA 61:10908.

Klimoski, Richard J. (1982). A nonnegotiable evaluation. [Review of Pruitt, 1981.] *Contemporary Psychology, 27,* 858-860.

Klimoski, Richard J.; & Ash, Ronald A. (1974).

Accountability and negotiator behavior. *Organizational Behavior and Human Performance, 11*, 409–425.

Kline, Linda M.; & Bell, Paul A. (1983). Privacy preference and interpersonal distancing. *Psychological Reports, 53*, 1214. PA 71:17754.

Kline, Linda M.; Harrison, Annemarie; Bell, Paul A.; Edney, Julian J.; & Hill, Ernie. (1984). Verbal reinforcement and feedback as solutions to a simulated commons dilemma. *Psychological Documents, 14*(2), 24. (Ms. No. 2648) PA 72:28026.

Klingberg, Haddon E. (1973). An evaluation of sensitivity training effects on self-actualization, purpose in life, and religious attitudes of theological students. *Journal of Psychology and Theology, 1*(4), 31–39. PA 52:5188.

Klinger, Eric; & McNelly, Frederick W. (1976). Self states and performances of preadolescent boys carrying out leadership roles inconsistent with their social status. *Child Development, 47*, 126–137. PA 56:7867.

Klopfer, Frederick J.; & Moran, Thomas. (1978). Influences of sex composition, decision rule, and decision consequences in small group policy making. *Sex Roles, 4*, 907–915. PA 63:9633. SA 80K8693.

Kmiecik, Cynthia; Mausar, Paula; & Banziger, George. (1979). Attractiveness and interpersonal space. *Journal of Social Psychology, 108*, 277–278. PA 65:1274.

Knapczyk, Dennis R.; & Yoppi, Judith O. (1975). Development of cooperative and competitive play responses in developmentally disabled children. *American Journal of Mental Deficiency, 80*, 245–255. PA 55:10357.

Knapp, Craig W.; & Harwood, B. Thomas. (1977). Factors in the determination of intimate same-sex friendship. *Journal of Genetic Psychology, 131*, 83–90. PA 60:3039.

Knapp, Mark L. (1978). *Nonverbal communication in human interaction* (2nd ed.). New York: Holt, Rinehart, & Winston.

Knapp, Mark L. (1984). *Interpersonal communication and human relationships.* Boston: Allyn & Bacon.

Knapp, Mark L.; & Miller, Gerald R. (Eds.). (1985). *Handbook of interpersonal communication.* Beverly Hills: Sage.

Knight, E. Leon; Alpert, Mark I.; & Witt, Robert E. (1976). Variation in group conformity influence. *Journal of Social Psychology, 98*, 137–138. PA 56:2307.

Knight, George P. (1980). Behavioral similarity, confederate strategy, and sex composition of dyad as determinants of interpersonal judgments and behavior in the Prisoner's Dilemma game. *Journal of Research in Personality, 14*, 91–103. PA 65:10385.

Knight, Patrick A.; & Saal, Frank E. (1984). Effects of gender differences and selection agent expertise on leader influence and performance evaluations. *Organizational Behavior and Human Performance, 34*, 225–243. PA 72:3999.

Knight, Patrick A.; & Weiss, Howard M. (1980). Effects of selection agent and leader origin on leader influence and group member perceptions. *Organizational Behavior and Human Performance, 26*, 7–21. PA 64:12458.

Knottnerus, J. David; & Greenstein, Theodore N. (1981). Status and performance characteristics in social interaction: A theory of status validation. *Social Psychology Quarterly, 44*, 338–349. PA 68:1094.

Knouse, Stephen B. (1980). Effects of sex of representative and quality of constituency's position in a technical negotiating task. *Perceptual and Motor Skills, 51*, 19–22. PA 66:8015.

Knowles, Eric S. (1975). Group risk taking shifts with a payoff response mode. *Journal of Social Psychology, 96*, 297–298. PA 55:726. SA 80K8694.

Knowles, Eric S. (1978a). A critique of figure placement procedures in studies of crowding. *Environmental Psychology and Nonverbal Behavior, 3*(1), 62–64. PA 63:9634.

Knowles, Eric S. (1978b). The gravity of crowding: Application of social physics to the effects of others. In A. Baum & Y. M. Epstein (Eds.), *Human response to crowding* (pp. 183–218). Hillsdale, NJ: Erlbaum.

Knowles, Eric S. (1980). An affiliative conflict theory of personal and group spatial behavior. In P. B. Paulus (Ed.), *Psychology of group influence* (pp. 133–188). Hillsdale, NJ: Erlbaum.

Knowles, Eric S. (1983). Social physics and the effects of others: Tests of the effects of audience size and distance on social judgments and behavior. *Journal of Personality and Social Psychology, 45*, 1263–1279. PA 71:15000.

Knowles, Eric S.; & Bassett, Rodney L. (1976). Groups and crowds as social entities: Effects of activity, size, and member similarity on nonmembers. *Journal of Personality and Social Psychology, 34*, 837–845. PA 57:12747.

Knowles, Eric S.; & Brickner, Mary A. (1981). Social cohesion effects on spatial cohesion. *Personality and Social Psychology Bulletin, 7*, 309–313. PA 67:5713.

Knowles, Eric S.; & Johnsen, Per K. (1974). Intrapersonal consistency in interpersonal distance. *Catalog of Selected Documents in Psychology, 4*, 124. PA 53:11583.

Knowles, Eric S.; Kreuser, Barbara; Haas, Susan; Hyde, Michael; & Schuchart, Guy E. (1976). Group size and the extension of social space boundaries. *Journal of Personality and Social Psychology, 33*, 647–654. PA 56:4050.

Knox, Robert E.; & Safford, R. Kirk. (1976). Group caution at the race track. *Journal of Experimental Social Psychology, 12*, 317–324. PA 56:5974.

Knudson, Roger M.; Sommers, Alison A.; & Golding, Stephen L. (1980). Interpersonal perception and mode of resolution in marital conflict. *Journal of Personality and Social Psychology, 38*, 751–763.

Knutson, Thomas J.; & Holdridge, William E. (1975). Orientation behavior, leadership and consensus: A possible functional relationship. *Speech Monographs, 42*(2), 107–114. PA 54:9566.

Kohen, Janet A. (1975a). The development of reciprocal self-disclosure in opposite-sex interaction. *Journal of Counseling Psychology, 22*, 404–410. PA 54:11667.

Kohen, Janet A. (1975b). Liking and self-disclosure in opposite sex dyads. *Psychological Reports, 36*, 695–698. PA 54:9604. SA 78J4691.

Kohn, Alfie. (1986). How to succeed without even vying. *Psychology Today, 20*(9), 22–28, 61.

Kohn, Martin; & Parnes, Barbara. (1974). Social interaction in the classroom: A comparison of apathetic-withdrawn and angry-defiant children. *Journal of Genetic Psychology, 125*, 165–175. PA 53:9481.

Kolb, Deborah M. (1983). *The mediators.* Cambridge, MA: MIT Press.

Kollock, Peter; Blumstein, Philip; & Schwartz, Pepper. (1985). Sex and power in interaction: Conversational privileges and duties. *American Sociological Review, 50*, 34–46.

Kolominskii, Ya. L. (1974). [The socio-psychological nature of children's groups]. *Voprosy Psikhologii,* No. 3, 31–40. PA 53:9305.

Komarovsky, Mirra. (1974). Patterns of self-disclosure of male undergraduates. *Journal of Marriage and the Family, 36*, 677–686. PA 55:727.

Komorita, Samuel S. (1974). A weighted probability model of coalition formation. *Psychological Review, 81*, 242–256. PA 52:9999.

Komorita, S[amuel] S. (1976). A model of the N-person Dilemma-Type Game. *Journal of Experimental Social Psychology, 12*, 357–373.

Komorita, Samuel S. (1977). Negotiating from strength and the concept of bargaining strength. *Journal for the Theory of Social Behaviour, 7*, 65–79. PA 61:5931.

Komorita, Samuel S. (1978). Evaluating coalition theories: Some indices. *Journal of Conflict Resolution, 22*, 691–706.

Komorita, Samuel S. (1979). An equal excess model of coalition formation. *Behavioral Science, 24*, 369–381. PA 65:1237. SA 81L3329.

Komorita, S. S. (1984). Coalition bargaining. *Advances in Experimental Social Psychology, 18*, 183–245.

Komorita, Samuel S.; & Barth, Joan M. (1985). Components of reward in social dilemmas. *Journal of Personality and Social Psychology, 48*, 364–373. PA 72:20114.

Komorita, Samuel S.; & Brinberg, David. (1977). The effects of equity norms in coalition formation. *Social Psychology Quarterly, 40*, 351–361. PA 61:8448. SA 78J4692.

Komorita, S. S.; & Ellis, Alan L. (1988). Level of aspiration in coalition bargaining. *Journal of Personality and Social Psychology, 54*, 421–431.

Komorita, Samuel S.; & Esser, James K. (1975). Frequency of reciprocated concessions in bargaining. *Journal of Personality and Social Psychology, 32*, 699–705. PA 56:2308.

Komorita, Samuel S.; Hamilton, Thomas P.; & Kravitz, David A. (1984). Effects of alternatives in coalition bargaining. *Journal of Experimental Social Psychology, 20*, 116–136. PA 71:31320.

Komorita, Samuel S.; & Kravitz, David A. (1979).

The effects of alternatives in bargaining. *Journal of Experimental Social Psychology, 15,* 147–157. PA 64:3254.

Komorita, Samuel S.; & Kravitz, David A. (1981). Effects of prior experience on coalition bargaining. *Journal of Personality and Social Psychology, 40,* 675–686. PA 67:5714.

Komorita, S. S.; & Kravitz, David A. (1983). Coalition formation. In H. H. Blumberg, A. P. Hare, V. Kent, & M. F. Davies (Eds.), *Small groups and social interaction* (Vol. 2, pp. 189–197). Chichester: John Wiley.

Komorita, Samuel S.; & Lapworth, C. William. (1982a). Alternative choices in social dilemmas. *Journal of Conflict Resolution, 26,* 692–708. PA 69:10402.

Komorita, Samuel S.; & Lapworth, C. William. (1982b). Cooperative choice among individuals versus groups in an N-person dilemma situation. *Journal of Personality and Social Psychology, 42,* 487–496. PA 68:8107.

Komorita, Samuel S.; Lapworth, C. William; & Tumonis, Toni M. (1981). The effects of certain vs risky alternatives in bargaining. *Journal of Experimental Social Psychology, 17,* 525–544. PA 67:12041.

Komorita, Samuel S.; & Leung, K. (1985). The effects of alternatives on the salience of reward allocation norms. *Journal of Experimental Social Psychology, 21,* 229–246. PA 73:14432.

Komorita, S. S.; & Meek, David D. (1978). Generality and validity of some theories of coalition formation. *Journal of Personality and Social Psychology, 36,* 392–404.

Komorita, Samuel S.; & Miller, Charles E. (1986). Bargaining strength as a function of coalition alternatives. *Journal of Personality and Social Psychology, 51,* 325–332. PA 73:29955.

Komorita, Samuel S.; & Moore, Danny. (1976). Theories and processes of coalition formation. *Journal of Personality and Social Psychology, 33,* 371–381. PA 56:7910.

Komorita, Samuel S.; & Nagao, Dennis. (1983). The functions of resources in coalition bargaining. *Journal of Personality and Social Psychology, 44,* 95–106. PA 70:3392.

Komorita, Samuel S.; Sweeney, James; & Kravitz, David A. (1980). Cooperative choice in N-person dilemma situation. *Journal of Personality and Social Psychology, 38,* 504–516. PA 65:10436.

Komorita, Samuel S.; & Tumonis, Toni M. (1980).

Extensions and tests of some descriptive theories of coalition formation. *Journal of Personality and Social Psychology, 39,* 256–268. PA 66:3594.

Konar-Goldband, Ellen; Rice, Robert W.; & Monkarsh, William. (1979). Time phased interrelationships of group atmosphere, group performance, and leader style. *Journal of Applied Psychology, 64,* 401–409. PA 64:7931.

Konecni, Vladimir J. (1975). The mediation of aggressive behavior: Arousal level versus anger and cognitive labelling. *Journal of Personality and Social Psychology, 32,* 706–712. PA 56:2361.

Konecni, Vladimir J.; Libuser, Lynn; Morton, Houston; & Ebbesen, Ebbe B. (1975). Effects of a violation of personal space on escape and helping responses. *Journal of Experimental Social Psychology, 11,* 288–299. PA 54:7516.

Koneya, Mele. (1977). Privacy regulation in small and large groups. *Group and Organization Studies, 2*(3), 324–335. PA 60:3040.

Koneya, Mele. (1978). The Steinzor effect revisited. *Small Group Behavior, 9,* 540–548. SA 80K4180.

König, René. (1983). Die Analytisch-praktische Doppelbedeutung des Gruppentherorems. Ein Blick in die Hintergründe [The analytical-practical double meaning of the theorem of groups: A glance at the background]. *Kölner Zeitschrift für Sociologie und Sozialpsychologie,* Supplement 25, 36–64. SA 84O2586.

Kool, V. K.; & Kumar, Vinai. (1979). Experimentally induced aggression levels of identical- and cross-sex dyads. *Journal of Social Psychology, 109,* 145–146. PA 65:3249.

Koomen, Willem. (1984). Zichzelf bevestigende en zichzelf vernietigende voorspellingen in interpersoonlijk gedrag [Self-fulfilling and self-defeating prophecies in interpersonal behavior]. *Nederlands Tijdschrift voor de Psychologie en haar Grensgebieden, 39*(8), 449–461. PA 72:28027.

Koomen, Willem; & Dijkstra, Wil. (1975). Effects of question length on verbal behavior in a bias-reduced interview situation. *European Journal of Social Psychology, 5,* 399–403. PA 58:3280.

Koomen, Willem; Ouweltjes, J.; Wester, A.; van Bovenkamp, J.; & Forma, H. (1979). De invloed van participeren en structureren op het toeschrijven van leiderschap in een groep [The effects of participation and organizational-integrative interaction on leadership-ratings in a group]. *Mens en Maatschappij*, *54*(3), 309–320. SA 801.0188.

Koomen, Willem; & Sagel, Piet K. (1977). The prediction of participation in two-person groups. *Sociometry*, *40*, 369–373. PA 61:8449. SA 78J4693.

Koomen, Willem; Van de Bovenkamp, J.; & Forma, H. (1980). [One's status in a group and his liking for the other group members]. *Nederlands Tijdschrift voor de Psychologie en haar Grensgebieden*, *35*(2), 121–126. PA 66:3606.

Koppelaar, Leendert. (1983). Interactie tussen politie en publiek: Invloed van spel en verbeelding op causale attributies [Police-public interaction: Influence of role-playing on causal attributes]. *Nederlands Tijdschrift voor de Psychologie en haar Grensgebieden*, *38*(5), 272–285. PA 71:12205.

Korte, Charles. (1980). Urban-nonurban differences in social behavior and social psychological models of urban impact. *Journal of Social Issues*, *36*(3), 29–51. PA 65:3126.

Korte, Charles; & Kerr, Nancy. (1975). Response to altruistic opportunities in urban and nonurban settings. *Journal of Social Psychology*, *95*, 183–184. PA 54:3023.

Korte, Charles; Ypma, Ido; & Toppen, Anneke. (1975). Helpfulness in Dutch society as a function of urbanization and environmental input level. *Journal of Personality and Social Psychology*, *32*, 996–1003. PA 55:12248.

Kostinskaya, A. G. (1976). Foreign investigations of risky decision-making in groups. *Voprosy Psikhologii*, No. 5, 171–178. PA 61:3539.

Kostinskaya, A. G. (1984). [Processes of social perception under conditions of group decision making]. *Voprosy Psikhologii*, No. 1, 75–80. PA 72:14473.

Kraft, Lee W.; & Vraa, Calvin W. (1975). Sex composition of groups and pattern of self-disclosure by high school females. *Psychological Reports*, *37*, 733–734. PA 55:12217.

Krail, Kristina A.; & Leventhal, Gloria. (1976). The sex variable in the intrusion of personal space. *Sociometry*, *39*, 170–173. PA 56:5996.

Krain, Mark. (1977). Effects of love and liking in premarital dyads. *Sociological Focus*, *10*(3), 249–262.

Kramarae, Cheris. (1981). *Women and men speaking: Frameworks for analysis*. Rowley, MA: Newbury House.

Kranas, Grazyna. (1982). Utility of outcomes and liking in ingroup conflict of interest. *Polish Psychological Bulletin*, *13*, 63–72. PA 71:6701.

Krantz, David S. (1979). A naturalistic study of social influences on meal size among moderately obese and nonobese subjects. *Psychosomatic Medicine*, *41*(1), 19–27. PA 64:3255.

Krantz, Murray; George, Susan Wanska; & Hursh, Kathleen. (1983). Gaze and mutual gaze of preschool children in conversation. *Journal of Psychology*, *113*, 9–15. PA 70:7795.

Kratcoski, Peter C. (1984). Perspectives on intrafamily violence. *Human Relations*, *37*, 443–454. PA 71:31581.

Kraut, Robert E. (1982). Social presence, facial feedback, and emotion. *Journal of Personality and Social Psychology*, *42*, 853–863. PA 68:12603.

Kraut, Robert E.; & Johnston, Robert E. (1979). Social and emotional messages of smiling: An ethological approach. *Journal of Personality and Social Psychology*, *37*, 1539–1553. PA 65:1226.

Kraut, Robert E.; Lewis, Steven H.; & Swezey, Lawrence W. (1982). Listener responsiveness and the coordination of conversation. *Journal of Personality and Social Psychology*, *43*, 718–731. PA 69:10404.

Kravitz, David A. (1981). Effects of resources and alternatives on coalition formation. *Journal of Personality and Social Psychology*, *41*, 87–98. PA 67:5716.

Kravitz, David A.; Cohen, Jerry L.; Martin, Barbara; Sweeney, James; McCarty, John; Elliott, Elaine; & Goldstein, Paul. (1978). Humans would do better without other humans. *Personality and Social Psychology Bulletin*, *4*, 559–560. PA 64:5561.

2436. Kravitz, David A.; & Iwaniszek, John. (1984). Number of coalitions and resources as sources of power in coalition bargaining. *Journal of Personality & Social Psychology*, *47*, 534–548. PA 72:04000.

Kravitz, David A.; & Martin, Barbara. (1986). Ringelmann rediscovered: The original article. *Journal of Personality and Social Psychology*, *50*, 936–941. PA 73:21914.

Krebs, Dennis L.; & Miller, Dale T. (1985). Altruism and aggression. In G. Lindzey & E.

Aronson (Eds.), *Handbook of social psychology* (3rd ed., Vol. 2, pp. 1-71). New York: Random House.

Kreeger, Lionel. (Ed.). (1975). *The large group: Dynamics and therapy*. Itasca, IL: Peacock. PA 54:11669.

Krege, Wolfgang. (1974). [On the cartography of groups]. *Gruppendynamik Forschung und Praxis*, *5*(4), 265-269. PA 54:9567.

Kremer, John M.; & Mack, David. (1983). Preemptive game behaviour and the emergence of leadership. *British Journal of Social Psychology*, *22*, 19-26. PA 70:12641. SA 8400953.

Krichevskii, R. L. (1977a, Jan.-Feb.). Determinanty rolevoi differentsiatsii liderstva v malykh gruppakh [Determining factors of the role differentiation of leadership in small groups]. *Voprosy psikhologii*, *1*, 28-38. PA 79J6850.

Krichevskii, R. L. (1977b). Sovremennye tendentsii v issledovanii liderstva v amerikanskoi sotsialnoi psikhologii [Modern trends in the study of leadership in american social psychology]. *Voprosy psikhologii*, *6*, 119-129. SA 79J8121.

Krichevskii, R. L. (1981). [Empiric verification of a model of leadership efficiency]. *Novye Issledovaniya v Psikhologii*, *2*(25), 89-94. PA 71:9485.

Krichevskii, R. L. (1984). [Leader authority and group effectiveness]. *Novye Issledovaniya v Psikhologii*, *31*(2), 57-62. PA 73:6338.

Kriss, Mitchel; Indenbaum, Eugene; & Tesch, Frederick. (1974). Message type and status of interactants as determinants of telephone helping behavior. *Journal of Personality and Social Psychology*, *30*, 856-859. PA 53:11612.

Kriss, Mitchel; Kinchla, R. A.; & Darley, John M. (1977). A mathematical model for social influences on perceptual judgments. *Journal of Experimental Social Psychology*, *13*, 403-420. PA 60:1076.

Krivohlavy, Jaro. (1976). [The psychology of cooperation and creative interpersonal conflict resolution]. *Przeglad Psychologiczny*, *19*(4), 491-509. PA 59:3336.

Krivohlavy, Jaro; & Klicperova, Martina. (1985). Stavba veze (Socialne psychologicka metoda zjist'ovani kooperace v dyade) [The building of a tower: A social-psychological method for assessment of a dyadic cooperation]. *Ceskoslovenska Psychologie*, *29*, 52-61. PA 74:6045.

Krivonos, Paul D.; Byrne, Donn; & Friedrich, Gustav W. (1976). The effect of attitude similarity on task performance. *Journal of Applied Social Psychology*, *6*, 307-313. PA 58:3327.

Krogius, Nikolai V. (1984). [People's cognition of one another in interpersonal conflict (using the example of chess game activity)]. *Psikologicheskii Zhurnal*, *5*(2), 54-61. PA 74:21912.

Krokoff, Lowell J.; & Gottman, John M. (1983). The structural model of marital interaction. In H. H. Blumberg, A. P. Hare, V. Kent, & M. F. Davies (Eds.), *Small Groups and Social Interaction* (Vol. 1, pp. 347-358). Chichester and New York: Wiley.

Kronik, A. A. (1981). [The mechanism of the perception of status structure in small groups: II. Perceived status in groups with varying levels of development]. *Novye Issledovaniya v Psikhologii*, No. 1 (24), 75-79. PA 70:5628.

Krop, Harry; Messinger, Jacqueline; & Reiner, Charles. (1973-1974). Increasing eye contact by covert reinforcement. *Interpersonal Development*, *4*(1), 51-57. PA 53:1065.

Krueger, Gerald P. (1977). *Conferencing and teleconferencing in three communication modes as a function of the number of conferees* (Tech. Rep. No. 6). Baltimore: Johns Hopkins University, Department of Psychology. PA 58:11660.

Krzemionka-Brozda, Dorota. (1984). Otwarcie sie—jego determinanty i konsekwencje dla funkcjonowania jednostki [Self-disclosure: Its determinants and consequences for the functioning of an individual]. *Przeglad Psychologiczny*, *27*(4), 915-931. PA 74:1057.

Kuethe, James L. (1975). Mapping into a structure: A method for studying social cognition. *Psychological Reports*, *37*, 1279-1283. PA 56:4052.

Kugihara, Naoki. (1985). [Conformity and fixation of escape behavior in emergency]. *Japanese Journal of Psychology*, *56*, 29-35. PA 73:14466.

Kugihara, Naoki; & Misumi, Jyuji. (1984). [An experimental study of the effect of leadership types on followers' escaping behavior in a fearful emergency maze-situation]. *Japanese Journal of Psychology*, *55*, 214-220. PA 72:25403.

Kugihara, Naoki; Misumi, Jyuji; & Sato, Seiichi. (1980). [Experimental study of escape behavior in a simulated panic situation: I]. *Japanese*

Journal of Experimental Social Psychology, 20, 55–67. PA 66:10332.

Kugihara, Naoki; Misumi, Jyuji; Sato, Seiichi; & Shigeoka, Kazunobu. (1982). [Experimental study of escape behavior in a simulated panic situation: II. Leadership in emergency situation]. *Japanese Journal of Experimental Social Psychology, 21,* 159–166. PA 68:10323.

Kuhlman, D. Michael; & Marshello, Alfred F. (1975). Individual differences in game motivation as moderators of preprogrammed strategy effects in prisoner's dilemma. *Journal of Personality and Social Psychology, 32,* 922–931. PA 55:4565.

Kuhlman, D. Michael; & Wimberley, David L. (1976). Expectations of choice behavior held by cooperators, competitors, and individualists across four classes of experimental games. *Journal of Personality and Social Psychology, 34,* 69–81. PA 56:5997.

Kuiken, Don. (1981). Nonimmediate language style and inconsistency between private and expressed evaluations. *Journal of Experimental Social Psychology, 17,* 183–196. PA 67:1231.

Kuiken, Don; Rasmussen, R. V.; & Cullen, Dallas. (1974). Some predictors of volunteer participation in human relations training groups. *Psychological Reports, 35,* 499–504. PA 53:7320.

Kukita, Jun. (1984). [Effects of intergroup relationships and level of performance on inter- and intra-group distribution]. *Japanese Journal of Experimental Social Psychology, 23,* 125–137. PA 71:28611.

Kulik, James A.; & Mahler, Heike I. M. (1986). Self-confirmatory effects of delay on perceived contribution to a joint activity. *Personality and Social Psychology Bulletin, 12,* 344–352. PA 74:34453.

Kumar, Pramod; & Kaur, Jasbir. (1976). Cooperation and competition: An experimental study. *Journal of Psychological Researches, 20*(1), 33–35. PA 65:1238.

Kumar, Pramod; & Sharma, Mukta. (1981). Norm formation: An experimental study. *Asian Journal of Psychology and Education, 7*(1), 27–30. PA 68:12616.

Kunzendorf, Robert G.; & Denney, Joseph. (1982). Definitions of personal space: Smokers versus nonsmokers. *Psychological Reports, 50,* 818. PA 69:1022.

Kuperminc, Murray; & Heimberg, Richard G. (1983). Consequence probability and utility as

factors in the decision to behave assertively. *Behavior Therapy, 14,* 637–646. PA 71:9506.

'2472. Kurdek, Lawrence A.; & Schmitt, J. Patrick. (1986). Relationship quality of partners in heterosexual married, heterosexual cohabiting, and gay and lesbian relationships. *Journal of Personality and Social Psychology, 51,* 711–720.

Kurecka, Paul M.; Austin, James M.; Johnson, Wanda; & Mendoza, Jorge L. (1982). Full and errant coaching effects on assigned role leaderless group discussion performance. *Personnel Psychology, 35,* 805–812. PA 69:7882.

Kurokawa, Masaru; & Misumi, Jyuji. (1975). [The effects of the size of working groups upon subordinates' perceptions of their supervisors' leadership functions]. *Japanese Journal of Experimental Social Psychology, 15*(1), 62–73. PA 58:1102.

Kushell, Elliot; & Newton, Rae. (1986). Gender, leadership style, and subordinate satisfaction: An experiment. *Sex Roles, 14,* 203–209. PA 74:10192.

Kushner, Harvey W.; & de Maio, Gerald. (1977). Using digraphs to determine the crucial actors in a voting body. *Social Psychology Quarterly, 40,* 361–369. PA 61:8450.

Kushnir, T. (1981). The status of arousal in recent social facilitation literature: A review and evaluation of assumptions implied by the current research model. *Social Behavior and Personality, 9,* 185–190. PA 68:8127.

Kushnir, T.; & Duncan, K. D. (1978). An analysis of social facilitation effects in terms of signal detection theory. *Psychological Record, 28,* 535–541. PA 62:3541.

Kuykendall, David; & Keating, John P. (1984). Crowding and reactions to uncontrollable events. *Population and Environment Behavioral and Social Issues, 7,* 246–259. PA 73:29957.

Kuypers, Bart C.; Davies, Don; & Hazewinkel, Aart. (1986). Developmental patterns in self-analytic groups. *Human Relations, 39,* 793–815. PA 74:1058.

Lacoursiere, Roy B. (1980). *The life cycle of groups: Group developmental stage theory.* New York: Human Sciences Press.

Lacy, William B. (1978). Assumptions of human nature, and initial expectations and behavior as mediators of sex effects in Prisoner's Dilemma research. *Journal of Conflict Resolution, 22,* 269–281. PA 62:10975.

Ladouceur, Robert; Tourigny, Marc; & Mayrand, Marie. (1986). Familiarity, group exposure, and risk-taking behavior in gambling. *Journal of Psychology*, *120*, 45–49. PA 74:21874.

LaFollette, William; & Belohlav, James A. (1982). The effect of motivational homogeneity on risk in decision making. *Journal of Psychology*, *112*, 53–61. PA 69:12663.

LaFrance, Marianne. (1979). Nonverbal synchrony and rapport: Analysis by the cross-lag panel technique. *Social Psychology Quarterly*, *42*, 66–70. PA 64:7932.

LaFrance, Marianne. (1985). Postural mirroring and intergroup relations. *Personality and Social Psychology Bulletin*, *11*, 207–217. PA 73:14434.

LaFrance, Marianne; & Broadbent, Maida. (1976). Group rapport: Posture sharing as a nonverbal indicator. *Group and Organization Studies*, *1*, 328–333. PA 58:1103.

LaFrance, Marianne; & Ickes, William. (1981). Posture mirroring and interactional involvement: Sex and sex typing effects. *Journal of Nonverbal Behavior*, *5*, 139–154. PA 67:1232.

LaFrance, Marianne; & Mayo, Clara. (1976). Racial differences in gaze behavior during conversations: Two systematic observational studies. *Journal of Personality and Social Psychology*, *33*, 547–552. PA 56:5998.

LaFreniere, Peter; & Charlesworth, William R. (1983). Dominance, attention, and affiliation in a preschool group: A nine-month longitudinal study. *Ethology and Sociobiology*, *4*, 55–67. SA 84N5652.

Laing, James D.; & Morrison, Richard J. (1973). Coalitions and payoffs in three-person sequential games: Initial tests of two formal models. *Journal of Mathematical Sociology*, *3*, 3–25. SA 75H5814.

Laing, James D.; & Slotznick, Benjamin. (1987). Viable alternatives to the status quo: A game-theoretic and laboratory study of four-fifths majority rule. *Journal of Conflict Resolution*, *31*, 63–85. PA 74:21875.

Laird, James D. (1974). Self-attribution of emotion: The effects of expressive behavior on the quality of emotional experience. *Journal of Personality and Social Psychology*, *24*, 475–486.

Laird, James D. (1984). The real role of facial response in the experience of emotion: A reply to Tourangeau and Ellsworth, and others.

Journal of Personality and Social Psychology, *47*, 909–917. PA 72:11389.

Lakin, Martin. (1985). *The helping group: Therapeutic principles and issues*. Reading, MA: Addison-Wesley.

LaKind, Elizabeth; & Hornstein, Harvey A. (1979). The effect of mood and social outlook on hypothetical juridic decisions. *Journal of Applied Social Psychology*, *9*, 548–559. PA 66:5808.

Lamb, Theodore A. (1980). Paralanguage hierarchies in dyads and triads: Talking first and talking the most. *Social Behavior and Personality*, *8*, 221–224. PA 66:10333. SA 82M4024.

Lamb, Theodore A. (1981). Nonverbal and paraverbal control in dyads and triads: Sex or power differences? *Social Psychology Quarterly*, *44*, 49–53. PA 67:1233. SA 82M1466.

Lamb, Theodore A. (1986). The familiarity effect in small-group-hierarchy research. *Journal of Social Psychology*, *126*, 51–56. PA 74:25051.

Lamb, Theodore A.; & Alsikafi, Majeed. (1980). Conformity in the asch experiment: Inner-other directedness and the "defiant subject". *Social Behavior and Personality*, *8*, 13–16. SA 81L3330.

Lamke, Leanne K.; & Bell, Nancy J. (1982). Sex-role orientation and relationship development in same-sex dyads. *Journal of Research in Personality*, *16*, 343–354. PA 70:1054.

Lamm, Helmut; & Kayser, Egon. (1976). [Negotiation preparation and conditions in situations with different communication and visual contact]. *Zeitschrift fur Sozialpsychologie*, *7*, 279–285. PA 63:11951.

Lamm, Helmut; & Kayser, Egon. (1978). The allocation of monetary gain and loss following dyadic performance: The weight given to effort and ability under conditions of low and high intra-dyadic attraction. *European Journal of Social Psychology*, *8*, 275–278. PA 62:3542. SA 79J9644.

Lamm, Helmut; & Myers, David G. (1976). Machiavellianism, discussion time, and group shift. *Social Behavior and Personality*, *4*, 41–48. SA 77I7504.

Lamm, Helmut; & Myers, David G. (1978). Group-induced polarization of attitudes and behavior. *Advances in Experimental Social Psychology*, *11*, 145–195.

Lamm, Helmut; Myers, David G.; & Ochsmann, Randolph. (1976). [On predicting group-induced shifts toward risk or caution: A second look at some experiments]. *Psychologische Beitrage, 18,* 288–296. PA 57:12750.

Lamm, Helmut; & Sauer, Claudius. (1974). Discussion-induced shift toward higher demands in negotiation. *European Journal of Social Psychology, 4,* 85–88. PA 54:02978.

Lamm, Helmut; & Trommsdorff, Gisela. (1973). Group versus individual performance on tasks requiring ideational proficiency (brainstorming): A review. *European Journal of Social Psychology, 3,* 361–388. PA 53:9483.

Lando, Harry A. (1976). Sex differences in response to differing patterns of attack. *Personality and Social Psychology Bulletin, 2,* 286–289.

Lando, Harry A.; Johnson-Payne, Elaine; Gilbert, Lucia A.; & Deutsch, Connie J. (1977). Sex differences in response to physical and nonphysical instigators. *Sex Roles, 3,* 523–535.

Lane, Irving M.; Mathews, Robert C.; Chaney, Courtland M.; Effmeyer, Robert C.; Reber, Robert A.; & Teddlie, Charles B. (1982). Making the goals of acceptance and quality explicit: Effects on group decisions. *Small Group Behavior, 13,* 542–554. PA 70:5629.

Lange, Hella; Mueller, Charles W.; & Donnerstein, Edward. (1979). The effects of social, spatial, and interference density on performance and mood. *Journal of Social Psychology, 109,* 283–287. PA 65:5419.

Lange, Jonathan I.; & Grove, Theodore G. (1981). Sociometric and autonomic responses to three levels of self-disclosure in dyads. *Western Journal of Speech Communication, 45,* 355–362. SA 84O2587.

Langer, Ellen J. (1978). Rethinking the role of thought in social interaction. In J. H. Harvey, W. J. Ickes, & R. F. Kidd (Eds.), *New directions in attribution research* (Vol. 2, pp. 35–58). Hillsdale, New Jersey: Erlbaum.

Langer, Ellen J.; Blank, Arthur; & Chanowitz, Benzion. (1978). The mindlessness of ostensibly thoughtful action: The role of "placebic" information in interpersonal interaction. *Journal of Personality and Social Psychology, 36,* 635–642.

Langer, Ellen J.; Chanowitz, Benzion; & Blank, Arthur. (1985). Mindlessness-mindfulness in perspective: A reply to Valerie Folkes. *Journal of Personality and Social Psychology, 48,* 605–607.

Langer, Ellen J.; & Imber, Lois. (1980). Role of mindlessness in the perception of deviance.

Journal of Personality and Social Psychology, 39, 360–367.

Langer, Ellen J.; & Saegert, Susan. (1977). Crowding and cognitive control. *Journal of Personality and Social Psychology, 35,* 175–182. PA 62:3662.

Lanyon, Richard I. (1984). Personality assessment. *Annual Review of Psychology, 35,* 667–701. PA 71:24921.

Lanzetta, John T.; & Orr, Scott P. (1986). Excitatory strength of expressive faces: Effects of happy and fear expressions and context on the extinction of a conditioned fear response. *Journal of Personality and Social Psychology, 50,* 190–194. PA 73:16329.

Larntz, Kinley. (1975). Reanalysis of Vidmar's data on the effects of decision alternatives on verdicts of simulated jurors. *Journal of Personality and Social Psychology, 31,* 123–125. PA 53:9484.

Larsen, Knud S. (1974). Conformity in the Asch experiment. *Journal of Social Psychology, 94,* 303–304. PA 53:9524.

Larsen, Knud S. (1982). Cultural conditions and conformity: The Asch effect. *Bulletin of the British Psychological Society, 35,* 347. PA 69:10406.

Larsen, Knud S.; Triplett, Jeff S.; Brant, William D.; & Langenberg, Don. (1979). Collaborator status, subject characteristics, and conformity in the Asch paradigm. *Journal of Social Psychology, 108,* 259–263.

Larwood, Laurie; & Blackmore, John. (1978). Sex discrimination in managerial selection: Testing predictions of the vertical dyad linkage model. *Sex Roles, 4,* 359–367. PA 63:3248.

Larwood, Laurie; & Lockheed, Marlaine. (1979). Women as managers: Toward second generation research. *Sex Roles, 5,* 659–666. PA 65:2406.

Larzelere, Robert E.; & Huston, Ted L. (1980). The dyadic trust scale: Toward understanding interpersonal trust in close relationships. *Journal of Marriage and the Family, 1980, 42,* 595–604. PA 66:3533.

Laschinsky, Dorte; & Koch, Uwe. (1975). [T-groups: Origin, participants and goals]. *Psychotherapy and Psychosomatics, 26*(1), 39–48. PA 54:11670.

Latané, Bibb. (1981). The psychology of social impact. *American Psychologist, 36,* 343–356.

Latané, Bibb; & Bidwell, Liane D. (1977). Sex and

affiliation in college cafeterias. *Personality and Social Psychology Bulletin, 3,* 571–574. PA 60:11694.

Latané, Bibb; & Dabbs, James M. (1975). Sex, group size and helping in three cities. *Sociometry, 38,* 180–194. PA 54:11671.

Latané, Bibb; & Darley, John M. (1968). Group inhibition of bystander intervention in emergencies. *Journal of Personality and Social Psychology, 10,* 215–221.

Latané, Bibb; & Darley, John M. (1970). *The unresponsive bystander: Why doesn't he help?* New York: Appleton-Century Crofts.

Latané, Bibb; & Harkins, Stephen. (1976). Cross-modality matches suggest anticipated stage fright a multiplicative power function of audience size and status. *Perception and Psychophysics, 20,* 482–488. PA 58:3296.

Latané, Bibb; & Nida, Steve. (1980). Social impact theory and group influence: A social engineering perspective. In P. B. Paulus (Ed.), *Psychology of group influence* (pp. 3–34). Hillsdale, New Jersey: Erlbaum. .

Latané, Bibb; & Nida, Steve. (1981). Ten years of research on group size and helping. *Psychological Bulletin, 89,* 308–324. PA 65:12743.

Latané, Bibb; Williams, Kipling; & Harkins, Stephen. (1979a). Many hands make light the work: The causes and consequences of social loafing. *Journal of Personality and Social Psychology, 37,* 822–832. PA 64:10335.

Latané, Bibb; Williams, Kipling; & Harkins, Stephen. (1979b, October). Social loafing. *Psychology Today, 13*(4), 104–110.

Latané, Bibb; & Wolf, Sharon. (1981). The social impact of majorities and minorities. *Psychological Review, 88,* 438–453. PA 66:12770.

Latham, Van M. (1987). Task type and group motivation: Implications for a behavioral approach to leadership in small groups. *Small Group Behavior, 18,* 56–71.

LaTour, Stephen; Houlden, Pauline; Walker, Laurens; & Thibaut, John. (1976). Some determinants of preference for modes of conflict resolution. *Journal of Conflict Resolution, 20,* 319–356. PA 56:7868.

Latta, R. Michael. (1978). Relation of status incongruence to personal space. *Personality and Social Psychology Bulletin, 4,* 143–146. PA 61:5933.

Latta, R. Michael; & Gorman, Michael E. (1984). The small group: A bridge between sociology

and social psychology. *Psychological Reports, 54,* 947–950. PA 72:3982.

Laufer, Robert S.; & Wolfe, Maxine. (1977). Privacy as a concept and a social issue: A multidimensional developmental theory. *Journal of Social Issues, 33*(3), 22–42. PA 62:836.

Laughlin, Patrick R. (1978). Ability and group problem solving. *Journal of Research and Development in Education, 12*(1), 114–120. PA 64:5562.

Laughlin, Patrick R. (1988). Collective induction: Group performance, social combination processes, and mutual majority and minority influence. *Journal of Personality and Social Psychology, 54,* 254–267.

Laughlin, Patrick R.; & Adamopoulos, John. (1980). Social combination processes and individual learning for six-person cooperative groups on an intellective task. *Journal of Personality and Social Psychology, 38,* 941–947. PA 65:12744.

Laughlin, Patrick R.; & Barth, Joan M. (1981). Group-to-individual and individual-to-group problem-solving transfer. *Journal of Personality and Social Psychology, 41,* 1087–1093. PA 67:12042.

Laughlin, Patrick R.; & Bitz, Deborah S. (1975). Individual versus dyadic performance on a disjunctive task as a function of initial ability level. *Journal of Personality and Social Psychology, 31,* 487–496. PA 54:1003.

Laughlin, Patrick R.; & Earley, P. Christopher. (1982). Social combination models, persuasive arguments theory, social comparison theory, and choice shift. *Journal of Personality and Social Psychology, 42,* 273–280. PA 68:5759.

Laughlin, Patrick R.; & Futoran, Gail C. (1985). Collective induction: Social combination and sequential transition. *Journal of Personality and Social Psychology, 48,* 608–613. PA 72:20078.

Laughlin, Patrick R.; & Jaccard, James J. (1975). Social facilitation and observational learning of individuals and cooperative pairs. *Journal of Personality and Social Psychology, 32,* 873–879. PA 55:7078.

Laughlin, Patrick R.; Kerr, Norbert; Davis, James H.; Halff, Henry M.; & Marciniak, Kenneth A. (1975). Group size, member ability, and social decision schemes on an intellective task. *Journal of Personality and Social Psychology, 31,* 522–535. PA 54:1002.

Laughlin, Patrick R.; Kerr, Norbert L.; Munch, Margaret M.; & Haggarty, Carol A. (1976). Social decision schemes of the same four-person groups on two different intellective tasks. *Journal of Personality and Social Psychology*, *33*, 80-88. PA 55:7079.

Laughlin, Patrick R.; & McGlynn, Richard P. (1986). Collective induction: Mutual group and individual influence by exchange of hypotheses and evidence. *Journal of Experimental Social Psychology*, *22*, 567-589.

Laughlin, Patrick R.; & Shippy, Thomas A. (1983). Collective induction. *Journal of Personality and Social Psychology*, *45*, 94-100. PA 71:6703.

Laughlin, Patrick R.; & Wong-McCarthy, William J. (1975). Social inhibition as a function of observation and recording of performance. *Journal of Experimental Social Psychology*, *11*, 560-571.

Lauth, Gerhard. (1980). [Reduction of social stress: Dominant variables and processes]. *Zeitschrift fur Sozialpsychologie*, *11*, 85-100. PA 66:3608.

Lawler, Edward J. (1975a). An experimental study of factors affecting the mobilization of revolutionary coalitions. *Sociometry*, *38*, 163-179. PA 54:11672. SA 76H9425.

Lawler, Edward J. (1975b). The impact of status differences on coalitional agreements. *Journal of Conflict Resolution*, *19*, 271-285. PA 55:730.

Lawler, Edward J. (1983). Cooptation and threats as "divide and rule" tactics. *Social Psychology Quarterly*, *46*, 89-98. PA 71:3978. SA 83N2358.

Lawler, Edward J. (Ed.). (1985). *Advances in group processes* (Vol. 2). Greenwich, CT: JAI.

Lawler, Edward J. (1986). Bilateral deterrence and conflict spiral: A theoretical analysis. *Advances in Group Processes*, *3*, 107-130.

Lawler, Edward J.; & MacMurray, Bruce K. (1980). Bargaining toughness: A qualification of level-of-aspiration and reciprocity hypotheses. *Journal of Applied Social Psychology*, *10*, 416-430. PA 66:3609.

Lawler, Edward J.; & Thompson, Martha E. (1978). Impact of leader responsibility for inequity on subordinate revolts. *Social Psychology*, *41*, 265-268. PA 63:3249 SA 79K1229.

Lawler, Edward J.; & Thompson, Martha E. (1979). Subordinate response to a leader's cooptation strategy as a function of the type of coalition power. *Representative Research in Social Psychology*, *9*, 69-80. PA 64:10336.

Lawler, Edward J.; & Youngs, George A. (1975). Coalition formation: An integrative model. *Sociometry*, *38*, 1-17. PA 54:07466.

Lawler, Edward J.; Youngs, George A.; & Lesh, Michael D. (1978). Cooptation and coalition mobilization. *Journal of Applied Social Psychology*, *8*, 199-214. PA 63:5425.

Lawlis, G. Frank; & Klein, Richard. (1973). Interpersonal cohesion and feeling orientation: An application of matrix algebra. *Psychological Reports*, *32*, 807-812. PA 56:1025.

Lawrence, John E. S. (1974). Science and sentiment: Overview of research on crowding and human behavior. *Psychological Bulletin*, *81*, 712-720. PA 53:3314.

Lay, Clarry; Allen, Marlene; & Kassirer, April. (1974). The responsive bystander in emergencies: Some preliminary data. *Canadian Psychologist*, *15*, 220-227. PA 53:2982.

Lazzerini, A. J.; Stephenson, G. M.; & Neave, H. (1978). Eye-contact in dyads: A test of the independence hypothesis. *British Journal of Social and Clinical Psychology*, *17*, 227-229. PA 63:976.

Lea, Martin. (1979). Personality similarity in unreciprocated friendships. *British Journal of Social and Clinical Psychology*, *18*, 393-394. PA 66:5754.

Lea, Martin; & Duck, Steve. (1982). A model for the role of similarity of values in friendship development. *British Journal of Social Psychology*, *21*, 301-310. PA 70:1055.

Leana, Carrie R. (1985). A partial test of Janis' groupthink model: Effects of group cohesiveness and leader behavior on defective decision making. *Journal of Management*, *11*, 5-17. PA 72:20079. SA 86Q3161.

Leary, Mark R. (1979). Interpersonal orientation and self-presentational style. *Psychological Reports*, *45*, 431-436. PA 65:7942.

Leary, Mark R.; Kowalski, Robin M.; & Bergen, David J. (1988). Interpersonal information acquisition and confidence in first encounters. *Personality and Social Psychology Bulletin*, *14*, 68-77.

Leary, Mark R.; Robertson, Rebecca B.; Barnes, Byron D.; & Miller, Rowland S. (1986). Self-presentations of small group leaders: Effects of role requirements and leadership orientation. *Journal of Personality and Social Psychology*, *51*, 742-748. PA 74:4008.

Leary, Mark R.; Rogers, Patricia A.; Canfield,

Robert W.; & Coe, Celine. (1986). Boredom in interpersonal encounters: Antecedents and social implications. *Journal of Personality and Social Psychology*, *51*, 968–975.

Leary, Mark R.; & Schlenker, Barry R. (1980). Self-presentation in task-oriented leadership situation. *Representative Research in Social Psychology*, *11*, 152–158. PA 69:3395.

Lebra, Takie S. (1975). An alternative approach to reciprocity. *American Anthropologist*, *77*, 550–565. PA 55:4508.

Lecuyer, Roger. (1976a). [Man's accommodation to space, man's accommodation of space]. *Travail Humain*, *39*, 195–206. PA 58:6513.

Lecuyer, Roger. (1976b). Social organization and spatial organization. *Human Relations*, *29*, 1045–1060. PA 57:12751.

Lee, Fred; & Bednar, Richard L. (1977). Effects of group structure and risk-taking disposition on group behavior, attitudes, and atmosphere. *Journal of Counseling Psychology*, *24*, 191–199. PA 58:11662.

Lee, Margaret T.; & Ofshe, Richard. (1981). The impact of behavioral style and status characteristics on social influence: A test of two competing theories. *Social Psychology Quarterly*, *44*, 73–82. PA 67:3538. SA 83N2359.

Lefcourt, Herbert M.; Martin, Rod A.; Fick, Carol M.; & Saleh, Wendy E. (1985). Locus of control for affiliation and behavior in social interactions. *Journal of Personality and Social Psychology*, *48*, 755–759. PA 72:20080.

Lefébvre, Luc M. (1973). An experimental approach to the use of ingratiation tactics under homogeneous and heterogeneous dyads. *European Journal of Social Psychology*, *3*, 427–445. PA 53:9526.

Lefébvre, Luc M. (1975). Encoding and decoding of ingratiation in modes of smiling and gaze. *British Journal of Social and Clinical Psychology*, *14*, 33–42. PA 54:1034.

Lefébvre, Luc M.; & Cunningham, John D. (1974). Competitive orientation among Belgian college students: Effects of nonpunitive and deterrent strategies on playing the allocation game. *Psychologica Belgica*, *14*, 261–272. PA 54:9568.

Lefébvre, Luc M.; & Cunningham, John D. (1977). The successful football team: Effects of coaching and team cohesiveness. *International Journal of Sport Psychology*, *8*, 29–41. PA 60:993.

Leffler, Ann; Gillespie, Dair L.; & Conaty, Joseph C. (1982). The effects of status differentiation on nonverbal behavior. *Social Psychology Quarterly*, *45*, 153–161. PA 69:10407.

Lehrer, Keith. (1976). When rational disagreement is impossible. *Noûs*, *10*(3), 327–332. SA 79J9645.

Lemaine, Gerard. (1975). Dissimilation and differential assimilation in social influence: Situations of "normalization." *European Journal of Social Psychology*, *5*, 93–120. PA 56:6000.

Lendenmann, Karl W.; & Rapoport, Anatol. (1980). Decision pressures in 2 * 2 games. *Behavioral Science*, *25*, 107–119. PA 65:7943. SA 81L4930.

Leng, Russell J.; & Walker, Stephen G. (1982). Comparing two studies of crisis bargaining: Confrontation, coercion, and reciprocity. *Journal of Conflict Resolution*, *26*, 571–591. PA 69:10408.

Lenney, Elizabeth. (1977). Women's self-confidence in achievement settings. *Psychological Bulletin*, *84*, 1–13. PA 57:12830.

Lennung, Sven Ake. (1974–1975). Implicit theories in experiential group practices: A pedagogical approach. *Interpersonal Development*, *5*(1), 37–49. PA 54:7468.

Lennung, Sven-Ake; & Ahlberg, Ake. (1975). The effects of laboratory training: A field experiment. *Journal of Applied Behavioral Science*, *11*, 177–188. SA 7714652.

Leonard, Kenneth E.; & Taylor, Stuart P. (1981). Effects of racial prejudice and race of target on aggression. *Aggressive Behavior*, *7*(3), 205–214. PA 67:9773.

Leonov, Alexei Arkhipovich; & Lebedev, Vladimir Ivanovich. (1972). K Probleme Psikhologicheskoi Sovmestimosti v Mezhplanetnom Polyote [On the problem of psychological compatibility in interplanetary flight]. *Voprosy filosofii*, *26*(9), 14–27. SA 774G9771.

Leplat, J.; & Savoyant, Alain. (1983–1984). Ordonnancement et coordination des activites dans les travaux individuels et collectifs [Sequencing and coordination of activities in the work of individuals and groups]. *Bulletin de Psychologie*, *37*, 271–278. PA 72:17316.

Lerner, Allan W.; Rundquist, Barry S.; & Cline, Mike. (1984). The effect of misperception on strategic behavior in legislative settings: Social psychology meets rational choice. *Political Behavior*, *6*, 111–127. PA 72:17317.

Lerner, Richard M.; & Frank, Phyllis. (1974). Relation of race and sex to supermarket helping behavior. *Journal of Social Psychology, 94,* 201-203. PA 53:9527.

Lesk, Steven; & Zippel, Bert. (1975). Dependency, threat, and helping in a large city. *Journal of Social Psychology, 95,* 185-186. PA 54:3024.

Lesko, Wayne A. (1977). Psychological distance, mutual gaze, and the affiliative-conflict theory. *Journal of Social Psychology, 103,* 311-312. PA 60:9306.

Lesko, Wayne A.; & Schneider, Frank W. (1978). Effects of speaking order and speaker gaze level on interpersonal gaze in a triad. *Journal of Social Psychology, 104,* 185-195. PA 61:13391.

Leung, Kwok. (1987). Some determinants of reactions to procedural models for conflict resolution: A cross-national study. *Journal of Personality and Social Psychology, 53,* 898-908.

Leung, Kwok; & Bond, Michael H. (1982). How Chinese and Americans reward task-related contributions: A preliminary study. *Psychologia An International Journal of Psychology in the Orient, 25,* 32-39. PA 69:1040.

Levenstein, Joseph; Jacobs, Alfred; & Cohen, Stanley H. (1977). The effects of feedback as interpersonal reciprocities. *Small Group Behavior, 8,* 415-432. PA 64:1003. SA 79K1098.

Leventhal, Gerald S. (1976). The distribution of rewards and resources in groups and organizations. *Advances in Experimental Social Psychology, 9,* 91-131.

Leventhal, Gloria; & Levitt, Lynn. (1979). Physical, social, and personal factors in the perception of crowding. *Journal of Nonverbal Behavior, 4,* 40-55. PA 66:1275.

Leventhal, Gloria; Lipshultz, Marsha; & Chiodo, Anthony. (1978). Sex and setting effects on seating arrangement. *Journal of Psychology, 100,* 21-26. PA 63:5426.

Leventhal, Gloria; & Matturro, Michelle. (1980). Differential effects of spatial crowding and sex on behavior. *Perceptual & Motor Skills, 51,* 111-120. PA 66:08016.

Leventhal, Gloria; Matturro, Michelle; & Schanerman, Joel. (1978). Effects of attitude, sex, and approach on nonverbal, verbal and projective measures of personal space. *Perceptual and Motor Skills, 47,* 107-118. PA 63:5451.

Leventhal, Gloria; Schanerman, Joel; & Matturro, Michelle. (1978). Effect of room size, initial approach distance and sex on personal space.

Perceptual and Motor Skills, 47, 792-794. PA 64:1004.

Levi, A. M.; & Benjamin, A. (1977). Focus and flexibility in a model of conflict resolution. *Journal of Conflict Resolution, 21,* 405-425. PA 60:3011.

Levin, Ellen M.; & Kurtz, Robert R. (1974). Structured and nonstructured human relations training. *Journal of Counseling Psychology, 21,* 526-531. PA 53:5174.

Levin, Martin L. (1976). Displaying sociometric structures: An application of interactive computer graphics for instruction and analysis. *Simulation and Games, 7,* 295-310. SA 77I4653.

Levine, Douglas W.; O'Neal, Edgar C.; Garwood, S. Gray; & McDonald, Peter J. (1980). Classroom ecology: The effects of seating position on grades and participation. *Personality and Social Psychology Bulletin, 6,* 409-412.

Levine, John M.; & Ruback, R. Barry. (1980). Reaction to opinion deviance: Impact of a fence straddler's rationale on majority evaluation. *Social Psychology Quarterly, 43,* 73-81. PA 65:10439.

Levine, John M.; Saxe, Leonard; & Harris, Hobart J. (1976). Reaction to attitudinal deviance: Impact of deviate's direction and distance of movement. *Sociometry, 39,* 97-107. PA 56:6043. SA 76I1694.

Levine, John M.; Saxe, Leonard; & Ranelli, Candice J. (1975). Extreme dissent, conformity education and the bases of social influence. *Social Behavior and Personality, 3,* 117-126. PA 56:4006.

Levine, John M.; Sroka, Karolyn R.; & Snyder, Howard N. (1977). Group support and reaction to stable and shifting agreement/disagreement. *Social Psychology Quarterly, 40,* 214-224. PA 60:5207. SA 78J4694.

Levine, Ron H. (1977). Why the ethogenic method and the dramaturgical perspective are incompatible. *Journal for the Theory of Social Behaviour, 7,* 237-247. PA 63:960.

Levinger, George. (1980). Toward the analysis of close relationships. *Journal of Experimental Social Psychology, 16,* 510-544. PA 66:12771.

Levitt, Lynn; & Kornhaber, Robert C. (1977). Stigma and compliance: A re-examination. *Journal of Social Psychology, 103,* 13-18. PA 60:5261.

Levitt, Lynn; & Leventhal, Gloria. (1978). Effect of density and environmental noise on perception of time, the situation, oneself and others. *Perceptual and Motor Skills, 47*, 999–1009. PA 64:1047.

Levy, Andre. (1983). La dynamique de groupe [Group dynamics]. *Connexions*, No. 41, 13–23. PA 74:1060.

Levy, Jeffrey C. (1978). Effects of contingencies of reinforcement on same-sexed and cross-sexed interpersonal interactions. *Psychological Reports, 43*, 1063–1069. PA 64:10337.

Levy, Leon H. (1976). Self-help groups: Types and psychological processes. *Journal of Applied Behavioral Science, 12*, 310–322.

Levy-Leboyer, C.; Moser, G.; Vedrenne, B.; & Veyssiere, M. (1976). [Fiedler's LPC Scale]. *Revue de Psychologie Appliquee, 28*, 1–14. PA 58:9449.

Lewicki, Roy J.; & Litterer, Joseph A. (1985). [Vol. 1:] *Negotiation*. [Vol. 2:] *Readings, exercises, and cases*. Homewood, IL: Irwin.

Lewin, Kurt. (1935). *A dynamic theory of personality: Selected papers*. New York: McGraw-Hill.

Lewin, Kurt. (1958). *Resolving social conflicts, selected papers on group dynamics* [1935–1946; Ed. by Gertrud Weiss Lewin]. New York: Harper.

Lewin, Miriam A.; & Kane, Maura. (1975). Impeachment of Nixon and the risky shift. *International Journal of Group Tensions, 5*, 171–176. PA 62:8598.

Lewis, Benjamin F. (1977). Group silences. *Small Group Behavior, 8*, 109–120. SA 78J0172.

Lewis, Benjamin F. (1978). An examination of the final phase of a group development theory. *Small Group Behavior, 9*, 507–517. SA 80K4182.

Lewis, Philip; Dawes, A. Stephen; & Cheney, Thomas. (1974). Effects of sensitivity training on belief in internal control of interpersonal relationships. *Psychotherapy Theory, Research and Practice, 11*, 282–284. PA 54:5199.

Lewis, Steven A.; & Fry, William R. (1977). Effects of visual access and orientation on the discovery of integrative bargaining alternatives. *Organizational Behavior and Human Performance, 20*, 75–92. PA 60:5234.

Li, Anita K. F. (1984). Peer interaction and activity setting in a high-density preschool environment. *Journal of Psychology, 116*, 45–54.

Libby, Robert; Trotman, Ken T.; & Zimmer, Ian. (1987). Member variation, recognition of exper-

tise, and group performance. *Journal of Applied Psychology, 72*, 81–87. PA 74:15530.

Liberman, Dov; & Meyerhoff, Michael K. (1986). Differential conformity rates to perceptual and logical tasks. *Journal of Social Psychology, 126*, 273–275. PA 74:25052.

Lieberman, Morton A. (1976). Change induction in small groups. *Annual Review of Psychology, 27*, 217–250. PA 56:10273.

Lieberman, Morton A.; & Bond, Gary R. (1978). Self-help groups: Problems of measuring outcome. *Small Group Behavior, 9*, 221–241. SA 79K2632.

Liebrand, Wim B. (1983a). A classification of social dilemma games. *Simulation and Games, 14*, 123–138. PA 71:6682.

Liebrand, Wim B. (1983b). Effecten van grootschaligheid op sociale dilemma's [Effects of large scale on social dilemmas]. *Gedrag Tijdschrift voor Psychologie, 11*(5), 236–250. PA 71:20452.

Liebrand, Wim B. (1984). The effect of social motives, communication and group size on behaviour in an N-person multi-stage mixed-motive game. *European Journal of Social Psychology, 14*, 239–264. PA 72:20117.

Liebrand, Wim B. G.; Jansen, Ronald W. T. L.; Rijken, Victor M.; & Suhre, Cor J. M. (1986). Might over morality: Social values and the perception of other players in experimental games. *Journal of Experimental Social Psychology, 22*, 203–215.

Liebrand, Wim B. [G.]; & Van Run, Godfried J. (1985). The effects of social motives on behavior in social dilemmas in two cultures. *Journal of Experimental Social Psychology, 21*, 86–102. PA 73:14467.

Liebrand, Wim B. [G.]; Wilke, Henk A.; Vogel, Rob; & Wolters, Fred J. (1986). Value orientation and conformity: A study using three types of social dilemma games. *Journal of Conflict Resolution, 30*, 77–97. PA 73:24480.

Likert, Rensis; & Likert, Jane G. (1978). A method for coping with conflict in problem-solving groups. *Group and Organization Studies, 3*, 427–434. PA 64:1005. SA 79J8025.

Liktorius, Alvita; & Stang, David J. (1975). Altruism, bystander intervention, and helping behavior: A bibliography. *Catalog of Selected Documents in Psychology, 5*, 326. PA 56:2365.

Lilienthal, Richard A.; & Hutchison, Sam L. (1979). Group polarization (risky shift) in led and leaderless group discussions. *Psychological Reports*, *45*, 168. PA 65:3252.

Lind, E. Allan; Kurtz, Susan; Musante, Linda; Walker, Laurens; & Thibaut, John W. (1980). Procedure and outcome effects on reactions to adjudicated resolution of conflicts of interest. *Journal of Personality and Social Psychology*, *39*, 643–653. PA 66:5810.

Lindholm, Lena-Pia; & Lundquist, Barbro. (1973). Cooperation and independence: studies of assessment techniques in observations of small groups. *Didakometry and Sociometry*, *5*(1), 9–26. SA 80K8695.

Lindow, Janet A.; Wilkinson, Louise Cherry; & Peterson, Penelope L. (1985). Antecedents and consequences of verbal disagreements during small-group learning. *Journal of Educational Psychology*, *77*, 658–667.

Lindsay, John S. (1976). On the number and size of subgroups. *Human Relations*, *29*, 1103–1114. PA 58:3297.

Lindsay, R. C.; Lim, Robert; Marando, Louis; & Cully, Deborah. (1986). Mock-juror evaluations of eyewitness testimony: A test of metamemory hypotheses. *Journal of Applied Social Psychology*, *16*, 447–459. PA 73:29982.

Lindskold, Svenn. (1978). Trust development, the GRIT proposal, and the effects of conciliatory acts on conflict and cooperation. *Psychological Bulletin*, *85*, 772–793. PA 62:3571.

Lindskold, Svenn. (1979). Conciliation with simultaneous or sequential interaction: Variations in trustworthiness and vulnerability in the prisoner's dilemma. *Journal of Conflict Resolution*, *23*, 704–714.

Lindskold, Svenn; Albert, Kevin P.; Baer, Robert; & Moore, Wayne C. (1976). Territorial boundaries of interacting groups and passive audiences. *Sociometry*, *39*, 71–76. PA 56:687.

Lindskold, Svenn; & Aronoff, Jonathan R. (1980). Conciliatory strategies and relative power. *Journal of Experimental Social Psychology*, *16*, 187–198. PA 65:10389.

Lindskold, Svenn; Betz, Brian; & Walters, Pamela S. (1986). Transforming competitive or cooperative climates. *Journal of Conflict Resolution*, *30*, 99–114. PA 73:24481.

Lindskold, Svenn; & Collins, Michael G. (1978). Inducing cooperation by groups and individuals: Applying Osgood's GRIT strategy. *Journal of Conflict Resolution*, *22*, 679–690.

Lindskold, Svenn; & Finch, Marta L. (1981). Styles of announcing conciliation. *Journal of Conflict Resolution*, *25*, 145–155. PA 65:12769.

Lindskold, Svenn; & Finch, Marta L. (1982). Anonymity and the resolution of conflicting pressures from the experimenter and from peers. *Journal of Psychology*, *112*, 79–86. PA 69:12664.

Lindskold, Svenn; Forte, Robert A.; Haake, Charles S.; & Schmidt, Edward K. (1977). The effects of directness of face-to-face requests and sex of solicitor on streetcorner donations. *Journal of Social Psychology*, *101*, 45–51. PA 58:9526.

Lindskold, Svenn; & Han, Gyuseog. (1988a). GRIT as a foundation for integrative bargaining. *Personality and Social Psychology Bulletin*, *14*, 335–345.

Lindskold, Svenn; & Han, Gyuseog. (1988b). Group resistance to influence by a conciliatory member. *Small Group Behavior*, *19*, 19–34.

Lindskold, Svenn; Han, Gyuseog; & Betz, Brian. (1986a). The essential elements of communication in the GRIT strategy. *Personality & Social Psychology Bulletin*, *12*, 179–186. PA 74:18757.

Lindskold, Svenn; Han, Gyuseog; & Betz, Brian. (1986b). Repeated persuasion in interpersonal conflict. *Journal of Personality and Social Psychology*, *51*, 1183–1188. PA 74:13093.

Lindskold, Svenn; McElwain, Douglas C.; & Wayner, Marc. (1977). Cooperation and the use of coercion by groups and individuals. *Journal of Conflict Resolution*, *21*, 531–550. PA 60:3042.

Lindskold, Svenn; Walters, Pamela S.; & Koutsourais, Helen. (1983). Cooperators, competitors, and response to GRIT. *Journal of Conflict Resolution*, *27*, 521–532. PA 71:3979.

Lindskold, Svenn; & Wayner, Marc. (1981). Territorial intrusions and perceptual distortion. *Perceptual and Motor Skills*, *53*, 298. PA 67:12069.

Lindzey, Gardner; & Aronson, Elliot. (Eds.). (1985). *Handbook of social psychology* (3rd ed., 2 vols.). New York: Random House.

Linimon, Diane; Barron, William L.; & Falbo, Toni. (1984). Gender differences in perceptions of leadership. *Sex Roles*, *11*, 1075–1089. PA 73:1148.

Lipman-Blumen, Joan; & Tickamyer, Ann R. (1975). Sex Roles in transition: A ten-year perspective. *Annual Review Of Sociology*, *1*, 297–337. PA 58:11609.

Lippa, Richard. (1976). Expressive control and the leakage of dispositional introversion-extraversion during role-played teaching. *Journal of Personality, 44*, 541–559. PA 58:3387.

Lippa, Richard. (1978). Expressive control, expressive consistency, and the correspondence between behavior and personality. *Journal of Personality, 46*, 438–461. PA 63:3319.

Lippitt, Ronald. (1986). The small group and participatory democracy: Comment on Graebner. *Journal of Social Issues, 42*(1), 155–156. PA 73:29960.

Lipshitz, Raanan; & Sherwood, John J. (1978). The effectiveness of third-party processes consultation as a function of the consultant's prestige and style of intervention. *Journal of Applied Behavioral Science, 14*, 493–509. PA 63:11952.

Liptak, F. (1980). Hodnotenie stylu tvorivej teamovej prace [Assessing the style of the creative group: Performance]. *Psychologie v Ekonomicke Praxi, 15*(2), 109–116. PA 68:3529.

Littlepage, Glenn; & Pineault, Tony. (1978). Verbal, facial, and paralinguistic cues to the detection of truth and lying. *Personality and Social Psychology Bulletin, 4*, 461–464. PA 64:3295.

Littlepage, Glenn E.; & Pineault, Martin A. (1981). Detection of truthful and deceptive interpersonal communications across information transmission modes. *Journal of Social Psychology, 114*, 57–68. PA 67:3541.

Littlepage, Glenn E.; & Pineault, Martin A. (1985). Detection of deception of planned and spontaneous communications. *Journal of Social Psychology, 125*, 195–201. PA 73:24518.

Littlepage, Glenn E.; & Whiteside, Harold D. (1976). Trick or treat: A field study of social class differences in altruism. *Bulletin of the Psychonomic Society, 7*, 491–492. PA 56:9819.

Lloyd, Sally; Cate, Rodney M.; & Henton, June. (1982). Equity and rewards as predictors of satisfaction in casual and intimate relationships. *Journal of Psychology, 110*, 43–48. PA 68:5760.

Lochman, John E.; & Allen, George. (1981). Nonverbal communication of couples in conflict. *Journal of Research in Personality, 15*, 253–269. PA 67:3542.

Lockard, J. S.; Allen, D. J.; Schiele, B. J.; & Wiemer, M. J. (1978). Human postural signals: Stance, weight-shifts and social distance as intention movements to depart. *Animal Behaviour, 26*, 219–224. PA 63:7566.

Lockard, J. S.; Fahrenbruch, C. E.; Smith, J. L.; & Morgan, C. J. (1977). Smiling and laughter: Different phyletic origins? *Bulletin of the Psychonomic Society, 10*, 183–186. PA 60:3012.

Lockard, Joan S.; McVittie, Renate; & Isaac, Lisa M. (1977). Functional significance of the affiliative smile. *Bulletin of the Psychonomic Society, 9*, 367–370. PA 59:7878.

Lockheed, Marlaine E. (1977). Cognitive style effects on sex status in student work groups. *Journal of Educational Psychology, 69*, 158–165. PA 58:11665.

Lockheed, Marlaine E. (1985). Sex and social influence: A meta-analysis guided by theory. In J. Berger & M. Zelditch (Eds.), *Status, rewards, and influence* (pp. 406–429). San Francisco: Jossey-Bass.

Lockheed, Marlaine E.; & Hall, Katherine P. (1976). Conceptualizing sex as a status characteristic: Applications to leadership training strategies. *Journal of Social Issues, 32*(3), 111–124. PA 57:5736.

Lockheed, Marlaine E.; Harris, Abigail M.; & Nemceff, William P. (1983). Sex and social influence: Does sex function as a status characteristic in mixed-sex groups of children? *Journal of Educational Psychology, 75*, 877–888.

Loevinger, Jane; & Knoll, Elizabeth. (1983). Personality: Stages, traits, and the self. *Annual Review of Psychology, 34*, 195–222. PA 70:5447.

Lofland, John. (1976). *Doing social life: The qualitative study of human interaction in natural settings.* New York: Wiley.

Lofland, John. (Ed.). (1978). *Interaction in everyday life: Social strategies.* Beverly Hills, CA: Sage.

Lombardo, John P.; & Catalano, John F. (1978). Failure and its relationship to the social facilitation effect: Evidence for a learned drive interpretation of the social facilitation effect. *Perceptual and Motor Skills, 46*, 823–829. PA 62:2871.

Lombardo, John P.; Franco, Raymond; Wolf, Thomas M.; & Fantasia, Saverio C. (1976). Interest in entering helping activities and self-disclosure to three targets on the Jourard Self-Disclosure Scale. *Perceptual & Motor Skills, 42*, 299–302. PA 56:09837.

Lomranz, Jacob. (1976). Cultural variations in personal space. *Journal of Social Psychology*, *99*, 21–27. PA 56:7914.

London, Manuel. (1975). Effects of shared information and participation on group process and outcome. *Journal of Applied Psychology*, *60*, 537–543. PA 55:731.

London, Manuel; & Oldham, Greg R. (1977). A comparison of group and individual incentive plans. *Academy of Management Journal*, *20*, 34–41. PA 58:5307.

London, Manuel; & Walsh, W. Bruce. (1975). The development and application of a model of long-term group process for the study of interdisciplinary teams. *Catalog of Selected Documents in Psychology*, *5*, 188. PA 53:11584.

Lonetto, Richard; & Williams, David. (1974). Personality, behavioural and output variables in a small group task situation: An examination of consensual leader and non-leader differences. *Canadian Journal of Behavioural Science*, *6*, 59–74. PA 52:5189.

Long, Gary T. (1984). Psychological tension and closeness to others: Stress and interpersonal distance preference. *Journal of Psychology*, *117*, 143–146. PA 72:9498.

Long, Gary T.; Selby, James W.; & Calhoun, Lawrence G. (1980). Effects of situational stress and sex on interpersonal distance preference. *Journal of Psychology*, *105*, 231–237. PA 66:3645.

Long, Susan. (1984). Early integration in groups: "A group to join, and a group to create." *Human Relations*, *37*, 311–332. PA 71:23064.

Long, Thomas J.; & Bosshart, Donald. (1974). The Facilitator Behavior Index. *Psychological Reports*, *34*, 1059–1068. PA 53:1067.

Long, Thomas J.; & Schultz, Edward W. (1973). Empathy: A quality of an effective group leader. *Psychological Reports*, *32*, 699–705. PA 56:1034.

Loo, Chalsa [M.]. (1973). Important issues in researching the effects of crowding on humans. *Representative Research in Social Psychology*, *4*, 219–226.

Loo, Chalsa M. (1978). Behavior problem indices: The differential effects of spatial density on low and high scorers. *Environment and Behavior*, *10*, 489–510. PA 63:11792.

Loo, Chalsa M. (1979). A factor analytic approach to the study of spatial density effects on preschoolers. *Journal of Population*, *2*, 47–68.

Loo, Chalsa M; & Kennelly, Denise. (1979). Social density: Its effects on behaviors and perceptions of preschoolers. *Environmental Psychology and Nonverbal Behavior*, *3*, 131–146. PA 64:5362.

Loo, Chalsa M.; & Smetana, Judi. (1978). The effects of crowding on the behavior and perception of 10-year-old boys. *Environmental Psychology and Nonverbal Behavior*, *2*, 226–249. PA 63:3251

Lopata, Helena Z. (1981). Friendship: Historical and theoretical introduction. *Research in the Interweave of Social Roles*, *2*, 1–19. PA 68:10325.

Lord, Robert G. (1976). Group performance as a function of leadership behavior and task structure: Toward an explanatory theory. *Organizational Behavior and Human Performance*, *17*, 76–96. PA 57:5800.

Lord, Robert G. (1977). Functional leadership behavior: Measurement and relation to social power and leadership perceptions. *Administrative Science Quarterly*, *22*, 114–133. PA 58:7452. SA 78J0284.

Lord, Robert G.; & Alliger, George M. (1985). A comparison of four information processing models of leadership and social perceptions. *Human Relations*, *38*, 47–65. PA 72:22606.

Lord, Robert G.; Binning, John F.; Rush, Michael C.; & Thomas, Jay C. (1978). The effect of performance cues and leader behavior on questionnaire ratings of leadership behavior. *Organizational Behavior and Human Performance*, *21*, 27–39. PA 61:104.

Lord, Robert G.; de Vader, Christy L.; & Alliger, George M. (1986). A meta-analysis of the relation between personality traits and leadership perceptions: An application of validity generalization procedures. *Journal of Applied Psychology*, *71*, 402–410. PA 73:29983.

Lord, Robert G.; Foti, Roseanne J.; & de Vader, Christy L. (1984). A test of leadership categorization theory: Internal structure, information processing, and leadership perceptions. *Organizational Behavior & Human Performance*, *34*, 343–378. PA 72:09519.

Lord, Robert G.; Phillips, James S.; & Rush, Michael C. (1980). Effects of sex and personality on perceptions of emergent leadership, influence, and social power. *Journal of Applied Psychology*, *65*, 176–182. PA 65:12726.

Lord, Robert G.; & Rowzee, Mary. (1979). Task interdependence, temporal phase, and cognitive heterogeneity as determinants of leadership behavior and behavior-performance reactions. *Organizational Behavior and Human Performance, 23,* 182–200. PA 64:5563.

Louche, Claude. (1974–1975). [The preparation of a group negotiation and its effects on the behavior of the negotiators and their attitudes]. *Bulletin de Psychologie, 28,* 113–117. PA 54:12684.

Louche, Claude; & Magnier, Jean Pierre. (1978). Group development: Effects on intergroup and intragroup relations. *European Journal of Social Psychology, 8,* 387–391. PA 63:3228.

Louvet, Catherine; Mogenet, Jean Luc; Vienat, Patricia; & Lemaine, Jean Marie. (1977–1978). [Approach distance as a function of sex and of a dimension of experimental personality study]. *Bulletin de Psychologie, 31,* 907–913. PA 64:1006.

Love, Kathleen D.; & Aiello, John R. (1980). Using projective techniques to measure interaction distance: A methodological note. *Personality and Social Psychology Bulletin, 6,* 102–104. PA 65:10390.

Love, Rhonda L.; Rozelle, Richard M.; & Druckman, Daniel. (1983). Resolving conflicts of interest and ideologies: A simulation of political decision-making. *Social Behavior and Personality, 11*(2), 23–28. PA 72:4001.

Lucker, G. William; Rosenfield, David; Sikes, Jev; & Aronson, Elliot (1977). Performance in the interdependent classroom: A field study. *American Educational Research Journal, 13,* 115–123. PA 58:8258.

Ludwig, Delores; Franco, Juan N.; & Malloy, Thomas E. (1986). Effects of reciprocity and self-monitoring on self-disclosure with a new acquaintance. *Journal of Personality and Social Psychology, 50,* 1077–1082. PA 73:24482.

Ludwig, Kurt; & Fontaine, Gary. (1978). Effect of witnesses' expertness and manner of delivery of testimony on verdicts on simulated jurors. *Psychological Reports, 42,* 955–961. PA 62:11005.

Luft, Joseph. (1984). *Group processes: An introduction to group dynamics* (3rd ed.). Palo Alto, CA: Mayfield.

Lujansky, Harald; & Mikula, Gerold. (1983). Can equity theory explain the quality and the stability of romantic relationships? *British Journal of Social Psychology, 22,* 101–112. PA 71:6704.

Lundberg, Craig; & Lundberg, Joan. (1974). Encounter co-training: Benefits and pitfalls. *Training and Development Journal, 28*(10), 20–26. PA 54:1005.

Lundgren, David C. (1974). Trainer-member influence in T groups: One-way or two-way? *Human Relations, 27,* 755–766. PA 54:3027.

Lundgren, David C. (1975). Interpersonal needs and member attitudes toward trainer and group. *Small Group Behavior, 6,* 371–388.

Lundgren, David C. (1977). Developmental trends in the emergence of interpersonal issues in T groups. *Small Group Behavior, 8,* 179–200. SA 78J4695.

Lundgren, David C.; & Bogart, Dodd H. (1974). Group size, member dissatisfaction, and group radicalism. *Human Relations, 27,* 339–355. PA 54:2980.

Lundgren, David C.; & Knight, David J. (1974). Leadership styles and member attitudes in T groups. *Personality and Social Psychology Bulletin, 1,* 263–266. PA 56:2605.

Lundgren, David C.; & Knight, David J. (1977). Trainer style and member attitudes toward trainer and group in T-groups. *Small Group Behavior, 8,* 47–64. PA 60:7855. SA 78J0285.

Lundgren, David C.; & Knight, David J. (1978). Sequential stages of development in sensitivity training groups. *Journal of Applied Behavioral Science, 14,* 204–222. SA 80K4183.

Lundgren, David C.; & Schaeffer, Catherine. (1976). Feedback processes in sensitivity training groups. *Human Relations, 29,* 763–782. PA 57:3899.

Lundgren, Terry D.; & Loar, R. Michael. (1978). CLUG: The spirit of capitalism and the success of a simulation. *Simulation and Games, 9,* 201–207. PA 63:989.

Lustig, Myron W. (1987). Bales's interpersonal rating forms: Reliability and dimensionality. *Small Group Behavior, 18,* 99–107.

Lynch, Michael. (1985). *Art and artifact in laboratory science: A study of shop work and shop talk in a research laboratory.* Boston: Routledge and Kegan Paul.

Lynn, Michael; & Oldenquist, Andrew. (1986). Egoistic and nonegoistic motives in social dilemmas. *American Psychologist, 41,* 529–534. PA 73:24461.

Lynn, Steven J. (1978). Three theories of self-disclosure exchange. *Journal of Experimental Social Psychology, 14,* 466–479. PA 63:3229.

Maass, Anne; & Clark, Russell D. (1983). Internalization versus compliance: Differential processes underlying minority influence and conformity. *European Journal of Social Psychology, 13,* 197–215. PA 71:9510.

Maass, Anne; & Clark, Russell D. (1984). Hidden impact of minorities: Fifteen years of minority influence research. *Psychological Bulletin, 95,* 428–450. PA 71:23065.

Maass, Anne; & Clark, Russell D., III. (1986). Conversion theory and simultaneous majority/minority influence: Can reactance offer an alternative explanation? *European Journal of Social Psychology, 16,* 305–309.

Maass, Anne; Clark, Russell D.; & Haberkorn, Gerald. (1982). The effects of differential ascribed category membership and norms on minority influence. *European Journal of Social Psychology, 12,* 89–104. PA 68:8130.

Mabry, Edward A. (1975). Exploratory analysis of a developmental model for task-oriented small groups. *Human Communication Research, 2,* 66–74. PA 60:1023.

Mabry, Edward A. (1985). The effects of gender composition and task structure on small group interaction. *Small Group Behavior, 16,* 75–96. PA 72:22584. SA 86Q4842.

Macaulay, Jacqueline. (1985). Adding gender to aggression research: Incremental or revolutionary change? In V. E. O'Leary, R. K. Unger, & B. S. Wallston (Eds.), *Women, gender, and social psychology* (pp. 191–224). Hillsdale, NJ: Erlbaum.

Maccoby, Eleanor E.; & Jacklin, Carol Nagy. (1974). *The psychology of sex differences.* Stanford, CA: Stanford Univ. Press. PA 53:9417.

MacCoun, Robert J.; & Kerr, Norbert L. (1988). Asymmetric influence in mock jury deliberation: Jurors' bias for leniency. *Journal of Personality and Social Psychology, 54,* 21–33.

Mace, David R. (1975). We call it ACME. *Small Group Behavior, 6,* 31–44. PA 54:7469.

Mack, David. (1976). Status and behavior in the reiterated Prisoner's Dilemma game. *Psychological Record, 26,* 529–532. PA 58:1167.

Mackey, Wade C. (1976). Parameters of the smile as a social signal. *Journal of Genetic Psychology, 129,* 125–130.

Mackie, Diane [M.]. (1980). A cross-cultural study of intra-individual and interindividual conflicts of centrations. *European Journal of Social Psychology, 10,* 313–318. SA 82M1467.

Mackie, Diane M. (1986). Social identification effects in group polarization. *Journal of Personality and Social Psychology, 50,* 720–728. PA 73:21915.

Mackie, Diane M. (1987). Systematic and nonsystematic processing of majority and minority persuasive communications. *Journal of Personality and Social Psychology, 53,* 41–52.

Mackie, Diane [M.]; & Cooper, Joel. (1984). Attitude polarization: Effects of group membership. *Journal of Personality and Social Psychology, 46,* 575–585. PA 71:17756.

MacKinnon, William J.; & Anderson, Linda M. (1976). The SPAN III computer program for synthesizing group decisions: Weighting participants' judgments in proportion to confidence. *Behavior Research Methods and Instrumentation, 8,* 409–410. PA 57:4690.

Mackintosh, Elizabeth; West, Sheree; & Saegert, Susan C. (1975). Two studies of crowding in urban public spaces. *Environment and Behavior, 7,* 159–184. PA 55:1697.

MacNeil, M[ark] K.; Davis, L. E.; & Pace, D. J. (1975). Group status displacement under stress: A serendipitous finding. *Sociometry, 38,* 293–307. PA 54:11673. SA 76H9427.

MacNeil, Mark K.; & Sherif, Muzafer. (1976). Norm change over subject generations as a function of arbitrariness of prescribed norms. *Journal of Personality and Social Psychology, 34,* 762–773.

Madsen, Daniel B. (1978). Issue importance and group choice shifts: A persuasive arguments approach. *Journal of Personality and Social Psychology, 36,* 1118–1127. PA 63:5429.

Madsen, Daniel B.; & Finger, John R. (1978). Comparison of a written feedback procedure, group brainstorming, and individual brainstorming. *Journal of Applied Psychology, 63,* 120–123. PA 62:1061.

Madsen, Millard C.; & Shapira, Ariella. (1977). Cooperation and challenge in four cultures. *Journal of Social Psychology, 102,* 189–195. PA 60:3044.

Madsen, Millard C., & Bunin Yi. (1975). Cooperation and competition of urban and rural children in the Republic of South Korea. *International Journal of Psychology, 10,* 269–274. PA 58:7454.

Maginn, Barbara K.; & Harris, Richard J. (1980). Effects of anticipated evaluation on individual brainstorming performance. *Journal of Applied Psychology, 65,* 219–225. PA 65:12727.

Magnusson, David. (Ed.). (1981). *Toward a psychology of situations: An interactional perspective.* Hillsdale, NJ: Erlbaum.

Magnusson, David; & Endler, Norman S. (Eds.). (1977). *Personality at the crossroads: Current issues in interactional psychology.* Hillsdale, NJ: Erlbaum.

Mahoney, E. R. (1974). Compensatory reactions to spatial immediacy. *Sociometry, 37,* 423-431. PA 53:5213.

Maier, Norman R. F.; Solem, Allen R.; & Maier, Ayesha A. (1975). *The roleplay technique: A handbook for management and leadership practice.* La Jolla, CA: University Associates.

Maines, David R. (1984). The sand and the castle: Some remarks concerning G. P. Stone's critique of small group research. *Studies in Symbolic Interaction, 5,* 23-34. SA 8402588

Maitland, Karen A.; & Goldman, Jacquelin R. (1974). Moral judgment as a function of peer group interaction. *Journal of Personality and Social Psychology, 30,* 699-704. PA 53:7325.

Major, Brenda; & Adams, Jeffrey B. (1983). Role of gender, interpersonal orientation, and self-presentation in distributive-justice behavior. *Journal of Personality and Social Psychology, 45,* 598-608. PA 71:12208.

Major, Brenda; & Adams, Jeffrey B. (1984). Situational moderators of gender differences in reward allocations. *Sex Roles, 11,* 869-880. PA 72:28028.

Major, Brenda; & Heslin, Richard. (1982). Perceptions of cross-sex and same-sex nonreciprocal touch: It is better to give than to receive. *Journal of Nonverbal Behavior, 6,* 148-162. PA 71:20486.

Maki, Judith E.; & McClintock, Charles G. (1983). The accuracy of social value prediction: Actor and observer influences. *Journal of Personality and Social Psychology, 45,* 829-838. PA 71:12209.

Mallinger, Mark A. (1981). Effective coping: A study of behavior in stressful small group situations. *Small Group Behavior, 12,* 269-284.

Malone, Thomas W. (1975). Computer simulation of two-person interactions. *Behavioral Science, 20,* 260-267. PA 55:4511.

Malouf, Michael W. K.; & Roth, Alvin E. (1981). Disagreement in bargaining: An experimental study. *Journal of Conflict Resolution, 25,* 329-348.

Mamali, Catalin; & Paun, Gheorghe. (1982). Group size and the genesis of subgroups: Objective restrictions. *Revue Roumaine des Sciences Sociales Serie de Psychologie, 26,* 139-148. PA 70:12642.

Mamola, Claire. (1979). Women in mixed groups:

Some research findings. *Small Group Behavior, 10,* 431-440. SA 80K8696.

Mandal, M. K.; & Maitra, S. (1985). Perception of facial affect and physical proximity. *Perceptual and Motor Skills, 60,* 782. PA 73:19802.

Mandel, Norman M.; & Shrauger, J. Sidney. (1980). The effects of self-evaluative statements on heterosocial approach in shy and nonshy males. *Cognitive Therapy and Research, 4,* 369-381. PA 66:1233.

Mander, Anthony M.; & Gaebelein, Jacquelyn W. (1977). Third party instigation of aggression as a function of noncooperation and veto power. *Journal of Research in Personality, 11,* 475-486. PA 60:9339.

Manderscheid, Ronald W.; Rae, Donald S.; McCarrick, Anne K.; & Silbergeld, Sam. (1982). A stochastic model of relational control in dyadic interaction. *American Sociological Review, 47,* 62-75. SA 82M3121.

Mangham, Iain. (1977). Definitions, interactions, and disengagement: Notes towards a theory of intervention processes in T-groups. *Small Group Behavior, 8,* 487-510. SA 79K1099.

Mangham, Iain L.; & Overington, Michael A. (1982). Performance and rehearsal: Social order and organizational life. *Symbolic Interaction, 5*(2), 205-222. SA 83N2360.

Mann, Brenda; & Murphy, Kevin C. (1975). Timing of self-disclosure, reciprocity of self-disclosure, and reactions to an initial interview. *Journal of Counseling Psychology, 22,* 304-308. PA 54:5201.

Mann, Leon. (1977). The effect of stimulus queues on queue-joining behavior. *Journal of Personality and Social Psychology, 35,* 437-442. PA 62:10977.

Mann, Leon. (1980). Cross-cultural studies of small groups. In H. C. Triandis & R. W. Brislin (Eds.), *Handbook of cross-cultural psychology* (Vol. 5, pp. 155-209). Boston: Allyn & Bacon.

Mann, Richard D. (1959). A review of the relationships between personality and performance in small groups. *Psychological Bulletin, 56,* 241-270.

Manninen, Vesa. (1977). Paenneet sankarit: piirteita eristyneen pienryhman elamasta ja dynamiikasta [Heroes in retreat: Aspects of the life and dynamics of an isolated small group]. *Sosiologia, 14,* 204-210. SA 81L8139.

Manning, Brad A.; Pierce-Jones, John; & Parelman, Rhona L. (1974). Cooperative, trusting behavior in a "culturally deprived" mixed ethnic-group population. *Journal of Social Psychology*, *92*, 133–141. PA 52:5190.

Manstead, A[ntony] S. R.; & Semin, Gün R. (1980). Social facilitation effects: Mere enhancement of dominant responses? *British Journal of Social and Clinical Psychology*, *19*, 119–136.

Manstead, Antony S. [R.]; Wagner, Hugh L.; & MacDonald, Christopher J. (1984). Face, body, and speech as channels of communication in the detection of deception. *Basic and Applied Social Psychology*, *5*, 317–332. PA 72:12027.

Mantell, David M.; & Panzarella, Robert. (1976). Obedience and responsibility. *British Journal of Social and Clinical Psychology*. *15*, 239–245. PA 57:5242.

Manz, Charles C.; & Sims, Henry P. (1982). The potential for "groupthink" in autonomous work groups. *Human Relations*, *35*, 773–784.

Maple, Frank. (1977). *Shared decision making*. Beverly Hills, CA: Sage. [Sage human services guides, Vol. 4].

Mar, Brian W.; & Wright, Jeff. (1978). Exchange mechanisms for policy analysis games. *Simulation and Games*, *9*, 393–412. PA 63:11953.

Marans, Robert W.; & Spreckelmeyer, Kent F. (1982). Evaluating open and conventional office designs. *Environment and Behavior*, *14*, 333–351. PA 68:9214.

Marcy, Michael R.; & Fromme, Donald K. (1979). Group modification of affective verbalizations: "here-and-now" and valence effects. *Small Group Behavior*, *10*, 547–556. SA 80L0088.

Mardellat, Rene. (1975). Relationship of the identification level of subjects to their behavior in potentially conflictive situations. *Cahiers de Psychologie*, *18*(4), 237–254. PA 61:5935.

Margulis, E. D. (1981). [Psychological features of group activity: II. Experimental research of group activity on the basis of problem-solving by computer]. *Novye Issledovaniya v Psikhologii*, *24*, 16–20. PA 70:5632.

Margulis, Stephen T. (1977). Conceptions of privacy: Current status and next steps. *Journal of Social Issues*, *33*(3), 5–21. PA 62:873.

Margulis, Ye. D. (1984). [Psychological characteristics of the teaching of group activity: I. Experimental teaching of group problem solving]. *Novye Issledovaniya v Psikhologii*, *30*, 65–69. PA 74:10195.

Markel, Norman N.; Long, Joseph F.; & Saine,

Thomas J. (1976). Sex effects on conversational interaction: Another look at male dominance. *Human Communication Research*, *2*, 356–364. PA 61:10910.

Markell, Richard A.; & Asher, Steven R. (1984). Children's interactions in dyads: Interpersonal influence and sociometric status. *Child Development*, *55*, 1412–1424. SA 86Q6536.

Markovsky, Barry; Smith, Le Roy F.; & Berger, Joseph. (1984). Do status interventions persist? *American Sociological Review*, *49*, 373–382. PA 72:12006.

Marks, Michael W.; & Vestre, Norris D. (1974). Self-perception and interpersonal behavior changes in marathon and time-extended encounter groups. *Journal of Consulting and Clinical Psychology*, *42*, 729–733. PA 53:2999.

Markus, Hazel. (1978). The effect of mere presence on social facilitation: An unobtrusive test. *Journal of Experimental Social Psychology*, *14*, 389–397. PA 63:977.

Markus, Hazel. (1981). The drive for integration: Some comments. *Journal of Experimental Social Psychology*, *17*, 257–261.

Markus Kaplan, Moriah; & Kaplan, Kalman J. (1984). A bidimensional view of distancing: Reciprocity versus compensation, intimacy versus social control. Special Issue: Nonverbal intimacy and exchange. *Journal of Nonverbal Behavior*, *8*, 315–326. PA 74:4009.

Marshall, Joan E.; & Heslin, Richard. (1975). Boys and girls together: Sexual composition and the effect of density and group size on cohesiveness. *Journal of Personality and Social Psychology*, *31*, 952–961. PA 54:7471.

Marshall, Nancy J. (1974). Dimensions of privacy preferences. *Multivariate Behavioral Research*, *9*, 255–271.

Marshall, Nelda P.; Pederson, Lucille M.; & Weiller, Ernest M. (1978). Interactional analysis of the task and maintenance behaviors of college men and women in problem-solving small-group interaction. *Catalog of Selected Documents in Psychology*, *8*, 61–62. [MS, 1720]. PA 62:10978.

Martens, Rainer; & White, Virginia. (1975). Influence of win-loss ratio on performance, satisfaction and preference for opponents. *Journal of Experimental Social Psychology*, *11*, 343–362.

Martin, Harry J.; & Greenstein, Theodore N. (1983). Individual differences in status generalization: Effects of need for social approval, anticipated interpersonal contact, and instrumental task abilities. *Journal of Personality and Social Psychology, 45,* 641–662. PA 71:12210.

Martin, J. David. (1979). Suspicion of confederacy by group members. *Small Group Behavior, 10,* 284–294. SA 80K8697.

Martin, John; Lobb, Brian; Chapman, Greg C.; & Spillane, Robert. (1976). Obedience under conditions demanding self-immolation. *Human Relations, 29,* 345–356. PA 58:3330.

Martin, Judith N.; & Craig, Robert T. (1983). Selected linguistic sex differences during initial school interactions of same-sex and mixed-sex student dyads. *Western Journal of Speech Communication, 47*(1), 16–28.

Martin, Linda; & Jacobs, Marion. (1980). Structured feedback delivered in small groups. *Small Group Behavior, 11,* 88–107. SA 80L0089.

Martin, Michael W.; & Sell, Jane. (1983). Self-awareness, information utilization, and social influence in cooperative task settings. *Sociological Focus, 16*(2), 147–153. SA 83N2361.

Martin, Michael W.; & Sell, Jane. (1985). The effect of equating status characteristics on the generalization process. *Social Psychology Quarterly, 48,* 178–182. PA 73:14435. SA 85Q1241.

Martin, Patricia Y.; & Shanahan, Kristin A. (1983). Transcending the effects of sex composition in small groups. *Social Work with Groups, 6*(3–4), 19–32. PA 71:20453.

Maruffi, Brian L. (1985). The impact of distributive systems and gender on perceptions of social relations. *Journal of Applied Social Psychology, 15,* 46–58. PA 72:28046.

Marwell, Gerald; & Ames, Ruth E. (1979). Experiments on the provision of public goods. I. Resources, Interest, Group Size, and the Free-Rider Problem. *American Journal of Sociology, 84,* 1335–1360. SA 80K5523.

Marwell, Gerald; & Schmitt, David R. (1975). *Cooperation: An experimental analysis.* New York: Academic Press.

Mason, Avonne; & Blankenship, Virginia. (1987). Power and affiliation motivation, stress, and abuse in intimate relationships. *Journal of Personality and Social Psychology, 52,* 203–210.

Massengill, Douglas; & DiMarco, Nicholas. (1979). Sex-role stereotypes and requisite management characteristics: A current replication. *Sex Roles, 5,* 561–570. PA 65:4260.

Matarazzo, Joseph D.; Wiens, Arthur N.; &

Manaugh, Thomas S. (1975). IQ correlates of speech and silence behavior under three dyadic speaking conditions. *Journal of Consulting and Clinical Psychology, 43,* 198–204. PA 54:1080.

Materska, Maria. (1982). Serial transmission and processing of information in chains of small task-solving groups. *Polish Psychological Bulletin, 13,* 53–61. PA 71:6705.

Mathes, Eugene W. (1975). The effects of physical attractiveness and anxiety on heterosexual attraction over a series of five encounters. *Journal of Marriage and the Family, 37,* 769–773. PA 56:6044.

Mathes, Eugene W.; Adams, Heather E.; & Davies, Ruth M. (1985). Jealousy: Loss of relationship rewards, loss of self-esteem, depression, anxiety, and anger. *Journal of Personality and Social Psychology, 48,* 1552–1561. PA 72:28029.

Mathes, Eugene W.; & Edwards, Linda L. (1978). Physical attractiveness as an input in social exchanges. *Journal of Psychology, 98,* 267–275. PA 61:10911.

Mathes, Eugene W.; & Guest, Thomas A. (1976). Anonymity and group antisocial behavior. *Journal of Social Psychology, 100,* 257–262. PA 58:1107.

Mathews, Kenneth E.; & Canon, Lance K. (1975). Environmental noise level as a determinant of helping behavior. *Journal of Personality and Social Psychology, 32,* 571–577. PA 56:688 [PsycLIT no. 57-03262].

Mathews, Kenneth E.; Canon, Lance K.; & Alexander, Kenneth R. (1974). The influence of level of empathy and ambient noise on body buffer zone. *Personality and Social Psychology Bulletin, 1,* 367–369. PA 56:2309.

Mathews, Robert C.; Lane, Irving M.; Reber, Robert A.; Buco, Steven M.; Chaney, Courtland M.; & Erffmeyer, Robert C. (1982). Toward designing optimal problem-solving procedures: Comparisons of male and female interacting groups. *Group and Organization Studies, 7,* 497–507. PA 69:10409.

Matson, David L. (1978). Public order in elevators: Environmental constraints on proxemic behavior. *Man-Environment Systems, 8*(4), 167–174. SA 82L9792.

Matsuda, Noriyuki. (1985). Strong, quasi-, and weak conformity among Japanese in the modified Asch. *Journal of Cross Cultural Psychology, 16,* 83–97. PA 74:4010. SA 85O9452.

Matsumoto, Yoshiyuki. (1980). [Experimental analyses of bargaining: Effects of communication in trucking game]. *Japanese Journal of Experimental Social Psychology*, 20, 45–53. PA 66:10335.

Matsumoto, Yoshiyuki. (1981). [Experimental analysis of bargaining: II. Effects of threat in trucking game]. *Japanese Journal of Experimental Social Psychology*, 21, 1–6. PA 68:1097.

Matthews, Byron A. (1979). Effects of fixed and alternated payoff inequity on dyadic competition. *Psychological Record*, 29, 329–339. PA 65:1239.

Matthews, Byron A.; Kordonski, William M.; & Shimoff, Eliot. (1983). Temptation and the maintenance of trust: Effects of bilateral punishment capability. *Journal of Conflict Resolution*, 27, 255–277. PA 70:10244.

Matthews, Byron A.; & Shimoff, Eliot. (1979). Expansion of exchange: Monitoring trust levels in ongoing exchange relations. *Journal of Conflict Resolution*, 23, 538–560.

Matthews, Robert W.; Paulus, Paul B.; & Baron, Robert A. (1979). Physical aggression after being crowded. *Journal of Nonverbal Behavior*, 4, 5–17. PA 66:1277.

Maxwell, Gabrielle M.; & Cook, Michael W. (1985). Postural congruence and judgements of liking and perceived similarity. *New Zealand Journal of Psychology*, 14, 20–26. PA 73:27161.

Mayer, Michael E. (1985). Explaining choice shift: An effects coded model. *Communication Monographs*, 52, 92–101. PA 72:30785.

Maynard, Douglas W. (Ed.). (1987). *Social Psychology Quarterly*, 50(2). [Special issue on "Language and social interaction."]

Maynard, Douglas W.; & Zimmerman, Don H. (1984). Topical talk, ritual and the social organization of relationships. *Social Psychology Quarterly*, 47, 301–316. PA 72:30786.

Mayo, Clara; & Henley, Nancy. (Eds.). (1981). *Gender and nonverbal behavior*. New York: Springer-Verlag.

Mazur, Allan. (1975). A model of behavior in Berger's standard experiment. *Journal of Mathematical Sociology*, 4, 83–92. PA 56:9838.

Mazur, Allan. (1977). Interpersonal spacing on public benches in "contact" vs. "noncontact" cultures. *Journal of Social Psychology*, 101, 53–58. PA 58:09486.

Mazur, Allan. (1985). A biosocial model of status in face-to-face primate groups. *Social Forces*, 64, 377–402. SA 86Q4843.

Mazur, Allan; Rosa, Eugene; Faupel, Mark; Heller, Joshua; Leen, Russell; & Thurman, Blake. (1980). Physiological aspects of communication via mutual gaze. *American Journal of Sociology*, 86, 50–74. SA 81L4931.

McAdams, Dan P.; & Constantian, Carol A. (1983). Intimacy and affiliation motives in daily living: An experience sampling analysis. *Journal of Personality and Social Psychology*, 45, 851–861. PA 71:12160.

McAdams, Dan P.; Healy, Sheila; & Krause, Steven. (1984). Social motives and patterns of friendship. *Journal of Personality and Social Psychology*, 47, 828–838. PA 72:12007.

McAdams, Dan P.; Jackson, R. Jeffrey; & Kirshnit, Carol. (1984). Looking, laughing, and smiling in dyads as a function of intimacy motivation and reciprocity. *Journal of Personality*, 52, 261–273. PA 72:20070. SA 86Q3072.

McAdams, Dan P.; & Powers, Joseph. (1981). Themes of intimacy in behavior and thought. *Journal of Personality & Social Psychology*, 40, 573–587. PA 66:12813.

McAllister, Ann; & Kiesler, Donald J. (1975). Interviewee disclosure as a function of interpersonal trust, task modeling, and interviewer self-disclosure. *Journal of Consulting and Clinical Psychology*, 43, 428. PA 54:7472.

McAllister, Hunter A.; & Bregman, Norman J. (1985). Reciprocity effects with intimate and nonintimate disclosure: The importance of establishing baseline. *Journal of Social Psychology*, 125, 775–776. PA 74:13094.

McAllister, Hunter A.; & Bregman, Norman J. (1986). Plea bargaining by defendants: A decision theory approach. *Journal of Social Psychology*, 126, 105–110. PA 74:25083.

McAndrew, Francis T.; Gold, Joel A.; Lonney, Ellen; & Ryckman, Richard M. (1984). Explorations in immediacy: The nonverbal system and its relationship to affective and situational factors. *Journal of Nonverbal Behavior*, 8, 210–228. PA 73:3680.

McAndrew, F[rancis] T.; Ryckman, Richard M.; Horr, William; & Solomon, Robin. (1978). The effects of invader placement of spatial markers on territorial behavior in a college population. *Journal of Social Psychology*, 104, 149–150.

McBride, Kevin J.; & Lao, Rosina C. (1978). The effects of locus of control on coalition formation among college females. *Psychology of Women Quarterly*, *3*, 203–206. PA 63:11954. SA 80K7131.

McCain, Garvin; Cox, Verne C.; & Paulus, Paul B. (1976). The relationships between illness complaints and degree of crowding in a prison environment. *Environment and Behavior*, *8*, 283–290. PA 57:4595.

McCain, Garvin; Cox, Verne C.; Paulus, Paul B.; Luke, Ann; & Abadzi, Helen. (1985). Some effects of reduction of extra-classroom crowding in a school environment. *Journal of Applied Social Psychology*, *15*, 503–515.

McCallum, Debra M.; Harring, Kathleen; Gilmore, Robert; Drenan, Sarah; Chase, Jonathan P.; Insko, Chester A.; & Thibaut, John W. (1985). Competition and cooperation between groups and between individuals. *Journal of Experimental Social Psychology*, *21*, 301–320. PA 73:19803.

McCallum, Richard; Rusbult, Caryl E.; Hong, George K.; Walden, Tedra A.; & Schopler, John. (1979). Effects of resource availability and importance of behavior on the experience of crowding. *Journal of Personality and Social Psychology*, *37*, 1304–1313. PA 64:12461.

McCann, C. Douglas; & Hancock, Rodney D. (1983). Self-monitoring in communicative interactions: Social cognitive consequences of goal-directed message modification. *Journal of Experimental Social Psychology*, *19*, 109–121. PA 70:12673.

McCann, C. Douglas; Ostrom, Thomas M.; Tyner, Linda K.; & Mitchell, Mark L. (1985). Person perception in heterogeneous groups. *Journal of Personality and Social Psychology*, *49*, 1449–1459. PA 73:11768.

McCanne, Lynn P. (1977). Dimensions of participant goals, expectations, and perceptions in small group experiences. *Journal of Applied Behavioral Science*, *13*, 533–541. PA 60:10499. SA 79K1100.

McCarrick, Anne K.; Manderscheid, Ronald W.; & Silbergeld, Sam. (1981). Gender differences in competition and dominance during married-couples group therapy. *Social Psychology Quarterly*, *44*, 164–177. SA 83N2362.

McCarthy, Barry; & Duck, Steven W. (1976). Friendship duration and responses to attitudinal agreement-disagreement. *British Journal of Social and Clinical Psychology*, *15*, 377–386. PA 58:1169.

McCarthy, Barry; & Duck, Steve. (1979). Studying friendship: Experimental and role-playing techniques in testing hypotheses about acquaintance. *British Journal of Social and Clinical Psychology*, *18*, 299–307. PA 64:12462.

McCarthy, Dennis; & Saegert, Susan. (1978). Residential density, social overload, and social withdrawal. *Human Ecology*, *6*, 253–272. PA 63:5452.

McCarthy, Henry. (1977). Some situational factors improving cognitive conflict reduction and interpersonal understanding. *Journal of Conflict Resolution*, *21*, 217–234. PA 59:12326.

McCauley, Clark; & Taylor, Janet. (1976). Is there overload of acquaintances in the city? *Environmental Psychology and Nonverbal Behavior*, *1*, 41–55. PA 60:849.

McClelland, Lou. (1976). Interaction level and acquaintance as mediators of density effects. *Personality and Social Psychology Bulletin*, *2*, 179–182. PA 56:6003.

McClelland, Lou; & Auslander, Nathan. (1978). Perceptions of crowding and pleasantness in public settings. *Environment and Behavior*, *10*, 535–553.

McClintock, Charles G. (Ed.). (1972). *Experimental social psychology*. New York: Holt, Rinehart and Winston.

McClintock, Charles G.; Kramer, Roderick M.; & Keil, Linda J. (1984). Equity and social change in human relationships. *Advances in Experimental Social Psychology*, *17*, 183–228.

McClintock, Charles G.; & Moskowitz, Joel M. (1976). Children's preferences for individualistic, cooperative, and competitive outcomes. *Journal of Personality and Social Psychology*, *34*, 543–555. PA 58:1059.

McClintock, Evie; & Sonquist, John A. (1976). Cooperative task-oriented groups in a college classroom: A field application. *Journal of Educational Psychology*, *68*, 588–596.

McComas, William C.; & Noll, Mark E. (1974). Effects of seriousness of charge and punishment severity on the judgments of simulated jurors. *Psychological Record*, *24*, 545–547. PA 53:9530.

McCorcle, Mitchell D. (1982). Critical issues in the functioning of interdisciplinary groups. *Small Group Behavior*, *13*, 291–310. PA 69:5577.

McCormick, Michael B.; Lundgren, Earl F.; & Cecil, Earl A. (1980). Group search and decision-making processes: A laboratory test of

Soelberg's confirmation hypothesis. *Journal of Social Psychology, 110*, 79–86. PA 65:10391.

McCroskey, James C.; & Daly, John A. (Eds.). (1987). *Personality and interpersonal communication.* Beverly Hills & London: Sage.

McCubbin, Hamilton I.; & Figley, Charles R. (Eds.). (1983). *Stress and the family* (Vol. 1). New York: Brunner/Mazel.

McCullagh, Penny D.; & Landers, Daniel M. (1976). Size of audience and social facilitation. *Perceptual and Motor Skills, 42*, 1067–1070. PA 57:3203.

McDowall, Joseph J. (1978). Interactional synchrony: A reappraisal. *Journal of Personality and Social Psychology, 36*, 963–975. PA 63:5430.

McElroy, James C.; & Shrader, Charles B. (1986). Attribution theories of leadership and network analysis. *Journal of Management, 12*, 351–362. PA 74:10196.

McFall, Miles E.; Winnett, Rochelle L.; Bordewick, Mark C.; & Bornstein, Philip H. (1982). Nonverbal components in the communication of assertiveness. *Behavior Modification, 6*, 121–140. PA 68:5796.

McGaffey, Thomas N. (1976). Motivational determinants of decision-making in a triadic coalition game. *Journal of General Psychology, 94*, 167–185. PA 59:3339.

McGillicuddy, Neil B.; Pruitt, Dean G.; & Syna, Helena. (1984). Perceptions of firmness and strength in negotiation. *Personality and Social Psychology Bulletin, 10*, 402–409. PA 72:22610.

McGillicuddy, Neil B.; Welton, Gary L.; & Pruitt, Dean G. (1987). Third-party intervention: A field experiment comparing three different models. *Journal of Personality and Social Psychology, 53*, 104–112.

McGlynn, Richard P. (1981). Effects of competition in concept attainment: Rivalry, coaction, and problem difficulty. *Journal of Social Psychology, 114*, 187–197. PA 67:7700.

McGlynn, Richard P.; Gibbs, Michael E.; & Roberts, Sam J. (1982). Effects of cooperative versus competitive set and coaction on creative responding. *Journal of Social Psychology, 118*, 281–282. PA 70:3394.

McGovern, Jana L.; & Holmes, David S. (1976). Influence of sex and dress on cooperation: An instance of "Person" chauvinism. *Journal of Applied Social Psychology, 6*, 206–210.

McGovern, Leslie P.; Ditzian, Jan L.; & Taylor, Stuart P. (1975). Sex and perceptions of dependency in a helping situation. *Bulletin of the Psychonomic Society, 5*, 336–338. PA 54:5251.

McGrath, Joseph Edward. (1984). *Groups: Interaction and performance.* Englewood Cliffs, NJ: Prentice-Hall.

McGrath, Joseph E[dward].; & Kravitz, David A. (1982). Group research. *Annual Review of Psychology, 33*, 195–230. PA 67:12045. SA 84N7290.

McGraw, Kathleen M.; & Bloomfield, Jeremy. (1987). Social influence on group moral decisions: The interactive effects of moral reasoning and sex role orientations. *Journal of Personality and Social Psychology, 53*, 1080–1087.

McGrew, Penny I.; & McGrew, W. C. (1975). Interpersonal Spacing Behavior of Preschool Children during Group Formation. *Man-Environment Systems, 5*(1), 43–48. SA 80K7132.

McGuire, Dennis; Thelen, Mark H.; & Amolsch, Thomas. (1975). Interview self-disclosure as a function of length of modeling and descriptive instructions. *Journal of Consulting and Clinical Psychology, 43*, 356–362. PA 54:5203.

McGuire, John M.; Graves, Sanford; & Blau, Burton. (1985). Depth of self-disclosure as a function of assured confidentiality and videotape recording. *Journal of Counseling and Development, 64*, 259–263. PA 73:11769.

McGuire, John M.; & Thomas, Margaret H. (1975). Effects of sex, competence, and competition on sharing behavior in children. *Journal of Personality and Social Psychology, 32*, 490–494. PA 54:11710.

McGuire, Martin. (1974, Summer). Group size, group homogeneity, and the aggregate provision of a pure public good under cournot behavior. *Public Choice, 18*, 107–126. SA 77I6196.

McGuire, Mary V.; & Bermant, Gordon. (1977). Individual and group decisions in response to a mock trial: A methodological note. *Journal of Applied Social Psychology, 7*, 220–226. PA 60.9217.

McGuire, Timothy W.; Kiesler, Sara; & Siegel, Jane. (1987). Group and computer-mediated discussion effects in risk decision making. *Journal of Personality and Social Psychology, 52*, 917–930.

McGuire, William J. (1985). Attitudes and attitude

change. In G. Lindzey and E. Aronson (Eds.), *Handbook of social psychology* (3rd ed., Vol. 2, pp. 233–346). New York: Random House.

McKelvey, Richard D.; & Ordeshook, Peter C. (1981). Experiments on the core: Some disconcerting results for majority rule voting games. *Journal of Conflict Resolution, 25*, 709–724. PA 67:9775.

McKenna, Ralph H. (1976). Good samaritanism in rural and urban settings: A nonreactive comparison of helping behavior of clergy and control subjects. *Representative Research in Social Psychology, 7*, 58–65. PA 56:6046.

McKenzie, I. K.; & Strongman, K. T. (1981). Rank (status) and interaction distance. *European Journal of Social Psychology, 11*, 227–230. PA 67:3543. SA 83M9102.

McKillip, Jack; DiMiceli, Anthony J.; & Luebke, Jerry. (1977). Group salience and stereotyping. *Social Behavior and Personality, 5*, 81–85. SA 78J3223.

McKinney, Mark E.; Gatchel, Robert J.; & Paulus, Paul B. (1983). The effects of audience size on high and low speech-anxious subjects during an actual speaking task. *Basic and Applied Social Psychology, 4*, 73–87. PA 71:20454.

McLachlan, Angus. (1986a). The effects of two forms of decision reappraisal on the perception of pertinent arguments. *British Journal of Social Psychology, 25*, 129–138.

McLachlan, Angus. (1986b). Polarization and discussion context. *British Journal of Social Psychology, 25*, 345–347.

McLaughlin, Margaret L.; & Cody, Michael J. (1982). Awkward silences: Behavioral antecedents and consequences of the conversational lapse. *Human Communication Research, 8*, 299–316. PA 69:3397.

McLaughlin, Margaret L.; Cody, Michael J.; Kane, Marjorie L.; & Robey, Carl S. (1981). Sex differences in story receipt and story sequencing behaviors in dyadic conversations. *Human Communication Research, 7*, 99–116. PA 67:1237.

McLaughlin, Margaret L.; & Jordan, William J. (1975). Impression formation in triads. *Speech Monographs, 42*, 47–55. PA 54:7521.

McLeish, John; & Martin, Jack. (1975). Verbal behavior: A review and experimental analysis. *Journal of General Psychology, 93*, 3–66. PA 54:11674.

McLeod, John. (1984). Group process as drama.

Small Group Behavior, 15, 319–332. SA 85O6026.

McMahon, Pamela M.; & Fehr, Lawrence A. (1984). Methodological problems in mock jury research. *Journal of Social Psychology, 123*, 277–278.

McNamara, J. Regis; & Blumer, Craig A. (1982). Role playing to assess social competence: Ecological validity considerations. *Behavior Modification, 6*, 519–549. PA 70:1057.

McNeel, Steven P.; & Reid, Edward C. (1975). Attitude similarity, social goals, and cooperation. *Journal of Conflict Resolution, 19*, 665–681. PA 56:7915.

McNeill, David M. (1985). So you think gestures are nonverbal? *Psychological Review, 92*, 350–371.

McWhirter, J. Jeffries; & Frey, Robert E. (1987). Group leader and member characteristics and attraction to initial and final group sessions and to the group and group leader. *Small Group Behavior, 18*, 533–547.

Meade, Robert D.; & Barnard, William A. (1975). Group pressure effects on American and Chinese females. *Journal of Social Psychology, 96*, 137–138. PA 54:7522.

Medlin, Steven M. (1976). Effects of grand coalition payoffs on coalition formation in three-person games. *Behavioral Science, 21*, 48–61. SA 7713063.

Mednick, Martha T.; & Weissman, Hilda J. (1975). The psychology of women - selected topics. *Annual Review of Psychology, 26*, 1–18. PA 54:2907.

Meeker, Barbara F. (1977). Interaction in a cooperative game: Status, sex roles and task behavior. *Pacific Sociological Review, 20*, 475–491. SA 78J1741.

Meeker, Barbara F. (1979). Exchange rules and goal structures. *Human Relations, 32*, 523–544. SA 82M1470.

Meeker, Barbara F. (1984). Cooperative orientation, trust, and reciprocity. *Human Relations, 37*, 225–243. PA 71:20455.

Meeker, Barbara F.; & Hornung, Carlton A. (1976). Strategies of interaction. *Social Science Research, 5*, 153–172. PA 56:7916.

Meeker, Barbara F.; & Weitzel O'Neill, P. A. (1977). Sex roles and interpersonal behavior in task-oriented groups. *American Sociological Review, 42*, 91–105. PA 58:3298. SA 7717505.

Meeks, John E. (1973). Structuring the early phase of group psychotherapy with adolescents. *Inter-*

national Journal of Child Psychotherapy, 2, 391-405. PA 53:7973.

Meglino, Bruce M. (1976). The effect of evaluation on dominance characteristics: An extension of social facilitation theory. Journal of Social Psychology, 92, 167-172.

Meile, Bruno. (1975). Zur Formalisierung Gruppendynamischer Konzepte [Inquiries in formalizing group-dynamic concepts]. Zeitschrift fur Soziologie, 4(2), 115-131. SA 7714654.

Melnick, Joseph; & Woods, Martha. (1976). Analysis of group composition research and theory for psychotherapeutic and growth-oriented groups. Journal of Applied Behavioral Science, 12, 493-512. PA 58:3775.

Melnick, Merrill J.; & Chemers, Martin M. (1974). Effects of group social structure on the success of basketball teams. Research Quarterly, 45, 1-8. PA 53:1068.

Mendoza, Jorge L.; & Graziano, William G. (1982). The statistical analysis of dyadic social behavior: A multivariate approach. Psychological Bulletin, 92, 532-540. PA 69:224.

Merbaum, Michael; & Osarchuk, Michael. (1975). Modification and generalization of verbal behavior as a function of direct verbal intervention. Psychological Reports, 36, 775-781. PA 54:9572.

Mercer, G. William; & Benjamin, M. L. (1980). Spatial behavior of university undergraduates in double-occupancy residence rooms: An inventory of effects. Journal of Applied Social Psychology, 10, 32-44. PA 66:5755.

Mesch, Debra; Lew, Marvin; Johnson, David W.; & Johnson, Roger. (1985). Isolated teenagers, cooperative learning, and the training of social skills. Journal of Psychology, 120, 323-334.

Messé, Lawrence A.; & Callahan Levy, Charlene. (1979). Sex and message effects on reward allocation behavior. Academic Psychology Bulletin, 1(2), 129-133. PA 65:1240.

Messé, Lawrence A.; & Sivacek, John M. (1979). Predictions of others' responses in a mixed-motive game: Self-justification or false consensus? Journal of Personality and Social Psychology, 37, 602-607. PA 64:8001.

Messé, Lawrence A.; Vallacher, Robin [R.]; & Phillips, James L. (1974). Equity and coalition formation in triads. Personality and Social Psychology Bulletin, 1, 249-251. PA 56:2310.

Messé, Lawrence A.; Vallacher, Robin R.; & Phillips, James L. (1975). Equity and the for-

mation of revolutionary and conservative coalitions in triads. Journal of Personality and Social Psychology, 31, 1141-1146. PA 54:9608.

Messick, David M.; & McClelland, Carol L. (1983). Social traps and temporal traps. Personality and Social Psychology Bulletin, 9, 105-110. PA 70:12644.

Messick, David M.; Wilke, Henk; Brewer, Marilynn B.; Kramer, Roderick H.; Zemke, Patricia English; & Lui, Layton. (1983). Individual adaptations and structural change as solutions to social dilemmas. Journal of Personality and Social Psychology, 44, 294-309. PA 70:5615.

Metcalfe, Beverly A. (1981). Model of psychological processes in social interaction. Perceptual and Motor Skills, 53, 254. PA 67:12046.

Mettee, David R.; & Riskind, John. (1974). Size of defeat and liking for superior and similar ability competitors. Journal of Experimental Social Psychology, 10, 333-351.

Meyer, John P.; & Pepper, Susan. (1977). Need compatibility and marital adjustment in young married couples. Journal of Personality and Social Psychology, 35, 331-342.

Michaels, James W.; Edwards, John N.; & Acock, Alan C. (1984). Satisfaction in intimate relationships as a function of inequality, inequity, and outcomes. Social Psychology Quarterly, 47, 347-357. PA 72:30787.

Michaels, James W.; & McCulloch, Donna H. (1976). Effects of differentially rewarding groups on cooperative task performance and satisfaction. Center for Social Organization of Schools Report, Johns Hopkins University (Rep. No. 211, 12 pages). PA 58:7456.

Michaels, James W.; & Wiggins, James A. (1976). Effects of mutual dependency and dependency asymmetry on social exchange. Sociometry, 39, 368-376. SA 7716197.

Michelini, Ronald L. (1975). Compliance to threat as a function of knowledge of the sources' prior losses. Bulletin of the Psychonomic Society, 5, 223-225. PA 54:3032.

Michelini, Ronald L.; Passalacqua, Robert; & Cusimano, John. (1976). Effects of seating arrangement on group participation. Journal of Social Psychology, 99, 179-186.

Michener, H. Andrew; & Burt, Martha R. (1975). Use of social influence under varying conditions of legitimacy. Journal of Personality and Social Psychology, 32, 398-407. PA 54:11675.

Michener, H. Andrew; Cohen, Eugene D.; &

Sørensen, Aage B. (1975). Social exchange: Predicting interpersonal outcomes in four-event, three-person systems. *Journal of Personality and Social Psychology, 32,* 283–293. PA 57:3344.

Michener, H. Andrew; Cohen, Eugene D.; & Sørensen, Aage B. (1977). Social exchange: Predicting transactional outcomes in five-event, four-person systems. *American Sociological Review, 42,* 522–535. PA 59:12327.

Michener, H. Andrew; Dettman, David C.; & Choi, Young C. (1984). The beta-core solution in cooperative non-sidepayment N-person games. *Advances in Group Processes, 1,* 145–181.

Michener, H. Andrew; Fleishman, John A.; & Vaske, Jerry J. (1976). A test of the bargaining theory of coalition formation in four-person groups. *Journal of Personality and Social Psychology, 34,* 1114–1126. PA 60:11696.

Michener, H. Andrew; Fleishman, John A.; Vaske, Jerry J.; & Statza, Gerald R. (1975). Minimum resource and pivotal power theories: A competitive test in four-person coalitional situations. *Journal of Conflict Resolution, 19,* 89–107. PA 54:5204.

Michener, H. Andrew; Ginsberg, Irving J.; & Yuen, Kenneth. (1979). Effects of core properties in four-person games with side-payments. *Behavioral Science, 24,* 263–280. PA 64:10338. SA 80L0090.

Michener, H. Andrew; & Lawler, Edward J. (1975). Endorsement of formal leaders: An integrative model. *Journal of Personality and Social Psychology, 31,* 216–223. PA 53:11586.

Michener, H. Andrew; Macheel, Greg B.; Depies, Charles G.; & Bowen, Chris A. (1986). Mollifier representation in non-constant-sum games: An experimental test. *Journal of Conflict Resolution, 30,* 361–382. PA 73:29961.

Michener, H. Andrew; & Potter, Kathryn (1981). Generalizability of tests in n-person sidepayment games. *Journal of Conflict Resolution, 25,* 733–749.

Michener, H. Andrew; Potter, Kathryn; Macheel, Greg B.; & Depies, Charles G. (1984). A test of the von Neumann-Morgenstern stable set solution in cooperative non-sidepayment *n*-person games. *Behavioral Science, 29,* 13–27.

Michener, H. Andrew; Sakurai, Melvin M.; Yuen, Kenneth; & Kasen, Thomas J. (1979). A competitive test of the M-sub-1-super((i)) and M-sub-1-super((im)) bargaining sets. *Journal of Conflict Resolution, 23,* 102–119. PA 64:1008.

Michener, H. Andrew; Vaske, Jerry J.; Schleifer, Steven L.; Plazewski, Joseph G.; & Chapman, Larry J. (1975). Factors affecting concession rate and threat usage in bilateral conflict. *Sociometry, 38,* 62–80. PA 54:7524.

Michener, H. Andrew; & Yuen, Kenneth. (1983). A test of M-sub-1-super((im)) bargaining sets in sidepayment games. *Journal of Conflict Resolution, 27,* 109–135. PA 70:5633.

Michener, H. Andrew; Yuen, Kenneth; & Geisheker, Stephen B. (1980). Nonsymmetry and core size in n-person sidepayment games. *Journal of Conflict Resolution, 24,* 495–523. PA 64:12463.

Michener, H. Andrew; Yuen, Kenneth; & Ginsberg, Irving J. (1977). A competitive test of the M1 bargaining set, kernel, and equal share models. *Behavioral Science, 22,* 341–355. SA 78J4697.

Mickelson, John S.; & Campbell, James H. (1975). Information behavior: Groups with varying levels of interpersonal acquaintance. *Organizational Behavior and Human Performance, 13,* 193–205. PA 54:2981.

Middlemist, R. Dennis; Knowles, Eric S.; & Matter, Charles F. (1976). Personal space invasions in the lavatory: Suggestive evidence for arousal. *Journal of Personality and Social Psychology, 33,* 541–546. PA 56:6047.

Midlarsky, Manus; & Midlarsky, Elizabeth. (1976). Status inconsistency, aggressive attitude, and helping behavior. *Journal of Personality, 44,* 371–391.

Miell, Dorothy; Duck, Steve; & la Gaipa, John. (1979). Interactive effects of sex and timing in self-disclosure. *British Journal of Social and Clinical Psychology, 18,* 355–362. PA 66:5756.

Miell, Dorothy; & le Voi, Martin. (1985). Self-monitoring and control in dyadic interactions. *Journal of Personality and Social Psychology, 49,* 1652–1661. PA 73:11737.

Mikula, Gerold. (1974). [Individual and group decisions concerning the sharing of commonly obtained winnings: A study of the influence of social responsibility.] *Psychologische Beiträge, 16,* 338–364. PA 54:11677.

Mikula, Gerold. (1984). Personal relationships: Remarks on the current state of research. *European Journal of Social Psychology, 14,* 339–352. PA 72:20082.

Mikula, Gerold; & Mueller, Guenter F. (1983).

Procedural preferences in the allocation of jointly produced gains and losses. *Journal of Social Psychology*, *121*, 117–124. PA 71:17758.

Mikula, Gerold; & Schwinger, Thomas. (1973). [Sympathy and the need for social approval as determinants for the allocation of common rewards]. *Psychologische Beitrage*, *15*, 396–407. PA 53:7326.

Milardo, Robert M. (1982). Friendship networks in developing relationships: Converging and diverging social environments. *Social Psychology Quarterly*, *45*, 162–172. PA 69:10410.

Milardo, Robert M.; Johnson, Michael P.; & Huston, Ted L. (1983). Developing close relationships: Changing patterns of interaction between pair members and social networks. *Journal of Personality and Social Psychology*, *44*, 964–976. PA 71:1322.

Miles, Matthew B. (1980). *Learning to work in groups: A practical guide for members and trainers* (2nd ed.). New York: Teachers College Press.

Milgram, Stanley. (1963). Behavioral study of obedience. *Journal of Abnormal and Social Psychology*, *67*, 371–378.

Milgram, Stanley. (1970). The experience of living in cities. *Science*, *167*, 1461–1468.

Milgram, Stanley. (1977). *Individual in a social world: Essays and experiments*. Reading, MA: Addison-Wesley.

Miller, Charles E. (1979a). Coalition formation in triads with single-peaked payoff curves. *Behavioral Science*, *24*, 75–84. PA 64:3256.

Miller, Charles E. (1979b). Probabilistic theories of coalition formation in groups. *Behavioral Science*, *24*, 359–368. PA 65:1241. SA 81L3331.

Miller, Charles E. (1980a). Coalition formation in characteristic function games: Competitive tests of three theories. *Journal of Experimental Social Psychology*, *16*, 61–76. PA 65:7945.

Miller, Charles E. (1980b). Effects of payoffs and resources on coalition formation: A test of three theories. *Social Psychology Quarterly*, *43*, 154–164. PA 66:1278. SA 83M7344.

Miller, Charles E. (1980c). A test of four theories of coalition formation: Effects of payoffs and resources. *Journal of Personality and Social Psychology*, *38*, 153–164.

Miller, Charles E. (1981). Coalition formation in triads: Effects of liking and resources. *Personality and Social Psychology Bulletin*, *7*, 296–301. PA 67:5720.

Miller, Charles E. (1985a). Coalition behaviour:

Effects of coalition values and monetary stakes. *British Journal of Social Psychology*, *24*, 249–258. PA 73:27145. SA 86Q4844.

Miller, Charles E. (1985b). Group decision making under majority and unanimity decision rules. *Social Psychology Quarterly*, *48*, 51–61. PA 73:6340. SA 85O7799.

Miller, Charles E.; & Anderson, Patricia D. (1979). Group decision rules and the rejection of deviates. *Social Psychology Quarterly*, *42*, 354–363. PA 65:10392. SA 83M7345.

Miller, Charles E.; Jackson, Patricia; Mueller, Jonathan; & Schersching, Cynthia. (1987). Some social psychological effects of group decision rules. *Journal of Personality and Social Psychology*, *52*, 325–332. PA 74:15531.

Miller, Charles E.; & Komorita, Samuel S. (1986). Changes in outcomes in coalition bargaining. *Journal of Personality and Social Psychology*, *51*, 721–729. PA 74:4012.

Miller, Charles E.; & Wong, Jane. (1986). Coalition behavior: Effects of earned versus unearned resources. *Organizational Behavior and Human Decision Processes*, *38*, 257–277. PA 74:4013.

Miller, Dale T.; & Holmes, John G. (1975). The role of situational restrictiveness on self-fulfilling prophecies: A theoretical and empirical extension of Kelley and Stahelski's triangle hypothesis. *Journal of Personality and Social Psychology*, *31*, 661–673. PA 54:11678.

Miller, Dale T.; & McFarland, Cathy. (1987). Pluralistic ignorance: When similarity is interpreted as dissimilarity. *Journal of Personality and Social Psychology*, *53*, 298–305. PA 74:34406.

Miller, Dale T.; & Turnbull, William. (1986). Expectancies and interpersonal processes. *Annual Review of Psychology*, *37*, 233–256. PA 73:21918.

Miller, Franklin G.; Hurkman, Marion F.; Robinson, Jennesse B.; & Feinberg, Richard A. (1979). Status and evaluation potential in the social facilitation and impairment of task performance. *Personality and Social Psychology Bulletin*, *5*, 381–385. PA 64:10387.

Miller, Frederick D. (1976). The problem of transfer of training in learning groups: Group cohesion as an end in itself. *Small Group Behavior*, *7*, 221–236. SA 77I8732.

Miller, Gerald R. (1975). Interpersonal communication: A conceptual perspective. *Communication*, *2*, 93–105. PA 61:8453. SA 81L6529.

Miller, Gerald R. (Ed.). (1976). *Explorations in interpersonal communication*. Beverly Hills & London: Sage.

Miller, Gerald R. (1978). The current status of theory and research in interpersonal communication. *Human Communication Research, 4,* 64–178. PA 61:5937.

Miller, Larry D. (1977). Dyadic perception of communicator style: Replication and confirmation. *Communication Research, 4,* 87–112. PA 58:5309.

Miller, Lisa; & Bart, William M. (1985). Patterns of nonverbal behavior among adolescents responding to a formal reasoning task. *Journal of Psychology, 120,* 51–57.

Miller, Lynn C.; Berg, John H.; & Archer, Richard L. (1983). Openers: Individuals who elicit intimate self-disclosure. *Journal of Personality and Social Psychology, 44,* 1234–1244. PA 71:1323.

Miller, Lynn C.; & Kenny, David A. (1986). Reciprocity of self-disclosure at the individual and dyadic levels: A social relations analysis. *Journal of Personality and Social Psychology, 50,* 713–719. PA 73:21919.

Miller, Norman; & Brewer, Marilynn B. (Eds.). (1984). *Groups in Contact: The Psychology of Desegregation*. Orlando, FL: Academic Press.

Miller, Norman; Brewer, Marilynn B; & Edwards, Keith. (1985). Cooperative interaction in desegregated settings: A laboratory analogue. *Journal of Social Issues, 41*(3), 63–79.

Miller, Norman; & Maruyama, Geoffrey. (1976). Ordinal position and peer popularity. *Journal of Personality and Social Psychology, 33,* 123–131. PA 56:648.

Miller, Philip Carnegie; Lefcourt, Herbert M.; Holmes, John G.; Ware, Edward E.; & Saleh, Wendy E. (1986). Marital locus of control and marital problem solving. *Journal of Personality and Social Psychology, 51,* 161–169.

Miller, Richard L.; & Suls, Jerry. (1977). Helping, self-attribution, and the size of an initial request. *Journal of Social Psychology, 103,* 203–208. PA 60:9342.

Miller, Rowland S.; Goldman, Howard J.; & Schlenker, Barry R. (1978). The effects of task importance and group performance on group members' attributions. *Journal of Psychology, 99,* 53–58. PA 62:1091.

Miller, Rowland S.; & Schlenker, Barry R. (1985). Egotism in group members: Public and private attributions of responsibility for group performance. *Social Psychology Quarterly, 48,* 85–89. PA 73:6341. SA 85O7800.

Miller, Scott A.; & Brownell, Celia A. (1976). Peers, persuasion, and Piaget: Dyadic interaction between conservers and nonconservers. *Child Development, 46,* 992–997. PA 57:7973.

Miller, Sherod; Nunnally, Elam W.; & Wackman, Daniel B. (1976). A communication training program for couples. *Social Casework, 57,* 9–18. PA 57:8696.

Miller, Stuart; & Nardini, Kathleen M. (1977). Individual differences in the perception of crowding. *Environmental Psychology and Nonverbal Behavior, 2,* 2–13. PA 60:11729.

Miller, Stuart; Rossbach, Jeanine; & Munson, Robert. (1981). Social density and affiliative tendency as determinants of dormitory residential outcomes. *Journal of Applied Social Psychology, 11,* 356–365.

Mills, Carol J.; & Bohannon, Wayne E. (1980). Character structure and jury behavior: Conceptual and applied implications. *Journal of Personality and Social Psychology, 38,* 662–667.

Mills, Judson; Belgrave, Faye Z.; & Boyer, Kathy M. (1984). Reducing avoidance of social interaction with a physically disabled person by mentioning the disability following a request for aid. *Journal of Applied Social Psychology, 14,* 1–11. PA 71:31340.

Mills, Theodore M. (1979). Changing paradigms for studying human groups. *Journal of Applied Behavioral Science, 15,* 407–423. SA 80K7133.

Mills, Theodore M. (1984). *The sociology of small groups* (2nd ed.). Englewood Cliffs, NJ: Prentice-Hall.

Milman, Donald S.; & Goldman, George D. (1974). *Group process today: Evaluation and perspective*. Springfield, IL: Charles C. Thomas.

Miner, Frederick C. (1979). A comparative analysis of three diverse group decision making approaches. *Academy of Management Journal, 22,* 81–93. PA 64:1009.

Miner, Frederick C. (1984). Group versus individual decision making: An investigation of performance measures, decision strategies, and process losses/gains. *Organizational Behavior and Human Performance, 33,* 112–124. PA 71:12161.

Miner, John B. (1982). The uncertain future of the leadership concept: Revisions and clarifications. *Journal of Applied Behavioral Science*, *18*, 293-307. PA 69:1001.

Minix, Dean A. (1982). *Small groups and foreign policy decision-making*. Washington, DC: University Press of America.

Mintz, Alexander. (1951). Non-adaptive group behavior. *Journal of Abnormal and Social Psychology*, *46*, 150-159. PA 25:8008

Minuchin, Salvador. (1974). *Families and family therapy*. Cambridge, MA: Harvard Univ. Press.

Misavage, Robert; & Richardson, James T. (1974). The focusing of responsibility: An alternative hypothesis in help-demanding situations. *European Journal of Social Psychology*, *4*, 5-15. PA 54:2982.

Mischel, Walter. (1968). *Personality and assessment*. New York; Wiley.

Mischel, Walter; & Peake, Philip K. (1982). Beyond deja-vu in the search for cross-situational consistency. *Psychological Review*, *89*, 730-755.

Mishara, Brian L.; Brawley, Patricia; Cheevers, Mary; Kitover, Rhonda M.; Knowles, Alice M.; Rautiala, Patricia; & Surjian, Ara. (1974). Encroachments upon the body buffer zones of the young and old woman: A naturalistic study. *International Journal of Aging and Human Development*, *5*, 3-5. PA 53:5218.

Mishra, Pravash K. (1983). Proxemics: Theory and research. *Perspectives in Psychological Researches*, *6*(1), 10-15. PA 71:17759.

Mishra, Pravash K.; & Das, Braja K. (1983) Group size and helping behavior: A comprehensive review. *Perspectives in Psychological Researches*, *6*(2), 60-64. PA 71:25830.

Misra, Sasi; & Kalro, Amar. (1979). Triangle effect and the connotative meaning of trust in Prisoner's Dilemma: A cross cultural study. *International Journal of Psychology*, *14*, 255-263. PA 65:7964.

Misumi, Jyuji. (1985). *The behavioral science of leadership: An interdisciplinary Japanese research program*. Ann Arbor: University of Michigan Press.

Misumi, Jyuji; & Ishida, Umeo. (1972). [An experimental study of "complementary effects" of leadership styles at two step supervisory levels]. *Japanese Journal of Experimental Social Psychology*, *11*, 148-158. PA 53:2079.

Misumi, Jyuji; & Sako, Hidekazu. (1982). [An experimental study of the effect of leadership behavior on followers' behavior of following after the leader in a simulated emergency situation]. *Japanese Journal of Experimental Social Psychology*, *22*, 49-59. PA 69:12665.

Misumi, Jyuji; Shinohara, Hirofumi; & Sato, Seiichi. (1974). Effect of PM leadership behavior patterns upon performance factors in perceptual-motor learning. *Japanese Journal of Experimental Social Psychology*, *14*, 31-47. PA 57:11203.

Mitchell, Herman E.; & Byrne, Donn. (1973). The defendant's dilemma: Effects of jurors' attitudes and authoritarianism on judicial decisions. *Journal of Personality and Social Psychology*, *25*, 123-129.

Mitchell, Ted; & Heeler, Roger. (1981). Toward a theory of acceptable outcomes. *Behavioral Science*, *26*, 163-176. PA 67:3545.

Mitchell, Terence R.; Larson, James R.; & Green, Stephen G. (1977). Leader behavior, situational moderators, and group performance: An attributional analysis. *Organizational Behavior and Human Performance*, *18*, 254-268. PA 59:5643.

Mixon, Don. (1976). Studying feignable behavior. *Representative Research in Social Psychology*, *7*, 89-104. PA 58:9451.

Moessinger, Pierre. (1974). [Developmental study of exchange and bargaining]. *Cahiers de Psychologie*, *17*(2), 119-124. PA 55:12027.

Molm, Linda D. (1979a). The development of social exchange under incompatible social contingencies. *Social Psychology Quarterly*, *42*, 324-340. PA 65:10394.

Molm, Linda D. (1979b). The effects of reinforcement differences and disruptions of social exchange in an alternative task situation. *Social Psychology Quarterly*, *42*, 158-171. PA 64:7935.

Molm, Linda D. (1980). The effects of structural variations in social reinforcement contingencies on exchange and cooperation. *Social Psychology Quarterly*, *43*, 269-282. PA 66:5757.

Molm, Linda D. (1981a). A contingency change analysis of the disruption and recovery of social exchange and cooperation. *Social Forces*, *59*(3), 729-751.

Molm, Linda D. (1981b). The conversion of power imbalance to power use. *Social Psychology Quarterly*, *44*, 151-163. PA 67:7701. SA 83N2364.

Molm, Linda D. (1981c). Power use in the dyad:

The effects of structure, knowledge, and interaction history. *Social Psychology Quarterly, 44*, 42–48. PA 67:1238. SA 82M1471.

Molm, Linda D. (1983). Changes in reinforcement contingencies and the disruption of social exchange. *Social Science Research, 12*, 330–352. PA 71:23068. SA 84N9147.

Molm, Linda D. (1984). The disruption and recovery of dyadic social interaction. *Advances in Group Processes, 1*, 183–227.

Molm, Linda D. (1985). Relative effects of individual dependencies: Further tests of the relation between power imbalance and power use. *Social Forces, 63*, 810–837. PA 72:28031.

Molm, Linda D.; & Wiggins, James A. (1979). A behavioral analysis of the dynamics of social exchange in the dyad. *Social Forces, 57*, 1157–1179. SA 80K7134.

Montano, Daniel; & Adamopoulos, John. (1984). The perception of crowding in interpersonal situations: Affective and behavioral responses. *Environment and Behavior, 16*, 643–666. PA 72:4024.

Montgomery, Barbara M. (1984). Individual differences and relational interdependencies in social interaction. *Human Communication Research, 11*, 33–60. PA 72:22585. SA 86Q3074.

Montgomery, Barbara M. (1986). An interactionist analysis of small group peer assessment. *Small Group Behavior, 17*, 19–37.

Montgomery, Robert L.; Hinkle, Stephen W.; & Enzie, Russell F. (1976). Arbitrary norms and social change in high- and low-authoritarian societies. *Journal of Personality and Social Psychology, 33*, 698–708.

Montmollin, Germaine de. (1977). *L'influence sociale: Phénomènes, facteurs et theories.* Paris, France: Presses Universitaires de France.

Mooij, Ton. (1980). Conflict behavior during cooperation within groups. *Nederlands Tijdschrift voor de Psychologie en haar Grensgebieden, 35*, 299–314. PA 66:3611.

Moore, Carl M. (1987). *Group techniques for idea building.* Newbury Park: Sage.

Moore, Christopher W. (1986). *The mediation process: Practical strategies for resolving conflict.* San Francisco: Jossey-Bass.

Moore, Danny L.; & Baron, Robert S. (1983). Social facilitation: A psychophysiological analysis. In J. T. Cacioppo & R. E. Petty (Eds.), *Social psychophysiology: A sourcebook* (pp. 434–466). New York: Guilford Press.

Moore, Danny L.; Byers, David A.; & Baron,

Robert S. (1981). Socially mediated fear reduction in rodents: Distraction, communication, or mere presence? *Journal of Experimental Social Psychology, 17*, 485–505. PA 67:5065.

Moore, Jeffrey C. (1974). Audience effects in a communication chain: An instance of ingratiation. *Personality and Social Psychology Bulletin, 1*, 58–60.

Moorhead, Gregory. (1982). Groupthink: Hypothesis in need of testing. *Group and Organization Studies, 7*, 429–444. PA 69:10411.

Moorhead, Gregory; & Montanari, John R. (1986). An empirical investigation of the groupthink phenomenon. *Human Relations, 39*, 399–410. PA 73:24485.

Moos, Rudolf H.; Van Dort, Bernice; Smail, Penny; & DeYoung, Alan J. (1975). A typology of university student living groups. *Journal of Educational Psychology, 67*, 359–367. PA 54:3992.

Moran, Gary; & Comfort, John Craig. (1982). Scientific jury selection: Sex as a moderator of demographic and personality predictors of impaneled felony jury behavior. *Journal of Personality and Social Psychology, 43*, 1052–1063.

Morasch, Bruce; Groner, Norman; & Keating, John P. (1979). Type of activity and failure as mediators of perceived crowding. *Personality and Social Psychology Bulletin, 5*, 223–226. PA 64:5611.

Moreland, Richard L. (1985). Social categorization and the assimilation of "new" group members. *Journal of Personality and Social Psychology, 48*, 1173–1190. PA 72:22586.

Moreland, Richard L.; & Levine, John M. (1982). Socialization in small groups: Temporal changes in individual-group relations. *Advances in Experimental Social Psychology, 15*, 137–192.

Moreno, Jacob L. (1953). *Who shall survive? Foundations of sociometry, group psychotherapy and sociodrama* (rev. ed.). Beacon, NY: Beacon House.

Morgan, Charles J. (1978). Bystander intervention: Experimental test of a formal model. *Journal of Personality and Social Psychology, 36*, 43–55. PA 62:5984.

Morgan, Cyril P.; & Aram, John D. (1975). The preponderance of arguments in the risky shift phenomenon. *Journal of Experimental Social Psychology, 11*, 25–34. PA 53:11587.

Morgan, Ross N.; & Evans, James F. (1977). Comparison of reinforcing and modeling techniques for promoting self-disclosure. *Psychological Reports*, *40*, 363-371. PA 59:3341.

Morgan, William R. (1975). Bales' role theory: An attribution theory interpretation. *Sociometry*, *38*, 429-444. SA 76H9429.

Morgan, William R.; & Sawyer, Jack. (1979). Equality, equity, and procedural justice in social exchange. *Social Psychology Quarterly*, *42*, 71-75. PA 64:7897.

Moriarty, Thomas. (1975). Crime, commitment, and the responsive bystander: Two field experiments. *Journal of Personality and Social Psychology*, *31*, 370-376. PA 53:11617.

Morley, Ian E.; & Stephenson, Geoffrey M. (1977). *The social psychology of bargaining.* London: Allen & Unwin.

Morran, D. Keith; & Hulse, Diana. (1984). Group leader and member reactions to selected intervention statements: A comparison. *Small Group Behavior*, *15*, 278-288. PA 72:1238.

Morrione, Thomas J. (1985). Situated interaction. *Studies in Symbolic Interaction*, Suppl. 1, 161-192. PA 73:19824.

Morris, William N.; & Miller, Robert S. (1975). The effects of consensus-breaking and consensus-preempting partners on reduction of conformity. *Journal of Experimental Social Psychology*, *11*, 215-223. PA 54:7526.

Morris, William N.; Miller, Robert S.; & Spangenberg, Scott. (1977). The effects of dissenter position and task difficulty on conformity and response conflict. *Journal of Personality*, *45*, 251-266. PA 59:9894.

Morris, William N.; Worchel, Stephen; Bois, Joyce L.; Pearson, Janine A.; Rountree, C. Alan; Samaha, Gary M.; Wachtler, Joel; & Wright, Sharon L. (1976). Collective coping with stress: Group reactions to fear, anxiety, and ambiguity. *Journal of Personality and Social Psychology*, *33*, 674-679. PA 56:6004.

Morrison, Richard J. (1974). Caplow's model: A reformulation. *Journal of Mathematical Sociology*, *3*, 215-230. PA 53:1042. SA 75H5815.

Morrison, Thomas L.; Greene, Les R.; & Tischler, Nancy G. (1979). Member learning in analytic self-study groups. *Journal of Social Psychology*, *109*, 59-67. PA 65:3253.

Morrissette, Julian O.; Hornseth, John P.; & Shellar, Kathy. (1975). Team organization and monitoring performance. *Human Factors*, *17*, 296-300. PA 54:11035.

Morse, John J.; & Caldwell, David F. (1979). Effects of personality and perception of the environment on satisfaction with task group. *Journal of Psychology*, *103*, 183-192. PA 65:1242.

Morse, Stanley J.; & Marks, Alan. (1985). "Cause Duncan's me mate": A comparison of reported relations with mates and with friends in Australia. *British Journal of Social Psychology*, *24*, 283-292. PA 73:27146.

Mortensen, C. David; & Arntson, Paul H. (1974). The effect of predispositions toward verbal behavior on interaction patterns in dyads. *Quarterly Journal of Speech*, *60*, 421-430. PA 53:11667.

Morton, Teru L. (1978). Intimacy and reciprocity of exchange: A comparison of spouses and strangers. *Journal of Personality and Social Psychology*, *36*, 72-81. PA 62:5985.

Morton, Teru L.; Alexander, James F.; & Altman, Irwin. (1976). Communication and relationship definition. In G. R. Miller (Ed.), *Explorations in interpersonal communication* (pp. 105-145). Beverly Hills, CA: Sage. PA 58:11670.

Moscovici, Serge. (1975). Reply to a critical note on two studies of minority influence. *European Journal of Social Psychology*, *5*, 261-263. PA 55:7152.

Moscovici, Serge. (1976). *Social influence and social change.* London: Academic Press.

Moscovici, Serge. (1979). A rejoinder. *British Journal of Social and Clinical Psychology*, *18*, 181. PA 64:7898.

Moscovici, Serge. (1980). Towards a theory of conversion behavior. *Advances in Experimental Social Psychology*, *13*, 209-239.

Moscovici, Serge; & Doms, Machteld. (1982). Compliance and conversion in a situation of sensory deprivation. *Basic and Applied Social Psychology*, *3*, 81-94. PA 69:1024.

Moscovici, Serge; & Faucheux, Claude. (1972). Social influence, conformity bias, and the study of active minorities. *Advances in Experimental Social Psychology*, *6*, 149-202.

Moscovici, Serge; & Lage, Elisabeth. (1976). Studies in social influence: III. Majority versus minority influence in a group. *European Journal of Social Psychology*, *6*, 149-174. PA 57:8208.

Moscovici, Serge; & Lage, Elisabeth. (1978). Studies in social influence: IV. Minority influence in a context of original judgments. *European Journal of Social Psychology*, *8*, 349-365. PA 63:3256.

Moscovici, Serge; Lage, E[lisabeth]; &

Naffrechoux, M. (1969). Influence of a consistent minority on the responses of a majority in a color-perception task. *Sociometry, 32,* 365–380.

Moscovici, Serge; Lage, Elisabeth; & Naffrechoux, Martine. (1973). Conflict in three-person groups: The relationship between social influence and cognitive style. In L. Rappoport and D. A. Summers (Eds.), *Human judgment and social interaction* (pp. 304–314). New York: Holt, Rinehart and Winston.

Moscovici, Serge; & Mugny, Gabriel. (1983). In P. B. Paulus (Ed.), *Basic group processes* (pp. 41–65). New York: Springer Verlag.

Moscovici, Serge; Mugny, Gabriel; & Papastamou, Stamos. (1981). Sleeper effect and/or minority effect? *Cahiers de Psychologie Cognitive, 1,* 199–221. PA 67:12047.

Moscovici, Serge; Mugny, Gabriel; & Van Avermaet, Eddy (Eds.). (1985). *Perspectives on minority influence.* New York: Cambridge University Press.

Moscovici, Serge; & Néve, Patricia. (1973a). Studies in social influence: II. Instrumental and symbolic influence. *European Journal of Social Psychology, 3,* 461–471. PA 53:9533.

Moscovici, Serge; & Néve, Patricia. (1973b). Studies on polarization of judgments: III. Majorities, minorities and social judgments. *European Journal of Social Psychology, 3,* 479–484. PA 53:11618.

Moscovici, Serge; & Paicheler, Geneviève. (1983). Minority or majority influences: Social change, compliance, and conversion. In H. H. Blumberg, A. P. Hare, V. Kent, & M. Davies (Eds.), *Small groups and social interaction* (Vol. 1, pp. 215–224). Chichester: John Wiley & Sons.

Moscovici, Serge; & Personnaz, Bernard. (1980). Studies in social influence: V. Minority influence and conversion behavior in a perceptual task. *Journal of Experimental Social Psychology, 16,* 270–282. PA 65:12728.

Moscovici, Serge; & Personnaz, Bernard. (1986). Studies on latent influence by the spectrometer method I: The impact of psychologization in the case of conversion by a minority or a majority. *European Journal of Social Psychology, 16,* 345–360.

Mossholder, Kevin W.; & Bedeian, Arthur G. (1983). Group interactional processes: Individual and group level effects. *Group and Organization Studies, 8,* 187–202. PA 70:10246.

Mossholder, Kevin W.; Bedeian, Arthur G.; & Armenakis, Achilles A. (1981). Role perceptions, satisfaction, and performance: Moderating effects of self-esteem and organizational level. *Organizational Behavior and Human Performance, 28,* 224–234.

Mowen, John C.; & Cialdini, Robert B. (1980). On implementing the door-in-the-face compliance technique in a business context. *Journal of Marketing Research, 17,* 253–258.

Moxnes, P. A.; & Engvik, H. A. (1973). Diagnosing the organization: The psychogram. *Interpersonal Development, 4,* 177–189. PA 53:11588.

Muehleman, J. T.; Bruker, Charles; & Ingram, Clara M. (1976). The generosity shift. *Journal of Personality and Social Psychology, 34,* 344–351.

Mueller, Ulrich. (1987). Optimal retaliation for optimal cooperation. *Journal of Conflict Resolution, 31,* 692–724.

Mugny, Gabriel. (1974–1975). Majority and minority: The level of their influence. *Bulletin de Psychologie, 28,* 831–835. PA 55:02312.

Mugny, Gabriel. (1975a). [Meaning of consistency in the case of influence through a concordant or discordant minority communication about social judgment-objects]. *Zeitschrift fur Sozialpsychologie, 6,* 324–332. PA 58:3337.

Mugny, Gabriel. (1975b). Negotiations, image of the other and the process of minority influence. *European Journal of Social Psychology, 5,* 209–228. PA 55:7153.

Mugny, Gabriel. (1976). What majority influence? What minority influence? *Psychologie Schweizerische Zeitschrift fur Psychologie und ihre Anwendungen, 35,* 255–268. PA 60:5210.

Mugny, Gabriel. (1979). A rejoinder to Paicheler: The influence of reactionary minorities. *European Journal of Social Psychology, 9,* 223–225. PA 64:7937.

Mugny, Gabriel. (1982). *The power of minorities.* London: Academic Press. [In collaboration with Stamos Papastamou].

Mugny, Gabriel. (1984a). Compliance, conversion and the Asch paradigm. *European Journal of Social Psychology, 14,* 353–368. PA 72:30788. SA 85O6027.

Mugny, Gabriel. (1984b). Complaisance et conversion dans le "paradigme de Asch" [Compliance and conversion in "Asch's paradigm"]. *Bulletin de Psychologie, 38,* 49–61. PA 72:28032.

Mugny, Gabriel. (1984–1985). Complaisance et

conversion dans le "paradigme de Asch" [Compliance and conversion in "Asch's paradigm"]. *Bulletin de psychologie*, 38, 49–61. PA 72:28032.

Mugny, Gabriel. (1985). Direct and indirect influence in the Asch paradigm: Effects of 'valid' or 'denied' information. *European Journal of Social Psychology*, 15, 457–461.

Mugny, Gabriel; & Doise, Willem. (1978). Sociocognitive conflict and structure of individual and collective performances. *European Journal of Social Psychology*, 8, 181–192.

Mugny, Gabriel; Kaiser, Claude; Papastamou, Stamos; & Perez, Juan A. (1984). Intergroup relations, identification and social influence. Special Issue: Intergroup processes. *British Journal of Social Psychology*, 23, 317–322. PA 72:28033. SA 8507871.

Mugny, Gabriel; & Papastamou, S. (1975–1976). [Study of Hollander's construct of social interdependence: Initial conformity or negotiation?]. *Bulletin de Psychologie*, 29, 970–976. PA 59:7853.

Mugny, Gabriel; & Papastamou, Stamos. (1976–1977). [New approach to minority influence: Psychosocial determinants of minority influence strategies]. *Bulletin de Psychologie*, 30, 573–579. PA 61:3501.

Mugny, Gabriel; & Papastamou, Stamos. (1980). When rigidity does not fail: Individualization and psychologization as resistances to the diffusion of minority innovations. *European Journal of Social Psychology*, 10, 43–61. PA 65:5424.

Mugny, Gabriel; & Papastamou, Stamos. (1982). Minority influence and psycho-social identity. *European Journal of Social Psychology*, 12, 379–394. PA 70:1058.

Mugny, Gabriel; [in collaboration with] Papastamou, Stamos; & [translated by] Sherrard, Carol. (1982). *The power of minorities*. London: Academic Press.

Mugny, Gabriel; Perez, Juan A.; Kaiser, Claude; & Papastamou, Stamos. (1984). Influence minoritaire et relations entre groupes: l'importance du contenu du message et des styles de comportement [Minority influence and between group relations: The importance of message content and behavior styles]. *Psychologie Schweizerische Zeitschrift fur Psychologie und ihre Anwendungen*, 43, 331–351. PA 73:3681.

Mugny, Gabriel; Rilliet, Diane; & Papastamou,

Stamos. (1981). Influence minoritaire et identification sociale dans des contextes d'originalite et de deviance [Minority influence and social identification in the context of the origin of deviance]. *Psychologie Schweizerische Zeitschrift fur Psychologie und ihre Anwendungen*, 40, 314–332. PA 68:3550.

Muirhead, Rosalind D.; & Goldman, Morton. (1979). Mutual eye contact as affected by seating position, sex, and age. *Journal of Social Psychology*, 109, 201–206. PA 65:5391.

Mukerji, Chandra. (1976). Having the authority to know: Decision-making on student film crews. *Sociology of Work and Occupations*, 3(1), 63–87. PA 56:649.

Mullen, Brian. (1982). Operationalizing the effect of the group on the individual: A self attention perspective. *Journal of Experimental Social Psychology*, 19, 295–322.

Mullen, Brian. (1985). Strength and immediacy of sources: A meta-analytic evaluation of the forgotten elements of social impact theory. *Journal of Personality and Social Psychology*, 48, 1458–1466. PA 72:28034.

Mullen, Brian. (1986). Effects of strength and immediacy in group contexts: Reply to Jackson. *Journal of Personality and Social Psychology*, 50, 514–516. PA 73:19804.

Mullen, Brian; & Goethals, George R. (Eds.). (1987). *Theories of group behavior*. New York: Springer-Verlag.

Müller, Gunter F. (1980). [Interpersonal conflict behavior: A comparison and an experimental study of two explanatory models]. *Zeitschrift fur Sozialpsychologie*, 11, 168–180. PA 66:8004.

Müller, Gunter F. (1981–1982). Motivationale, Kognitive und affektive komponenten von Gerechtigkeit bei sozialer Interaktion und gemeinsamer Gewinnaufteilung [Motivational, cognitive, and affective components of justice in social interaction and joint distribution of rewards]. *Archiv fur Psychologie*, 134, 219–235. PA 70:3395.

Müller, Gunter F.; & Autenrieth, Uwe. (1985). Koalitionsbildung in 3-Personen-Gruppen und ihre Vorhersagbarkeit durch sozialpsychologische Interaktionstheorien [Coalition formation in 3-person groups and its predictability on the basis of social psychological interaction theory]. *Zeitschrift fur Sozialpsychologie*, 16, 206–218. PA 73:21920.

Mumford, Mary S. (1974). A comparison of inter

personal skills in verbal and activity groups. *American Journal of Occupational Therapy, 28*(5), 281–283. PA 52:10031.

Mummendey, Amelie. (Ed.). (1984). *Social psychology of aggression: From individual behavior to social interaction.* Berlin: Springer-Verlag.

Munne, Frederic. (1985). ?Dinamica de Grupos o Actividad del Grupo? [Group dynamics or group activity?]. *Boletin de Psicologia Spain,* No. 9, 29–48. PA 74:15532.

Munroe, Robert L.; & Munroe, Ruth H. (1977). Cooperation and competition among East African and American children. *Journal of Social Psychology, 101,* 145–146. PA 58:9372.

Murata, Koji. (1982). Attribution processes in a mixed-motive interaction: The role of active observer's behavior. *Behaviormetrika,* No. 12, 47–61. PA 72:4028.

Murnighan, J. Keith. (1978a). Models of coalition behavior: Game theoretic, social psychological, and political perspectives. *Psychological Bulletin, 85,* 1130–1153. PA 62:5960.

Murnighan, J. Keith. (1978b). Strength and weakness in four coalition situations. *Behavioral Science, 23,* 195–208. PA 64:1011. SA 79K1101.

Murnighan, J. Keith. (1981). Defectors, vulnerability, and relative power: Some causes and effects of leaving a stable coalition. *Human Relations, 34,* 589–609. PA 67:1239. SA 83N2365.

Murnighan, J. Keith. (1982). Evaluating Theoretical Predictions in the Social Sciences: Coalition Theories and Other Models. *Behavioral Science, 27,* 125–130. SA 83N4034.

Murnighan, J. Keith. (1985). Coalitions in decision-making groups: Organizational analogs. *Organizational Behavior and Human Decision Processes, 35,* 1–26. PA 72:20083.

Murnighan, John K.; & Castore, Carl H. (1975). An experimental test of three choice shift hypotheses. *Memory and Cognition, 3,* 171–174. PA 54:7527.

Murnighan, J. Keith; Komorita, S. S.; & Szwajkowski, Eugene. (1977). Theories of coalition formation and the effects of reference groups. *Journal of Experimental Social Psychology, 13,* 166–181. PA 58:9455.

Murnighan, J. Keith; & Leung, Thomas K. (1976). The effects of leadership involvement and the importance of the task on subordinates' performance. *Organizational Behavior and Human Performance, 17,* 299–310. PA 58:1109.

Murnighan, J. Keith; & Roth, Alvin E. (1978). Large group bargaining in a characteristic function game. *Journal of Conflict Resolution, 22,* 299–317. PA 62:10980.

Murnighan, J. Keith; & Roth, Alvin E. (1980). Effects of group size and communication availability on coalition bargaining in a veto game. *Journal of Personality and Social Psychology, 39,* 92–103. PA 66:3612.

Murnighan, J. Keith; & Roth, Alvin E. (1983). Expecting continued play in prisoner's dilemma games: A test of several models. *Journal of Conflict Resolution, 27,* 279–300. PA 70:10247.

Murnighan, J. Keith; & Szwajkowski, Eugene. (1979). Coalition bargaining in four games that include a veto player. *Journal of Personality and Social Psychology, 37,* 1933–1946. PA 65:5392.

Murphy Berman, Virginia; & Berman, John. (1978). The importance of choice and sex in invasions of interpersonal space. *Personality and Social Psychology Bulletin, 4,* 424–428. PA 64:3298.

Murray, Edward J.; & Vincenzo, Joseph. (1976). Bystander intervention in a mild need situation. *Bulletin of the Psychonomic Society, 7*(2), 133–135. PA 56:6049.

Murstein, Bernard I.; Cerreto, Mary; & MacDonald, Marcia G. (1977). A theory and investigation of the effect of exchange-orientation on marriage and friendship. *Journal of Marriage and the Family, 39,* 543–548. PA 60:1026.

Murstein, Bernard I.; Wadlin, Robert; & Bond, Charles F., Jr. (1987). The revised exchange-orientation scale. *Small Group Behavior, 18,* 212–223.

Musante, Linda; Gilbert, Marcia A.; & Thibaut, John. (1983). The effects of control on perceived fairness of procedures and outcomes. *Journal of Experimental Social Psychology, 19,* 223–238. PA 71:1352.

Musick, Susan A.; Beehr, Terry A.; & Gilmore, David C. (1981). Effects of perceptions of presence of audience and achievement instructions on performance of a simple task. *Psychological Reports, 49,* 535–538. PA 67:12071.

Musser, Steven J. (1982). A model for predicting the choice of conflict management strategies by subordinates in high-stakes conflicts. *Organizational Behavior and Human Performance*, 29, 257-269.

Myers, David G. (1973). Summary and bibliography of experiments on group-induced response shift. *Catalog of Selected Documents in Psychology*, 3, 123-124. PA 52:5194.

Myers, David G. (1975). Discussion-induced attitude polarization. *Human Relations*, 28, 699-714. PA 55:7083.

Myers, David G. (1978). Polarizing effects of social comparison. *Journal of Experimental Social Psychology*, 14, 554-563. PA 63:9636.

Myers, David G.; & Bach, Paul J. (1974). Discussion effects on militarism-pacifism: A test of the group polarization hypothesis. *Journal of Personality and Social Psychology*, 30, 741-747. PA 53:9487.

Myers, David G.; & Bach, Paul J. (1976). Group discussion effects on conflict behavior and self-justification. *Psychological Reports*, 38, 135-140. PA 56:2312.

Myers, David G.; & Kaplan, Martin F. (1976). Group-induced polarization in simulated juries. *Personality and Social Psychology Bulletin*, 2, 63-66. PA 56:4060.

Myers, David G.; & Lamm, Helmut. (1975). The polarizing effect of group discussion. *American Scientist*, 63, 297-303. PA 55:02328.

Myers, David G.; & Lamm, Helmut. (1976). The group polarization phenomenon. *Psychological Bulletin*, 83, 602-627. PA 56:6005.

Myers, Jerome L., DiCecco, Joseph V.; & Lorch, Robert F., Jr. (1981). Group dynamics and individual performances: Pseudogroup and quasi-*F* analyses. *Journal of Personality and Social Psychology*, 40, 86-98.

Mynatt, Clifford; & Sherman, Steven J. (1975). Responsibility attribution in groups and individuals: A direct test of the diffusion of responsibility hypothesis. *Journal of Personality and Social Psychology*, 32, 1111-1118. PA 55:7154.

Naar, Ray. (1982). *A primer of group psychotherapy*. New York: Human Sciences Press.

Nacci, Peter L.; & Tedeschi, James T. (1976). Liking and power as factors affecting coalition choices in the triad. *Social Behavior and Personality*, 4, 27-32. SA 7717506.

Nachman, Sidney; Dansereau, Fred; & Naughton, Thomas J. (1985). Levels of analysis and the Vertical Dyad Linkage approach to leadership.

Psychological Reports, 57, 661-662. PA 74:1062.

Nadler, Arie; Goldberg, Marta; & Jaffe, Yoram. (1982). Effect of self-differentiation and anonymity in group on deindividuation. *Journal of Personality and Social Psychology*, 42, 1127-1136. PA 69:1025.

Nadler, Arie; Shapira, Rina; & Ben Itzhak, Shulamit. (1982). Good looks may help: Effects of helper's physical attractiveness and sex of helper on males' and females' help-seeking behavior. *Journal of Personality and Social Psychology*, 42, 90-99. PA 68:3551.

Nadler, David A. (1979). The effects of feedback on task group behavior: A review of the experimental research. *Organizational Behavior and Human Performance*, 23, 309-338.

Nagao, Dennis H.; & Davis, James H. (1980). The effects of prior experience on mock juror case judgments. *Social Psychology Quarterly*, 43, 190-199. PA 66:1280.

Nagar, Dinesh; & Pandey, Janak. (1987). Affect and performance on cognitive task as a function of crowding and noise. *Journal of Applied Social Psychology*, 17, 147-157.

Nagata, Yoshiaki. (1973). [Structure of classroom interpersonal relations in terms of interpersonal attraction and perceived similarity of the amount of resources among the classroom members]. *Japanese Journal of Experimental Social Psychology*, 13, 105-115. PA 54:5255.

Nagata, Yoshiaki. (1980). [Status as a determinant of conformity to and deviation from the group norm]. *Japanese Journal of Psychology*, 51, 152-159. PA 66:8020.

Nagel, Trevor W.; & O'Driscoll, Michael P. (1978). Group polarization in a real-life context: Analysis of choice shifts in an educational situation. *Australian Journal of Psychology*, 30, 229-240. PA 63:11933.

Nahemow, Lucille; & Lawton, M. Powell. (1975). Similarity and propinquity in friendship formation. *Journal of Personality and Social Psychology*, 32, 205-213. PA 57:3042.

Nail, Paul R. (1986). Toward an integration of some models and theories of social response. *Psychological Bulletin*, 100, 190-206. PA 74:1042.

Nail, Paul R.; & Cole, Steven G. (1985a). A critical comparison of bargaining theory and the weighted probability model of coalition behaviour. *British Journal of Social Psychology*, *24*, 259–266. PA 73:27147.

Nail, Paul; & Cole, Steven G. (1985b). Three theories of coalition behaviour: A probabilistic extension. *British Journal of Social Psychology*, *24*, 181–190. PA 73:21921.

Naiman, Thomas H.; & Breed, George. (1974). Gaze duration as a cue for judging conversational tone. *Representative Research in Social Psychology*, *5*, 115–122. PA 53:1099.

Nakanishi, Masayuki. (1988). Group motivation and group task performance: The expectancy-valence theory approach. *Small Group Behavior*, *19*, 35–55.

Napier, Rodney W.; & Gershenfeld, Matti K. (1983). *Making groups work: A guide for group leaders*. Boston: Houghton Mifflin.

Napier, Rodney W.; & Gershenfeld, Matti K. (1985). *Groups, theory and experience* (3rd ed.). Boston: Houghton Mifflin.

Narayanan, V. K.; & Nath, Raghu. (1984). The influence of group cohesiveness on some changes induced by flexitime: A quasi-experiment. *Journal of Applied Behavioral Science*, *20*, 265–276.

Nascimento-Schulze, Clelia Maria. (1981). Towards situational classification. *European Journal of Social Psychology*, *11*, 149–159. SA 83M9103.

Nasu, Kosyo. (1975). [Study of a social affiliation motive as it is affected by the presence of another person in an anxiety situation]. *Japanese Journal of Educational Psychology*, *23*, 143–153. PA 55:7229.

Natale, Michael. (1975a). Convergence of mean vocal intensity in dyadic communication as a function of social desirability. *Journal of Personality and Social Psychology*, *32*, 790–804. PA 55:7084.

Natale, Michael. (1975b). Social desirability as related to convergence of temporal speech patterns. *Perceptual and Motor Skills*, *40*, 827–830. PA 54:7474.

Natale, Michael. (1976). Need for social approval as related to speech interruption in dyadic communication. *Perceptual and Motor Skills*, *42*, 455–458. PA 58:05425.

Natale, Michael. (1977). Induction of mood states and their effect on gaze behaviors. *Journal of Consulting and Clinical Psychology*, *45*, 960. PA 60:1028.

Natale, Michael; Entin, Elliot; & Jaffe, Joseph.

(1979). Vocal interruptions in dyadic communication as a function of speech and social anxiety. *Journal of Personality and Social Psychology*, *37*, 865–878. PA 64:10340.

NATO Conference on role transitions. (1982 [copyright 1984]). [*Proceedings of … conference … held … at the University of Wisconsin.*] New York: Plenum.

Nau, Ekkehard. (1983). Gruppendynamik in Deutschland-Ein Uberblick [Group dynamics in Germany—An overview]. *Kolner Zeitschrift fur Soziologie und Sozialpsychologie*, Supplement 25, 126–143. SA 84O2590.

Navarre, Davida. (1982). Posture sharing in dyadic interaction. *American Journal of Dance Therapy*, *5*, 28–42. PA 70:3396.

Neal, Arthur G.; Ivoska, William J.; & Groat, H. Theodore. (1976). Dimensions of family alienation in the marital dyad. *Sociometry*, *39*, 396–405.

Neale, Margaret A. (1984). The effects of negotiation and arbitration cost salience on bargainer behavior: The role of the arbitrator and constituency on negotiator judgment. *Organizational Behavior and Human Performance*, *34*, 97–111.

Neale, Margaret A.; & Bazerman, Max H. (1985a). The effect of externally set goals on reaching integrative agreements in competitive markets. *Journal of Occupational Behaviour*, *6*, 19–32. PA 72:17320.

Neale, Margaret A.; & Bazerman, Max H. (1985b). Perspectives for understanding negotiation: Viewing negotiation as a judgmental process. *Journal of Conflict Resolution*, *29*, 33–55. PA 72:17319.

Neale, Margaret A.; Huber, Vandra L.; & Northcraft, Gregory B. (1987). The framing of negotiations: Contextual versus task frames. *Organizational Behavior and Human Decision Processes*, *39*, 228–241.

Neale, Margaret A.; & Northcraft, Gregory B. (1986). Experts, amateurs, and refrigerators: Comparing expert and amateur negotiators in a novel task. *Organizational Behavior and Human Decision Processes*, *38*, 305–317. PA 74:7168.

Near, Janet P. (1978). Comparison of developmental patterns in groups. *Small Group Behavior*, *9*, 493–506. SA 80K4184.

Neidhardt, Friedhelm. (1979). Das innere System sozialer Gruppen. Ansatze zur Gruppensoziologie [The inner system of social groups

Preliminaries toward a sociology of groups]. *Kolner Zeitschrift fur Soziologie und Sozialpsychologie, 31,* 639–660. SA 80K7135.

Neidhardt, Friedhelm. (1983). Themen und Thesen zur Gruppensoziologie [Themes and theses on the sociology of groups]. *Kolner Zeitschrift fur Soziologie und Sozialpsychologie,* Supplement 25, 12–34. SA 84O2592.

Neimeyer, Greg J.; & Banikiotes, Paul G. (1981). Self-disclosure flexibility, empathy, and perceptions of adjustment and attraction. *Journal of Counseling Psychology, 28,* 272–275. PA 66:1281.

Neimeyer, Greg J.; & Merluzzi, Thomas V. (1982). Group structure and group process: Personal construct theory and group development. *Small Group Behavior, 13,* 150–164. PA 68:12618.

Nelson, Stephen D. (1975). Nature/nurture revisited: II. Social, political, and technological implications of biological approaches to human conflict. *Journal of Conflict Resolution, 19,* 734–761. PA 56:7873.

Nelson-Jones, Richard; & Dryden, Windy. (1979). Anticipated risk and gain from negative and positive self-disclosure. *British Journal of Social and Clinical Psychology, 18,* 79–80. PA 64:1049.

Nemeth, Charlan [Jean] (Ed.). (1974). *Social Psychology: Classic and contemporary integrations.* Chicago: Rand McNally.

Nemeth, Charlan J[eanne]. (1975). Understanding minority influence: A reply and a digression. *European Journal of Social Psychology, 5,* 265–267. PA 55:7155.

Nemeth, Charlan [Jeanne]. (1977). Interaction between jurors as a function of majority vs. unanimity decision rules. *Journal of Applied Social Psychology, 7,* 38–56.

Nemeth, Charlan J[eanne]. (1979). The role of an active minority in intergroup relations. In W. G. Austin & S. Worchel (Eds.), *The social psychology of intergroup relations* (pp. 225–236). Monterey, California: Brooks/Cole.

Nemeth, Charlan Jeanne. (1981). Jury trials: Psychology and law. *Advances in Experimental Social Psychology, 14,* 309–367.

Nemeth, Charlan J[eanne]. (1983). Reflections on the dialogue between status and style: Influence processes of social control and social change. *Social Psychology Quarterly, 46,* 70–74. PA 70:10248.

Nemeth, Charlan Jeanne. (1985). Dissent, group process, and creativity: The contribution of minority influence. *Advances in Group Processes, 2,* 57–75.

Nemeth, Charlan J[eanne]. (1986). Differential contributions of majority and minority influence. *Psychological Review, 93,* 23–32.

Nemeth, Charlan [Jeanne]; Endicott, Jeffrey; & Wachtler, Joel. (1976). From the '50s to the '70s: Women in jury deliberations. *Sociometry, 39,* 293–304.

Nemeth, Charlan J[eanne].; & Kwan, Julianne L. (1985). Originality of word associations as a function of majority vs. minority influence. *Social Psychology Quarterly, 48,* 277–282. PA 73:24486.

Nemeth, Charlan Jeanne; & Kwan, Julianne L. (1987). Minority influence, divergent thinking and detection of correct solutions. *Journal of Applied Social Psychology, 17,* 788–799.

Nemeth, Charlan J[eanne]; Swedlund, Mark; & Kanki, Barbara. (1974). Patterning of the minority's responses and their influence on the majority. *European Journal of Social Psychology, 4,* 53–64. PA 54:2983.

Nemeth, Charlan J[eanne].; & Wachtler, Joel. (1974). Creating the perceptions of consistency and confidence: A necessary condition for minority influence. *Sociometry, 37,* 529–540. PA 53:9425. SA 76H9431.

Nemeth, Charlan J[eanne].; & Wachtler, Joel. (1983). Creative problem solving as a result of majority vs minority influence. *European Journal of Social Psychology, 13,* 45–55. PA 70:10249. SA 83N0761.

Nemeth, Charlan J[eanne].; Wachtler, Joel; & Endicott, Jeffrey. (1977). Increasing the size of the minority: Some gains and some losses. *European Journal of Social Psychology, 7,* 15–27. PA 60:7419.

Nemiroff, Paul M.; & King, Donald C. (1975). Group decision-making performance as influenced by consensus and self-orientation. *Human Relations, 28,* 1–21. PA 54:5206.

Nemov, R. L.; & Shestakov, A. G. (1981). [Cohesion as a factor of group efficiency] *Voprosy Psikhologii,* No. 3, 113–118. PA 68:5763.

Neuberger, Oswald; & Roth, Bernhard. (1974). [Leadership style and group performance: A test of the contingency model and the LPC concept]. *Zeitschrift fur Sozialpsychologie, 5,* 133–144. PA 53:8501.

Néve, Patricia; & Gautier, Jean Michel. (1977-1978). Phenomena of polarization in group decisions: Experimental study of the effects of contradiction. *Bulletin de Psychologie*, *31*, 361-370. PA 63:978.

Néve, Patricia; & Moscovici, Serge. (1982). Implication et decisions en groupe [Contradiction and group decisions]. *Bulletin de Psychologie*, *35*, 317-323. PA 71:1325.

Neville, Bernard W. (1978). Interpersonal functioning and learning in the small group. *Small Group Behavior*, *9*, 349-361. SA 79K2633.

Neville, Bernie W. (1983). Carkhuff, Maslow, and interpersonal perception in small groups. *Small Group Behavior*, *14*, 211-226. PA 71:12162. SA 84O0835.

Newcomb, Michael D. (1986). Nuclear attitudes and reactions: Associations with depression, drug use, and quality of life. *Journal of Personality and Social Psychology*, *50*, 906-920. PA 73:21805.

Newcomb, Theodore M. (1981). Heiderian balance as a group phenomenon. *Journal of Personality and Social Psychology*, *40*, 862-867. PA 67:3548.

Newcomer, Laurel L. (1985). Limitations of Fiedler's contingency model of leadership styles. *Wisconsin Sociologist*, *22*(2-3), 79-84. SA 85Q1313.

Newman, Alexander; Dickstein, Renie; & Gargan, Michele. (1978). Developmental effects in social facilitation and in being a model. *Journal of Psychology*, *99*, 143-150. PA 62:13440.

Newman, Helen. (1981). Communication within ongoing intimate relationships: An attributional perspective. *Personality and Social Psychology Bulletin*, *7*, 59-70. PA 67:3549.

Newman, Joseph; & McCauley, Clark. (1977). Eye contact with strangers in city, suburb, and small town. *Environment and Behavior*, *9*, 547-558.

Newman, Oscar. (1972). *Defensible space: Crime prevention through urban design*. New York: Macmillan.

Ng, Sik Hung. (1977). Structural and non-structural aspects of power distance reduction tendencies. *European Journal of Social Psychology*, *7*, 317-345. PA 60:7439. SA 79J6851.

Nguyen, Michelle L.; Heslin, Richard; & Nguyen, Tuan. (1976). The meaning of touch: Sex and marital differences. *Representative Research in Social Psychology*, *7*, 13-18. PA 56:4061.

Nichol, Hamish. (1977). A developmental hierarchy of dyadic relationships. *Canadian Psychiatric Association Journal/La Revue de l'Association des Psychiatres du Canada*, *22*(1), 3-9. SA 80K8700.

Nicholls, J. R. (1985). A new approach to situational leadership. *Leadership and Organization Development Journal*, *6*(4), 2-7. PA 74:18737.

Nichols, Albert L. (1977). Coalitions and learning: Applications to a simple game in the triad. *Behavioral Science*, *22*, 391-402. PA 60:11698. SA 78J4699.

Nichols, Mary L.; & Day, Victoria E. (1982). A comparison of moral reasoning of groups and individuals on the "Defining Issues Test." *Academy of Management Journal*, *25*, 201-208. PA 67:12048.

Nicholson, Nigel; Cole, Steven G.; & Rocklin, Thomas. (1985). Conformity in the Asch situation: A comparison between contemporary British and US university students. *British Journal of Social Psychology*, *24*, 59-63. PA 73:3682.

Nicholson, Nigel; Cole, Steven G.; & Rocklin, Thomas. (1986). Coalition formation in parliamentary situations as a function of simulated ideology, resources, and electoral systems. *Political Psychology*, *7*, 103-116. PA 74:18738.

Nicosia, Gregory J.; Hyman, Douglas; Karlin, Robert A.; Epstein, Yakov M.; & Aiello, John R. (1979). Effects of bodily contact on reactions to crowding. *Journal of Applied Social Psychology*, *9*, 508-523. PA 66:5758.

Niebuhr, Robert E.; & Davis, Kermit R. Jr. (1984). Self-esteem: Relationship with leader behavior perceptions as moderated by the duration of the superior-subordinate dyad association. *Personality and Social Psychology Bulletin*, *10*, 51-59. PA 71:32909.

Nilsen, Alleen P. (1983). WIT: An alternative to force. *Etc.*, *40*, 445-450. PA 71:25832.

Ninane, Paul. (1980). Groups and individuals. *Connexions*, No. 31, 113-143. PA 66:5759.

Nirenberg, Theodore D.; & Gaebelein, Jacquelyn W. (1979). Third party aggression: Traditional versus liberal sex role attitudes. *Personality and Social Psychology Bulletin*, *5*, 348-351.

Nishikawa, Masayuki. (1985). The effects of help intentionality and harm doing on restitution. *Japanese Journal of Experimental Social Psychology*, *24*, 161-165. PA 73:11740.

Nishikawa, Masayuki; & Hirata, Kimiyoshi.

(1978). The experimental investigation of equity norm under inequitable distribution. *Japanese Journal of Experimental Social Psychology, 18,* 57–65. PA 64:10318.

Nitz, Lawrence H. (1976). Resource theory and ameliorative strategy in a minimal information political convention game. *Behavioral Science, 21,* 161–172. PA 57:5803.

Nixon, Howard L. (1976). Team orientations, interpersonal relations, and team success. *Research Quarterly, 47,* 429–435. PA 58:7459.

Nixon, Howard L., II. (1977). Reinforcement effects of sports team success cohesiveness-related factors. *International Review of Sport Sociology, 12,* 17–38. SA 79J6852.

Nixon, Howard L. (1979). *The small group.* Englewood Cliffs, NJ: Prentice Hall.

Noe, Francis P.; McDonald, Cary D.; & Hammitt, William E. (1983). Comparison of perceived risk taking in groups and implications drawn from the risky-shift paradigm. *Perceptual and Motor Skills, 56,* 199–206. PA 70:12647.

Noesjirwan, Jennifer. (1977). Contrasting cultural patterns of interpersonal closeness in doctors' waiting rooms in Sydney and Jakarta. *Journal of Cross-Cultural Psychology, 8,* 357–368. PA 60:2903.

Noesjirwan, Jennifer. (1978). A laboratory study of proxemic patterns of Indonesians and Australians. *British Journal of Social and Clinical Psychology, 17,* 333–334. PA 63:7567.

Noesjirwan, Jennifer; & Freestone, Colin. (1979). The culture game: A simulation of culture shock. *Simulation and Games, 10,* 189–206. PA 63:9637.

Nogami, Glenda Y. (1976). Crowding: Effects of group size, room size, or density? *Journal of Applied Social Psychology, 6,* 105–125. PA 57:5827.

Noller, Patricia. (1980). Misunderstandings in marital communication: A study of couples' nonverbal communication. *Journal of Personality and Social Psychology, 39,* 1135–1148. PA 66:5650.

Noller, Patricia. (1982). Channel consistency and inconsistency in the communications of married couples. *Journal of Personality and Social Psychology, 43,* 732–741. PA 69:10415.

Noller, Patricia. (1984). *Nonverbal communication and marital interaction: International series in experimental social psychology* (Vol. 9). Oxford, England: Pergamon Press.

Noller, Patricia; & Gallois, Cynthia. (1986). Sending emotional messages in marriage: Nonverbal behaviour, sex and communication ability. *British Journal of Social Psychology, 25,* 287–297.

Noma, Elliot; & Smith, D. Randall. (1978). SHED: A FORTRAN IV program for the analysis of small group sociometric structure. *Behavior Research Methods and Instrumentation, 10,* 60–62. SA 80K8701.

Nordholm, Lena A. (1975). Effects of group size and stimulus ambiguity on conformity. *Journal of Social Psychology, 97,* 123–130. PA 55:7085.

Norland, Stephen. (1978, Fall). Unacknowledged accounts and the negotiation of deviant identity in small groups. *Sociological Forum, 1,* 60–71. SA 7918026.

Norman, Warren T. (1963). Toward an adequate taxonomy of personality attributes: Replicated factor structure in peer nomination personality ratings. *Journal of Abnormal and Social Psychology, 66,* 574–583.

Normoyle, Janice; & Lavrakas, Paul J. (1984). Fear of crime in elderly women: Perceptions of control, predictability, and territoriality. *Personality and Social Psychology Bulletin, 10,* 191–202. PA 72:17392.

Norton, Robert W. (1979). The Coalition game: Isolating social system subgroups. *Simulation and Games, 10,* 385–402. PA 66:3615. SA 81L1668.

Norton-Ford, Julian D.; & Hogan, Douglas R. (1980). Role of nonverbal behaviors in social judgments of peers' assertiveness. *Psychological Reports, 46,* 1085–1086. PA 66:3651.

Norvell, Nancy; & Forsyth, Donelson R. (1984). The impact of inhibiting or facilitating causal factors on group members' reactions after success and failure. *Social Psychology Quarterly, 47,* 293–297. PA 72:25405.

Norvell, Nancy; & Worchel, Stephen. (1981). A reexamination of the relation between equal status contact and intergroup attraction. *Journal of Personality and Social Psychology, 41,* 902–908. PA 67:9777.

Nowakowska, Maria. (1978). A model of participation in group discussions. *Behavioral Science, 23,* 209–212. PA 64:1013. SA 79K1102.

Nurmi, Hannu. (1984). On the strategic properties of some modern methods of group decision making. *Behavioral Science, 29,* 248–257.

Nydegger, Rudy V. (1975a). Information processing complexity and leadership status. *Journal of Experimental Social Psychology, 11,* 317–328. PA 54:8821.

Nydegger, Rudy V. (1975b). Leadership in small groups: A rewards-cost analysis. *Small Group Behavior, 6,* 353–368. PA 55:4516. SA 7718827.

Nydegger, Rudy V. (1980). The effects of information processing complexity and interpersonal cue availability on strategic play in a mixed-motive game. *Journal of Personality, 48,* 38–53. PA 65:10442.

Nydegger, Rudy V.; & Owen, Guillermo. (1977). The norm of equity in a three-person majority game. *Behavioral Science, 22,* 32–37. PA 59:1043. SA 78J0173.

Nyquist, Linda V.; & Spence, Janet T. (1986). Effects of dispositional dominance and sex role expectations on leadership behaviors. *Journal of Personality and Social Psychology, 50,* 87–93. PA 73:17212.

Oberschall, Anthony. (1978). Theories of social conflict. *Annual Review of Sociology, 4,* 291–315. PA 63:979.

Obozov, Nikolay N.; & Obosova, A. N. (1981). [Three approaches to the study of psychological compatibility]. *Voprosy Psikhologii,* No. 6, 98–101. PA 68:10326.

O'Brien, Gordon E.; & Gross, W. F. (1981). Structural indices for potential participation in groups. *Australian Journal of Psychology, 33,* 135–148. PA 68:3531.

O'Brien, Gordon E.; & Harary, Frank. (1977). Measurement of the interactive effects of leadership style and group structure upon group performance. *Australian Journal of Psychology, 29,* 59–71. PA 59:9867.

O'Brien, Gordon E.; & Kabanoff, Boris. (1981). The effects of leadership style and group structure upon small group productivity: A test of a discrepancy theory of leader effectiveness. *Australian Journal of Psychology, 33,* 157–168. PA 68:3532.

Ochsman, Robert B.; & Chapanis, Alphonse. (1974). The effects of 10 communication modes on the behavior of teams during co-operative problem-solving. *International Journal of Man Machine Studies, 6,* 579–619. PA 53:5274.

O'Connell, Michael J.; Cummings, Larry L.; & Huber, George P. (1976). The effects of environmental information and decision unit structure on felt tension. *Journal of Applied Psychology, 61,* 493–500. PA 56:10815.

O'Connell, Walter E. (1975, January). Encouragement labs: A didactic-experiential approach to courage. *Individual Psychologist,* pp. 8–12. PA 54:11679.

O'Connor, Gerald G. (1980). Small groups: A general system model. *Small Group Behavior, 11,* 145–174.

Offermann, Lynn R. (1984). Short-term supervisory experience and LPC score: Effects of leader's sex and group sex composition. *Journal of Social Psychology, 123,* 115–121. SA 8507873.

Offermann, Lynn R.; & Schrier, Pamela E. (1985). Social influence strategies: The impact of sex, role and attitudes toward power. *Personality and Social Psychology Bulletin, 11,* 286–300.

Ofshe, Richard; & Lee, Margaret T. (1981). Reply to Greenstein. *Social Psychology Quarterly, 44,* 383–385. PA 68:1100.

Ofshe, Richard; & Lee, Margaret T. (1983). "What are we to make of all this?" Reply to Berger and Zelditch. *Social Psychology Quarterly, 46,* 63–65. PA 70:10250.

Ogilvie, John R.; & Haslett, Beth. (1985). Communicating peer feedback in a task group. *Human Communication Research, 12,* 79–98. PA 73:21922.

Ogunlade, James O. (1977). Some effects of asymmetry of rewards on productivity in simulated industrial groups. *Social Behavior and Personality, 5,* 73–80. PA 60:9345.

O'Hair, Henry D.; Cody, Michael J.; & McLaughlin, Margaret L. (1981). Prepared lies, spontaneous lies, Machiavellianism, and nonverbal communication. *Human Communication Research, 7,* 325–339. PA 67:5722.

Ohbuchi, Kennichi. (1982). Effects of endogenous and exogenous attributions of attack upon retaliation. *Psychologia An International Journal of Psychology in the Orient, 25,* 53–58. PA 69:1044.

Ohbuchi, Kennichi; & Izutsu, Toshinobu. (1984). Retaliation by male victims: Effects of physical attractiveness and intensity of attack of female attacker. *Personality and Social Psychology Bulletin, 10,* 216–224. PA 72:17321.

Ohbuchi, Kennichi; & Saito, Megumi. (1986). Power imbalance, its legitimacy, and aggression. *Aggressive Behavior, 12*(1), 33–40. PA 74:4018.

Okanes, Marvin; & Stinson, John E. (1974). Machiavellianism and emergent leadership in a management simulation. *Psychological Reports*, *35*, 255–259. PA 56:7874.

O'Keefe, Barbara J.; Delia, Jesse G.; & O'Keefe, Daniel J. (1980). Interaction analysis and the analysis of interactional organization. *Studies in Symbolic Interaction*, *3*, 25–57. PA 69:10416.

O'Keefe, R. D.; Kernaghan, J. A.; & Rubenstein, A. H. (1975). Group Cohesiveness: A Factor in the Adoption of Innovations among Scientific Work Groups. *Small Group Behavior*, *6*, 282–292. SA 7718734.

O'Kelley, Faith R.; & Schuldt, W. John. (1981). Self-disclosure as a function of experimenter's self-disclosure, experimenter's sex and subject's sex. *Perceptual and Motor Skills*, *52*, 557–558. PA 67:5723.

Okuda, Hidetaka. (1985). [Self-interest in reward allocation and interpersonal attraction]. *Japanese Journal of Psychology*, *56*, 153–159. PA 74:25056.

Okun, Morris A; & di Vesta, Francis J. (1975). Cooperation and competition in coacting groups. *Journal of Personality and Social Psychology*, *31*, 615–620. PA 54:11680.

Okwuanaso, Sam I. (1985). Teachers' and principals' perceptions of effective supervisory practices in Nigerian secondary schools. *Education*, *105*, 449–450. PA 73:12921.

O'Leary, Virginia E. (1974). Some attitudinal barriers to occupational aspirations in women. *Psychological Bulletin*, *81*, 809–826. PA 53:5110.

Oliva, Terence A.; & Leap, Terry L. (1981a). A taxonomy of bargaining models. *Human Relations*, *34*, 935–946.

Oliva, Terence A.; & Leap, Terry L. (1981b). A typology of metamodels in collective bargaining. *Behavioral Science*, *26*, 337–345. PA 67:9779.

Oliva, Terence A.; Peters, Michael H.; & Murthy, H. S. (1981). The preliminary empirical test of a cusp catastrophe model in the social sciences. *Behavioral Science*, *26*, 153–162. PA 67:3550.

Oliver, Pamela. (1980). Selective incentives in an apex game. *Journal of Conflict Resolution*, *24*, 113–141.

Oliver, Pamela. (1984). Rewards and punishments as selective incentives: An apex game. *Journal of Conflict Resolution*, *28*, 123–148. PA 71:20457.

Oltman, Philip K.; Goodenough, Donald R.;

Witkin, Herman B.; Freedman, Norbert; & Friedman, Florence. (1975). Psychological differentiation as a factor in conflict resolution. *Journal of Personality and Social Psychology*, *32*, 730–736. PA 56:2375.

Olvera, Dennis R.; & Hake, Don F. (1976). Producing a change from competition to sharing: Effects of large and adjusting response requirements. *Journal of the Experimental Analysis of Behavior*, *26*, 321–333. PA 58:1110.

O'Malley, Michael N.; & Davies, Daniel K. (1984). Equity and affect: The effects of relative performance and moods on resource allocation. *Basic and Applied Social Psychology*, *5*, 273–282.

O'Malley, Michael N.; & Schubarth, Glena. (1984). Fairness and appeasement: Achievement and affiliation motives in interpersonal relations. *Social Psychology Quarterly*, *47*, 364–371. PA 72:30792.

O'Neal, Edgar C.; Brunault, Mark A.; Marquis, James F.; & Carifio, Michael. (1979). Anger and the body-buffer zone. *Journal of Social Psychology*, *108*, 135–136. PA 64:7938.

O'Neal, Edgar [C.]; Caldwell, Christine; & Gallup, Gordon G. (1977). Territorial invasion and aggression in young children. *Environmental Psychology and Nonverbal Behavior*, *2*, 14–25. PA 60:11529.

O'Neal, Edgar C.; Brunault, Mark A.; Carifio, Michael S.; Troutwine, Robert; & Epstein, Jane. (1980). Effect of insult upon personal space preferences. *Journal of Nonverbal Behavior*, *5*, 56–92. PA 65:12746.

O'Neill, Patrick; & Levings, Diane E. (1979). Inducing biased scanning in a group setting to change attitudes toward bilingualism and capital punishment. *Journal of Personality and Social Psychology*, *37*, 1432–1438.

Oomkes, Frank R.; & Bakker, Adriaan I. J. (1984). *Groepstrainingen: ....* Meppel, Netherlands: Boom.

O'Quin, Karen; & Aronoff, Joel. (1981). Humor as a technique of social influence. *Social Psychology Quarterly*, *44*, 349–357. PA 68:1132. SA 83N2366.

Orbell, John M.; van de Kragt, Alphons J. C.; & Dawes, Robyn M. (1988). Explaining discussion-induced cooperation. *Journal of Personality and Social Psychology*, *54*, 811–819.

Orcutt, James D.; & Harvey, Lynn K. (1985).

Deviance, rule-breaking and male dominance in conversation. *Symbolic Interaction*, *8*, 15–32. PA 73:17213.

Orford, Jim. (1986). The rules of interpersonal complementarity: Does hostility beget hostility and dominance, submission? *Psychological Review*, *93*, 365–377. PA 73:29963.

Organ, Dennis W. (1974). Social exchange and psychological reactance in a simulated superior-subordinate relationship. *Organizational Behavior and Human Performance*, *12*, 132–142. PA 53:3001.

Orive, Ruben. (1984). Group similarity, public self-awareness, and opinion extremity: A social projection explanation of deindividuation effects. *Journal of Personality and Social Psychology*, *47*, 727–737. PA 72:12030.

Orkin, Michael. (1987). Balanced strategies for Prisoner's Dilemma. *Journal of Conflict Resolution*, *31*, 186–191. PA 74:21880.

Orne, Martin T. (1962). On the social psychology of the psychological experiment: With particular reference to demand characteristics and their implications. *American Psychologist*, *17*, 776–783.

Osato, Eiko. (1983). [The effects competition and cooperation between two participants on a third one's heart rate, problem solving, and cognitive responses in triad]. *Japanese Journal of Psychology*, *54*, 293–299. PA 71:25834.

Osborn, Richard N.; & Vicars, W. M. (1976). Sex stereotypes: An artifact in leader behavior and subordinate satisfaction analysis? *Academy of Management Journal*, *19*, 439–449.

Oskamp, Stuart; & Spacapan, Shirlynn. (Eds.). (1987). *Interpersonal processes*. Newbury Park: Sage.

Osman, Liesl M. (1982). Conformity or compliance? A study of sex differences in pedestrian behavior. *British Journal of Social Psychology*, *21*, 19–21.

Osmond, Humphrey. (1957). Function as the basis of psychiatric ward design. *Mental Hospitals*, *8*, 23–30.

Otani, Darlene; & Dixon, Paul W. (1976). Power function between duration of friendly interaction and conformity in perception and judgments. *Perceptual and Motor Skills*, *43*, 975–978. PA 58:1111.

Pace, D. J.; & MacNeil, M. K. (1974). Comparison of social norms across four judgment situations. *Perceptual and Motor Skills*, *39*, 575–582. PA 56:09841.

Packel, Edward W. (1980). Transitive permutation groups and equipotent voting rules. *Mathematical Social Sciences*, *1*, 93–100. SA 81L4932.

Paczkowska, Maria; & Zaborowski, Zbigniew. (1975). [Effect of rewarding and punishing information on interpersonal equilibrium.] *Psychologia Wychowawcza*, *18*, 99–106. PA 58:11674.

Page, R. A. (1977). Noise and helping behavior. *Environment and Behavior*, *9*, 311–334. PA 60:2075.

Pagerey, Peter D.; & Chapanis, Alphonse. (1983). Communication control and leadership in telecommunications by small groups. *Behaviour and Information Technology*, *2*, 179–196. PA 71:9487.

Paicheler, Geneviève. (1976). Norms and attitude change: I. Polarization and styles of behaviour. *European Journal of Social Psychology*, *6*, 405–427. PA 59:5614.

Paicheler, Geneviève. (1977a). [Argumentation, negotiation, and polarization]. *Bulletin de Psychologie*, *31*, 923–931. PA 64:1015.

Paicheler, Geneviève. (1977b). Norms and attitude change: II. The phenomenon of bipolarization. *European Journal of Social Psychology*, *7*, 5–14. PA 60:7440.

Paicheler, Geneviève. (1979a). On the comparability of experimental results. *European Journal of Social Psychology*, *9*, 227–228. PA 64:7939.

Paicheler, Geneviève. (1979b). Polarization of attitudes in homogeneous and heterogeneous groups. *European Journal of Social Psychology*, *9*, 85–96. PA 64:1014. SA 80K5526.

Paicheler, G[eneviève].; & Darmon, G. (1977). [Majority and minority representations and intergroup relations]. *Bulletin de Psychologie*, *31*, 170–180. PA 61:10912.

Palisi, Anthony T.; & Ruzicka, Mary F. (1974–1975). Panel analysis, comparison of theories of group development. *Interpersonal Development*, *5*, 234–244. PA 56:5978.

Pallak, Michael S.; Cook, David A.; & Sullivan, John J. (1980). Commitment and energy conservation. *Applied Social Psychology Annual*, *1*, 235–253. PA 66:4596.

Paloutzian, Raymond F. (1974). Some consequences of individuation and deindividuation: Aggression and altruism as functions of responsibility and group size. *Catalog of Selected Documents in Psychology*, *4*, 124–125. PA 53:11589.

Paloutzian, Raymond F. (1975). Effects of deindividuation, removal of responsibility, and coaction on impulsive and cyclical aggression. *Journal of Psychology*, *90*, 163–169. PA 54:9611.

Pandey, Janak. (1976). Effects of leadership style, personality characteristics and method of leader selection on members' and leaders' behavior. *European Journal of Social Psychology*, *6*, 475–489. PA 59:5646. SA 78J0286.

Pandey, Janak; & Griffitt, William. (1977). Benefactor's sex and nurturance need, recipient's dependency, and the effect of number of potential helpers on helping behavior. *Journal of Personality*, *45*, 79–99. PA 59:1083.

Paniotto, Vladimir Il'ich. (1976). Sotsiometricheskie metody izucheniya malykh sotsial'nykh grupp [Sociometric methods of studying small social groups]. *Sotsiologicheskie Issledovaniya*, *3*(3), 141–152. SA 81L4933.

Pantin, Hilda M.; & Carver, Charles S. (1982). Induced competence and the bystander effect. *Journal of Applied Social Psychology*, *12*, 100–111. PA 70:10251.

Papastamou, Stamos. (1985). Effets de la psychologisation sur l'influence d'un groupe et d'un "leader" minoritaires [The effects of psychologization on the influence exerted by minority groups and leaders]. *Annee Psychologique*, *85*, 361–381. PA 74:1095.

Papastamou, Stamos. (1986). Psychologization and processes of minority and majority influence. *European Journal of Social Psychology*, *16*, 165–180.

Pape, Thomas; & Bolle, Ilona. (1984). Einfallsproduktion von Individuen und Dyaden unter "Brainstorming"-Bedingungen. Replikation einer Studie und allgemeine Probleme eines Forschungsgebietes [Brainstorming in group (dyadic) and individual conditions: A replication of Barkowski et al.]. (1982). *Psychologische Beitrage*, *26*, 459–468. PA 73:17215.

Parcel, Toby L.; & Cook, Karen S. (1977). Status characteristics, reward allocation, and equity. *Social Psychology Quarterly*, *40*, 311–324. PA 61:8455. SA 78J4701.

Pareek, Udai; & Banerjee, Debadatta. (1974). Developmental trends in the dimensions of cooperative and competitive game behaviour in some sub-cultures. *Indian Educational Review*, *9*(1), 11–37. PA 56:7718.

Pareek, Udai; & Banerjee, Debadatta. (1976). Achievement motive and competitive behaviour. *Manas*, *23*(1), 9–15. PA 59:7856.

Parke, B. K.; & Houben, H. C. (1985). An objective analysis of group types. *International Journal of Small Group Research*, *1*, 131–149.

Parker, Kevin C. H. (1988). Speaking turns in small group interaction: A context-sensitive event sequence model. *Journal of Personality and Social Psychology*, *54*, 965–971.

Parks, Malcolm R.; Stan, Charlotte M.; & Eggert, Leona L. (1983). Romantic involvement and social network involvement. *Social Psychology Quarterly*, *46*, 116–131. PA 71:3963.

Parrillo, Vincent N.; Stimson, John; & Stimson, Ardyth. (1985). Rationalization and ritualism in committee decision making. *Small Group Behavior*, *16*, 355–371. SA 86Q4845.

Parsons, Arthur S. (1973). Constitutive phenomenology: Schutz's theory of the We-relation. *Journal of Phenomenological Psychology*, *4*, 331–361. PA 53:8564.

Pasternack, Thomas L. (1973). Qualitative differences in development of yielding behavior by elementary school children. *Psychological Reports*, *32*, 883–896. PA 56:538.

Patchen, Martin (1987). Strategies for eliciting cooperation from an adversary: Laboratory and internation findings. *Journal of Conflict Resolution*, *31*, 164–185.

Patrick, Christopher; Craig, Kenneth D; & Prkachin, Kenneth M. (1986). Observer judgments of acute pain: Facial action determinants. *Journal of Personality and Social Psychology*, *50*, 1291–1298. PA 73:23913.

Patterson, Arthur H. (1978). Territorial behavior and fear of crime in the elderly. *Environmental Psychology and Nonverbal Behavior*, *2*, 131–144. PA 62:8190.

Patterson, Arthur H.; & Boles, William E. (1974). The effects of personal space variables upon approach and attitudes toward the other in a Prisoner's Dilemma game. *Personality and Social Psychology Bulletin*, *1*, 364–366. PA 56:2313.

Patterson, David L.; & Smits, Stanley J. (1974). Communication bias in black-white groups. *Journal of Psychology*, *88*, 9–25. PA 53:5178.

Patterson, Miles L. (1975). Eye contact and distance: A re-examination of measurement problems. *Personality and Social Psychology Bulletin*, *1*, 600–603. PA 56:4008.

Patterson, Miles L. (1976). An arousal model of

interpersonal intimacy. *Psychological Review, 83*, 235–245. PA 57:10264.

Patterson, Miles L. (1977). Interpersonal distance, affect, and equilibrium theory. *Journal of Social Psychology, 101*, 205–214. PA 59:3343.

Patterson, Miles L. (1978). Arousal change and cognitive labeling: Pursuing the mediators of intimacy exchange. *Environmental Psychology and Nonverbal Behavior, 3*, 17–22. PA 63:9638.

Patterson, Miles L. (1982). A sequential functional model of nonverbal exchange. *Psychological Review, 89*, 231–249. PA 68:3533.

Patterson, Miles L. (1983). *Nonverbal behavior: A functional perspective.* New York: Springer-Verlag.

Patterson, Miles L. (Ed.). (1984). *Journal of Nonverbal Behavior, 8*(4). [Special issue on "Nonverbal intimacy and exchange"].

Patterson, Miles L.; Jordan, Andrew; Hogan, Michael B.; & Frerker, Daved. (1981). Effects of nonverbal intimacy on arousal and behavioral adjustment. *Journal of Nonverbal Behavior, 5*, 184–198. PA 67:1240.

Patterson, Miles L.; Kelly, Carl E.; Kondracki, Bruce A.; & Wulf, Linda J. (1979). Effects of seating arrangement on small-group behavior. *Social Psychology Quarterly, 42*, 180–185. PA 64:7940. SA 81L1670.

Patterson, Miles; & Mahoney, E. R. (1975). Compensatory reactions to spatial intrusion: An examination of contradictory findings. *Sociometry, 38*, 420–427. PA 54:11713.

Patterson, Miles L.; Roth, Charles P.; & Schenk, Claire. (1979). Seating arrangement, activity, and sex differences in small group crowding. *Personality and Social Psychology Bulletin, 5*, 100–103. PA 64:3301.

Patterson, Miles L.; & Schaeffer, Russell E. (1977). Effects of size and sex composition on interaction distance, participation, and satisfaction in small groups. *Small Group Behavior, 8*, 433–442. PA 64:1016. SA 79K1103.

Paulsell, S.; & Goldman, M. (1984). The effect of touching different body areas on prosocial behavior. *Journal of Social Psychology, 122*, 269–273. PA 72:6633.

Paulus, Paul B. (1980). Crowding. In P. B. Paulus (Ed.), *Psychology of group influence* (pp. 245–289). Hillsdale, NJ: Erlbaum.

Paulus, Paul B. (Ed.). (1983). *Basic group processes.* New York and Berlin: Springer-Verlag.

Paulus, Paul B. (Ed.). (1989). *Psychology of group influence.* (2nd ed.). Hillsdale, NJ: Erlbaum.

Paulus, Paul B.; Annis, Angela B.; Seta, John J.; Schkade. Janette K.; & Matthews, Robert W. (1976). Density does affect task performance. *Journal of Personality and Social Psychology, 34*, 248–253. PA 56:7876.

Paulus, Paul [B].; Cox, Verne; McCain, Garvin; & Chandler, Jane. (1975). Some effects of crowding in a prison environment. *Journal of Applied Social Psychology, 5*, 86–91.

Paulus, Paul B.; & Matthews, Robert W. (1980a). When density affects task performance. *Personality and Social Psychology Bulletin, 6*, 119–124. PA 65:10444.

Paulus, Paul B.; & Matthews, Robert W. (1980b). Crowding, attribution, and task performance. *Basic and Applied Social Psychology, 1*, 3–13.

Paulus, Paul B.; & McCain, Garvin. (1983). Crowding in jails. *Basic and Applied Social Psychology, 4*, 89–107.

Paulus, Paul B.; McCain, Garvin; & Cox, Verne. (1978). Death rates, psychiatric commitments, blood pressure, and perceived crowding as a function of institutional crowding. *Environmental Psychology and Nonverbal Behavior, 3*, 107–116.

Paulus, Paul B.; Shannon, John C.; Wilson, Dexter L.; & Boone, Thomas D. (1972). The effect of spectator presence on gymnastic performance in a field situation. *Psychonomic Science, 29*, 88–90. PA 53:4387.

Payne, Roy. (1981). Stress in task-focused groups. *Small Group Behavior, 12*, 253–268.

Payne, Roy; & Cooper, Cary L. (Eds.). (1981). *Groups at work.* Chichester, England: Wiley.

Peabody, Dean; & Goldberg, Lewis R. (1989). Some determinants of factor structures from personality-trait descriptors. *Journal of Personality and Social Psychology, 57*, 552–567.

Pearce, John A., II; & Ravlin, Elizabath C. (1987). The design and activation of self-regulating work groups. *Human Relations, 40*, 751–782.

Pearce, W. Barnett; & Sharp, Stewart M. (1973). Self-Disclosing Communication. *Journal of Communication, 23*, 409–425. SA 7717507.

Pearson, Judy C. (1981). The effects of setting and gender on self-disclosure. *Group and Organization Studies, 6*, 334–340. PA 67:1241.

Peay, Marilyn Y. (1980). Changes in attitudes and beliefs in two-person interaction situations. *European Journal of Social Psychology, 10*, 367–377. PA 66:10337. SA 82M1474.

Peay, Marilyn Y.; & Peay, Edmund R. (1983). The effects of density, group size, and crowding on behavior in an unstructured situation. *British Journal of Social Psychology, 22*, 13-18. PA 70:12648. SA 84O0836.

Pedersen, Darhl M. (1973). Self-disclosure, body-accessibility, and personal space. *Psychological Reports, 33*, 975-980. PA 52:5196.

Pedersen, Darhl M. (1977). Factors affecting personal space toward a group. *Perceptual and Motor Skills, 45*, 735-743. PA 60:11699. SA 79K2635.

Pedersen, Darhl M. (1978). Effects of group characteristics on social space. *Perceptual and Motor Skills, 47*, 1307-1321. PA 64:7941. SA 81L4934.

Pedersen, Darhl M ; Keithly, Sheila; & Brady, Karie. (1986). Effects of an observer on conformity to handwashing norm. *Perceptual and Motor Skills, 62*, 169 170. PA 74:21916.

Pedersen, Darhl M.; & Sabin, Lisa. (1982). Personal space invasion: Sex differentials for near and far proximities. *Perceptual and Motor Skills, 55*, 1060-1062. PA 70:7962.

Pedersen, Darhl M; & Shears, Loyda M. (1973). A review of personal space research in the framework of general systems theory. *Psychological Bulletin, 80*, 367-388.

Pedersen, Darhl M.; & Shears, Loyda M. (1974). Effects of an interpersonal game and of confinement on personal space. *Journal of Personality and Social Psychology, 30*, 838-845. PA 53:9488.

Pedersen, Paul B. (1985). Decision making in a multicultural group. *Journal for Specialists in Group Work, 10*(3), 164-174. PA 73:9097.

Pedigo, James M.; & Singer, Barton. (1982). Group process development: A psychoanalytic view. *Small Group Behavior, 13*, 496-517. PA 70:5635.

Peery, J. Craig. (1978). Magnification of affect using frame-by-frame film analysis. *Environmental Psychology and Nonverbal Behavior, 3*, 58-61. PA 63:9661.

Peery, J. Craig; & Crane, Paul M. (1980). Personal space regulation: Approach-withdrawal-approach proxemic behavior during adult-preschooler interaction at close range. *Journal of Psychology, 106*, 63-75.

Pellegrini, Robert J.; Hicks, Robert A.; & Meyers-Winton, Susan. (1978). Effects of simulated approval-seeking and avoiding on self-disclosure, self-presentation, and interpersonal attraction. *Journal of Psychology, 98*, 231-240. PA 61:10913.

Pellegrini, Robert J.; Hicks, Robert A.; Meyers-Winton, Susan; & Antal, Bruce G. (1978). Physical attractiveness and self-disclosure in mixed-sex dyads. *Psychological Record, 28*, 509-516. PA 62:3577.

Pendleton, Mark G.; & Batson, C. Daniel. (1979). Self-presentation and the door-in-the-face technique for inducing compliance. *Personality and Social Psychology Bulletin, 5*, 77-81. PA 64:3304.

Pennington, Donald C. (1987). Confirmatory hypothesis testing in face-to-face interaction: An empirical refutation. *British Journal of Social Psychology, 26*, 225-235.

Penrod, Stephen; & Hastie, Reid. (1980). A computer simulation of jury decision making. *Psychological Review, 87*, 133-159.

Pepitone, Albert. (1976). Toward a normative and comparative biocultural social psychology. *Journal of Personality and Social Psychology, 34*, 641-653.

Pepitone, Albert. (1981). Lessons from the history of social psychology. *American Psychologist, 36*, 972-985. PA 67:5692 [Also, PA 68:5752].

Pepitone, Emmy A. (1977). Patterns of interdependence in cooperative work of elementary children. *Contemporary Educational Psychology, 2*, 10-24. PA 58:4266.

Pepitone, Emmy A. (Ed.). (1980). *Children in cooperation and competition: Toward a developmental social psychology*. Lexington, MA: Lexington.

Peretti, Peter O. (1980). Perceived primary group criteria in the relational network of closest friendships. *Adolescence, 15*, 555-565. PA 65:3254.

Perez Yera, Armando. (1984). Confeccion de un modelo para el analisis del nivel de desarrollo de los colectivos [Making a model for the analysis of stage of development of collectives]. *Boletin de Psicologia Cuba*. PA 74:13095.

Perinbanayagam, R. S. (1985). *Signifying acts: Structure and meaning in everyday life*. Carbondale: Southern Illinois Univ. Press.

Perju-Liiceanu, Aurora. (1973). [Cognitive role differentiation in dyadic problem solving]. *Revista de Psihologie, 19*, 55-68. PA 55:734.

Perju-Liiceanu, Aurora. (1977). [Psychosocial factors of research team stability]. *Revista de Psihologie, 23*, 291-303. PA 63:7568.

Perkins, David V. (1982). Individual differences

and task structure in the performance of a behavior setting: An experimental evaluation of Barker's manning theory. *American Journal of Community Psychology, 10,* 617–634. PA 70:3399.

Perrin, Stephen; & Spencer, Christopher P. (1981). Independence or conformity in the Asch experiment as a reflection of cultural and situational factors. *British Journal of Social Psychology, 20,* 205–209. PA 68:1133.

Perrin, Steven; & Spencer, Christopher. (1980). The Asch effect—a child of its time? *Bulletin of the British Psychological Society, 33,* 405–406.

Perry, David G.; & Perry, Louise C. (1976). A note on the effects of prior anger arousal and winning or losing a competition on aggressive behaviour in boys. *Journal of Child Psychology and Psychiatry and Allied Disciplines, 17,* 145–149. PA 56:4063.

Perry, Nick. (1974). Conflict on board ship: An interpretation. *Sociological Review, 22,* 557–580. SA 75H4716.

Personnaz, Bernard. (1979). Niveau de resistance a l'influence de reponses nomiques et anomiques: Etude de phenomenes de referents clandestins et de conversion [Level of resistance to public and private responses: A study of the phenomena of clandestine referents and of conversion]. *Recherches de Psychologie Sociale, 1,* 5–27. PA 67:1262.

Personnaz, Bernard. (1981). Study in social influence using the spectrometer method: Dynamics of the phenomena of conversion and covertness in perceptual responses. *European Journal of Social Psychology, 11,* 431–438. PA 67:12074.

Pervin, Lawrence, A. (1985). Personality: Current controversies, issues, and directions. *Annual Review of Psychology, 36,* 83–114. PA 72:17394.

Peteroy, Edward T. (1980). Expectational composition and development of group cohesiveness across time periods. *Psychological Reports, 47,* 243–249. PA 66:10338. SA 83N2368.

Peters, Joseph J. (1973). Do encounter groups hurt people? *Psychotherapy: Theory, Research & Practice. 10*(1), 33–35.

Peters, Roger W.; & Torrance, E. Paul. (1973). Effects of triadic interaction on performance of five-year-old disadvantaged children. *Psychological Reports, 32,* 755–758. PA 56:1458.

Peterson, Lizette. (1984). The influence of donor competence to aid on bystander intervention.

British Journal of Social Psychology, 21, 85–86. PA 71:28615.

Peterson, Penelope L.; & Swing, Susan R. (1985). Students' cognitions as mediators of the effectiveness of small-group learning. *Journal of Educational Psychology, 77,* 299–312.

Peterson, Roger L. (1973). Small groups: Selected bibliography. *Catalog of Selected Documents in Psychology, 3,* 47. PA 52:5198.

Petri, Herbert L.; Huggins, Richard G.; Mills, Carol J.; & Barry, Linda S. (1974). Variables influencing the shape of personal space. *Personality and Social Psychology Bulletin, 1,* 360–361. PA 56:2314.

Petronio, Sandra; Martin, Judith; & Littlefield, Robert. (1984). Prerequisite conditions for self-disclosing: A gender issue. *Communication Monographs, 51,* 268–273. PA 72:25406.

Petrovskii, A. V. (1976). [On some phenomena of interpersonal relations in a collective]. *Voprosy Psikhologii,* No. 3, 16–25. PA 60:3046.

Petrovskii, A. V. (1980). [Theory of activity mediation and the problem of leadership]. *Voprosy Psikhologii,* No. 2, 29–41. PA 65:10396.

Petrovskii, A. V. (1983). The new status of psychological theory concerning groups and collectives. *Soviet Psychology, 21*(4), 57–78. PA 71:23070.

Petrovskii, A. V. (1985). Some new aspects of the development of the stratometric concept of groups and collectives. *Soviet Psychology, 23*(4), 51–67. PA 74:1063.

Petrovskii, A. V. (1986). A "contrasting position grid" as a diagnostic measure of the level of development of interpersonal relations. *Soviet Psychology, 24*(3), 43–54. PA 74:21881.

Petty, Richard E.; Brock, T. C.; & Brock, S. (1978). Hecklers: Boon or bust for speakers. *Public Relations Journal, 34,* 10–12.

Petty, Richard E.; & Cacioppo, John T. (1981). *Attitudes and persuasion: Classic and contemporary approaches.* Dubuque, IA: William C. Brown.

Petty, Richard E.; & Cacioppo, John T. (1986). The elaboration likelihood model of persuasion. *Advances in Experimental Social Psychology, 19,* 123–205.

Petty, Richard E.; Cacioppo, John T.; & Harkins, Stephen G. (1983). Group size effects on cognitive effort and attitude change. In H. H. Blumberg, A. P. Hare, V. Kent, & M. F. Davies

(Eds.), *Small groups and social interaction* (Vol. 1). Chichester: John Wiley & Sons.

Petty, Richard E.; Harkins, Stephen G.; & Williams, Kipling D. (1980). The effects of group diffusion of cognitive effort on attitudes: An information-processing view. *Journal of Personality and Social Psychology, 38,* 81–92. PA 65:5394.

Petty, Richard E.; Harkins, Stephen G.; Williams, Kipling D.; & Latané, Bibb. (1977). The effects of group size on cognitive effort and evaluation. *Personality and Social Psychology Bulletin, 3,* 579–582. PA 60:11700.

Petty, Richard E.; & Mirels, Herbert L. (1981). Intimacy and scarcity of self-disclosure: Effects on interpersonal attraction for males and females. *Personality and Social Psychology Bulletin, 7,* 493–503. PA 67:9780.

Petty, Richard E.; Williams, Kipling D.; Harkins, Stephen G.; & Latané, Bibb. (1977). Social inhibition of helping yourself: Bystander response to a cheeseburger. *Personality and Social Psychology Bulletin, 3,* 575–578. PA 60:11734.

Petzel, Thomas P.; Johnson, James E.; Johnson, Homer H.; & Kowalski, Janice. (1981). Behavior of depressed subjects in problem solving groups. *Journal of Research in Personality, 15,* 389–398. PA 67:7705.

Peuckert, Rudiger. (1975). [Sex-specific differences in conformity behavior]. *Zeitschrift fur Sozialpsychologie, 6,* 112–121. PA 54:9719.

Pfeiffer, J. William; & Jones, John E. (1974). Structured experiences for human relations training: A reference guide. La Jolla, CA: University Associates.

Pfister, Gordon. (1975). Outcomes of laboratory training for police officers. *Journal of Social Issues, 31*(1), 115–121. PA 55:7597.

Phares, E. Jerry; & Lamiell, James T. (1977). Personality. *Annual Review of Psychology, 28,* 113–140.

Philipsen, Gerry; Mulac, Anthony; & Dietrich, David. (1979). The effects of social interaction on group idea generation. *Communication Monographs, 46,* 119–125. SA 82L9794.

Phillips, Gerald M.; & Erickson, Eugene C. (1970). *Interpersonal dynamics in the small group.* New York: Random House.

Phillips, Gerald M.; & Wood, Julia T. (Eds.). (1984). *Emergent issues in human decision making.* Carbondale, IL: Southern Illinois University Press.

Phillips, James S.; & Lord, Robert G. (1981). Causal attributions and perceptions of leadership. *Organizational Behavior and Human Performance, 28,* 143–163. PA 67:1263.

Piché, André; & Sachs, Michael L. (1982). Influence of friendship on performance on a noncompetitive task. *Perceptual and Motor Skills, 54,* 1212–1214. PA 69:3398.

Piliavin, Jane A.; Dovidio, J. F.; Gaertner, S. L.; & Clark, R. D., III. (1981). *Emergency intervention.* New York: Academic Press.

Pilisuk, Marc; & Uren, Emmanuel. (1975). Deriving a language for interaction sequences. *Journal of Conflict Resolution, 19,* 484–502.

Pincus, Jeffrey; & Bixenstine, V. Edwin. (1977). Cooperation in the decomposed Prisoner's Dilemma game: A question of revealing or concealing information. *Journal of Conflict Resolution, 21,* 519–530. PA 60:3047.

Pincus, Jeffrey; & Bixenstine, V. Edwin. (1979). Cognitive factors and cooperation in the Prisoner's Dilemma game. *Psychological Record, 29,* 463–471. PA 65:1246.

Pines, Ayala. (1976). The shift to competition in the Prisoner's Dilemma game. *Social Behavior and Personality, 4,* 177–186. PA 58:7460.

Pines, Malcolm. (1983). *The evolution of group analysis.* London: Routledge & Kegan Paul.

Pines, Malcolm; & Rafaelson, Lise. (Eds.). (1982). *The individual and the group: Boundaries and interrelationships* (2 Vols.). New York: Plenum.

Piper, William E.; Debbane, Elie G.; Garant, Jacques; & Bienvenu, Jean Pierre. (1979). Pretraining for group psychotherapy: A cognitive-experiential approach. *Archives of General Psychiatry, 36,* 1250–1256. PA 65:1745.

Piper, William E.; Jones, Barry D.; Lacroix, Renée; Marrache, Myriam; & Richardsen, Astria M. (1984). Pregroup interactions and bonding in small groups. *Small Group Behavior, 15,* 51–62. PA 71:28617.

Piper, William E.; Marrache, Myriam; Lacroix, Renée; Richardsen, Astria M.; & Jones, Barry D. (1983). Cohesion as a basic bond in groups. *Human Relations, 36,* 93–108. PA 70:1060. SA 84N7292.

Planalp, Sally; & Honeycutt, James M. (1985). Events that increase uncertainty in personal relationships. *Human Communication Research, 11,* 593–604. PA 73:14438.

Platt, John. (1973). Social traps. *American Psychologist, 28,* 641–651.

Plax, Timothy G.; & Rosenfeld, Lawrence B. (1976). Dogmatism and decisions involving risk. *Southern Speech Communication Journal*, *41*, 266–277. SA 81L3334.

Pleck, Joseph H. (1976). Male threat from female competence. *Journal of Consulting and Clinical Psychology*, *44*, 608–613. PA 56:7918.

Pliner, Patricia; Hart, Heather; Kohl, Joanne; & Saari, Dory. (1974). Compliance without pressure: Some further data on the foot-in-the-door technique. *Journal of Experimental Social Psychology*, *10*, 17–22.

Plous, S. (1987). Perceptual illusions and military realities: Results from a computer-simulated arms race. *Journal of Conflict Resolution*, *31*, 5–33. PA 74:21882.

Pluckham, Margaret L. (1973). An investigation of sociometric choices in various behavioral settings. *Handbook of International Sociometry*, *7*, 43–51. PA 53:5180.

Plutchik, Robert; & Landau, H. (1973). Perceived dominance and emotional states in small groups. *Psychotherapy Theory, Research and Practice*, *10*, 341–342. PA 52:10037.

Podmore, David; Chaney, David; & Golder, Paul. (1975). Third parties in the interview situation: Evidence from Hong Kong. *Journal of Social Psychology*, *95*, 227–231. PA 54:2920.

Podsakoff, Philip; & Schriesheim, Chester A. (1985). Field studies of French and Raven's bases of power: Critique, reanalysis, and suggestions for future research. *Psychological Bulletin*, *97*, 387–411. PA 72:22587

Polit, Denise; & LaFrance, Marianne. (1977). Sex differences in reaction to spatial invasion. *Journal of Social Psychology*, *102*, 59–60. PA 59:7881.

Polivy, Janet; Herman, C. Peter; Hackett, Rick; & Kuleshnyk, Irka. (1986). The effects of self-attention and public attention on eating in restrained and unrestrained subjects. *Journal of Personality and Social Psychology*, *50*, 1253–1260.

Pollack, Lance M.; & Patterson, Arthur H. (1980). Territoriality and fear of crime in elderly and nonelderly homeowners. *Journal of Social Psychology*, *111*, 119–129. PA 66:1287.

Polley, Richard B. (1983). Dimensions of political reality. *Journal of Applied Social Psychology*, *13*, 66–77. PA 70:10272.

Polley, Richard Brian. (1987). The dimensions of social interaction: A method for improving rating scales. *Social Psychology Quarterly*, *50*, 72–82.

Polley, Richard B[rian]; Hare, A. Paul; & Stone, Philip J. (Eds.). (1988). *The SYMLOG practitioner: Applications of small group research*. New York: Praeger.

Pollio, Howard R.; & Bainum, Charlene K. (1983). Are funny groups good at solving problems? A methodological evaluation and some preliminary results. *Small Group Behavior*, *14*, 379–404. PA 71:23071.

Polozova, T. A. (1980). Methodological problems in the study of interpersonal conflicts within groups. *Voprosy Psikhologii*, No. 4, 123–129. PA 66:1235.

Polozova, T. A. (1981). [Methodological principles of the study of intragroup conflict]. *Novye Issledovaniya v Psikhologii*, *25*, 94–98. PA 71:9488.

Pood, Elliott A. (1980). Functions of communication: An experimental study in group conflict situations. *Small Group Behavior*, *11*, 76–87. SA 80L0092.

Pool, Jonathan. (1976). Coalition formation in small groups with incomplete communication networks. *Journal of Personality and Social Psychology*, *34*, 82–91. PA 56:6007.

Poole, M. Scott; & Folger, Joseph P. (1981). Modes of observation and the validation of interaction analysis schemes. *Small Group Behavior*, *12*, 477–493.

Poole, Marshall S. (1981). Decision development in small groups: I. A comparison of two models. *Communication Monographs*, *48*, 1–24. PA 67:3551.

Poole, Marshall S. (1983a). Decision development in small groups: II. A study of multiple sequences in decision making. *Communication Monographs*, *50*, 206–232. PA 71:12164.

Poole, Marshall S. (1983b). Decision development in small groups: III. A multiple sequence model of group decision development. *Communication Monographs*, *50*, 321–341. PA 71:28618.

Poole, Marshall S.; McPhee, Robert D.; & Seibold, David R. (1982). A comparison of normative and interactional explanations of group decision-making: Social decision schemes versus valence distributions. *Communication Monographs*, *49*, 1–19. PA 68:12620.

Poole, Marshall S.; Seibold, David R.; & McPhee, Robert D. (1985). Group decision-making as a structurational process. *Quarterly Journal of Speech*, *71*, 74–102. PA 72:28035.

Poppe, Matthijs; & Utens, Lisbeth. (1986). Effects of greed and fear of being gypped in a social dilemma situation with changing pool size. *Journal of Economic Psychology*, 7, 61–73. PA 74:10201.

Porter, Natalie; Geis, Florence L.; Cooper, Ellen; & Newman, Eileen. (1985). Androgyny and leadership in mixed-sex groups. *Journal of Personality and Social Psychology*, 49, 808–823. PA 73:3639.

Posner-Weber, Cheryl. (1987). Update on groupthink. *Small Group Behavior*, 18, 118–125. PA 75:16802.

Poteet, Don; & Weinberg, Robert S. (1980). Competition trait anxiety, state anxiety, and performance. *Perceptual and Motor Skills*, 50, 651–654. PA 66:1236.

Potter, Jonathan; & Wetherell, Margaret. (1987). *Discourse and social psychology: Beyond attitudes and behaviour.* Beverly Hills & London: Sage.

Powell, Gary N.; & Butterfield, D. Anthony. (1980). The female leader: Attributional effects of group performance. *Psychological Reports*, 47, 891–897. PA 66:12820.

Powell, Gary N.; & Butterfield, D. Anthony. (1982). Sex, attributions, and leadership: A brief review. *Psychological Reports*, 51, 1171–1174. PA 70:7986. SA 83N4123.

Powell, Gary N.; & Butterfield, D. Anthony. (1984). The female leader and the "high-high" effective leader stereotype. *Journal of Psychology*, 117, 71–76. SA 8402728.

Powell, J. P. (1974). Small group teaching methods in higher education. *Educational Research*, 16(3), 163–171. PA 53:10459.

Powell, Patricia H; & Dabbs, James M. (1976). Physical attractiveness and personal space. *Journal of Social Psychology*, 100, 59–64. PA 57:10266.

Powers, Edward A.; & Bultena, Gordon L. (1976). Sex differences in intimate friendships of old age. *Journal of Marriage and the Family*, 38, 739–747. PA 57:12567.

Powers, Richard B.; & Boyle, William. (1983). Generalization from a commons-dilemma game: The effects of a fine option, information, and communication on cooperation and defection. *Simulation and Games*, 14, 253–274. PA 71:17739.

Powers, William G. (1977). The rhetorical interrogative: Anxiety or control? *Human Communication Research*, 4, 44–47. PA 60:9280.

Powers, William G.; & Guess, Delana. (1976). Research note on invasion of males' personal space by feminists and non-feminists. *Psychological Reports*, 38, 1300. PA 56:7921.

Poyatos, Fernando. (1985). The deeper levels of face-to-face interaction. *Language and Communication*, 5, 111–131. PA 73:24488.

Prabhu, John C.; & Singh, P. (1975). Small group research and risky shift: A review of research findings. *Management and Labour Studies*, 1(1), 61–72. PA 61:1001.

Pratt, Linda K.; Uhl, Norman P.; & Little, Elizabeth R. (1980). Evaluation of games as a function of personality type. *Simulation and Games*, 11, 336–346. PA 66:5764.

Prein, Hugo. (1984). A contingency approach for conflict intervention. *Group and Organization Studies*, 9, 81–102. PA 71:20458.

Prentice-Dunn, Steven; & Rogers, Ronald W. (1980). Effects of deindividuating situational cues and aggressive models on subjective deindividuation and aggression. *Journal of Personality and Social Psychology*, 39, 104–113. PA 66:3618.

Prentice-Dunn, Steven; & Rogers, Ronald W. (1982). Effects of public and private self-awareness on deindividuation and aggression. *Journal of Personality and Social Psychology*, 43, 503–513. PA 69:7888.

Prentice-Dunn, Steven; & Spivey, Cashton B. (1986). Extreme deindividuation in the laboratory: Its magnitude and subjective components. *Personality and Social Psychology Bulletin*, 12, 206–215. PA 74:18740.

Prerost, Frank J. (1981). Positive mood-inhibiting potential of human crowding. *Psychological Reports*, 48, 43–48. PA 67:3552.

Prerost, Frank J. (1982). The development of the mood-inhibiting effects of crowding during adolescence. *Journal of Psychology*, 110, 197–202.

Press, S. J.; Ali, M. W.; & Yang, Chung-Fang Elizabath. (1979). An empirical study for a new method for forming group judgments: Qualitative controlled feedback. *Technological Forecasting and Social Change*. 15(3), 171–189. SA 82M1475.

Preston, Joan M. (1984). Referential communication: Some factors influencing communication efficiency. *Canadian Journal of Behavioural Science*, 16, 196–207. PA 72:12008.

Price, Gay H.; & Dabbs, James M. (1974). Sex, setting, and personal space: changes as children grow older. *Personality and Social Psychology Bulletin, 1*, 362–363. PA 56:2168.

Price, Kenneth H. (1987). Decision responsibility, task responsibility, identifiability, and social loafing. *Organizational Behavior and Human Decision Processes, 40*, 330–345.

Price, Kenneth H.; & Garland, Howard. (1978). Leader interventions to ameliorate the negative consequences of collective group failure. *Journal of Management, 4*, 7–15. PA 64:1017. SA 80L0093.

Price, Kenneth H.; & Garland, Howard. (1981a). Compliance with a leader's suggestions as a function of perceived leader/member competence and potential reciprocity. *Journal of Applied Psychology, 66*, 329–336. PA 66:8023.

Price, Kenneth H.; & Garland, Howard. (1981b). Influence mode and competence: Compliance with leader suggestions. *Personality and Social Psychology Bulletin, 7*, 117–122. PA 67:3553.

Price, Richard. (1986). Cooperation dilemmas. In A. Furnham (Ed.), *Social behavior in context* (pp. 195–207). Boston: Allyn and Bacon.

Pridham, Karen F. (1975). Acts of turning as stress-resolving mechanisms in work groups: With special reference to the work of W. R. Bion. *Human Relations, 28*, 229–248. PA 54:11681.

Prokop, Charles K. (1983). Responses to interpersonal confrontation: Interactions with human movement and color perception. *Journal of Personality and Social Psychology, 44*, 1297–1303.

Propst, Lois R. (1979). Effects of personality and loss of anonymity on aggression: A reevaluation of deindividuation. *Journal of Personality, 47*, 531–545. PA 64:12467.

Proshansky, Harold M.; Ittelson, William H.; & Rivlin, Leanne G. (Eds.). (1976). *Environmental psychology: People and their physical settings* (2nd ed.). New York: Holt, Rinehart, and Winston.

Pruitt, Dean G. (1981). *Negotiation behavior.* New York: Academic Press.

Pruitt, Dean G. (1983a). Experimental gaming and the goal/expectation hypothesis. In H. H. Blumberg, A. P. Hare, V. Kent, & M. F. Davies (Eds.), *Small groups and social interaction* (Vol. 2, pp. 107–121). Chichester: John Wiley.

Pruitt, Dean G. (1983b). Strategic choice in negotiation. *American Behavioral Scientist, 27*, 167–194. PA 71:23072.

Pruitt, Dean G.; Carnevale, Peter J. D.; Forcey,

Blythe; & Van Slyck, Michael. (1986). Gender effects in negotiation: Constituent surveillance and contentious behavior. *Journal of Experimental Social Psychology, 22*, 264–275.

Pruitt, Dean G.; & Cosentino, Charles. (1975). The role of values in the choice shift. *Journal of Experimental Social Psychology, 11*, 301–316.

Pruitt, Dean G.; & Gleason, James M. (1978). Threat capacity and the choice between independence and interdependence. *Personality and Social Psychology Bulletin, 4*, 252–255. PA 64:5569.

Pruitt, Dean G.; & Kimmel, Melvin J. (1977). Twenty years of experimental gaming: critique, synthesis, and suggestions for the future. *Annual Review of Psychology, 28*, 363–392.

Pruitt, Dean G.; & Lewis, Steven A. (1975). Development of integrative solutions in bilateral negotiation. *Journal of Personality and Social Psychology, 31*, 621–633. PA 55:735.

Pruitt, Dean G.; & Syna, Helena. (1985). Mismatching the opponent's offers in negotiation. *Journal of Experimental Social Psychology, 21*, 103–113. PA 73:6345.

Pryor, John B.; & Merluzzi, Thomas V. (1985). The role of expertise in processing social interaction scripts. *Journal of Experimental Social Psychology, 21*, 362–379. PA 73:19805.

Pugh, M. D.; & Wahrman, Ralph. (1983). Neutralizing sexism in mixed-sex groups: Do women have to be better than men? *American Journal of Sociology, 88*, 746–762. PA 70:10252. SA 83N0762.

Pulkowski-Rebellius, Hanne B. (1973). [Conflict and sociometric status: Game theory investigation of 6th-8th grade pupils from 30 elementary schools]. *Archiv fur Psychologie, 125*, 113–138. PA 54:2986.

Purvis, James A.; Dabbs, James M.; & Hopper, Charles H. (1984). The "opener": Skilled user of facial expression and speech pattern. *Personality and Social Psychology Bulletin, 10*, 61–66. PA 71:31321.

Putnam, Linda L. (1983). Small group work climates: A lag-sequential analysis of group interaction. *Small Group Behavior, 14*, 465–494. PA 71:23073.

Putnam, Linda L.; & Jones, Tricia S. (1982). The role of communication in bargaining. *Human Communication Research, 8*, 262–280. PA 68:10330.

Pyke, S. W.; & Neely, C. A. (1975). Training and

evaluation of communication skills. *Canadian Counsellor*, 9(1), 20–30. PA 54:7476.

Quereshi, M. Y.; & Strauss, Lloyd A. (1980). Immunization of a controverted belief through group discussion. *Social Behavior and Personality*, 8, 229–232. PA 66:10339.

Quigley-Fernandez, Barbara; Malkis, Farrell S.; & Tedeschi, James T. (1985). Effects of first impressions and reliability of promises on trust and cooperation. *British Journal of Social Psychology*, 24, 29–36. PA 73:3713.

Quinn, Robert E. (1977). Coping with Cupid: The formation, impact, and management of romantic relationships in organizations. *Administrative Science Quarterly*, 22, 30–45. PA 58:8519.

Quirk, Thomas J.; & DiMarco, Nicholas. (1979). Relationship between operation inventory scores and overt small-group problem-solving behavior. *Group and Organization Studies*, 4, 103–115. SA 80K4185.

Rabbie, J[acob] M. (1974). [Effects of a competitive and cooperative intergroup orientation on within- and between-group behavior]. *Nederlands Tijdschrift voor de Psychologie en haar Grensgebieden*, 29, 239–257. PA 53:2985.

Rabbie, Jacob M.; Benoist, Frits; Oosterbaan, Henk; & Visser, Lieuwe. (1974). Differential power and effects of expected competitive and cooperative intergroup interaction on intragroup and outgroup attitudes. *Journal of Personality and Social Psychology*, 30, 46–56.

Rabbie, J[acob] M.; Visser, L.; & Tils, J. (1976). [The representative and his constituency: An explorative study]. *Nederlands Tijdschrift voor de Psychologie en haar Grensgebieden*, 31, 253–268. PA 58:7464.

Racine, Luc. (1978). Acces differentiel au materiel de jeu chez des enfants d'age scolaire [Differential access to game materials among school-age children]. *Sociologie et Societes*, 10(1), 65–86. SA 79K1104.

Radecki, Catherine; & Jennings, Joyce. (1980). Sex as a status variable in work settings: Female and male reports of dominance behavior. *Journal of Applied Social Psychology*, 10, 71–85. PA 66:6809.

Raden, David. (1980). Authoritarianism and overt aggression. *Psychological Reports*, 47, 452–454. PA 66:5765.

Radford, Linda M.; & Larwood, Laurie. (1982). A field study of conflict in psychological exchange: The California taxpayers' revolt.

Journal of Applied Social Psychology, 12, 60–69. PA 68:10331.

Radocy, Rudolf E. (1975). A naive minority of one and deliberate majority mismatches of tonal stimuli. *Journal of Research in Music Education*, 23(2), 120–133. PA 55:147.

Rae, Donald S.; Vathally, Stephen T.; Manderscheid, Ronald W.; & Silbergeld, Sam. (1976). Hill Interaction Matrix (HIM) scoring and analysis programs. *Behavior Research Methods and Instrumentation*, 8, 520–521. PA 58:2480.

Raffagnino, Rosalba. (1982). La comunicazione non verbale tra equilibrio e reciprocit [Nonverbal communication between equilibriuym and reciprocity]. *Bolletino di Psicologia Applicata*, No. 161–164, 23–31. PA 71:9489.

Raiffa, Howard. (1983). Mediation of conflicts. *American Behavioral Scientist*, 27, 195–210. PA 71:23075.

Rajecki, D. W.; Ickes, William; Corcoran, Christine; & Lenerz, Kathy. (1977). Social facilitation of human performance: Mere presence effects. *Journal of Social Psychology*, 102, 297–310. PA 60:3015.

Rajecki, D. W.; Ickes, William; & Tanford, Sarah. (1981). Locus of control and reactions to strangers. *Personality and Social Psychology Bulletin*, 7, 282–289.

Rajecki, D. W.; Kidd, Robert F.; & Ivins, Barbara. (1976). Social facilitation in chickens: A different level of analysis. *Journal of Experimental Social Psychology*, 12, 233–246.

Rall, Marilyn; Greenspan, Abbie; & Neidich, Ellen. (1984). Reactions to eye contact initiated by physically attractive and unattractive men and women. *Social Behavior and Personality*, 12, 103–109. PA 72:25407.

Ramirez, Albert. (1977). Social influence and ethnicity of the communicator. *Journal of Social Psychology*, 102, 209–213. PA 60:3049.

Rand, Thomas M.; & Wexley, Kenneth N. (1975). Demonstration of the effect, "similar to me," in simulated employment interviews. *Psychological Reports*, 36, 535–544. PA 55:13662.

Rands, Marylyn; & Levinger, George. (1979). Implicit theories of relationship: An intergenerational study. *Journal of Personality and Social Psychology*, 37, 645–661. PA 64:8008.

Rapoport, Amnon. (1984). Variability in payoff disbursement in coalition formation experiments. *European Journal of Social Psychology*, *14*, 265–280. PA 72:20072.

Rapoport, Amnon; & Kahan, James P. (1974). Computer controlled research on bargaining and coalition formation. *Behavior Research Methods and Instrumentation*, *6*, 87–93. PA 52:10039.

Rapoport, Amnon; & Kahan, James P. (1976). When three is not always two against one: Coalitions in experimental three-person cooperative games. *Journal of Experimental Social Psychology*, *12*, 253–273. PA 56:6008.

Rapoport, Amnon; & Kahan, James P. (1981). The power of a coalition and payoff disbursement in three-person negotiable conflicts. *Journal of Mathematical Sociology*, *8*, 193–224. SA 83N0763.

Rapoport, Amos. (1975). Toward a redefinition of density. *Environment and Behavior*, *7*, 133–158.

Rapoport, Anatol. (1985). Editorial comment on articles by Diekmann and Molander. *Journal of Conflict Resolution*, *29*, 619–622. PA 73:14440.

Rapoport, Anatol; Frenkel, Oded; & Perner, Josef. (1977). Experiments with cooperative 2 * 2 games. *Theory & Decision*, *8*, 67–92. PA 60:03050.

Rapoport, Rhona; Rapoport, Robert; & Thiessen, Victor. (1974). Couple symmetry and enjoyment. *Journal of Marriage and the Family*, *36*, 588–591. PA 54:11682.

Ratajczak, Zofia; & Jagoda, Irmina. (1984). Ufnosc a efektywnosc i sposob komunikowania sie w grupie zadaniowej [Trust and effectiveness and means of communication in a task group]. *Przeglad Psychologiczny*, *27*, 601–615. PA 73:21925.

Ratner, R. S.; & Hathaway, Craig T. (1984). Mutuality between men and women in self-analytic groups. *Small Group Behavior*, *15*, 471–495. SA 85O6029.

Rauch, Herbert. (1983). Partizipation und Leistung in Grossgruppen-Sitzungen; Qualitative und Quantitative Vergleichsanalyse von 20 Fallstudien zum Sitzungsprozess entscheidungsfindender Grossgruppen [Participation and achievement in meetings of large groups: a qualitative and quantitative comparative analysis of twenty case studies on the meeting process of large decision-making groups]. *Kolner Zeitschrift fur Soziologie und Sozialpsychologie*, Supplement 25, 256–274. SA 84O2593.

Raush, Harold L. (1976). Intra- or interaction: Discussion. *Small Group Behavior*, *7*, 65–72. SA 77I8735.

Rawlins, William K. (1983a). Negotiating close friendship: The dialectic of conjunctive freedoms. *Human Communication Research*, *9*, 255–266. PA 70:10253.

Rawlins, William K. (1983b). Openness as problematic in ongoing friendships: Two conversational dilemmas. *Communication Monographs*, *50*, 1–13. PA 70:10254. SA 85O2594.

Rayko, Donald S. (1977). Does knowledge matter? Psychological information and bystander helping. *Canadian Journal of Behavioural Science*, *9*, 295–304. PA 61:3547.

Reason, Peter. (1980). Human interaction as exchange and encounter: A dialectical exploration. *Small Group Behavior*, *11*, 3–12. SA 80L0094.

Reddy, Diane M.; Baum, Andrew; Fleming, Raymond; & Aiello, John R. (1981). Mediation of social density by coalition formation. *Journal of Applied Social Psychology*, *11*, 529–537. PA 68:5764.

Reddy, W. Brendan. (1973). The impact of sensitivity training on self-actualization: A one-year follow-up. *Small Group Behavior*, *4*, 407–413. PA 52:5201.

Reddy, W. Brendan. (1975). Diagnosing team problem-solving effectiveness: A comparison of four populations. *Small Group Behavior*, *6*, 174–186. PA 55:2329.

Reed, Beth G. (1983). Women leaders in small groups: Social-psychological perspectives and strategies. *Social Work with Groups*, *6*(3–4), 35–42. PA 71:20460.

Reed, Beth G.; & Garvin, Charles D. (Eds.). (1983). *Groupwork with women/groupwork with men: An overview of gender issues in social groupwork practice*. New York: Haworth Press.

Rees, C. Roger; & Segal, Mady W. (1984). Role differentiation in groups: The relationship between instrumental and expressive leadership. *Small Group Behavior*, *15*, 109–123. PA 71:28620. SA 85O6030.

Reggio, F. (1980–1981). De quelques processus en oeuvre dans la dynamique des groupes [On several processes at work in the dynamics of groups]. *Bulletin de Psychologie*, *34*, 343–348. PA 70:3400.

Reichner, Richard F. (1979). Differential responses to being ignored: The effects of architectural design and social density on interpersonal behavior. *Journal of Applied Social Psychology, 9,* 13–26. PA 64:5570.

Reid, Edward; & Novak, Patricia. (1975). Personal space: An unobtrusive measures study. *Bulletin of the Psychonomic Society, 5,* 265–6. PA 54:2956.

Reingen, Peter H. (1976). Do subjects understand the choice dilemma questionnaire? *Journal of Social Psychology, 99,* 303–304.

Reingen, Peter H. (1977). Effects of skewness of initial choices on the risky shift: An experimental test with the use of consumer stimuli. *Psychological Reports, 40,* 95–101. PA 58:9458.

Reingen, Peter H.; & Kernan, Jerome B. (1977). Risky shift or confused subjects? *Journal of Social Psychology, 101,* 311–312. PA 59:3390.

Reis, Harry T.; & Gruzen, Joan. (1976). On mediating equity, equality, and self interest: The role of self-presentation in social exchange. *Journal of Experimental Social Psychology, 12,* 487–503. PA 56:9842.

Reis, Harry T.; & Jackson, Linda A. (1981). Sex differences in reward allocation: Subjects, partners, and tasks. *Journal of Personality and Social Psychology, 40,* 465–478. PA 66:12776.

Reis, Harry T.; Nezlek, John; & Wheeler, Ladd. (1980). Physical attractiveness in social interaction. *Journal of Personality and Social Psychology, 38,* 604–617. PA 65:10397.

Reis, Harry T.; Senchak, Marilyn; & Solomon, Beth. (1985). Sex differences in the intimacy of social interaction: Further examination of potential explanations. *Journal of Personality and Social Psychology, 48,* 1204–1217. PA 72:22590.

Reis, Harry T.; Wheeler, Ladd; Spiegel, Nancy; Kernis, Michael; Nezlek, John; & Perri, Michael. (1982). Physical attractiveness in social interaction: II. Why does appearance affect social experience? *Journal of Personality and Social Psychology, 43,* 979–996. PA 70:1061.

Reiser, Robert A.; & Gerlach, Vernon S. (1977). Research on simulation games in education: A critical analysis. *Educational Technology, 17*(12), 13–18. PA 60:12577.

Reisman, John M. (1984). Friendliness and its correlates. *Journal of Social and Clinical Psychology, 2,* 143–155. PA 72:22591.

Reizenstein, Janet E; & Ostrander, Edward R. (1981). Design for independence: Housing for the severely disabled. *Environment and Behavior, 13,* 633–639. PA 67:1825.

Remland, Martin S. (1984). Leadership Impressions and Nonverbal Communication in a Superior-Subordinate Interaction. *Communication Quarterly, 32*(1), 41–48. SA 85O9454.

Rempel, John K.; Holmes, John G.; & Zanna, Mark P. (1985). Trust in close relationships. *Journal of Personality and Social Psychology, 49,* 95–112. PA 72:30794.

Remus, William; & Jenner, Steve. (1979). Playing business games: Attitudinal differences between students playing singly and as teams. *Simulation and Games, 10,* 75–85. SA 80K4186.

Renzulli, Joseph S.; Owen, Steven V.; & Callahan, Carolyn M. (1974). Fluency, flexibility, and originality as a function of group size. *Journal of Creative Behavior, 8,* 107–113. PA 58:5336.

Rettig, Solomon. (1975). Conjunctive, affiliation and ethical risk taking. *Journal of Social and Economic Studies, 3*(2), 213–223. PA 59:3346.

Reychler, Luc. (1979). The effectiveness of a pacifist strategy in conflict resolution: An experimental study. *Journal of Conflict Resolution, 23,* 228–260.

Reynolds, Paul D. (1984). Leaders never quit: Talking, silence, and influence in interpersonal groups. *Small Group Behavior, 15,* 404–413. PA 72:9501. SA 85O6171.

Rice, Peter. (1979). The finite negotiation problem: A solution theory. *Journal of Conflict Resolution, 23,* 561–576.

Rice, Robert W. (1978). Construct validity of the Least Preferred Co-worker score. *Psychological Bulletin, 85,* 1199–1237. PA 62:5129.

Rice, Robert W. (1981). Leader LPC and follower satisfaction: A review. *Organizational Behavior and Human Performance, 28,* 1–25. PA 66:10340.

Rice, Robert W.; Bender, Lisa Richer; & Vitters, Alan G. (1980). Leader sex, follower attitudes toward women, and leadership effectiveness: A laboratory experiment. *Organizational Behavior and Human Performance, 25,* 46–78. PA 65:7910.

Rice, Robert W.; Bender, Lisa R[icher]; & Vitters, Alan G. (1982). Testing the validity of the contingency model for female and male leaders. *Basic and Applied Social Psychology, 3,* 231–247. PA 70:5636.

Rice, Robert W.; Instone, D.; & Adams, J. (1984). Leader sex, leader success, and leadership process: Two field studies. *Journal of Applied Psychology, 69*, 12–31. PA 71:13684.

Rice, Robert W.; & Kastenbaum, Denise R. (1983). The contingency model of leadership: Some current issues. *Basic and Applied Social Psychology, 4*, 373–392.

Rice, Robert W.; Marwick, Nancy J.; Chemers, Martin M.; & Bentley, Joseph C. (1982). Task performance and satisfaction: Least Preferred Coworker (LPC) as a moderator. *Personality and Social Psychology Bulletin, 8*, 534–541. PA 69:12667.

Rice, Robert W.; Seaman, F. James; & Garvin, Deborah J. (1978). An empirical examination of the esteem for Least Preferred Co-worker (LPC) construct. *Journal of Psychology, 98*, 195–205. PA 61:10134.

Rice, Robert W.; Yoder, Jan D.; Adams, Jerome; Priest, Robert F.; Prince, Howard T., II. (1984). Leadership ratings for male and female military cadets. *Sex Roles, 10*, 885–901. SA 85O6172.

Richardson, Deborah C.; Bernstein, Sandy; & Taylor, Stuart P. (1979). The effect of situational contingencies on female retaliative behavior. *Journal of Personality and Social Psychology, 37*, 2044–2048. PA 65:5427.

Richardson, Deborah; Leonard, Kenneth; Taylor, Stuart; & Hammock, Georgina. (1985). Male violence toward females: Victim and aggressor variables. *Journal of Psychology, 119*, 129–135. PA 73:24489.

Richardson, Stephen A.; Ronald, Linda; & Kleck, Robert E. (1974). The social status of handicapped and nonhandicapped boys in a camp setting. *Journal of Special Education, 8*(2), 143–152. PA 53:01563.

Richmond, Bert O.; & Vance, John J. (1974). Cooperative-competitive game strategy and personality characteristics of Black and White children. *Interpersonal Development, 5*, 78–85. PA 55:2216.

Richmond, Virginia P. (1978). The relationship between trait and state communication apprehension and interpersonal perceptions during the acquaintance stages. *Human Communication Research, 4*, 338–349. PA 63:7597.

Ridgeway, Cecilia L. (1978). Conformity, group-oriented motivation, and status attainment in small groups. *Social Psychology, 41*, 175–188. PA 63:3258. SA 79K1105.

Ridgeway, Cecilia L. (1981). Nonconformity, competence, and influence in groups: A test of

two theories. *American Sociological Review, 46*, 333–347. SA 81L8140.

Ridgeway, Cecilia L. (1982). Status in groups: The importance of motivation. *American Sociological Review, 47*, 76–88. SA 82M3122.

Ridgeway, Cecilia L. (1983). *Dynamics of small groups.* New York: St. Martin's Press.

Ridgeway, Cecilia L. (1984). Dominance, performance, and status in groups: A theoretical analysis. *Advances in Group Processes, 1*, 59–93.

Ridgeway, Cecilia L.; Berger, Joseph; & Smith, LeRoy. (1985). Nonverbal cues and status: An expectation states approach. *American Journal of Sociology, 90*, 955–978.

Ridgeway, Cecilia L.; & Jacobson, Cardell K. (1977). Sources of status and influence in all female and mixed sex groups. *Sociological Quarterly, 18*, 413–425. PA 60:9282. SA 78J3225.

Ridley, Dennis R.; Young, Paul D.; & Johnson, David E. (1981). Salience as a dimension of individual and group risk taking. *Journal of Psychology, 109*, 283–291. PA 68:1101. SA 83N 2369.

Riedesel, Paul L. (1974). Bales reconsidered: A critical analysis of popularity and leadership differentiation. *Sociometry, 37*, 557–564. PA 53:9489. SA 76H9518.

Riedesel, Paul L.; & Seem, John. (1976). Establishing the convergent validity of role and leadership differentiation through causal modeling. *Free Inquiry, 4*, 10–25. SA 78J5976.

Riggio, Ronald E.; & Friedman, Howard S. (1983). Individual differences and cues to deception. *Journal of Personality and Social Psychology, 45*, 899–915. PA 71:12165.

Riggio, Ronald E.; & Friedman, Howard S. (1986). Impression formation: The role of expressive behavior. *Journal of Personality and Social Psychology, 50*, 421–417. PA 73:14515.

Riggio, Ronald E.; Friedman, Howard S.; & DiMatteo, M. Robin. (1981). Nonverbal greetings: Effects of the situation and personality. *Personality and Social Psychology Bulletin, 7*, 682–689. PA 68:3534.

Riggio, Ronald E.; Tucker, Joan; & Throckmorton, Barbara. (1987). Social skills and deception ability. *Personality and Social Psychology Bulletin, 13*, 568–577.

Riggs, Janet M.; & Cantor, Nancy. (1984). Getting acquainted: The role of the self-concept and preconceptions. *Personality and Social Psychology Bulletin, 10*, 432–445. PA 72:22612.

Rijsman, J.; & Poppe, M. (1977). Power difference between players and level of matrix as determinants of competition in a MDG. *European Journal of Social Psychology, 7*, 347–367. PA 60:7422. SA 79J6854.

Rim, Y. (1977). Personality variables and interruptions in small discussions. *European Journal of Social Psychology, 7*, 247–251. SA 78J4702.

Rimé, Bernard. (1974). [Spatial and relational structures]. *Revue de Psychologie et des Sciences de l'Education, 9*, 263–278. PA 54:11717.

Rimé, Bernard. (1977). [The determinants of visual behavior in social interaction]. *Annee Psychologique, 77*, 497–523. PA 62:10982.

Rimé, Bernard. (1982). The elimination of visible behaviour from social interactions: Effects on verbal, nonverbal and interpersonal variables. *European Journal of Social Psychology, 12*, 113–129. PA 69:1026.

Rimé, Bernard; & Leyens, Jacques Philippe. (1974). [Effect of ecological factors and nonverbal signals on affective structures in small groups]. *Annee Psychologique, 74*, 487–500. PA 54:2987. SA 7714658.

Rimé, Bernard; & McCusker, Lex. (1976). Visual behaviour in social interaction: The validity of eye-contact assessments under different conditions of observation. *British Journal of Psychology, 67*, 507–514. PA 58:1117.

Rinn, William E. (1984). The neuropsychology of facial expression: A review of the neurological and psychological mechanisms for producing facial expressions. *Psychological Bulletin, 95*, 52–77. PA 71:11565.

Riordan, Cornelius; & Ruggiero, Josephine. (1980). Producing equal-status interracial interaction: A replication. *Social Psychology Quarterly, 43*, 131–136. PA 65:10399.

Rittle, Robert H. (1981). Changes in helping behavior: Self- versus situational perceptions as mediators of the foot-in-the-door effect. *Personality and Social Psychology Bulletin, 7*, 431–437. PA 67:9824.

Rittle, Robert H.; & Bernard, Nickolas. (1977). Enhancement of response rate by the mere physical presence of the experimenter. *Personality and Social Psychology Bulletin, 3*, 127–130. PA 58:7465.

Ritvo, Roger A.; & Sargent, Alice G. (Eds.). (1983). *The NTL managers' handbook*. Arlington, VA: NIL Institute.

Rivano-Fischer, Marcelo. (1984). Interactional space: Invasion as a function of the type of social interaction. *Psychological Research Bulletin, Lund U., 24*, 15 p.

Rivera, Alba N.; & Tedeschi, James T. (1976). Competitive behavior and perceived aggression. *Perceptual and Motor Skills, 42*, 485–486. PA 58:5312.

Robbins, Owen; Devoe, Shannon; & Wiener, Morton. (1978). Social patterns of turn-taking: Nonverbal regulators. *Journal of Communication, 28*, 38–46. PA 64:7945.

Roberts, Glyn C. (1974). Effect of achievement motivation and social environment on risk taking. *Research Quarterly, 45*, 42–55. PA 53:1215.

Robertson, Roby D. (1980). Small group decision making: The uncertain role of information in reducing uncertainty. *Political Behavior, 2*, 163–188. SA 82M4025.

Robins, George L.; & Wexley, Kenneth N. (1975). Modification through modeling and reinforcement in leaderless groups. *Journal of Psychology, 91*, 87–91. PA 55:4519.

Robinson, Mike. (1984). *Groups*. New York: Wiley.

Robinson, Robbie. (1978). Individual difference and performance measures in crowding research. *Environmental Psychology and Nonverbal Behavior, 3*, 123–124. PA 63:9640.

Robinson, W. LaVome; & Calhoun, Karen S. (1984). Assertiveness and cognitive processing in interpersonal situations. *Journal of Behavioral Assessment, 6*(1), 81–96. PA 72:25409.

Rocha, Rene; & Rogers, Ronald W. (1976). Ares and Babbitt in the classroom: Effects of competition and reward on children's aggression. *Journal of Personality and Social Psychology, 33*, 588–593. PA 56:7924.

Roco, Mihaela. (1977). [Psychosocial behavior and group creativity]. *Revista de Psihologie, 23*, 279–290. PA 63:7570.

Rodin, Judith. (1976). Density, perceived choice and response to controlled and uncontrolled outcomes. *Journal of Experimental Social Psychology, 12*, 564–578. PA 57:14144.

Rodin, Judith; Solomon, Susan K.; & Metcalf, John. (1978). Role of control in mediating perceptions of density. *Journal of Personality and Social Psychology, 36*, 988–999. PA 63:5435.

Rodrigues, Aroldo; & de la Coleta, Jose A. (1983). The prediction of preferences for triadic interpersonal relations. *Journal of Social Psychology, 121*, 73–80. PA 71:17762.

Roering, Kenneth J.; Slusher, E. Allen; & Schooler, Robert D. (1975). Commitment to future interaction in marketing transactions. *Journal of Applied Psychology, 60*, 386–388. PA 54:4297.

Rofé, Yacov. (1984). Stress and affiliation: A utility theory. *Psychological Review, 91*, 235–250. PA 71:17740.

Roger, D. B. (1976). Personal space, body image, and leadership: An exploratory study. *Perceptual and Motor Skills, 43*, 25–6. PA 57:6903.

Roger, D. B.; & Reid, R. L. (1978). Small group ecology revisited: Personal space and role differentiation. *British Journal of Social and Clinical Psychology, 17*, 43–46. PA 61:5938. SA 79K1106.

Roger, D. B.; & Reid, R. L. (1982). Role differentiation and seating arrangements: A further study. *British Journal of Social Psychology, 21*, 23–29. PA 68:5766. SA 84N7295.

Roger, D. B.; & Schaelerkamp, E. E. (1976). Body-buffer zone and violence: a cross-cultural study. *Journal of Social Psychology, 98*, 153–158. PA 56:5886.

Roger, Derek [B.]; & Nesshoever, Willfried. (1987). Individual differences in dyadic conversational strategies: A further study. *British Journal of Social Psychology, 26*, 247–255.

Roger, Derek B.; & Schumacher, Andrea. (1983). Effects of individual differences on dyadic conversational strategies. *Journal of Personality and Social Psychology, 45*, 700–705. PA 71:12166.

Rogers, Carl R. (1982, August). Nuclear war: A personal response. *APA Monitor, 13*(8), 6–7.

Rogers, Peter; Rearden, John J.; & Hillner, William. (1981). Effects of distance from interviewer and intimacy of topic on verbal productivity and anxiety. *Psychological Reports, 49*, 303–307. PA 67:9781.

Rogers, Richard; & Wright, E. Wayne. (1976). Preliminary study of perceived self-disclosure. *Psychological Reports, 38*, 1334. PA 56:7972.

Rogers, Ronald W. (1980). Expressions of aggression: Aggression-inhibiting effects of anonymity to authority and threatened retaliation. *Personality and Social Psychology Bulletin, 6*, 315–320. PA 66:1238.

Rogers, Ronald W.; & Prentice-Dunn, Steven. (1981). Deindividuation and anger-mediated interracial aggression: Unmasking regressive rac-

ism. *Journal of Personality & Social Psychology, 41*, 63–73. PA 67:5725.

Rogozinska, Hanna. (1981). Spostrzeganie zachowania i jego wynikow przez wykonawce i obserwatora [Perceiving behavior and its results by actor and observer]. *Przeglad Psychologiczny, 24*, 517–535. PA 70:10275.

Rohde, Kermit J. (1974). Polarization–What is it? *Personality and Social Psychology Bulletin, 1*, 207–209.

Rohe, William M. (1982). The response to density in residential settings: The mediating effects of social and personal variables. *Journal of Applied Social Psychology, 12*, 292–303.

Rohrbaugh, John W. (1979). Improving the quality of group judgment: Social judgment analysis and the Delphi technique. *Organizational Behavior and Human Performance, 24*, 73–92. PA 64:10343.

Rohrbaugh, John [W.]. (1981). Improving the quality of group judgment: Social judgment analysis and the nominal group technique. *Organizational Behavior and Human Performance, 28*, 272–288. PA 67:1244.

Rokach, Amiram. (1982). Sex differences and locus of control in cooperative behaviour. *Ontario Psychologist, 14*(2), 7–11. PA 68:12621.

Roloff, Michael E. (1976). Communication strategies, relationships, and relational change. In G. R. Miller (Ed.), *Explorations in interpersonal communication* (pp. 173–195). Beverly Hills, CA: Sage. PA 58:11680.

Roloff, Michael E. (1981). *Interpersonal communication: The social exchange approach.* Beverly Hills & London: Sage.

Roloff, Michael E.; & Miller, Gerald R. (Eds.). (1987). *Interpersonal processes: New directions in communication research.* Beverly Hills & London: Sage.

Romer, Daniel. (1983). Effects of own attitude on polarization of judgment. *Journal of Personality and Social Psychology, 44*, 273–284. PA 70:5647.

Rosa, Eugene; & Mazur, Allan. (1979). Incipient status in small groups. *Social Forces, 58*, 18–37. SA 80K8703.

Rose, Gary R.; & Bednar, Richard L. (1980). Effect of positive and negative self-disclosure and feedback on early group development. *Journal of Counseling Psychology, 27*, 63–70. PA 63:7571.

Rose, Gerald L.; Menasco, Michael B.; & Curry,

David J. (1982). When disagreement facilitates performance in judgment tasks: Effects of different forms of cognitive conflict, information environments, and human information processing characteristics. *Organizational Behavior and Human Performance, 29,* 287–306. PA 68:5767.

Rose, Suzanna M. (1985). Same- and cross-sex friendships and the psychology of homosociality. *Sex Roles, 12,* 63–74. PA 73:3686.

Rose, Yaacov J.; & Tryon, Warren W. (1979). Judgments of assertive behavior as a function of speech loudness, latency, content, gestures, inflection, and sex. *Behavior Modification, 3,* 112–123. PA 65:10449.

Rosen, Benson; & Jerdee, Thomas H. (1974). Influence of sex role stereotypes on personnel decisions. *Journal of Applied Psychology, 59,* 9–14.

Rosen, Benson; Jerdee, Thomas H.; & Prestwich, Thomas L. (1975). Dual-career marital adjustment: Potential effects of discriminatory managerial attitudes. *Journal of Marriage and the Family, 37,* 565–572. PA 56:3919.

Rosen, Sidney; Powell, Evan R.; & Schubot, David B. (1977). Peer-tutoring outcomes as influenced by the equity and type of role assignment. *Journal of Educational Psychology, 69,* 244–252.

Rosenbaum, Max; & Snadowsky, Alvin. (Eds.). (1976). *The intensive group experience.* New York: Free Press.

Rosenbaum, Milton E.; Moore, Danny L.; Cotton, John L.; Cook, Michael S.; Hieser, Rex A.; Shovar, M. Nicki; & Gray, Morris J. (1980). Group productivity and process: Pure and mixed reward structures and task interdependence. *Journal of Personality and Social Psychology, 39,* 626–642. PA 66:5767.

Rosenblatt, Paul C.; & Budd, Linda G. (1975). Territoriality and privacy in married and unmarried cohabiting couples. *Journal of Social Psychology, 97,* 67–76. PA 55:6968.

Rosenfeld, Howard M.; Breck, Barbara E.; Smith, Stephanie H.; & Kehoe, Sara. (1984). Intimacy-mediators of the proximity-gaze compensation effect: Movement, conversational role, acquaintance, and gender. [Special Issue: Nonverbal intimacy and exchange]. *Journal of Nonverbal Behavior, 8,* 235–249. PA 74:4024.

Rosenfeld, Lawrence B.; & Fowler, Gene D. (1976). Personality, sex, and leadership style.

Communication Monographs, 43, 320–324. SA 78J1863.

Rosenfield, David; Stephan, Walter G.; & Lucker, G. William. (1981). Attraction to competent and incompetent members of cooperative and competitive groups. *Journal of Applied Social Psychology, 11,* 416–433. PA 68:5768.

Rosenthal, Robert W.; & Landau, Henry J. (1979). A game-theoretic analysis of bargaining with reputations. *Journal of Mathematical Psychology, 20,* 233–255. PA 65:7935.

Rosenthal, Robert W.; & Landau, Henry J. (1981). Repeated bargaining with opportunities for learning. *Journal of Mathematical Sociology, 8,* 61–74. PA 67:7707.

Rosenthal, Saul F. (1978). The relationship of attraction and sex composition to performance and nonperformance experimental outcomes in dyads. *Sex Roles, 4,* 887–898. PA 63:9641. SA 80K8704.

Rosenzweig, S. (1983). Vers une definition et une classification d'ensemble de l'agression [Towards a definition and a classification of the general effect of aggression]. *Revue de Psychologie Appliquee, 33,* 157–162. PA 71:20487.

Ross, Lee; Bierbrauer, Günter; & Hoffman, Susan. (1976). The role of attribution processes in conformity and dissent: Revisiting the Asch situation. *American Psychologist, 31,* 148–157.

Rossel, Robert D. (1981). Word play: Metaphor and humor in the small group. *Small Group Behavior, 12,* 116–136.

Rossignol, Christian. (1975). Experimental approach to the dynamics of the domain of representation with respect to the concept of a group. *Bulletin du C.E.R.P., 23,* 31–41. PA 59:7882.

Roth, Alvin E.; & Malouf, Michael W. K. (1979). Game-theoretic models and the role of information in bargaining. *Psychological Review, 86,* 574–594.

Roth, Byron M. (1979). Competing norms of distribution in coalition games. *Journal of Conflict Resolution, 23,* 513–537.

Roth, Marvin; & Kuiken, Don. (1975). Communication immediacy, cognitive compatibility, and immediacy of self-disclosure. *Journal of Counseling Psychology, 22,* 102–107. PA 53:12112.

Rothbart, Myron; & Hallmark, William. (1988). In-group—out-group differences in the perceived efficacy of coercion and conciliation in resolving social conflict. *Journal of Personality and Social Psychology, 55,* 248–257.

Rotheram, Mary; la Cour, Jean; & Jacobs, Alfred. (1982). Variations in group process due to valence, response mode, and directness of feedback. *Group and Organization Studies, 7*(1), 67–75. PA 68:1102.

Rotton, James. (1977). Sex, residential location, and altruism. *Psychological Reports, 40,* 102. PA 58:5313.

Rotton, James. (1983). Affective and cognitive consequences of malodorous pollution. *Basic and Applied Social Psychology, 4,* 171–191. PA 71:24741.

Rotton, James; Barry, Timothy; Frey, James; & Soler, Edgardo. (1978). Air pollution and interpersonal attraction. *Journal of Applied Social Psychology, 8,* 57–71. PA 62:3579.

Rotton, James; & Frey, J. (1985). Air pollution, weather, and violent crimes: Concomitant time-series analysis of archival data. *Journal of Personality and Social Psychology, 49,* 1207–1220. PA 73:12106.

Rotton, James; Frey, James; Barry, Timothy; Mulligan, M.; & Fitzpatrick, M. (1979). The air pollution experience and physical aggression. *Journal of Applied Social Psychology, 9,* 397–412. PA 66:5769.

Rotton, James; Olszewski, Donald; Charleton, Marc; & Soler, Edgardo. (1978). Loud speech, conglomerate noise, and behavioral aftereffects. *Journal of Applied Psychology, 63,* 360–365. PA 61:12433.

Roweton, William E. (1982). Creativity and competition. *Journal of Creative Behavior, 16,* 89–96. PA 69:10417.

Royce, W. Stephen. (1982). Behavioral referents for molar ratings of heterosocial skill. *Psychological Reports, 50,* 139–146. PA 68:8137.

Ruback, R. Barry. (1987). Deserted (and nondeserted) aisles: Territorial intrusion can produce persistence, not flight. *Social Psychology Quarterly, 50,* 270–276.

Ruback, R. Barry; Dabbs, James M. Jr.; & Hopper, Charles H. (1984). The process of brainstorming: An analysis with individual and group vocal parameters. *Journal of Personality and Social Psychology, 47,* 558–567. PA 72:4007.

Ruben, Brent D. (1984). *Communication and human behavior.* New York: Macmillan.

Rubenstein, Franklin D.; Watzke, Gerard;

Doktor, Robert H.; & Dana, Jonathan. (1975). The effect of two incentive schemes upon the conservation of shared resource by five-person groups. *Organizational Behavior and Human Performance, 13,* 330–338. PA 54:7478.

Rubin, Jeffrey Z. (1980). Experimental research on third-party intervention in conflict: Toward some generalizations. *Psychological Bulletin, 87,* 379–391. PA 63:9642.

Rubin, Jeffrey Z. (1981). Psychological traps. *Psychology Today, 15*(3), 52–63.

Rubin, Jeffrey Z. (1983). Negotiation: An introduction to some issues and themes. *American Behavioral Scientist, 27,* 135–147. PA 71:23077.

Rubin, Jeffrey Z.; Brockner, Joel; Eckenrode, John; Enright, Margaret A.; & Johnson-George, Cynthia. (1980). Weakness as strength: Test of a "my hands are tied" ploy in bargaining. *Personality and Social Psychology Bulletin, 6,* 216–221.

Rubin, Jeffrey Z.; & Brown, Bert R. (1975). *The social psychology of bargaining and negotiation.* New York: Academic Press.

Rubin, Jeffrey Z.; Greller, Martin; & Roby, Thornton B. (1974). Factors affecting the magnitude and proportionality of solutions to problems of coordination. *Perceptual and Motor Skills, 39,* 599–618. PA 56:9872.

Rubin, Zick. (1975). Disclosing oneself to a stranger: Reciprocity and its limits. *Journal of Experimental Social Psychology, 11,* 233–260. PA 54:7479.

Rubin, Zick. (1976). Naturalistic studies of self-disclosure. *Personality and Social Psychology Bulletin, 2,* 260–263. PA 57:1177.

Rubin, Zick; Hill, Charles T.; Peplau, Letitia A.; & Dunkel Schetter, Christine. (1980). Self-disclosure in dating couples: Sex roles and the ethic of openness. *Journal of Marriage and the Family, 42,* 305–317. PA 65:12749.

Rubin, Zick; & Shenker, Stephen. (1978). Friendship, proximity, and self-disclosure. *Journal of Personality, 46,* 1–22. PA 61:10917.

Rubinstein, David; & Timmins, Joan F. (1978). Depressive dyadic and triadic relationships. *Journal of Marriage and Family Counseling, 4,* 13–23. SA 78J3226.

Ruble, Diane N. (1975). Visual orientation and self-perceptions of children in an external-cue-relevant or cue-irrelevant task situation. *Child Development, 46,* 669–676. PA 57:07904.

Ruble, Diane N.; & Higgins, E. Tory. (1976).

Effects of group sex composition on self-presentation and sex-typing. *Journal of Social Issues, 32*(3), 125–132. PA 57:5807.

Ruble, Thomas L. (1976). Effects of one's locus of control and the opportunity to participate in planning. *Organizational Behavior and Human Performance, 16,* 63–73. PA 56:7926.

Ruble, Thomas L. (1983). Sex stereotypes: Issues of change in the 1970s. *Sex Roles, 9,* 397–402. PA 71:1283.

Ruble, Thomas L.; & Thomas, Kenneth W. (1976). Support for a two-dimensional model of conflict behavior. *Organizational Behavior and Human Performance, 16,* 142–155. PA 56:7925.

Rucker, M. H.; & King, D. C. (1985). Reactions to leadership style as a function of locus of control and ascendancy of subordinates. *Social Behavior & Personality, 13,* 91–107. PA 73:29965.

Rudestam, Kjell Erik. (1982). *Experiential groups in theory and Practice.* Monterey, CA: Brooks/Cole.

Rugel, Robert P.; & Meyer, Darrell J. (1984). The Tavistock group: Empirical findings and implications for group therapy. *Small Group Behavior, 15,* 361–374. PA 72:9503.

Ruhe, John A.; & Allen, W. R. (1977, April). Differences and similarities between Black and White leaders. *Proceedings of the American Institute of Decision Sciences, NorthEast Division,* pp. 30–35.

Ruhe, John, & Eatman, John. (1977). Effects of racial composition on small work groups. *Small Group Behavior, 8,* 479–486. PA 64:1021. SA 79K1108.

Rule, Brendan G.; & Gareau, Andre. (1977). Polarization as a function of meaning and consequences. *European Journal of Social Psychology, 7,* 307–315. PA 60:7442. SA 79J6855.

Rumelhart, Marilyn A. (1983). When in doubt: Strategies used in response to interactional uncertainty. *Discourse Processes, 6,* 377–402. SA 86Q3075.

Rumsey, Michael G.; Allgeier, Elizabeth R.; & Castore, Carl H. (1978). Group discussion, sentencing judgments, and the leniency shift. *Journal of Social Psychology, 105,* 249–257. PA 63:5458.

Rumsey, Michael G.; & Castore, Carl H. (1980). Group discussion, commitment, and penalty shifts. *Small Group Behavior, 11,* 108–119. SA 80L0095.

Rumsey, Nichola; Bull, Ray; & Gahagan, Denis. (1982). The effect of facial disfigurement on the proxemic behavior of the general public. *Journal of Applied Social Psychology, 12,* 137–150. PA 70:10255.

Rusbult, Caryl E. (1980). Commitment and satisfaction in romantic associations: A test of the investment model. *Journal of Experimental Social Psychology, 16,* 172–186. PA 65:10400.

Rusbult, Caryl E. (1983). A longitudinal test of the investment model: The development (and deterioration) of satisfaction and commitment in heterosexual involvements. *Journal of Personality and Social Psychology, 45,* 101–117. PA 71:6711.

Rusbult, Caryl E.; Johnson, Dennis J.; & Morrow, Gregory D. (1986a). Determinants and consequences of exit, voice, loyalty, and neglect: Responses to dissatisfaction in adult romantic involvements. *Human Relations, 39,* 45–63. PA 73:14441.

Rusbult, Caryl E.; Johnson, Dennis J.; & Morrow, Gregory D. (1986b). Impact of couple patterns of problem solving on distress and nondistress in dating relationships. *Journal of Personality and Social Psychology, 50,* 744–753. PA 73:21927.

Rusbult, Caryl E.; Morrow, Gregory D.; & Johnson, Dennis J. (1987). Self-esteem and problem-solving behaviour in close relationships. *British Journal of Social Psychology, 26,* 293–303.

Rusbult, Caryl E.; Musante, Linda; & Solomon, Michael R. (1982). The effects of clarity of decision rule and favorability of verdict on satisfaction with resolution of conflicts. *Journal of Applied Social Psychology, 12,* 304–317. PA 69:5584.

Rusbult, Caryl E.; & Zembrodt, Isabella M. (1983). Responses to dissatisfaction in romantic involvements: A multidimensional scaling analysis. *Journal of Experimental Social Psychology, 19,* 274–293. PA 71:1327.

Rusbult, Caryl E.; Zembrodt, Isabella M.; & Gunn, Lawanna K. (1982). Exit, voice, loyalty, and neglect: Responses to dissatisfaction in romantic involvements. *Journal of Personality and Social Psychology, 43,* 1230–1242. PA 70:1063.

Rush, Michael C.; Phillips, James S.; & Lord, Robert G. (1981). Effects of a temporal delay in rating on leader behavior descriptions: A laboratory investigation. *Journal of Applied Psychology, 66*, 442–450. PA 66:10358.

Rush, Michael C.; Thomas, Jay C.; & Lord, Robert G. (1977). Implicit leadership theory: A potential threat to the internal validity of leader behavior questionnaires. *Organizational Behavior and Human Performance, 20*, 93–110. PA 60:6507.

Rushton, J. Philippe. (1978). Urban density and altruism: Helping strangers in a Canadian city, suburb, and small town. *Psychological Reports, 43*, 987–990. PA 64:7948.

Rushton, J. Phillippe; & Sorrentiino, Richard M. (Eds.). (1981). *Altruism and helping behavior: Social, personality, and developmental perspectives*. Hillsdale, NJ: L. Erlbaum.

Russ, Raymond C.; & Gold, Joel A. (1975). Task expertise and group communication. *Journal of Psychology, 91*, 187–196. PA 56:2316.

Russell, J. Curtis; Firestone, Ira J.; & Baron, Reuben M. (1980). Seating arrangement and social influence: Moderated by reinforcement meaning and internal-external control. *Social Psychology Quarterly, 43*, 103–109. PA 65:10401. SA 83M7346.

Russell, J. Curtis; & Hubbard, W. Dale. (1977). Expectancy violation and choosing whom to help. *Psychological Reports, 41*, 831–836. PA 60:09348.

Russell, James A.; & Ward, Lawrence M. (1982). Environmental psychology. *Annual Review of Psychology, 33*, 651–688. PA 67:13260.

Russo, Nancy F. (1975). Eye contact, interpersonal distance, and the equilibrium theory. *Journal of Personality and Social Psychology, 31*, 497–502. PA 54:1009.

Rutkowski, Gregory K.; Gruder, Charles L.; & Romer, Daniel. (1983). Group cohesiveness, social norms, and bystander intervention. *Journal of Personality and Social Psychology, 44*, 545–552. PA 70:10233.

Rutte, C. G.; & Wilke, H. A. (1984). Social dilemmas and leadership. *European Journal of Social Psychology, 14*, 105–121. PA 72:6634.

Rutte, C. G.; & Wilke, H. A. (1985). Preference for decision structures in a social dilemma situation. *European Journal of Social Psychology, 15*, 367–370. PA 73:11773.

Rutte, Christel G.; Wilke, Henk A. M.; & Messick, David M. (1987a). The effects of framing social dilemmas as give-some or take-some games. *British Journal of Social Psychology, 26*, 103–108.

Rutte, Christel G.; Wilke, Henk A. M.; & Messick, David M. (1987b). Scarcity or abundance caused by people or the environment as determinants of behavior in the resource dilemma. *Journal of Experimental Social Psychology, 23*, 208–216.

Rutter, David R. (1976). Visual interaction in recently admitted and chronic long-stay schizophrenics patients. *British Journal of Social and Clinical Psychology, 15*, 295–303. PA 57:8417.

Rutter, D[avid] R. (1978). Visual interaction in schizophrenic patients: The timing of looks. *British Journal of Social and Clinical Psychology, 17*, 281–282. PA 63:1136.

Rutter, D[avid] R.; & Stephenson, G. M. (1977). The role of visual communication in synchronising conversation. *European Journal of Social Psychology, 7*, 29–37. PA 60:7443. SA 78J4703.

Rutter, D[avid] R.; & Stephenson, Geoffrey M. (1979a). The functions of looking: Effects of friendship on gaze. *British Journal of Social and Clinical Psychology, 18*, 203–205. PA 64:7949.

Rutter, D[avid] R.; & Stephenson, Geoffrey M. (1979b). The role of visual communication in social interaction. *Current Anthropology, 20*(1), 124–125. PA 64:5571.

Rutter, D[avid] R.; Stephenson, G. M.; Ayling, K.; & White, P. A. (1978). The timing of looks in dyadic conversation. *British Journal of Social and Clinical Psychology, 17*, 17–21. PA 61:5939. SA 79K1109.

Rutter, D[avid] R.; Stephenson, G. M.; Lazzerini, A. J.; Ayling, K.; & White, P. A. (1977). Eye-contact: A chance product of individual looking? *British Journal of Social and Clinical Psychology, 16*, 191–192. PA 59:12330.

Ruzicka, Mary F.; Palisi, Anthony T.; & Berven, Normal L. (1979). Use of Cattell's three panel model: Remedying problems in small group research. *Small Group Behavior, 10*, 40–48. SA 80K5528.

Ruzicka, Mary F.; Palisi, Anthony T.; Kelly, Mary D.; & Corrado, Nancy R. (1979). The relation of perceptions by leaders and members to creative group behavior. *Journal of Psychology, 103*, 95–101. PA 65:1249.

Ryen, Allen H.; & Kahn, Arnold. (1975). Effects of intergroup orientation on group attitudes and proxemic behavior. *Journal of Personality and Social Psychology, 31,* 302–310. PA 53:11591.

Ryff, Carol D. (1987). The place of personality and social structure research in social psychology. *Journal of Personality and Social Psychology, 53,* 1192–1202.

Ryzhov, V. V. (1981). [The relationship between social interaction and social perception]. *Voprosy Psikhologii,* No. 2, 58–67. PA 67:5765.

Saaty, Thomas L.; & Vargas, Luis G. (1980). Hierarchical analysis of behavior in competition: Prediction in chess. *Behavioral Science, 25,* 180–191. PA 65:12750. SA 82L9795.

Sabatelli, Ronald M.; Buck, Ross; & Dreyer, Albert. (1980). Communication via facial cues in intimate dyads. *Personality and Social Psychology Bulletin, 6,* 242–247. PA 66:1241.

Sabatelli, Ronald M.; Buck, Ross; & Dreyer, Albert. (1982). Nonverbal communication accuracy in married couples: Relationship with marital complaints. *Journal of Personality and Social Psychology, 43,* 1088–1097. PA 70:986.

Sabatelli, Ronald M.; Buck, Ross; & Dreyer, Albert. (1983). Locus of control, interpersonal trust, and nonverbal communication accuracy. *Journal of Personality and Social Psychology, 44,* 399–409. PA 70:5637.

Sabatelli, Ronald M ; Dreyer, Albert S.; & Buck, Ross. (1983). Cognitive style and relationship quality in married dyads. *Journal of Personality, 51,* 192–201. PA 71:6572.

Sacks, Colin Hamilton; & Bugenthal, Daphne Blunt. (1987). Attributions as moderators of affective and behavioral responses to social failure. *Journal of Personality and Social Psychology, 53,* 939–947.

Sadalla, Edward K.; Burroughs, W. Jeffrey; & Staplin, Lorin J. (1978). The experience of crowding. *Personality and Social Psychology Bulletin, 4,* 304–308.

Sadava, S. W.; & Forsyth, R. (1976). Decisions about drug use: An application of the choice-shifts paradigm. *Psychological Reports, 38,* 1119–1133. PA 56:7845.

Saegert, Susan. (1973). Crowding: Cognitive overload and behavioral constraint. In W. F. E. Preiser (Ed.), *Environmental design research:*

Vol. 2. Symposia and workshops [proceedings of the fourth International Environmental Design Research Conference] (pp. 254–260). Stroudsberg, PA: Dowden, Hutchinson, & Ross.

Safer, Martin A. (1980). Attributing evil to the subject, not the situation: Student reaction to Milgram's film on obedience. *Personality and Social Psychology Bulletin, 6,* 205–209. PA 66:1291.

Safilios-Rothschild, Constantina. (1981). Toward a social psychology of relationships. *Psychology of Women Quarterly, 5,* 377–384. PA 67:3558.

Sagan, Keith; Pondel, Marc; & Wittig, Michele A. (1981). The effect of anticipated future interaction on reward allocation in same- and opposite-sex dyads. *Journal of Personality, 49,* 438–449. PA 68:1136.

Saha, Sudhir K. (1979). Contingency theories of leadership: A study. *Human Relations, 32,* 313–322. SA 81L5010.

St. Jean, Richard. (1979). Role of potential gain and loss in choice-dilemma decisions. *Perceptual and Motor Skills, 49,* 617–618. PA 65:5397.

Sakamaki, Yoshio. (1974). [The effects of the factors of group structure and the degree of task performance on the group members' perceptions of leadership functions]. *Japanese Journal of Experimental Social Psychology, 14,* 139–146. PA 54:11718.

Sakamoto, Shiori. (1980). Contingency severity and individual performance in a probabilistic game setting. *Human Relations, 33,* 687–709. PA 65:3282.

Saltzstein, Herbert D. (1975). Effect of rejection and acceptance from a group on conformity to two types of social influence. *Psychological Reports, 37,* 839–848. PA 55:12266. SA 78J4704.

Saltzstein, Herbert D.; & Ast, Shelley. (1975). The influence of males and females on the psychophysical judgments of females. *Journal of Psychology, 90,* 259–268. PA 54:9613.

Saltzenstein, Herbert D.; & Sandberg, Lewis. (1979). Indirect social influence: Change in judgmental process or anticipatory conformity? *Journal of Experimental Social Psychology, 15,* 209–216.

Samerotte, George C.; & Harris, Mary B. (1976).

Some factors influencing helping: The effects of a handicap, responsibility, and requesting help. *Journal of Social Psychology, 98*, 39–45. PA 56:2384.

Samuelson, Charles D.; & Messick, David M. (1986a). Alternative structural solutions to resource dilemmas. *Organizational Behavior and Human Decision Processes, 37*, 139–155.

Samuelson, Charles D.; & Messick, David M. (1986b). Inequities in access to and use of shared resources in social dilemmas. *Journal of Personality and Social Psychology, 51*, 960–967. PA 74:7172.

Samuelson, Charles D.; Messick, David M.; Rutte, Christel; & Wilke, Henk. (1984). Individual and structural solutions to resource dilemmas in two cultures. *Journal of Personality & Social Psychology, 47*, 94–104. PA 71:31323.

Sanchez, Heriberto; & Clark, Nathan T. (1981). Test of Weiss and Miller's social facilitation hypothesis: Are audiences aversive? *Perceptual and Motor Skills, 53*, 767–772. PA 68:5800.

Sande, Gerald N.; Ellard, John H.; & Ross, Michael. (1986). Effect of arbitrarily assigned status labels on self-perceptions and social perceptions: The mere position effect. *Journal of Personality and Social Psychology, 50*, 684–689. PA 73:21945.

Sanders, Glenn S. (1978). An integration of shifts toward risk and caution in gambling situations. *Journal of Experimental Social Psychology, 14*, 409–416. PA 63:980.

Sanders, Glenn S. (1980). What do gambling and advice-giving have in common? *Personality and Social Psychology Bulletin, 6*, 293–298. PA 66:01242.

Sanders, Glenn S. (1981a). Driven by distraction: An integrative review of social facilitation theory and research. *Journal of Experimental Social Psychology, 17*, 227–251.

Sanders, Glenn S. (1981b). Toward a comprehensive account of social facilitation: Distraction/conflict does not mean theoretical conflict. *Journal of Experimental Social Psychology, 17*, 262–265.

Sanders, Glenn S. (1983). Attentional processes and social facilitation: How much, how often, how long-lasting? In H. H. Blumberg, A. P. Hare, V. Kent, & M. F. Davies (Eds.), *Small groups and social interaction* (Vol. 1, pp. 155–163). Chichester: John Wiley & Sons.

Sanders, Glenn S. (1984). Self-presentation and drive in social facilitation. *Journal of Experimental Social Psychology, 20*, 312–322.

Sanders, Glenn S.; & Baron, Robert S. (1975). Motivating effects of distraction on task performance. *Journal of Personality and Social Psychology, 32*, 956–963.

Sanders, Glenn S.; & Baron, Robert S. (1977). Is social comparison irrelevant for producing choice shifts? *Journal of Experimental Social Psychology, 13*, 303–314. PA 59:9900.

Sanders, Glenn S.; Baron, Robert S.; & Moore, Danny L. (1978). Distraction and social comparison as mediators of social facilitation effects. *Journal of Experimental Social Psychology, 14*, 291–303. PA 61:10894.

Sanders, Jeffrey L.; Hakky, Ulfat M.; & Brizzolara, Mary M. (1985). Personal space amongst Arabs and Americans. *International Journal of Psychology, 20*, 13–17. PA 73:6347.

Santee, Richard T.; & Maslach, C. (1982). To agree or not to agree: Personal dissent amid pressure to conform. *Journal of Personality and Social Psychology, 42*, 690–700.

Santi, Angelo; & Wells, Roger. (1975). Strategy choices in three variants of a threat-vulnerable game. *Journal of Personality and Social Psychology, 31*, 776–786. PA 55:2353.

Sapolsky, Barry S.; & Zillmann, Dolf. (1978). Enjoyment of a televised sport contest under different social conditions of viewing. *Perceptual and Motor Skills, 46*, 29–30. PA 61:8458.

Sappington, A. A.; & Farrar, W. E. (1982). Brainstorming vs. critical judgment in the generation of solutions which conform to certain reality constraints. *Journal of Creative Behavior, 16*, 68–73. PA 69:5585.

Sarafino, Edward P.; & Helmuth, Holly. (1981). Development of personal space in preschool children as a function of age and day-care experience. *Journal of Social Psychology, 115*, 59–63. PA 67:9642.

Saravay, Stephen M. (1978). A psychoanalytic theory of group development. *International Journal of Group Psychotherapy, 28*, 481–507. SA 80L0096.

Saraydar, Edward. (1984). Modeling the role of conflict and conciliation in bargaining. *Journal of Conflict Resolution, 28*, 420–450. PA 72:6636.

Sarges, Werner. (1975). [Test of Fiedler's contingency model of leadership effectiveness with co-acting groups]. *Zeitschrift fur Experi-*

mentelle und Angewandte Psychologie, 22, 241–262. PA 55:13725.

Sasaki, Kaoru. (1979). Present status of research on group norms in Japan. *American Journal of Community Psychology*, 7, 147–158. PA 64:5572.

Sato, Kaori. (1985). [An experimental simulation of the tragedy of the commons]. *Japanese Journal of Experimental Social Psychology*, 24, 149–159. PA 73:11774.

Sato, Kaori. (1987). Distribution of the cost of maintaining common resources. *Journal of Experimental Social Psychology*, 23, 19–31.

Sato, Seiichi; Kugihara, Naoki; Misumi, Jyuji; & Shigeoka, Kunzunobu. (1984). [Experimental study of escape behavior in a simulated panic situation: III. Effect of the PM leadership conditions]. *Japanese Journal of Experimental Social Psychology*, 24, 83–91. PA 72:14496.

Satow, Kay L. (1975). Social approval and helping. *Journal of Experimental Social Psychology*, 11, 501–509.

Sauer, Claudius. (1974). [The investigation of group polarization after discussion]. *Zeitschrift fur Sozialpsychologie*, 5, 255–273. PA 54:5213.

Sauermann, Heinz. (Ed.). (1978a). *Bargaining behavior*. Tübingen, West Germany: Mohr.

Sauermann, Heinz. (Ed.). (1978b). *Coalition forming behavior*. Tübingen, West Germany: Mohr.

Savin-Williams, Ritch C. (1982). A field study of adolescent social interactions: Developmental and contextual influences. *Journal of Social Psychology*, 117, 203–209. PA 69:5453.

Scapinello, K. F.; & Sibbald, C. P. (1976). Structured group interaction: An evaluation of Bales' and Leary's methods of scoring interactions of first incarcerates. *Ontario Psychologist*, 8(1), 22–25. PA 58:2528.

Schachter, Stanley. (1951). Deviation, rejection, and communication. *Journal of Abnormal and Social Psychology*, 46, 190–207.

Schachter, Stanley. (1959). *The psychology of affiliation: Experimental studies of the sources of gregariousness*. Stanford, CA: Stanford University Press.

Schaefer, Earl S.; & Burnett, Charles K. (1987). Stability and predictability of quality of women's marital relationships and demoralization. *Journal of Personality and Social Psychology*, 53, 1129–1136.

Schaeffer, Gerald H.; & Patterson, Miles L.

(1980). Intimacy, arousal, and small group crowding. *Journal of Personality and Social Psychology*, 38, 283–290. PA 65:7946.

Schafer, Robert B.; & Keith, Patricia M. (1985). A causal model approach to the symbolic interactionist view of the self-concept. *Journal of Personality and Social Psychology*, 48, 963–969.

Schaffer, Ralf E. (1978). Eine entscheidungstheoretische Analyse des Risky Shift Phanomens [A decision-theory analysis of the risky shift phenomenon]. *Zeitschrift fur Sozial Psychologie*, 9, 186–205. SA 80L0097.

Schaible, Todd, D.; & Jacobs, Alfred. (1975) Feedback III: Sequence effects: Enhancement of feedback acceptance and group attractiveness by manipulation of the sequence and valence of feedback. *Small Group Behavior*, 6, 151–173. PA 55:2330.

Scheidlinger, Saul. (1974). On the concept of the "mother-group." *International Journal of Group Psychotherapy*, 24, 417–428. PA 54:2989.

Scheidlinger, Saul. (Ed.). (1980). *Psychoanalytic group dynamics: Basic readings*. New York: International Universities Press.

Scheidt, Fredrick J.; & Smith, Mary E. (1974). Same-sex dyads and Toman's theory of birth-order compatibility. *Psychological Reports*, 34, 1174. PA 53:1073.

Scheidt, Fredrick J., & Smith, Mary E. (1976). Birth-order compatibility and same-sex dyads: A replication. *Journal of Social Psychology*, 99, 291–292. PA 57:6904.

Schellenberg, James A. (1974). The effect of pretesting upon the risky shift. *Journal of Psychology*, 88, 197–200.

Schellenberg, James A. (1976). Is there a pessimistic shift?. *Psychological Reports*, 39, 359–362. SA 81L6531.

Schellenberg, James A. (1985). Behavioral differences between structures with rank-order equivalence. *Journal of Conflict Resolution*, 29, 531–542. PA 73:3687.

Scherer, Klaus R. (1978). Personality inference from voice quality: The loud voice of extraversion. *European Journal of Social Psychology*, 8, 467–487. PA 63:7599.

Scherer, Klaus R. (1986). Vocal affect expression: A review and model for further research. *Psychological Bulletin*, 99, 143–165. PA 73:16849.

Scherer, Shawn E. (1974). Influence of proximity

and eye contact on impression formation. *Perceptual and Motor Skills, 38*, 538. PA 53:1074.

Schettino, Andrew P.; & Borden, Richard J. (1976). Sex differences in responses to naturalistic crowding: Affective reactions to group size and group density. *Personality and Social Psychology Bulletin, 2*, 67–70. PA 56:3985.

Schiavo, R. Steven; Schiffenbauer, Allen; & Roberts, Jean. (1977). Methodological factors affecting interpersonal distance in dyads. *Perceptual and Motor Skills, 44*, 903–906. PA 59:9869. SA 79J8027.

Schick, Connie; & McGlynn, Richard P. (1976). Cooperation versus competition in group concept attainment under conditions of information exchange. *Journal of Social Psychology, 100*, 311–312. PA 58:1119.

Schiffenbauer, Allen; & Schiavo, R. Steven. (1976). Physical distance and attraction: An intensification effect. *Journal of Experimental Social Psychology, 12*, 274–282. PA 56:6057.

Schindler-Rainman, Eva; & Lippitt, Ronald. (1975). *Taking your meetings out of the doldrums.* Columbus, OH: Association of Professional Directors.

Schlenker, Barry R. (1975a). Group members' attributions of responsibility for prior group performance. *Representative Research in Social Psychology, 6*, 96–108. PA 55:9747.

Schlenker, Barry R. (1975b). Liking for a group following initiation: Impression management or dissonance reduction? *Sociometry, 38*, 99–118. PA 54:7530.

Schlenker, Barry R. (1975c). Self-presentation: Managing the impression of consistency when reality interferes with self-enhancement. *Journal of Personality and Social Psychology, 32*, 1030–1037. PA 55:9804.

Schlenker, Barry R. (1980). *Impression management: The self-concept, social identity, and interpersonal relations.* Monterey, CA: Brooks/Cole.

Schlenker, Barry R. (Ed.). (1985). *Self and social life.* New York: McGraw-Hill.

Schlenker, Barry R.; & Bonoma, Thomas V. (1978). Fun and games: The validity of games for the study of conflict. *Journal of Conflict Resolution, 22*, 7–38. PA 61:10918.

Schlenker, Barry R.; Forsyth, Donelson R.; Leary, Mark R.; & Miller, Rowland S. (1980). Self-presentational analysis of the effects of incen-

tives on attitude change following counterattitudinal behavior. *Journal of Personality and Social Psychology, 39*, 553–577.

Schlenker, Barry R.; & Goldman, Howard J. (1978). Cooperators and competitors in conflict: A test of the "triangle model." *Journal of Conflict Resolution, 22*, 393–410. PA 64:1023.

Schlenker, Barry R.; & Miller, Rowland S. (1977). Group cohesiveness as a determinant of egocentric perceptions in cooperative groups. *Human Relations, 30*, 1039–1055. PA 60:9310.

Schlenker, Barry R.; Miller, Rowland S.; & Leary, Mark R. (1983). Self-presentation as a function of self-monitoring and the validity and quality of past performance. *Representative Research in Social Psychology, 13*, 2–14. PA 71:20461.

Schlenker, Barry R.; Soraci, Salvatore; & McCarthy, Bernard. (1976). Self-esteem and group performance as determinants of egocentric perceptions in cooperative groups. *Human Relations, 29*, 1163–1176. PA 58:3301.

Schlenker, Barry R.; Soraci, Salvatore, Jr.; & Schlenker, Patricia A. (1974). Self-presentation as a function of performance expectations and performance anonymity. *Personality and Social Psychology Bulletin, 1*, 152–154.

Schlesinger, I. M. (1974). Towards a structural analysis of discussions. *Semiotica, 11*(2), 109–122. PA 55:7088.

Schmid, Tom L.; & Hake, Don F. (1983). Fast acquisition of cooperation and trust: A two-stage view of trusting behavior. *Journal of the Experimental Analysis of Behavior, 40*, 179–192. PA 71:15016.

Schmidt, Donald E. (1983). Personal control and crowding stress: A test of similarity in two cultures. *Journal of Cross-Cultural Psychology, 14*, 221–239. SA 84N9150.

Schmidt, Donald E.; & Keating, John P. (1979). Human crowding and personal control: An integration of the research. *Psychological Bulletin, 86*, 680–700. PA 62:11011.

Schmidt, Stuart M.; & Kipnis, David. (1987, November). The perils of persistence. *Psychology Today*, pp. 32, 34.

Schmitt, Bernd H.; Gilovich, Thomas; Goore, Natan; & Joseph, Lisa. (1986). Mere presence and social facilitation: One more time. *Journal of Experimental Social Psychology, 22*, 242–248.

Schmitt, David R. (1976). Some conditions affecting the choice to cooperate or compete. *Journal of the Experimental Analysis of Behavior, 25,* 165-178. PA 56:4071.

Schmitt, David R. (1984). Interpersonal relations: Cooperation and competition. *Journal of the Experimental Analysis of Behavior, 42,* 377-383. PA 72:30795.

Schmitt, David R. (1986). Competition: Some behavioral issues. *Behavior Analyst, 9*(1), 27-34. PA 74:10202.

Schneider, David J.; & Blankmeyer, Bonnie L. (1983). Prototype salience and implicit personality theories. *Journal of Personality and Social Psychology, 44,* 712-722. PA 70:12680.

Schneider, David J.; Hastorf, Albert H.; & Ellsworth, Phoebe C. (1979). *Person perception* (2nd ed.), New York: Random House.

Schneider, Frank W.; Coutts, Larry M.; & Garrett, William A. (1977). Interpersonal gaze in a triad as a function of sex. *Perceptual and Motor Skills, 44,* 184. PA 58:9491.

Schneider, Frank W.; & Hansvick, Christine L. (1977). Gaze and distance as a function of changes in interpersonal gaze. *Social Behavior and Personality, 5,* 49-53. PA 60:9311.

Schneider, Frank W.; Lesko, Wayne R.; & Garrett, William A. (1980). Helping behavior in hot, comfortable, and cold temperatures. *Environment and Behavior, 12,* 231-240. PA 64:13636.

Schneider, Frank W.; & Mockus, Zig. (1974). Failure to find a rural-urban difference in incidence of altruistic behavior. *Psychological Reports, 35,* 294. PA 56:7927.

Schneider, Hans-Dieter. (1977). Koalitionstendenzen in der Tetrade [Coalition tendencies in the tetrad]. *Zeitschrift fur Soziologie, 6*(1), 77-90. SA 78J4705.

Schneider, Hans Dieter. (1978). [What determines coalition tendencies in small groups – resources or similarity of partners? Results of a study on the coalition behavior of triadic and tetradic groups]. *Zeitschrift fur Experimentelle und Angewandte Psychologie, 25,* 153-168. PA 61:13396

Schneider, Katherine S. (1977). Personality correlates of altruistic behavior under four experimental conditions. *Journal of Social Psychology, 102,* 113-116. PA 59:7916.

Schneider, Walter; & Shiffrin, Richard M. (1977). Controlled and automatic human information

processing. 1. Detection, search and attention. *Psychological Review, 84,* 1-66.

Schneier, Craig E. (1978). The contingency model of leadership: An extension to emergent leadership and leader's sex. *Organizational Behavior and Human Performance, 21,* 220-239. PA 61:1004.

Schneier, Craig E.; & Bartol, Kathryn M. (1980). Sex effects in emergent leadership. *Journal of Applied Psychology, 65,* 341-345. PA 65:1250.

Schneier, Craig Eric; & Goktepe, Janet R. (1983). Issues in emergent leadership: The contingency model of leadership, leader sex, and leader behavior. In H. H. Blumberg, A. P. Hare, V. Kent, & M. F. Davies (Eds.), *Small groups and social interaction* (Vol. 2, pp. 413-421). Chichester: John Wiley.

Schofield, Janet W.; & Sagar, H. Andrew. (1977). Peer interaction patterns in an integrated middle school. *Sociometry, 40,* 130-138. PA 59:11097.

Schönemann, Peter H. (1979). Alternative decision schemes for six-person mock juries. *Organizational Behavior and Human Performance, 23,* 388-398.

Schopler, John; & Stockdale, Janet E. (1977). An interference analysis of crowding. *Environmental Psychology and Nonverbal Psychology, 1,* 81-88. PA 60:4247.

Schriesheim, Chester A.; Kinicki, Angelo J.; & Schriesheim, Janet F. (1979). The effect of leniency on leader behavior descriptions. *Organizational Behavior and Human Performance, 23,* 1-29. PA 64:2274.

Schreiber, Elliott. (1979). Bystanders' intervention in situations of violence. *Psychological Reports, 45,* 243-246. PA 65:3255.

Schroder, Keith H. (1981). Social styles and heterosexual pair relationships. *American Journal of Family Therapy, 9*(3), 65-74. PA 67:9782.

Schroeder, David A. (1983). Promoting cooperation in social trap situations. *Academic Psychology Bulletin, 5,* 237-246. PA 71:12169.

Schroeder, David A.; Jensen, Thomas D.; Reed, Andrew J.; Sullivan, Debra K.; & Schwab, Michael. (1983). The actions of others as determinants of behavior in social trap situations. *Journal of Experimental Social Psychology, 19,* 522-539. PA 71:20462.

Schroeder, David A.; & Johnson, David E. (1982). Utilization of information in a social-trap situation. *Psychological Reports, 50*, 107–113. PA 68:8111.

Schul, Yaacov; & Benbenishty, Rami. (1985). Preferences, expectations, and behaviours in interpersonal interaction. *European Journal of Social Psychology, 15*, 345–352. PA 73:12406.

Schuler, Randall S. (1977). The effects of role perceptions on employee satisfaction and performance moderated by employee ability. *Organizational Behavior & Human Performance, 18*, 98–107. PA 58:6445.

Schullo, Stephen A.; & Alperson, Burton L. (1984). Interpersonal phenomenology as a function of sexual orientation, sex, sentiment, and trait categories in long-term dyadic relationships. *Journal of Personality and Social Psychology, 47*, 983–1002.

Schultz, Beatrice. (1978). Predicting emergent leaders: An exploratory study of the salience of communicative functions. *Small Group Behavior, 9*, 109–114.

Schultz, Beatrice. (1980). Communicative correlates of perceived leaders. *Small Group Behavior, 11*, 175–191. SA 82M1631.

Schultz, Beatrice. (1986). Communicative correlates of perceived leaders in the small group. *Small Group Behavior, 17*, 51–65.

Schultz, Beatrice; & Anderson, Judith. (1984). Training in the management of conflict: A communication theory perspective. *Small Group Behavior, 15*, 333–348. PA 72:9504.

Schulz, Justin W.; & Pruitt, Dean G. (1978). The effects of mutual concern on joint welfare. *Journal of Experimental Social Psychology, 14*, 480–492. PA 63:3259.

Schulz, Richard; & Barefoot, John. (1974). Nonverbal responses and affiliative conflict theory. *British Journal of Social and Clinical Psychology, 13*, 237–243. PA 59:3347.

Schulz, Ulrich; & Hesse, Werner. (1978). A model for gaming behavior in sequences of Prisoner's Dilemma games in consideration of expectations. *Psychologische Beitrage, 20*, 551–570. PA 64:3259.

Schumacker, Randall E. (1981). Differences in comprehension are important in studies of conformity, influence, and persuasion. *Psychological Reports, 48*, 583–586. PA 67:3559.

Schutz, W. C. (1958). *FIRO: A three-dimensional theory of interpersonal behavior*. New York: Rinehart.

Schwanenberg, Enno; & Huth, Wolfgang. (1977). The hard and the soft in interdependence: Locating game behavior in semantic space. *Perceptual and Motor Skills, 45*, 131–153. PA 60:5213. SA 79K2637.

Schwartz, Barry; Tesser, Abraham; & Powell, Evan. (1982). Dominance cues in nonverbal behavior. *Social Psychology Quarterly, 45*, 114–120. PA 68:12622.

Schwartz, Larry M.; Foa, Uriel G.; & Foa, Edna B. (1983). Multichannel nonverbal communication: Evidence for combinatory rules. *Journal of Personality and Social Psychology, 45*, 274–281. PA 71:6757.

Schwartz, Shalom H.; & Gottlieb, Avi. (1976). Bystander reactions to a violent theft: Crime in Jerusalem. *Journal of Personality and Social Psychology, 34*, 1188–1199. PA 60:11740.

Schwartz, Shalom H.; & Gottlieb, Avi. (1980a). Bystander anonymity and reactions to emergencies. *Journal of Personality and Social Psychology, 39*, 418–430. PA 66:5772.

Schwartz, Shalom H.; & Gottlieb, Avi. (1980b). Participation in a bystander intervention experiment and subsequent everyday helping: Ethical considerations. *Journal of Experimental Social Psychology, 16*, 161–171. PA 65:10403.

Schwartz, T. M.; Wullwick, V. J.; & Shapiro, H. J. (1980). Self-esteem and group decision making: An empirical study. *Psychological Reports, 46*, 951–956. PA 66:3620.

Schwarzwald, Joseph; Bizman, Aharon; & Raz, Moshe. (1983). The foot-in-the-door paradigm: Effects of second request size on donation probability and donor generosity. *Personality and Social Psychology Bulletin, 9*, 443–450. PA 71:12170.

Schwarzwald, Joseph; & Yinon, Yoel. (1978). Physical aggression: Effects of ethnicity of target and directionality of aggression. *European Journal of Social Psychology, 8*, 367–376. PA 63:3281.

Schwinger, Thomas; Kayser, Egon; & Muller, Thomas. (1981–1982). Was rechtfertigt ungleichmabige Guterverteilung? [Under which circumstances will unequal distribution of resources be taken to be just?]. *Archiv fur Psychologie, 134*, 303–314. PA 70:12681.

Scioli, Frank P.; Dyson, James W.; & Fleitas, Daniel W. (1974). The relationship of personality and decisional structure to leadership. *Small Group Behavior, 5*, 3–22. PA 52:10040.

Scott, Joseph A. (1974). Awareness of informal

space: A longitudinal analysis. *Perceptual and Motor Skills, 39,* 735-738. PA 53:9541.

Scott, W. E.; & Cherrington, David J. (1974). Effects of competitive, cooperative, and individualistic reinforcement contingencies. *Journal of Personality and Social Psychology, 30,* 748-758. PA 53:9490.

Scott, William A.; & Cohen, Robert D. (1978). Sociometric indices of group structure. *Australian Journal of Psychology, 30,* 41-57. PA 63:981. SA 821.9796.

Scott, William A.; & Scott, Ruth. (1981). Intercorrelations among structural properties of primary groups. *Journal of Personality and Social Psychology, 41,* 279-292.

Sebba, Rachel; & Churchman, Arza. (1983). Territories and territoriality in the home. *Environment and Behavior, 15,* 191-210. PA 70:4583.

Sechrest, Lee. (1976). Personality. *Annual Review of Psychology, 27,* 1-27.

Seeborg, Irmtraud; Lafollette, William; & Belohlav, James. (1980). An exploratory analysis of effect of sex on shift in choices *Psychological Reports, 46,* 499-504. PA 65:12751.

Seeman, Daniel C. (1982). Leader style and anxiety level: Their relation to autonomic response. *Small Group Behavior, 13,* 192-203.

Segal, Jonathan. (1979). Coalition formation in tetrads: A critical test of four theories. *Journal of Psychology, 103,* 209-219. PA 65:1251. SA 82M1476.

Segal, Jonathan. (1981). Coalition formation and players' incentives. *Journal of Psychology, 107,* 261-266. PA 67:3560. SA 83N2370.

Segal, Mady W. (1974). Alphabet and attraction: An unobtrusive measure of the effect of propinquity in a field setting. *Journal of Personality and Social Psychology, 30,* 654-657. PA 53:7300.

Segal, Mady W. (1977). A reconfirmation of the logarithmic effect of group size. *Social Psychology Quarterly, 40,* 187-190. PA 59:9870. SA 78J1744.

Segal, Mady W. (1979). Varieties of interpersonal attraction and their interrelationships in natural groups. *Social Psychology Quarterly, 42,* 253-261. PA 65:10404. SA 83M7347.

Segal, Uma A. (1982a). The cyclical nature of decision making: An exploratory empirical investigation. *Small Group Behavior, 13,* 333-348. PA 69:05586.

Segal, Uma A. (1982b). Micro-behaviors in group

decision-making: An exploratory study. *Journal of Social Service Research, 5*(1-2), 1-14. PA 70:3402.

Seholm, Kenneth J.; Walker, James L.; & Esser, James K. (1985). A choice of alternative strategies in oligopoly bargaining. *Journal of Applied Social Psychology, 15,* 345-353. PA 72:30796.

Seibold, David R.; & Steinfatt, Thomas M. (1979). The Creative Alternative game: Exploring interpersonal influence processes. *Simulation and Games, 10,* 429-457. PA 66:3621.

Seidner, Constance J.; & Dukes, Richard L. (1976). Simulation in social-psychological research. A methodological approach to the study of attitudes and behavior. *Simulation and Games, 7,* 3-20. PA 57:11501.

Seiler, Marilyn. (1974). Some effects of an imbalance between power and motivation in a cooperative dyad. *Personality and Social Psychology Bulletin, 1,* 219-221. PA 56:2317.

Seldman, Martin L.; McBrearty, John F.; & Seldman, Shari L. (1974). Deification of marathon encounter group leaders. *Small Group Behavior, 5,* 80-91. PA 52:10093.

Seligman, Clive; Bush, Malcolm; & Kirsch, Kenneth. (1976). Relationship between compliance in the foot-in-the-door paradigm and size of first request. *Journal of Personality and Social Psychology, 33,* 517-520. PA 56:6009.

Seligman, Martin E. P. (1975). *Helplessness: On depression, development, and death.* San Francisco: Freeman.

Sell, Jane; & Freese, Lee. (1984). The process of eliminating status generalization. *Social Forces, 63,* 538-554. SA 85O4356.

Selten, Reinhard. (1978). The chain store paradox. *Theory and Decision, 9,* 127-159. PA 63:3261.

Selye, H. (1976). *The stress of life.* 2nd Ed. New York: McGraw-Hill.

Semin, Gun R. (1975). Two studies on polarization. *European Journal of Social Psychology, 5,* 121-131. PA 56:6010.

Semin, Gun R.; & Strack, Fritz. (1980). The plausibility of the implausible: A critique of Snyder and Swann (1978). *European Journal of Social Psychology, 10,* 379-388. PA 66:10362.

Sengupta, Manimay; & Dutta, Bhaskar. (1979). A condition for Nash-stability under binary and democratic group decision functions. *Theory and Decision, 10,* 293-309. SA 80L0098.

Senneker, Phyllis; & Hendrick, Clyde. (1983).

Androgyny and helping behavior. *Journal of Personality and Social Psychology*, 45, 916-925. PA 71:12171.

Serpe, Richard T.; & Stryker, Sheldon. (1987). The construction of self and the reconstruction of social relationships. *Advances in Group Processes*, 4, 41-66.

Seta, John J. (1982). The impact of comparison processes on coactors' task performance. *Journal of Personality and Social Psychology*, 42, 281-291. PA 68:5769.

Seta, John J.; & Schkade, Janette K. (1976). Effects of group size and proximity under cooperative and competitive conditions. *Journal of Personality and Social Psychology*, 34, 47-53. PA 56:6011.

Sevigny, Robert. (1977). Intervention psychosociologique: reflexion critique [Psychological intervention: a critical reflection]. *Sociologie et Societes*, 9(2), 7-33. SA 79J9651.

Shaffer, David R.; & Case, Thomas. (1982). On the decision to testify in one's own behalf: Effects of withheld evidence, defendant's sexual preferences, and juror dogmatism on juridic decisions. *Journal of Personality and Social Psychology*, 42, 335-346. PA 68:5734.

Shaffer, David R.; Case, Thomas; & Brannen, Lanier. (1979). Effects of withheld evidence on juridic decisions: Amount of evidence withheld and its relevance to the case. *Representative Research in Social Psychology*, 10, 2-15. PA 66:1292.

Shaffer, David R.; & Ogden, J. Kirby. (1986). On sex differences in self-disclosure during the acquaintance process: The role of anticipated future interaction. *Journal of Personality and Social Psychology*, 51, 92-101. PA 73:27150.

Shaffer, David R.; Plummer, D.; & Hammock, Georgina (1986). Hath he suffered enough? Effects of jury dogmatism, defendant similarity, and defendant's pretrial suffering on juridic decisions. *Journal of Personality and Social Psychology*, 50, 1059-1067 PA 73:21929.

Shaffer, David R.; & Sadowski, Cyril. (1975). This table is mine: Respect for marked barroom tables as a function of gender or spatial marker and desirability of locale. *Sociometry*, 38, 408-419. PA 54:11722.

Shaffer, David R.; Smith, Jonathan E.; & Tomarelli, Michele. (1982). Self-monitoring as a determinant of self- disclosure reciprocity during the acquaintance process. *Journal of*

Personality and Social Psychology, 43, 163-175. PA 69:3400.

Shaffer, Leigh S. (1978). On the current confusion of group-related behavior and collective behavior: A reaction to Buys. *Personality and Social Psychology Bulletin*, 4, 564-567. PA 64:5573.

Shah, M. A.; & Dembla, Pratibha. (1985). A study of social status as related to territoriality among the adolescents. *Psycho Lingua*, 15(1), 49-63. PA 74:21884.

Shalinsky, William. (1983). One-session meetings: Aggregate or group? *Small Group Behavior*, 14, 495-514. PA 71:23079.

Shambaugh, Philip W. (1978). The development of the small group. *Human Relations*, 31, 283-295. PA 61:10920 SA 79J9652.

Shanab, Mitri E.; & Isonio, Steven A. (1980). The effects of delay upon compliance with socially undesirable requests in the foot-in-the-door paradigm. *Bulletin of the Psychonomic Society*, 15, 76-78. PA 66:2812.

Shanab, Mitri E.; & Isonio, Steven A. (1982). The effects of contrast upon compliance with socially undesirable requests in the foot-in-the-door paradigm. *Bulletin of the Psychonomic Society*, 20, 180-182. PA 69:10419.

Shanab, Mitri E.; & O'Neill, Pamela. (1979). The effects of contrast upon compliance with socially undesirable requests in the door-in-the-face paradigm. *Canadian Journal of Behavioural Sciences/Revue canadienne des sciences du comportement*, 11, 236-244. SA 80K8705.

Shanab, Mitri E.; & O'Neill, Pamela J. (1982). The effects of self-perception and perceptual contrast upon compliance with socially undesirable requests. *Bulletin of the Psychonomic Society*, 19, 279-281. PA 69:10438.

Shanab, Mitri E.; & Yahya, Khawla A. (1977). A behavioral study of obedience in children. *Journal of Personality and Social Psychology*, 35, 530-536.

Shane, Barry. (1979). Open and rigid communication networks: A reevaluation by simulation. *Small Group Behavior*, 10, 242-262. SA 80K8706.

Shapira, Ariella. (1976). Developmental differences in competitive behavior of kibbutz and city children in Israel. *Journal of Social Psychology*, 98, 19-26. PA 56:2171.

Shapiro, Arnold; & Swensen, Clifford H. (1977). Self-disclosure as a function of self-concept and sex. *Journal of Personality Assessment, 41,* 144-149. PA 59:1047.

Shapiro, Rodney J.; & Klein, Robert H. (1975). Perceptions of the leaders in an encounter group. *Small Group Behavior, 6,* 238-248. PA 55:2335.

Sharan, Shlomo. (1984). *Cooperative learning in the classroom: Research in desegregated schools.* Hillsdale, NJ: Earlbaum.

Shaver, Philip. (Ed.). (1985). Self, situations, and social behavior. *Review of personality and social psychology* (Vol. 6). Beverly Hills, CA: Sage.

Shaver, Philip; & Klinnert, Mary. (1982). Schachter's theories of affiliation and emotion: Implications of developmental research. In L. Wheeler (Ed.), *Review of personality and social psychology* (Vol. 3, pp. 37-72). Beverly Hills, CA: Sage.

Shaver, Phillip; & Liebling, Barry A. (1976). Explorations in the drive theory of social facilitation. *Journal of Social Psychology, 99,* 259-271.

Shaw, Jerry I. (1975). Effects of response contingent rewards on cooperative game behavior. *Goteborg Psychological Reports, 5*(26), 15. PA 56:6012.

Shaw, Jerry I. (1976). Response-contingent payoffs and cooperative behavior in the Prisoner's Dilemma Game. *Journal of Personality and Social Psychology, 34,* 1024-1033.

Shaw, Jerry I.; & Thorslund, Christer. (1973). Effects of varying patterns of rewards on cooperation in a Prisoner's Dilemma game. *Goteborg Psychological Reports, 3*(5), 14. PA 52:10041.

Shaw, Jerry I.; & Thorslund, Christer. (1975). Varying patterns of reward cooperation: The effects in a Prisoner's Dilemma game. *Journal of Conflict Resolution, 19,* 108-122. PA 54:5214.

Shaw, Marvin E. (1981). *Group dynamics: The psychology of small group behavior* (3rd ed.). New York: McGraw-Hill.

Shaw, Marvin E.; Ackerman, Bette; McCown, Nancy E.; Worsham, Annette Pearce; Haugh, Larry D.; Gebhardt, Bryan M.; & Small, Parker A., Jr. (1979). Interaction patterns and facilitation of peer learning. *Small Group Behavior, 10,* 214-223. SA 80K8707.

Shaw, Marvin E.; & Ashton, Nancy. (1976). Do assembly bonus effects occur on disjunctive tasks? A test of Steiner's theory. *Bulletin of the Psychonomic Society, 8,* 469-471. PA 58:1121.

Shaw, Marvin E.; & Harkey, Blaze. (1976). Some effects of congruency of member characteristics and group structure upon group behavior. *Journal of Personality and Social Psychology, 34,* 412-418.

Shaw, Marvin E.; & Small, Parker A., Jr. (1981). Interaction patterns and facilitation of peer learning: Two replications. *Small Group Behavior, 12,* 233-240.

Shaw, Marvin E.; & Wagner, Peggy J. (1975). Role selection in the service of self-presentation. *Memory and Cognition, 3,* 481-484. PA 54:11723.

Shaw, Marvin E.; & Webb, Jeaninne N. (1982). When compatibility interferes with group effectiveness. *Small Group Behavior, 13,* 555-564. PA 70:5638.

Shea, Gregory P. (1980). The study of bargaining and conflict behavior: Broadening the conceptual arena. *Journal of Conflict Resolution, 24,* 706-741. [Review of five books.]

Shea, Marilyn; & Rosenfeld, Howard M. (1976). Functional employment of nonverbal social reinforcers in dyadic learning. *Journal of Personality and Social Psychology, 34,* 228-239. PA 56:7928.

Sheehan, Joseph J. (1979). Conformity prior to the emergence of a group norm. *Journal of Psychology, 102,* 121-127. PA 65:1352.

Sheehan, Peter W.; & Marsh, M. C. (1974). Demonstration of the effect of "faking subjects' knowledge that others are aware of their pretense" on perception of role-playing performance: A methodological comment. *International Journal of Clinical and Experimental Hypnosis, 22*(1), 62-67. PA 52:5260.

Sheikh, Anees A.; & Koch, Richard J. (1977). Recall of group tasks as a function of group cohesiveness and interruption of tasks. *Psychological Reports, 40,* 275-278. PA 58:5339.

Shelby, Bo; Heberlein, Thomas A.; Vaske, Jerry J.; & Alfano, Geraldine. (1983). Expectations, preferences, and feeling crowded in recreation activities. *Leisure Sciences, 6,* 1-14. PA 71:25857.

Sheley, Kathy; & Shaw, Marvin E. (1979). Social power: To use or not to use? *Bulletin of the Psychonomic Society, 13,* 257-260. PA 64:10344.

Sheppard, Blair H.; Saunders, David M.; &

Minton, John W. (1988). Procedural justice from the third-party perspective. *Journal of Personality and Social Psychology, 54*, 629–637.

Sheppard, Blair H.; & Vidmar, Neil. (1980). Adversary pretrial procedures and testimonial evidence: Effects of lawyer's role and Machiavellianism. *Journal of Personality and Social Psychology, 39*, 320–332.

Sherif, Muzafer. (1935). A study of some social factors in perception. *Archives of Psychology, 27*, No. 187, 1–60.

Sherman, Steven J. (1983). Expectation-based and automatic behavior: A comment on Lee and Ofshe, and Berger and Zelditch. *Social Psychology Quarterly, 46*, 66–70. PA 70:10256.

Sherman, Thomas M.; & Smith, Brenda V. (1976). Application of behavioral technology to small group discussion with university students. *Instructional Science, 5*(1), 93–105. PA 55:13241.

Sherrod, Drury R. (1974). Crowding, perceived control, and behavioral aftereffects. *Journal of Applied Social Psychology, 4*, 171–186. PA 53:2989.

Sherrod, Drury R.; & Downs, Robin. (1974a). Environmental determinants of altruism: The effects of stimulus overload and perceived control on helping. *Journal of Experimental Social Psychology, 10*, 468–479. PA 53:3044.

Sherrod, Drury R.; & Downs, Robin. (1974b). Environmental determinants of altruism: Stimulus overload, perceived control, and helping. *Personality and Social Psychology Bulletin, 1*, 180–182. PA 56:2385.

Sherwin, Ronald G. (1975). Structural balance and the sociomatrix: Finding triadic valence structures in signed adjacency matrices. *Human Relations, 28*, 175–189. PA 54:11659.

Shiflett, Samuel. (1976). Dyadic performance on two tasks as a function of task difficulty, work strategy, and member ability. *Journal of Applied Psychology, 61*, 455–462. PA 56:9844.

Shiflett, Samuel. (1979a). Temporal changes in the prediction of group performance. *Journal of Social Psychology, 108*, 185–191. PA 65:1253.

Shiflett, Samuel. (1979b). Toward a general model of small group productivity. *Psychological Bulletin, 86*, 67–79. PA 62:10985.

Shimizu, Jun. (1973). [Group-members' behaviors caused by their judgments between the group goal and their outputs]. *Japanese Journal of Experimental Social Psychology, 13*, 141–147. PA 54:5215.

Shindelman, Harvey. (1980). Demonstration of coalition formation. *International Journal of Group Tensions, 10*, 153–178. PA 71:1328.

Shinohara, Hirofumi; & Misumi, Jyuji. (1977). [A study of the group process of the PM-sensitivity development program: In relation to the meeting attractiveness and the cognitive discrepancy between self-rating and rating-by-others on discussion group]. *Japanese Journal of Experimental Social Psychology, 16*, 136–154. PA 64:10345.

Shiota, Yoshihisa; et al. (1974). [A study of group problem-solving: The effects of grouping method and problem-solving strategy]. *Bulletin of the Faculty of Education, U. Nagoya, 21*, 169–191. PA 58:10435.

Shirakashi, Sanshiro. (1984). Social loafing of Japanese students. *Hiroshima Forum for Psychology, 10*, 35–40. PA 74:21886.

Shirakashi, Sanshiro; & Yoshida, Michio. (1975). The effects of success vs. failure and leader's LPC on member reactions. *Psychologia An International Journal of Psychology in the Orient, 18*, 22–29. PA 55:2354.

Short, J. A. (1974). Effects of medium of communication on experimental negotiation. *Human Relations, 27*, 225–234. PA 54:6451.

Short, James F.; & Strodtbeck, Fred L. (1974). *Group process and gang delinquency* (4th impression with new preface and bibliography). Chicago: University of Chicago Press.

Shotland, R. Lance; & Heinold, William D. (1985). Bystander response to arterial bleeding: Helping skills, the decision-making process, and differentiating the helping response. *Journal of Personality and Social Psychology, 49*, 347–356. PA 73:1156.

Shotland, R. Lance; & Huston, Ted L. (1979). Emergencies: What are they and do they influence bystanders to intervene? *Journal of Personality and Social Psychology, 37*, 1822–1834. PA 65:1287.

Shotland, R. Lance; & Straw, Margaret K. (1976). Bystander response to an assault: When a man attacks a woman. *Journal of Personality and Social Psychology, 34*, 990–999. PA 57:10327.

Shrivastava, R. S. (1973). Formation and functioning of friendship groups: A sociological study among prison inmates. *Sociological Bulletin, 22*(1), 98–111. SA 74G7448.

Shrout, Patrick E.; & Fiske, Donald W. (1981). Nonverbal behaviors and social evaluation.

Journal of Personality, 49, 115–128. SA 82M1477.

Shubik, Martin. (1986). Cooperative game solutions: Australian, Indian, and U.S. opinions. *Journal of Conflict Resolution, 30*, 63–76. PA 73:24492.

Shubik, Martin; Wolf, Gerrit; & Poon, Byron. (1974). Perception of payoff structure and opponent's behavior in related matrix games. *Journal of Conflict Resolution, 18*, 646–655. PA 53:9491.

Shulghina, B. A. (1974). [Some characteristics of the acceptance by school children of a peer's opinion in a conflict situation]. *Voprosy Psikhologii*, No. 2, 145–149. PA 53.9544.

Shumaker, Sally A.; & Brownell, Arlene. (1984). Toward a theory of social support: Closing conceptual gaps. *Journal of Social Issues, 40*(4), 11–36. PA 72:30799.

Shuter, Robert. (1976). Proxemics and tactility in Latin America. *Journal of Communication, 26*(3), 46–52.

Shuter, Robert. (1982). Initial interaction of American Blacks and Whites in interracial and intraracial dyads. *Journal of Social Psychology, 117*, 45–52. PA 69:3401.

Sieber, Sam D. (1974). Toward a theory of role accumulation. *American Sociological Review, 39*, 567–578. PA 53:1104.

Siegel, Jane; Dubrovsky, Vitaly; Kiesler, Sara; & McGuire, Timothy W. (1986). Group processes in computer-mediated communication. *Organizational Behavior and Human Decision Processes, 37*, 157–187. PA 73:19807.

Siegel, Judith M.; & Mitchell, Herman E. (1979). The influence of expectancy violations, sex, and authoritarianism on simulated trial outcomes. *Representative Research in Social Psychology, 10*, 37–47. PA 66:1215.

Siegel, Judith M.; & Steele, Claude M. (1980). Environmental distraction and interpersonal judgments. *British Journal of Social and Clinical Psychology, 19*, 23–32. PA 65:7974.

Siegman, Aron W. (1976). Do noncontingent interview mm-hmms facilitate interviewee productivity? *Journal of Consulting and Clinical Psychology, 44*, 171–182. PA 56:9845.

Siegman, Aron W. (1978). The telltale voice: Nonverbal messages of verbal communication. In A. W. Siegman & S. Feldstein (Eds.), *Nonverbal behavior and communication* (pp. 183–243). Hillsdale, NJ: Erlbaum.

Siegman, Aron W.; & Feldstein, Stanley. (Eds.). (1978). *Nonverbal behavior and communication*. Hillsdale, NJ: Erlbaum.

Siegman, Aron W.; & Feldstein, Stanley. (1979). *Of speech and time: Temporal speech patterns in interpersonal contexts*. Hillsdale, NJ: Erlbaum.

Siegman, Aron W.; & Reynolds, Mark A. (1983a). Effects of mutual invisibility and topical intimacy on verbal fluency in dyadic communication. *Journal of Psycholinguistic Research, 12*, 443–455. PA 71:14971.

Siegman, Aron W.; & Reynolds, Mark A. (1983b). Self-monitoring and speech in feigned and unfeigned lying. *Journal of Personality and Social Psychology, 45*, 1325–1333. PA 71:15076.

Siegman, Aron W.; & Reynolds, Mark A. (1984). The facilitating effects of interviewer rapport and the paralinguistics of intimate communications. *Journal of Social and Clinical Psychology, 2*, 71–88. PA 72:12009.

Siem, Frederick M.; & Spence, Janet T. (1986). Gender-related traits and helping behaviors. *Journal of Personality and Social Psychology, 51*, 615–621. PA 74:1101.

Sievers, Walter; & Langthaler, Werner U. (1974). [Analysis of polylogue conversation sequences]. *Zeitschrift für Experimentelle und Angewandte Psychologie, 21*, 299–325. PA 53:7301.

Sigman, Stuart J. (1984). Talk and interaction strategy in a task oriented group. *Small Group Behavior, 15*, 33–50. PA 71:28631. DA 85O6032.

Sigman, Stuart J. (1987). *A perspective on social communication*. Lexington, Mass.: D. C. Heath and Co.

Sillars, Alan L. (1980). Attributions and communication in roommate conflicts. *Communication Monographs, 47*, 180–200. PA 66:5774.

Sillars, Alan [L.]; & Parry, Doug. (1982). Stress, cognition, and communication in interpersonal conflicts. *Communication Research, 9*, 201–226. PA 68:10335.

Sillars, Alan L.; & Scott, Michael D. (1983). Interpersonal perception between intimates: An integrative review. *Human Communication Research, 10*, 153–176. PA 71:14972.

Silver, Steven D.; Cohen, Bernard P.; & Rainwater, Julie. (1988). Group structure and information exchange in innovative problem solving. *Advances in Group Processes, 5*, 169–194.

Silverstein, C. Harris; & Stang, David J. (1976). Seating position and interaction in triads: A field study. *Sociometry, 39,* 166–170. PA 56:7929. SA 76I1695.

Silzer, Robert F.; & Clark, Russell D., III. (1977). The effects of proportion, strength and value orientation of arguments on decision-making. *European Journal of Social Psychology, 7,* 451–464. SA 79J6856.

Simkin, David K.; Lederer, Jan P.; & Seligman, Martin E. (1983). Learned helplessness in groups. *Behaviour Research & Therapy, 21,* 613–622. PA 71:12172.

Simmons, Carolyn H.; King, Cheryl Simrell; Tucker, Suzette Settle; & Wehner, Elizabeth A. (1986). Success strategies: Winning through cooperation or competition. *Journal of Social Psychology, 126,* 437–444.

Simon, Armando. (1976). Chivalry on the road: Helping stalled drivers. *Psychological Reports, 39,* 883–886. PA 58:1188.

Simon, Gerald; Langmeyer, Daniel; & Boyer, Ronald K. (1974). Perceptual style as a determinant in the solution of a group task. *Personality and Social Psychology Bulletin, 1,* 252–255. PA 56:2318.

Simon, Rita J. (1974). An assessment of racial awareness, preference, and self identity among white and adopted non-white children. *Social Problems, 22*(1), 43–57. PA 54:9454.

Simonton, Dean K. (1985). Intelligence and personal influence in groups: Four nonlinear models. *Psychological Review, 92,* 532–547. PA 73:14442.

Simpson, Douglas B.; & Punwani, Prem A. (1975). The effect of risk and pressure on coalition behavior in a triadic situation. *Behavioral Science, 20,* 174–178. PA 54:9579. SA 76I0643.

Sims, Henry P.; & Manz, Charles C. (1984). Observing leader behavior: Toward reciprocal determinism in leadership theory. *Journal of Applied Psychology, 69,* 222–232. PA 71:23080.

Singer, David L.; Astrachan, Boris M.; Gould, Laurence J.; & Klein, Edward B. (1975). Boundary management in psychological work with groups. *Journal of Applied Behavioral Science, 11,* 137–176. PA 54:7482. SA 77I4659.

Singh, Ramadhar. (1983). Leadership style and reward allocation: Does Least Preferred Coworker scale measure task and relation orientation? *Organizational Behavior and Human Performance, 32,* 178–197. PA 71:5441.

Singleton, Royce. (1979). Another look at the conformity explanation of group-induced shifts in choice. *Human Relations, 32,* 37–56. PA 63:11958.

Sinha, T. N.; & Sinha, Jai B. (1977). Styles of leadership and their effects on group productivity. *Indian Journal of Industrial Relations, 13*(2), 209–223. PA 62:1069.

Sipek, Jiri. (1974). [Soviet social psychological research into the relationship of individuals and small groups]. *Ceskoslovenska Psychologie, 18,* 391–400. PA 64:5575.

Siperstein, Gary N.; Bak, John J.; & Gottlieb, Jay. (1977). Effects of group discussion on children's attitudes toward handicapped peers. *Journal of Educational Research, 70,* 131–134, PA 58:3349.

Sissons, Mary. (1981). Race, sex and helping behaviour. *British Journal of Social Psychology, 20,* 285–292.

Sistrunk, Frank; & McDavid, John W. (1971). Sex variable in conforming behavior. *Journal of Personality and Social Psychology, 17,* 200–207.

Six, Bernd; Martin, Peter; & Pecher, Monika. (1983). A cultural comparison of perceived crowding and discomfort: The United States and West Germany. *Journal of Psychology, 114,* 63–67. SA 84N7297.

Skolnick, Paul. (1977). Helping as a function of time of day, location, and sex of victim. *Journal of Social Psychology, 102,* 61–62. PA 59:7859.

Skolnick, Paul; Frasier, Lana; & Hadar, Ilana. (1977). Do you speak to strangers? A study of invasions of personal space. *European Journal of Social Psychology, 7,* 375–381. PA 60:07444.

Skotko, Vincent P.; & Langmeyer, Daniel. (1977). The effects of interaction distance and gender on self-disclosure in the dyad. *Social Psychology Quarterly, 40,* 178–182. PA 59:9871. SA 78J1746.

Skotko, Vincent; Langmeyer, Daniel; & Lundgren, David. (1974). Sex differences as artifact in the Prisoner's Dilemma game. *Journal of Conflict Resolution, 18,* 707–713. PA 53:9545.

Skvoretz, John. (1981). Extending expectation states theory: Comparative status models of participation in N person groups. *Social Forces, 59,* 752–770. SA 81L8141.

Skvoretz, John. (1988). Models of participation in status-differentiated groups. *Social Psychology Quarterly, 51,* 43–57.

Slavin, Robert E. (1975). *Classroom reward structure: An analytical and practical review.* Center for Social Organization of Schools Report, Johns Hopkins University, No. 207, 25 pages. PA 55:10948.

Slavin, Robert E. (1977). How student learning teams can integrate the desegregated classroom. *Integrated Education,* 15(6), 56–58.

Slavin, Robert E. (1985). Cooperative learning: Applying contact theory in desegregated schools. *Journal of Social Issues,* 41(3), 45–62.

Slavin, Robert; Sharan, Shlomo; Kagan, Spencer; Hertz-Lazarowitz, Rachel; Webb, Clark; & Schmuck, Richard. (Eds.). (1985). *Learning to cooperate, cooperating to learn.* New York: Plenum.

Slepicka, P. (1975). Interpersonal behaviour and sports group effectiveness. *International Journal of Sport Psychology,* 6, 14–27. PA 55:2336.

Sloan, William W.; & Solano, Cecilia H. (1984). The conversational styles of lonely males with strangers and roommates. *Personality and Social Psychology Bulletin,* 10, 293–301. PA 72:17324.

Slugoski, Ben R.; Marcia, James E.; & Koopman, Raymond F. (1984). Cognitive and social interactional characteristics of ego identity statuses in college males. *Journal of Personality and Social Psychology,* 47, 646–661.

Slusher, E. Allen. (1978). Counterpart strategy, prior relations, and constituent pressure in a bargaining simulation. *Behavioral Science,* 23, 470–477. PA 63:9643. SA 80K4187.

Slusher, E. Allen; Rose, Gerald L.; & Roering, Kenneth J. (1978). Commitment to future interaction and relative power under conditions of interdependence. *Journal of Conflict Resolution,* 22, 282–298. PA 62:10986.

Small Group Behavior. (1987). 18(3 and 4), 291–367, 443–547. [Special "theme section" on "Research on outcomes of sensitivity training groups."]

Smedley, Joseph W.; & Bayton, James A. (1978). Evaluative race-class stereotypes by race and perceived class of subjects. *Journal of Personality and Social Psychology,* 36, 530–535. PA 61:13432.

Smetana, J.; Bridgeman, D. L.; & Bridgeman, B. (1978). A field study of interpersonal distance in early childhood. *Personality and Social Psychology Bulletin,* 4, 309–313.

Smith, Althea. (1983). Nonverbal communication among Black female dyads: An assessment of intimacy, gender, and race. *Journal of Social Issues,* 39(3), 55–67. PA 71:12173. SA 84O0838.

Smith, D. Leasel; Pruitt, Dean G.; & Carnevale, Peter J. (1982). Matching and mismatching: The effect of own limit, other's toughness, and time pressure on concession rate in negotiation. *Journal of Personality and Social Psychology,* 42, 876–883. PA 68:12624.

Smith, David E.; Willis, Frank N.; & Gier, Joseph A. (1980). Success and interpersonal touch in a competitive setting. *Journal of Nonverbal Behavior,* 5, 26–34. PA 65:12752.

Smith, Eliot R.; & Miller, Frederick D. (1983). Mediation among attributional inferences and comprehension processes: Initial findings and a general method. *Journal of Personality and Social Psychology,* 44, 492–505. PA 70:10277.

Smith, Frank J.; & Lawrence, John E. (1978). Alone and crowded: The effects of spatial restriction on measures of affect and simulation response. *Personality and Social Psychology Bulletin,* 4, 139–142. PA 61:5940.

Smith, H. W. (1981). Territorial spacing on a beach revisited: A cross-national exploration. *Social Psychology Quarterly,* 44, 132–137. SA 83N2371.

Smith, H. Wayne; & George, Clay E. (1980). Gender effects in two gender-oriented appointed leader situations. *Catalog of Selected Documents in Psychology,* 10, 58–59. [MS. 2072]. PA 66:5721.

Smith, Herman W. (1977). Small group interaction at various ages: Simultaneous talking and interruptions of others. *Small Group Behavior,* 8, 65–74. PA 60:7445. SA 78J0174.

Smith, J. L. (1975). A games analysis for attitude change: Use of role enactment situations for model development. *Journal for the Theory of Social Behaviour,* 5, 63–79. PA 55:2356.

Smith, Karl; Johnson, David W.; & Johnson, Roger T. (1981). Can conflict be constructive? Controversy versus concurrence seeking in learning groups. *Journal of Educational Psychology,* 73, 651–663.

Smith, Karl A.; Johnson, David W.; & Johnson, Roger T. (1984). Effects of controversy on learning in cooperative groups. *Journal of Psychology,* 122, 199–209.

Smith, Karl A.; Petersen, Renee P.; Johnson, David W.; & Johnson, Roger T. (1986). The effects of controversy and concurrence seeking on effective decision making. *Journal of Social Psychology, 126*, 237–248. PA 74:25058.

Smith, Kenwyn K.; & Berg, David N. (1987a). *Paradoxes of group life: Understanding conflict, paralysis, and movement in group dynamics*. San Francisco: Jossey-Bass.

Smith, Kenwyn K.; & Berg, David N. (1987b). A paradoxical conception of group dynamics. *Human Relations, 40*, 633–658.

Smith, Kenwyn K.; & White, Gregory L. (1983). Some alternatives to traditional social psychology of groups. *Personality and Social Psychology Bulletin, 9*, 65–73. PA 70:12651.

Smith, Mary J.; Reinheimer, Robert E.; & Gabbard-Alley, Anne. (1981). Crowding, task performance, and communicative interaction in youth and old age. *Human Communication Research, 7*, 259–272. PA 67:3563. SA 82M5654.

Smith, Nancy S.; Vernon, Charles R.; & Tarte, Robert D. (1975). Random strategies and sex differences in the Prisoner's Dilemma game. *Journal of Conflict Resolution, 19*, 643–658. PA 56:7930.

Smith, Peter B. (1974). Group composition as a determinant of Kelman's social influence modes. *European Journal of Social Psychology, 4*, 261–277. PA 54:5216. SA 75H4717.

Smith, Peter B. (1975). Controlled studies of the outcome of sensitivity training. *Psychological Bulletin, 82*, 597–622.

Smith, Peter B. (1976a). Social influence processes and the outcome of sensitivity training. *Journal of Personality and Social Psychology, 34*, 1087–1094. PA 60:12157.

Smith, Peter B. (1976b). Sources of influence in the sensitivity training laboratory. *Small Group Behavior, 7*, 331–348. SA 77I8737.

Smith, Peter B. (Ed.). (1980). *Small groups and personal change*. London: Methuen.

Smith, Peter B. (1983). Back-home environment and within-group relationships as determinants of personal change. *Human Relations, 36*, 53–68.

Smith, Peter B.; & Peterson, Mark F. (1988). *Leadership, organizations and culture: An event management model*. London: Sage.

Smith, Robert C.; Parker, Elizabeth S.; & Noble, Ernest P. (1975). Alcohol and affect in dyadic social interaction. *Psychosomatic Medicine, 37*, 25–40. PA 54:2569.

Smith, Robert J.; & Knowles, Eric S. (1978).

Attributional consequences of personal space invasions. *Personality and Social Psychology Bulletin, 4*, 429–433.

Smith, Robert J.; & Knowles, Eric S. (1979). Affective and cognitive mediators of reactions to spatial invasions. *Journal of Experimental Social Psychology, 15*, 437–452. PA 64:12437.

Smith, William P. (1987). Conflict and negotiation: Trends and emerging issues. *Journal of Applied Social Psychology, 17*, 641–677.

Smith, William P.; & Anderson, A. James. (1975). Threats, communication, and bargaining. *Journal of Personality and Social Psychology, 32*, 76–82. PA 54:7535.

Smith-Lovin, Lynn; Skvoretz, John V.; & Hudson, Charlotte G. (1986). Status and participation in six-person groups: A test of Skvoretz's comparative status model. *Social Forces, 64*, 992–1005. PA 74:15534.

Smithson, Michael; Amato, Paul R.; & Pearce, Philip. (1983). *Dimensions of helping behavior*. Oxford, England: Pergamon.

Smuts, Barbara B.; Cheney, Dorothy L.; Seyfarth, Robert M.; Wrangham, Richard W.; & Struhsaker, Thomas T. (Eds.). (1987 [copyright 1986]). *Primate societies*. Chicago: University of Chicago Press.

Snapka, Petr. (1976). [A contribution to the model of unification of views on problem solving in a group in relation to the decision-making process]. *Sociologicky Casopis, 12*(2), 176–189. PA 58:7474.

Snodgrass, Sara E. (1985). Women's intuition: The effect of subordinate role on interpersonal sensitivity. *Journal of Personality and Social Psychology, 49*, 146–155. PA 72:30800.

Snodgrass, Sara E.; & Rosenthal, Robert. (1984). Females in charge: Effects of sex of subordinate and romantic attachment status upon self-ratings of dominance. *Journal of Personality, 52*, 355–371. SA 86Q3163.

Snortum, John R.; Klein, Jeff S.; & Sherman, Wynn A. (1976). The impact of an aggressive juror in six- and twelve-member juries. *Criminal Justice and Behavior, 3*(3), 255–262. PA 57:5714.

Snow, Robert P.; & Brissett, Dennis. (1986). Pauses: Explorations in social rhythm. *Symbolic Interaction, 9*, 1–18. PA 74:25060.

Snyder, C. R.; Lassegard, MaryAnne; & Ford, Carol E. (1986). Distancing after group success and failure: Basking in reflected glory and cutting off reflected failure. *Journal of Personality and Social Psychology*, *51*, 382–388. PA 73:29969.

Snyder, C. R.; & Newburg, Cheryl L. (1981). The Barnum effect in a group setting. *Journal of Personality Assessment*, *45*, 622–629. PA 67:7710.

Snyder, Mark. (1974). Self-monitoring of expressive behavior. *Journal of Personality and Social Psychology*, *30*, 526–537.

Snyder, Mark. (1979). Self-monitoring processes. *Advances in Experimental Social Psychology*, *12*, 85–128.

Snyder, Mark. (1983). The influence of individuals on situations: Implications for understanding the links between personality and social behavior. *Journal of Personality*, *51*, 497–516. PA 71:12294.

Snyder, Mark. (1984). When belief creates reality. *Advances in Experimental Social Psychology*, *18*, 247–305.

Snyder, Mark; Berscheid, Ellen; & Glick, Peter. (1985). Focusing on the exterior and the interior. Two investigations of the initiation of personal relationships. *Journal of Personality and Social Psychology*, *48*, 1427–1439. PA 72:28053.

Snyder, Mark; & Campbell, Bruce. (1980). Testing hypotheses about other people: The role of the hypothesis. *Personality and Social Psychology Bulletin*, *6*, 421–426. PA 66:5829.

Snyder, Mark; & Cunningham, Michael R. (1975). To comply or not comply: Testing the self-perception explanation of the "foot-in-the-door" phenomenon. *Journal of Personality and Social Psychology*, *31*, 64–67. PA 53:9546.

Snyder, Mark; & Gangestad, Steven. (1982). Choosing social situations: Two investigations of self-monitoring processes. *Journal of Personality and Social Psychology*, *43*, 123–135. PA 69:3402.

Snyder, Mark; & Gangestad, Steve. (1986). On the nature of self-monitoring: Matters of assessment, matters of validity. *Journal of Personality and Social Psychology*, *51*, 125–139. PA 73:26250.

Snyder, Mark; Gangestad, Steve; & Simpson, Jeffry A. (1983). Choosing friends as activity partners: The role of self-monitoring. *Journal of Personality and Social Psychology*, *45*, 1061–1072. PA 71:12174.

Snyder, Mark; & Monson, Thomas C. (1975).

Persons, situations, and the control of social behavior. *Journal of Personality and Social Psychology*, *32*, 637–644. PA 56:699.

Snyder, Mark; & Simpson, Jeffry A. (1984). Self-monitoring and dating relationships. *Journal of Personality and Social Psychology*, *47*, 1281–1291. PA 72:12011.

Snyder, Mark; & Swann, William, B., Jr. (1978a) Behavioral confirmation in social interaction: From social perception to social reality. *Journal of Experimental Social Psychology*, *14*, 148–162. PA 61:1038.

Snyder, Mark; & Swann, William, B., Jr. (1978b) Hypothesis-testing processes in social interaction. *Journal of Personality and Social Psychology*, *36*, 1202–1212. PA 63:9663.

Snyder, Mark; Tanke, Elizabeth D.; & Berscheid, Ellen. (1977). Social perception and interpersonal behavior: On the self-fulfilling nature of social stereotypes. *Journal of Personality and Social Psychology*, *35*, 656–666. PA 62:6014.

Snyder, Mark; & White, Phyllis. (1981). Testing hypotheses about other people: Strategies of verification and falsification. *Personality and Social Psychology Bulletin*, *7*, 39–43. PA 67:3694.

Snyder, Melvin L. (1976). The inverse relationship between restaurant party size and tip percentage: Diffusion of responsibility or equity? *Personality and Social Psychology Bulletin*, *2*, 308.

Sobel, Robert S.; & Lillith, Nancy. (1975). Determinants of nonstationary personal space invasion. *Journal of Social Psychology*, *97*, 39–45. PA 55:7094.

Soble, Sharon L.; & Strickland, Lloyd H. (1974). Physical stigma, interaction, and compliance. *Bulletin of the Psychonomic Society*, *4*(2-B), 130–132. PA 53:3003.

Sodikoff, Charles L.; Firestone, Ira J.; & Kaplan, Kalman J. (1974). Distance matching and distance equilibrium in the interview dyad. *Personality and Social Psychology Bulletin*, *1*, 243–245. PA 56:2389.

Sohn, David. (1980). Critique of Cooper's meta-analytic assessment of the findings on sex differences in conformity behavior. *Journal of Personality and Social Psychology*, *39*, 1215–1221. PA 66:5722.

Solano, Cecilia H.; & Dunham, Mina. (1985). Two's company: Self-disclosure and reciprocity in triads versus dyads. *Social Psychology Quarterly*, *48*, 183–187. PA 73:14443. SA 85Q1242.

Solem, Allen R. (1976). The effect of situational vs. behavioral problem statements on solution quality. *Human Relations*, *29*, 249–255. PA 58:3302.

Solomon, George T.; & Winslow, Erik K. (Eds.). (1983). *Group dynamics: An annotated bibliography*. Washington, DC: George Washington University (Department of Management Science).

Solomon, Linda Z.; Solomon, Henry; & Maiorca, Joseph. (1982). The effects of bystander's anonymity, situational ambiguity, and victim's status on helping. *Journal of Social Psychology*, *117*, 285–294. PA 69:5587.

Solomon, Linda Z.; Solomon, Henry; & Stone, Ronald. (1978). Helping as a function of number of bystanders and ambiguity of emergency. *Personality and Social Psychology Bulletin*, *4*, 318–321. PA 64:5576.

Solomon, Manson J. (1981). Dimensions of interpersonal behavior: A convergent validation within a cognitive interactionist framework. *Journal of Personality*, *49*, 15–26. PA 67:1246.

Solomon, Warren E. (1982). *SASP Newsletter*, *8*(6), p. 24. [Review of Gergen, Greenberg, & Willis, 1980.]

Sommer, Robert. (1959). Studies in personal space. *Sociometry*, *22*, 247–260.

Sommer, Robert. (1962). The distance for comfortable conversation: A further study. *Sociometry*, *25*, 111–116.

Sommer, Robert. (1969). *Personal space: The behavioral basis of design*. Englewood Cliffs, NJ: Prentice-Hall.

Sommer, Robert. (1974). *Tight spaces: Hard architecture and how to humanize it*. Englewood Cliffs, NJ: Prentice-Hall.

Sommer, Robert. (1982). The district attorney's dilemma: Experimental games and the real world of plea bargaining. *American Psychologist*, *37*, 526–532.

Sommer, Robert. (1983). *Social Design: Creating Buildings with People in Mind*. Englewood Cliffs, NJ: Prentice-Hall.

Sommers, Shula. (1984). Social cognition and interpersonal affect: Correlates of role-taking skills in young adulthood. *Journal of Genetic Psychology*, *144*, 233–239. PA 71:25859.

Soper, W. Barlow; & Karasik, Russell. (1977). Use of spatial cues with regard to the invasion of group space. *Psychological Reports*, *40*, 1175–1178. PA 59:9872.

Sorensen, Gail; & McCroskey, James C. (1977). The prediction of interaction behavior in small groups: Zero history vs intact groups. *Communication Monographs*, *44*, 73–80. PA 59:7885. SA 79K2638.

Sorrels, J. Paul; & Kelley, Jeanette. (1984). Conformity by omission. *Personality and Social Psychology Bulletin*, *10*, 302–305. PA 72:17325.

Sorrels, J. Paul; & Myers, Bettye. (1983). Comparison of group and family dynamics. *Human Relations*, *36*, 477–492. PA 70:10258.

Sorrentino, Richard M.; & Boutillier, Robert G. (1975). The effect of quantity and quality of verbal interaction on ratings of leadership ability. *Journal of Experimental Social Psychology*, *11*, 403–411. PA 55:4575.

Sorrentino, Richard M.; & Field, Nigel. (1986). Emergent leadership over time: The functional value of positive motivation. *Journal of Personality and Social Psychology*, *50*, 1091–1099. PA 73:24526.

Sorrentino, Richard M.; King, Gillian; & Leo, Gloria. (1980). The influence of the minority on perception: A note on a possible alternative explanation. *Journal of Experimental Social Psychology*, *16*, 293–301. PA 65:12730.

Sorrentino, Richard M.; & Sheppard, Blair H. (1978). Effects of affiliation-related motives on swimmers in individual versus group competition: A field experiment. *Journal of Personality and Social Psychology*, *36*, 704–714. PA 63:993.

Sosnowski, Tytus. (1978). Reactivity, level of stimulation, and some features of verbal behavior in small, task-oriented groups. *Polish Psychological Bulletin*, *9*, 129–137. PA 64:3260.

Sossin, K. Mark; Esser, Aristide H.; & Deutsch, Robert D. (1978). Ethological studies of spatial and dominance behavior of female adolescents in residence. *Man-Environment Systems*, *8*(1), 43–48. SA 81L4936.

Spector, Bertram I. (1977). Negotiation as a psychological process. *Journal of Conflict Resolution*, *21*, 607–618. PA 61:3554.

Spector, Paul E.; Cohen, Stephen L.; & Penner, Louis A. (1976). The effects of real vs. hypothetical risk on group choice-shifts. *Personality and Social Psychology Bulletin*, *2*, 290–293.

Spector, Paul E.; & Sistrunk, Frank. (1978). Does the presence of others reduce anxiety? *Journal of Social Psychology*, *105*, 301–302. PA 63:5436.

Spector, Paul E.; & Sistrunk, F[rank] (1979).

Reassurance—mechanism by which the presence of others reduces anxiety. *Journal of Social Psychology*, *109*, 119–126.

Spence, Janet T.; Deaux, Kay; & Helmreich, Robert L. (1985). Sex roles in contemporary American society. In G. Lindzey and E. Aronson (Eds.), *Handbook of social psychology* (3rd ed., Vol. 1, pp. 149–177). New York: Random House.

Spence, Janet T.; & Helmreich, Robert L. (1978). *Masculinity and femininity: Their psychological dimensions, correlates and antecedents*. Austin: University of Texas Press.

Spencer, Christopher; Williams, Marylin; & Oldfield-Box, Hilary. (1974). Age, group decisions on risk-related topics and the prediction of choice shifts. *British Journal of Social and Clinical Psychology*, *13*, 375–381. PA 53:7335.

Spich, Robert S.; & Keleman, Kenneth. (1985). Explicit norm structuring process: A strategy for increasing task-group effectiveness. *Group and Organization Studies*, *10*, 37–59. PA 72:30801.

Spillane, Robert. (1983). Authority in small groups: A laboratory test of a Machiavellian observation. *British Journal of Social Psychology*, *22*, 51–59. PA 70:12653. SA 84O0839.

Spillman, Bonnie; Spillman, Richard; & Reinking, Kim. (1981). Leadership emergence-dynamic analysis of the effects of sex and androgyny. *Small Group Behavior*, *12*, 139–157. SA 82M4120.

Spindler, Z. A. (1976, Winter). Endogenous bargaining power and the theory of small group collective choice. *Public Choice*, *28*, 67–78. SA 78J0175.

Spitzo, Craig E.; & Davis, James H. (1978). Mutual social influence in dynamic groups. *Social Psychology*, *41*, 24–33. PA 64:5578. SA 79J6857.

Spitzer, Dean R. (1975a). Effect of group discussion on teachers' attitudes toward risk taking in educational situations. *Journal of Educational Research*, *68*, 371–374. PA 54:10464.

Spitzer, Dean R. (1975b). Reviving the risky shift phenomenon: Applications of group dynamics research to educational practice. *Improving Human Performance A Research Quarterly*, *4*(1), 1–11. PA 55:7095.

Spoelders-Claes, Rita. (1973). Small-group effectiveness on an administrative task as influenced by knowledge of results and sex composition of

the group. *European Journal of Social Psychology*, *3*, 389–401. PA 53:9492. SA 75H2587.

Srivastava, Ashok K. (1985). Cooperation and competition in Prisoner's Dilemma game. *Psychological Studies*, *30*(2), 116–120. PA 73:24493.

Stake, Jayne E. (1981). Promoting leadership behaviors in low performance-self-esteem women in task-oriented mixed-sex dyads. *Journal of Personality*, *49*, 401–414. PA 68:1105. SA 84N7462.

Stake, Jayne E. (1983). Factors in reward distribution: Allocator motive, gender, and Protestant ethic endorsement. *Journal of Personality and Social Psychology*, *44*, 410–418. PA 70:5649.

Stake, Jayne E. (1985). Exploring the basis of sex differences in third-party allocations. *Journal of Personality and Social Psychology*, *48*, 1621–1629.

Stamm, Keith R.; & Pearce, W. Barnett. (1974). Message locus and message content: Two studies in communication behavior and coorientational relations. *Communication Research*, *1*, 184–203. PA 53:1076.

Stamps, Louis W.; & Teevan, Richard C. (1974). Fear of failure and conformity in the Asch and Crutchfield situations. *Psychological Reports*, *34*, 1327–1330. PA 53:1077.

Stanfield, Gary G. (1974). A critique and integration of the major social psychological approaches to the study of coalition formation. *Kansas Journal of Sociology*, *10*(1), 5–17. PA 53:1078.

Stanfield, Gary G.; Jenks, Richard J.; & McCartney, James L. (1975). Nonutilitarian consideration of coalition theory. *Sociology and Social Research*, *60*(1), 58–76. PA 55:7044.

Stanton, Wilbur W.; & Morris, Michael H. (1987). The identification of coalitions in small groups using multidimensional scaling: A methodology. *Small Group Behavior*, *18*, 126–137.

Starke, Frederick A.; & Notz, William W. (1981). Pre- and post-intervention effects of conventional versus final offer arbitration. *Academy of Management Journal*, *24*, 832–850. PA 67:7711.

Stasser, Garold; & Davis, James H. (1977). Opinion change during group discussion. *Personality and Social Psychology Bulletin*, *3*, 252–256. PA 59:3352.

Stasser, Garold; & Davis, James H. (1981). Group decision making and social influence: A social interaction sequence model. *Psychological Review, 88*, 523–551. PA 67:3564.

Stasser, Garold; & Titus, William. (1985). Pooling of unshared information in group decision making: Biased information sampling during discussion. *Journal of Personality and Social Psychology, 48*, 1467–1478. PA 72:28037.

Stasser, Garold; & Titus, William. (1987). Effects of information load and percentage of shared information on the dissemination of unshared information during group discussion. *Journal of Personality and Social Psychology, 53*, 81–93.

Staub, Ervin. (1978). *Positive social behavior and morality*. (Vol. 1). *Social and personal influences*. New York: Academic Press.

Staub, Ervin. (1979). *Positive social behavior and morality*. (Vol. 2). *Socialization and development*. New York: Academic Press.

Steblay, Nancy Mehrkens. (1987). Helping behavior in rural and urban environments: A meta-analysis. *Psychological Bulletin, 102*, 346–356.

Stech, Frank; & McClintock, Charles G. (1981). Effects of communication timing on duopoly bargaining outcomes. *Journal of Personality and Social Psychology, 40*, 664–674. PA 67:5726.

Stech, Frank J.; McClintock, Charles G.; & Moss, Barry F. (1984). The effectiveness of the carrot and the stick in increasing dyadic outcomes during duopolistic bargaining. *Behavioral Science, 29*, 1–12. SA 85O7803.

Steck, R.; & Sundermann, J. (1978). The effects of group size and cooperation on the success of interdisciplinary groups in R & D. *R and D Management, 8*(2), 59–64. PA 61:10927.

Steele, Claude M. (1975). Name-calling and compliance. *Journal of Personality and Social Psychology, 31*, 361–369. PA 53:11628.

Stefànsson, Bjorn S. (1974). Mathematical aggregation of preferences. *Quality and Quantity, 8*(2), 121–138. SA 75H5817.

Steffen, John J.; & Reckman, Richard F. (1978). Selective perception and interpretation of interpersonal cues in dyadic interactions. *Journal of Psychology, 99*, 245–248. PA 62:13635.

Steffen, John J.; & Redden, Joan. (1977). Assessment of social competence in an evaluation-interaction analogue. *Human Communication Research, 4*, 30–37. PA 60:9314.

Steigleder, Michele K.; Weiss, Robert F.; Balling, Susan B.; Wenninger, V. L.; & Lombardo, John P. (1980). Drivelike motivational properties of competitive behavior. *Journal of Personality and Social Psychology, 38*, 93–104. PA 65:5430.

Steigleder, Michele K.; Weiss, Robert Frank; Cramer, Robert Ervin; & Feinberg, Richard A. (1978). Motivating and reinforcing functions of competitive behavior. *Journal of Personality and Social Psychology, 36*, 1291–1301.

Stein, Arthur A. (1976). Conflict and cohesion: A review of the literature. *Journal of Conflict Resolution, 20*, 143–172.

Stein, Morris I. (1984). A minority of one, a crackpot (?), in an introductory psychology textbook. *Perceptual and Motor Skills, 59*, 730.

Stein, R. Timothy. (1975). Identifying emergent leaders from verbal and nonverbal communications. *Journal of Personality and Social Psychology, 32*, 125–135. PA 54:7484.

Stein, R. Timothy. (1977). Accuracy of process consultants and untrained observers in perceiving emergent leadership. *Journal of Applied Psychology, 62*, 755–759. PA 60:6309.

Stein, R. Timothy. (1980). Experimental investigations of the relationship between status level and conformity: A review of the literature. *Catalog of Selected Documents in Psychology, 10*, 13. (Ms. No. 2000). PA 64:10347.

Stein, R. Timothy. (1982). High-status group members as exemplars: A summary of field research on the relationship of status to congruence conformity. *Small Group Behavior, 13*, 3–21.

Stein, R. Timothy; & Heller, Tamar. (1979). An empirical analysis of the correlations between leadership status and participation rates reported in the literature. *Journal of Personality and Social Psychology, 37*, 1993–2002. PA 65:5398.

Stein, R. Timothy; & Heller, Tamar. (1983). The relationship of participation rates to leadership status: A meta-analysis. In H. H. Blumberg, A. P. Hare, V. Kent, & M. F. Davies (Eds.), *Small groups and social interaction* (Vol. 1, pp. 401–406). Chichester, UK: Wiley & Sons.

Steiner, Ivan D. (1974). Whatever happened to the group in social psychology? *Journal of Experimental Social Psychology, 10*, 94–108.

Steiner, Ivan D. (1986). Paradigms and groups. *Advances in Experimental Social Psychology, 19*, 251–289.

Steinfatt, Thomas M.; & Miller, Gerald R. (1974). Communication in game theoretic models of conflict. In G. R. Miller & H. W. Simons

(Eds.), *Perspectives on communication in social conflict* (pp. 14–75). Englewood Cliffs, NJ: Prentice-Hall.

Stephan, Cookie. (1974). Sex prejudice in jury simulation. *Journal of Psychology, 88,* 305–312. PA 54:1054.

Stephan, Cookie; Burnam, M. Audrey; & Aronson, Elliot. (1979). Attributions for success and failure after cooperation, competition, or team competition. *European Journal of Social Psychology, 9,* 109–114. PA 64:987

Stephan, Cookie; Kennedy, James C.; & Aronson, Elliot. (1977). The effects of friendship and outcome on task attribution. *Sociometry, 40,* 107–112. PA 59:09904.

Stephan, Cookie; Presser, Nan R.; Kennedy, James C.; & Aronson, Elliot. (1978). Attributions to success and failure after cooperative or competitive interaction. *European Journal of Social Psychology, 8,* 269–274. PA 62:3617

Stephan, Walter G. (1985). Intergroup relations. In G. Lindzey & E. Aronson (Eds.), *Handbook of Social Psychology* (Vol. 2, pp. 599–658). New York: Random House.

Stephan, Walter G.; & Feagin, Joe R. (Eds). (1980). *School desegregation: Past, present, and future.* New York: Plenum.

Stephan, Walter G.; & Kennedy, James C. (1975). An experimental study of interethnic competition in segregated schools. *Journal of School Psychology, 13*(3), 234–247. PA 55:5630.

Stephan, Walter G.; Lucker, G. William; & Aronson, Elliot. (1976). The interpersonal consequences of self-disclosure and internal attributions for success. *Personality and Social Psychology Bulletin, 2,* 252–255. PA 57:1182.

Stephen, Timothy D. (1984). A symbolic exchange framework for the development of intimate relationships. *Human Relations, 37,* 393–408.

Stephen, Timothy D.; & Harrison, Teresa M. (1985). A longitudinal comparison of couples with sex-typical and non-sex-typical orientations to intimacy. *Sex Roles, 12,* 195–206. PA 73:3688.

Stephenson, Blair; & Wicklund, Robert A. (1984). The contagion of self-focus within a dyad. *Journal of Personality and Social Psychology, 46,* 163–168. PA 71:28625.

Stephenson, G[eoffrey] M.; Ayling, K.; & Rutter, D. R. (1976). The role of visual communication in social exchange. *British Journal of Social Psychology, 15,* 113–120. PA 57:1183.

Stephenson, Geoffrey M.; Brandstatter, Hermann; & Wagner, Wolfgang. (1983). An experimental study of social performance and delay on the testimonial validity of story recall. *European Journal of Social Psychology, 13,* 175–191. PA 71:3982.

Stephenson, G[eoffrey] M.; & Brotherton, C. J. (1975). Social progression and polarization: A study of discussion and negotiation in groups of mining supervisors. *British Journal of Social and Clinical Psychology, 14,* 241–252. PA 55:7096. SA 78J0176.

Stephenson, G[eoffrey] M.; Clark, N. K.; & Wade, G. S. (1986). Meetings make evidence? An experimental study of collaborative and individual recall of a simulated police interrogation. *Journal of Personality and Social Psychology, 50,* 1113–1122. PA 73:24494.

Stephenson, Geoffrey M.; & Kniveton, Bromley K. (1978). Interpersonal and interparty exchange: An experimental study of the effect of seating position on the outcome of negotiations between teams representing parties in dispute. *Human Relations, 31,* 555–566. PA 62:10987. SA 79K2639.

Stephenson, Geoffrey M.; Kniveton, Bromley K.; & Morley, Ian E. (1977). Interaction analysis of an industrial wage negotiation. *Journal of Occupational Psychology, 50,* 231–241. PA 60:12849.

Stephenson, Geoffrey M.; Skinner, Martin; & Brotherton, C. J. (1976). Group participation and intergroup relations: An experimental study of negotiation groups. *European Journal of Social Psychology, 6,* 51–70. SA 78J0177.

Steptoe, Andrew; & Fidler, Helen. (1987). Stage fright in orchestral musicians: A study of cognitive and behavioural strategies in performance anxiety. *British Journal of Psychology, 78,* 241–249.

Stern, Paul C. (1976). Effect of incentives and education on resource conservation decisions in a simulated common dilemma. *Journal of Personality and Social Psychology, 34,* 1285–1292. PA 60:11750.

Sternberg, Robert J.; & Barnes, Michael L. (1985). Real and ideal others in romantic relationships: Is four a crowd? *Journal of Personality and Social Psychology, 49,* 1586–1608. PA 73:11742.

Sternberg, Robert J.; & Smith, Craig. (1985). Social intelligence and decoding skills in nonverbal communication. *Social Cognition, 3,* 168–192. PA 73:29992.

Sternberg, Robert J.; & Soriano, Lawrence J. (1984). Styles of conflict resolution. *Journal of Personality and Social Psychology, 47,* 115–126. PA 71:31325.

Steuden, Stanislawa. (1979). [Psychological analysis of behaviour in emotionally balanced and imbalanced groups in conflict situations]. *Przeglad Psychologiczny, 22,* 507–515. PA 65:7948.

Stevens, Michael J.; Rice, Mary B.; & Johnson, James J. (1986). Effect of eye gaze on self-disclosure. *Perceptual and Motor Skills, 62,* 939–942. PA 74:25062.

Stevenson, William B.; Pearce, Jone L.; & Porter, Lyman W. (1985). The concept of "coalition" in organization theory and research. *Academy of Management Review, 10,* 256–267.

Stewart, Abigail J.; & Rubin, Zick. (1976). The power motive in the dating couple. *Journal of Personality and Social Psychology, 34,* 305–309. PA 56:7932.

Stewart, David W.; & Latham, Donald R. (1986). On some psychometric properties of Fiedler's contingency model of leadership. *Small Group Behavior, 17,* 83–94.

Stier, Deborah S.; & Hall, Judith A. (1984). Gender differences in touch: An empirical and theoretical review. *Journal of Personality and Social Psychology, 47,* 440–459. PA 72:1241.

Stiles, William B. (1978). Verbal response modes and dimensions of interpersonal roles: A method of discourse analysis. *Journal of Personality and Social Psychology, 36,* 693–703. PA 63:982.

Stiles, William B.; Waszak, Cynthia S.; & Barton, Laine R. (1979). Professorial presumptuousness in verbal interactions with university students. *Journal of Experimental Social Psychology, 15,* 158–169. PA 64:3261.

Stingle, Sandra F.; & Cook, Harold. (1985). Age and sex differences in the cooperative and non-cooperative behavior of pairs of American children. *Journal of Psychology, 119,* 335–345.

Stinson, J.; & Tracy, L. (1974). Some disturbing characteristics of the LPC score. *Personnel Psychology, 27,* 477–485. PA 54:6486.

Stires, Lloyd. (1980). Classroom seating location, student grades, and attitudes. *Environment and Behavior, 12,* 241–254. PA 64:13365.

Stitt, Christopher; Schmidt, Stuart; Price, Karl; & Kipnis, David. (1983). Sex of leader, leader behavior, and subordinate satisfaction. *Sex Roles, 9,* 31–42. PA 70:12654.

Stix, Allen H. (1974). Chlordiazepoxide (Librium): The effects of a minor tranquilizer on strategic choice behavior in the Prisoner's Dilemma. *Journal of Conflict Resolution, 18,* 373–394. PA 53:6875.

Stock, Dorothy; & Thelen, Herbert A. (1958). *Emotional dynamics and group culture: Experimental studies of individual and group behavior.* Washington: National Training Laboratories.

Stockton, Rex. (1978). Reviews and bibliographies of experiential small group research: Survey and perspective. *Small Group Behavior, 9,* 435–448.

Stokes, Joseph P. (1983). Components of group cohesion: Intermember attraction, instrumental value, and risk taking. *Small Group Behavior, 14,* 163–173. PA 71:12176. SA 84O0840.

Stokes, Joseph [P.]; Childs, Laurence; & Fuehrer, Ann. (1981). Gender and sex roles as predictors of self-disclosure. *Journal of Counseling Psychology, 28,* 510–514. PA 67:3565.

Stokes, Joseph P.; Fuehrer, Ann; & Childs, Laurence. (1983). Group members' self-disclosures: Relation to perceived cohesion. *Small Group Behavior, 14,* 63–76. PA 71:1362.

Stokes, Joseph [P.]; & Levin, Ira. (1986). Gender differences in predicting loneliness from social network characteristics. *Journal of Personality and Social Psychology, 51,* 1069–1074.

Stokols, Daniel. (1972). On the distinction between density and crowding: Some implications for future research. *Psychological Review, 79,* 275–278.

Stokols, Daniel. (1976). The experience of crowding in primary and secondary environments. *Environment and Behavior, 8,* 49–86.

Stokols, Daniel. (Ed.). (1977). *Perspectives on environment and behavior.* New York: Plenum.

Stokols, Daniel. (1978). Environmental psychology. *Annual Review of Psychology, 29,* 253–295. PA 62:12495.

Stokols, Daniel; & Altman, Irwin. (Eds.). (1987). *Handbook of environmental psychology* (2 vols.). New York: Wiley.

Stokols, Daniel; Rall, Marilyn; Pinner, Berna; & Schopler, John. (1973). Physical, social, and personal determinants of the perception of crowding. *Environment and Behavior, 5,* 87–115.

Stoll, Francois C.; Hoecker, Douglas G.; Krueger,

Gerald P.; & Chapanis, Alphonse. (1976). The effects of four communication modes on the structure of language used during cooperative problem solving. *Journal of Psychology, 94,* 13–26. PA 57:9910.

Stolte, John F. (1978a). Positional power and interpersonal evaluation in bargaining networks. *Social Behavior and Personality, 6,* 73–80. PA 63:5466.

Stolte, John F. (1978b). Power structure and personal competence. *Journal of Social Psychology, 106,* 83–92. PA 63:7575. SA 82M1480.

Stolte, John F. (1983). Positional power, personality, and perceptions of fairness in exchange. *Journal of Social Psychology, 120,* 287–288. PA 71:12177.

Stone, Gregory P. (1984). Conceptual problems in small group research. *Studies in Symbolic Interaction, 5,* 3–21. PA 72:4011. SA 84O2596.

Storm, P. (1978). Literatuurbeschouwing: leiderschap; een kritische beschouwing van enkele recente publikaties [Literature review: Leadership; a critical review of some recent publications]. *Mens en Onderneming, 32*(4), 204–224. SA 79K2769.

Storms, Michael D.; & Thomas, George C. (1977). Reactions to physical closeness. *Journal of Personality and Social Psychology, 35,* 412–418. PA 62:5992.

Strack, Stephen; & Coyne, James C. (1983). Social confirmation of dysphoria: Shared and private reactions to depression. *Journal of Personality and Social Psychology, 44,* 798–806. PA 70:12655.

Straffin, Philip D. (1977). Majority rule and general decision rules. *Theory and Decision, 8,* 351–360. PA 61:13398.

Strassberg, Donald S.; Gabel, Harris; & Anchor, Kenneth N. (1976). Patterns of self-disclosure in parent discussion groups. *Small Group Behavior, 7,* 369–378. PA 59:9874.

Straub, Helga H. (1975). [Developmental processes dependent upon leader behavior in psychodramatic groups]. *Gruppendynamik Forschung und Praxis, 2*(6), 104–108. PA 56:2597.

Straub, William F. (1975). Team cohesiveness in athletics. *International Journal of Sport Psychology, 6,* 125–133. PA 58:5341.

Strayer, F. F.; & Trudel, M. (1984). Developmental changes in the nature and function of social dominance among young children.

Ethology and Sociobiology, 5, 279–295. SA 85O6034.

Streater, Alicia L.; & Chertkoff, Jerome M. (1976). Distribution of rewards in a triad: A developmental test of equity theory. *Child Development, 47,* 800–805. PA 57:8045.

Street, Warren R. (1974). Brainstorming by individuals, coacting and interacting groups. *Journal of Applied Psychology, 59,* 433–436.

Strickland, Lloyd H.; Guild, Paul D.; Barefoot, John C.; & Paterson, Stuart A. (1978). Teleconferencing and Leadership Emergence. *Human Relations, 31,* 583–596. SA 79K2641.

Strodtbeck, F; & Hook, L. H. (1961). The social dimensions of a 12-man jury table. *Sociometry, 24,* 397–415.

Strodtbeck, Fred L.; & Lipinski, Richard M. (1985). Becoming first among equals: Moral considerations in jury foreman selection. *Journal of Personality and Social Psychology, 49,* 927–936.

Stroebe, Wolfgang; & Frey, Bruno S. (1982). Self-interest and collective action: The economics and psychology of public goods. *British Journal of Social Psychology, 21,* 121–137. PA 69:3429.

Strong, Stanley R.; Hills, Hope I.; Kilmartin, Christopher T.; DeVries, Helen; Lanier, Keith; Nelson, Blair N.; Strickland, Deborah; & Meyer, Charles W. III. (1988). The dynamic relations among interpersonal behaviors: A test of complementarity and anticomplementarity. *Journal of Personality and Social Psychology, 54,* 798–810.

Strube, Michael J.; & Garcia, Joseph E. (1981). A meta-analytic investigation of Fiedler's contingency model of leadership effectiveness. *Psychological Bulletin, 90,* 307–321. PA 66:10341.

Strube, Michael J.; & Garcia, Joseph E. (1983). On the proper interpretation of empirical findings: Strube and Garcia. (1981) revisited. *Psychological Bulletin, 93,* 600–603. PA 70:5639.

Strube, Michael J.; Miles, Margo E.; & Finch, William H. (1981). The social facilitation of a simple task: Field tests of alternative explanations. *Personality and Social Psychology Bulletin, 7,* 701–707. PA 68:3556.

Strube, Michael J.; & Werner, Carol. (1982). Interpersonal distance and personal space: A conceptual and methodological note. *Journal of Nonverbal Behavior, 6,* 163–170. PA 71:20438.

Stults, Daniel M.; & Messé, Lawrence A. (1985).

Behavioral consistency: The impact of public versus private statements of intentions. *Journal of Social Psychology*, *125*, 277-278. PA 73:24527.

Subbarao, A. V. (1978). The impact of binding interest arbitration on negotiation and process outcome: An experimental study. *Journal of Conflict Resolution*, *22*, 79-103. PA 61:10929.

Sue, Stanley; Smith, Ronald E.; & Pedroza, George. (1975). Authoritarianism, pretrial publicity, and awareness of bias in simulated jurors. *Psychological Reports*, *37*, 1299-1302. PA 56:4077.

Suenaga, Toshiro; Andow, Kiyoshi; & Ohshima, Takashi. (1981) [Social facilitation: History, current studies, and future perspectives]. *Japanese Psychological Review*, *24*, 423-457. PA 71:14956.

Sugiman, Toshio. (1977). [A study of the effect of participation in decision-making]. *Japanese Journal of Experimental Social Psychology*, *16*, 121-126. PA 64:10348.

Sugiman, Toshio. (1979). A study on the effects of equality of influence in group decision making. *Japanese Journal of Experimental Social Psychology*, *19*, 33-39. PA 65:5399.

Sugiman, Toshio; & Misumi, Jyuji. (1984). [Action research on evacuation method in emergent situation: II. Effects of leader: Evacuee ratio on efficiency of follow-direction method and follow-me method]. *Japanese Journal of Experimental Social Psychology*, *23*, 107-115. PA 71:28626.

Summerfield, Angela B. (1975). Effects of vocal expression and instructions on bargaining performance. *European Journal of Social Psychology*, *5*, 395-398. PA 58:3350.

Summerfield, Angela B.; & Lake, J. A. (1977). Non-verbal and verbal behaviours associated with parting. *British Journal of Psychology*, *68*, 133-136.

Sundel, Martin; Glasser, Paul; Sarri, Rosemary; & Vinter, Robert. (Eds.). (1985). *Individual change through small groups* (2nd ed.). New York: Free Press.

Sundstrom, Eric. (1975). An experimental study of crowding: Effects of room size, intrusion, and goal blocking on nonverbal behavior, self-disclosure, and self-reported stress. *Journal of Personality and Social Psychology*, *32*, 645-654. PA 56:702.

Sundstrom, Eric. (1978a). Crowding as a sequen-

tial process: Review of research on the effects of population density on humans. In A. Baum, & Y. M. Epstein (Eds.), *Human response to crowding* (pp. 31-116). Hillsdale, NJ: Erlbaum.

Sundstrom, Eric. (1978b). A test of equilibrium theory: Effects of topic intimacy and proximity on verbal and nonverbal behavior in pairs of friends and strangers. *Environmental Psychology and Nonverbal Behavior*, *3*(1), 3-16. PA 63:9647.

Sundstrom, Eric; & Altman, Irwin. (1976). Interpersonal relationships and personal space: Research review and theoretical model. *Human Ecology*, *4*, 47-67. PA 56:9848.

Sundstrom, Eric; Herbert, R. Kring; & Brown, David W. (1982). Privacy and communication in open-plan offices. *Environment and Behavior*, *14*, 379-392. PA 68:9219.

Sundstrom, Eric; & Sundstrom, Mary G. (1977). Personal space invasions: What happens when the invader asks permission? *Environmental Psychology and Nonverbal Behavior*, *2*, 76-82. PA 61:13399.

Sundstrom, Eric; Town, Jerry P; Brown, David W.; Forman, A.; & McGee, C. (1982). Physical enclosure, type of job, and privacy in the office. *Environment and Behavior*, *14*, 543-559. PA 69:4594.

Sundstrom, Gerdt. (1986). Intergenerational mobility and the relationship between adults and their aging parents in Sweden. *Gerontologist*, *26*, 367-371. PA 75:1268.

Surazska, Wieslawa. (1986). Normative and instrumental functions of equity criteria in individual choices of the input-payoff distribution pattern. *Journal of Conflict Resolution*, *30*, 532-550. PA 74:7176.

Surra, Catherine A. (1985). Courtship types: Variations in interdependence between partners and social networks. *Journal of Personality and Social Psychology*, *49*, 357-375.

Sussman, Nan M.; & Rosenfeld, Howard M. (1978). Touch, justification, and sex: Influences on the aversiveness of spatial violations. *Journal of Social Psychology*, *106*, 215-225. PA 64:5579.

Sussman, Nan M.; & Rosenfeld, Howard M. (1982). Influence of culture, language, and sex on conversational distance. *Journal of Personality and Social Psychology*, *42*, 66-74. PA 68:3536.

Sussman, Stephen A. (1977). Body disclosure and

self-disclosure: Relating two modes of interpersonal encounter. *Journal of Clinical Psychology*, *33*, 1146–1148. PA 60:9315.

Swain, Janet; Stephenson, Geoffrey M.; & Dewey, Michael E. (1982). 'Seeing a stranger': Does eye-contact reflect intimacy? *Semiotica*, *42*(2–4), 107–118. SA 84N7298.

Swann, William B. Jr. (1987). Identity negotiation: Where two roads meet. *Journal of Personality and Social Psychology*, *53*, 1038–1051.

Swann, William B.; & Ely, Robin J. (1984). A battle of wills: Self-verification versus behavioral confirmation. *Journal of Personality and Social Psychology*, *46*, 1287–1302. PA 71:28628.

Swann, William B.; Giuliano, Toni; & Wegner, Daniel M. (1982). Where leading questions can lead: The power of conjecture in social interaction. *Journal of Personality and Social Psychology*, *42*, 1025–1035. PA 69:1004.

Swann, William, B.; & Hill, Craig, A. (1982). When our identities are mistaken: Reaffirming self-conceptions through social interaction. *Journal of Personality and Social Psychology*, *43*, 59–66. PA 69:3495.

Swann, William B.; & Predmore, Steven C. (1985). Intimates as agents of social support: Sources of consolation or despair? *Journal of Personality and Social Psychology*, *49*, 1609–1617. PA 73:11778.

Swann, William, B.; & Read, Stephen, J. (1981a). Acquiring self-knowledge: The search for feedback that fits. *Journal of Personality and Social Psychology*, *41*, 1119–1128. PA 67:12142.

Swann, William B.; & Read, Stephen J. (1981b). Self-verification processes: How we sustain our self-conceptions. *Journal of Experimental Social Psychology*, *17*, 351–372. PA 67:7712. PA 67:7712.

Swanson, Elizabeth B.; Sherman, Martin F.; & Sherman, Nancy. (1982). Anxiety and the foot-in-the-door technique. *Journal of Social Psychology*, *118*, 269–275.

Swanson, Marcia A.; Tjosvold, Dean. (1979). The effects of unequal competence and sex on achievement and self-presentation. *Sex Roles*, *5*, 279–285. PA 64:7887.

Swanson, Ronald G.; & Johnson, Douglas A. (1975). Relation between peer perception of leader behavior and instructor-pilot performance. *Journal of Applied Psychology*, *60*, 198–200. PA 54:2075.

Swap, Walter C.; & Associates. (1984). *Group decision making*. Beverly Hills, CA: Sage.

Sweeney, John W., Jr (1974). Altruism, the Free Rider Problem and Group Size. *Theory and Decision*, *4*, 259–275. SA 75H5818.

Swerts, A.; Peeters, R.; & d'Ydewalle, Gery. (1983). Group size: A possible distorting factor in learning experiments. *Bulletin of the Psychonomic Society*, *21*, 93–96. PA 71:1330.

Swinth, Robert L. (1981). The personal responsibility group. *Small Group Behavior*, *12*, 21–36.

Sykes, Richard E. (1983). Initial interaction between strangers and acquaintances: A multivariate analysis of factors affecting choice of communication partners. *Human Communication Research*, *10*, 27–53. PA 71:14974.

Sykes, Richard E.; Larntz, Kinley; & Fox, James C. (1976). Proximity and similarity effects on frequency of interaction in a class of naval recruits. *Sociometry*, *39*, 263–269. SA 7714660.

Syna, Helena; & Pruitt, Dean G. (1986). Impact of the total equality norm on social conflict. *Journal of Social Behavior and Personality*, *1*, 143–148. PA 74:10204. SA 86Q6537.

Sypher, Beverly Davenport; & Sypher, Howard E. (1983). Perceptions of communication ability: Self-monitoring in an organizational setting. *Personality and Social Psychology Bulletin*, *9*, 297–304.

Szmajke, Andrzej. (1984). Anticipation of task cooperation with an actor and causal attribution of his failures: Effects of locus of control *Polish Psychological Bulletin*, *15*, 245–256. PA 73:24528.

Szymanski, Kate; & Harkins, Stephen G. (1987). Social loafing and self-evaluation with a social standard. *Journal of Personality and Social Psychology*, *53*, 891–897.

Tack, Werner H. (1987). The real-estate broker's problem: Coalition formation and conflict resolution in an experimental game. *International Journal of Small Group Research*, *3*, 61–86.

Tajfel, Henri. (1970, November). Experiments in intergroup discrimination. *Scientific American*, *223*(5), 96–102.

Tajfel, Henri. (Ed.). (1978). *Differentiation between social groups: Studies in the social psychology of intergroup relations*. London: Academic Press.

Tajfel, Henri. (1979). Individuals and groups in social psychology. *British Journal of Social and Clinical Psychology*, *18*, 183–190. PA 64:7903.

Tajfel, Henri. (1983). Experiments in intergroup discrimination. In H. H. Blumberg, A. P. Hare, V. Kent, & M. F. Davies (Eds.), *Small groups and social interaction* (Vol. 1, pp. 109–118). Chichester: John Wiley. [Revised and abridged by the author from Tajfel, 1970.]

Takigawa, Tetsuo. (1985). [An analysis of decision making processes in a multi-person experimental game: The effect of payoff matrices introduced in a voting situation]. *Japanese Journal of Experimental Social Psychology*, *24*(2), 143–148. PA 73:11779.

Tallman, Irving; & Miller, Gary. (1974). Class differences in family problem solving: The effects of verbal ability, hierarchical structure, and role expectations. *Sociometry*, *37*, 13–37. PA 52:10045.

Tammivaara, Julie Stulac. (1982). The effects of task structure on beliefs about competence and participation in small groups. *Sociology of Education*, *55*, 212–222. SA 83M9104.

Tanaka, Koji. (1975). [An experimental study on the effects of changing task structure in the contingency model: An exercise in situational engineering]. *Japanese Journal of Experimental Social Psychology*, *15*, 74–85. PA 58:1122.

Tanford, Sarah; & Penrod, Steven. (1983). Computer Modeling of Influence in the Jury: The Role of the Consistent Juror. *Social Psychology Quarterly*, *46*, 200–212. SA 84N7299.

Tanford, Sarah; & Penrod, Steven. (1984a). Social Influence Model: A formal integration of research on majority and minority influence processes. *Psychological Bulletin*, *95*, 189–225. PA 71:14975.

Tanford, Sarah; & Penrod, Steven. (1984b). Social inference processes in jury judgments of multiple-offense trials. *Journal of Personality and Social Psychology*, *47*, 749–765.

Tanford, Sarah; & Penrod, Steven. (1986). Jury deliberations: Discussion content and influence processes in jury decision making. *Journal of Applied Social Psychology*, *16*, 322–347. PA 73:27152.

Tanur, Judith M. (1975). Strategic interaction in children: An experiment in role-taking and expression management. *Sociometry*, *38*, 558–572.

Tao, Masao. (1974). [Effects of status inconsistency upon the cooperative working]. *Japanese Journal of Psychology*, *44*, 296–304. PA 52:10046.

Tartter, Vivien C. (1983). The effects of symmetric and asymmetric dyadic visual access on attribution during communication. *Language and Communication*, *3*, 1–10. PA 71:17763.

Taylor, Dalmas A.; & Altman, Irwin. (1975). Self-disclosure as a function of reward-cost outcomes. *Sociometry*, *38*, 18–31. PA 54:7485. SA 76H9439.

Taylor, Dalmas A.; & Altman, Irwin. (1983). Environment and interpersonal relationships: privacy, crowding, and intimacy. In H. H. Blumberg, A. P. Hare, V. Kent, & M. F. Davies (Eds.), *Small groups and social interaction* (Vol. 1, pp. 17–41). Chichester, UK: Wiley.

Taylor, Dalmas A.; & Belgrave, Faye Zollicoffer. (1986). The effects of perceived intimacy and valence on self-disclosure reciprocity. *Personality and Social Psychology Bulletin*, *12*, 247–255.

Taylor, Dalmas A.; Gould, Robert J.; & Brounstein, Paul J. (1981). Effects of personalistic self-disclosure. *Personality and Social Psychology Bulletin*, *7*, 487–492. PA 67:9784.

Taylor, Dalmas A.; & Hinds, Melissa. (1985). Disclosure reciprocity and liking as a function of gender and personalism. *Sex Roles*, *12*, 1137–1153. PA 73:21931.

Taylor, Donald M.; & Doria, Janet R. (1981). Self-serving and group-serving bias in attribution. *Journal of Social Psychology*, *113*, 201–211. PA 67:3624.

Taylor, Donald M.; Doria, Janet; & Tyler, J. Kenneth. (1983). Group performance and cohesiveness: An attribution analysis. *Journal of Social Psychology*, *119*, 187–198. PA 71:1331.

Taylor, Irving A. (1975). An emerging view of creative actions. In I. A. Taylor & J. W. Getzels (Eds.), *Perspectives in creativity* (pp. 297–325). Chicago: Aldine.

Taylor, Ralph B. (1981). Perception of density: Individual differences? *Environment and Behavior*, *13*, 3–21. PA 65:7976.

Taylor, Ralph B.; & Brooks, Debra Kaye. (1980). Temporary territories? Responses to intrusions in a public setting. *Population and Environment*, *3*, 135–145. SA 82M4027.

Taylor, Ralph B.; De Soto, Clinton B.; & Lieb, Robert. (1979). Sharing secrets: Disclosure and discretion in dyads and triads. *Journal of Personality and Social Psychology*, *37*, 1196–1203. PA 64:12475.

Taylor, Ralph B.; & Ferguson, Glenn. (1980).

Solitude and intimacy: Linking territoriality and privacy experiences. *Journal of Nonverbal Behavior, 4,* 227–239. PA 66:1244.

Taylor, Ralph B.; Gottfredson, Stephen D.; & Brower, Sidney. (1980). The defensibility of defensible space. In T. Hirschi, & M. Gottfredson (Eds.), *Understanding crime: Current theory and research.* Beverley Hills, CA: Sage.

Taylor, Ralph B.; Gottfredson, Stephen D.; & Brower, Sidney. (1981). Territorial cognitions and social climate in urban neighborhoods. *Basic and Applied Social Psychology, 2,* 289–303. PA 68:1106.

Taylor, Ralph B.; & Lanni, Joseph C. (1981). Territorial dominance: The influence of the resident advantage in triadic decision making. *Journal of Personality and Social Psychology, 41,* 909–915. PA 67:9785.

Taylor, Ronald D.; Messick, David M.; Lehman, Gary A.; & Hirsch, Jeffrey K. (1982). Sex, dependency, and helping revisited. *Journal of Social Psychology, 118,* 59–65. PA 69:12691.

Taylor, Stuart P.; Shuntich, Richard J.; & Greenberg, Andrew. (1979). The effects of repeated aggressive encounters on subsequent aggressive behavior. *Journal of Social Psychology, 107,* 199–208. PA 64:3263.

Taylor, Stuart P.; & Smith, Ian. (1974). Aggression as a function of sex of victim and male subject's attitude toward women. *Psychological Reports, 35,* 1095–1098. PA 53:11629.

Tedeschi, James T. (1979). Frustration, fantasy aggression, and the exercise of coercive power. *Perceptual and Motor Skills, 48,* 215–219. PA 64:3264.

Tedeschi, James T. (Ed.). (1981). *Impression management theory and social psychological research.* New York: Academic Press.

Tedeschi, James T.; & Lindskold, Svenn. (1976). *Social psychology: Interdependence, interaction, and influence.* New York: Wiley. PA 56:3988.

Tedeschi, James T.; & Norman, Nancy M. (1985). A social psychological interpretation of displaced aggression. *Advances in Group Processes, 2,* 29–56.

Tedeschi, James T.; Riordan, Catherine A.; Gaes, Gerald G.; & Kane, Thomas. (1983). Verbal accounts and attributions of social motives. *Journal of Research in Personality, 17,* 218–225. PA 71:3996.

Tedeschi, James T.; Schlenker, Barry R.; & Bonoma, Thomas V. (1975). Compliance to threats as a function of source attractiveness and esteem. *Sociometry, 38,* 81–98. PA 54:7539.

Teichman, Meir; & Foa, Uriel G. (1975). Effect of resources similarity on satisfaction with exchange. *Social Behavior and Personality, 3,* 213–224. PA 56:6062.

Tennis, Gay H.; & Dabbs, James M. (1975). Sex, setting and personal space: First grade through college. *Sociometry, 38,* 385–394. PA 54:11730.

Tennis, Gay H.; & Dabbs, James M., Jr. (1976). Race, setting, and actor-target differences in personal space. *Social Behavior and Personality, 4,* 49–55. SA 7717509.

Terborg, James R. (1977). Women in management: A research review. *Journal of Applied Psychology, 62,* 647–664. PA 60:6320.

Terborg, James R.; Castore, Carl; & DeNinno, John A. (1976). A longitudinal field investigation of the impact of group composition on group performance and cohesion. *Journal of Personality and Social Psychology, 34,* 782–790.

Terhune, Kenneth W. (1974). "Wash-in," "wash-out," and systemic effects in extended Prisoner's Dilemma. *Journal of Conflict Resolution, 18,* 656–685. PA 53:9493.

Tesser, Abraham. (1980a). Self-esteem maintenance in family dynamics. *Journal of Personality and Social Psychology, 39,* 77–91.

Tesser, Abraham. (1980b). When individual dispositions and social pressure conflict: A catastrophe. *Human Relations, 33,* 393–407. SA 82M5655.

Tesser, Abraham; Campbell, Jennifer; & Mickler, Susan. (1983). The role of social pressure, attention to the stimulus, and self-doubt in conformity. *European Journal of Social Psychology, 13,* 217–233. PA 71:9517. SA 8400841.

Tesser, Abraham; & Conlee, Mary C. (1975). Some effects of time and thought on attitude polarization. *Journal of Personality and Social Psychology, 31,* 262–270. PA 53:11630.

Tetlock, Philip E. (1979). Identifying victims of groupthink from public statements of decision makers. *Journal of Personality and Social Psychology, 37,* 1314–1324. PA 64:12511.

Thalhofer, Nancy N. (1980). Violation of a spacing norm in high social density. *Journal of Applied Social Psychology, 10,* 175–183.

Theodory, George C. (1982). The validity of Fiedler's contingency logic. *Journal of Psychology, 110*, 115–120. PA 68:6624.

Thibaut, John; Friedland, Nehemia; & Walker, Laurens. (1974). Compliance with rules: Some social determinants. *Journal of Personality and Social Psychology, 30*, 792–801. PA 53:9494.

Thibaut, John W.; & Kelley, Harold H. (1986). *Social psychology of groups* (rev. ed.). New Brunswick, NJ: Transaction Books. [Reprint of 1959 edition, with a new introduction by the authors]

Tholey, Paul. (1973). *Zur Einzel-und Gruppenleistung unter eingeschränkten Kommunikationsbedingungen* [Individual and group performance under limited conditions of communication]. Frankfurt-on-Main, West Germany: Waldemar Kramer. PA 53:3111.

Thomas, Andrew P.; & Bull, Peter. (1981). The role of pre-speech posture change in dyadic interaction. *British Journal of Social Psychology, 20*, 105–111. PA 67:5727.

Thomas, David R. (1976). Cooperation and competition among Polynesian and European children. *Child Development, 46*, 948–953. PA 57:8089.

Thomas, Ewart A.; & Malone, Thomas W. (1979). On the dynamics of two-person interactions. *Psychological Review, 86*, 331–360. PA 62:13637.

Thomas, Kenneth W.; & Pondy, Louis R. (1977). Toward an intent model of conflict management among principal parties. *Human Relations, 30*, 1089–1102. PA 60:12830.

Thomas, Veronica G.; & Littig, Lawrence W. (1985). A typology of leadership style: Examining gender and race effects. *Bulletin of the Psychonomic Society, 23*, 132–134. PA 73:14445.

Thompson, Donna E.; Aiello, John R.; & Epstein, Yakov M. (1979). Interpersonal distance preferences. *Journal of Nonverbal Behavior, 4*, 113–118. PA 66:1245.

Thompson, Henry L.; & Richardson, Deborah R. (1983). The rooster effect: Same-sex rivalry and inequity as factors in retaliative aggression. *Personality and Social Psychology Bulletin, 9*, 415–425. PA 71:12178.

Thompson, John E.; & Carsrud, Alan L. (1976). The effects of experimentally induced illusions of invulnerability and vulnerability on decisonal risk taking in triads. *Journal of Social Psychology, 100*, 263–267. PA 58:1123.

Thompson, Leigh L.; Mannix, Elizabeth A.; & Bazerman, Max H. (1988). Group negotiation: Effects of decision rule, agenda, and aspiration. *Journal of Personality and Social Psychology, 54*, 86–95.

Thompson, William C.; Fong, Geoffrey T.; & Rosenhan, D. L. (1981). Inadmissible evidence and juror verdicts. *Journal of Personality and Social Psychology, 40*, 453–463.

Thornton, Billy. (1977). Effect of rape victim's attractiveness in a jury simulation. *Personality and Social Psychology Bulletin, 3*, 666–669. PA 60:11752.

Thornton, Billy; & Ryckman, Richard M. (1979). Actor-observer attributions for success and failure in public or private disclosure situations. *Representative Research in Social Psychology, 10*, 87–96. PA 66:1294.

Thornton, Russell; & Nardi, Peter M. (1975). The dynamics of role acquisition. *American Journal of Sociology, 80*, 870–885. SA 75H4760.

Thune, Elizabeth S.; Manderscheid, Ronald W.; & Silbergeld, Sam. (1980). Status or sex roles as determinants of interaction patterns in small, mixed-sex groups. *Journal of Social Psychology, 112*, 51–65. PA 66:8026. SA 83N2372.

Thurman, Blake. (1979). In the office: Networks and coalitions. *Social Networks, 2*, 47–63. SA 81L3340.

Tice, Dianne M.; & Baumeister, Roy F. (1985). Masculinity inhibits helping in emergencies: Personality does predict the bystander effect. *Journal of Personality and Social Psychology, 49*, 420–428. PA 73:1161.

Timney, Brian; & London, Harvey. (1973). Body language concomitants of persuasiveness and persuasibility in dyadic interaction. *International Journal of Group Tensions, 3*, 48–67. PA 54:2991.

Tindale, R. Scott; & Davis, James H. (1983). Group decision making and jury verdicts. In H. H. Blumberg, A. P. Hare, V. Kent, & M. F. Davies (Eds.), *Small groups and social interaction* (Vol. 2, pp. 9–37). Chichester: John Wiley.

Tindale, R. Scott; & Davis, James H. (1985). Individual and group reward allocation decisions in two situational contexts: Effects of relative need and performance. *Journal of Personality and Social Psychology, 48*, 1148–1161. PA 72:22594.

Tindall, Jeffry. (1979). Time-limited and time-extended encounter groups: Descriptive stage development. *Small Group Behavior*, *10*, 402–413. SA 80K8710.

Tindall, Jeffry H.; Houtz, John C.; Hausler, Regina; & Heimowitz, Shelly. (1982). Processes of creative problem solvers in groups. *Small Group Behavior*, *13*, 109–116.

Tjosvold, Dean. (1977a). Commitment to justice in conflict between unequal status persons. *Journal of Applied Social Psychology*, *7*, 149–162. PA 60:1002.

Tjosvold, Dean. (1977b). The effects of the constituent's affirmation and the opposing negotiator's self-presentation in bargaining between unequal status groups. *Organizational Behavior and Human Performance*, *18*, 146–157. PA 58:5343.

Tjosvold, Dean. (1977c). Low power person's strategies in bargaining: Negotiability of demand, maintaining face, and race. *International Journal of Group Tensions*, *7*, 29–41. PA 65:3259.

Tjosvold, Dean. (1978a). Affirmation of the high-power person and his position: Ingratiation in conflict. *Journal of Applied Social Psychology*, *8*, 230–243. PA 63:5471.

Tjosvold, Dean. (1978b). Control strategies and own group evaluation in intergroup conflict. *Journal of Psychology*, *100*, 305–314. PA 63:9648.

Tjosvold, Dean. (1981). Unequal power relationships within a cooperative or competitive context. *Journal of Applied Social Psychology*, *11*, 137–150. PA 67:3628.

Tjosvold, Dean. (1982). Effects of cooperative and competitive interdependence and task complexity on subordinates' productivity, perception of leader, and group development. *Canadian Journal of Behavioural Science*, *14*, 24–34. PA 69:7890.

Tjosvold, Dean. (1983). Social face in conflict: A critique. *International Journal of Group Tensions*, *13*, 49–64. PA 72:25413.

Tjosvold, Dean. (1985). Power and social context in superior-subordinate interaction. *Organizational Behavior and Human Decision Processes*, *35*, 281–293. PA 72:25412.

Tjosvold, Dean; & Fabrey, Lawrence J. (1980). Motivation for perspective taking: Effects of interdependence and dependence on interest in learning others' intentions. *Psychological Reports*, *46*, 755–765. PA 66:3663.

Tjosvold, Dean; & Field, Richard H. (1983). Effects of social context on consensus and majority vote decision making. *Academy of Management Journal*, *26*, 500–506. PA 71:1332.

Tjosvold, Dean; & Field, Richard H. (1985). Effect of concurrence, controversy, and consensus on group decision making. *Journal of Social Psychology*, *125*, 355–363. PA 74:1067.

Tjosvold, Dean; & Huston, Ted L. (1978). Social face and resistance to compromise in bargaining. *Journal of Social Psychology*, *104*, 57–68.

Tjosvold, Dean; Johnson, David; & Johnson, Roger T. (1981). Effect of partner's effort and ability on liking for partner after failure on a cooperative task. *Journal of Psychology*, *109*, 147–152.

Tjosvold, Dean; Johnson, David W.; & Johnson, Roger. (1984). Influence strategy, perspective-taking, and relationships between high- and low-power individuals in cooperative and competitive contexts. *Journal of Psychology*, *116*, 187–202. PA 72:4012.

Tjosvold, Dean; Johnson, David W.; & Lerner, Jacqueline V. (1981). Effects of affirmation and acceptance on incorporation of opposing information in problem-solving. *Journal of Social Psychology*, *114*, 103–110. PA 67:3567.

Tjosvold, Dean; & Okun, Morris. (1979). Effects of unequal power on cooperation in conflict. *Psychological Reports*, *44*, 239–242. PA 64:3265.

Tjosvold, Dean; & Sagaria, Sabato D. (1978). Effects of relative power on cognitive perspective-taking. *Personality and Social Psychology Bulletin*, *4*, 256–259. PA 64:5627.

Tobiasen, Joyce M.; & Allen, Andrea. (1983). Influence of gaze and physical closeness: A delayed effect. *Perceptual and Motor Skills*, *57*, 491–495. PA 71:15021.

Toder, Nancy L. (1980). The effect of the sexual composition of a group on discrimination against women and sex-role attitudes. *Psychology of Women Quarterly*, *5*, 292–310. PA 66:12779. SA 82M4028.

Toder, Nancy L.; & Marcia, James E. (1973). Ego identity status and response to conformity pressure in college women. *Journal of Personality and Social Psychology*, *26*, 287–294. PA 50:11281.

Tognoli, Jerome. (1975). Reciprocation of generosity and knowledge of game termination in the decomposed Prisoner's Dilemma game. *European Journal of Social Psychology*, *5*, 297–313. PA 58:9546.

Tolor, Alexander; Cramer, Marie; D'Amico,

Denis; & O'Marra, Margaret M. (1975). The effects of self-concept, trust, and imagined positive or negative self-disclosures on psychological space. *Journal of Psychology*, 89, 9–24. PA 54:1058.

Tolstedt, Betsy E.; & Stokes, Joseph P. (1984). Self-disclosure, intimacy, and the depenetration process. *Journal of Personality and Social Psychology*, 46, 84–90. PA 71:28629.

Törnblom, Kjell Y.; Fredholm, Eva M.; & Jonsson, Dan R. (1987). New and old friendships: Attributed effects of type and similarity of transacted resources. *Human Relations*, 40, 337–360.

Toseland, Ron; Krebs, Anne; & Vahsen, John. (1978). Changing group interaction patterns. *Journal of Social Service Research*, 2(2), 219–232. PA 64:3266.

Tourangeau, Roger; & Ellsworth, Phoebe C. (1979). The role of facial response in the experience of emotion. *Journal of Personality and Social Psychology*, 37, 1519–1531. PA 65:499.

Touzard, H. (1975–1976). [Ideological and technical negotiation themes and effective mediator behavior]. *Bulletin de Psychologie*, 29, 824–847. PA 58:9498.

Touzard, H. (1977–1978). [Mediation and resolution of conflicts]. *Bulletin de Psychologie*, 31, 193–196. PA 61:10931.

Touzard, Hubert. (1974–1975). [The influence of the behavior of the mediator on the performance of negotiation groups and the process of resolution of conflict]. *Bulletin de Psychologie*, 28, 471–487. PA 54:11688.

Town, Jerri P.; & Harvey, John H. (1981). Self-disclosure, attribution, and social interaction. *Social Psychology Quarterly*, 44, 291–300. PA 68:1140.

Towson, Shelagh M. J.; & Zanna, Mark P. (1982). Toward a situational analysis of gender differences in aggression. *Sex Roles*, 8, 903–914.

Traupmann, Jane; Hatfield, Elaine; & Wexler, Philip. (1983). Equity and sexual satisfaction in dating couples. *British Journal of Social Psychology*, 22, 33–40. PA 70:12656.

Tresemer, David. (1976). Observing Social Interaction: Methodological Models. *Small Group Behavior*, 7, 47–58. SA 7718739.

Trope, Yaacov; & Bassok, Miriam. (1982). Confirmatory and diagnosing strategies in social information gathering. *Journal of Personality and Social Psychology*, 43, 22–34. PA 69:3433.

Trope, Yaacov; Bassok, Miriam; & Alon, Eve. (1984). The questions lay interviewers ask. *Journal of Personality*, 52, 91–106. PA 72:14529.

Tropp, Karen J.; & Landers, Daniel M. (1979). Team interaction and the emergence of leadership and interpersonal attraction in field hockey. *Journal of Sport Psychology*, 1, 228–240. PA 65:3260.

Trow, Donald B. (1977). Status equilibration: Fueled by uncertainty, frustration, or anxiety. *Human Relations*, 30, 721–736. PA 60:3054.

Trujillo, Nick. (1986). Toward a taxonomy of small group interaction-coding systems. *Small Group Behavior*, 17, 371–394.

Truscott, Janice C.; Parmelee, Pat; & Werner, Carol. (1977). Plate-touching in restaurants: preliminary observations of a food-related marking behavior in humans. *Personality and Social Psychology Bulletin*, 3, 425–428. PA 59:12311.

Tscherbo, Nataliya P. (1984). [Characteristics of individual and group solution of problems where there is interaction]. *Voprosy Psikhologii*, No. 2, 107–112. PA 73:6350.

Tubbs, Stewart L. (1984). *A systems approach to small group interaction* (2nd ed.). Reading, MA: Addison-Wesley.

Tuchman, Paula Susan. (1981). Efecto de algunas caracteristicas individuales sobre la toma de riesgo. *Revista de la Asociacion Latinoamericana de Psicologia Social*, 1(1), 109–133. SA 85Q1243.

Tuckman, Bruce W.; & Jensen, Mary A. (1977). Stages of small-group development revisited. *Group and Organization Studies*, 2, 419–427. PA 60:11706. SA 78J3227.

Tuma, Nancy Brandon; & Hallinan, Maureen T. (1979) The effects of sex, race, and achievement on schoolchildren's friendships. *Social Forces*, 57, 1265–1285.

Turnbull, Allen A.; Strickland, Lloyd H.; & Shaver, Kelly G. (1974). Phasing of concessions, differential power, and medium of communication: Negotiating success and attributions of the opponent. *Personality and Social Psychology Bulletin*, 1, 228–230. PA 56:2319.

Turnbull, Allen A.; Strickland, Lloyd [H.]; & Shaver, Kelly G. (1976). Medium of communication, differential power, and phasing of concessions: Negotiating success and attributions to the opponent. *Human Communication Research*, 2, 262–270. PA 60:3055.

Turner, John C. (1981). Towards a cognitive redefinition of the social group. *Cahiers de Psychologie Cognitive, 1*(2), 93–118. PA 67:12053.

Turner, John C. (1985). Social categorization and the self-concept: A social-cognitive theory of group behavior. *Advances in Group Processes, 2*, 77–121.

Turner, John C. (1987). *Rediscovering the social group. A self categorization theory*. Oxford, England: Basil Blackwell.

Turner, John C.; & Giles, Howard. (Eds.). (1981). *Intergroup behaviour*. Chicago: University of Chicago Press.

Turner, J[ohn] C.; Hogg, M. A.; Turner, P. J.; & Smith, P. M. (1984). Failure and defeat as determinants of group cohesiveness. *British Journal of Social Psychology, 23*, 97–111. PA 72:14501. SA 8506035.

Turner, Ralph H.; & Colomy, Paul. (1988). Role differentiation: Orienting principles. *Advances in Group Processes, 5*, 1–27.

Turovskaya, A. A. (1976). [An experimental study of group behavior as a function of the degree of identification with group goals]. *Voprosy Psikhologii*, No. 2, 42–49. PA 60:1035.

Tuthill, Douglas M.; & Forsyth, Donelson R. (1982). Sex differences in opinion conformity and dissent. *Journal of Social Psychology, 116*, 205–210. PA 68:10359

Tuzlak, Aysan; & Moore, James C., Jr. (1984). Status, demeanor and influence: An empirical reassessment. *Social Psychology Quarterly, 47*, 178–183. SA 8400842.

Tyerman, Andrew; & Spencer, Christopher. (1983). A critical test of the Sherifs' robber's cave experiments: Intergroup competition and cooperation between groups of well-acquainted individuals. *Small Group Behavior, 14*, 515–531. PA 71:23081.

Tyler, Tom R.; Rasinski, Kenneth A.; & Spodick, Nancy. (1985). Influence of voice on satisfaction with leaders: Exploring the meaning of process control. *Journal of Personality and Social Psychology, 48*, 72–81. PA 72:17356.

Tyler, Tom R., & Sears, David O. (1977) Coming to like obnoxious people when we must live with them. *Journal of Personality and Social Psychology, 35*, 200–211. PA 62:3621.

Tyrell, Hartmann. (1983). Zwischen Interaktion und Organisation I: Gruppe als Systemtyp [Between interaction and organization I: Group as system type]. *Kolner Zeitschrift fur Soziologie und Sozialpsychologie*, Supplement 25, 75–87. SA 8402599.

Tyszka, Tadeusz; & Grzelak, Janusz L. (1976). Criteria of choice in non-constant-sum games. *Journal of Conflict Resolution, 20*, 357–376.

Tziner, Aharon. (1982a). Differential effects of group cohesiveness types: A clarifying overview. *Social Behavior and Personality, 10*, 227–239. PA 71:6716.

Tziner, Aharon. (1982b). Group cohesiveness: A dynamic perspective. *Social Behavior and Personality, 10*, 205–211. PA 71:6715.

Ueno, Tokumi; & Yokogawa, Kazuaki. (1982). [The role of social comparison in group polarization phenomenon]. *Japanese Journal of Experimental Social Psychology, 21*, 167–173. PA 68:10360.

Ugwuegbu, Denis C.; & Anusiem, A. U. (1982). Effects of stress on interpersonal distance in a simulated interview situation. *Journal of Social Psychology, 116*, 3–7.

Ulvila, Jacob W. (1983). On the value of assessing preferences explicitly for bargaining. *IEEE Transactions on Systems, Man, and Cybernetics, SMC-13*, 125–136. PA 70:5640.

Umino, Michio. (1983). [Reexamination of French-Harary model on social power]. *Japanese Journal of Experimental Social Psychology, 22*, 123–132. PA 71:9496.

Uray, Hans. (1976). [Causes of performance, ascription of responsibility, and division of winnings]. *Zeitschrift fur Sozialpsychologie, 7*, 69–80. PA 59:3633.

Urruti, Giselle; & Miller, Charles E. (1984). Test of the bargaining and equal excess theories of coalition formation: Effects of experience, information about payoffs, and monetary stakes. *Journal of Personality and Social Psychology, 46*, 825–836. PA 71:23082.

Vaisman, R. S. (1977). Svyaz mezhlichnostnykh otnoshenii s gruppovoi effektivnostyu deyatelnosti [The connection between interpersonal relations and group efficiency]. *Voprosy psikhologii, 4*, 64–73. SA 79J8030.

Valenti, Angelo; & Downing, Leslie. (1974). Six versus twelve member juries. An experimental test of the Supreme Court assumption of functional equivalence. *Personality and Social Psychology Bulletin, 1*, 273–275. PA 56:2250.

Valenti, Angelo C.; & Downing, Leslie L. (1975). Differential effects of jury size on verdicts following deliberation as a function of the apparent guilt of a defendant. *Journal of Personality and Social Psychology, 32,* 655-663. PA 57:3283 [PsycLIT No. 56-00598].

Valentine, Kristin B.; & Fisher, B. Aubrey. (1974). An interaction analysis of verbal innovative deviance in small groups. *Speech Monographs, 41,* 413-420. PA 54:9580.

Valentine, Mary E. (1980). The attenuating influence of gaze upon the bystander intervention effect. *Journal of Social Psychology, 111,* 197-203. PA 66:5777.

Valentine, Mary E.; & Ehrlichman, Howard. (1979). Interpersonal gaze and helping behavior. *Journal of Social Psychology, 107,* 193-198. PA 64:3267.

Valentinova, N. G.; & Myedvyedyev, V. V. (1973). Selected problems of small groups in sports teams. *International Review of Sport Sociology, 8,* 69-77. SA 75H1337.

Valiant-Dyckoff, G. L. (1977). A British-American contrast of coalition strategies in four-person groups of unequal pivotal power. *Journal of Cross Cultural Psychology, 8,* 465-476. PA 60:9316. SA 79J6859.

Valins, Stuart; & Baum, Andrew. (1973). Residential group size, social interaction, and crowding. *Environment and Behavior, 5,* 421-439.

Vallacher, Robin R.; Callahan-Levy, Charlene M.; & Messé, Lawrence A. (1979). Sex effects on bilateral bargaining as a function of interpersonal context. *Personality and Social Psychology Bulletin, 5,* 104-108. PA 64:3268.

Valle, Valerie A.; DeGood, Douglas E.; & Valle, Ronald S. (1978). Physiological response and task performance in like- and cross-sex competition. *Sex Roles, 4,* 445-454. PA 63:3265.

Vallerand, Robert J.; Gauvin, Lise I.; & Halliwell, Wayne R. (1986). Effects of zero-sum competition on children's intrinsic motivation and perceived competence. *Journal of Social Psychology, 126,* 465-472.

van Asperen, G. M. (1981). Normatieve theorie en kollektieve beslissingen [Normative theories and collective decisions]. *Algemeen Nederlands Tijdschrift voor Wijsbegeerte, 73*(2), 94-106. SA 84O2600.

Van Blerkom, Malcolm; & Tjosvold, Dean. (1981). Effects of social context and other's competence on engaging in controversy. *Journal of Psychology, 107,* 141-145. PA 66:12780.

Vance, Robert J.; & Biddle, Thomas F. (1985). Task experience and social cues: Interactive

effects on attitudinal reactions. *Organizational Behavior and Human Decision Processes, 35,* 252-265. PA 72:20092.

Van den Berghe, Pierre L. (1977). Territorial behavior in a natural human group. *Social Science Information, 16*(3-4), 419-430. PA 62:3582.

Vanderslice, Virginia J.; Rice, Robert W.; & Julian, James W. (1987). The effects of participation in decision-making on worker satisfaction and productivity: An organizational simulation. *Journal of Applied Social Psychology, 17,* 158-170.

Van de Ven, Andrew H. (1980). Problem solving, planning, and innovation: II. Speculations for theory and practice. *Human Relations, 33,* 757-779. PA 65:3261.

Van de Ven, Andrew H.; & Delbecq, André L. (1974). The effectiveness of nominal, delphi, and interacting group decision making processes. *Academy of Management Journal, 17,* 605-621. PA 53:9495.

Van de Vliert, Evert. (1981). Siding and other reactions to a conflict: A theory of escalation toward outsiders. *Journal of Conflict Resolution, 25,* 495-520. PA 67:3568.

Van de Vliert, Evert. (1985). Escalative intervention in small-group conflicts. *Journal of Applied Behavioral Science, 21,* 19-36. SA 85O9455.

Van Egeren, Lawrence F. (1979). Cardiovascular changes during social competition in a mixed-motive game. *Journal of Personality and Social Psychology, 37,* 858-864. PA 64:10349.

van Kreveld, D.; & Menckeberg, H. W. (1974). Status congruency as a cognitive schema in dyad-learning. *Nederlands Tijdschrift voor de Psychologie en haar Grensgebieden, 29,* 583-599. PA 53:7337.

Van Kreveld, David; Willigers, Fred J. M.; Gloudemans, Theo; Rancuret, Frans; Van der Wiel, Kiek; & Poot, Ruud. (1974). The importance of status congruency in interaction processes. *European Journal of Social Psychology, 4,* 137-158. PA 54:5220. SA 75H4718.

van Nieuwenhuizen, E. F. J. (1983). Group cohesion in small task groups / Groepskohesie in kleintaakgroepe. *Suid-Afrikaanse Tydskrif vir Sosiologie/The South African Journal of Sociology, 14*(4), 132-142. SA 84N5653.

Van Tuinen, Mark; & McNeel, Steven P. (1975). A test of the social facilitation theories of Cottrell and Zajonc in a coaction situation. *Personality* and Social Psychology Bulletin, 1, 604–607. PA 56:4082.

Varca, Philip E.; & Levy, Jodie C. (1984). Individual differences in response to unfavorable group feedback. Organizational Behavior and Human Performance, 33, 100–111. PA 71:12180.

Varghese, Raju. (1982). Eriksonian personality variables and interpersonal behavior in groups. Small Group Behavior, 13, 133–149. PA 68:12626.

Vassiliou, Vasso G.; & Vassiliou, George. (1974). Variations of the group process across cultures. International Journal of Group Psychotherapy, 24, 55–65. PA 52:5167.

Vecchio, Robert P. (1977). An empirical examination of the validity of Fiedler's model of leadership effectiveness. Organizational Behavior and Human Performance, 19, 180–206. PA 59:5654.

Vecchio, Robert P. (1980). Alternatives to the Least Preferred Co-worker construct. Journal of Social Psychology, 112, 261–269. PA 66:4470.

Vecchio, Robert P. (1981). A test based on the contingency model of leadership. Small Group Behavior, 12, 107–115. SA 82M4129.

Vecchio, Robert P. (1982). A further test of leadership effects due to between-group variation and within-group variation. Journal of Applied Psychology, 67, 200–208. PA 68:1109.

Vecchio, Robert P. (1983). Assessing the validity of Fiedler's contingency model of leadership effectiveness: A closer look at Strube and Garcia. Psychological Bulletin, 93, 404–408. PA 70:1113.

Vedder, P. H. (1985). Cooperative learning: A study of processes and effects on cooperation between primary school children. New York: Taylor and Francis.

Veno, Arthur E. (1976). Response to approach: A preliminary process oriented study of human spacing. Social Science Information, 15(1), 93–115. PA 58:3306.

Verbrugge, Lois M. (1977). The structure of adult friendship choices. Social Forces, 56, 576–597. PA 60:9317.

Verbrugge, Lois M. (1983). A research note on adult friendship contact: A dyadic perspective. Social Forces, 62, 78–83. PA 71:14978. SA 83N4036.

Verma, Jyoti; & Sinha, Jai B. (1981). Cultural invariance in risky shift and its determinants.

Psychologia An International Journal of Psychology in the Orient, 24, 235–238. PA 68:8141.

Vernon, Glenn M. (1978). Symbolic aspects of interaction. Washington: University Press of America.

Vertommen, Hans. (1980). [The structure and conformity of meaning of interpersonal behaviors in different forms of relationships]. Psychologica Belgica, 20, 91–108. PA 65:12753.

Vestewig, Richard E.; & Moss, Martin K. (1976). The relationship of extraversion and neuroticism to two measures of assertive behavior. Journal of Psychology, 93, 141–146.

Vicino, Franco L.; Krusell, Judith; Bass, Bernard M.; Deci, Edward L.; & Landy, David A. (1973). The impact of PROCESS: Self-administered exercises for personal and interpersonal development. Journal of Applied Behavioral Science, 9, 737–756. PA 52:5206.

Vidal, J. P. (1978). [Collective acting-out and the rule of abstention in training groups]. Bulletin de Psychologie, 32, 65–73. PA 65:1254.

Vinokur, Amiram; & Burnstein, Eugene. (1978a). Depolarization of attitudes in groups. Journal of Personality and Social Psychology, 36, 872–885. PA 63:965.

Vinokur, Amiram; & Burnstein, Eugene. (1978b). Novel argumentation and attitude change: The case of polarization following group discussion. European Journal of Social Psychology, 8, 335–348. PA 63:3233. SA 80K4188.

Vinokur, Amiram; Burnstein, Eugene; Sechrest, Lee; & Wortman, Paul M. (1985). Group decision making by experts: Field study of panels evaluating medical technologies. Journal of Personality and Social Psychology, 49, 70–84. PA 72:30805.

Vinokur, Amiram; Trope, Yaacov; & Burnstein, Eugene. (1975). A decision-making analysis of persuasive argumentation and the choice-shift effect. Journal of Experimental Social Psychology, 11, 127–148. PA 54:2992.

Vinsel, Anne; Brown, Barbara B.; Altman, Irwin; & Foss, Carolyn. (1980). Privacy regulation, territorial displays, and effectiveness of individual functioning. Journal of Personality and Social Psychology, 39, 1104–1115. PA 66:5778.

Virk, J.; Aggarwal, Y. P.; & Bhan, R. N. (1983). Similarity versus complementarity in clique formation. Journal of Social Psychology, 120, 27–34. PA 71:6717.

Vlaander, G. P.; & Van Rooijen, L. (1985). Independence and conformity in Holland: Asch's experiment three decades later. *Gedrag Tijdschrift voor Psychologie, 13*(1), 49–55. PA 73:1138.

Voicu, Maria. (1973). [The influence of active communication on efficiency of group problem-solving by students]. *Revista de Psihologie, 19*, 193–208. PA 54:2993.

Von Baeyer, Carl L.; Sherk, Debbie L.; & Zanna, Mark P. (1981). Impression management in the job interview: When the female applicant meets the male (chauvinist) interviewer. *Personality and Social Psychology Bulletin, 7*, 45–51. PA 67:3502.

Von Cranach, Mario; Ochsenbein, Guy; & Valach, Ladislav. (1986). The group as a self-active system: Outline of a theory of group action. *European Journal of Social Psychology, 16*, 193–229.

von Grumbkow, J.; & Wilke, H. (1978). Extreme underpayment in a simple and a complex comparison situation. *European Journal of Social Psychology, 8*, 129–133. PA 63:7603.

Vorob'ev, N. N. [Compiler?]. (1980). *Teoriia igr: … Leningrad: Nauka.*

Vraa, Calvin W. (1974). Emotional climate as a function of group composition. *Small Group Behavior, 5*, 105–120. PA 52:10047.

Vroman, H. William. (1975). An application of the nominal group technique in educational systems analysis. *Educational Technology, 15*(6), 51–53. PA 55:13093.

Wadington, James. (1975). Social decision schemes and two-person bargaining. *Behavioral Science, 20*, 157–165. PA 54:9581.

Wagner, David G.; & Berger, Joseph. (1982). Paths of relevance and the induction of status-task expectancies: A research note. *Social Forces, 61*, 575–586. PA 70:3372.

Wagner, H.; Clarke, A. H.; & Ellgring, J. H. (1983). Eye-contact and individual looking: The role of chance. *British Journal of Social Psychology, 22*, 61–62. PA 70:12657.

Wagner, Hugh L.; MacDonald, C. J.; & Manstead, A. S. R. (1986). Communication of individual emotions by spontaneous facial expressions. *Journal of Personality and Social Psychology, 50*, 737–743. PA 73:21950.

Wagner P., Isis. (1972). [Research problems related to the results of laboratory training]. *Cuadernos de Psicologia*, No. 2, 59–61. PA 52:10048.

Wagner, R. Harrison. (1979). On the unification of two-person bargaining theory. *Journal of Conflict Resolution, 23*, 71–101. PA 64:1027.

Wagner, Richard V. (1975). Complementary needs, role expectations, interpersonal attraction, and the stability of working relationships. *Journal of Personality and Social Psychology, 32*, 116–124. PA 54:7486.

Wahrman, Ralph. (1977). Status, deviance, sanctions, and group discussion. *Small Group Behavior, 8*, 147–168. PA 62:3583.

Wahrman, Ralph; & Pugh, M. D. (1972). Competence and conformity: Another look at Hollander's study. *Sociometry, 35*, 376–386.

Wahrman, Ralph; & Pugh, Meredith D. (1974). Sex, nonconformity and influence. *Sociometry, 37*, 137–147.

Walden, Tedra A.; & Forsyth, Donelson R. (1981). Close encounters of the stressful kind: Affective, physiological, and behavioral reactions to the experience of crowding. *Journal of Nonverbal Behavior, 6*, 46–64. PA 67:9788.

Walker, Betty A.; & Robinson, Rick. (1979). Utilizing dimensions of the Rotter Interpersonal Trust Scale in investigations of trust: Validation of suggested methods. *Psychological Reports, 44*, 423–429. PA 64:10350.

Walker, David N. (1975). A dyadic interaction model for nonverbal touching behavior in encounter groups. *Small Group Behavior, 6*, 308–324. SA 7718740.

Walker, John W.; & Borden, Richard J. (1976). Sex, status, and the invasion of shared space. *Representative Research in Social Psychology, 7*, 28–34. PA 56:4013.

Walker, Laurens; LaTour, Stephen; Lind, F. Allan; & Thibaut, John. (1974). Reactions of participants and observers to modes of adjudication. *Journal of Applied Social Psychology, 4*, 295–310. PA 54:3047.

Walker, Lilly S.; & Wright, Paul H. (1976). Self-disclosure in friendship. *Perceptual and Motor Skills, 42*, 735–742. PA 56:9881.

Walker, Michael B. (1982). Smooth transitions in conversational turn-taking: Implications for theory. *Journal of Psychology, 110*, 31–37. PA 68:5771.

Walker, Michael B.; & Bragg, Brian W. (1981). On testing the equilibrium model of intimacy. *Italian Journal of Psychology, 8*(2), 133–147. PA 68:8112.

Walker, Thomas G. (1974). The decision-making superiority of groups: A research note. *Small Group Behavior, 5*, 121–128. PA 52:10004.

Wall, James A. (1974). Intergroup bargaining

studied as a dynamic process: The effects of constituent trust and representative bargaining visibility. *Personality and Social Psychology Bulletin, 1*, 225–227. PA 56:2320.

Wall, James A. (1975a). Effects of constituent trust and representative bargaining orientation on intergroup bargaining. *Journal of Personality and Social Psychology, 31*, 1004–1012. PA 54:9582.

Wall, James A. (1975b). The effects of constituent trust and representative bargaining visibility on intergroup bargaining. *Organizational Behavior and Human Performance, 14*, 244–256. PA 55:7098.

Wall, James A. (1976). Effects of sex and opposing representative's bargaining orientation on intergroup bargaining. *Journal of Personality and Social Psychology, 33*, 55–61. PA 55:7099.

Wall, James A. (1977a). Intergroup bargaining: Effects of opposing constituent stances, opposing representative's bargaining, and representative's locus of control. *Journal of Conflict Resolution, 21*, 459–474. PA 60:3020.

Wall, James A. (1977b). Operantly conditioning a negotiator's concession making. *Journal of Experimental Social Psychology, 13*, 431–440. PA 60:1036.

Wall, James A. (1979). The effects of mediator rewards and suggestions upon negotiations. *Journal of Personality and Social Psychology, 37*, 1554–1560. PA 65:1255.

Wall, James A. (1981a). An investigation of reciprocity and reinforcement theories of bargaining behavior. *Organizational Behavior and Human Performance, 27*, 367–385. PA 66:1247.

Wall, James A. (1981b). Mediation: An analysis, review, and proposed research. *Journal of Conflict Resolution, 25*, 157–180. PA 65:12755.

Wall, James A. (1985). *Negotiation, theory and practice*. Glenview, IL: Scott, Foresman.

Wall, Shavaun M.; Pickert, Sarah M.; & Paradise, Louis V. (1984). American men's friendships: Self-reports on meaning and changes. *Journal of Psychology, 116*, 179–186. PA 72:4015.

Wall, Victor D., Jr.; Galanes, Gloria J.; & Love, Sue Beth. (1987). Small, task-oriented groups: Conflict, conflict management, satisfaction, and decision quality. *Small Group Behavior, 18*, 31–55.

Wall, Victor D.; & Nolan, Linda L. (1986). Perceptions of inequity, satisfaction, and conflict in task-oriented groups. *Human Relations, 39*, 1033–1051. PA 74:15536.

Walsh, Debra G.; & Hewitt, Jay. (1985). Giving men the come-on: Effect of eye contact and smiling in a bar environment. *Perceptual and Motor Skills, 61*, 873–874. PA 74:7210.

Walter, Gordon A. (1975a). Acted versus natural models for performance-oriented behavior change in task groups. *Journal of Applied Psychology, 60*, 303–307. PA 54:5221.

Walter, Gordon A. (1975b). Effects of video tape feedback and modeling on the behaviors of task group members. *Human Relations, 28*, 121–138. PA 54:11689.

Walter, Gordon A. (1975c). Effects of videotape training inputs on group performance. *Journal of Applied Psychology, 60*, 308–312. PA 54:6289.

Wankel, Leonard M. (1975). The effects of social reinforcement and audience presence upon the motor performance of boys with different levels of initial ability. *Journal of Motor Behavior, 7*, 207–216. PA 55:6020.

Warehime, Robert G. (1981). Interactional gestalt therapy. *Small Group Behavior, 12*, 37–54.

Warner, Rebecca M.; Kenny, David A.; & Stoto, Michael. (1979). A new round robin analysis of variance for social interaction data. *Journal of Personality and Social Psychology, 37*, 1742–1757. PA 65:303.

Warnick, Dell H.; & Sanders, Glenn S. (1980). The effects of group discussion on eyewitness accuracy. *Journal of Applied Social Psychology, 10*, 249–259. PA 65:3236.

Watkins, John T.; Noll, Gary A.; & Breed, George R. (1975). Changes toward self-actualization. *Small Group Behavior, 6*, 272–281. SA 7718741.

Watson, Warren; & Michaelsen, Larry. (1984). Task performance information and leader participation behavior: Effect on leader-subordinate interaction, frustration, and future productivity. *Group and Organization Studies, 9*, 121–144. PA 71:20467.

Watson, Warren E.; & Michaelsen, Larry K. (1985). Effect of disclosure of performance data in role-played interviews appraising performance. *Psychological Reports, 56*, 67–80. PA 73:9119.

Watts, Barbara L.; & Messé, Lawrence A. (1982). The impact of task inputs, situational context, and sex on evaluations of reward allocators.

Social Psychology Quarterly, *45*, 254–262. PA 70:3429.

Weathers, James E.; Messé, Lawrence A.; & Aronoff, Joel. (1984). The effects of task-group experiences on subsequent prosocial behavior. *Social Psychology Quarterly*, *47*, 287–292. PA 72:25414.

Webb, Bill; Worchel, Stephen; Riechers, Lisa; & Wayne, Wendy. (1986). The influence of categorization on perceptions of crowding. *Personality and Social Psychology Bulletin*, *12*, 539–546.

Webb, Janette. (1982). Arbitration: Semi-judicial process or negotiation? *Current Psychological Reviews*, *2*, 251–268. PA 70:10259.

Webb, Noreen M. (1984a). Microcomputer learning in small groups: Cognitive requirements and group processes. *Journal of Educational Psychology*, *76*, 1076–1088.

Webb, Noreen M. (1984b). Stability of small group interaction and achievement over time. *Journal of Educational Psychology*, *76*, 211–224. PA 71:24494.

Webb, Noreen M. (1984c). Sex differences in interaction and achievement in cooperative small groups. *Journal of Educational Psychology*, *76*, 33–44.

Weber, Hans Jurgen. (1977). [On the level of aspiration theory in repetitive decision situations]. *Zeitschrift fur Experimentelle und Angewandte Psychologie*, *24*, 649–670. PA 61:5942.

Webster, Murray. (1977). Equating characteristics and social interaction: Two experiments. *Sociometry*, *40*, 41–50. PA 58:9500.

Webster, Murray; & Driskell, James E. (1978). Status generalization: A review and some new data. *American Sociological Review*, *43*, 220–236. PA 61:10932.

Webster, Murray; & Driskell, James E. (1983). Processes of status generalization. In H. H. Blumberg, A. P. Hare, V. Kent, & M. F. Davies (Eds.), *Small groups and social interaction* (Vol. 1, pp. 57–67). Chichester and New York: Wiley & Sons.

Webster, Murray, Jr.; & Smith, Le Roy F. (1978). Justice and revolutionary coalitions: A test of two theories. *American Journal of Sociology*, *84*, 267–292. SA 79J8031.

Weckerle, G. R. (1976). Vertical village: Social contacts in a singles high-rise complex. *Sociological Forces*, *9*, 299–315.

Weed, Stan E.; Mitchell, Terence R.; & Moffitt, Weldon. (1976). Leadership style, subordinate personality, and task type as predictors of performance and satisfaction with supervision. *Journal of Applied Psychology*, *61*, 58–66. PA 55:11180.

Weeks, Gerald D.; & Chapanis, Alphonse. (1976). Cooperative versus conflictive problem solving in three telecommunication modes. *Perceptual and Motor Skills*, *42*, 879–917. PA 56:9617.

Wegner, Daniel M.; & Crano, William D. (1975). Racial factors in helping behavior: An unobtrusive field experiment. *Journal of Personality and Social Psychology*, *32*, 901–905. PA 55:4582.

Wegner, Daniel M.; & Schaefer, Donna. (1978). The concentration of responsibility: An objective self-awareness analysis of group size effects in helping situations. *Journal of Personality and Social Psychology*, *36*, 147–155. PA 61:5943.

Weigel, Richard G.; & Corazzini, John G. (1978). Small group research: Suggestions for solving common methodological and design problems. *Small Group Behavior*, *9*, 193–220. SA 79K2642.

Weigel, Ronald M. (1984). The application of evolutionary models to the study of decisions made by children during object possession conflicts. *Ethology and Sociobiology*, *5*, 229–238. SA 85O6036.

Weigel, Russell H.; & Quinn, Thomas E. (1977). Ethnic differences in cooperative behavior: A non-confirmation. *Psychological Reports*, *40*, 666. PA 59:5655.

Weigel, Russell H.; Wiser, Patricia L.; & Cook, Stuart W. (1975). The impact of cooperative learning experiences on cross-ethnic relations and attitudes. *Journal of Social Issues*, *31*, 219–244. PA 55:7604.

Weight, David G. (1974). Interviewer's locus of control and conditioning of interviewee's self-reference statements. *Psychological Reports*, *35*, 1307–1316. PA 53:11595.

Weinberg, R. S.; Poteet, Don; Morrow, James R.; & Jackson, Allen. (1982). Effect of evaluation on causal and trait attribution of males and females. *International Journal of Sport Psychology*, *13*, 163–175. PA 70:7992.

Weinberg, Robert S.; Yukelson, David; & Jackson, Allen. (1980). Effect of public and private efficacy expectations on competitive performance. *Journal of Sport Psychology, 2,* 340 349. PA 65:7981.

Weinberg, Sanford B.; Smotroff, Larry J.; & Pecka, John C. (1978). Communication factors of group leadership. *Journal of Applied Communication Research, 6*(2), 85–91. SA 81L1747.

Weiner, Ferne H. (1976). Altruism, ambiance, and action: The effects of rural and urban rearing on helping behavior. *Journal of Personality and Social Psychology, 34,* 112–124. PA 56.6066.

Weinstein, Malcolm S.; & Hanson, Robert. (1975). Leader experience level and patterns of participation in sensitivity training groups. *Small Group Behavior, 6,* 123–140. PA 55:2337.

Weisfeld, Carol C. (1986). Female behavior in mixed-sex competition: A review of the literature. *Developmental Review, 6,* 278–299. PA 73:29972.

Weisfeld, Glenn E. (1972). Violations of social norms as inducers of aggression. *International Journal of Group Tensions, 2*(4), 53–70. PA 52:5209.

Weiss, Howard M. (1977). Subordinate imitation of supervisor behavior: The role of modeling in organizational socialization. *Organizational Behavior and Human Performance, 19,* 89–105. PA 59:6798.

Weiss, Howard M. (1978). Social learning of work values in organizations. *Journal of Applied Psychology, 63,* 711–718. PA 63:10798.

Weiss, Howard M.; & Nowicki, Christine E. (1981). Social influences on task satisfaction: Model competence and observer field dependence. *Organizational Behavior and Human Performance, 27,* 345–366. PA 66:1296.

Weiss, Robert F.; & Miller, Franklin G. (1971). The drive theory of social facilitation. *Psychological Review. 78,* 44–57. PA 45:8157.

Weiss, Robert F.; Weiss, Joyce J.; Wenninger, V. L.; & Balling, Susan S. (1981). Sex differences in social influence: Social learning. *Bulletin of the Psychonomic Society, 18,* 233–236. PA 68:3515.

Weitz, Shirley. (Ed.). (1979). *Nonverbal communication: Readings with commentary.* New York: Oxford University Press.

Weldon, Elizabeth. (1984). Deindividualization, interpersonal affect and productivity in laboratory task groups. *Journal of Applied Social Psychology, 14,* 469–485. PA 72:17328.

Weldon, Elizabeth; & Gargano, Gina M. (1985).

Cognitive effort in additive task groups: The effects of shared responsibility on the quality of multiattribute judgments. *Organizational Behavior and Human Decision Processes, 36,* 348–361. PA 73:9120.

Wellens, A. Rodney; & Goldberg, Myron L. (1978). The effects of interpersonal distance and orientation upon the perception of social relationships. *Journal of Psychology, 99,* 39–47. PA 62.1108.

Welton, Gary L.; & Pruitt, Dean G. (1980). The mediation process: The effects of mediator bias and disputant power. *Personality and Social Psychology Bulletin, 13,* 123–133.

Wener, Richard E.; & Kaminoff, Robert D. (1983). Improving environmental information: Effects of signs on perceived crowding and behavior. *Environment and Behavior, 15,* 3–20.

Wentworth, Diane K.; & Anderson, Lynn R. (1984). Emergent leadership as a function of sex and task type. *Sex Roles, 11,* 513–524. PA 72:20095.

Werner, Carol M.; Kagehiro, Dorothy K.; & Strube, Michael J. (1982). Conviction proneness and the authoritarian juror: Inability to disregard information or attitudinal bias? *Journal of Applied Psychology, 67,* 629–636. PA 69:3351.

Werner, Carol; & Parmelee, Pat. (1979). Similarity of activity preferences among friends: Those who play together stay together. *Social Psychology Quarterly, 42,* 62–66. PA 64:7953.

Werner, Carol M.; Strube, Michael J.; Cole, Allen M.; & Kagehiro, Dorothy K. (1985). The impact of case characteristics and prior jury experience on jury verdicts. *Journal of Applied Social Psychology, 15,* 409–427.

West, Stephen G.; Whitney, Glayde; & Schnedler, Robert. (1975). Helping a motorist in distress: The effects of sex, race, and neighborhood. *Journal of Personality and Social Psychology, 31,* 691–698. PA 55:777.

Westbrook, Franklin D. (1985). Third-party consultation, mediation, and coercive bargaining. *Journal of Counseling and Development, 63,* 535–536. PA 72:20096.

Westen, T. Edward; & Buckley, James J. (1974). Toward an explanation of experimentally obtained outcomes to a simple, majority rule game. *Journal of Conflict Resolution, 18,* 198–236. PA 53:5183.

Wetzel, Christopher G.; Schwartz, David; & Vasu,

Ellen S. (1979). Roommate compatibility: Is there an ideal relationship? *Journal of Applied Social Psychology, 9,* 432–445. PA 66:5726.

Wetzel, Christopher G.; & Wright-Buckley, Carol. (1988). Reciprocity of self-disclosure: Breakdowns of trust in cross-racial dyads. *Basic and Applied Social Psychology, 9,* 277–288.

Wexley, Kenneth N.; Fugita, Stephen S.; & Malone, Michael P. (1975). An applicant's nonverbal behavior and student-evaluators' judgments in a structured interview setting. *Psychological Reports, 36,* 391–394. PA 54:7542.

Whalen, Carol K.; Flowers, John V.; Fuller, Mary J.; & Jernigan, Terry. (1975). Behavioral studies of personal space during early adolescence. *Man-Environment Systems, 5*(5), 289–297. PA 57:8047.

Wheaton, Blair. (1974). Interpersonal conflict and cohesiveness in dyadic relationships. *Sociometry, 37,* 328–348. PA 53:5152.

Wheeler, Ladd; & Nezlek, John. (1977). Sex differences in social participation. *Journal of Personality and Social Psychology, 35,* 742–754. PA 62:9764.

Wheeler, Ladd; Reis, Harry; & Nezlek, John B. (1983). Loneliness, social interaction, and sex roles. *Journal of Personality and Social Psychology, 45,* 943–953. PA 71:12181.

Wheeless, Lawrence R. (1976). Self-disclosure and interpersonal solidarity: Measurement, validation, and relationships. *Human Communication Research, 3,* 47–61. PA 60:5244.

Wheeless, Lawrence R. (1978). A follow-up study of the relationships among trust, disclosure, and interpersonal solidarity. *Human Communication Research, 4,* 143–157. PA 61:5944.

Wheeless, Lawrence R.; Wheeless, Virginia E.; & Dickson-Markman, Fran. (1982). A research note: The relations among social and task perceptions in small groups. *Small Group Behavior, 13,* 373–384. PA 69:5589.

Whitaker, Dorothy S. (1975). Some conditions for effective work with groups. *British Journal of Social Work, 5,* 423–439. PA 56:656.

Whitaker, Dorothy S. (1985). *Using groups to help people.* London: Routledge.

Whitcher, Sheryle J.; & Fisher, Jeffrey D. (1979). Multidimensional reaction to therapeutic touch in a hospital setting. *Journal of Personality and Social Psychology, 37,* 87–96.

White, Gregory L. (1980). Physical attractiveness and courtship progress. *Journal of Personality*

and Social Psychology, 39, 660–668. PA 66:5779.

White, Jacquelyn Weygandt. (1983). Sex and gender issues in aggression research. In R. G. Geen & E. I. Donnerstein (Eds.), *Aggression: Theoretical and empirical reviews* (Vol. 2, pp. 1–26). New York: Academic Press.

White, James H. (1974). Justice and generosity in social exchange: An experimental study of reactions to winning or losing a game. *British Journal of Social and Clinical Psychology, 13,* 369–373. PA 53:7340.

White, James M. (1982). Dyadic systems analysis. *Behavioral Science, 27,* 104–117. SA 83N4037.

White, Jerome D.; & White, Terry. (1974). TA psychohistory: Adapting, scripting, and cultural scripting. *Transactional Analysis Journal, 4*(3), 5–17. PA 54:2744.

White, Karl R. (1974). T-groups revisited: Self-concept change and the "fish-bowling" technique. *Small Group Behavior, 5,* 473–485. PA 54:9548.

White, Lynn K.; & Brinkerhoff, David B. (1978). Measuring dyadic properties: An exploratory analysis. *International Journal of Sociology of the Family, 8*(2), 219–229. SA 79K1111.

White, Michael J. (1975). Interpersonal distance as affected by room size, status, and sex. *Journal of Social Psychology, 95,* 241–249. PA 54:2994.

White, Michael J. (1977). Counternormative behavior as influenced by deindividuating conditions and reference group salience. *Journal of Social Psychology, 103,* 75–90. PA 60:5246.

White, Ralph K. (Ed.). (1986). *Psychology and the prevention of nuclear war.* New York: New York University Press.

White, Willard P. (Ed.). (1978). *Resources in environment and behavior.* Washington, DC: APA.

Whitley, Bernard E.; Schofield, Janet W.; & Snyder, Howard N. (1984). Peer preferences in a desegregated school: A round-robin analysis. *Journal of Personality and Social Psychology, 46,* 799–810. PA 71:22877.

Wicker, Allan W. (1975). An application of the multitrait-multimethod logic to the reliability of observational records. *Personality and Social Psychology Bulletin, 1,* 575–579. PA 56:3203.

Wicker, Allan W.; Kirmeyer, Sandra L.; Hanson, Lois; & Alexander, Dean. (1976). Effects of manning levels on subjective experiences, performance, and verbal interaction in groups.

Organizational Behavior and Human Performance, 17, 251–274. PA 58:1124.

Widmar, Neil. (1974). Effects of group discussion on category width judgments. *Journal of Personality and Social Psychology, 29,* 187–195. PA 52:5210.

Wiemann, John M. (1977). Explication and test of a model of communicative competence. *Human Communication Research, 3,* 195–213. PA 60:3022.

Wiemann, John M.; & Harrison, Randall P. (Eds.). (1983). *Nonverbal interaction.* Beverly Hills: Sage.

Wiener, E. (1976). Altruism, ambience, and action: The effects of rural and urban rearing on helping behavior. *Journal of Personality and Social Psychology, 34,* 112–124.

Wiesenthal, David L.; Edwards, J.; Endler, N. S.; Koza, P.; Walton, A.; & Emmott, S. (1978). Trends in conformity research. *Canadian Psychological Review, 19,* 41–58. PA 61:10896.

Wiesenthal, David L.; Endler, Norman S.; Coward, Teresa R.; & Edwards, Jean. (1976). Reversibility of relative competence as a determinant of conformity across different perceptual tasks. *Representative Research in Social Psychology, 7,* 35–43. PA 56:4084.

Wiewiorowski, Krzysztof. (1975). Information, communication and productivity in conditions of team work. *Polish Psychological Bulletin, 6,* 95–100. PA 55:738.

Wilcox, Brian L.; & Holahan, Charles J. (1976). Social ecology of the megadorm in university student housing. *Journal of Educational Psychology, 68,* 453–458. PA 56:8760.

Wild, Cynthia M.; Shapiro, Linda N.; & Abelin, Theodor. (1977). Communication patterns and role structure in families of male schizophrenics: A study using automated techniques. *Archives of General Psychiatry, 34,* 58–70. PA 58:3514.

Wilder, David A. (1977). Perception of groups, size of opposition, and social influence. *Journal of Experimental Social Psychology, 13,* 253–268. PA 59:3354.

Wilder, David A.; & Allen, Vernon L. (1977). Veridical social support, extreme social support, and conformity. *Representative Research in Social Psychology, 8,* 33–41. PA 60:3059.

Wilke, H[enk A. M]. (1974). [Polarization]. *Nederlands Tijdschrift voor de Psychologie en haar Grensgebieden, 29,* 259–280. PA 53:3052.

Wilke, Henk A. M. (Ed.). (1985). *Coalition formation.* Amsterdam: North-Holland/Elsevier.

Wilke, Henk A. [M]; de Boer, Karst L.; & Liebrand, Wim B. (1986). Standards of justice and quality of power in a social dilemma situation. *British Journal of Social Psychology, 25,* 57–65. PA 74:13100.

Wilke, Henk A. [M.]; Liebrand, W. B.; Lotgerink, B.; & Buurma, B. (1986). Equity and individual preferences in an MDG. *European Journal of Social Psychology, 16,* 131–148. PA 74:21925.

Wilke, Henk [A. M.]; & Meertens, Roel. (1973). Individual risk taking for self and others. *European Journal of Social Psychology, 3,* 403–413. PA 53:9552.

Wilke, Henk [A. M.]; & Mulder, Mauk. (1974). A comparison of rotation versus non-rotation in coalition formation experiments. *European Journal of Social Psychology, 4,* 99–102. PA 54:2995.

Wilke, Henk [A. M.]; Pruyn, Jean; & de Vries, Gerjan. (1978). Coalition formation: Political attitudes and power. *European Journal of Social Psychology, 8,* 245–261. SA 79J9654.

Wilke, H[enk A. M.]; & Van Knippenberg, A. (1983). Integration, differentiation and coalition formation. *Journal for the Theory of Social Behaviour, 13,* 181–194. PA 71:14979.

Wilke, H[enk] A. [M.]; Van Knippenberg, A. F.; & Bruins, J. (1986). Conservative coalitions: An expectation states approach. *European Journal of Social Psychology, 16,* 51–63. PA 74:7211.

Williams, Carolyn L. (1981). Assessment of social behavior: Behavioral role play compared with Si scale of the MMPI. *Behavior Therapy, 12,* 578–584. PA 67:1248.

Williams, Daniel C.; & Mueller, Ronald H. (1975). Attributed motivation and decision making in mixed-motive dyadic interaction. *Representative Research in Social Psychology, 6,* 13–23. PA 54:4620.

Williams, Ederyn. (1975). Medium or message? Communications medium as a determinant of interpersonal evaluation. *Sociometry, 38,* 119–130. PA 54:7488.

Williams, J. Sherwood; Gray, Louis N.; & von Broembsen, Maxmilian H. (1976). Proactivity and reinforcement: The contingency of social behavior. *Small Group Behavior, 7,* 317–330. PA 59:9877.

Williams, J. Sherwood; Martin, J. David; & Gray, Louis N. (1975). Norm formation or condition ing? A study in divergence. *Small Group Behavior, 6*, 141–150. PA 55:2338.

Williams, J. Sherwood; Singh, B. Krishna; Gray, Louis N.; & Von Broembsen, Maximillian H. (1974). Small groups as simulates of formal organizations. *International Journal of Contemporary Sociology, 11*(1), 44–51. SA 79K1112.

Williams, Janice G.; & Solano, Cecilia H. (1983). The social reality of feeling lonely: Friendship and reciprocation. *Personality and Social Psychology Bulletin, 9*, 237–242. PA 71:6719.

Williams, Jennifer A. (1984). Gender and intergroup behaviour: Towards an integration. [Special Issue: Intergroup processes]. *British Journal of Social Psychology, 23*, 311–316. PA 72:28040.

Williams, John M. (1984). Assertiveness as a mediating variable in conformity to confederates of high and low status. *Psychological Reports, 55*, 415–418. PA 72:17330.

Williams, John M.; & Warchal, Judith. (1981). The relationship between assertiveness, internal-external locus of control, and overt conformity. *Journal of Psychology, 109*, 93–96.

Williams, Karen B.; & Williams, Kipling D. (1983). Social inhibition and asking for help: The effects of number, strength, and immediacy of potential help givers. *Journal of Personality and Social Psychology, 44*, 67–77. PA 70:3404.

Williams, Kipling; Harkins, Stephen G.; & Latané, Bibb. (1981). Identifiability as a deterrant to social loafing: Two cheering experiments. *Journal of Personality and Social Psychology, 40*, 303–311. PA 66:12831.

Williams, Robert H.; McCandless, Peter H.; Hobb, Dennis A.; & Williams, Sharon A. (1986). Changing attitudes with "identification theory." *Simulation and Games, 17*, 25–43. PA 74:25091.

Williams, Sarah; & Ryckman, Richard M. (1984). The effects of sensation seeking and misattribution of arousal on dyadic interactions between similar or dissimilar strangers. *Journal of Mind and Behavior, 5*, 337–349. PA 72:20097.

Williams, Timothy P.; & Sogon, Shunya. (1984). Group composition and conforming behavior in Japanese students. *Japanese Psychological Research, 26*, 231–234. PA 73:1139.

Williamson, Robert C. (1981). Adjustment to the highrise: Variables in a German sample. *Environment and Behavior, 13*, 289–310.

Willis, Frank N.; Carlson, Roger; & Reeves, Dennis. (1979). The development of personal space in primary school children. *Environmental Psychology and Nonverbal Behavior, 3*, 195–204. PA 64:10216.

Willis, Frank N.; & Hamm, Helen K. (1980). The use of interpersonal touch in securing compliance. *Journal of Nonverbal Behavior, 5*, 49–55. PA 65:12756.

Willke, Helmut. (1976). Funktionen und Konstitutionsbedingungen des Normativen Systems der Gruppe [Functions and contingencies of the normative system of the group]. *Kolner Zeitschrift fur Soziologie und Sozialpsychologie, 28*, 426–450. SA 7717512.

Wills, Thomas Ashby. (Ed.). (1982). *Basic processes in helping relationships.* New York: Academic Press.

Wilshire, Bruce. (1982). *Role playing and identity: The limits of theatre as metaphor.* Bloomington: Univ. of Indiana Press.

Wilson, David W.; & Donnerstein, Edward. (1977). Guilty or not guilty? A look at the "simulated" jury paradigm. *Journal of Applied Social Psychology, 7*, 175–190.

Wilson, David W.; & Kahn, Arnold. (1975). Rewards, costs, and sex differences in helping behavior. *Psychological Reports, 36*, 31–34. PA 54:7489.

Wilson, Gerald L.; & Hanna, Michael S. (1986). *Groups in context: Leadership and participation in small groups.* New York: Random House.

Wilson, John P.; Aronoff, Joel; & Messé, Lawrence A. (1975). Social structure, member motivation, and group productivity. *Journal of Personality and Social Psychology, 32*, 1094–1098. PA 55:9756.

Wilson, Lorene; & Rogers, Ronald W. (1975). The fire this time: Effects of race of target, insult, and potential retaliation on Black aggression. *Journal of Personality and Social Psychology, 32*, 857–864. PA 55:7102.

Wilson, Melvin N.; & Rappaport, Julian. (1974). Personal self-disclosure: Expectancy and situational effects. *Journal of Consulting and Clinical Psychology, 42*, 901–908. PA 53:9496.

Wilson, Stephen. (1978). *Informal groups: An introduction.* Englewood Cliffs, NJ: Prentice-Hall.

Wilson, Thomas P.; Wiemann, John M.; &

Zimmerman, Don H. (1984). Models of turn taking in conversational interaction. *Journal of Language and Social Psychology*, *3*, 159–183. PA 73:11745.

Wilson, Timothy D.; & Capitman, John A. (1982). Effect of script availability on social behavior. *Personality and Social Psychology Bulletin*, *8*, 11–19. PA 68:10338.

Wimer, Scott; & Derlega, Valerian J. (1983). At tributions in T-groups: A test of Kelley's ANOVA model. *Small Group Behavior*, *14*, 50–62. PA 71:1364.

Wine, Jeri D. (1975). Test anxiety and helping behaviour. *Canadian Journal of Behavioural Science*, *7*, 216–222. PA 55:778.

Wineman, Jean D. (1982). Office design and evaluation: an overview. *Environment and Behavior*, *14*, 271–298. PA 68:9220.

Winstead, Barbara A.; & Derlega, Valerian J. (1985). Benefits of same-sex friendships in a stressful situation. *Journal of Social and Clinical Psychology*, *3*, 378–384. PA 73:24497.

Winter, Marlene S. (1976). The rehabilitation team: A catalyst to risky rehabilitation decisions? *Rehabilitation Counseling Bulletin*, *19*, 580–586. PA 56:8544.

Winton, Ward M. (1986). The role of facial response in self-reports of emotion: A critique of Laird. *Journal of Personality and Social Psychology*, *50*, 808–812. PA 73:21206.

Winum, Paul C.; & Banikiotes, Paul G. (1983). The effects of similarity and actual levels of self-disclosure and self-disclosure flexibility on perceptions of interpersonal attraction and adjustment. *Social Behavior and Personality*, *11*, 17–22. PA 72:4032.

Wisdom, J. O. (1978). Three types of groups. *Israel Annals of Psychiatry and Related Disciplines*, *16*(2), 103–123. PA 64:1028.

Wisdom, J. O. (1985). Types of groups: Transitions and cohesion; emergent properties. *International Review of Psycho Analysis*, *12*(1), 73–85. PA 72:30806.

Wish, M.; D'Andrade, R. G.; & Goodnow, J. E. (1980). Dimensions of interpersonal communication: Correspondences between structures for speech acts and bipolar scales. *Journal of Personality and Social Psychology*, *39*, 848–860. PA 66:7729.

Wish, Myron; Deutsch, Morton; & Kaplan, Susan J. (1976). Perceived dimensions of interpersonal relations. *Journal of Personality and Social Psychology*, *33*, 409–420. PA 56:7989.

Wish, Myron; & Kaplan, Susan J. (1977). Toward an implicit theory of interpersonal communication. *Social Psychology Quarterly*, *40*, 234–246. PA 60:5247.

Witkin, Herman A.; & Goodenough, Donald R. (1977). Field dependence and interpersonal behavior. *Psychological Bulletin*, *84*, 661–689.

Wittig, Michele A.; & Skolnick, Paul. (1978). Status versus warmth as determinants of sex differences in personal space. *Sex roles*, *4*, 493–503. PA 63:3267.

Wofford, Jerry C. (1985). Experimental examination of the contingency model and the Leader-Environment-Follower Interaction Theory of leadership. *Psychological Reports*, *56*, 823–832. PA 73:19809.

Wofford, Jerry C.; & Srinivasan, T. N. (1983). Experimental tests of the leader-environment-follower interaction theory of leadership. *Organizational Behavior and Human Performance*, *32*, 35–54. PA 71:2683.

Wogan, Michael; Getter, Herbert; Amdur, Millard J.; Nichols, Margaret F.; & Okman, Guler. (1977). Influencing interaction and outcomes in group psychotherapy. *Small Group Behavior*, *8*, 25–46. PA 60:7848.

Wohlwill, Joachim F.; & Weisman, Gerald D. (1981). *The physical environment and behavior: An annotated bibliography and guide to the literature*. New York: Plenum.

Wolf, Gerrit. (1974). Some conversational conditions and processes of brief encounters. *Communication Research*, *1*, 167–183. PA 53:1079.

Wolf, Gerrit; & Shubik, Martin. (1977). Beliefs about coalition formation in multiple resource three-person situations. *Behavioral Science*, *22*, 99–106. PA 59:12336.

Wolf, Sharon. (1979). Behavioural style and group cohesiveness as sources of minority influence. *European Journal of Social Psychology*, *9*, 381–395. PA 65:3262.

Wolf, Sharon. (1985). Manifest and latent influence of majorities and minorities. *Journal of Personality and Social Psychology*, *48*, 899–908. PA 72:20098.

Wolf, Sharon; & Latané, Bibb. (1981). If laboratory research doesn't square with you, then Qube it: The potential of interactive TV for social psychological research. *Personality and Social Psychology Bulletin*, *7*, 344–352. PA 67:5695.

Wolfe, Maxine. (1975). Room size, group size, and density: Behavior patterns in a children's psychiatric facility. *Environment and Behavior*, 7, 199–224. PA 55:1174.

Wolfson, Sandra L. (1981). Effects of Machiavellianism and communication on helping behavior during an emergency. *British Journal of Social Psychology*, 20, 189–195. PA 68:1111.

Wolosin, Robert J.; Sherman, Steven J.; & Cann, Arnie. (1975). Predictions of own and other's conformity. *Journal of Personality*, 43, 357–378. PA 55:7177.

Wolosin, Robert J.; Sherman, Steven J.; & Mynatt, Clifford R. (1975). When self-interest and altruism conflict. *Journal of Personality and Social Psychology*, 32, 752–760. PA 56:2395.

Won-Doornink, Myong J. (1979). On getting to know you: The association between the stage of a relationship and reciprocity of self-disclosure. *Journal of Experimental Social Psychology*, 15, 229–241. PA 64:7956.

Wood, Julia T. (1981). Sex differences in group communication: Directions for research in speech communications and sociometry. *Journal of Group Psychotherapy, Psychodrama and Sociometry*, 34, 24–31. PA 71:6721.

Wood, Wendy. (1987). Meta-analytic review of sex differences in group performance. *Psychological Bulletin*, 102, 53–71.

Wood, Wendy; & Karten, Stephen J. (1986). Sex differences in interaction style as a product of perceived sex differences in competence. *Journal of Personality and Social Psychology*, 50, 341–347. PA 73:14481.

Wood, Wendy; Polek, Darlene; & Aiken, Cheryl. (1985). Sex differences in group task performance. *Journal of Personality and Social Psychology*, 48, 63–71. PA 72:17331.

Worchel, Stephen; Andreoli, Virginia A.; & Folger, Robert. (1977). Intergroup cooperation and intergroup attraction: The effect of previous interaction and outcome of combined effort. *Journal of Experimental Social Psychology*, 13, 131–140. PA 58:9501.

Worchel, Stephen; Axsom, Danny; Ferris, Frances; Samaha, Gary; & Schweizer, Susan. (1978). Determinants of the effect of intergroup cooperation on intergroup attraction. *Journal of Conflict Resolution*, 22, 429–439.

Worchel, Stephen; & Norvell, Nancy. (1980). Effect of perceived environmental conditions during cooperation on intergroup attraction.

Journal of Personality and Social Psychology, 38, 764–772. PA 65:12757.

Worchel, Stephen; & Teddlie, Charles. (1976). The experience of crowding: A two-factor theory. *Journal of Personality and Social Psychology*, 34, 30–40. PA 56:6017.

Worchel, Stephen; & Yohai Steven M. (1979). The role of attribution in the experience of crowding. *Journal of Experimental Social Psychology*, 15, 91–104. PA 64:5537.

Worringham, Charles J.; & Messick, David M. (1983). Social facilitation of running: An unobtrusive study. *Journal of Social Psychology*, 121, 23–29. PA 71:17782.

Worth, Leila T.; Allison, Scott T.; & Messick, David M. (1987). Impact of a group decision on perception of one's own and others' attitudes. *Journal of Personality and Social Psychology*, 53, 673–682.

Worthington, Mary E. (1974). Personal space as a function of the stigma effect. *Environment and Behavior*, 6, 289–294. PA 53:11631.

Wortman, Camille B.; Adesman, Peter; Herman, Elliot; & Greenberg, Richard. (1976). Self-disclosure: An attributional perspective. *Journal of Personality and Social Psychology*, 33, 184–191. PA 56:705.

Wright, Edward F.; & Wells, Gary L. (1985). Does group discussion attenuate the dispositional bias? *Journal of Applied Social Psychology*, 15, 531–546. PA 73:3690.

Wright, Fred. (1976). The effects of style and sex of consultants and sex of members in self-study groups. *Small Group Behavior*, 7, 433–456. SA 78J0180.

Wright, George (Ed.). (1985). *Behavioral decision making*. New York: Plenum.

Wright, Jack C.; Giammarino, Mary; & Parad, Harry W. (1986). Social status in small groups: Individual-group similarity and the social misfit. *Journal of Personality and Social Psychology*, 50, 523–536.

Wright, Paul H. (1974). The delineation and measurement of some key variables in the study of friendship. *Representative Research in Social Psychology*, 5, 93–96. PA 53:1111.

Wright, Paul H. (1978). Toward a theory of friendship based on a conception of self. *Human Communication Research*, 4, 196–207. PA 62:1077.

Wright, Thomas L.; & Duncan, Douglas. (1986). Attraction to group, group cohesiveness, and individual outcome: A study of training groups. *Small Group Behavior, 17*, 487–492.

Wright, Thomas L.; & Ingraham, Loring J. (1985). Simultaneous study of individual differences and relationship effects in social behavior in groups. *Journal of Personality and Social Psychology, 48*, 1041–1047. PA 72:20099.

Wright, Thomas L.; & Ingraham, Loring J. (1986). A social relations model test of the interpersonal circle. *Journal of Personality and Social Psychology, 50*, 1285–1290. PA 73:24498.

Wrightsman, Lawrence S. (1960). Effects of waiting with others on changes in level of felt anxiety. *Journal of Abnormal and Social Psychology, 61*, 216–222.

Wrightsman, Lawrence S. (1975). The presence of others does make a difference—sometimes. *Psychological Bulletin, 82*, 884–885. PA 55:7103.

Wyant, Kerry W.; & Gardner, Glenn W. (1977). Interpersonal evaluations, attitudes and attraction. *Journal of Research in Personality, 11*, 356–367. PA 60:3089.

Yager, Stuart; Johnson, Roger T.; Johnson, David W.; & Snider, Bill. (1986). The impact of group processing on achievement in cooperative learning groups. *Journal of Social Psychology, 126*, 389–397.

Yamada, Elaine M.; Tjosvold, Dean; & Draguns, Juris G. (1983). Effects of sex-linked situations and sex composition on cooperation and style of interaction. *Sex Roles, 9*, 541–553. PA 71:1333.

Yamagishi, Toshio. (1984). Development of distribution rules in small groups. *Journal of Personality and Social Psychology, 46*, 1069–1078. PA 71:25837.

Yamagishi, Toshio. (1986a). The provision of a sanctioning system as a public good. *Journal of Personality and Social Psychology, 51*, 110–116. PA 73:27153.

Yamagishi, Toshio. (1986b). The structural goal/expectation theory of cooperation in social dilemmas. *Advances in Group Processes, 3*, 51–87.

Yamaguchi, Susumu; Okamoto, Koichi; & Oka, Takashi. (1985). Effects of coactor's presence: Social loafing and social facilitation. *Japanese Psychological Research, 27*, 215–222. PA 74:10222.

Yamauchi, Takahisa. (1982). The effect of face-to-face playing on choice behavior in Prisoner's Dilemma game. *Japanese Journal of Psychology, 52*, 337–343. PA 68:8113.

Yanoushek, Ya. (1982). [Problems of communication under conditions of common activity]. *Voprosy Psikhologii, 6*, 57–65. PA 70:10261.

Yantis, Betty; & Nixon, John E. (1982). Interpersonal compatibility: Effect on simulation game outcomes. *Simulation and Games, 13*, 337–349. PA 69:12669.

Yarczower, Matthew; & Daruns, Laura. (1982). Social inhibition of spontaneous facial expressions in children. *Journal of Personality and Social Psychology, 43*, 831–837.

Yarkin, Kerry L.; Harvey, John H.; & Bloxom, Bruce M. (1981). Cognitive sets, attribution, and social interaction. *Journal of Personality and Social Psychology, 41*, 243–252. PA 67:7742.

Yarkin-Levin, Kerry. (1983). Anticipated interaction, attribution, and social interaction. *Social Psychology Quarterly, 46*, 302–311. PA 71:23102.

Yarnold, Paul R.; Grimm, Laurence G.; & Mueser, Kim T. (1986). Social conformity and the Type A behavior pattern. *Perceptual and Motor Skills, 62*, 99–104. PA 74:21894.

Yasui, Yasuo. (1985). [Dynamic conformity process in perceptual judgment]. *Japanese Journal of Psychology, 55*, 335–341. PA 73:3692.

Yerby, Janet. (1975). Attitude, task, and sex composition as variables affecting female leadership in small problem-solving groups. *Speech Monographs, 42*, 160–168. PA 54:11691.

Yetton, Philip W.; & Bottger, Preston C. (1982). Individual versus group problem solving: An empirical test of a best-member strategy. *Organizational Behavior and Human Performance, 29*, 307–321. PA 68:5772.

Yetton, Philip [W.]; & Bottger, Preston. (1983). The relationships among group size, member ability, social decision schemes, and performance. *Organizational Behavior and Human Performance, 32*, 145–159. PA 71:3984.

Yinon, Yoel; & Bizman, Aharon. (1974). The nature of effective bonds and the degree of personal responsibility as determinants of risk taking for "self and others." *Bulletin of the Psychonomic Society, 4*(2-A), 80–82. PA 53:3054.

Yinon, Yoel; & Bizman, Aharon. (1980). Noise, success, and failure as determinants of helping behavior. *Personality and Social Psychology Bulletin, 6*, 125-130. PA 65:10462.

Yinon, Yoel; Jaffe, Yoram; & Feshbach, Seymour. (1975). Risky aggression in individuals and groups. *Journal of Personality and Social Psychology, 31*, 808-815. PA 54:5222.

Yinon, Yoel; & Sharon, Irit. (1985). Similarity in religiousness of the solicitor, the potential helper, and the recipient as determinants of donating behavior. *Journal of Applied Social Psychology, 15*, 726-734. PA 73:11783.

Yinon, Yoel; Sharon, Irit; Gonen, Yitzhak; & Adam, Ron. (1982). Escape from responsibility and help in emergencies among persons alone or within groups. *European Journal of Social Psychology, 12*, 301-305. PA 69:10387.

Yoder, Janice D. (1981). The effects of disagreement on the continuation of an interpersonal relationship. *Human Relations, 34*, 195-205. PA 66:1250.

Yoshida, Fujio. (1984). [Intergroup orientations and intergroup perceptions in a Prisoner's Dilemma Game]. *Japanese Journal of Psychology, 55*, 282-288. PA 73:3722.

Yoshida, Fujio; & Ohmoto, Susumu. (1985). [Comparison between interpersonal and intergroup behaviors and perceptions in a Prisoner's Dilemma Game]. *Japanese Journal of Psychology, 56*, 86-92. PA 73:17220.

Yoshida, Michio; & Shirakashi, Sanshiro. (1973). [The effect of success vs. failure and leaders' LPC on the group process]. *Japanese Journal of Experimental Social Psychology, 13*, 1-10. PA 54:2996.

Yoshitake, Kumuko. (1985). [The effects of opinion's reality on conformity in the changing situations of majority opinion]. *Japanese Journal of Experimental Social Psychology, 24*, 121-126. PA 73:11784.

Young, Jerald W. (1977). Behavioral and perceptual differences between structurally equivalent, two-person games: A rich versus poor context comparison. *Journal of Conflict Resolution, 21*, 299-322. PA 59:12375.

Youngs, George A. (1986). Patterns of threat and punishment reciprocity in a conflict setting. *Journal of Personality and Social Psychology, 51*, 541-546. PA 74:1070.

Yuferova, T. I. (1975). [The behavior of "affective" children in conflict situations]. *Voprosy Psikhologii*, No. 2, 113-123. PA 54:5516.

Yukl, Gary. (1974). Effects of the opponent's initial offer, concession magnitude, and concession frequency on bargaining behavior. *Journal of Personality and Social Psychology, 30*, 323-335.

Yukl, Gary A. (1976). Effects of information, payoff magnitude, and favorability of alternative settlement on bargaining outcomes. *Journal of Social Psychology, 98*, 269-282. PA 56:6067.

Yukl, Gary A.; Malone, Michael P.; Hayslip, Bert; & Pamin, Thomas A. (1976). The effects of time pressure and issue settlement order on integrative bargaining. *Sociometry, 39*, 277-281.

Zaborowski, Zbigniew. (1977). [A theory of interpersonal equilibrium and its application]. *Przeglad Psychologiczny, 20*, 243-257. PA 61:986.

Zaccaro, Stephen J. (1984). Social loafing: The role of task attractiveness. *Personality and Social Psychology Bulletin, 10*, 99-106. PA 71:31327.

Zaccaro, Stephen J.; Peterson, Christopher; & Walker, Steven. (1987). Self-serving attributions for individual and group performance. *Social Psychology Quarterly, 50*, 257-263.

Zachary, Wayne W. (1977). An information flow model for conflict and fission in small groups. *Journal of Anthropological Research, 33*, 452-473. SA 80L0099.

Zajonc, Robert B. (1965). Social facilitation. *Science, 149*, 269-274.

Zajonc, Robert B. (1980). Feeling and thinking: Preferences need no inferences. *American Psychologist, 35*, 151-175. PA 63:9733.

Zajonc, Robert B. (1985). Emotion and facial efference: A theory reclaimed. *Science, 228*, 15-21. PA 73:5516.

Zaleska, Maryla. (1974). The effects of discussion on group and individual choices among bets. *European Journal of Social Psychology, 4*, 229-250. PA 54:5223.

Zaleska, Maryla. (1976). Majority influence on group choices among bets. *Journal of Personality and Social Psychology, 33*, 8-17.

Zaleska, Maryla. (1978). Individual and group choices among solutions of a problem when solution verifiability is moderate or low. *European Journal of Social Psychology, 8*, 37-53. SA: 79J9655.

Zaleska, Maryla. (1980). [Climate of interpersonal relations and polarization of attitudes in groups]. *Psychologie Française*, *25*, 183–193. PA 66:3625.

Zaleska, M[aryla]; & Askevis-Leherpeux, F. (1973–1974). [The influence of unanimous group error on the response of the individual]. *Bulletin de Psychologie*, *27*, 526–535. PA 53:7341.

Zamarripa, Perrin O.; & Krueger, Dorothy L. (1983). Implicit contracts regulating small group leadership: The influence of culture. *Small Group Behavior*, *14*, 187–210. PA 71:12182.

Zander, Alvin F. (1974). Productivity and group success: Team spirit vs. the individual achiever. *Psychology Today*, *8*(6), 64–68. PA 54:4362.

Zander, Alvin. (1976). The psychology of removing group members and recruiting new ones. *Human Relations*, *29*, 969–987. PA 57:14130.

Zander, Alvin. (1977). *Groups at work*. San Francisco: Jossey-Bass.

Zander, Alvin. (1979a). The psychology of group processes. *Annual Review of Psychology*, *30*, 417–451. PA 62:8610.

Zander, Alvin. (1979b). The study of group behavior during four decades. *Journal of Applied Behavioral Science*, *15*, 272–282. SA: 80K7138.

Zander, Alvin. (1982). *Making groups effective*. San Francisco: Jossey-Bass. [2nd printing has 1983 imprint.]

Zander, Alvin. (1983). The value of belonging to a group in Japan. *Small Group Behavior*, *14*, 3–14. PA 71:1334.

Zander, Alvin. (1985a). *The purposes of groups and organizations*. San Francisco: Jossey-Bass.

Zander, Alvin. (1985b). Whatever became of group dynamics? *Contemporary Social Psychology*, *11*(4), 128–132.

Zanna, Mark P.; & Pack, Susan J. (1975). On the self-fulfilling nature of apparent sex differences in behavior. *Journal of Experimental Social Psychology*, *11*, 583–591. PA 55:12275.

Zartman, I. William. (Ed.). (1978). *The negotiation process: Theories and Applications*. Beverly Hills, CA: Sage.

Zeedyk-Ryan, Janice; & Smith, Gene F. (1983). The effects of crowding on hostility, anxiety, and desire for social interaction. *Journal of Social Psychology*, *120*, 245–252. PA 71:12183.

Zelditch, Morris; Lauderdale, Patrick; & Stublarec, Stephen. (1980). How are inconsistencies between status and ability resolved? *Social Forces*, *58*, 1025–1043.

Zemore, Robert; & Dell, Lewis W. (1983). Interpersonal problem-solving skills and depression-proneness. *Personality and Social Psychology Bulletin*, *9*, 231–235. PA 71:6722.

Zerschling, Greg; & Palisi, Bartolomeo J. (1975). Rationality of Coalition Formation in the Triad. *Western Sociological Review*, *6*, 61–71. SA 78J1748.

Ziffo, P. M. (1977). Communication sequence in small groups: Persuasion as a two-step process. *Journal of Social Psychology*, *102*, 291–296. PA 60:3024.

Ziller, Robert C. (1977). Group dialectics: The dynamics of groups over time. *Human Development*, *20*, 293–308. PA 60:7449.

Zillmann, Dolf; Baron, Robert A.; & Tamborini, Ron. (1981). Social costs of smoking: Effects of tobacco smoke on hostile behavior. *Journal of Applied Social Psychology*, *11*, 548–561. PA 68:5773.

Zimbardo, Philip G. (1973). On the ethics of intervention in human psychological research: With special reference to the Stanford prison experiment. *Cognition*, *2*, 243–256. PA 53:1311.

Zimmer, Jacqueline L.; & Sheposh, John P. (1975). Effects of high status and low status actor's performance on observers' attributions of causality and behavioral intentions. *Sociometry*, *38*, 395–407. PA 54:11734.

Zimmerman, Barry J.; & Brody, Gene, H. (1975). Race and modeling influences on the interpersonal play patterns of boys. *Journal of Educational Psychology*, *67*, 591–598. PA 55:4532.

Zlate, M. (1983). Groupe et collectif [The group and the collective]. *Revue Roumaine des Sciences Sociales Serie de Psychologie*, *27*, 141–154. PA 74:7179.

Zlate, M. (1984). Un procedeu de analiza a comportamentului interpersonal [A technique for the analysis of interpersonal behaviour]. *Revista de Psihologie*, *30*, 120–132. PA 72:22596.

Zlate, M. (1985). [A new method for diagnosing interpersonal behavior]. *Revue Roumaine des Sciences Sociales Serie de Psychologie*, *29*(1), 29–37. PA 74:13101.

Zuber, Irena. (1977). [An attempt to classify and determine the regulatory power of cognitive schemes in relations: I. Others]. *Przeglad Psychologiczny, 20,* 3–19. PA 60:1040.

Zuckerman, Miron; Amidon, Mary D.; Bishop, Shawn E.; & Pomeranz, Scott D. (1982). Face and tone of voice in the communication of deception. *Journal of Personality and Social Psychology, 43,* 347–357. PA 69:5591.

Zuckerman, Miron; DePaulo, Bella M.; & Rosenthal, Robert. (1981). Verbal and nonverbal communication of deception. *Advances in Experimental Social Psychology, 14,* 1–59.

Zuckerman, Miron; Driver, Robert; & Koestner, Richard. (1982). Discrepancy as a cue to actual and perceived deception. *Journal of Nonverbal Behavior, 7,* 95–100. PA 71:20496.

Zuckerman, Miron; Koestner, Richard; & Colella, Michele J. (1985). Learning to detect deception from three communication channels. *Journal of Nonverbal Behavior, 9,* 188–194. PA 73:27167.

Zuckerman, Miron; Larrance, Deborah [T.]; Hall, Judith; DeFrank, R.; & Rosenthal, Robert. (1979). Posed and spontaneous communication of emotion via facial and vocal cues. *Journal of Personality, 47,* 712–733. PA 65:5434.

Zuckerman, Miron; Larrance, Deborah T.; Spiegel, Nancy H.; & Klorman, Rafael. (1981). Controlling nonverbal displays: Facial expressions and tone of voice. *Journal of Experimental Social Psychology, 17,* 506–524. PA 67:5781.

Zuckerman, Miron; Lazzaro, Michele M.; &

Waldgeir, Diane. (1979). Undermining effects of the foot-in-the-door technique with extrinsic rewards. *Journal of Applied Social Psychology, 9,* 292–296.

Zuckerman, Miron; Lipets, Marsha S.; Koivumaki, Judith H.; & Rosenthal, Robert. (1975). Encoding and decoding nonverbal cues of emotion. *Journal of Personality and Social Psychology, 32,* 1068–1076. PA 55:7180.

Zuckerman, Miron; Schmitz, Marie; & Yosha, Andrew. (1977). Effects of crowding in a student environment. *Journal of Applied Social Psychology, 7,* 67–72.

Zuckerman, Miron; Spiegel, Nancy H.; DePaulo, Bella M.; & Rosenthal, Robert. (1982). Nonverbal strategies for decoding deception. *Journal of Nonverbal Behavior, 6,* 171–187. PA 71:20497.

Zur, Ofer (1987). Neither doves nor hawks: Marking the territory covered by the field of the psychology of peace and war: Part I. *Contemporary Social Psychology, 12,* 89–100.

Zurcher, Louis A. (1983). *Social roles: Conformity, conflict and creativity.* Beverly Hills: Sage.

Zurcher, Louis A.; & Wilson, Kenneth L. (1981). Role satisfaction, situational assessment, and scapegoating. *Social Psychology Quarterly, 44,* 264–271. PA 67:7745.

Zwick, Rami; & Rapoport, Amnon. (1985). Relative gain maximization in sequential 3-person characteristic function games. *Journal of Mathematical Psychology, 29,* 333–359. PA 74:7180.

Name Index

This is a name index, not a person index. The same person may be listed more than once if the person's name appears differently in different sources — whereas the entries for two different people having identical names may be interfiled.

Aamodt, Michael G, 53
Abadzi, Helen, 35
Abascal, Juan, 53
Abbey, David S, 222
Abdel-Halim, Ahmed A, 51
Abele, Andrea, 91, 97
Ahelin, Theodor, 290
Abelson, Robert P, 3, 111
Abraham, Ada, 159, 179, 284
Abramo, Joseph L, 204
Abrams, Dominic, 86
Accolla, Patrick, 159, 284
Ackerman, Bette, 182
Acock, Alan C, 152
Adam, Ron, 93
Adamopoulos, John, 35, 76, 265, 266
Adams, Claire A, 34
Adams, David, 224
Adams, Gerald R, 76, 118, 123
Adams, Heather E, 152
Adams, J, 66
Adams, Jeffrey B, 67, 159
Adams, Jerome, 158, 159
Adams, Kathrynn A, 56, 63, 75
Adato, Albert, 141
Adelman, Leonard, 71
Adelson, Joseph P, 192
Aderman, Morris, 157
Adesman, Peter, 187
Adler, Alfred, 262
Adler, Leonore L, 25

Adler, Nancy E, 289
Adler, Nancy L, 152
Adler, Patricia A, 3
Adler, Peter, 3
Adsit, Laury, 70
Aebischer, Verena, 134
Agazarian, Yvonne, 289
Ager, Joel W, 285
Aggarwal, Y P, 245
Ahlberg, A'ke, 289
Ahlgren, Andrew, 3
Ahmed, S M, 22, 25, 76, 93
Aho, Lynn, 24
Ahrentzen, Sherry, 38
Aiello, John R, 21, 22, 25, 26, 30, 31, 33-35, 37, 185, 245, 286
Aikawa, Atsushi, 279
Aiken, Cheryl, 57, 68
Akama, Midori, 191
Alagna, Sheryle W, 66, 158
Alagna, Sheryle Whitcher, 63, 220
Alba, Richard D, 286
Albers, Wulf, 245, 257
Albert, Kevin P, 20, 25
Albert, Stuart, 184
Alblas, Gert, 6
Albrecht, Gary L, 284
Alcock, J E, 253
Alcock, James E, 241
Alden, Lynn E, 43
Alderfer, Clayton P, 288

Subject Index